Reference Books Bulletin 1994-95

A compilation of evaluations
September 1, 1994, through August 1995

Prepared by the American Library Association
Reference Books Bulletin Editorial Board

Edited by Sandy Whiteley
Compiled by Kim Dillon

BOOKLIST Publications
Chicago, 1995

Copyright 1994, 1995 by the American Library Association.
Permission to quote any review in full or in part must be obtained
from the Office of Rights and Permissions of the American Library
Association. Permission to quote a review in full will be granted
only to the publisher of the work reviewed.

Library of Congress Catalog Card Number 73-159565

International Standard Book Number 0-8389-7816-9
International Standard Serial Number 8755-0962

Printed in the United States of America

Cover design by Ellen Pettengell

Contents

v	Preface
vii	Reference Books Bulletin Editorial Board
ix	Alumni
	Omnibus Articles
1	1994 Annual Encyclopedia Update
10	Trivia Books for the Reference Shelf
12	American Ethnicity
14	Environmental Reference Sources
18	Reference Sources for Persons with Physical and Learning Disabilities
21	Reference Sources for Children's Literature
	Featured Reviews and Reviews
26	Generalities
34	Philosophy, Psychology, Religion
42	Social Sciences
54	Business, Economics
59	Law, Public Administration, Social Problems and Services
66	Education, Communication, Customs
75	Language
82	Science
90	Medicine, Health, Technology, Management
100	Fine Arts, Decorative Arts, Music
110	Performing Arts, Recreation
115	Literature
126	Geography, Biography
138	History
149	Index to Type of Material
152	Subject Index
160	Title Index

Preface

This past year was a milestone for *Reference Books Bulletin* for a number of reasons. It marked the ninetieth anniversary of *Booklist*, the publication where RBB reviews are published as a separate section; the sixty-fifth anniversary of *RBB* and its predecessors, *Reference and Subscription Books Review* and *Subscription Books Bulletin*; and the tenth anniversary of Sandy Whiteley's tenure as editor of *RBB*. Although the name of the publication has changed over the years, one thing has remained constant—*RBB* is the source of quality reference reviews. Reviews in *RBB* are unsigned and published in the name of the Reference Books Bulletin Editorial Board.

This 1994–95 cumulation of *RBB*, the twenty-seventh to be published, includes reviews from the pages of the September 1994–August 1995 issues of *Booklist*. The Board reviewed 500 reference sources in volume 91. This included 24 featured reviews, in-depth assessments of significant reference sources (e.g., *Britannica Online, Exegy, Encyclopedia of Bioethics, The Oxford Encyclopedia of the Modern Islamic World*). The Board recognizes the impact in libraries of electronic reference tools (CD-ROMs, diskettes, online services) and continues to review these media. *RBB* reviewed 26 electronic products in 1994–95.

The Board also publishes omnibus reviews—annotated lists of reference sources on a subject. Five omnibus reviews, plus the eleventh "Annual Encyclopedia Update" (which included CD-ROM encyclopedias for the first time), were published in 1994–95. The omnibus reviews were "Facts, Miscellaneous: Trivia Books for the Reference Shelf"; "American Ethnicity: Recent Sources"; "Environmental Reference Sources"; "Reference Sources for Persons with Physical and Learning Disabilities: A Selective List"; and "Reference Sources for Children's Literature." A special thanks to the Board members and alumni reviewers who compiled the omnibus reviews, members of the Omnibus Reviews Task Force (ORTF) who read and revised them, and Sarah Watstein who chaired the ORTF.

Sandy Whiteley's guidance and editorial expertise continue to be a stabilizing force to members of the Board. Kim Dilion and Lisa Orzepowski, *RBB* publishing assistants, had the unenviable task of organizing and mailing hundreds of review copies and manuscripts to Board members across the country. A special thanks to Kim who compiled this year's cumulation.

I personally want to thank the Board members, alumni reviewers, and *RBB* interns for all of their time and hard work. Their efforts continue *Reference Books Bulletin*'s 65-year tradition as an essential collection-development resource for librarians. Finally, I want to thank the administration of the Arts and Sciences Library of Tufts University for their support during the past year.

Jim Walsh
Chair, *Reference Books Bulletin* Editorial Board
1994–1995

Reference Books Bulletin Editorial Board

Jim Walsh, Head of Reference, Tufts University, Medford, Massachusetts, Chairperson

Ken Black, Head of Public Services, Rosary College, River Forest, Illinois

Robert Craig Bunch, Librarian, Jones H.S. Library, Coldspring, Texas

Jerry Carbone, Director of Library, Brooks Memorial Library, Brattleboro, Vermont

Ronald Chepesiuk, Head, Special Collections, Dacus Library, Winthrop College, Rock Hill, South Carolina

Sharon E. Cohen, New York, New York

Bryna Coonin, Asst. Head, Reference Dept., D.H. Hill Library, N.C. State University, Raleigh, North Carolina

Barbara Flynn, Library Director, Park Forest Public Library, Park Forest, Illinois

Naomi Galbreath, Branch Librarian, Archdale Public Library, Archdale, North Carolina

Rochelle Glantz, Library Media Specialist, Arlington High School, Arlington, Massachusetts

Carol Sue Harless, Stone Mountain High School, Stone Mountain, Georgia

Dona Helmer, Director, Curriculum Resource Library, Montana State University Library, Billings, Montana

Robin Hoelle, Librarian, Badin High School, Hamilton, Ohio

Sarah Sartain Jane, Head of Reference, Fort Meyers/Lee County Public Library, Fort Meyers, Florida

Sue Kamm, Associate Librarian, Audio-Visual/Circulation Divisions, Inglewood Public Library, Inglewood, California

Marlene M. Kuhl, Baltimore County Public Library, Reisterstown, Maryland

Marilyn L. Long, Palma High School, Salinas, California

Kathleen M. McBroom, Media Specialist, Fordson Media Center, Dearborn, Michigan

William A. McHugh, Reference Collection Librarian, Northwestern University Library, Evanston, Illinois

Carolyn Mulac, Assistant Head, Information Center, Chicago Public Library, Chicago, Illinois

Elizabeth Nibley, Reference Librarian, American University Library, Washington, DC

Deborah Rollins, Reference Department, Univeristy of Maine, Orono, Maine

Esther Sinofsky, Library Media Teacher, Alexander Hamilton High School, Los Angeles, California

Kathleen Stipek, Adult Services Librarian, Alachua County Library District, Gainesville, Florida

Fannette Thomas, Coordinator of Collection Development, James A. Newpher Library, Baltimore County, Maryland

Sarah Barbara Watstein, James Branch Cabell Library, Virginia Commonwealth University, Richmond, Virginia

Alumni

James D. Anderson, Associate Dean and Professor, Rutgers University, New Bruswick, New Jersey

Hilda Arnold, Drakesboro, Kentucky

Skip Auld, Chesterfield County Public Library, Chesterfield, Virginia

Susan Awe, Manager, Arvada Branch, Jefferson County Library System, Arvada, Colorado

Barbara Bibel, Reference Librarian, Oakland Public Library, Oakland, CA

Christine Bulson, Head of Reference, Milne Library, State University of New York, Oneonta, Oneonta, New York

Ann E. Cohen, Assistant Division Head, Reynolds Information Center, Rochester Public Library, Rochester, New York

Brian E. Coutts, Head, Department of Public Service, Helm-Cravens Library, Western Kentucky University, Bowling Green, Kentucky

Milton H. Crouch, Assistant Director for Reader Services, Bailey/Howe Library, University of Vermont, Burlington, Vermont

Donald G. Davis, Jr., Professor, Graduate School of Library and Information Service, University of Texas at Austin, Austin, Texas

Winifred F. Dean, Business/Social Science Librarian, Cleveland State University Library, Cleveland, Ohio

Carole C. Deily, Reference Librarian, Plano Public Library System, Plano, Texas

Marie Ellis, English and American Literature Bibliographer, History and Humanities Department, University of Georgia Libraries, Athens, Georgia

Lesley S.J. Farmer, Library Director, Redwood High School, Larkspur, California

Jack Forman, Reference/Bibliographic Service Librarian, Mesa College Library, San Diego, California

Elizabeth L. Fraser, Reference/Foundation/ILL Librarian, Kanawha County Public Library, Charleston, West Virginia

Gary Golden, Director, Camden Arts and Science Library, Rutgers University, Camden, New Jersey

Susan Gooden, Librarian, Concord High School, Wilmington, Delaware

Ruth M. Hadlow, Head, Children's Literature Department, Cleveland Public Library, Cleveland, Ohio

Nancy Huntley, Assistant Director, Lincoln Library, Springfield, Illinois

Vincent J. Jennings, Documents and Map Librarian, Hofstra University Library, Hempstead, New York

Rashelle Karp, Associate Professor, College of Library Science, Clarion University of Pennsylvania, Clarion, Pennsylvania

Abbie Vestal Landry, Head, Reference Division, Watson Library, Northwestern State University, Natchitoches, Louisiana

John C. Larsen, Baltimore, Maryland

Arthur Lichtenstein, Reference Librarian, Torreyson Library, University of Central Arkansas, Conway, Arkansas

Judith Yankielun Lind, Director, Roseland Free Public Library, Roseland, New Jersey

Josephine McSweeney, Professor, Reference Librarian, Pratt Institute Library, Brooklyn, New York

H. Robert Malinowsky, Professor and Bibliographer of Science and Engineering, University of Illinois–Chicago Library, Chicago, Illinois

Arthur S. Meyers, Library Director, Hammond Public Library, Hammond, Indiana

Margaret C. Power, Reference Department Head, DePaul University Library, Chicago, IL

Mary Ellen Quinn, Chicago Public Library, Uptown Branch, Chicago, IL

James R. Rettig, Assitant Dean of University Libraries for Reference and Information Services, Earl Gregg Swem Library, College of William and Mary, Williamsburg, Pennsylvania

Stewart P. Schneider, Associate Professor, Graduate School of Library and Information Studies, University of Rhode Island, West Kingston, Rhode Island

Martin D. Sugden, Reference Librarian, Business, Science and Industry Department, Haydon Burns Library, Jacksonville, Florida

Terri Tomchyshyn, Status of Disabled Persons Secretariat, National Clearinghouse on Disabled Issues, Quebec, Canada

David A. Tyckoson, Head, Reference Deaprtment, State University of New York–Albany, Albany, New York

Bobbi Walters, Houston, Texas

Christine A. Whittington, Reference Department, Raymond H. Folger Library, University of Maine, Orono, Maine

Wiley J. Williams, Chapel Hill, North Carolina

A. Virginia Witucke, Central Michigan University, Merrifield Center, Falls Church, Virginia

Raymund F. Wood, Encino, California

Omnibus Reviews

ENCYCLOPEDIA UPDATE, 1994

Reference Books Bulletin has a long history of reviewing encyclopedias. The first issue of *Subscription Books Bulletin*, our predecessor publication, published in January 1930, contained reviews of *Encyclopaedia Britannica* (the price of the library edition was $129.50) and *World Book* ($62.50). This is our eleventh "Encyclopedia Update," reviewing the 1994 editions of the 10 annually revised general encyclopedias, and, for the first time, CD-ROM encyclopedias. Reviews appear in alphabetical order, except that electronic products are listed following their print counterparts.

The rapid pace of world events is reflected in these sets. For example, they all note the division of Czechoslovakia into two separate states and the independence of Eritrea. The instability of many nations continues to make the encyclopedia editor's task a difficult one. For example, in 1991 most sets were revised to show the reunification of North and South Yemen. Now the civil war there has reignited.

The number of print encyclopedias sold in recent years is declining, while sales of electronic titles have grown rapidly. This year about 600,000 sets of print encyclopedias will be sold (down from approximately 900,000 several years ago); an estimated 4,000,000 CD-ROM encyclopedias have been sold since the inception of this technology. Many of the CD-ROMs are bundled with the purchase of a CD-ROM drive, so figures may not reflect the deliberate purchase of an encyclopedia, but these sales do cut into the sales of print sets.

The text of CD-ROM encyclopedias doesn't always completely correlate with the print sets. For example, articles that have to be shortened in the print set because of space limitations may appear in their entirety on CD-ROM. Because some CD-ROM versions are issued months after the print set, they may also be more up-to-date. For example, the 1994 *Grolier Multimedia Encyclopedia* contains some information that will be in the 1995 *Academic American Encyclopedia*. Microsoft maintains an editorial staff to create additional articles to add to *Encarta* to supplement the text from *Funk & Wagnalls*.

Two tables accompany this article. The one for print sets no longer includes the consumer price. Because encyclopedias are now sold in many ways and at many prices, it seemed to us that the consumer prices provided to us by publishers were sometimes misleading. The prices on the table for CD-ROM versions are the suggested retail price. These sets are often discounted in stores.

For information on encyclopedia yearbooks, see the article in the February 15, 1994, issue of RBB. —*Sandy Whiteley*

Academic American Encyclopedia. 21v. Lawrence T. Lorimer, editorial director; K. Anne Ranson, editor in chief. Grolier, 1994. (0-7172-2053-2).

HISTORY: Created by a Dutch firm in 1980, *Academic American Encyclopedia* (AAE) was first published by Grolier in 1982. Various versions are sold under other titles: *Lexicon Universal Encyclopedia*, *Grolier International Encyclopedia*, etc.

SCOPE AND TREATMENT: Written for students from middle school through college and adults, AAE added 57 new contributors in 1994, including Stanton Glantz, professor of medicine at the University of California, San Francisco (*Smoking*); Deborah Daro, director of the Center on Child Abuse Prevention Research (*Child Abuse*); and Foster Hirsch, professor of film at Brooklyn College (*Allen, Woody*). Approximately 75 percent of the articles, even very short ones, are signed by the contributor. The word-by-word alphabetization is the same as that used in phone books and library catalogs, so that *Radio Galaxies* appears before *Radioactivity*. During the past several years, AAE has been changing the transliteration of Chinese names to the pinyin system; this process is nearly completed.

QUALITY AND CURRENCY: This year's set has 106 new articles for a total of 32,000 entries. There are 203 new four-color photos and 78 new or revised maps out of the total 17,000 illustrations. Among the new maps provided by Rand McNally are those for Armenia, Azerbaijan, Slovenia, and Uzbekistan. The revised "World: A Physical-Political Map" is particularly useful, as the boundaries of the new countries of Eastern Europe are shown.

Major world events were followed through mid-December 1993. Examples include reporting the results of the Russian parliamentary elections, the passage of the Brady bill, the meeting of the Convention for a Democratic South Africa, the flight of the *Endeavor*, and the signing by Bush and Yeltsin of the START II nuclear arms pact. Currency is definitely a strong point in AAE. *Artificial Life*, *Muslim Brotherhood*, *Star Trek*, *Yoga*, and *Yugoslav War* are examples of new articles on subjects of current interest. There is a new entry for *Ayodha*, the site in India of recent violence between Hindus and Muslims. New biographical subjects include Les Aspin, Caryl Churchill, Frank Gehry, Rosa Parks, Sting, and Robin Williams. AAE is the only set to have biographies of some people (e.g., Harvey Swados, Kurt Wolff).

Among the 72 replacement articles are *Child Abuse*, *Religious Cults*, *Suicide*, and *Telecommunications*. A replacement article on Bill Clinton takes stock of his first year in office. *United Nations* was rewritten to reflect dramatic changes in current politics. Environmental issues are addressed in rewritten coverage of *Pesticides and Pest Control*, *Water Resources*, and *Zoological Gardens*. Almost 3,000 additional articles were revised along with 1,893 bibliographies. The coverage of *Weather* has been reorganized, and an array of illustrations regarding impending weather has been added. Expanded health-related articles include *Antioxidants*, *Autoimmune Diseases*, *Hypertension*, *Smoking*, *Sports Medicine*, and *Virus*. Deaths noted include those of Roy Campanella, Cesar Chavez, Lillian Gish, and Frank Zappa. However, Eoraptor, the dog-sized dinosaur fossil found in Argentina, is not mentioned.

AAE's illustrations include excellent tables, graphs, artwork, and maps, besides outstanding photographs. *Aerospace Industry* has an exploded view of the new Boeing 777. Nature has not been kind lately, and AAE added new pictures of the Mississippi basin under *Floods and Flooding* and Hurricane Andrew's devastation under *Hurricane and Typhoon*. Other new photos include an African mask (*Chokwe*), a portrait of Thurgood Marshall, and the Tomb of the Unknowns (*Arlington National Cemetary*). The index, with 201,000 entries, provides access to bibliographies, illustrations, and maps.

ELECTRONIC VERSIONS: AAE was the first encyclopedia to be available on compact disc; the CD-ROM version of the complete set is sold as the *New Grolier Electronic Encyclopedia* (see below). Versions are also available for CDTV, CD-I, and Data Discman. The index to the set is available on CD-ROM as part of the *Grolier Master Encyclopedia Index*, along with the indexes to *Encyclopedia Americana* and *The New Book of Knowledge*. The text is online, updated quarterly, with Prodigy, GEnie, Delphi, and CompuServe (with no illustrations). It can also be leased on tape and mounted on a library network.

CONCLUSION: *Attractive* and *current* describe the *Academic American Encyclopedia*. Especially useful in ready-reference work for its exceptionally current brief-overview articles, it will start many students and researchers on their way.

The New Grolier Multimedia Encyclopedia. Grolier, 1994.

HARDWARE: Versions are available for DOS, Windows, and Macintosh. The Windows version requires a 386 computer, a hard disk with 1.5MB free, 4MB RAM, a VGA monitor (SVGA recommended), a mouse, a Windows-compatible sound card, and headphones or speakers.

HISTORY: First released in a text-only version in 1985 as *The New Electronic Encyclopedia*, the 1990 edition added illustrations and was retitled *The New Grolier Electronic Encyclopedia* [RBB D 15 90]. In 1992, Grolier added sound and video, and the title was changed to *The New Grolier Multimedia Encyclopedia*. The 1995 edition to be published this October will be titled *The Grolier Multimedia Encyclopedia*. It is also sold as *Software Toolworks Illustrated Encyclopedia*.

SCOPE AND TREATMENT: NGME contains almost one million more words than the print set. It has 3,250 still pictures and maps, 80 video clips, and 70 minutes of audio. It has no dictionary. New this year is a list of contributors and their affiliations.

DATABASE STRUCTURE: It is possible to browse article titles or do a keyword search using Boolean operators. In keyword searches, word relationships (same paragraph, ___ of words apart, exact order), and parts of the database to be searched (all, bibliographies, fact boxes, etc.) can be specified. All cross references are hotlinked and using "Search for Selection," a keyword search of the database can be done on any word in an article. Longer articles have outlines which can be used to jump to the appropriate section. "Knowledge Tree" lists articles in a topical hierarchy. Icons for fact boxes, tables, and various forms of media accompany articles. Indexes of pictures, maps, animations, sound, and video can also be searched. New to this release is "Knowledge Explorer," 12 audiovisual essays (with no text) on such topics as Painting and Sculpture and Space Exploration that are each several minutes long. Also new are "Multimedia Maps," sound and animation on maps showing, for example, the spread of prehistoric humans around the world or the growth of the Roman Empire.

CONCLUSION: *The New Grolier Multimedia Encyclopedia* continues to be an attractive and useful reference tool for students in the middle grades and up and for adults. Academic, school, and public libraries will find it a useful source.

Children's Britannica. 20v. Margaret Sutton, editorial director; James Somerville, editor. Encyclopaedia Britannica, 1994. (0-85229-239-2).

HISTORY: This encyclopedia has been published in the U.K. since 1960. The fourth edition, published in 1988, was the first one issued in the U.S.

SCOPE AND TREATMENT: Contributors tend to be British experts. With more than 4,000 articles, the set's strength is in the social sciences and biography (particularly British politicos; Richard Nixon and Al Gore are not included). There are separate entries for counties of the U.K. as well as for U.S. states. American professional sports are particulary lacking in coverage; the only name mentioned in the basketball article is the founder of the game (nine players have brief biographies in the index). Perhaps because of its audience of upper elementary and middle-school children, controversial topics are given little treatment. There is no article on birth control, but a separate AIDS article is new this year.

The extensive index includes thumbnail sketches of people and geographic locations that don't have separate entries in the body of the set. Cross-references are frequent and useful, such as those that point to the treatment of Prince Charles and Princess Diana under *Wales, Prince of*. An atlas in the last volume provides up-to-date maps, especially for Europe.

QUALITY AND CURRENCY: The 1994 copyright marks another year of minor changes. Among the eight new articles are *Dahl, Roald* and *Global Warming*. The new country of *Macedonia* is given about a page of treatment. Four articles were rewritten (e.g., *Magazine, Sun*), 49 extensively revised, and 237 updated in some way. Deaths in 1993 were noted for Arthur Ashe, Dizzy Gillespie, and William Golding, but not for Thurgood Marshall. Coverage is uneven; for example, the Olympic Games are treated up to 1988; Academy Award winners are listed through 1990. *Palestine* has nothing about the peace talks; indeed, it says that the Israeli government refuses to negotiate with the PLO. Coverage of South Africa needs updating, and there is no mention of NAFTA.

Thirty-seven articles were reillustrated this year, and most of the new photographs are in color. However, half the set's illustrations are black and white. Eighteen new maps were added, most of them for republics of the former Soviet Union. There are no bibliographies for further reading.

Writing is simple and objective (although some British topics are treated in too great detail for an American audience). Spelling is American. Volume size is manageable for young hands, and binding and printing are excellent.

CONCLUSION: If you own the 1993 *Children's Britannica*, you probably don't need this year's. Libraries that need a supplementary children's encyclopedia will find this a noncontroversial and usable set.

Collier's Encyclopedia. 24v. Lauren S. Bahr, editorial director; Bernard Johnston, editor in chief. P. F. Collier, 1994.

HISTORY: Published since 1950, *Collier's Encyclopedia* is a "scholarly, systematic, continuously revised summary of the knowledge that is most significant to mankind." The preface states that *Collier's* is aimed at both professionals and nonspecialists, at college and high school students. Until recently, *Collier's* was owned by Macmillan; it was purchased by Editorial Planeta-De Agostini, a consortium of European publishers.

SCOPE AND TREATMENT: *Collier's* contains more than 25,000 entries, some of them quite lengthy. A number of the longer articles, such as *Dance*, *Baseball*, and *Television*, include glossaries, a useful feature unique to *Collier's*. Contributors, who are listed in volume 1, include such distinguished names as Ada Louise Huxtable, who wrote *House Architecture in the United States*, psychiatrist Robert Coles on *Erickson, Erik*, Gay Wilson Allen on *Whitman, Walt*, and Craig Claiborne on *Cooking*. Eighty-eight of the contributors to the 1994 set are new. Almost all entries are signed.

This edition of *Collier's* has approximately 14,450 illustrations, about 30 more than in 1993. This is the fourth year of a program to replace black-and-white illustrations with four-color ones. About 36 percent of the illustrations are in color, up from 28 percent in 1993 and 17 percent in 1991. The appearance of the set is greatly enhanced by these illustrations, although there are still stretches of pages with no illustrations at all. Volume 24 contains a classified bibliography of 11,500 titles and the index. Most entries do not include bibliographies, although it is *Collier's* policy to add reading lists to new, replacement, and revised articles. Bibliographies were added to the new *Telecommunications* article, as well as to several rewritten articles, including *Aerospace Industry*, *Business Machines and Equipment*, and *Camera*. A number of existing bibliographies were revised.

QUALITY AND CURRENCY. The 1994 edition of *Collier's* includes 51 new entries (plus nine capsule biographies), 88 rewritten articles, 1,534 updated or otherwise revised articles, 844 new illustrations, 84 revised maps, and 3 new maps. Among the new articles are *Chemotherapy*, *DNA Fingerprinting*, *Landscape Painting*, and *Reincarnation*. The 24 new biographical entries include *Ashe, Arthur*; *Friedan, Betty*; and *Thomas, Clarence*. Two sections, "The Science of Baseball" and "Women in Baseball," have been added to *Baseball*, which is now 37 pages in length, with 40 four-color illustrations. Among the articles that have been completely rewritten are *Hoover, J. Edgar*; *Exceptional Children*; *Food Additives*; *Science Fiction*; and *Skating*. *Basketball* has been rewritten and totally redesigned and now includes 25 four-color illustrations, as well as such current information as Michael Jordan's retirement. The 15 articles on countries that were formerly part of the Soviet Union have been revised to include developments to mid-1993.

Parts of *Europe* have been extensively revised to reflect developments in the early 1990s. The section on the economy discusses changes in the former Soviet bloc, and there is a new section on European integration. The section on race and ethnicity now emphasizes "genetic unity" rather than "accepted racial types" listed in previous editions. However, the section on European history has not been revised, and ends with the Cold War.

A number of articles have benefitted from the addition of four-color illustrations, including *Dinosaurs*. Seventeen new color illustrations have been added to *Painting*, which at 43 pages, typifies *Collier's* lengthy treatment of some topics. Another is the completely rewritten *Museum*, with 44 color illustrations.

Collier's has done a good job of keeping up with recent changes. For example, there is mention of the floods in Illinois during the summer of 1993, ousted Haitian President Aristide's address to the United Nations in October 1993; the appointment of Ruth Bader Ginsburg to the Supreme Court; the signing of the peace agreement between Israel and the PLO in September 1993; the election of Jean Chrétien as Canadian prime minister in November; the flight of the space shuttle *Discovery* in September; and the attack on the Russian congress building by troops loyal to Yeltsin in October. The deaths of Wallace Stegner, Marian Anderson, General Matthew Ridgeway, and Cesar Chavez are noted, though not that of Thurgood Marshall. However, there is still out-of-date information in *Collier's*. The article on the telephone makes no mention of cellular phones; the latest advance discussed is the introduction of direct distance calling. The article *Deafness* does not mention TDDs. *Audio Visual Instructional Materials* does not mention video. There is no reference to air bags in the list of safety features in *Automobile*. *Consumerism* appears to have had no new information added since the 1970s. *Cold War* seems to be current through 1992, with no mention of the Cold War's end. Some illustrations are out of date. *Civil Defense* still illustrates how to build and stock a basic fallout shelter. However, two of the illustrations the Board mentioned in its review of the 1993 edition, the picture of the chain gang in *Criminology* and one of an old computer in *Banking, Commercial*, have been removed. Instead of the chain gang picture, there is an illustration of a boot camp in the article *Criminal Law*.

CONCLUSION. *Collier's* can present some problems in terms of currency of information. *Immigration* and *Cold War* are typical examples: although current information on both subjects can be found elsewhere in the set, the *Immigration* and *Cold War* articles themselves are misleading. On the other hand, the authoritative information in newly or recently revised articles, the program to add more color illustrations, and the extensive treatment of subjects make *Collier's* worth considering for high school, public, and academic libraries.

Compton's Encyclopedia. 26v. Dale Good, editorial director. Compton's Learning Co., 1994. (0-944262-00-7).

HISTORY: Published for many years by Encyclopaedia Britannica, *Compton's* was bought last year by the Tribune Company. Librarians can purchase *Compton's* from representatives of Marshall Cavendish, Follett Library Book Company, and the Wright Group.

SCOPE AND TREATMENT: Aimed at children in upper elementary grades and up, *Compton's* 5,274 articles are supplemented by another 29,322 brief entries in the *Fact-Index*, the final volume. Longer articles are signed with the contributor's name and credentials. New contributors this year include Karen Collins and Judith Davidson (*Hockey, Field*), both affiliated with the U.S. Field Hockey Association, and Richard Ulack (*Philippines*), department of geography, University of Kentucky. A section at the beginning of each volume, "Exploring Volume . . . ," poses questions and cites the location of answers in each. Some articles include questions for students to consider.

QUALITY AND CURRENCY: This year *Compton's* has 12 new articles in the main text. Seven treat places (most of them in Eastern Europe), and four are biographies (*Dillinger, John*; *Dinesen, Isak*). The other new article, *Dinosaur*, mentions the recent discovery of Eoraptor in South America. This article is heavily illustrated. This year, the editors have added nearly 200 new photographs and drawings and almost 100 new or revised maps. Approximately 65 percent of the illustrations are in full color. Another 165 articles have been replaced or extensively rewritten, for example, *Food and Nutrition* (which includes the new USDA food pyramid), *Mississippi River* (which discusses the 1993 floods), and *Palestine Liberation Organization* (which covers the Israeli-PLO accord). More than 350 additional articles were updated in some way, including AIDS and *European Communities*. *Canada* notes the agreement for a self-governing homeland for the Inuit. *Yeltsin, Boris* notes his dissolution of the Russian parliament in September 1993. The bibliographies generally reflect the audience for this set, as most suggest titles for children and young adults. This year six bibliographies were added to entries that didn't have them previously, and 40 were updated.

Although librarians generally urge users to employ an encyclopedia's index, it is essential for *Compton's* readers to utilize the *Fact-Index*. Not only does this volume provide a guide to the main text, but it includes brief articles on topics not covered there. For example, Roy Campanella and Don Drysdale merit short biographies in the *Fact-Index*, not in the main text. Among the 327 new articles added to the *Fact-Index* this year are biographies of Marian Wright Edelman and Menachem Mendel Schneerson, *Gaia Hypothesis, Infomercial, Maastricht Treaties, North American Free Trade Agreement*, and *Shock Radio*. Among the more than 70 *Fact-Index* entries updated are 20 Midwest cities to note the 1993 flood. Deaths are noted in *Fact-Index* entries for William Golding, Helen Hayes, and Thurgood Marshall. There are many tables in the *Fact-Index* as well, such as those listing presidential cabinets (and that of Jefferson Davis), concise properties of chemical elements, members of athletic halls of fame, and lists of countries' rulers. New tables this year include "Major Computer Languages," "Solar Eclipses," and "Rock and Roll Hall of Fame."

There are some shortcomings to *Compton's*. The letter-by-letter arrangement may be confusing to young readers accustomed to word-by-word alphabetization. The article *Library* has an added section with information about online catalogs and other electronic sources, but this information needs to be incorporated into the rest of the article. Given the prominence of the gay rights movement, it is surprising that *Compton's* does not have an article on homosexuality. It is discussed under "Sexual Orientation" in the article *Sexuality*, and there is a one-sentence definition in the *Fact-Index*, but with no recognition of the political and social issues surrounding gays and lesbians. A few articles (*Opera, Nursery Rhyme*) still have a dull appearance because of their illustrations.

ELECTRONIC VERSIONS: *Compton's* is available in several electronic formats. *Compton's Interactive Encyclopedia*, for Macintosh and Windows (see below), sold to consumers; *Compton's MultiMedia Encyclopedia*, for Macintosh, DOS, and Windows, sold to schools; and *Compton's Interactive Encyclopedia* for the CD-I player and the Sega CD-ROM player. In addition, the text is available online through America Online, updated annually.

CONCLUSION: Up-to-date and attractive, *Compton's* is a sound purchase at a reasonable price for public and school libraries. Consumers may also find it a useful addition to a home library.

Compton's Interactive Encyclopedia. Compton's Learning Co., 1995.

HARDWARE AND SOFTWARE REQUIREMENTS: The Windows version requires a 386 computer (486 recommended), Windows 3.1, 4MB RAM (8MB recommended), SVGA monitor, mouse, speakers or headphones, and Sound Blaster or 100% compatible sound card. A Macintosh version will be available later this year.

HISTORY: Released in 1989 as *Compton's MultiMedia Encyclopedia*, this was the first multimedia encyclopedia [RBB Je 15 90]. A version under that title is still sold to schools, accompanied by three teacher's guides with lesson plans, suggested assignments, worksheets, and answer keys. It also has science feature articles not found in CIE. It is available in a DOS version ($99) as well as Windows and Macintosh versions.

SCOPE AND TREATMENT: CIE has more than 33,000 articles, 7,000 pictures, 100 videos and animations, and 14 hours of sound, plus a dictionary. *Star Trek's* Patrick Stewart serves as guide to CIE in an introductory video tour. He also appears when the Explain button is touched.

QUALITY AND CURRENCY: This new release has a totally redesigned interface. The screen has three windows. Their functions vary somewhat, but generally one is used for formulating the search, one displays the article, and the third is the media viewer. Each window can be blown up to full screen. All directions appear on the screen; there are no pull-down boxes. Icons accompany many articles, leading to maps, pictures, sound, and video. Icons are also provided for "quick facts," related articles from the print set's Fact-Index. Cross references within articles are hotlinked, so one need only click on them to go the related entry. Outlines can be invoked for lengthy articles, so the reader can jump to the appropriate part of the entry.

DATABASE STRUCTURE: CIE has many forms of access. "Contents" searches on article, picture, movie, sound, and table titles. You can also specify a particular medium (movies, for example) and browse through a list of titles. "Idea Search" searches on keywords but has no Boolean capability. "Topic Tree" provides a hierarchical arrangement of article titles under topics and subtopics. The "Timeline" has two visual displays of events, one for the world, the other for the U.S. "Info Pilot" leads from one article to related ones. If pursued too far, it gets off track. For example, searching on South Africa, there are four choices, one of which is Durban. Clicking on that, there are four more related articles, one of which is Alan Paton. Clicking on Paton, the choices include other people with the first name Alan. "Explore" is a large picture with labeled parts, such as Dictionary, Atlas, Timeline, etc. Clicking on the appropriate part of the picture is another way to get to these features. The atlas allows one to zoom in and out, but maps are not very detailed. The only place labeled on Maine, for instance, is the capital. When the dictionary is invoked, a box opens in which the word is typed. Definitions can also be accessed by clicking on a word in an article.

MULTIMEDIA FEATURES: One special feature is "Slide Shows," collections of pictures on a topic. "Editing Room" allows users to bookmark various items in the encyclopedia and create their own multimedia presentation.

CONCLUSION: The new interface for Compton's Interactive Encyclopedia should prove to be very attractive to children. The many means of access to text and media will keep them interested for hours. Elementary and middle school libraries and public libraries will want to consider this new version of CIE.

Encyclopedia Americana. 30v. Lawrence T. Lorimer, editorial director; Mark Cummings, editor. Grolier, 1994. (0-7172-0125-2).

HISTORY: The Encyclopedia Americana was first published 1829–33. The current 30-volume format appeared in 1920. Grolier acquired Americana in 1945 and has revised it annually since then.

SCOPE AND TREATMENT: Americana is written for secondary school students and adults. Although international in scope, its coverage of American and Canadian subjects is especially strong. The current edition contains 52,000 entries and 23,000 illustrations, 17 percent of which are in color. Most articles are signed. There are 84 new contributors, among them John A. Rock, Emory University School of Medicine (Human Reproduction); Susan Tumarkin Goodman, chief curator of the Jewish Museum (Yaacov Agam); and Marc Redfield, Claremont Graduate School (Deconstruction, Poststructuralism). The editorial advisory board has 17 new members including Emily J. Sano (Asian art), James M. Poterba (economics), and Andrew Colin Renfrew (archaeology).

QUALITY AND CURRENCY: The 1994 edition has 40 new articles, 96 replacement entries, 51 major revisions, and minor revisions to 500 entries. In addition, bibliographies accompanying 401 other entries have been updated. Four new maps have been added, and 28 others have been revised. More than 170 photographs, 87 in color, have been added. New articles include biographies of Stella Adler, Jacob Lawrence, Ruth Bader Ginsburg, and Satyajit Ray. African American Religion, Semiotics, and Structuralism in both literary theory and anthropology are new topics in the humanities. Current political developments are represented by the articles European Community, North American Free Trade Agreement, and Maastricht Treaty. Replaced articles include Dead Sea Scrolls, Fundamentalism, Political Science, and Public Health. The replacement articles Archaeology and Furniture are well-illustrated, comprehensive overviews of the historical developments and current trends in these areas. Some subjects have been divided and covered in separate articles, Cancer, Oncology, and Tumors; Diet and Nutrition. These would be more useful if combined into single entries.

Current events are well treated for the most part. The signing of the North American Free Trade Agreement and START II Treaty, the attempted impeachment of Boris Yeltsin, and new heads of state in Canada and South Korea are noted. The accord between Israel and the PLO is covered in the article on Israel, but not in the PLO entry. South Africa notes the end of apartheid, but elections are not mentioned. The end of El Salvador's civil war and the continued fighting in Bosnia are covered. The deaths of Thurgood Marshall, Cesar Chavez, Wallace Stegner, and Marian Anderson are noted.

There are still many articles that need updating. Population figures for many countries and cities are old: Spain, 1974; Turkey, 1977; Stockholm, 1970. Population figures from the 1991 Canadian census have still not been added to text (they are found on map indexes). Historical coverage of many countries stops in the early 1980s. Entries for German states, cities, and natural features still locate them in either East or West Germany. Prague is identified as the capital of Czechoslovakia. The computer article talks about punched cards. Sexually transmitted diseases are still called venereal diseases. Outdated statistics are found in Fluoridation and Foundation. Sound Recording and Reproduction goes into great detail about the process of making records but doesn't mention CDs.

Americana illustrations are mostly black and white. Although color pictures have been added, the quality, especially of the art reproductions, is mediocre. Many photographs of places are outdated. A diagram of the female reproductive tract illustrating the article on the menstrual cycle is unfortunately placed on the next page facing an article on mental illness. The overall layout and appearance of the set is gray and old-fashioned. The Americana index is comprehensive and easy to use. Maps and illustrations are indexed.

ELECTRONIC VERSIONS: In addition to the print index, this encyclopedia is indexed in the Grolier Master Encyclopedia Index, a CD-ROM product for DOS, Windows, or Macintosh computers. This tool indexes The New Book of Knowledge and the Academic American Encyclopedia in addition to Americana. It is easy to use and offers online help screens for assistance. Users may browse the entire index alphabetically, search by specific subject, or combine terms using Boolean operators and parentheses. Truncation is also permitted. This index is easier to use with a mouse than with keyboard commands. It is a useful tool for libraries that own all three encyclopedia sets, although each set reaches a different group of readers. Grolier has announced that next year the full text of Americana will be released on CD-ROM.

CONCLUSION: The Encyclopedia Americana offers comprehensive coverage of North American history and culture, the arts, and humanities, but it needs to improve its currency with further revision and provide a more contemporary layout with better-quality illustrations. Americana is now produced with an electronic publishing system. The Board hopes that this will result in better revision of the set, including eliminating the awkward pagination resulting from added and deleted material.

Funk & Wagnalls New Encyclopedia. 29v. Leon L. Bram, editorial director; Norma H. Dickey, editor in chief. Funk & Wagnalls, 1994. (0-8343-0094-X).

HISTORY: Funk & Wagnalls, published since 1912, is available to the public through "book-a-week" programs in supermarkets, and to schools and libraries through World Almanac Education.

SCOPE AND TREATMENT: F&W is intended as a resource for junior and senior high school students and nonspecialist adults. Most of the 25,000 articles are brief and unsigned. Lengthy, signed articles go into greater depth on countries, social and economic issues, and historical periods. The brief essays "How to Use the Library" and "How to Write a Term Paper" are followed by a bibliography section, in which more than 9,000 annotated entries are grouped into more than 1,500 reading lists.

QUALITY AND CURRENCY: Seven biographies (including Margaret Drabble, Stephen King, and H. Norman Schwarzkopf) and 13 other new articles (Wallawalla Indians, Social Darwinism) were added to this edition; nearly 2,000 articles were revised. For the most part, deaths (Arthur Ashe, John Hersey, Albert Sabin) and other events through the first few months of 1993 have been noted. German reunification is noted at the beginning of Germany, but changes since 1990 are primarily dealt with under Germany, West. Many of the history sections in entries on countries have undergone extensive revision. Telecommunications mentions E-mail and Compuserve, but not the Internet. The advent of electronic publishing goes unnoticed in Dictionary and Book Trade, though Encyclopedia acknowledges its existence.

Thirty-six of the 300-plus Hammond maps have been updated. The small page size continues to force some tight double-page spreads as well as very small maps for some countries. It's interesting to note, however, that the maps do provide greater detail, with more cities, towns, and geographic features, than those in Encarta, the multimedia encyclopedia based on F&W. Articles on West Germany and the USSR contain maps of reunited Germany and "Russia and neighboring countries," respectively.

Almost half of the 9,000-plus illustrations and photographs are now in color, including all birds and flowers as of this edition. Charts, tables, diagrams, and highlighted lists (geologic time scale, wind patterns, Oscar winners, state economic profiles) are used when appropriate. The bibliography in volume 28 provides useful reading lists organized by number; longer encyclopedia articles conclude with references to the appropriate numbered reading list(s). The bibliography needs content headings, as noted in the last RBB review. Each numbered list must be studied to determine its focus; after looking at several titles, list 606, for example, appears to be a bibliography of cookery.

The index, q.v. cross-references within article text, and see references at the ends of articles provide adequate access to F&W.

ELECTRONIC VERSIONS: The text of F&W was licensed by Microsoft for use in *Encarta* (see below). This fall another multimedia encyclopedia based on F&W will be released, *Infopedia*, from InterActive Publishing.

CONCLUSION: F&W will meet the needs of many encyclopedia users in the home and school, and at a bargain price.

Microsoft Encarta Multimedia Encyclopedia. CD-ROM. Microsoft, 1994.

HARDWARE AND SOFTWARE REQUIREMENTS: A 386SX or faster PC, Windows 3.1, a VGA monitor, a sound card, and speakers or headphones. Four MB of RAM recommended. A Macintosh version is also available.

HISTORY: Microsoft first published *Encarta* in early 1993 [RBB Ag 93].

SCOPE AND TREATMENT: *Encarta*'s target audience is ages nine to adult. Many of its 26,000 articles are taken from *Funk & Wagnalls New Encyclopedia*, but additional content is written by the *Encarta* editorial staff. The disc also contains a dictionary and a thesaurus that are always available on a pull-down menu, an atlas, and a time line of world history. Microsoft takes full advantage of the multimedia possibilities of CD-ROM technology, with more than 8,000 color photographs and graphics, as well as animations, videos, charts, and sound clips. "Highlights" gives a tour of some of the most interesting media segments. "MindMaze" is a fun single or multiplayer quiz game based on and linked to *Encarta* entries.

QUALITY AND CURRENCY: *Encarta* has 170 new articles, including 39 new biographies (including Hillary Rodham Clinton, Shaquille O'Neal, Mae Jemison, and others not in the print set). The publisher says that revisions were made to 25 percent of the topics. Any omissions in F&W are likely to be missing from *Encarta* as well, though with another group of editors at Microsoft, there are differences. Although *Encarta* notes the September 1993 Israeli-PLO accords, which occurred too late for inclusion in this year's F&W, its table listing Oscar winners is current only through 1991 (through 1992 in F&W). F&W notes terrorist attacks at the Uffizi and the World Trade Center bombing, but *Encarta* does not. *Encarta*'s illustrations were all added by Microsoft, and there are usually more per article than in F&W.

DATABASE STRUCTURE: Several search options are available. Click on "Contents" and you get a picture of an encyclopedia lined up A to Z, a traditional approach that allows the user to type in a request. If the request does not match any items in the alphabetical listing of articles, another search technique should be used. The "Find Wizard" is the most flexible, allowing Boolean searching, truncation, and use of proximity operators in the full text of the database. The "Gallery" comprises all illustrations, animation, sound, and video; a search in "Gallery Find" (which can be limited by format and/or broad subject area) will retrieve multimedia items, which have links to articles. Finally, the "Category Browser" has nine broad subject areas, each of which is further divided.

Some media items, such as sample license plates and pictures and song clips of state birds, are not easily identified unless one knows that the information is there. For instance, although there is a picture and good-quality audio clip of a chickadee in several state fact boxes, a "Gallery Find" search on *chickadee* results in no hits, and the "Find Wizard" gives seven text hits, omitting the occurrence of *chickadee* in the state fact box for Massachusetts. "Gallery Find" discovers the word *license* as part of the credits for a number of music clips, but not for state plates. Another problem, which should be easy to correct by making appropriate hotlinks, is that all gallery items relevant to a particular subject are not obvious when looking at the article text. For instance, the entry on Andy Warhol provides an image of "Marilyn Diptych" but does not indicate the famous Campbell's Soup can found in *Painting*. Only eight media items come up when reading about Mozart, but "Gallery Find" brings up 23, most of them sound clips. An animated sequence showing basic steps in social dance appears within *Dance*, but there is no way anyone reading the articles *Popular and Social Dance, Tango,* or *Waltz* would know it exists.

Cross-references in the electronic world of *Encarta* take the form of some 300,000 hotlinks. *Encarta* editors have added 275,000 cross references to the *q.v.* and *see* references provided by F&W. Simply click on a text word, map location, bibliographic entry, or author name that appears in red to see more information on that item.

MULTIMEDIA FEATURES: The maps in *Encarta* are much less detailed than those found in print encyclopedias; no latitude or longitude is indicated. Only major cities and landmarks are included; the map of Maine, for example, names only 17 places and physical features. There are 798 maps in all, with 25 new urban maps (Cairo, New York City, Seoul).

Eight hours of high-quality audio clips include phrases for 60 languages (14 new to this edition), music from traditional Ashanti to Verdi to George Jones, and the voice of Martin Luther King. Animation, video, and illustrations have accompanying sound, too. More than 100 video and animation segments, such as an interactive earth-moon orbit simulation, news footage of a hurricane, and honeybee dances, provide data in a way that transcends any written description.

Articles, maps, and pictures can be copied to the clipboard and incorporated in a report (with proper credit, of course). "Slide shows" of favorite images and charts comparing the climate or population of up to four states can be created. A teacher's activity guide and accompanying literature increase *Encarta*'s usefulness for schools.

CONCLUSION: A large part of *Microsoft Encarta*'s appeal is in its slick format and multimedia features. Hours can and will be spent clicking away in *Encarta*. It is recommended for school and public library use.

The New Book of Knowledge. 21v. Lawrence T. Lorimer, editorial director; Gerry Gabianelli, editor in chief. Grolier, 1994. (0-7172-0525-8).

HISTORY: In 1908, the topically arranged *Children's Encyclopedia*, the first major encyclopedia for young readers, was published in Great Britain. A U.S. version was published from 1910 until 1965 as *The Book of Knowledge*. Since 1966, *The New Book of Knowledge* has been arranged alphabetically.

SCOPE AND TREATMENT: More than 1,800 experts have contributed to the encyclopedia. Among the 28 new contributors to the 1994 edition are Robert W. Noyes, Harvard professor of astronomy (*Sun*); Marvin Schwartz, lecturer at the Metropolitan Museum of Art (*Furniture*); and Stanley Atkinson, chairman, A.A.U. Gymnastics Committee (*Gymnastics*). Most articles in NBK are signed by contributing authors, reviewers, or both; a list of these people appear at the end of volume 20.

Written primarily for children ages 7 to 14, NBK combines information relevant to both the elementary school curriculum and the after-school interests of children. NBK highlights areas of interest with special boxed "wonder questions," such as "Why do leaves change color in the autumn?" (*Plants*) or "Was Mother Goose a real person?" (*Nursery Rhymes*). NBK also excels at illustrating such projects as "How to Build a Kaleidoscope." A clear strength is the set's coverage of children's hobbies with articles on airplane models and jacks. Also unique is its frequent inclusion of such literature as Kipling's *The Elephant Child* or an excerpt from *Peter Pan*. Given NBK's broad coverage, two areas continue to be weak: contemporary children's authors and such controversial topics as abortion and animal rights. Biographical coverage of children's authors clearly emphasizes classic writers and a few contemporary standouts such as Maurice Sendak and Beverly Cleary, but ignored are contemporary favorites such as Peter Spier and Patricia MacLachlan. NBK does address some controversial topics in a factual and balanced manner. For example, *Racism* and *Prohibition* were added in 1994. However, it also covers others, like abortion, in a minimal fashion and totally ignores gambling.

QUALITY AND CURRENCY: In 1992, NBK editors began a major five-year revision project that is significantly changing the content, design, and illustrations of the set. For this edition, the letters E, F, N, P, and S were substantially rewritten. In addition to creating a more contemporary encyclopedia, this project will result in the elimination of the brief dictionary entries located in a separate index at the end of each NBK volume and the creation of more short articles. This improves access by integrating entries into the main alphabetical sequences of the encyclopedia. Biographies are the exception to this trend to more direct access. Brief biographical profiles are more frequently being placed within topical articles that provide relevant in-context information. For example, rather than being listed under their last names, John Jacob Astor is found under *Fur Trade in America*, and current Supreme Court Justices are included in *Supreme Court of the United States*. However, many new separate biographies were added this year, including Robert Penn Warren, Jane Goodall, and Malcolm X.

Thirty-five articles are new this year, including *Kurds, Persian Gulf War,*

Encyclopedia Summary Chart, 1994

Encyclopedia	Approximate entries	Pages	Approximate illustrations	School & Library Price, 1994*
Academic American Encyclopedia (21v.)	28,975	9,896	17,000	$719
Children's Britannica (20v.)	4,200	6,832	14,417	$369
Collier's Encyclopedia (24v.)	25,00	19,878	14,450	$999
Compton's Encyclopedia (26v.)	5,274 29,322 (Fact-Index)	10,692	22,510	$395
Encyclopedia Americana (30v.)	52,000	26,740	23,000	$999
Funk & Wagnall's New Encyclopedia (29v.)	25,000	13,056	9,500	$250
The New Book of Knowledge (21v.)	9,097	10,576	24,600	$679
The New Encyclopedia Britannica (32v.)	65,000	32,000	23,800	$1,099 until Sept. 30; $1,299 thereafter
New Standard Encyclopedia (20v.)	17,497	10,926	12,000	$549.95
The World Book Encyclopedia (22v.)	17,050	14,124	28,000	$559

*Prices exclude shipping and handling costs.

and *Protozoans*. The 44 replaced articles include *Arkansas*, *Earthquakes*, *Endangered Species*, and *Solar Energy*. Another 36 articles were heavily revised, including *Races, Human* and *Soccer*. In addition, 309 articles were updated in some fashion. In this edition, 778 new photographs, 159 pieces of color artwork, and 54 new maps were added. More than 90 percent of NBK illustrations are in color, and the editors estimate one-third of the set is devoted to illustrations.

In the 1994 edition, the death of Marian Anderson, the November congressional approval of NAFTA, and the December repair of the Hubble Space Telescope are noted. The Israeli-PLO agreement is mentioned. However, the majority of NBK is written so that it does not appear to grow out of date quickly. Families looking for an encyclopedia that will benefit their children during elementary school may benefit from this approach, while librarians will find NBK less useful for quick reference questions.

The paperback *Home and School Reading and Study Guides* is included with the set. The reading guide is a subject bibliography of further readings, which can be used with children of varying reading abilities. The study guide is an overview of school curriculum for parents and teachers of children in kindergarten through ninth grade. It lists articles within NBK that can be used with children at given ages and subject areas. Also included is *Teaching Basic Reference Skills with . . . The New Book of Knowledge*.

ELECTRONIC VERSIONS: The index to NBK is available on CD-ROM as part of the *Grolier Master Encyclopedia Index*, along with the indexes to *Academic American Encyclopedia* and *Encyclopedia Americana*.

CONCLUSION: With excellent and attractive articles, the academic and recreational information needs of school-age children are authoritatively and reliably answered in *The New Book of Knowledge*. Children through middle school, as well as their parents, teachers, and librarians, will find it a valuable reference source.

The New Encyclopaedia Britannica. 32v. 15th ed. Robert McHenry, editor in chief. Encyclopaedia Britannica, 1994. (0-85229-591-X).

HISTORY: First published in 1768–71, *The New Encyclopaedia Britannica* is the oldest and largest encyclopedia in English. Published in America since 1900, the set adopted its three-part arrangement with the fifteenth edition in 1974. With the 1985 printing, the current arrangement was established: the 12-volume *Micropaedia*, shorter articles suitable for ready reference; the 17-volume *Macropaedia*, 672 scholarly articles that range from 2 to 309 pages; the one-volume *Propaedia*, an outline of knowledge; and a two-volume index.

SCOPE AND TREATMENT: Sold around the world, Britannica has less of an American bias than other American encyclopedias. The most scholarly of any general encyclopedia, it is aimed at educated adults, college students, and advanced high-school students.

QUALITY AND CURRENCY: The *Micropaedia* features 64,351 articles, 153 of them new this year. Another 1,088 articles were rewritten or revised. The publisher notes that more than 350 pages alone were handled to account for the dissolution of Czechoslovakia. New entries include *Chronic Fatigue Syndrome*, *Czech Literature*, *Higgs Particle*, *Renormalization*, *Strong Nuclear Force*, and *Velociraptor*. Interestingly, 15 of the new entries are dinosaur-related topics. The *Sporting Record* entry has at long last been updated, with all tables covering through 1992 or 1993. Biographies are a strength in the *Micropaedia*, accounting for about 35 percent of the entries. New entries this printing include *Abu Nidal*; *Dahl, Roald*; *Durocher, Leo*; *Ginsburg, Ruth Bader*; *Hesburgh, Theodore M.*; *Ramos, Fidel*; and *Theroux, Paul Edward*.

The *Micropaedia* had 82 color, 42 black-and-white photographs, and 6 new maps added. Only slightly more than 25 percent of its illustrations are in color. The lack of color is particularly evident in the *Micropaedia*'s art entries. That for Lyonel Feininger describes his "lyrical use of colour," yet has a black-and-white reproduction. Although the majority of entries in the *Micropaedia* do not have bibliographies, this year's revision features five new and 189 revised bibliographies.

The 1994 *Macropaedia* features one new article: *Materials Science*. In addition, 10 entries have new text, 27 are revised, and another 142 underwent minor changes. *Czech and Slovak Republics* is among the articles with new text. While there is a separate article *Slovakia* in the *Micropaedia*, the new *Macropaedia* article was obviously written to fill the space taken up by the old *Czechoslovakia*. There is no *see* reference under *Slovakia* in the *Macropaedia*. All entries are signed and feature extensive bibliographies. This year's printing has 45 new contributors, all from academic backgrounds. Some articles in the *Macropaedia* are above the reading level of most high school students. The entry *Protists*, for example, mentions that they "embrace a number of forms of syncytial (coenocytic) or multicellular composition, generally manifest as filaments, colonies, coenobia . . . or thalli."

CD-ROM Summary Chart, 1994

CD-ROM	Print Title	System	Price*	Online
Britannica CD	New Encyclopaedia Britannica	Windows	$995	Internet
Compton's Interactive Encyclopedia	Compton's Encyclopedia	Windows	$149.95	America Online
Microsoft Encarta	Funk & Wagnalls New Encyclopedia	Windows Macintosh	$99.95	NA
The New Grolier Multimedia Encyclopedia	Academic American Encyclopedia	DOS Windows Macintosh	$259 DOS; $149.95 Windows and Macintosh	Dow Jones Compuserve GEnie Prodigy
The World Book Multimedia Encyclopedia	The World Book Encyclopedia	DOS Windows Macintosh	$395 ($99 with purchase of print set)	NA

*Prices here are list prices. Most CD-ROMS are sold in retail stores and prices may vary.

Some of the revised articles reflect up-to-the-minute technology. *Computers* includes mention of the Pentium chip and multimedia. *Information Processing and Information Systems* mentions the Internet. On the other hand, though the publisher cites the entry *Enyclopaedias and Dictionaries* as being updated with this printing, the article mentions that Grolier "has proposed to make its [*Academic American*] complete computerized text available to anyone subscribing to certain data-transmission services, such as *The New York Times' Information Bank.*" In fact, *Academic American* has been available online for some time, and the *Information Bank* has been defunct for years. Other articles and bibliographies are still in need of updating. The entry *Growth and Development* cites nothing after the 1970s in its bibliography. *Sex and Sexuality* still does not mention AIDS. *Telecommunications Systems* refers to "push-button dialing now being introduced." The *Macropaedia*, like the *Micropaedia*, does not have an abundance of illustrations, though Britannica has been increasing their number slowly. The 1994 printing features 51 new photographs (28 in color) and seven new maps. Approximately one-third of the *Macropaedia's* illustrations are in color.

The *Propaedia* was updated in accordance with changes throughout the set but is not likely to see much use in libraries. With more than 231,000 entries and more than 720,000 cross-references, the two-volume index remains an essential part of *Britannica*, given the set's divided arrangement. The *Britannica Book of the Year/Britannica World Data*, in addition to the standard coverage of events of the past year, also gives updated statistical information on the countries of the world. Unfortunately, the volume often contains important information not incorporated into the main set. Subjects such as the floods in the Midwest, the signing of the NAFTA agreement, the Group of Seven's economic assistance to the former Soviet republics, and the issue of homosexuals in the military are all dealt with solely in the *Book of the Year*.

The combination of what are essentially two separate sets plus a yearbook, which is virtually a requirement for up-to-date information on countries, results in a work that may leave users confused as to where to turn first. Although one would expect the *Micropaedia*—since it is more easily updated—to contain more current information than the *Macropaedia*, this is not always the case. Mention of both the Internet and the discovery of the dinosaur Eoraptor, for example, are found solely in the *Macropaedia*.

ELECTRONIC VERSIONS: The *Britannica Electronic Index*, a CD-ROM index to the set, offers several searching capabilities beyond the printed index. The user may perform an "Idea Search" using phrases or Boolean operators, which provides a list of articles in order of probability that they contain the requested information. One drawback to this search is that the user must search either the *Micropaedia* or *Macropaedia* individually. The "People, Places, Things" search will list terms by those search options. The "People" search will allow one to search by geographic/ethnic/religious association as well as by activity. Unfortunately, these searches provide only a list of terms and not actual volume and page numbers where they may be found, thus necessitating a second search. The *Electronic Index* also allows a user to look up a word from *Webster's Ninth New Collegiate Dictionary*.

Britannica CD. Encyclopaedia Britannica, 1994.

HARDWARE AND SOFTWARE REQUIREMENTS: A 386/25-based PC or higher, Windows 3.1 or higher, a VGA display card and monitor, mouse, 4MB RAM, and 5MB of hard drive space.

SCOPE AND TREATMENT: *Britannica* CD represents the first time that the entire text of *Britannica* is available directly from a CD-ROM, without having to download first onto a hard drive (as is the case with *Britannica Instant Research System* which is on two CDs). *Britannica* has thus become the first of the three large adult encyclopedias to be available in this format. This is strictly a text-only product, with no pictures or sound.

DATABASE STRUCTURE: *Britannica* CD is relatively easy to use. The user may search the *Macropaedia*, *Micropaedia*, or both using the "idea search" retrieval method, which allows the user to type in natural language phrases rather than use a special command language. As such, it is similar to the "idea search" employed by *Compton's* on CD and uses the same SmarTrieve search engine. After the user types in a search, the system responds with a list of article titles ranked from highest to lowest based on their relevance ranking (called "score"). Obviously, many false hits result but with enough looking a relevant hit will usually be found. For example, for the search *America's first compact car*, the user will find the correct answer in the 11th article title listed. (The first article retrieved is on William Powell Lear of Lear jet fame.) Each search term is highlighted in red within the text of the article. One drawback, however, is that for longer articles there is no "go to" feature to go directly to the first highlighted word; instead, the user must scroll through the article. Double-clicking a word within an article will invoke the appropriate definition from the *Merriam-Webster's Collegiate Dictionary*, which is included along with a thesaurus. The dictionary and thesaurus can also be searched independently of the encyclopedia.

More precise searching is available by enclosing the search within parentheses, which will automatically truncate all terms but also will ensure that all terms are present within the article (a Boolean AND). The previous search, for example, yields 50 items, but the search (*com-*

pact car) retrieves only 18. For users who simply wish to find a specific article, the program also allows one to scroll through a list of article titles in either the *Macropaedia* or *Micropaedia*.

Articles may be printed out directly from within the program by clicking the "File" pull-down menu, but downloading is only allowed via the Windows clipboard, which is cumbersome, at best, and requires using the mouse to highlight all text to be copied to the clipboard. A 7-minute instructional video on installing the CD-ROM is included, along with a user's manual. A minor irritation is the inclusion of a "hardware key" that must be attached to the computer's parallel port for the program to run. The user unplugs the printer cable, plugs the device into the parallel port, then plugs the printer into the device. There were no problems with the printer or with any other CD-ROM programs run on the same machine. When trying to invoke the program without the hardware key, an error message was displayed in Windows. This security device is obviously intended to ensure that no pirating occurs, but considering that other CD-ROM products in the same price category as *Britannica* (such as *Contemporary Authors* or the OED) do not use such devices, it seems overly cautious on the part of the publisher to include it.

CONCLUSION: Pote tial purchasers may well wish to wait for version 2.0 of the *Britannica* CD—due to be released late this year or early 1995—which the publisher claims will include graphic elements. However, the video indicates that purchasers of version 1.0 will be entitled to a free upgrade to 2.0, so those who have long waited for *Britannica* to appear on CD need not wait any longer.

New Standard Encyclopedia. 20v. Douglas W. Downey, editor in chief. Standard Educational Corp., 1994. (0-87392-199-2).

HISTORY: Begun in 1910, *New Standard Encyclopedia* expanded to its present 20 volumes in 1989, including for the first time a separate index. It is designed for basic reference use by the general reader from middle school to adult.

SCOPE AND TREATMENT: Most articles are drafted by editorial staff and are unsigned; authenticators review these entries for accuracy. Ten new authenticators were added this year, including Stephen Ambrose of the University of New Orleans (*Eisenhower, Dwight D.*), Charles Brown of the Fermi Accelerator Laboratory (*Nuclear Physics*), and Lewis Gould of the University of Texas (*Johnson, Lyndon B.*).

While most articles are only a few paragraphs in length, multipage coverage is given to such topics as *Astronomy*, *Russia*, and *Television*. Pronunciation is provided for foreign and difficult words. The index contains more than 100,000 entries; in addition, the text volumes contain approximately 13,600 *see* entries and 40,000 cross-references.

QUALITY AND CURRENCY: Of the set's nearly 17,500 articles, 101 are new. These include *Animal Rights Movement*, *Electronic Mail*, and *New Age* plus biographical articles on such individuals as Jean Chrétien, Kim Campbell, Hillary Rodham Clinton, Michael Jordan, Janet Reno, and Clarence Thomas. Typical rewritten articles (37 in all) include AIDS, *Bosnia*, and *Electronic Eavesdropping*. Among the 38 articles with extensive revision are *Canada* (*Government & History*), *Euthanasia*, and *Johnson, Lyndon B.* In addition, more than 1,400 articles were updated in some way, such as changing population figures for countries, revising the areas of all 50 states to reflect a resurvey, and expanding and reillustrating the Academy Awards table.

Other events of the previous year are unevenly covered. The article *Flood* indicates that in 1993 10 Midwestern states were ravaged by flooding from the Mississippi River and its western tributaries. The signing on December 17, 1992, of the North American Free Trade Agreement is recorded. The only mention of homosexuals in the military is not in *Homosexuality* but in *Clinton, William Jefferson*. Readers searching for treatment of terrorism may begin by scanning the 27-line overview in *Terrorism*, then looking elsewhere for "attacks by right-wing extremists on foreigners" (*Germany*) and the bombing of *Uffizi Gallery* and its partial reopening. The attempted impeachment of Yeltsin is not covered, nor is the signing by Bush and Yeltsin in Moscow of the START II nuclear arms pact in January. The renewed unrest in Cambodia and the return of Sihanouk as its king is covered. There is no mention of the fact that by 1999 the Canadian government plans to give the Inuit a new territory, Nunavut. The deaths of many notable personalities—Willy Brandt, Dizzy Gillespie, Lillian Gish, Helen Hayes, John Hersey, Thurgood Marshall, Rudolf Nureyev, General Matthew Ridgway, and Albert Sabin—are duly recorded.

More than 160 bibliographies, usually including titles for adults and children, were updated this year. Titles from the 1980s and 1990s predominate throughout the set. Seventeen maps were added. Revisions were made on 79 maps, and there are 409 new color illustrations (e.g., *Canada*, *Flowering Plants*, *Furniture*, *Motion Pictures*). The publisher continues to update illustrations and to increase the use of full color, which now is found in 37 percent of the illustrations.

CONCLUSION. *New Standard Encyclopedia* provides basic factual information on a large variety of topics and continues to be a good source for home or library use by middle- and high-school students and adults.

The World Book Encyclopedia. 22v. Ed. by Dale W. Jacobs. World Book, 1994. (0-7166-0094-3).

HISTORY: First published in 1917, *World Book* aims to present information "in the most accessible and usable form." Its primary audience is students through the high-school level, though adults will find it useful, too. For general information needs, librarians everywhere will attest to its efficacy.

SCOPE AND TREATMENT: One strength of *World Book* is its readability and appropriateness for users at all levels. Its interesting visual presentation, which includes 24,000 color and 5,000 black-and-white illustrations (time lines, photos, diagrams, art) and 2,300 maps, gives this encyclopedia great appeal.

More than 3,900 scholars and experts serve as contributors, authenticators, reviewers, and consultants. Among this year's 193 new contributors are Richard Frankel of California Polytechnic State University and Brian Schwartz of Brooklyn College and the American Physical Society (*Magnetism*), Graham Fraser of the Toronto *Globe and Mail* (*Campbell, Kim* and *Chrétien, Jean*), and Laurel Rasplica Rodd of Arizona State University (*Japanese Language* and *Japanese Literature*).

The final volume, the *Research Guide/Index*, has 150,000 index entries, 200 reading and study guides (suggested paper topics and bibliographies), and brief articles on speaking, writing, and researching. Liberal use of cross-references between articles saves extra index checking for many information searches. *See also* references within articles and "Related Articles" lists at the end of many articles enhance *World Book*'s usability.

QUALITY AND CURRENCY: *World Book* does a good job of keeping current. Of its 17,050 articles, 97 are new this year, 288 were extensively revised, and 2,300 were partially revised. New to this edition are *Desktop Publishing*, *Certificate of Deposit*, *Grateful Dead*, *Tyrannosaurus*, *Vietnam Veterans Memorial*, and *Virtual Reality*. Forty-five of the new articles are biographies, including ones for Robert Bly, Benjamin Chavis, Dale Earnhardt, Tony Hillerman, and Garrison Keillor. Extensively revised articles include those on 27 kings, *Compact Disc*, *Laser*, and *Sears, Roebuck and Co.* (which notes the demise of its catalog). Deaths are noted for Cesar Chavez, Dizzy Gillespie, Thurgood Marshall, and others. More than 350 bibliographies were reviewed and revised as necessary, and bibliographies were added to eight articles that didn't have them before. Also, 75 maps were added and 105 were revised. Approximately 450 photographs, diagrams, or other illustrations were added; *United Kingdom*, for example, has many new color photographs. All statistics are reviewed and revised regularly. For example, this year's *World Book* provides the 1994 population estimate and 1999 projection, in addition to the actual 1990 census figure, for the U.S. Every year, one or two special features are included for just that printing. This year an eight-page foldout section on *Endangered Animals* was added as part of the newly revised *Animal* article.

Despite the attention to revision, some need for updating is evident. For example, *Interior Decoration* features outdated furnishings, and *Pioneer Life in America* uses an old-fashioned style of illustration. But general updating of events is good. The World Trade Center bombing is noted in the articles *New York City* and *Terrorism*. The ceding of the Nunavut territory by Canada to Inuit people is noted in *Eskimo*. The Midwest floods and the signing of the agreement between Israel and the PLO are also covered.

ELECTRONIC VERSIONS: *World Book* is available on CD-ROM as *The Information Finder* (see below).

CONCLUSION: *World Book* remains an outstanding encyclopedia for a general audience, with highly engaging and instructive graphics and text.

The World Book New Illustrated Information Finder. World Book, 1994.

HARDWARE AND SOFTWARE REQUIREMENTS: Requirements for the Windows version include a 386 PC with 4 MB RAM, a hard drive with 5 MB available, and a VGA monitor. For the Mac version, a Mac LC with 4 MG RAM running system 6.0.5 and a 12-inch color monitor are necessary (a 14-inch monitor is recommended).

HISTORY: *Information Finder* was first released in 1989 [RBB Je 1 90]. The search software remains virtually the same.

SCOPE AND TREATMENT: The CD-ROM contains all the text of *World Book* and *World Book Dictionary*. This year, for the first time, illustrations have been added to the disc for the Mac and Windows versions. (A DOS version without illustrations is still available.) The Windows version was examined for this review.

DATABASE STRUCTURE: *Information Finder* can be searched by topic and by keyword. Topic searching uses *World Book*'s extensive index; keyword searching looks through every word in the encyclopedia to find exact matches. Boolean operators can be used, as can truncation and proximity searching. After an entry is selected, an outline of it appears to the left of the article on the screen. *World Book*'s 60,000 cross-references are all hotlinked so that users can jump to related articles. Any word in the text of the encyclopedia can be looked up in the dictionary, a fine feature of *Information Finder*. It is also very handy to click between text and maps or pictures or other related text. *Information Finder* now includes 3,000 of the 29,000 pictures from the print set and 260 maps created specifically for this CD-ROM. It is possible to browse through *Information Finder*'s pictures by using the Gallery feature, where all the illustrations have been classified into 37 categories. Also, when doing a keyword search, relevant pictures and maps are listed in the search results list and users can go directly to them, without calling up the related article. Seventy percent of the pictures and all the maps can be printed. Photographs and diagrams have a crisp, high-resolution quality.

CONCLUSION: Though it has fewer paths for accessing information than other CD-ROM encyclopedias, *Information Finder* serves as a great browsing tool, and students will happily print articles, diagrams, and pictures to use in their assignments. The addition of illustrations is an improvement, though the number is small relative to the parent set and to other CD-ROM encyclopedias.

Omnibus Reviews

FACTS, MISCELLANEOUS: TRIVIA BOOKS FOR THE REFERENCE SHELF

by Carolyn Mulac

"Miscellanea," "curiosa," in other words, "trivia." Variously classified as "handbooks," "compendiums," "pocket companions," or "vade mecums," these are the books that occupy the AG or 031 sections of library shelves everywhere. Board games such as Trivial Pursuit, game shows like television's *Jeopardy!* and radio's *Whad'ya Know?* and such columns as "The Straight Dope" and "Harper's Index" all demonstrate our fascination with fact and factoid. Most reference collections, then, will need to acquire at least a few of these titles. Some books considered staples of the general reference collection also might be characterized as trivia books. This article will categorize trivia books under three headings: "Questions and Answers," "Curiosities and Wonders," and "Miscellaneous Facts."

Questions and Answers:

Ask Me Something I Don't Know. By Bill Adler and Beth Pratt-Dewey. Avon, 1993. 201p. paper $4.99 (0-380-76782-1).
The Book of Answers: The New York Public Library Telephone Reference Service's Most Unusual and Entertaining Questions. By Barbara Berliner and others. Prentice Hall, 1990. 311p. $21.45 (0-13-957432-8); paper $9.95 (0-13-406554-9).
Do Penguins Have Knees? An Imponderables Book. By David Feldman. Harper, 1991. 263p. paper $10 (0-06-092327-X).
History's Trickiest Questions. By Paul Kuttner. Dawnwood Press, 1990. 311p. $14.95 (0-911025-10-3); Holt, paper $10.95 (0-8050-2127-2).
How Did They Do That? By Caroline Sutton. Quill, 1984. 332p. paper $9 (0-688-05935-X).
How Do They Do That? By Caroline Sutton. Quill, 1982. 292p. paper $9 (0-688-01111-X).
How Does Aspirin Find a Headache? An Imponderables Book. By David Feldman. Harper, 1993. 269p. $20 (0-06-016923-0).
More How Do They Do That? By Caroline Sutton and Kevin Markey. Morrow, 1993. 256p. $18 (0-688-10129-1).
More of the Straight Dope. By Cecil Adams. Ballantine, 1988. 502p. paper $8.95 (0-345-38111-4).
Return of the Straight Dope. By Cecil Adams. Ballantine, 1994. paper $10 (0-345-38111-4).
Science Trivia: From Anteaters to Zeppelins. By Charles J. Cazeau. Plenum, 1986. 296p. $19.95 (0-306-42353-7); Berkeley, 1992, paper $4.99 (0-425-13306-0).
The Straight Dope. By Cecil Adams. Ballantine, 1986. paper $5.95 (0-345-33315-2).
When Do Fish Sleep? And Other Imponderables of Everyday Life. By David Feldman. Harper, 1989. 260p. paper $10 (0-06-092011-4).
Why Do Clocks Run Clockwise? And Other Imponderables. By David Feldman. Harper, 1987. 251p. paper $10 (0-06-091515-3).
Why Do Dogs Have Wet Noses? And Other Imponderables of Everyday Life. By David Feldman. Harper, 1990. 249p. paper $10 (0-06-09211-0).

This is a popular format for trivia books. Individual questions may be followed by answers, or questions may be printed in one part of the book with the answers in another. At its worst, this type of trivia book is nothing more than a board game in book form. At its best, it can offer a convenient way to locate a bit of information, particularly when the questions are those frequently asked. This is certainly the case with *The Book of Answers*, which is based on questions asked of the New York Public Library's Telephone Reference Service staff. A quick glance through this book is like replaying a day in any reference department. Although the 26 broad subject categories from *American History* to *World History* offer relatively easy access to questions and their answers, a general index is also included. Unfortunately, no sources are indicated for any of the answers given. The authors of *Ask Me Something I Don't Know* contacted more than 70 American institutions, organizations, and tourist attractions and asked for their most frequently asked questions, and, of course, the answers. The entries are arranged alphabetically, from *Alcatraz Island* to *Zero Population Growth*. An index would have been helpful, but the alphabetical arrangement and relatively modest number of entries makes scanning the table of contents easy.

Science Trivia: From Anteaters to Zeppelins offers nearly 400 questions and answers on the solar system, evolution, plants, UFOs, and many other scientific and quasiscientific topics. These are presented in chapters by subject, and there is also an index of subjects and names. *History's Trickiest Questions* is a collection of more than 400 posers that span recorded human history. The first half of the book consists of numbered questions in five categories: *General History*, *World War II and the Nazis*, *Political World*, *Places*, and *Religion*. The second half contains the answers, correspondingly numbered. The questions are quite challenging; there is no indication of sources for the answers. With *How Do They Do That?* Caroline Sutton began a series of books intended to explain wonders past and present. The table of contents lists more than 100 questions, in no apparent order. Then, in the main part of the book, each question is printed with an answer, sometimes brief, sometimes running to more than a page. The questions represent a broad range of topics: business, science, history, the arts, etc. What makes Sutton's works unique among trivia books is the practice of listing under each question the sources for its answer. In many case, more than one source is cited. A fairly detailed index is also appended.

Another author of a popular series of trivia books is David Feldman. In humorously titled collections like *Do Penguins Have Knees?* and *How Does Aspirin Find a Headache?* he addresses the perplexing questions of everyday life, for example "Why does pasta create foam when boiling?" Each collection includes questions on matters animal, vegetable, mineral, and more. Questions and answers are not arranged by subject, but reference use is made easier by the inclusion of an index. Any discussion of trivia books would be incomplete without a mention of Cecil Adams, self-proclaimed "world's smartest human being." There are now three compilations of the "The Straight Dope" column carried by several alternative newspapers. In each, the questions are organized into categories, and their answers run from one paragraph to several. The range of topics represented is broad and often touches on topics not mentioned in family newspapers.

Curiosities and Wonders

The Browser's Book of Beginnings: Origins of Everything under (and including) the Sun. By Charles Panati. Houghton, 1984. 427p. paper $9.95 (0-395-36099-4).
The Guinness Book of Records, 1994. Ed. by Peter Matthews. Facts On File, 1993. 330p. $23.95 (0-8160-2645-9).
Panati's Extraordinary Endings of Practically Everything and Everbody. By Charles Panati. Harper, 1989. 470p. paper $10.95 (0-06-055181-X).
Panati's Parade of Fads, Follies, and Manias: The Origins of Our Most Cherished Obsessions. By Charles Panati. Harper, 1991. 491p. $25 (0-06-055191-7); paper $13 (0-06-096477-4).

These books document the weirdness, wackiness, and even wondrousness of the world. The *Guinness Book of Records* has been the standard work in this category for years. Arranged by broad categories including *Human Achievement*, *Buildings and Structures*, and *Earth and Space*, the longest, tallest, fastest, heaviest, and more are recorded, often accompanied by color photographs. The table of contents breaks down each of the broad categories into more manageable topics; for example, under *Buildings and Structures* one finds *Bridges*, *Canals*, *Tunnels*, *Specialized Structures*, etc. This feature, and the two indexes (name and subject) make it easy to locate the 10,000 records in this latest edition. Charles Panati, "the foremost specialist on everything," is another serial author of trivia books. Since *The Browser's Book of Beginnings*, he has addressed myriad topics dear to the hearts of trivia enthusiasts. *Panati's Extraordinary Endings of Practically Everything and Everybody* is a curious compendium devoted to the demise of famous people, modes of execution, and dreaded diseases. A detailed table of contents sets out every topic and subtopic covered. There is also a fairly detailed index. References for each of the chapters are included between the end of the text and the index. Trivia in a lighter vein is on display in *Panati's Parade of Fads, Follies, and Manias*, which covers popular culture in the U.S. for the last century. Arranged by decade, each of the lengthy chapters covers fads, fairs and expos, dance crazes, popular songs, best-selling books, and, for later periods, radio and television hits. There is a selected reading list to round off this amusing aggregation.

Miscellaneous Facts

Baseballistics. Ed. by Bert Randolph Sugar. St. Martin's, 1990. 387p. paper $16.95 (0-312-03789-9).

The Book of Odds. By Michael D. Shook and Robert L. Shook. Penguin/Plume, 1991. 222p. paper $8.95 (0-452-26692-0).

Facts about the Presidents. 6th ed. By Joseph Nathan Kane. Wilson. 1993. 432p. $55 (0-8242-0845-5).

Famous First Facts. 4th ed. By Joseph Nathan Kane. Wilson, 1981. 1,350p. $80 (0-8242-0661-4).

Five Rings, Six Crises, Seven Dwarfs, and 38 Ways to Win an Argument: Numerical Lists You Never Knew or Once Knew and Probably Forgot. By John Boswell and Daniel Starer. Viking, 1990. 241p. $14.95 (0-670-83240-5); paper $9 (0-14-013195-7).

The Guinness Book of Movie Facts and Feats. 5th ed. By Patrick Robertson. Abbeville, 1991. 240p. $19.95 (1-55859-236-9).

The Guinness Book of Sports Records, 1994–1995. By Mark Young. Facts On File, 1994. 250p. $20.95 (0-8160-2655-6); paper $13.95 (0-8160-2654-4).

The New York Public Library Desk Reference. 2d ed. Prentice Hall, 1993. 836p. $40 (0-671-85014-8).

The Ultimate TV Trivia Book. By Vincent Terrace. Faber, 1991. 207p. paper $13.95 (0-571-12913-7).

What Counts: The Complete Harper's Index. Ed. by Charis Conn and Ilena Silverman. Holt, 1991. 288p. $24.95 (0-8050-1279-6).

The World Almanac and Book of Facts. Ed. by Robert Famighetti. World Almanac, 1993. 976p. $19.95 (0-88687-746-6); paper $8.95 (0-88687-745-8).

The World Almanac of Presidential Facts. Rev. ed. By Lu Ann Paletta and Fred L. Worth. World Almanac, 1993. 256p. paper $10.95 (0-88687-713-X).

To paraphrase Mark Twain quoting Disraeli, there are three kinds of facts: facts, miscellaneous facts, and statistics. Annual rainfall, earned-run averages, presidential nicknames, yards gained, Academy Award nominations: these are the stuff of which reference questions are made. Several of these titles are standard works in reference collections. Miscellaneous facts and tidbits of information about the presidents of the U.S. are the subject of many a reference question, and not only during an election year. Since 1959, one standard source for this information has been *Facts about the Presidents*. With uniformly designed chapters devoted to each president, this is the work to turn to with a presidential query. Though quite comprehensive, *Facts about the Presidents* has some competition in a relatively recent publication, *The World Almanac of Presidential Facts*. Taking a slightly different approach, each presidential chapter is divided into "The Straight Facts" and "The More Colorful Facts," a more informal and personal account, including nicknames, astrological signs, favorite foods, and the like. The "Intriguing Miscellaneous Facts" section includes a list of who played the presidents in the movies and on television.

Another traditional title in general reference collections is *Famous First Facts*. Outstanding in its organization, it contains extensive cross-references and no less than four separate indexes (years, days of the month, personal names, and geography). *The World Almanac and Book of Facts* is another staple—it is hard to imagine answering reference questions without it. Everything from the proper gift for wedding anniversaries to the date of Easter 2001 to the capital of any nation can be found in this compact volume.

Although there are quite a few sports statistics in the *World Almanac*, there are not enough to satisfy the seemingly insatiable need for such numbers. Baseball fans in particular are on a constant quest for the most obscure figure. *Baseballistics* is the title to turn to for an answer to those queries. Although there is no index per se, the table of contents is so descriptive that locating notable numbers is an easy task. Superlatives are practically synonymous with the name *Guinness*, and for still more sports statistics there is *The Guinness Book of Sports Records*. Sports from aerobatics to yachting are represented in this handy volume. Another topic subjected to the *Guinness* treatment is the cinema. *The Guinness Book of Movie Facts and Feats* documents many firsts, longests, and most expensives in statistics and anecdotes. Indexes by name, movie title, and subject and special lists of several kinds add to the box-office value of this production. Television trivia buffs can match baseball fans in their zeal for a particular fact. *The Ultimate TV Trivia Book* is a treasure trove of more than 10,000 bits of trivia. It covers shows from the 1940s to the 1990s. Cast lists, (TV) addresses and telephone numbers, pet names, family members, and many other points of interest along with a general idea of the story line are provided for more than 300 television shows.

As every reference librarian knows, there is virtually no limit to the number of subjects covered in a typical workday's worth of reference questions. *The New York Public Library Desk Reference* is organized around 26 broad subject categories that will ring familiar to any reference generalist, for example, *Symbols and Signs*, *Time and Dates*, *Useful Addresses*. Specific topics found in each of those categories are included in the detailed table of contents. There is also a general index. Another source of familiar material is *Five Rings, Six Crises, Seven Dwarfs, and 38 Ways to Win an Argument*. Consisting entirely of lists that will stir up many a schoolday memory, this indexed book is fun to browse. Where else would you find Nixon's Six Crises and the Seven Wonders of the Ancient World in one volume? "What are the odds that . . . ?" is an often-asked question. *The Book of Odds* is another browsable (read: no index) book of statistics expressed in percentages. Its 13 chapters highlight some of the favorite topics of contemporary conversation, for example, crime, sports, sex. Sources are indicated for each of the statistics quoted.

Not only regular readers of the magazine will be familiar with the "Harper's Index," since it is reprinted in a number of newspapers. Each month this single page of statistics is offered as a measure of what Lewis H. Lapham calls "the drifting tide of events." *What Counts: The Complete Harper's Index* is a compilation of the first seven years of the index. The editors have created 81 categories organized into 10 broad sections similar to a typical high-school curriculum (e.g., social studies, science, home economics). In addition to this easily scanned arrangement is a fairly detailed index. The editor's introduction and the foreward by Lapham offer some background information on the way the index is compiled each month. A list of sources corresponds to the 81 categories used.

There are numerous trivia titles of local and narrow interest: cities, states, sports, television programs, and films are some of the most popular subjects covered. Individual reference collections will need to seek these out and add them when appropriate.

Carolyn Mulac is assistant head of the Information Center at the Chicago Public Library.

Omnibus Reviews

AMERICAN ETHNICITY: RECENT SOURCES

by Arthur S. Meyers

"My fellow immigrants"—this was the way FDR began an address to the Daughters of the American Revolution. A nation of immigrants, we have an opportunity to become better informed about our rich diversity through excellent reference resources.

The following list consists of titles published since 1991 that have broad, popular appeal, particularly for class assignments. With a few outstanding exceptions, the list does not include bibliographies, guides to the literature, and specialized works. In the 1990s, a redressing of past neglect is shown in the publication of more titles on people of color and less emphasis on ethnic groups of European origin. RBB published a list of ethnic travel guides [Ap 15 94]; special lists appeared on ethnic resources on black, Asian, and Hispanic Americans [Jl 90] and on Native Americans [Je 1 & 15 93].

Multicultural Sources

Against Borders: Promoting Books for a Multicultural World. By Hazel Rochman. ALA, 1993. paper $18.95 (0-8389-0601-X).

An insightful examination of the universality of literature for young people through essays and annotated bibliography, showing the richness of our transnational fabric.

American Ethnic Literatures: Native American, African American, Chicano/Latino, and Asian American Writers and Their Backgrounds. By David R. Peck. Salem, 1992. $40 (0-89356-685-5). [RBB Ap 15 93]

Although primarily an annotated bibliography, this important reference tool will also provide secondary and undergraduate students with the historical and social context for understanding different literary traditions.

Encyclopedia of Multiculturalism. 6v. By Susan Auerbach. Marshall Cavendish, 1993. $449.95 (1-85435-670-4). [RBB My 1 94]

In no other resource is so much information gathered that recognizes and celebrates the nation's diversity, thus recommending this set highly for middle- and high-school libraries and public libraries.

Ethnic NewsWatch. CD-ROM. Softline Information, 1991– . $1,360–$3,689 (separate price schedules for school, academic, and public libraries). [RBB My 15 94]

Full-text access to local, national, and international news in ethnic and minority newspapers and magazines which capture the broad range of the nation's diversity.

Guide to Multicultural Resources, 1993/1994. Ed. by Charles A. Taylor. Highsmith, 1993. $49 (0-917846-18-4). [RBB F 15 94]

A useful work for all types of libraries—lists 3,000 organizations, associations, resources, and government agencies covering African American, Asian or Pacific American, Hispanic American, Native American, and multicultural sources.

Multicultural Projects Index: Things to Make and Do to Celebrate Festivals, Cultures, and Holidays around the World. By Mary Anne Pilger. Libraries Unlimited, 1992. $35 (0-87287-867-8). [RBB N 15 92]

A valuable compilation of 15,000 projects for elementary and middle-school teachers to incorporate into the curriculum, and for students using public libraries to choose for school projects.

The Multicultural Student's Guide to Colleges: What Every African-American, Asian-American, Hispanic, and Native American Applicant Needs to Know about America's Top Schools. By Robert Mitchell. Farrar/Noonday, 1993. $25 (0-374-52362-2). [RBB N 15 93]

A wide range of information to help minority students make wise decisions about schools, such as scholarships, academic support services, and ethnic studies programs.

Multiculturalism in the United States: A Comparative Guide to Acculturation and Ethnicity. Ed. by John D. Buenker and Lorman A. Ratner. Greenwood, 1992. $55 (0-313-25374-9). [RBB Je 1 92]

Essays on the historical, social, political, and psychological factors affecting Native Americans and Americans of African, German, Irish, Scandinavian, Polish, Jewish, Italian, Chinese, and Mexican descent.

Our Family, Our Friends, Our World: An Annotated Guide to Significant Multicultural Books for Children and Teenagers. By Lyn Miller-Lachmann. Bowker, 1992. $44.95 (0-8352-3025-2). [RBB My 1 92]

An excellent, useful annotated bibliography.

Videos for Understanding Diversity: A Core Selection and Evaluative Guide. By Gregory I. Stevens. ALA, 1993. paper $31.50 (0-8389-0612-5). [RBB N 1 93]

Bibliographic information, evaluation, and suggestions on classroom use for academic, public, and secondary school libraries.

African American Sources

African American Biographies: Profiles of 558 Current Men and Women. By Walter L. Hawkins. McFarland, 1992. $39.95 (0-89950-664-X). [RBB Ag 92]

Readable essays on persons in a variety of fields, who are either currently living or who died since 1968, but who have not always been nationally known.

African American Biography. 4v. Gale, 1994. $112 (0-8103-9234-8). [RBB Ap 1 94]

Profiles of 300 persons, past and present, for middle- and high-school students, in the *African American Reference Library* (which includes *African American Chronology*, below, and the recently published *African American Almanac*).

African American Chronology. By Alton Hornsby and Deborah Gillan Straub. Gale, 1994. $55 (0-8103-9231-3). [RBB F 15 94]

The author's *Chronology of African-American History: Significant Events and People from 1619 to the Present* (1991) was designed for adults, while the new work is aimed at middle-school students.

African American Encyclopedia. 6v. Ed. by Michael W. Williams. Marshall Cavendish, 1993. $479.95 (1-85435-545-7). [RBB Jl 93]

With 2,900 entries encompassing several thousand years and a wide range of topics, this comprehensive, well-written work will be useful in high-school, public, and college libraries.

America's Black & Tribal Colleges. By J. Wilson Bowman. Sandcastle, 1994. paper $19.95 (0-883995-02-7). [RBB O 15 94]

A handy, inexpensive guide to the 100 historically and/or predominantly African American institutions and 24 American Indian colleges.

Black American Colleges & Universities: Profiles of Two-year, Four-year, & Professional Schools. Ed. by Levirn Hill. Gale, 1994. $55 (0-8103-9166-X). [RBB O 15 94]

Detailed profiles of 118 colleges that are traditionally or predominantly black.

Black Americans: A Statistical Sourcebook. Ed. by Louise L. Hornor. Information Publications, 1994. $50 (0-929960-16-5). [RBB My 15 93]

Tables of data, drawn mostly from government publications, are useful for comparative purposes.

Black History Month Resource Book. Ed. by Mary Ellen Snodgrass. Gale, 1993. $34.95 (0-8103-9151-1). [RBB N 1 93]

A useful compilation of activities for schools and public libraries, arranged in such subject areas as math, sewing, fashion, and storytelling, to enrich curriculum and community programming.

Black Women in America: An Historical Encyclopedia. 2v. Ed. by Darlene Clark Hine and others. Carlson, 1993. $195 (0-926019-61-9); paper, Indiana Univ., 1994. $49.95 (0-253-32774-1). [RBB My 1 93]

A resource for high-school, public, and academic libraries on 800 women who have played a national role or typify the contributions of women in local communities, as well as organizations, educational institutions, organizations, and topics important in our history.

A Century of Musicals in Black and White: An Encyclopedia of Musical Stage Works by, about, or involving African Americans. By Bernard L. Peterson. Greenwood, 1993. $85 (0-313-26657-3). [RBB Ja 1 94]

A comprehensive, accessible work on the tremendous impact of African Americans on the musical stage.

My Soul Looks Back, 'Less I Forget: A Collection of Quotations by People of Color. Ed. by Dorothy Winbush Riley. HarperCollins, 1993. $27.50 (0-06-270086-3); paper, Feb. 1995, $12 (0-06-272057-0). [RBB N 15 93]

This first collection of quotations by African Americans and other people of color is timely and useful for a wide variety of users, recommending it to all types of libraries.

Notable Black American Women. Ed. by Jessie Carney Smith. Gale, 1992. $75 (0-8103-4749-0). [RBB Ap 15 92]

Broadly representative geographically, historically, and professionally, these sketches convey the past and present contributions of 500 women in our history, many of whom are unknown.

Asian American Sources

Asian Americans Information Directory. Ed. by Karen Backus and Julia C. Furtaw. Gale, 1992. $75 (0-8103-8332-2; ISSN 1059-2458). [RBB Mr 1 92]

Similar to earlier Gale directories on black and Hispanic Americans, this volume covers 19 nationalities, with a wide range of information and easy access, making it useful for public and academic libraries.

Japanese American History: An A-to-Z Reference from 1868 to the Present. Ed. by Brian Niiya. Facts On File, 1993. $45 (0-8160-2680-7). [RBB N 1 93]

Valuable for high-school, public, and academic libraries, this informative work will add to the general community's knowledge of the contributions of this group in our history, as well as the challenges they have faced.

Statistical Record of Asian Americans. Ed. by Susan B. Gall and Timothy L. Gall. Gale, 1993. $89.50 (0-8103-8918-5). [RBB O 15 93]

This compilation of data from a wide range of U.S. government publications and other sources provides a comprehensive portrait of the group.

Who's Who among Asian Americans. Ed. by Amy Unterburger. Gale, 1994. $75 (0-8103-9433-2). [RBB O 1 94]

Gale has published similar biographical dictionaries for black and Hispanic Americans.

Hispanic/Latino American Sources

Handbook of Hispanic Cultures in the United States. 4v. Ed. by Nicolas Kanellos and Claudio Esteva-Fabregat. Arte Publico, 1994. $200/set or $60/vol. (1-55885-074-0). [RBB My 15 94]

Separate authoritative volumes of essays on history, literature and art, anthropology, and sociology cover historical contributions and contemporary issues.

Hispanic Americans: A Statistical Sourcebook. Ed. by Louise L. Hornor. Information Publications, 1994. $50 (0-929960-17-3). [RBB My 15 93]

Draws data mainly from federal government sources, putting the information into easily accessed tables, so trends can be identified and comparisons made with the total population.

The Hispanic-American Almanac: A Reference Work on Hispanics in the United States. By Nicolas Kanellos. Gale, 1993. $99.50 (0-8103-7944-9). [RBB Ap 15 93]

A unique compendium of information on the background, history, and contributions of the 22 million people who make the U.S. one of the largest Spanish-speaking countries. Thus the book is an essential purchase for high-school, public, and academic libraries.

The Hispanic Presence in North America: From 1492 to Today. By Carlos M. Fernandez-Shaw. Facts On File, 1991. $45 (0-8160-2133-3). [RBB Ap 15 92]

Originally published in Spain in 1987, this work records the influence of Spain and persons of Hispanic descent on the U.S. Primarily arranged by region, it is useful in high-school, public, and academic libraries.

Notable Hispanic American Women. Ed. by Diane Telgen and Jim Kamp. Gale, 1993. $59.95 (0-8103-7578-8). [RBB O 15 93]

This outstanding resource chronicles the achievements of more than 300 women from the eighteenth century to the present and will be useful in all libraries.

Statistical Record of Hispanic Americans. Ed. by Marlita A. Reddy. Gale, 1993. $89.50 (0-8103-8962-2). [RBB O 15 93]

Data drawn mostly from government publications is displayed in tables.

U.S. Latino Literature: An Essay and Annotated Bibliography. By Marc Zimmerman. MARCH/Abrazo Press, 1992. $10.95 (1-877636-01-0). [RBB Je 15 92]

While primarily an annotated bibliography on writers since the 1970s, a long essay on Latino literature makes this inexpensive book useful for libraries where there is growing interest in the field.

Native American Sources

The American Indian: A Multimedia Encyclopedia. CD-ROM. Facts On File, 1993. $295 (0-8160-2835-4). [RBB Je 1 & 15 93]

Incorporates the contents of four Facts On File publications plus 1,000 images and maps.

The Encyclopedia of Native American Religions. By Arlene Hirschfelder and Paulette Molin. Facts On File, 1992. $45 (0-8160-2017-5). [RBB My 15 92]

Religious ceremonies, biographies of leaders and missionaries, and summaries of major court cases make this readable work important for most academic and public libraries and many high schools.

The Native American Almanac: A Portrait of Native America Today. By Arlene Hirschfelder and Martha Kreipe de Montano. Prentice Hall, 1993. $25 (0-671-85012-1). [RBB Ja 15 94]

A comprehensive guide to understanding how the cultural, social, and political world of Native America developed.

Native Americans Information Directory. Ed. by Julia C. Furtaw. Gale, 1993. $69.50 (0-8103-8854-5). [RBB Je 1 & 15 93]

Information on 4,500 organizations, agencies, institutions, programs, and publications.

The Native North American Almanac. Ed. by Duane Champagne. Gale, 1994. $95 (0-8103-8865-0). [RBB My 1 94]

Historical and current perspectives, maps, photographs, a chronology, directory information, a biographical dictionary of 500 persons, a glossary, and a bibliography make this a valuable addition.

Statistical Record of Native North Americans. Ed. by Marlita A. Reddy. Gale, 1993. $89.50 (0-8103-8963-0). [RBB O 15 93]

Similar to the volumes on black and Hispanic Americans.

Arthur S. Meyers is library director at the Hammond (Indiana) Public Library.

Omnibus Reviews

ENVIRONMENTAL REFERENCE SOURCES

by Betty Nibley

Earth Day, UNCED, *eco-feminism, ecotourism, ecowarriors, ecogophers, biodiversity, the environmental literacy movement*—these terms have all become part of our vocabulary. As Vice President Al Gore stated in the foreword to Environmental Profiles, "Happily, a new way of thinking about our responsibility to the global environment is gaining momentum. Young people today think this is the number one issue facing the world, and the community of nations is beginning to move toward a commitment of following sustainable patterns of development."

To meet this commitment, it is important for libraries to collect a wide variety of materials in this area. Due to the amount of environment-related material in print and electronic form, this list is limited to reference works published in the 1990s for adults and young adults. Although the list is arranged by format, an effort was made to provide coverage of as many environmental topics as possible. Many of the works, especially atlases, dictionaries, and encyclopedias, treat a broad spectrum of topics. Others are more specialized, treating only one aspect of the environment, such as recycling, environmental education, consumer behavior, or wildlife.

Directories and Sourcebooks

Conservation Directory. National Wildlife Federation, 1968– . $18 (ISSN 0069-911X).

An annual guide to U.S. and Canadian agencies, national, and international organizations. The latest edition includes a useful list of electronic sources on the environment.

Environmental Profiles: A Global Guide to Projects and People. Garland, 1993. 1,083p. $125 (0-8153-0063-8).

A comprehensive global directory of environmental organizations. Provides names, addresses, and program descriptions for government, NGO, private, and university programs.

Gale Environmental Sourcebook: A Guide to Organizations, Agencies, and Publications. Ed. by Karen Hill and Annette Piccarelli. Gale, 1992. 688p. $75 (0-8103-8403-5).

In addition to organizations, agencies, and publications, includes awards, honors, and prizes, a glossary, a list of endangered and threatened wildlife and plants, EPA national priorities, and Superfund sites.

The Greenpeace Guide to Anti-environmental Organizations. By Carl Deal. Odonian Press, 1993. paper $5 (1-878825-05-4).

Designed to unmask organizations that appear to be "green" but whose actions have proven otherwise. Funding sources included.

Official World Wildlife Fund Guide to Endangered Species of North America. 2v. By David W. Lowe and others. Beacham, 1990. 1,258p. $195 (0-933833-17-2); v.3, 1992. 546p. $85 (0-933833-29-6); v.4, 1994. 690p. $85 (0-933833-33-4).

Issued by the World Wildlife Fund and the Nature Conservancy, volumes treat habitat, appearance, behavior, biology, conservation status, and date species added to list. Volume 3 updates through 1991; volume 4 has species added to the list since 1991. Good color photos.

World Directory of Environmental Organizations: A Handbook of National & International Organizations & Programs. 4th ed. By Thaddeus C. Trzyna and Roberta Childers. California Institute of Public Affairs, 1992. 232p. paper $45 (0-912102-97-7).

Published in cooperation with the Sierra Club and the International Union for the Conservation of Nature (IUCN), this book includes more than 2,600 organizations in 200 countries and lists landmark events and "who's doing what" on more than 50 environmental issues.

WorldWIDE Directory of Women in Environment. 5th ed. WorldWIDE Network, 1331 H St. NW, Ste. 903, Washington, DC 20005, 1992. 468p. $22.50.

A unique directory devoted to identifying key women contacts in the environmental field throughout the world.

Bibliographies

The Environmentalist's Bookshelf: A Guide to the Best Books. By Robert Meredith. G. K. Hall, 1993. 272p. $40 (0-8161-7359-1).

Guide to 500 "best books" on the environment, based on a questionnaire sent to a variety of professionals. Books published from the turn of the century to 1990. Good for collection development and readers' advisory services.

The Island Press Bibliography of Environmental Literature. Comp. by Joseph A. Miller and others. Island, 1993. 396p. $48 (1-55963-189-9).

Comprehensive annotated bibliography covers almost every major environmental topic. More than 3,000 entries, mainly from the 1980s, include books, periodicals, conference proceedings, report literature, abstracts, and databases.

Reading about the Environment: An Introductory Guide. By Pamela E. Jansma. Libraries Unlimited, 1993. 252p. paper $27.50 (0-87287-985-2).

Nonspecialist's guide to popular magazine articles and books on environmental issues with annotations that note "especially noteworthy entries" as overview, scholarly, or factual.

Dictionaries and Encyclopedias

Concise Oxford Dictionary of Ecology. Ed. by Michael Allaby. Oxford, 1994. $35 (0-19-211699-4); paper $12.95 (0-19-286160-3).

Many entries derived from the *Oxford Dictionary of Natural History*. Plant and animal physiology, animal behavior, pollution, conservation, climatology, meteorology, and oceanography included in short citations.

Dictionary of Environment and Development: People, Places, Ideas, and Organizations. By Andy Crump. MIT, 1993. 272p. $40 (0-262-03207-4); paper $16.95 (0-262-53117-8).

Treats environmental protection and economic development. Entries include organizations, treaties, persons, and events from a nonspecialist's point of view.

Dictionary of Environmental Quotations. Comp. by Barbara K. Rodes and Rice Odell. Simon & Schuster, 1992. 335p. $30 (0-13-210576-4).

More than 3,700 diverse quotations collected from ancient to modern writers arranged chronologically in 143 categories.

Dictionary of Environmental Science and Technology. By Andrew Porteous. Wiley, 1992. 420p. $29.95 (0-471-93544-1).

To be "dipped into, as well as read straight through." Selected terms from the fields of ecology, economics, sociology, technology, physics, and chemistry. Basic definitions and data.

Dictionary of the Environment. 3d ed. By Michael Allaby. New York Univ., 1991. 304p. $75 (0-8147-0591-X); paper $18.50 (0-8147-0597-9).

Originally published in 1977, the third edition has been updated to include more nuclear terms. Agencies, organizations, and legislation included. Brief entries.

The Encyclopedia of Environmental Studies. By William Ashworth. Facts On File, 1992. 470p. $60 (0-8160-1531-7).

Covers a wide range of disciplines, especially chemistry, biology, geology, and ecology. For laypersons, public libraries, and undergraduate studies.

The Encyclopedia of the Environment. Ed. by Ruth A. Eblen and William R. Eblen. Houghton, 1994. 800p. $49.95 (0-395-55041-8).

Nontechnical essays by 350 specialists on topics relating to humans and their relationship to their environment. Brief historical reviews of legislation, biographies, and an overview of organizations.

Environment Encyclopedia & Directory. Europa; dist. by Gale, 1994. 381p. $325 (0-946653-94-1).

Serves as an international directory, a glossary of environmental terms, a bibliography, and a who's who of environmental contacts.

Environmental Encyclopedia. Ed. by William P. Cunningham. Gale, 1993. 981p. $195 (0-8103-4986-8).

Covers a broad spectrum of environmental issues for the layperson in 1,200 articles varying in length from a paragraph to two pages. Biographical sketches and environmental organizations with addresses.

The Environmentalists: A Biographical Dictionary from the 17th Century to the Present. By Alan Axelrod and Charles Phillips. Facts On File, 1993. 258p. $45 (0-8160-2715-3).

Six hundred biographical sketches of people and organizations, including those from earlier centuries.

The Facts On File Dictionary of Environmental Science. By L. Harold Stevenson and Bruce Wyman. Facts On File, 1991. 294p. $24.95 (0-8160-2317-4).

Easy-to-read definitions taken from a wide variety of publications. Stresses nontechnical scientific aspects of environmental science.

The Green Encyclopedia. By Irene Franck and David Brownstone. Prentice Hall, 1992. 486p. $35 (0-13-365685-3); paper $20 (0-13-365677-2).

Excellent source of information on environmental issues, events, and laws for people of all ages. Packaged well for easy lookup. Includes action guides useful for term-paper topics.

McGraw-Hill Encyclopedia of Environmental Science & Engineering. 3d ed. Ed. by Sybil P. Parker and Robert A. Corbitt. McGraw-Hill, 1992. 749p. $84.50 (0-07-051396-1).

Most material taken from the *McGraw-Hill Encyclopedia of Science and Technology* or its yearbook. Some articles have been updated.

Atlases

Atlas of the Environment. By Geoffrey Lean and Don Hinrichsen. ABC-Clio, 1994. 192p. $39 (0-87436-768-9).

An updated version of an atlas published by Prentice-Hall in 1990. Subjects include demographics, social issues, literacy rates, land issues, disasters, and more. Good color illustrations. Some statistics more up-to-date than others.

Atlas of United States Environmental Issues. By Robert J. Mason and Mark T. Mattson. Macmillan, 1991. 252p. $90 (0-02-897261-9).

A physical and political overview of wetlands, forests, air, water, toxic waste, energy, parks and wildlife, agriculture, and environmental politics. Substantial essays, maps, photos, and graphs in clear colors. Oversize pages.

The Conservation Atlas of Tropical Forests: Asia and the Pacific. By N. Mark Collins and others. Simon & Schuster, 1991. $95 (0-13-179227-X).

More than 50 color maps and current statistics from government agencies, the United Nations, and the World Bank. Includes text on "closed canopy" forests.

The Conservation Atlas of Tropical Forests: Africa. Ed. by Jeffrey A. Sayer and others. 282p. Simon & Schuster, $95 (0-13-175332-0).

Background and overview of forests emphasizing conservation, population, agriculture, and timber trade. Color maps, statistics, and tables on individual countries.

Deserts: The Encroaching Wilderness: A World Conservation Atlas. Ed. by Tony Allan and Andrew Warren. Oxford, 1993. 176p. $35 (0-19-520941-9).

Mainly comprises large photographs, maps, and descriptions of the deserts on Earth. Ecosystems, impact on human societies, and challenges for sustainable use.

The Last Rain Forests: A World Conservation Atlas. Ed. by Mark Collins. Oxford, 1990. 200p. $29.95 (0-19-520836-6).

Beautiful color photos. Treats why we need rain forests, the pressures on rain forests such as the impact of logging and cattle ranching, ecology, human population, and the need for cooperation.

Wetlands: A World Conservation Atlas. Ed. by Patrick Dugan. Oxford, 1993. 187p. $35 (0-19-520942-7).

Beautiful color photos, three-dimensional color diagrams of wetland areas, definition of wetlands, and losses. Species index.

Abstracts and Indexes

Environment Abstracts. CIS, 1975– . Also online, on CD-ROM, and on magnetic tape. CD-ROM includes the former Energy Information Abstracts and Acid Rain Abstracts. Prices vary.

Abstracts more than 800 scientific journals plus conference papers and proceedings and selected special reports. Available in a monthly print format, an annual cumulative volume, a CD-ROM updated quarterly, and as Enviroline on Dialog. Many full-text documents available on accompanying monthly microfiche, *Envirofiche*. Contact Congressional Information Service for prices. Previously published by Bowker and EIC/Intelligence.

Environmental Periodicals Bibliography. International Academy at Santa Barbara, Environmental Studies Institute, 1973– . Price varies. (ISSN 0046-2306).

Covers tables of contents of more than 400 international periodicals on human ecology, air, energy, land resources, water, nutrition, and health. Available in print, published six times a year; as EBCD CD-ROM; EBCD Jr., covering the most recent 5 years; and online on Dialog. Popular and scientific journals covered.

Statistical Sources

Environmental Data Report: United Nations Environment Programme. 3d ed. Blackwell, 1991. 408p. $74.95 (0-631-18083-4).

Data on pollution, population, health, ecotourism, climate, waste, natural disasters, and energy. Focuses on international cooperation.

Statistical Record of the Environment. By Arsen J. Darnay. Gale, 1992. 855p. $89.50 (0-8103-8374-8).

More than 850 statistical tables cover pollution and legal and political issues, mainly in the U.S. Most information is from federal and state government documents and periodicals.

World Development Report, 1992: Development and the Environment. Oxford, 1992. 308p. $37.95 (0-19-520877-3); paper $19.95 (0-19-520876-5); diskette, $70 (0-685-59174-3).

Fifteenth in an annual series published by the World Bank. Explores links between economic development and the environment. Includes essays on sustainable development and policy issues, tables, graphs, and statistics.

World Resources. Oxford, 1986– . 400p. $35 (0-19-521044-1); paper $21.95 (0-19-521045-X); diskette $119.95 (0-685-55003-6).

Stresses sustainable development. Background information on water, population, energy, climate, forests, wildlife, food, and statistical data on countries worldwide. The diskette allows user to create worksheets with variables.

Guides, Handbooks, Almanacs

ABC-Clio Companion to the Environmental Movement. By Mark Grossman. ABC-Clio, 1994. 300p. $55 (0-87436-714-X).

Groups, individuals, legislation, and events related to conservation and environmental concerns in the U.S. since 1789 with emphasis on the twentieth century.

Access EPA. U.S. Environmental Protection Agency. GPO, 1993. $24.

The best source for information on the EPA and other publicly accessible sources. Complete directory available online through the Internet. See "Electronic Resources" below.

Contemporary World Issues. ABC-Clio, $39.50 each.
- Environmental Hazards: Marine Pollution. By Martha Gorman. 1993. (0-87436-641-0).
- Environmental Hazards: Toxic Waste and Hazardous Material. E. Willard Miller and Ruby M. Miller. 1991. (0-87436-591-1).
- Global Warming. By David E. Newton. 1993. (0-87436-711-5).
- Energy and American Society. By E. Willard Miller and Ruby M. Miller. (0-87436-689-5).
- Rainforests of the World. By Kathlyn Gay. 1993. (0-87436-712-3).
- Recycling in America. By Debi Kimball. 1992. (0-87436-663-1).
- Wilderness Preservation. Kenneth A. Rosenberg. 1994. (0-87436-731-X).

The Contemporary World Issues series offers similar formats: essay, chronology, biographies, tables, a directory, an annotated list of print sources, nonprint sources including electronic, and subject, author, and title indexes.

The Earth Care Annual. National Wildlife Federation, 1990– . (0-89596-136-3; ISSN 1054-0067).

Dedicated to making this the "Decade of the Environment," documents vivid examples of what has been done throughout the year. Projects include coral reefs, endangered species, garbage, etc. Black-and-white photos.

Earth Journal: Environmental Almanac and Resource Directory. By the editors of Buzzworm Magazine. Buzzworm Books, 1992. 447p. paper $7.95 (0-9603722-9-6).

Inexpensive, popular ready-reference guide covers the year in review, topical entries on such subjects as ecotravel, and a section on regions of the world.

Gale Environmental Almanac. Ed. by Russ Hoyle. Gale, 1993. 684p. $79.95 (0-8103-8877-4).

Authoritative chapters on historical, political, legal, scientific, and media aspects of environmental issues. Good background reading on personalities, issues, and events in the U.S. environmental movement.

Green Index: A State-by-State Guide to the Nation's Environmental Health. By Bob Hall and Mary Lee Kerr. Island, 1991. 162p. $29.95 (1-55963-115-5); paper $18.95 (1-55963-114-7).

Uses 256 indicators to rank each state: air, water, energy, auto abuse, waste, workplace health, farms, forests, fish and recreation, and state initiatives and policies.

Hazardous Substances Resource Guide. Gale, 1994. 510p. $175 (0-8103-8494-6).

Written in clear language for the layperson, identifies hazardous substances in the home, community, and workplace. Profiles of chemicals, chemical names, CAS numbers, and listings for further information.

The Information Please Environmental Almanac. Comp. by World Resources Institute. Houghton, 1992– . annual. paper $9.95 (ISSN 1057-8293).

Excellent annual treats a broad spectrum of national, global, and local environmental issues in essays, graphs, tables, windows of advice, and statistics. A "green cities" rating and more than 140 country profiles.

The McGraw-Hill Recycling Handbook. Ed. by Herbert F. Lund. McGraw-Hill, 1993. $84.50 (0-07-039096-7).

User-friendly handbook directed to individuals who develop recycling programs. All aspects: recyclable materials, processing, and case studies written by experts.

The National Audubon Society Almanac of the Environment: The Ecology of Everyday Life. By Valerie Haras. Putnam, 1994. 304p. $16.95 (0-399-13942-7).

Ecology defined in terms of the body, the home, the community, land and ocean, and culture, with plentiful advice from familiar personalities.

Recycling Sourcebook. Ed. by Thomas J. Cichonski and Karen Hill. Gale, 1993. 600p. $75 (0-8103-8855-3; ISSN 1064-4938).

Essays on recycling household, office, and other waste. Information on starting a recycling program, references to other published sources on recycling, and directory information on approximately 3,000 organizations and on recyclable materials.

Toxics A to Z: A Guide to Everyday Pollution Hazards. By John Harte and others. Univ. of California, 1991. 576p. $75 (0-520-07223-5); paper $30 (0-520-07224-3).

Covers more than 100 toxics found in air, water, food, and products. Balanced treatment and helpful tables.

Miscellaneous

Education for the Earth: The College Guide for Careers in the Environment. 2d ed. Peterson's, 1994. 319p. paper $14.95 (1-56079-407-0).

Profiles more than 350 undergraduate and 240 graduate programs in environmental engineering and design, health, science, environmental studies, and natural-resource management in the U.S. and Canada. Essays discuss careers.

The Green Pages: Your Everyday Shopping Guide to Environmentally Safe Products. Random, 1990. $8.95 (0-67973-130-X).

Based on the idea that individual efforts make a difference, here are supermarket shopper's and mail-order shopper's guides and a guide to environmental issues.

The New Complete Guide to Environmental Careers. By Bill Sharp. Island, 1993. 364p. $29.95 (1-55963-179-1); paper $15.95 (1-55963-178-3).

Job hunting, on-the-job training, and important volunteer programs and internships in environmental protection and resource management.

Opposing Viewpoints. Greenhaven Press. $17.95; paper $9.95.
The Environmental Crisis: Opposing Viewpoints. By Neal Bernards. 1993. 288p. $17.95 (0-89908-175-40); paper $9.95 (0-89908-150-9).
Global Resources: Opposing Viewpoints. Ed. by Matthew Polesetsky. 1991. 264p. $17.95 (0-89908-177-0); paper $9.95 (0-89908-152-5).

The Opposing Viewpoints series from Greenhaven Press reprints magazine articles, books, newspapers, statements, and position papers to help develop reading and critical thinking skills.

Peterson's Job Opportunities in the Environment, 1994. Peterson's, 1993. $18.95 (1-56079-244-2; ISSN 1071-183X).

Employer profiles, strategies for job searching, top companies, industry and geographic indexes, and a directory of associations and government organizations with contacts and expertise needed.

State of the World, 1994: A Worldwatch Institute Report on Progress toward a Sustainable Society. By Lester R. Brown. Norton, 1994.

A serial publication that includes economic information and population and environment policy for nations of the world.

Electronic Sources

Ecolinking: Everyone's Guide to Online Environmental Information. By Don Rittner. Peachpit, 1992. 352p. paper $18.95 (0-938151-35-5).

A handy guide for "econauts." Contains a wealth of information on getting online, networks, bulletin boards (BBS), commercial access, CD-ROMs, and environmental information on the Internet.

A Guide to Environmental Resources on the Internet. By Carol Briggs-Erickson and Toni Murphy.

An invaluable resource. Address on the World Wide Web: Gopher: // una.hh.lib.umich.edu or telnet to the same address.

The Consortium for International Earth Science Information Network (CIESIN).

Offers excellent information for researchers and teachers. Address: gopher gopher.ciesin.org. CIESIN's Classroom Earth offers topics for curriculum development and exchange of ideas. Telnet classroom_earth ciesin.org 2010, login as ce.

The Environmental Protection Agency (EPA).

Offers its Online Library System. Address: telnet epaibm.rt-pnc.epa.gov, login as public,OLS or gopher gopher.epa.gov or ftp // ftp.epa.gov.

The Envirolink Network.

Offers a gopher that leads to EnviroGopher at Carnegie Mellon and to many other excellent sources. Address: telnet envirolink.org, login as gopher.

EcoGopher at UVA.

Has a multitude of choices. Katie, a keyword search of document contents, is a unique and especially useful choice on the menu. Address: gopher: // ecosys.drdr.Virginia.edu.

United Nations Development Programme (UNDP).

Gopher leads to the all-important U.N. Environment Programme (UNEP) gopher. Address: gopher.undp.org. Choose UNEP from the menu.

Newsgroups and listservs offer other ways to communicate. Newsgroups do not require you to join and thus do not clog up your E-mail. Two such groups are sci.environment and clari.tw.environment. A number of listservs are listed in the Murphy/Briggs document (above). ENVINF-L for environmental information and ENVST-L for environmental studies are two of the many listservs that offer subscriptions. To subscribe, send a message to Listserv@HEARN with the message SUBSCRIBE ENVIRON-L [your name], or to Listserv@BROWN with the message SUBSCRIBE ENVST-L [your name].

Betty Nibley is a reference librarian at American University in Washington, D.C.

Omnibus Reviews

REFERENCE SOURCES FOR PERSONS WITH PHYSICAL AND LEARNING DISABILITIES: A SELECTIVE LIST

by Barbara Flynn

Since the passage of the Americans with Disabilities Act in 1990, a wealth of information has become available to help persons with disabilities, their families, employers, and care and service providers. The following is a sample of some of the types of sources available.

Americans with Disabilities Act Handbook. U.S. Equal Employment Opportunity Commission and the U.S. Department of Justice. GPO, 1992. index. loose-leaf $34 (SN 052-015-00074-0).

Provides the text of the ADA and descriptions and interpretations of its provisions. Includes specific information on and illustrations of space, height and width, and other measurement requirements.

Americans with Disabilities Act: Questions and Answers. U.S. Equal Employment Opportunity Commission and the U.S. Department of Justice. GPO, 1992. 32p. paper. free.

Uses a simple question-and-answer format to answer the most-asked questions about the ADA. Includes telephone numbers for ADA information.

Americans with Disabilities Act: Title II Technical Assistance Manual. U.S. Department of Justice, Civil Rights Division, Office of the ADA. GPO, 1992. index. loose-leaf $24.

Focuses on the requirements of Title II, which applies to the operations of state and local government.

Complying with the ADA: A Small Business Guide to Hiring and Employing the Disabled. By Jeffrey G. Allen. Wiley, 1993. 210p. bibliog. index. paper $17.95 (0-471-59051-7).

Designed to help small business owners understand their obligations under ADA, this guide offers detailed information and resources for hiring and employing persons with disabilities.

Disability Rights Guide: Practical Solutions to Problems Affecting People with Disabilities. 2d ed. By Charles D. Goldman. Westport/Media Publications, 1991. 250p. paper $14.95 (0-939644-77-0).

Offers practical information on dealing with everyday problems affecting people with disabilities. Discusses additional barriers, employment, housing, and transportation. Also information on state laws and contracts and a selection on AIDS information sources.

How Libraries Must Comply with the Americans with Disabilities Act (ADA). Comp. by Donald D. Foos and Nancy C. Pack. Oryx, 1990. 168p. bibliog. index. paper $30 (0-89774-760-7).

Provides information on compliance for libraries along with case studies and exercises. Gives legal implications for libraries and lists potential problem areas within ADA.

Legal Rights: The Guide for Deaf and Hard of Hearing People. 4th. Ed. by Sy DuBow. Gaulladet Univ. Press, 1992. 270p. bibliog. illus. index. paper $20 (1-56368-000-9).

A guide to the legal rights and remedies available for the deaf and the hard-of-hearing. Includes addresses of state commissions and councils for deaf and hard-of-hearing people.

A Technical Assistance Manual on the Employment Provisions (Title I) of the Americans with Disabilities Act. 2v. U.S. Equal Employment Opportunity Commission. GPO, 1992. various paginations. index. paper $25 (EEOC-M-1B).

Published in two volumes, this manual covers key legal requirements of the ADA, presented in practical terms. Volume 2 is a resource directory that lists public and private agencies and organizations that provide information on employing people with disabilities.

Accent on Living. quarterly. Cheever, 1956-. $10/y. (ISSN 0001-4508).

Provides news and information in articles aimed at people with disabilities.

Accent on Living Buyer's Guide, 1994-95 Edition. Ed. by Betty Garee. Cheever, 1994. biennial. illus. index. paper $12 (0-915708-35-3).

Catalog of equipment for disabled individuals, including such items as sports equipment and various computer accessories.

AFB Directory of Services for Blind and Visually Impaired Persons in the United States and Canada. 24th ed. American Foundation for the Blind, 1993. 531p. indexes. $75 (0-89128-242-4; ISSN 1067-5833).

Lists thousands of services for education, information, rehabilitation, low vision, and aging, arranged by state or province.

The Complete Directory for People with Disabilities. Ed. by Leslie Mackenzie and Amy Lignor. Gale, 1991. 580p. indexes. $99.95(0-93900-12-5); Grey House, paper $69.95 (0-939300-09-5).

The more than 5,600 entries include institutions (camps, associations, housing); media; products (assistive devices, clothing, computer products); and programs (education, rehabilitation, recreation, and travel). Covers a wide range of disabilities, including mental illness and substance abuse.

Complete Directory for People with Learning Disabilities. Ed. by Leslie Mackenzie. Grey House, 1993. 535p. indexes. paper $125(0-939300-24-9).

Lists almost 6,000 resources, products, books, and services. Includes videos, toys, computer software, camps, employment programs, etc.

Computer Resources for People with Disabilities: A Guide to Exploring Today's Assistive Technology. Comp. by Alliance for Technology Access. Hunter House, 1994. 282p. index. $24.95(0-89793-111-4); paper $14.95 (0-89793-112-2).

Offers information on equipment selection and screening and buying tips. Includes descriptions of software, processing aids, and specialized products.

Disability Information at Your Fingertips: A Guide to Toll-Free Telephone Resources. Disability Resources, 4 Glatter Ln., Centereach, NY 11720-1032, 1994. 13p. paper $3.

Arranged alphabetically by subject/disability, this small but information-packed guide lists toll-free numbers for national organizations providing information about disabilities and disability-related topics.

The First Whole Rehabilitation Catalog: A Comprehensive Guide to Products and Services for the Physically Disadvantaged. By A. Jay Abrams and Margaret Ann Abrams. Betterway, 1990. 240p. bibliog. illus. index. paper $16.95 (1-55870-131-1).

Offers information about independent-living aids and services for disabled individuals, arranged in nine major subject categories. Included in the appendix is information on support groups, independent-living centers, and organizations of general interest.

Living with Low Vision: A Resource Guide for People with Sight Loss. Resources for Rehabilitation, 1993. 271p. index. paper $35 (0-929718-09-7).

Contains information about national organizations, laws, self-help groups, high-tech aids, and services. Designed to help those with sight loss live independently. Updated regularly.

Resource Directory for the Disabled. By Richard Neil Shrout. Facts On File, 1991. 392p. bibliog. index. $45 (0-8160-2216-X).

Sections for the mobility, hearing, and visually impaired list appliances and assistive aids; travel, recreation, and sports opportunities; education; publications, employment and training; computers; and organizations.

Resource Guide for the Disabled. By Gayle Backstrom. Taylor, 1994. 155p. index. paper $10.95 (0-87833-845-4).

An alphabetically arranged overview of 500 resources available for persons with disabilities. Includes practical tips on finding information, making contacts, and getting what one needs once the contacts have been made.

Resources for Elders with Disabilities. Resources for Rehabilitation, 1993. 303p. index. paper $43.95 (0-929718-11-9).

Grouped by specific needs, this book provides information about organizations, services, and assistive devices. Includes information about strokes, osteoporosis, and "everyday living made easier."

The Special Education Sourcebook: A Teacher's Guide to Programs, Materials, and Information Sources. By Michael S. Rosenberg and Irene Edmond-Rosenberg. Woodbine House, 1994. 325p. indexes. paper $21.95 (0-933149-52-2).

Special education resources for the resource specialist, the mainstream teacher, and the parent. Books, periodicals, media, and organizations are listed by disability.

A Woman's Guide to Coping with Disability. Resources for Rehabilitation, 1994. 224p. bibliog. index. paper $39.95 (0-9297 18-15-1).

Comprehensive overview of how disability affects all aspects of a woman's life. Provides information on federal law, housing, and coping at home and in the workplace. Includes information on lupus, diabetes, and epilepsy.

Yes You Can: A Helpbook for the Physically Disabled. By Helynn Hoffa and Gary Morgan. Pharos, 1990. 309p. index. paper $12.95 (0-88687-480-7).

Offers encouragement and information on employment, education, travel, and independent living.

The American Sign Language Dictionary on CD-ROM. By Martin L. A. Sternberg. HarperCollins, 1994. Windows version $69.95 (0-06-279015-3); Macintosh version $69.95 (0-06-279014-5).

Signs for 2,200 words and phrases are provided using text, graphics, audio, and video. Special sections provide ways to test skills by playing a game.

Directory of Disability Media in Canada. Katz Communications, 5877A Park Ave., Montreal, Quebec H2V 4H4, 1992.

A province-by-province listing of journals, serials, and newsletters on disability.

Everyone Can Win: Opportunities and Programs in the Arts for the Disabled. By Anne Allen and George Allen. EPM Publications, 1988. 272p. illus. paper $13.95 (0-939009-09-9).

Explores the importance of the visual and performing arts and how people with disabilities are becoming part of the arts. Includes personal accounts of artists and performers as well as information on VSA ("Very Special Arts"), state organizations, and arts organizations and publications.

Fun and Games: Practical Leisure Ideas for People with Profound Disabilities. By Judy Denziloe. Butterworth/Heinemann, 1994. 153p. bibliog. illus. index. paper $23 (0-7506-0571-5).

A sourcebook of ideas and instructions for helping adults with profound disabilities enter into leisure activities at their level.

Gopen's Guide to Closed Captioned Video. By Stuart Gopen. Caption Database, 1 Walker's Way, Framingham, MA 01701-9640, 1993. 547p. index. paper $29.95 (0-9635726-0-1).

Lists more than 5,000 closed-captioned videos by subject for the hearing impaired.

Random House American Sign Language Dictionary. By Elaine Costello. Random, 1994. 1,067p. illus. $50 (0-394-58580-1).

A compendium of more than 5,600 words and signs. Gives definitions and instructions on how to form the sign. Includes slang and computer terms.

Special Recreations: Opportunities for Persons with Disabilities. By Don W. Kennedy and others. Brown, 1991. 371p. bibliog. illus. index. $32 (0-697-10965-8).

Designed primarily for students preparing for work in special recreation, this text includes information on program and facility planning, camping, competitive sports, and current legislation.

BOSC Directory: Facilities for People with Learning Disabilities. Ed. by Irene Slovak. BOSC, P.O. Box 305, Congers, NY 10920-0305, 1995. 300p. loose-leaf $65 (0-9613860-6-1).

A directory of schools, independent-living programs, colleges, vocational-training programs, and clinics and agencies.

Financial Aid for the Disabled and Their Families, 1992–1994. By Gail Ann Schlachter and R. David Weber. Reference Service Press, 1992. 315p. $35 (0-918276-16-0).

Provides a listing of scholarships, fellowships, awards, grants, loans, and internships for disabled persons and their families. Revised bienially.

Peterson's Colleges with Programs for Students with Learning Disabilities. 4th ed. Ed. by Charles T. Mangrum and Stephen S. Strichart. Peterson's, 1994. 800p. index. paper $26.95 (1-56079-400-3).

Provides information on nearly 1,600 two-and four-year colleges in the U.S. Arranged alphabetically in two sections: colleges with comprehensive programs and colleges with special programs.

Job Hunting Tips for the So-Called Handicapped or People Who Have Disabilities: A Supplement to "What Color is Your Parachute?" By Richard Nelson Bolles. Ten Speed, 1991. 61p. bibliog. illus. paper $5.95 (0-89815-471-5).

Discusses positive ways in which people with disabilities can do job searching while emphasizing that "everyone is employable."

Job Strategies for People with Disabilities: Enable Yourself for Today's Job Market. By Melanie Astaire Witt. Peterson's, 1992. 292p. bibliog. index. paper $14.95 (1-56079-143-8).

Combines career decision-making and job-finding techniques. Includes information on identifying the job market, uncovering marketable skills, matching skills and jobs, and researching job families. Includes self-assessment exercises and information on ADA Technical Assistance Program.

Meeting the Needs of Employees with Disabilities. 2d ed. Resources for Rehabilitation, 1993. 208p. bibliog. index. paper $42.95 (0-929718-13-5).

Provides information on a variety of organizations, assistive devices, and publications. Includes chapters on older workers and persons with chronic conditions.

Able to Travel: True Stories by and for People with Disabilities. Ed. by Alison Walsh. Rough Guides, 1992. 603p. bibliog. paper $19.95 (1-85828-110-5).

Arranged by geographic region, this guide offers information on each country based on the first-hand accounts of travelers with disabilities. Offers solid information and tips for easier travel worldwide.

Access Travel U.S.A.: A Directory for People with Disabilities. By Candida H. Cremona. Creative Hospitality Concepts, P.O. Box 70152-333, Ft. Lauderdale, FL 33307, 1994. 170p. index. paper $19.95 (0-9642279-0-8).

A directory of travel information for travelers with disabilities including information on cruises, hotels and resorts, travel-information sources, ski areas, transportation, and a listing of TTY numbers. Arranged alphabetically by state or service.

Omnibus Reviews

Easy Access to National Parks: The Sierra Club Guide for People with Disabilities. By Wendy Roth and Michael Tompane. Sierra Club, 1992. 404p. bibliog. illus. paper $16 (0-87156-620-6).

Offers specific information for persons with mobility problems, deafness and hearing impairments, and blindness and vision impairments. Begins with the 15 best vacation spots and then lists all other parks alphabetically by region. Also lists parks recreation support groups.

Great American Vacations for Travelers with Disabilities. Fodor's, 1994. 600p. illus. paper $18 (0-679-02591-X).

Details on essential accessibility information are incorporated into the recognized Fodor format. Vacation spots are listed alphabetically. The appendix lists national, state, and city sources of travel information.

Wheels and Waves: A Cruise Ferry, River, and Canal Barge Guide for the Physically Handicapped. By Genie Aroyan and George Aroyan. Wheels Aweigh Publishing, 17105 San Carlos Blvd., Ste. 1-6107, Ft. Meyers Beach, FL 33931, 1993. 179p. illus. index. $19.95 (0-9635698-1-3).

Provides reports on cruise lines, cruise ships, ferries, river cruises, etc., including floor and deck plans for some of the vessels. Worldwide in scope.

Access Foundation for the Disabled

This organization is compiling a list of online sources for the disabled. Send an E-mail message to danyaon@savvy.com for further information.

USENET Groups
misc.handicap, items of interest for and about the disabled.

BITNET Listservs
bit.listserv.blindnws, blindness issues and discussion.
bit.listserv.deaf-l, deafness list.
bit.listserv.l-hcap, disabilities list.

Handicap News BBS
List of bulletin boards for the disabled: 203-926-6168.

Barbara Flynn is director of the Park Forest, Illinois, Public Library.

Omnibus Reviews

REFERENCE SOURCES FOR CHILDREN'S LITERATURE

By Deborah Rollins

What do you recommend for the 10-year-old who asks for "monster books"? For the social studies teacher who needs novels about the Civil War? For the education student seeking reviews of the works of Dr. Seuss? The field of children's literature is so large that finding the best books to answer these and other questions can be difficult. This review describes some important tools on literature for children from preschool through sixth grade that can be used for reference and readers' advisory, curriculum planning, and collection development in elementary-school, public, and academic libraries. It is not comprehensive, particularly in the area of specialized bibliographies, but is an attempt to represent the variety of tools available. RBB will publish a companion list of young adult literature sources in 1996.

Selection Tools

These bibliographies provide subject, author, and title access to thousands of children's books. A limited reference budget may preclude purchase of some of the more specialized titles in this review, but all libraries should purchase at least one of these.

Best Books for Children: Preschool through Grade 6. 5th ed. By John T. Gillespie and Corinne J. Naden. Bowker, 1994. $58 (0-8352-3455-X).
 Lists 15,500 titles, each of which has been recommended in at least two leading review sources. Provides review citations, Dewey numbers, one-line plot descriptions, and extensive subject indexing conveniently divided by grade level. Fiction and nonfiction are arranged by genre or subject.

Children's Books in Print. 2v. Bowker, 1995. annual. $149.95 (0-8352-3593-9).
El-Hi Textbooks and Serials in Print. Bowker, 1995. annual. $139.95 (0-8352-3618-8).
Subject Guide to Children's Books in Print. Bowker, 1995. annual. $149.95 (0-8352-3596-3).
 These bibliographies of materials currently available from publishers contain full citation and price.

Children's Catalog. 16th ed. Wilson, 1991. main volume plus four annual supplements. $90 (0-8242-0805-6).
 Each of the 6,000 entries in the base volume contains complete bibliographic citation, grade level, subject headings, and descriptive and critical annotations; each annual update lists several hundred titles. Nonfiction arranged by Abridged Dewey Decimal Classification; fiction by author. Series titles are provided.

Children's Reference Plus. CD-ROM. Bowker. annual. $595.
 This electronic product includes entries from *Children's Books in Print*, *El-Hi Textbooks and Serials in Print*, and other Bowker bibliographies; from 29 Bowker children's literature reference titles (*Best Books for Children*, etc.); and full-text reviews from 12 journals.

The Elementary School Library Collection: A Guide to Books and Other Media, Phases 1-2-3. 19th ed. Ed. by Lauren K. Lee. Brodart, 1994. $99.95 (0-87272-096-9); CD-ROM, $249 (0-87272-097-7).
 This standard tool covers 12,000 print and nonprint materials for preschool through grade 6. Detailed selection policies are the foundation of this bibliography's authority for use in school library collection development. Provides evaluative comments and content description of each title. Phase notations for each entry indicate suggested priorities for acquisition. Foreign-language, braille, sound, and videocassette versions are noted. Detailed subject index.

Helping Kids Cope

Children who identify with book characters gain insight as they see those characters coping with issues relevant to their own lives. These specialized bibliographies can assist librarians in finding the right read for the right need. Bibliotherapy, the use of books as part of the therapeutic process, is discussed in most of them.

Best of the Bookfinder: A Guide to Children's Literature about the Interests and Concerns of Youth Aged 2-18. By Sharon Spredemann Dreyer. American Guidance Service, 1992. $89.95 (0-88671-440-0); paper $49.95 (0-88671-439-7).
 Detailed annotated entries for 676 titles (mostly fiction) dealing with families, human development, school, and social and behavioral issues. Books, all of which appeared in three earlier volumes of *The Bookfinder*, were published before 1983. Other formats (braille, cassette, talking book) are listed if known.

Books to Help Children Cope with Separation and Loss: An Annotated Bibliography. 4th ed. By Masha K. Rudman and others. Bowker, 1994. $49 (0-8352-3412-6).
 More than 700 fiction, nonfiction, poetry, and folklore titles for ages 3-16 on themes such as illness, death, disrupted friendship, and homelessness are described. Contains useful introductory matter on bibliotherapy and on children's concepts of separation and loss.

Portraying Persons with Disabilities: An Annotated Bibliography of Fiction for Children and Teenagers. By Debra Robertson. Bowker, 1992. $39.95 (0-8352-3023-6).
 Critical annotations of 650 recent titles; also cites the best books from two earlier bibliographies published under the title *Notes from a Different Drummer*. Excellent coverage of health problems; orthopedic, hearing, and visual impairments; emotional disturbances, mental retardation, and learning disabilities.

Portraying Persons with Disabilities: An Annotated Bibliography of Nonfiction for Children and Teenagers. By Joan Brest Friedberg and others. Bowker, 1992. $39.95 (0-8352-3022-8).
 Companion to the above book, this covers 350 nonfiction titles published between 1984 and 1991. Includes AIDS narratives. Earlier edition was called *Accept Me as I Am*.

Sensitive Issues: An Annotated Guide to Children's Literature K–6. By Timothy V. Rasinski and Cindy S. Gillespie. Oryx, 1992. paper $29.95 (0-89774-777-1).
 The introduction discusses various strategies (directed reading, reciprocal questioning, creative writing) in using books to explore sensitive issues. Annotations for fiction and nonfiction titles are arranged in chapters on dealing with divorce, substance abuse, prejudice, moving, and disability.

Survival Themes in Fiction for Children and Young People. 2d ed. By Binnie Tate Wilkin. Scarecrow, 1993. $27.50 (0-8108-2676-3).
 Social/psychological commentary is given here for 300 titles on themes of the individual (e.g., aloneness, feelings, sexuality), pairings and groupings (friendship, peer pressure, families), and world views (environment, religion, politics). Includes programming ideas and related film listings.

Multicultural Awareness

The diversity of cultures and traditions in communities and schools is increasingly well represented in books for children. Readers can gain a deeper understanding of their own and others' heritages through the titles listed in these bibliographies.

Africa in Literature for Children and Young Adults: An Annotated Bibliography of English-Language Books. By Meena Khorana. Greenwood, 1994. $59.95 (0-313-25488-5).
 Nearly 700 books published from 1873 to 1994 are described in this guide. Arranged by genres within geographic regions, the titles, many of which were published in Africa, are evaluated for sensitivity to mul-

ticultural issues. Khorana also authored *The Indian Subcontinent in Literature for Children and Young Adults* (Greenwood, 1991, $55, 0-313-25489-3).

American Indian Reference Books for Children and Young Adults. By Barbara J. Kuipers. Libraries Unlimited, 1991. $25 (0-87287-745-0).

Detailed evaluation criteria used here could be applied for reviews of other materials on Native American cultures. Listed under Dewey numbers, the 200 titles in the annotated bibliography include both children's and young adult selections. The word *Reference* in the title is a misnomer, since most of the books would be placed in a circulating collection.

Books by African-American Authors and Illustrators for Children and Young Adults. By Helen E. Williams. ALA, 1991. $43 (0-8389-0570-6).

Annotated entries on titles with a black perspective published in the twentieth century.

Kaleidoscope: A Multicultural Booklist for Grades K–8. Ed. by Rudine Sims Bishop. National Council of Teachers of English, 1994. paper $14.95 (0-8141-2543-3).

Includes nearly 400 fiction and nonfiction titles published between 1990 and 1992. Titles are grouped by genre, such as poetry, folktales, celebrations, anthologies, and biography, rather than by culture, in order to draw connections between cultures. Subject index.

Literature for Children about Asians and Asian Americans: Analysis and Annotated Bibliography with Additional Readings for Adults. By Esther C. Jenkins and Mary C. Austin. Greenwood, 1987. $49.95 (0-313-25970-4).

Provides an informed discussion of the folk and contemporary literature of each culture, followed by a bibliography of children's books and recommended background readings for adults. Covers folk literature in single tales and collections, picture books, fiction, nonfiction, biography, poetry, and songs of the Chinese, Japanese, Koreans, Filipinos, Vietnamese, Cambodians, Laotians, Thais, Indonesians, and Malaysians.

Multicultural Picture Books: Art for Understanding Others. By Sylvia Marantz and Kenneth Marantz. Linworth, 1994. paper $28.95 (0-938865-22-6).

A description of each book's artistic style, medium, and fit with the story is a major feature of this source. Both traditional literature (e.g., folktales) and stories about contemporary life are included for each world area. Includes many titles not in *Our Family, Our Friends, Our World*.

Our Family, Our Friends, Our World: An Annotated Guide to Significant Multicultural Books for Children and Teenagers. By Lyn Miller-Lachmann. Bowker, 1992. $46 (0-8352-3025-2).

Arranged by grade level within each cultural group, this guide lists 1,000 fiction and nonfiction titles about ethnic groups of the U.S. as well as the cultures of other lands. Critical annotations note strengths and weaknesses and tell how the books further multicultural understanding. The selection and evaluation criteria found in the introduction will be useful to librarians and teachers.

This Land Is Our Land: A Guide to Multicultural Literature for Children and Young Adults. By Alethea K. Helbig and Agnes Regan Perkins. Greenwood, 1994. $49.95 (0-313-28742-2).

Includes critical annotations for nearly 600 books of poetry and oral tradition (not so well represented or labeled in other bibliographies) as well as fiction for African, Native, Asian, and Hispanic American cultures. Titles were published from 1985 to 1993.

Venture into Cultures: A Resource Book of Multicultural Materials and Programs. Ed. by Carla D. Hayden. ALA, 1992. $25 (0-8389-0579-1).

Annotated bibliography with suggested programming, activities, illustrations, and resource lists. Includes Arabic, Jewish, and Persian cultures in addition to Asian, African, Hispanic, and Native American groups. Some titles are in foreign languages.

Other Specialized Subject Bibliographies

Book Links: Connecting Books, Libraries, and Classrooms, published six times a year, has annotated bibliographies of children's books in every issue on topics ranging from grandparents to Egypt to the seasons. (Booklist Publications/ALA, $16.95, ISSN 1055-4742). Unless otherwise noted, the reference sources below have subject indexes.

A to Zoo: Subject Access to Children's Picture Books. 4th ed. By Carolyn W. Lima and John A. Lima. Bowker, 1993. $55 (0-8352-3201-8).

Nearly 800 subject headings provide access to more than 14,000 children's titles in which pictures occupy as much or more space than text. Books are suitable for preschool through grade 2.

American History for Children and Young Adults: An Annotated Bibliographic Index. By Vandelia VanMeter. Libraries Unlimited, 1990. $32.50 (0-87287-731-0). Available on disk: Apple $25, Mac $26, IBM $25.50.

World History for Children and Young Adults: An Annotated Bibliographic Index. By Vandelia VanMeter. Libraries Unlimited, 1992. $32 (0-87287-732-9).

Each of these books briefly describes 2,000 K-12 recommended fiction and nonfiction titles. *World History* is arranged by continent and nation; *American History* by subject within chronological periods.

Books in Spanish for Children and Young Adults, Series VI: An Annotated Guide. By Isabel Schon. Scarecrow, 1993. $35 (0-8108-2622-4).

Updates earlier bibliographies by this author; most titles listed have been published since 1989. Includes critical evaluation of Spanish and Spanish-English books from Latin American countries as well as the U.S. and Europe. Books are listed under general headings (fiction, biography, folklore) within each country; no subject index.

E for Environment: An Annotated Bibliography of Children's Books with Environmental Themes. By Patti K. Sinclair. Bowker, 1992. $42 (0-8352-3028-7).

Especially useful in schools, with more than 500 fiction and nonfiction titles grouped by subject (recycling, pollution, endangered species, etc.) and a section on background reading and classics for adult or advanced readers.

Exploring the United States through Literature. Oryx, 1994. Ed. by Kathy Howard Latrobe. $24.95/v. Regions: Great Lakes (0-89774-731-3), Pacific (0-89774-771-2), Southeast (0-89774-770-4), Southwest (0-89774-765-8), Plains (0-89774-762-3), Mountain (0-89774-783-6), and Northeast (0-89774-779-8).

This series, useful for collection development and K–8 curriculum planning, provides citations to fiction, nonfiction, media, and professional materials.

Fantasy Literature for Children and Young Adults: An Annotated Bibliography. 4th ed. By Ruth Nadelman Lynn. Bowker, 1995. $52 (0-8352-3456-8).

Books recommended by at least two review sources are arranged in chapters on witchcraft, time travel, alternate worlds, allegorical fantasy, and more. Also provides bibliographies for reference, history and criticism, teaching resources, and individual authors.

Gender Positive! A Teachers' and Librarians' Guide to Nonstereotyped Children's Literature. By Patricia L. Roberts and others. McFarland, 1993. paper $24.95 (0-89950-816-2).

This guide for use with K–8 children lists more than 200 books in which gender roles are positively and nonstereotypically portrayed. One or more target activities for classroom use are discussed for each book.

It's the Story That Counts: More Children's Books for Mathematical Learning, K-6. By David J. Whitin and Sandra Wilde. Heinemann, 1995. $21.50 (0-435-08369-4).

Math through Children's Literature: Making the NCTM Standards Come Alive. By Kathryn L. Braddon and others. Libraries Unlimited, 1993. $23.50 (0-87287-932-1).

Read Any Good Math Lately? Children's Books for Mathematical Learning, K-6. By David J. Whitin and Sandra Wilde. Heinemann, 1992. paper $18.50 (0-435-08334-1).

These list books and related activities for grades K–6 on such subjects as counting, fractions, estimation, and geometry.

The Literature of Delight: A Critical Guide to Humorous Books for Children. By Kimberly Olson Fakih. Bowker, 1993. $40 (0-8352-3027-9).

More books—approximately 800—will fit into one of this guide's categories of humor (healing humor, cautionary tales, anthropomorphism, send-ups, riddles) than you might imagine!

My Name in Books: An Annotated Guide to Children's Literature. By Katharyn Tuten-Puckett. Libraries Unlimited, 1993. $24 (0-87287-979-8).

Children who want to read books starring characters with their own first name can consult this unique source listing 2,000 titles.

Popular Reading for Children III: A Collection of Booklist Columns. Ed. by Sally Estes. ALA, 1992. $4.95 (0-8389-7599-2).

Reprints 16 annotated bibliographies from *Booklist* on topics ranging from dragons to humor. Author/title indexes only.

Recreating the Past: A Guide to American and World Historical Fiction for Children and Young Adults. By Lynda G. Adamson. Greenwood, 1994. $55 (0-313-29008-3).

Approximately 70 percent of the 970 works of fiction described here cover the British Isles, the American colonies, and the U.S.

Science & Technology in Fact and Fiction: A Guide to Children's Books. By DayAnn M. Kennedy and others. Bowker, 1990. $38 (0-8352-2708-1).

Books for children preschool to grade 6 are given a lengthy summary and critical evaluation based on several review sources. Covers physical and earth sciences, excludes life sciences. Categorized by fiction or nonfiction; includes a subject index.

Science Books & Films' Best Books for Children, 1988-91. Ed. by Maria Sosa and Shirley M. Malcom. American Association for the Advancement of Science, 1992. $40 (0-87168-505-1).

A bibliography of recommended K–9 books and AV materials based upon reviews in the AAAS journal *Science Books & Films*. Categorized by such subjects as sex education, psychology, and ethics as well as mathematics, ecology, animals, etc. Critical annotations focus on scientific accuracy.

Teachers' Favorite Books for Kids: Teachers' Choices, 1989-1993. International Reading Association, 1994. paper $8 (0-87207-389-0).

This compilation of annual columns from *The Reading Teacher* describes outstanding trade books for use in the K–8 curriculum grouped by suggested reading levels.

War and Peace Literature for Children and Young Adults: A Resource Guide to Significant Issues. By Virginia A. Walter. Oryx, 1993. paper $27.50 (0-89774-725-9).

Conflict resolution as well as real and fictional conflicts are the focus of this bibliography of books for preschool through grade 9.

The Ways of War: The Era of World War II in Children's and Young Adult Fiction: An Annotated Bibliography. By M. Paul Holsinger. Scarecrow, 1995. $57.50 (0-8108-2925-X).

This narrowly focused bibliography rates and describes in depth more than 1,000 titles. Includes geographic and thematic indexes.

Wordless/Almost Wordless Picture Books: A Guide. By Virginia H. Richey and Katharyn E. Puckett. Libraries Unlimited, 1992. $27.50 (0-87287-878-3).

Use this guide to identify books in which pictures tell the story. Each of 600 titles, published through mid-1991, is described in terms of plot, characters, format, and illustrations.

Young People's Books in Series: Fiction and Non-Fiction, 1975–1991. By Judith K. Rosenberg. Libraries Unlimited, 1992. $27.50 (0-87287-882-1).

This detailed resource lists series published 1975–91. It must be used in conjunction with Rosenberg's earlier bibliography for volumes in a series published before these dates. Other reference titles (*Something about the Author, Elementary School Library Collection*, and others) also list series information.

What Kids Want to Read

Do children actually read all these recommended and award-winning books? Yes, but they also love books from such series as Fear Street, The Baby-Sitters Club, and Goosebumps, which do not always meet with critical acclaim or merit entries in bibliographies. A look at annual bestseller lists reveals that children's books with movie and television tie-ins are among the biggest sellers.

BookBrain. Diskette. Oryx. $195.

Software available for grades 1-3, grades 4-6, and grades 7-9 allows kids to select their own books using the "Book Detective." It contains descriptions of thousands of books selected for their appeal to children. (Most of the titles were also recommended by major selection aids.) The librarian can add additional titles to the system, and children can add their comments to the records of books they've read.

More Exciting, Funny, Scary, Short, Different, and Sad Books Kids Like about Animals, Science, Sports, Families, Songs, and Other Things. By Frances Laverne Carroll and Mary Meacham. ALA, 1992. paper $18 (0-8389-0585-4).

Chapter headings such as "I Want a Skinny Book," "Do You Have Any Books like The Baby-Sitters Club?" and "I Need to Do a Science Project" reflect things librarians hear every day. This guide gives brief annotations of fiction and nonfiction titles for 75 topics. Suitable for grades 2-5, the books were designated as children's favorites by librarians in ALA's Association for Library Service to Children.

More Kids' Favorite Books: A Compilation of Children's Choices, 1992-1994. Children's Book Council/International Reading Association, 1995. $8 (0-87207-130-8).

Compilation of annual lists from *The Reading Teacher*. Books were evaluated by 10,000 schoolchildren from different regions of the U.S.; their annotations are arranged by age level.

What Do Children Read Next? A Reader's Guide to Fiction for Children. Ed. by Candy Colborn. Gale, 1994. $39.95 (0-8013-8886-3).

For readers' advisory purposes, the major feature of this title is the listing of five "other books you might like," which concludes each of the 2,000 annotated title entries. Book reviews for main entries are cited. Indexes by subject, award, time period, geography, character name, character description (e.g., cats, detectives), age level, illustrator, author, and title. For use with grades 1–8.

Indexes to Children's Literature in Collections

Index to Fairy Tales, 1987-1992: Including 310 Collections of Fairy Tales, Folktales, Myths, and Legends with Significant Pre–1987 Titles Not Previously Indexed. Comp. by Joseph W. Sprug. Scarecrow, 1994. $59.50 (0-8108-2750-6).

Approximately 25 percent of the collections indexed here by subject, author, and title are suitable for children. Stories for children are marked with an asterisk in the subject index.

Index to Poetry for Children and Young People: 1989-1992. Comp. by Meredith Blackburn. Wilson, 1994. $58 (0-8242-0861-7).

This indispensable book, latest in a series, indexes nearly 8,000 poems in 123 collections by title, author, subject, and first line.

Read-Alouds and Booktalking

Reading aloud to kids is one of the best ways to get them interested in reading for themselves. The following sources all describe characters, plot, and ideas for reading aloud or booktalking.

Books Kids Will Sit Still For: The Complete Read-Aloud Guide. 2d ed. By Judy Freeman. Bowker, 1990. $45 (0-8352-3010-4).

Covers more than 2,100 titles for pre-K-6. Grade-level lists are categorized into fiction, nonfiction and biography, poetry, and traditional literature. Recommended projects, props, and related titles are a bonus. Detailed subject index. *More Books Kids Will Sit Still For* will be published this month. (Bowker, $45, 0-8352-3520-3)

The Latest and Greatest Readalouds. By Sharron L. McElmeel. Libraries Unlimited, 1993. paper $24.50 (1-56308-140-7).

Annotations for more than 150 recent picture books or novels also discuss other titles of interest. Includes a useful list of suggestions on how to encourage reading both at home and at school.

The New Read-Aloud Handbook. 2d ed. By Jim Trelease. Penguin, 1989. paper $10.95 (0-14-046881-1).

Outlines the whys and hows and do's and don'ts of reading aloud and concludes with a treasury of several hundred recommended titles. Every library serving teachers, parents, and others who work with children should own a copy of this book. A new edition will be published in September as *The Read-Aloud Handbook*. (Penguin, $12.95, 0-14-046971-0).

Primaryplots 2: A Book Talk Guide for Use with Readers Ages 4–8. By Rebecca L. Thomas. Bowker, 1993. $42 (0-8352-3411-8).
Middleplots 4: A Book Talk Guide for Use with Readers Ages 8-12. By John T. Gillespie and Corinne J. Naden. Bowker, 1994. $42 (0-8352-3446-0).

A plot summary, thematic material, booktalk suggestions, descriptions of related titles, and citations to reviews and biographical material are included in these listings of 150 and 80 titles, respectively. The booktalk suggestions range from specific episodes for reading aloud, complete with page numbers, for the longer books in *Middleplots 4* to creative writing and hands-on activities for those in *Primaryplots 2*.

Reading Rainbow Guide to Children's Books: The 101 Best Titles. By Twila C. Liggett and Cynthia Mayer Benfield. Citadel, 1994. $19.95 (1-55972-222-3); paper $12.95 (0-8065-1493-0).

Lists tried-and-true read-alouds from the popular PBS TV show.

Media Adaptations

Media adaptations of books can be used to get reluctant readers interested in a story or to reinforce its message. Many bibliographies in this review, such as *Elementary School Library Collection*, *Best of the Bookfinder*, *Something about the Author*, and *Primaryplots*, cite audio-and videocassette versions of children's books; the following titles are useful if nonprint media are of primary consideration.

American Library Association Best of the Best for Children. By Denise Perry Donavin. Random, 1992. $30 (0-679-40450-3); paper $20 (0-679-74250-6).

This excellent guide to recommended books, magazines, audio, video, software, toys, and travel lists "connections" to books in its video listings. For infants through age 14. Especially useful for parents.

From Page to Screen: Children's and Young Adult Books on Film and Video. By Joyce Moss and George Wilson. Gale, 1992. $35 (0-8103-7893-0).

Rates 1,400 pre-K-12 films on their adherence to the book and on their own merits. Descriptive entries also cite reviews.

Newbery and Caldecott Medal and Honor Books in Other Media. By Paulette B. Sharkey and James W. Roginski. Neal-Schuman, 1992. $29.95 (1-55570-119-1).

Award-winning books in filmstrip, video, large print, audio, braille, and other formats.

Awards

The plethora of awards in the field of children's literature means that there are more juvenile titles with a little seal or exclamatory banner than one might suppose. A number of books are devoted exclusively to the best-known awards, the Newbery (fiction) and Caldecott (illustration). Most libraries will meet their needs with the bibliography from the Children's Book Council, *Children's Books: Awards and Prizes*.

Children's Book Awards International: A Directory of Awards and Winners, from Inception through 1990. By Laura Smith. McFarland, 1992. $82 (0-89950-686-0).

The most comprehensive source for awards given in foreign countries. Includes discontinued awards.

Children's Books: Awards and Prizes. Rev. ed. Children's Book Council, 1993. $85 (0-933633-01-7); paper $57.50 (0-933633-02-5); (ISSN 0069-3472).

Lists awards from the U.S., the U.K., Australia, New Zealand, and Canada and selected international awards.

Children's Literature Awards and Winners. 3d ed. By Dolores B. Jones. Gale, 1994. $94 (0-8103-6900-1).

Awards for English-language books. Includes a separate listing by author of winning titles.

The Coretta Scott King Awards Book: From Vision to Reality. Ed. by Henrietta Smith. ALA, 1994. paper $25 (0-8389-3441-2).

Attractively illustrated, this guide has annotations for each winning book, as well as a photograph, brief biography, and bibliography for each author.

The Newbery and Caldecott Awards: A Guide to the Medal and Honor Books. ALA, 1995. paper $15 (0-8389-3453-6).

For those interested in just these awards, this inexpensive paperback describes the plot, characters, and illustrative technique of each book.

Authors and Illustrators

Librarians are constantly inundated with requests for biographical material, and many reference titles focus solely on children's authors and illustrators. The most comprehensive of these is Gale's *Something about the Author* series. Libraries with limited budgets may find Wilson's *Junior Authors and Illustrators* series of six volumes sufficient for their needs.

Authors of Books for Young People. 3d ed. By Martha E. Ward and others. Scarecrow, 1990. $59.50 (0-8108-2293-8).

Authors about whom information was hard to find were given preference for inclusion in this source. Includes 3,708 very brief entries based on an author file at the Quincy, Illinois, Public Library.

Biographical Index to Children's and Young Adult Authors and Illustrators. By David V. Loertscher. Hi Willow; dist. by Libraries Unlimited, 1992. $45 (0-931510-40-6).

Indexes more than 13,000 persons in more than 1,500 works, including single biographies, autobiographies, and audiovisual resources, as well as collective biographies.

The Birthday Book. By Mary H. Munroe and Judith R. Banja. Neal-Schuman, 1991. $49.95 (1-55570-051-9).

Use this title to find out who was born on a certain date or in a state; cites other sources of biographical information.

Children's Authors and Illustrators: An Index to Biographical Dictionaries. 5th ed. Gale, 1994. $156 (0-8103-2899-2).
Indexes more than 200,000 biographical citations to 30,000 persons in 650 reference books.

Dictionary of Literary Biography. v.52: American Writers for Children since 1960: Fiction, 1986 (0-8103-1730-3); v.61: Nonfiction, 1987 (0-8103-1739-7); v.22: American Writers for Children, 1900-60, 1983 (0-8103-1146-1); v.42: American Writers for Children Before 1900, 1983 (0-8103-1720-6). Gale. $120/v.
Libraries without a subscription to this series might want to purchase these titles, which provide biobibliographic essays for more than 150 authors.

Illustrators of Children's Books. Horn Book, 1945-. v.1: 1946-56, o.p.; v.2: 1958, $30.95 (0-87675-016-1); v.3: 1957-66, o.p.; v.4: 1967-76, o.p.; v.5: 1978. $35.95 (0-87675-018-8).
Essays on aspects of children's book illustration, biographies (some with comments from the illustrator), and bibliographies.

Sixth Book of Junior Authors and Illustrators. Ed. by Sally Holmes Holtze. Wilson, 1989. $48 (0-8242-0777-7).
More than 200 biographical sketches (with photo and bibliography) of prominent authors and illustrators, as well as a cumulative index to the more than 1,500 biographies in the Junior Authors and Illustrators series.

Something about the Author. Gale. $85/v. More than 80 volumes.
One hundred or more biographies per volume have a comprehensive bibliography of the author's or illustrator's works, photographs, illustrations or cover art, and additional sources. Entries for Carolyn Keene ("author" of Nancy Drew books) and other collective pseudonyms, often omitted from other sources, are useful.

Something about the Author Autobiography Series. Gale. $85/v. 20 volumes in print.
Authors and illustrators of children's and young adult books write about their own lives, influences, and techniques.

Twentieth Century Children's Writers. 4th ed. Ed. by Laura Standley Berger. St. James, 1995. $132 (1-558-62177-6).
This edition focuses on authors for children ages 10 and under.

Reviews/Criticisms

In addition to such standard sources as *Book Review Digest*, *Book Review Index*, and *MLA Bibliography*, which may be used to identify citations to reviews and criticism, there are a number of specialized reference tools.

Children's Book Review Index. Gale, annual. $114 (ISSN 0147-5681).
Citations to reviews of children's and young adult literature, professional resources, and reference books are indexed in this series. A letter code designates book type next to each citation.

Children's Literature: A Guide to the Criticism. By Linnea Hendrickson. G. K. Hall, 1987. $38.50 (0-8161-8670-7).
Cites criticism in books and periodicals of individual authors' works and provides subject bibliographies on a wide range of topics.

Children's Literature Review. Gale. 34v. in print. $110/v.
Illustrated entries for each major author or illustrator (approximately 500 to date) include a list of major works, critical introduction, author's commentary, and excerpts of reviews and criticism from books, essays, and periodicals. Especially useful in small collections without ready access to the original sources.

Horn Book Index, 1924-1989. Ed. by Serenna F. Day. Oryx, 1991. $65 (0-89774-156-0).
Index to reviews in the *Horn Book Magazine*.

General References

Dictionary of American Children's Fiction, 1859-1959: Books of Recognized Merit. By Alethea K. Helbig and Agnes Regan Perkins. Greenwood, 1985. $69.50 (0-313-22590-7).
Dictionary of American Children's Fiction, 1960-1984: Recent Books of Recognized Merit. By Alethea K. Helbig and Agnes Regan Perkins. Greenwood, 1986. $75 (0-313-25233-5).
Dictionary of American Children's Fiction, 1985-1989: Books of Recognized Merit. By Alethea K. Helbig and Agnes Regan Perkins. Greenwood, 1993. $55 (0-313-27719-2).
Entries for books, their authors and illustrators, their characters, and other topics. Detailed subject and setting indexes. Helbig and Perkins have also compiled a similar series on British children's fiction.

Literature Activity Books: An Index to Materials for Whole Language and Shared Literature. By Marybeth Green and Beverly Williams. Libraries Unlimited, 1993. paper $27 (1-56308-011-7).
More than 1,000 books that list activities and teaching suggestions associated with individual children's books are indexed by subject, title, and author. Using this index a teacher can identify 11 books that contain activities related to *Johnny Tremain* without searching through dozens of individual indexes.

Oxford Companion to Children's Literature. By Humphrey Carpenter and Mari Prichard. Oxford, 1984. $49.95 (0-19-211582-0).
Focused primarily on British and American children's literature, this illustrated guide has entries for titles, authors and illustrators, characters, literature types and formats (fairy tales, penny dreadful), countries, and more. Essential for general reference.

Special Collections in Children's Literature. By Dee Jones. ALA, July 1995. paper $40 (0-8389-3454-4).
A greatly expanded version of Carolyn Field's 1982 directory.

Deborah Rollins is a reference librarian at the University of Maine, Orono.

Featured Reviews & Reviews

Generalities

The Columbia Dictionary of Modern Literary and Cultural Criticism. Ed. by Joseph Childers and Gary Hentzi. Columbia Univ., 1995. 362p. bibliog. index. $49.50 (0-231-07243-0); paper $19.50 (0-231-07242-2).
001.3'03 Criticism—Dictionaries || Humanities—Philosophy—Dictionaries || Social sciences—Philosophy—Dictionaries [CIP] 94-42535

Modern literary and cultural criticism has tended to express itself in terms unfamiliar to the nonspecialist (e.g., *gynesis*, *metalanguage*, *semiotics*). This dictionary provides succinct definitions of more than 450 terms relating to criticism and theory in literature, film, linguistics, psychoanalysis, philosophy, feminist studies, media studies, and related areas. Major concepts and schools of thought receive somewhat longer treatment (e.g., two pages for *deconstruction*). Pronunciation is provided for terms when necessary.

While the needs of the nonspecialist receive special consideration, the dictionary also aims to serve as a useful reference for users with some background in modern criticism and theory. The compilers omitted terms too narrowly associated with a single discipline or adequately treated in sources covering specific fields. The bibliographies that follow most entries direct the user to fuller treatments of the topics. A comprehensive bibliography of 25 pages lists all the works cited in the entry bibliographies. Cross-references within entries direct users to related entries. An index of names includes critics and theoreticians, ranging from Freud to Foucault, cited or discussed in the entries.

Recommended, as appropriate, for academic and large public libraries.

UFO: The Definitive Guide to Unidentified Flying Saucers and Related Phenomena. By David Ritchie. Facts On File, 1994. 272p. bibliog. illus. index. $40 (0-8160-2894-X).
001.9'42 Unidentified flying objects—Encyclopedias [CIP] 93-31037

In the preface to this guide to UFO phenomena, Ritchie rejects the view that extraterrestrials are visiting earth. Knowledge of surrounding planets indicates none can support life even remotely similar to Earth, the distances to other solar systems are too vast for visitors, and no solid evidence has ever been discovered to support the existence of life beyond Earth. He does believe UFOs are real but relies on paranormal or spiritual explanations. He cites the similarities between accounts of UFO pilots with demonic visitations.

Arranged in alphabetical order by subject, the entries include accounts of UFO sightings, both unexplained and hoaxes. Also included are other phenomena such as the appearance of the Virgin Mary at Fatima and accounts of encounters with demons by early church writers. Ritchie also discounts the theories of Erich Van Daniken, who postulated that the ancient "gods" were actually space travelers. Ritchie thinks the Nazca lines in Peru, which can be seen only from the air, were drawn by primitives using hot air balloons. He does not give a reference for this bit of information. He also covers "crop circles," which have puzzled Europeans for decades, but does not mention the two elderly men who claimed responsibility for those in England. A selected bibliography with 36 titles is included at the end of this work. More than 50 black-and-white illustrations are included. Although most articles include cross-references to related topics, there is an index as well.

Jerome Clark's three-volume UFO Encyclopedia series (Omnigraphics, 1990–93) covers the earliest sightings to the present. The articles are longer, and sources are cited at the end of most entries. Clark avoids the easy answers, while not ruling out any possibility, including extraterrestrials. Ritchie's work is an interesting interpretation of some very puzzling phenomena, but it is not up to the quality of Clark. UFO is not a necessary purchase for libraries already holding Clark's encyclopedia, but libraries where demand is high for information on UFOs, the paranormal, and New Age or spiritual information may want a copy for the circulating collection.

Computers: A Visual Encyclopedia. By Sherry Kinkoph and others. Alpha Books, 1994. 371p. illus. index. paper $25 (1-56761-464-7).
004 Computers || Computers—Encyclopedias || Microcomputers [OCLC] 93-74398

The publisher describes this book as different from other computer books because it emulates an encyclopedia, offering description, histories, and illustrations. Certainly it is different from the how-to book, but it's certainly not the first computer-related dictionary or encyclopedia available, though it may well be the first with such sumptuous, full-color illustrations. All are sharp; even those taken from a computer screen are highly readable. The large format (8 by 11 inches), appropriate font sizes, and plenty of white space make for easy readability.

Entries are arranged alphabetically, from *Access* (a popular database program) to WYSIWYG ("What you see is what you get"). Entries run one to four pages, with most on a two-page spread. Illustrations accompany every entry. Related terms are defined in a separate area on the page so readers don't need to constantly flip pages. The table of contents and index make it easy to find entries. Entries include companies, software, hardware, and such terms as CONFIG.SYS and RAM that are frequently mentioned in computer magazines. IBM, *Apple*, *Borland*, *Microsoft*, and *Hewlett-Packard* have entries but not *Tandy* or *Dell*. *WordPerfect*, *Word*, *dBase*, *PrintShop*, and *Lotus* 1-2-3 are here. "How Does It Work" boxes appear throughout the book to further explain topics. Cross-references to other entries are liberally provided. (But why doesn't *Electronic Mail* include a reference to *Internet*?) Honest appraisals of a product's status (e.g., popularity waning due to lack of Windows version) help readers consider the appropriateness of a product for purchase. Alas, no suggestions for further reading appear. A run through a spell checker and grammar checker should have caught the two errors noted (*earlly* for *early*; *Apple'* for *Apple's*).

Recommended for readers of all ages who want to learn computer basics. Consider a copy for circulating collections, although the paperback binding might prove a drawback.

The Large Print Computer Dictionary. By Donald D. Spencer. Camelot, P.O. Box 1357, Ormond Beach, FL 32175, 1995. 196p. paper $24.95 (0-89218-242-3).
004'.03 Computers—Dictionaries || Large type books [CIP] 94-32000

Spencer's *The Large Print Computer Dictionary* is especially welcome to computer users with tired eyes from sitting in front of their screens all day. Based on the author's other computer books, this volume culls 1,200 of the most popular computer terms and includes a few line drawings to help the reader understand its brief definitions. Type size is 18pt Times Roman.

Geared to the nontechnical user, each term is given 1 to 20 lines of simple explanation. Some cross-references exist to link like terms. While many of the definitions are the same as in Spencer's *Computer Dictionary* [RBB Ap 15 93], some changes have been made to reflect current usage. For example, the definition of *access* is broadened, and *Pentium* is included for the first (maybe last?) time. A few terms are listed in different ways (e.g., *Adobe Illustrator* is listed under A rather than under I as in the older book.) On the other hand, the entry *baud rate* states that common rates are 300, 1200, and 2400; these are being eclipsed by 9600 and 14,400 rates.

The title-page drawing shows an older user, which reflects the probable target for this book. Very elementary, this dictionary will prove useful to those public libraries with visually challenged computer novices.

Classroom Prodigy. Online. Prodigy Services, 445 Hamilton Ave., White Plains, NY 10601. Subscriptions range from $99/yr. for 5 hours/month in a 9-month year to $449/yr. for 25 hours/month in a 12-month year.
005.7'1369 Prodigy (Videotex system) [BKL]

The consumer online service Prodigy, with more than 2 million home subscribers, now has a special version for K–12 schools. Since most classrooms don't have telephone lines, this service—though titled *Classroom Prodigy*—is more likely to be used in libraries.

There are DOS, Windows, and Macintosh versions, all of which require a 2400 or 9600 bps modem to link the library's computer over a telephone line to Prodigy's computer. The DOS and Windows versions require an IBM-compatible computer with 640K memory, one disk drive, and a VGA/MCGA/EGA monitor. The Mac version requires a Macintosh Plus or higher with 1MB RAM and a disk drive. A floppy disk containing the software needed to run the service is provided by Prodigy. Each subscription comes with six passwords, five for student use weekdays until 5 p.m., and one for the teacher/librarian that can be used at any time. An on-screen clock tells how much time has been used and how much remains for the month.

Many features will look familiar to anyone who has used the consumer version of Prodigy. There is the same colorful graphical interface. Headline news is updated frequently during the day. Often news articles are hotlinked to a related article from the *Academic American Encyclopedia*, which is updated four times a year. In September, for example, 191 new articles were added. For Windows and Mac users, some news articles have accompanying sound and photographs. Here's where you will want a 9600 bps modem; watching these photos fill the screen is painfully slow at 2400 bps. There are science articles from *National Geographic* and Public Television's *Nova*. "White House Memo" provides the full text of recent presidential speeches and briefings. There are games, mostly with an educational slant. There is Internet access, both for E-mail and newsgroups. Mail-manager software downloaded from Prodigy enables users to write and read mail offline, thereby saving connect hours.

Prodigy has installed special features, too, for this classroom version. In the "Teacher's Corner" is "Teacher's Journal Reviews," a news service. There's "Internet Digest," a weekly overview of educational materials on the Internet, and a list of grants for special projects in education. "Connecting Kids," the special section for children, has peer support groups, "Adopt-a-Cause," and reading and writing projects children can work on with partner schools. "Learning Adventures" allows classes to follow a real-time adventure, such as an ocean voyage or a bicycle trip across Central America. The adventurers check in online several times a week to answer student questions. There are separate bulletin boards for elementary, middle-school, and high-school students, plus one for teachers. (All messages are run through a filter to remove any objectionable language before they are posted on bulletin boards.) Children's authors sometimes appear on a bulletin board. For example, in October the author and the illustrator of *The Stinky Cheese Man* answered queries from kids. (Publishers take note: Viking had a screen that described how to order the book.)

Subscribers get a notebook with suggestions for curriculum use of *Classroom Prodigy*. Some curriculum areas aren't as well served as others. For example, while there is lots of information for current events and science, there is little math material, especially for older students.

How is *Classroom Prodigy* different from the consumer version? First, there is no advertising. You can't buy anything online, make plane reservations, or read travel bulletin boards. Some of the columnists on investing and computers aren't available. While the consumer version has a low monthly fee for unlimited hours, some features carry an extra charge. There are no extra charges with the classroom version.

Some schools are accessing the Internet directly, and it has a much wider range of material than Prodigy, though some of it is unsuitable for students. But the Internet doesn't have much material specifically for children in the lower grades, and it is much harder to navigate. For schools, especially elementary and middle schools, that haven't been able to get on the information superhighway, *Classroom Prodigy* may be an excellent way to start. Call 1-800-PRODIGY, ext. 176, for further information. —*Sandy Whiteley*

The Cyberspace Lexicon: An Illustrated Dictionary of Terms from Multimedia to Virtual Reality. By Bob Cotton and Richard Oliver. Phaidon; dist. by Chronicle, 1994. 223p. bibliog. illus. paper $29.99 (0-7148-3267-7).
006'.03 Multimedia systems—Dictionaries || Virtuality reality—Dictionaries [BKL]

MIDI? MPC? MPEG? These are some examples of the specialized vocabulary of multimedia. The more than 800 concise definitions in this book go beyond the limits of most computer dictionaries to explain existing and emerging multimedia technologies, from video games to virtual reality. Terms are defined in language laypeople can understand; for example, "MIDI [Musical Instrument Digital Interface]—A standard for music information interchange adopted by the electronic music industry in 1983." Longer feature entries for such terms as *full-motion video* and *infotainment and edutainment* are scattered throughout the book and color illustrations crowd every page. An excellent cross-reference structure links related terms, and a lengthy bibliography ends the volume. The authors are British, but this is such an international industry that the book is appropriate for American audiences. Highly recommended for high-school, public, and academic libraries. —*Sandy Whiteley*

Young Adult Literature and Nonprint Material: Resources for Selection. By Millicent Lenz and Mary Meacham. Scarecrow, 1994. 336p. indexes. $37.50 (0-8108-2906-1).
011.62'5 Teenagers—U.S.—Books and reading—Bibliography || Bibliography—Bibliography—Young adult literature || Young adult literature—Bibliography || Audio-visual materials—U.S.—Bibliography [BKL] 94-13774

This annotated bibliography of resources useful to librarians and teachers working with students in grades 6–12 includes assessments of more than 600 books, periodicals, and electronic databases that will help educators select print and nonprint resources. Most of the sources listed have copyrights between 1988 and 1993, with some earlier works listed that have not been revised or updated.

Entries are divided into seven general topics, and subdivided by type of resource or subject area covered. The sections include research material, selection aids for print and audiovisual materials, and the longest sections on specific genres or subjects. Titles falling under more than one category are cross-referenced with the full annotation appearing in the primary location. Author, title, and subject indexes also refer to material only mentioned in an annotation. A publisher's directory includes phone numbers.

Bibliographic citations include publication information, price, and ISBN. Periodical citations also include subscription price, number of issues per year, address, and phone number. Annotations include scope of the work, arrangement, indexes, and special features. The longer annotations give a general overview of the contents and years covered, suggested uses, and comparisons with related works or previous editions. The annotations are very helpful to users unfamiliar with the title.

Both authors have taught children's literature on the college level. Their knowledge of the field is extensive, as evidenced by the informative annotations and depth of coverage in most of the sections. Omissions include Gale's CD-ROM *Literary Index* under "Indexes—Serial Publications," and general periodical indexes aside from the *Reader's Guide* under "Research—Print and Computerized Formats." In the section "Using Books with Young Adults," many of the titles cover books for younger children.

Guides to Library Collection Development [RBB Fe 1 95] includes resources for building young adult collections. Most of the bibliographies in *Young Adult Literature* are also found in *Guides*. But *Young Adult Literature* lists more sources for the selection of nonprint media, especially computer software. Middle- and high-school librarians and young adult public librarians will find *Young Adult Literature* a valuable resource for collection assessment and selection.

U.S. Government Periodicals Index. Congressional Information Service, 1993– . quarterly. paper (plus hardcover annual cumulation) $795/yr. (ISSN 1076-3163).
016 Government publications—U.S.—Indexes || American periodicals—Indexes [OCLC] 94-356

Periodicals produced by agencies of the U.S. government consti-

Generalities

tute one of the most varied sources of information available. With the publication of *Infordata's Index to U.S. Government Periodicals* beginning in 1974, these periodicals were accorded the recognition they merit. However, *Infordata's Index* ceased with the 1987 volume. With the publication of *U.S. Government Periodicals Index* (USGPI), access is once again available on a quarterly basis to articles presenting research results, discussions of programs or policies, or materials of general-interest value that have appeared in periodicals published by the government.

Examples of the 170 periodicals indexed are *Background Notes on Countries of the World, Business America, Children Today, Design,* and the *Social Security Bulletin.* A few titles are indexed in the *Readers' Guide* or other Wilson indexes, but the majority are not indexed elsewhere. Articles are indexed by subject and name. Index terms and cross-references have been selected primarily from a controlled vocabulary developed for USGPI. Noncontrolled vocabulary terms are used as subject entries when article-specific terms are warranted. Titles are cited as they appear in the source publication but are often followed by a brief USGPI-provided amplifying annotation enclosed in brackets. Most academic and public libraries have holdings of many journals in USGPI, such as *Monthly Labor Review, Occupational Outlook Quarterly,* and *Survey of Current Business.* Users identifying articles contained in periodicals that are not part of their library's holdings may request paper copies for a fee directly from the CIS Documents on Demand Service. The USGPI Accession Number is all that is needed to order copies.

USGPI is also available on CD-ROM for $795 a year and may be licensed on magnetic tape. The Board did not have the opportunity to preview either of these alternative formats. One feature of the CD-ROM format is that libraries can add periodical holdings information for their institution.

The first issue of USGPI covers October–December 1993. In late 1994, CIS will publish an annual volume with coverage back to January 1993. In addition to ongoing indexing, one additional year of retrospective coverage will be published each year, until the 1988–92 gap in coverage is filled. CIS is to be credited for bringing back an index whose utility promises to be great in both depository and nondepository libraries.

The Humanities: A Selective Guide to Information Sources. 4th ed. By Ron Blazek and Elizabeth Aversa. Libraries Unlimited, 1994. 525p. indexes. hardcover $45 (1-56308-167-9); paper $35 (1-56308-168-7).
016.0160013 Bibliography—Bibliography—Humanities || Humanities—Bibliography || Reference books—Humanities—Bibliography || Humanities—Information services—Directories [CIP] 87-33907

Last published in 1988, this guide to the literature lists more than 1,200 resources for research in philosophy, religion, the visual and performing arts, and literature. History is not covered. For each discipline there are two chapters. One has essays on major divisions of the discipline, the use of computers in the field, and important organizations, information centers, and special collections. The second annotates reference works arranged by form: bibliographies, indexes, biographical sources, etc. While the book's arrangement is basically unchanged, some new subtopics have been added; for example, in the religion sources chapter, the section "New Alternatives: New Age, Occult, Etc." The annotations are helpful and often cite related sources. Coverage is admirably current, with many 1993 and even 1994 sources listed. More than 25 percent of the sources included are new to this edition. The editors have also done an excellent job of noting electronic sources. Author/title and subject indexes aid access.

More detailed guides to the literature of these disciplines exist, some of them published by Libraries Unlimited, for example, *Reference Works in British and American Literature* (1990–91) and *The Performing Arts: A Guide to the Reference Literature* (1994). However, for a very up-to-date overview, *The Humanities* is highly recommended for public and academic libraries. —*Sandy Whiteley*

Guides to Library Collection Development. By John T. Gillespie and Ralph J. Folcarelli. Libraries Unlimited, 1994. 450p. indexes. $49.50 (1-56308-173-3).
025.2'1 Bibliography—Bibliography || Collection development (Libraries)—U.S.—Handbooks, manuals, etc. [CIP] 94-13621

The term *collection development* has taken on new meaning in recent years. The development of massive library networks and the increased use of electronic technology across library functions are among the contributing factors. As a result of these developments, "even the smallest of libraries is now able to give its patrons access to a tremendous amount of resources hitherto unavailable."

Guides to Library Collection Development is a bibliography of more than 1,600 bibliographies that will be useful in book selection. Most are completely bibliographic in nature, but other works are included where deemed by the authors to contain sufficiently extensive bibliographic content (ALA-RASD's RQ magazine, for example). The bibliographies were published from 1985 through late 1993.

The book is divided into three major parts. The first, "Periodicals and Serials," is an annotated list of review journals useful in collection development, arranged by intended audience (children or adults), then alphabetically by title. Titles cover both print and nonprint media. The other two sections list bibliographies, again divided into sections for children and adults. These sections are further broken down by subject. Materials are listed only once, so the subject index should be consulted for items that may contain material suitable for more than one age group. Symbols before each entry note type of audience (children, youth, adult), and asterisks note highly recommended works. Entries are critically annotated. After each entry are listed the subject headings under which the item is listed in the subject index. There is also an author-title index.

Inevitably in any printed resource there will be items omitted, if only due to publication deadlines. This book is not immune. Lorna Daniells' *Business Information Sources* is represented by the second edition (Univ. of California, 1985) rather than the third, which apparently appeared too late in 1993 for inclusion. This is in the nature of the beast, however, and does not detract from the overall usefulness of *Guides.*

The authors have many years of experience of writing about libraries and library literature. Gillespie is former dean and instructor of library science at Long Island University and the author of such books as *Juniorplots* and the Best Books series; Folcarelli is professor emeritus at the same institution.

Guides to Library Collection Development will be helpful for library staff in selecting materials and for collection evaluation. It should also prove useful in identifying items for reference, reader's advisory, and interlibrary loan. It is recommended for school, public, and academic libraries, with the caveat that research libraries will need more specialized bibliographies.

Great New Nonfiction Reads. By Sharron L. McElmeel. Libraries Unlimited, 1995. 224p. illus. indexes. paper $21 (1-56308-228-4).
028.1'62 Children—Books and reading || Oral reading [CIP] 94-20258

This latest book by library media specialist McElmeel features more than 140 nonfiction titles that can be used as read-alouds or shared by readers through sixth grade. The selection of books was based on the author's preferences.

McElmeel provides a detailed introduction for the librarian and teacher on choosing and using information books. The first of two main sections, "Seeking Information," lists more than 120 books under subjects from *Adopting* to *Wounds and Injuries.* Though only one book is included for each topic, McElmeel's "Connections" section after each main entry includes suggestions for further reading. The second section, "Biographies," follows the same format and includes 22 main entries, each followed by additional readings. Included for each title are publication data, target audience, and a detailed summary of the story. Black-and-white reproductions of book jackets are provided as illustrations.

At the end of each of the two main sections are author and title indexes for that particular section. At the end of the book, the user finds author-title-illustrator and subject indexes that include all the "Connections" titles as well, for a total of more than 500 books. Although somewhat limited in scope, teachers and librarians will find this a valuable stepping-stone for nonfiction book choices.

Microsoft Bookshelf '94. CD-ROM. Microsoft, 1994. $99.
030 Encyclopedias and dictionaries—Databases [BKL]

If there was ever a product in the CD-ROM marketplace that firmly establishes that the same item can find equal use at home or in the library—apart from the multimedia encyclopedias—it is this one. Integrating seven popular reference works into one CD-ROM at an extremely competitive price, *Bookshelf '94* is radically redesigned from previous versions.

Bookshelf '94 requires a PC with 386SX/25Hz or higher processor, 4MB of RAM, at least 2MB free hard drive space, Windows 3.1, a mouse, an audio board, headphones or speakers, and VGA or higher resolution display (256-color display recommended). The program creates a "QuickShelf" tool bar that appears at the top of every Windows application after installation. This tool bar enables one to call up any or all books in Bookshelf from within any other Windows application at the click of the mouse. Printed documentation consists solely of a three-page manual; users must rely on the help screens within the program, which operate like other Windows-based pull-down help screens and are not context-sensitive.

Bookshelf '94 includes several new volumes or editions. The third edition (1992) of The American Heritage Dictionary (Bookshelf '93 had the second edition) is perhaps the most noteworthy inclusion. Also included is The Original Roget's Thesaurus (Bookshelf '93 had Roget's II), The Columbia Dictionary of Quotations (1993; Bookshelf '93 had the concise version), and The People's Chronology (1992)—an entirely new addition. As in previous versions of Bookshelf, the latest edition of The World Almanac is included, as are The Concise Columbia Encyclopedia (2d ed.) and maps from Hammond Intermediate World Atlas. Dropped from this edition is Bartlett's Familiar Quotations.

Users may search the contents of any one or all seven books in the program. When all seven works are searched simultaneously, icons next to each article title indicate the work of origin. Double-click a word in a Windows word processing program and Bookshelf will search a given reference work for that word after the proper QuickShelf icon is clicked. About two-thirds of the screen is devoted to text from the work being searched, and one-third contains the searching menu and list of articles retrieved for a search. There are two primary ways of searching: Contents, basically a search on main entries, and Find, a keyword search on all words within entries using Boolean operators. There is also a Gallery search where users may search all pictures, animation clips, and motion picture clips (there are more than 60 animation and video clips in the program).

The program is relatively easy to learn, though more sophisticated features are learned about only through the many help screens. The Find feature appears to truncate terms even when the user does not use any truncation symbols, and often in seemingly random places. A Find search on toleran* in the quotations dictionary, for example, retrieves but one hit. On the other hand, a search on tolerant retrieves 72 hits, including quotations with words such as tolerable, tolerably, and tolerated. A Find search in the dictionary on d*r, which allows for unlimited letters between the d and the r correctly retrieves such words as dour and dealer, but also retrieves decarburize and dorsiventral among its 2,000 hits, indicating the program truncates after the last letter on its own. As proof, a search on d*r* also retrieves 2,000 hits—though it takes more than twice as long as the first search. Such peculiarities also occur with Boolean searching. A search on all seven books for basketball NEAR champion retrieves seven hits, yet basketball* NEAR champion* retrieves none, making it appear that truncation cannot be used with Boolean operators. On the other hand, a search for rain* NEAR cat* retrieves 31 hits. Although not indicated in the help screens, an asterisk at the beginning of letters also will retrieve words. A search on *phobi* retrieves 43 hits for various phobias, albeit at the expense of an extraordinarily long 17-minute search on a double-speed CD-ROM drive. (Most searches lasted no longer than a minute or so at the most.)

Though librarians may be frustrated with such inconsistencies, Bookshelf is nevertheless a fine program. There are some 80,000 spoken pronunciations in the dictionary, and all parts of a definition, including idioms, run-on entries, inflections, and words in the etymologies are retrieved with a Find search. A user double-clicking on any word within any of the seven books will retrieve a definition from the dictionary on that word and can even execute a further search of all seven works on that word with a click of the right mouse button. There are also pronunciations for various cities and countries in the atlas, along with national flags and anthems. Thanks to the inclusion of The People's Chronology, a phrase search on a specific date will retrieve articles featuring events on that day. Again, however, some programming inconsistencies arise. A Find search on all books on February 25 accurately retrieves 23 articles; a Find search on February 2 retrieves 697 articles, including one that mentions the date February 14.

Bookshelf allows one to copy an article to the Windows clipboard for pasting into another Windows program, and—an increasing rarity in Windows programs—has a print function within the program itself. As for the usability of the reference works included, such purely textual works as Original Roget's Thesaurus, People's Chronology, and Columbia Dictionary of Quotations are particularly easy to incorporate into this type of media. Even World Almanac and Concise Columbia Encyclopedia make the transition reasonably well. The American Heritage Dictionary is a minor casualty, since the Bookshelf version features about 2,000 images rather than the some 4,000 in the printed work. Nevertheless, the spoken pronunciations and the fact that there are illustrations at all give it an advantage over the recently released Random House Unabridged Dictionary on CD-ROM [RBB F 1 94], which is larger in content but has neither pronunciations nor illustrations. The weakest book of the seven is the Hammond Atlas. Like the maps in electronic encyclopedias, its maps go into virtually no detail. A Find search on Chicago, for example, brings up one regional map depicting seven states and parts of five others.

Libraries with the necessary hardware will likely find Bookshelf a useful ready-reference tool. The price is much lower than stand-alone versions of similar works (the recently reviewed Columbia Dictionary of Quotations on floppy disk [RBB My 15 94] alone costs almost the same as Bookshelf's seven works). Despite the jitters some librarians may feel about the lack of security within Windows programs, the fact that there is a printing utility within the program itself helps tremendously. Regardless of the occasional glitches in some Find searches, Bookshelf is proof that several disparate reference works can make a successful transition to multimedia.

Britannica Online: Academic Access. Encyclopaedia Britannica, 1994– . Annual subscription. Single-campus colleges and universities: 5,000 or fewer FTE students, $5,000; 5,001–35,000 FTEs, $1 per FTE; 35,001 FTEs, $35,000. Multicampus institutions: 35,000 or fewer FTEs, $1 per FTE; 35,001 FTEs, $35,000 plus $.50 per student over 35,000 FTEs.

031 Encyclopedias and dictionaries [BKL]

Right on the heels of its recent Britannica CD [RBB S 15 94], Encyclopaedia Britannica is again carving a new path of electronic access, this time via the World Wide Web on the Internet. Although other encyclopedias such as Academic American and Compton's have been available online for some time through services such as CompuServe (even Britannica had a brief fling in the early 1980s on Mead Data Central), Britannica Online (BOL) marks the first appearance of a major multivolume encyclopedia available through the Internet. BOL's more than 44 million words dwarf the other online encyclopedias, which have 9–10 million words. The product also breaks new ground by providing cross-references from the encyclopedia to other Internet resources. Britannica plans to update the database quarterly; the current version contains some information from the 1995 print set.

System requirements for running BOL include a dedicated Internet connection with some version of the World Wide Web browser Mosaic running. It will also run on a SLIP or PPP connection (albeit more slowly). Britannica recommends several packages in an on-screen help file. Among the NCSA Mosaic packages, Britannica lists WinMosaic version 2.07 alpha for 32-bit machines (version 2.02 alpha for 16-bit machines), Mosaic version 1.03 for Macintoshes, and Mosaic version 2.04 for XWindow systems. Britannica also lists other packages: MacWeb (for Macintoshes), Spry Air Mosaic or Spyglass Enhanced NCSA Mosaic (for Windows), and LYNX (for VT100 terminals). The system was tested on a PC running WinMosaic version 2.07 alpha.

Any user comfortable with basic Windows commands and a mouse will have little difficulty adapting to searching BOL. After accessing the system, the user sees the "home page," where various searches may be selected and where help screens can be accessed. The Frequently Asked Questions help screen claims there are "over 700,000 hypertext links" in the database. These links to other screens are displayed in blue underlined type on the screen. Users may input searches in an Index search box or a Text search box. Either path will search the Macropaedia, the Micropaedia, and the Book of the Year. There are also options for browsing the Book of the Year separately and searching Merriam-Webster's Collegiate Dictionary (10th ed.), Nations of the World (which provides access to the flag, map, 1993 events, and statistics of countries gleaned from Britannica World Data Annual), and the Propaedia. Boolean operators (AND, OR, NOT, and ADJ) and truncation (*) are allowed in either the Index or Text search.

The Index search, similar to a search in the printed index, searches index entries to retrieve a list of those likely to be of interest to the searcher. Like the Text search, the listing retrieved will be based on relevancy ranking. Unlike the Text search, however, the system will not automatically depluralize a word. Typing in *floods*, for example, retrieves no hits, whereas typing in *flood* or *flood** will. All index entries retrieved are hot-linked to articles, so the full article is retrieved simply by clicking the mouse on the appropriate entry. There is, however, no navigation device so a user can go from entry to entry quickly—one must always press a "back arrow" icon on the screen to move back to the list of index entries.

The Text search allows one to type in single words or complex phrases (such as *America's first compact car*) or Boolean searches to search the full text of the encyclopedia. The user may set the maximum number of article matches desired as well as the number of matches that will display the first paragraph of the article to provide an idea of how relevant the hit is. The system lists articles based on relevance, with the article's length (in bytes) to give an idea how long retrieval may take. Obviously, using a Boolean operator such as ADJ (adjacency) provides more relevant hits than simply typing in a phrase. A Text search on *operation restore hope* retrieves several articles with any of those words in it (though the top few were indeed relevant hits). A Text search on *operation* ADJ *restore* ADJ *hope* retrieves but one hit. The system will automatically depluralize words, so that the search *novas* AND *astronomy* retrieves an article on Anders Celsius, who was a professor of astronomy and wrote a work titled *Dissertation de Nova Methodo*. ... (It should be pointed out the software does allow for parenthetical Boolean searches: (*michelangelo* OR *raphael*) AND *painting*).

When articles are displayed, BOL will display a few screens of text that may be scrolled through. If the article is particularly long, however, an icon labeled Next Section appears that must be clicked with the mouse to move on. Bearing in mind that this is an online system, this can make viewing a very long article quite time-consuming. To help avoid this problem, users can click on a Table of Contents icon for *Macropaedia* articles; clicking on a part of the contents list takes you directly to that part of the article. Hot links to the index appear scattered throughout articles in the usual blue underlined type surrounded by brackets. On occasion, this appears quite odd. For example, a section of the article *History of Western Painting* begins: "During [Index] [Index] the Upper Paleolithic Period," with the first link leading to the index entry for *Stone Age*, the second to the entry for *Paleolithic Period*. A nice touch is that the author's initials at the end of an article are hot-linked to the biographical information that appears on them in the *Propaedia*. In addition, articles have hot links to related topics listed in the *Propaedia—a publication that is not on the CD version at all*.

If the software used by the local system permits, articles may be printed out on a local printer by clicking a print icon in the program, or downloaded using the standard Windows menus. A downloaded file, however, is saved in HyperText Markup Language format (.HTML), which—though it can be read as ASCII text—has many special codes scattered throughout the text.

BOL currently includes 2,200 illustrations plus maps. For example, the periodic table of elements is shown in color. Clicking on any element leads to more information about that element. Links to illustrations within various articles can cause potential problems for users. Identified by bracketed, underlined blue type (such as [Image], [Map], or [Table]), these links open another window featuring .GIF-based illustrations. For many articles that begin with several links to images (such as the section on the Andes in the article *South America*), the error message "Failed to find internal anchor" often came up when the article was initially retrieved. Clicking the [Image] link after the article did come up simply retrieves an illustration box with the words "Under Construction"—indicating that the image has not yet been added to the database.

Maps and illustrations of flags that were retrieved were quite clear; the maps were more detailed than those in CD-ROM encyclopedias but not as detailed as those in print sets. The Board was frustrated in not being able to find any other images in the database besides maps, flags, or tables. Browsing through several sections of *The History of Western Painting* revealed no images at all.

Links to related Internet resources are provided at the ends of several hundred articles. For example, clicking on "NASA Home Page" at the end of the *National Aeronautics and Space Administration* article connects the user directly to that rich resource. Success in reaching these resources is dependent on the host computer that is running them. For example, if all the ports at NASA were busy, BOL would not be able to make a connection. There are 400 of these references at this writing; this is an area of the system that Britannica plans to continue developing.

The other major component of BOL—*the dictionary*—offers straightforward word lookup only. Unlike CD-ROM dictionaries, words within definitions are not hot-linked to each other nor can one jump from a word in the encyclopedia to the dictionary. The program also offers little help on misspellings. A user typing in *online* will retrieve no hits, as *Merriam-Webster's* has the word entered as *on-line*.

A potential headache for users will be BOL's use of British spelling (as in the parent work). BOL makes note of this in a special help file that lists British equivalents to American words, indicating that "we plan to add technology to the search engine that equates British and American spellings. In the meantime, if one cannot find the information desired, one may need to enter British equivalents." Indeed, a Text search on *encyclopedias* AND *cd-rom* retrieves 6 hits; a search on *encyclopaedias* AND *cd-rom* retrieves 10.

BOL's retrieval speed is very much dependent on the speed of one's hookup to the Internet. One can also never be certain that when retrieval time is slow which computer is at fault—one's host system or Britannica's. (Retrieval of illustrations seems to cause more crashes and/or system slowdowns than anything else.) One annoyance is the use of relatively large .GIF files that display automatically on certain screens (such as the home page or in the dictionary, where the *Merriam-Webster* logo takes up almost one-third of the screen), which slows retrieval time for those screens. (This art can be turned off by the host institution.)

Still, any new system such as this is likely to experience some teething pains. Despite its high price, academic libraries with the proper facilities may find this a useful reference tool for their students and faculty, with the subscription permitting unlimited use within the campus domain. Many libraries may simply want to stick with the recent CD-ROM version, which—though it as yet contains no illustrations nor the *Propaedia* or *Book of the Year*—has all of the main text and is *much less expensive*. But, though it has not yet achieved its full potential and some bugs remain, BOL is an easy-to-use system that bodes well for information delivered in this format. Using the encyclopedia to index relevant parts of the Internet is another innovative step by Britannica.

Internet users with the appropriate connection who would like to sample the product can do so at http://www.eb.com. They will be able to view the home page, try a demo, and get information on how to subscribe to *Britannica Online*.

The Top 10 of Everything. By Russell Ash. Dorling Kindersley, 1994. 287p. illus. index. $24.95 (1-56458-721-5); paper $14.95 (1-56458-703-7).
031.02 Curiosities and wonders || Questions and answers [CIP] 94-6324

Though it was originally compiled by a British packager, a U.S. editor has done a good job of adding American material to this book of lists. Topics covered range from the universe and the human body to the commercial world and travel and tourism. Some of this information is easily found in an encyclopedia or the *Guinness Book of World Records*: Oscar winners, sports records, tallest waterfalls and longest rivers. However, some information is more elusive: top films by studio, longest running programs on National Public Radio, top fairs by attendance, most- and least-visited states, fastest fighter aircraft of World War II, best-selling Ben & Jerry's flavors. But sources for the information here are not given consistently, and many tables aren't even dated. This is a problem in verifying facts. For example, the list of the 10 most-visited zoos in the U.S. differs dramatically from a similar list in *Gale City & Metro Rankings Reporter*. Gale gives a source for its information, *Top 10* does not. Though there are pictures on most pages, this attractive book is not as heavily illustrated as the typical DK title. A brief index lists the topics of tables, not the names on the tables.

The Top 10 of Everything is a fascinating book to browse and will be popular in school and public libraries, but it doesn't have the authority to serve as a reference book.—*Sandy Whiteley*

The Concise Columbia Encyclopedia. 3d ed. Ed. by Paul G. Lagassé. Columbia; dist. by Houghton, 1994. 973p. charts. illus. maps. tables. $49.95 (0-395-62439-8).
031 Encyclopedias and dictionaries [CIP] 94-16721

This new edition of *The Concise Columbia Encyclopedia* has 2,000 more entries than the second, published in 1989 [RBB Ja 1 90]. But it is not just updated relative to that edition but also to the fifth edition of *The*

Columbia Encyclopedia [RBB S 15 93]. The Concise Columbia has never been just a spin-off of The Columbia Encyclopedia; it has always had some unique material. The editors of this new edition have taken advantage of the extra year since the publication of the parent work to update articles and to add some new topics. Editor Lagassé worked on both previous editions of the Concise.

The most obvious change since the second edition of the Concise is in the illustrations. The color insert of maps has been replaced by black-and-white maps accompanying country articles. One hundred black-and-white photographs, mostly portraits of such people as Aretha Franklin and Gertrude Stein, have been added. Some articles new to this edition (which weren't in the The Columbia Encyclopedia either) include Campbell, Kim; multimedia; network (which mentions the Internet); and Jordan, Michael. Entries updated over The Columbia Encyclopedia include the table of Justices of the Supreme Court, which now lists Ruth Bader Ginsburg; Euthanasia, which notes Jack Kevorkian; and a table accompanying Olympic Games, which includes Sydney as the site for the 2000 games. European Union replaces European Community, reflecting the name change since the Maastricht Treaty.

What does The Columbia Encyclopedia have that The Concise Columbia doesn't? It has 50,000 entries versus 17,000 (many entries for places and people were dropped in the Concise), bibliographies at the ends of longer entries, and pronunciation given more consistently. It also has a bargain price of $99.

The Concise Columbia Encyclopedia is admirably up-to-date and will prove useful in libraries and as a home and office desk reference. —Sandy Whiteley

InfoPedia. CD-ROM. Future Vision Multimedia, 300 Airport Executive P., Spring Valley, NY 10977, 1994. $79.95 (1-57213-047-4).
031 Encyclopedias and dictionaries, English [BKL]

This new multimedia reference tool adds animation, video, pictures, and sound clips to the contents of Funk & Wagnall's New Encyclopedia (1994), Hammond Atlas, New Biographical Dictionary, 1994 World Almanac, Roget's 21st Century Thesaurus, and Merriam Webster's Dictionary, Dictionary of English Usage, and Dictionary of Quotations. Intended primarily for school or home use, it comes with a book on term-paper and report writing.

Hardware requirements for the Windows version include an IBM or compatible PC with 486 processor, 4MB RAM (8MB recommended), Windows 3.1 or later, SVGA graphics card, Windows-compatible sound card, double-speed CD-ROM drive, and a mouse. Macintosh requirements are a 68030 running System 7.1 or later, 4MB of RAM (8MB recommended), 13-inch color monitor, double-speed CD-ROM drive, and a mouse. The Windows version was used for this review. InfoPedia comes with a 20-page "Quick Start Guide" that explains the structure of the database and how to get around in it. There are also help screens.

InfoPedia appears to contain the same text as its print sources, with updates provided by video for some entries. For instance, the text of Rwanda describes events through 1991, while the accompanying video clip contains information on the 1994 ethnic conflict between the Hutu and Tutsi. Omissions noticed in Funk & Wagnalls are also noted here; there is no entry for Hillary Clinton, for example. Sound clips, from birds to national anthems to famous speakers, are of excellent quality. Many illustrations of animals are beautiful old color engravings rather than photographs. Videos are for the most part well chosen, accompanying such topics as Cyclone, Hitler, and Astaire, Fred, although they "float" within articles without captions (which movie did that clip of Fred and Ginger come from?). Animations are provided for many topics in the biological and physical sciences. Like other multimedia encyclopedias, the maps are much less detailed than those found in print. The publisher claims that InfoPedia has more animations (90), video clips (60), and sounds (500) than Microsoft Encarta, The New Grolier Multimedia Encyclopedia, or Compton's Interactive Encyclopedia.

InfoPedia's search options include Index, Search, Gallery, Subject, and Links and Project "Browsers." The Index allows searching for a single term in any or all of the eight reference sources from a single combined alphabetical list. A split screen is used, with the index in the left third and text and pictures on the right two-thirds. Vocabulary is not controlled in the Index, so that a search for Colorado will bring up links to the atlas, dictionary, and almanac, but Colorado (State of the U.S.) must be chosen to link to the encyclopedia entry. An "active book icon" always indicates which source is being displayed. The Search option allows Boolean combinations (AND, OR, NOT) of two words.

Within the Gallery, a click on Video, Animation, Sounds, Pictures, or Maps brings up an alphabetical list of items in that category. Each of these items then links to the appropriate text entry or entries. Under Subject, articles are grouped in broad categories such as "Arts and Architecture," which are then further subdivided. The Links Browser gives a list of words in the currently displayed article that have links to other articles. Hypertext links also appear in blue text in the body of the entry. (Links to a dictionary definition can also be made by clicking on any word in the text.) Finally, the Projects Browser can be used to save marked text and create personalized subject folders for reports that can be printed out.

A better cross-reference structure is one of the most appealing features of the best electronic reference tools. Unfortunately, although it does search a single term in up to eight different reference titles, InfoPedia is not a significant improvement over print in terms of cross-references within entries. Many more hypertext links could be added to each article. While there are links from maps in the atlas to the encyclopedia articles on countries, there are no hotlinks on the maps themselves. With Encarta, for example, clicking on Chicago on a map of Illinois leads to a more detailed map of the city. An annoying feature is the inability to jump immediately to the part of an article that contains the text that was typed into the search field: a search for the word Mandela and a click on the article South Africa brings one to the top of that long article, not to the section with information on Mandela. Finally, many hypertext links to alternate names within the New Biographical Dictionary did not work at all.

There are many bugs in the display of sounds and pictures. Beethoven lists three options under Sounds: "Beethoven," "Beethoven," and "Beethoven String Quartet." All three play the same music, which is not identified. The sound for telephone does not work (don't they all sound different now anyway?). Pictures for two kinds of wood warblers are offered; one displays a blank screen when chosen. An entry for Moose River from the dictionary brings up the picture from the entry for the animal. Captions for pictures do not display unless the screen is enlarged. Other annoyances in the database: instead of a cursor displaying in the box where text is typed (which seems to be a standard feature in Windows programs), the box is outlined in red. Needing improvement are the tiny icons for multimedia items and tiny print that identifies the icon when it is clicked.

Potentially this work could be the equivalent of a combination of Microsoft Encarta [RBB S 15 94], which is also based on Funk & Wagnall's Encyclopedia, and Microsoft Bookshelf [RBB O 1 94], which contains the text of seven similar (in two cases, identical) reference tools. But this first version of InfoPedia falls short of its potential.

The Kingfisher Young World Encyclopedia. Ed. by Sue Grabham. Kingfisher, 1995. 488p. illus. index. $29.95 (1-85697-519-3).
031 Children's encyclopedias and dictionaries [CIP] 94-29226

This book for children ages 5–8 provides a wealth of information organized in 10 thematic sections: "The Universe," "Our Planet Earth," "The Sea," "All Kind of Animals," "Plants," "When Dinosaurs Lived," "My Body," "Machines," "Science," and "People and Places." At the onset of each section, a table of contents lists the topics covered. Most topics are discussed in two-page spreads with quizzes, activities, stories, and word boxes to aid in better understanding of the content. For example, "The Sea" discusses waves and tides and includes the legend of King Canute and the tides, a quiz, and an activity. More than 2,500 full-color photographs, diagrams, cross-sections, maps, and artwork will make the book appealing to children. The index notes main entries in bold type. Illustrations are not indexed. In "Machines," under the subsection "Other Aircraft," one finds an activity on how to make a gyrocopter. However, nowhere is there a definition of such an aircraft, and the index does not include the term gyrocopter.

This book is not arranged alphabetically and thus does not serve to introduce young readers to the concept of reference books, but it may encourage browsing in school and public libraries.

Kister's Best Encyclopedias: A Comparative Guide to General and Specialized Encyclopedias. By Kenneth F. Kister. Oryx, 1994. 506p. index. $42.50 (0-89774-744-5).
031 Encyclopedias and dictionaries—Book reviews || Encyclopedias and dictionaries—Bibliography || Encyclopedias and dictionaries—History and criticism || Bibliography—Best books—Encyclopedias and dictionaries [BKL] 94-11282

A man whose name is virtually synonymous with encyclopedia reviewing, Kister here presents his opinions on every encyclopedia likely to be considered for purchase by either a librarian or a consumer. Much has changed in the encyclopedia industry in the eight years since this work was last published, and Kister has not missed a beat. The volume is current (Kister even devotes some space to the upcoming Britannica on the Internet), though the 1993 rather than 1994 sets of most encyclopedias were reviewed. Kister's Best Encyclopedias features well-written reviews of more than 77 general encyclopedias (up from 52 in the last edition), as well as briefer reviews of more than 800 subject encyclopedias (up from 450) and 44 foreign-language encyclopedias in 9 languages (up from 27).

After a preface in which the author explains the criteria he used in judging the works, the volume opens with a section titled "About Encyclopedias," where Kister answers such questions as "How are encyclopedias bought and sold?" and "What should you look for when choosing an encyclopedia?"

The part of the book likely to be of greatest interest to librarians and consumers alike is "General Encyclopedias," which is sub-divided into five categories by size of encyclopedia and intended reader (such as "Small Encyclopedias for Adults and Older Students") as well as the two categories "Electronic Encyclopedias" and "Out-of-Print Encyclopedias." Reviews range from under a page (primarily for works that are reprinted under different titles) to 11 pages for the New Encyclopaedia Britannica. Each review includes basic facts about the work, an evaluation, and where other reviews may be found. New to this edition is a "Report Card" feature, where sample articles from each work are graded on an A to F scale on coverage, accuracy, recency, and clarity. At the end of each section is a useful comparison chart of all encyclopedias in that category, listing for each the number of words, pages, articles, illustrations and maps, cross-references, and index entries, as well as retail price and a rating on an A to F scale. The only drawback to these charts is that there is no separate column for black-and-white as opposed to color illustrations, nor does this information appear in the reviews themselves.

The section "Electronic Encyclopedias" alone is practically worth the cost of the book—though this part will age the quickest. Just one error was spotted: Encarta is noted as being available in three versions, but there is no DOS version. The comparison chart at the conclusion of this section will help the frustrated librarian distinguish between, for example, the four CD-ROMs going by the name of Compton's.

The section of the book on subject encyclopedias is divided into 30 categories ("Computer and Electronic Sciences," "Music," etc.), with brief reviews of standard works, usually citing other reviews. Although Kister's Best Encyclopedias will (justifiably) be better known for its reviews of general encyclopedias, librarians should not overlook the fine reviews in this section. The volume concludes with appendixes featuring a bibliography on evaluating and making encyclopedias, a directory of encyclopedia publishers and distributors, and an index.

Any reader wanting to make sense of the often confusing world of encyclopedia publishing will benefit from this work. Librarians in all public and academic libraries will want to place this on their "must buy" list and may want separate copies for their reference and circulating collections.

Life's Big Instruction Book: The Almanac of Indispensible Information. By Carol Orsag Madigan and Ann Elwood. Warner, 1995. 881p. illus. index. tables. paper $29.95 (0-446-51757-7).
031.02 Handbooks, vade-mecums, etc. || Conduct of life—Miscellanea—Handbooks, manuals, etc. [CIP] 94-26523

Life, as R. B. Fuller said of Spaceship Earth, does not come with an instruction manual. At least it didn't until the publication of this book, the purpose of which is to provide some of the practical information needed for everyday survival. Helpful hints on topics as diverse as etiquette, first aid, volunteering, parenting, and cooking fill its pages. Like a good reference librarian, it answers specific questions or suggests sources for further information but never offers legal, medical, or financial advice. The material is presented under 17 broad subject banners, for example, Health, Crime, Pets, Travel, and further divided into more manageable sections. Money Matters, for example, is broken down into "Sizing Up Your Finances," "Credit and Debt," "Saving and Investing," and so on. All the sections and subsections are listed in the main table of contents, and each of the 17 chapters begins with a repeat of the section's page breakdown. An index helps locate specific points of information. This book is not related in any way to Life's Little Instruction Book (Rutledge Hill, 1992).

Although the compliers say they did not want "to include the kind of information easily found in lots of other reference books," they have. Such items as a perpetual calendar, U.S. flag etiquette, a map of U.S. time zones, metric-U.S. conversions, a list of Roman numerals, all standard features of many an almanac, are included here. But what almanac also includes a guide to basic pasta shapes, opera for beginners, and six tips to make one a better dancer? In order to have the same coverage of the topics represented here, one would have to have at least a small shelf of reference works. This would make a useful addition to a home library as well as to the ready-reference desk in public libraries.

Visual Encyclopedia of Science. Kingfisher, 1994. 320p. illus. index. $22.95 (1-85697-998-9).
031.02 Curiosities and wonders—Juvenile literature [CIP] 93-43118

This overview for readers ages 9–13 covers a wide variety of topics, with sections on the planet Earth, the living world, stars and planets, and technology. Written by popular-science writers, each section covers several topics in a format for intermediate and middle-school students. The book relies heavily on visuals, mostly well-labeled color drawings. Maps, cutaway diagrams, and charts are also included. Occasional photographs, many too small in which to see details, are included. Topics where photographs would be useful, such as Apollo 11's moon landing, are represented by drawings.

Most topics are covered on a two-page spread with very little white space. These pages are filled with illustrations and boxed areas that contain vital statistics or factoids on the topic. Brief text is placed wherever there is space. Some text goes across a page, other text goes down, and sometimes it is printed in three-column format. Sizes of illustrations also seem based on available space, and unrealistic size comparisons, such as leaves much larger than adjacent trees, will lead to confusion for young readers.

Some information is incomplete for the sake of simplicity and reading level of younger users. However, readers might want to know that the illustration of "Australian's most famous building" is the Sydney Opera House. Readers will be fascinated by some of the material offered. In the pages on life in space, they will get answers to questions about how the astronauts eat, go to the bathroom, and move about outside of their spacecraft. They will also enjoy browsing the chronology of inventions, which begins with pottery in 7000 B.C. and ends with the Macintosh computer in 1984. The index indicates illustrations by using italics, but these page numbers are difficult to discern from the regular type used for text references.

Young people will enjoy browsing through this volume, but serious students will not find enough depth on a particular topic to hold their interest or satisfy their needs. Libraries would better serve their patrons with titles covering individual fields of science or specific topics within those fields. This book's value will be in the home or in the circulating collection.

Primary Search. CD-ROM. EBSCO, 83 Pine St., Peabody, MA, 01960, 1994– . quarterly. $549.
051 Children's periodicals—Indexes [BKL]

EBSCO's Primary Search, an electronic periodical index intended for children, is updated quarterly. It is designed especially for use in library children's rooms and school media centers. The IBM-compatible version requires a 386 computer with 640K RAM and 5MB hard disk space available running DOS 3.3 or higher (5.0 recommended). The Macintosh version requires system 6.05 or higher, 1.5MB RAM available, and 1MB disk space.

As of the August 1994 disc, Primary Search indexed and abstracted 107 titles, including 3-2-1 Contact and Boy's Life, and contained 27 titles full text, including Cobblestone and Highlights for Children. In order to fit all the data on one disc, only the three most recent years of the full-text magazines are included. Indexing coverage of periodicals varies; for some titles it goes back to 1988, for others it begins with 1994. More than half the periodicals are indexed since 1988 or 1989. In addition to magazines for children, Primary Search indexes titles for teachers and librarians, such as Book Links and Arithmetic Teacher. Also, it has 52 full-text pamphlets on such topics as sports and health. The CD is accompanied by a list of these magazines and pamphlets.

The disc is both IBM/PC and Macintosh compatible. The accompanying reference manual is not particularly helpful, but *Primary Search* is fairly self-explanatory. Searching is easy enough for children to handle on their own. Space is provided for entering the topic of choice, and opportunity is given for adding or eliminating other topics. When the search is completed, a list of the results is given and the searcher is told whether or not full text is available and how to view it. Many graphics from full-text articles can be easily viewed. During a search under the topic *dogs*, an article on animal actors from *Boy's Life* came up that included a beautiful full-color still from the movie *The Lion King*, as well as two photographs of animal actors and their trainers. When an unusual term, *Samhain* (the Celtic word for Halloween), was searched, it yielded the full text of an Irish folk tale from *Cricket* with four gorgeous illustrations. The searcher also came across a "Calvin and Hobbes" comic strip as well as the full text of a pamphlet on smoke-free daycare centers. The full-text feature is particularly helpful since children's magazines in libraries are always missing pages, especially if everyone in the class is assigned the same topic. Printing and exiting are both extremely easy.

Children's Magazine Guide (Bowker), published nine times a year, indexes 45 periodicals; all but five of them are in *Primary Search*. Thirty-five of the adult periodicals in *Primary Search* are also indexed in the *Readers' Guide* (e.g., *American History, Consumer Reports, Ebony, Time*). But the powerful search engine and the inclusion of full text for some magazines make *Primary Search* a useful and reliable tool for elementary-school libraries that have the necessary equipment.

An expanded version of this CD-ROM, *Middle Search*, was not seen by the Board. It includes all the titles indexed in *Primary Search*, plus an additional 55 periodicals of interest to older students, such as *Car & Driver* and *Astronomy*. *Middle Search* contains 36 magazines full text, titles aimed at older and younger children. A 10-month academic year subscription is $899. Middle schools and K-8 schools will want to learn more about *Middle Search*.

International Book Publishing: An Encyclopedia. Ed. by Philip G. Altbach and Edith S. Hoshino. Garland, 1995. 736p. bibliog. charts. index. tables. $95 (0-8153-0786-1).
070.503 Publishers and publishing—Encyclopedias [CIP] 94-10027

American book publishing is a relatively small industry, with revenues only 13 percent larger than the video-rental business, but it is of special interest to librarians. The first half of this encyclopedia has articles on U.S. publishing and some general topics such as *International Copyright* and *The Societal Context of Book Publishing*. Special areas such as children's, feminist, reference, and university-press publishing are treated. *Education for Publishing*, *The Paperback*, and *Libraries and Publishers* are among other topics covered. The second half of the volume is arranged by regions of the world and contains articles on publishing in 26 countries, plus such survey articles as *Francophone Africa*. These articles are not in any standard format but often touch on government relations, literacy, imports and exports, copyright, distribution, and authorship. Some of these entries have statistical tables.

In both parts of the book, the lengthy articles are signed, and many of the authors are well known in the field (John Dessauer, Bernie Rath, John Tebbel, Nat Bodian). Most close with notes and/or a select bibliography. Statistical tables appear in such entries as *Book Marketing in the United States* and *Mergers and Acquisitions*. Appendixes include tables of world book production, production by language, children's-book production, and school-textbook production for 1970–90. A detailed index concludes the book.

It's ironic that so little has been published in book form about book publishing. This fascinating overview of the industry will be of interest to librarians and other book people. —*Sandy Whiteley*

Gale's Quotations: Who Said What? CD-ROM. Gale, 1995. $400; 2–8 user single-site version $500 (0-8103-9989-X).
080 Quotations, English—Databases [BKL]

Multiple points of access are offered to the more than 117,000 quotations stored on this CD-ROM. Simple searches can be done using author/speaker name, quotation, or keyword; an extended-search feature allows searching using a number of other elements, including nationality, occupation, and birth or death year. The biographical information about the authors/speakers, when available, comes from Gale's *Almanac of Famous People*. It is also possible to search on the source of a quotation; for example, all quotations from the *New York Times*.

Both DOS and Windows versions are available on the same disc. The DOS version used for this review has a graphical user interface similar to Windows. The minimum system requirements include an IBM or compatible PC with 286 processor, DOS version 3.3 or higher, Windows 3.0 or higher (for that version), 640k bytes of RAM (520K available), hard disk with a minimum of 2.5MB of free space, and a VGA graphics card and monitor. A mouse and printer are considered optional, but actual use recommends them. The instructions for installation are clearly written, and the process itself is fairly straightforward. The accompanying manual is not indexed and is therefore not very helpful. There are context-sensitive help screens.

One of the advantages of this format is that information unused when searching conventional author-keyword indexes can now be used to perform an extended search. One can search for "quotations on death by a Russian author" or "quotations by teachers" with some success. Searching *prince* as an occupation, *English* as a nationality, and *architecture* as a keyword yielded Prince Charles' infamous remarks about modern architecture. One access point missing from the extended-search function is the sex of the author/speaker. Such a feature would save the time it takes to consult the several collections of quotations by women that are needed to supplement the standard quotation sources. There are many quotations from contemporary figures: Maya Angelou (59 quotations), Tom Stoppard (21), Chinua Achebe (11), and Margaret Atwood (4).

The use of a mouse speeds up the actual searching process, as using keyboard arrows and combinations (e.g., ALT-M) is a bit cumbersome. Screen design and layouts are visually appealing, if not colorful. Although a printer is considered optional equipment, use of one saves a lot of time. This copy was "field tested" in a closed telephone-reference area, where it was quite helpful to be able to print off the requested quotation and dash back to the phone with page in hand.

In addition to identifying specific quotations, it is possible to generate custom-tailored lists of quotations using the extended-search function. This would be one feature to recommend this product for public use, especially in a setting where there is not a large collection of quotation books available.

Two of the standard print quotation dictionaries are available on diskette: *The Columbia Electronic Dictionary of Quotations* [RBB My 15 94] and *The Oxford Dictionary of Quotations & Modern Quotations* [RBB O 1 94]. Taken together, they have only about one-quarter the number of quotations as *Gale's Quotations*. However, they are also considerably less expensive. *The Oxford English Dictionary* on CD-ROM contains 2 million quotations that can be searched. However, they were chosen to illustrate the use of a word, not for their quotability. As the first stand-alone quotation collection on CD-ROM, *Gale's* is a good product. (*The Columbia Dictionary of Quotations* is available on CD-ROM as part of *Microsoft Bookshelf*.) The addition of access points by sex of author/speaker would make it even better.

Metaphors Dictionary. Ed. by Elyse Sommer and Dorrie Weiss. Gale, 1994. 833p. bibliog. indexes. $65 (0-8103-9149-X).
081 English language—Terms and phrases || Metaphor—Dictionaries [CIP] 94-36728

In the words of Christopher Fry, "There's not a devil / In the length of the land could pick such a posy of words / And not swoon smelling it." These words appear under the subject heading *Language* and serve as an apt description of *Metaphors Dictionary*. The editors bring unique qualifications to the volume: Sommer compiled the *Similes Dictionary* (Gale, 1988), and Weiss is a retired English teacher. Intended for browsing, as "inspiration for writers and speakers," for the enhancement of the understanding and appreciation of metaphor, and as a quotation finder, the work meets the compilers stated goals. More than 6,500 metaphors under 600 subject headings make this the most comprehensive work of its kind.

An informative introduction discusses types of metaphor: mixed, extended, personification, allusion, metonymy, and antonomasia. A brief bibliography for further reading on these topics follows. A table of subject headings serves as an outline of contents. Subjects range from such abstract ideas as *Abandonment*, *Enthusiasm*, and *Guilt* to the concrete: *Rainbows*, *Pets*, and *Diaries*. Entries are arranged alphabetically by subject and then by author. Brief annotations that include background information, variants, or related metaphors accompany many entries. The source is given for most metaphors. The metaphors are from all periods of history, Homer to Bill Clinton, and represent the words of poets, speech writers, journalists, scientists, philosophers, business people, actors, and "just plain folks." There are author-speaker and subject indexes, a list of one- or two-word "common" metaphors, and a section of 600 metaphors from Shakespeare. A lengthy bibliography lists the works from which the authors chose the metaphors. Literary and classical metaphors predominate; many others are from newspapers and speeches.

Future editions would benefit from a word index such as those found in quotation dictionaries, which would make the location of specific quotations much easier. Metaphors Dictionary is a valuable addition to reference works on words. A complementary dictionary of familiar metaphors with unknown origins is Loose Cannons & Red Herrings: A Book of Lost Metaphors (Norton, 1988), with no attributions but useful explanations of derivation. Libraries will also want to collect specialized metaphor dictionaries such as Robert Palmatier's Sports Talk: A Dictionary of Sports Metaphors (Greenwood, 1989) and his Speaking of Animals: A Dictionary of Animal Metaphors (Greenwood, 1995).

The Oxford Dictionary of Quotations & Modern Quotations. 3-diskette. Oxford, 1994. $75 (Windows 0-19-268134-6; Macintosh 0-19-268115-X).
082 Quotations, English—Dictionaries [BKL]

The second major quotations dictionary to appear in a disk-based version this year (the first was Columbia Dictionary of Quotations [RBB My 15 94]), this product consists of the electronic equivalent of two works: the fourth edition of The Oxford Dictionary of Quotations [RBB D 1 92] and The Oxford Dictionary of Modern Quotations [RBB My 1 91]. Minimum hardware requirements are a 386SX PC, 4MB RAM, a VGA monitor or better, Windows 3.1, and hard drive space of 7MB. A mouse is recommended. A Macintosh version is also available.

The Oxford Dictionary of Quotations & Modern Quotations (ODQ&MQ) is part of what Oxford is calling its CompLex series and is apparently the first of several Oxford works that will appear with the same searching interface, with such titles as The Concise Oxford Dictionary and The Oxford Thesaurus to follow. According to help screens in the program, The Oxford Dictionary of Quotations (ODQ) consists of "some 17,500 quotations from roughly 2,500 authors," and The Oxford Dictionary of Modern Quotations (ODMQ) has "about 5,000 quotations," which "all originate from people who were still alive after 1900." There is some overlap between the two works; Gore Vidal, for example, has six quotes in each, three being identical. Both works can be searched simultaneously or separately.

Upon starting the program, a "bookshelf" appears with icons for ODQ and ODMQ, below which are icons for invoking the various search commands. Like many Windows-based programs, the search commands can be called upon by clicking the icons or by pulling down a Windows menu. Unlike other programs, the pull-down menu is, oddly, the "Tools" menu; there is no pull-down menu labeled "Search." The default search when the program is started is the "Entry Window," which allows one to search by author or full text. The same search may be invoked by clicking the "Show Entries" icon, which is—somewhat oddly—a book with its pages being turned. The author search simply brings up a quotation window with the first quotation by that author. Moving on to the next quote requires clicking a right arrow key next to the "Show Entries" icon, which allows one to move through the entire work by author's name, one quote at a time. The full-text search brings up a listing of authors that used the word being searched. The user may double-click a particular name, or simply start at the beginning and move through the list. To move through these quotations, however, requires clicking the right arrow key next to the "Show Results" icon. This use of two different arrow icons to move forward through results may be confusing to some. The program has an easy-to-spot "Print" icon, which allows one to print within the program rather than having to paste a quote and print it in another Windows program. The "Edit" pull-down menu also allows one to cut and paste quotations to the clipboard if desired.

The most powerful tool is "Search," which allows the user to perform a full-text search using Boolean operators (AND, OR, NOT), single or multiple character truncation (? and *, respectively), and proximity searching (a # sign and a number between words). Boolean operators, however, must be enclosed in brackets, and "" must be used together to exclude the second term in a search statement (heart love). The proximity operator is problematic. According to the manual, "characters are counted (left to right) from the beginning of the first word to the space before the first letter of the second," rather than the traditional number of words between two words. A searcher looking for quotations from the Times Literary Supplement, for example, will retrieve no hits with the search times #1 literary, but must instead use the strategy times #6 literary to account for the number of letters in the first word. Oddly, the search times AND literary retrieves two hits that should have been retrieved with the proximity search but were not. On the plus side, both left- and right-handed truncation may be used, though at the cost of time. A search on *lov* #25 heart* took more than three minutes on a 386/33 PC with 8MB of RAM but retrieved relevant hits.

There are differences between ODQ&MQ and the Columbia Dictionary of Quotations on floppy disk. Columbia has a more American bent, while ODQ&MQ is more British-oriented. Shakespeare, for example, has 245 quotations in Columbia, but 1,186 in ODQ. On the other hand, Hemingway has 97 in Columbia, but six in ODQ and 12 in ODMQ. Columbia gets the nod for being a bit easier to use initially, primarily because of ODQ&MQ's rather odd symbols on its icons. ODQ&MQ certainly has lengthier documentation with a 42-page booklet, but some sort of a "help card" would be a terrific enhancement given the icons. With the exception of the third edition of ODQ being searchable on Dialog as The Quotations Database, the Oxford works are not available in any other machine-readable form, unlike Columbia, which is also available on CD-ROM in Microsoft Bookshelf '94 (see review in this issue). At $75, ODQ&MQ is not prohibitively expensive, but libraries will have to determine if the differences between Columbia and the present work are sufficient enough for the investment in yet another machine-readable quotations dictionary.

Philosophy, Psychology, Religion

The Oxford Dictionary of Philosophy. By Simon Blackburn. Oxford, 1994. 408p. $35 (0-19-211694-0).
103 Philosophy—Dictionaries [CIP] 94-8832

Blackburn designed The Oxford Dictionary of Philosophy "as a playground for browsers and a resource for anyone interested in general intellectual movements, as well as a simple work of reference." He was editor of the journal Mind from 1984 through 1990 and is currently a distinguished professor of philosophy at the University of North Carolina. He is author of Essays in Quasi-Realism (1993) and Spreading the Word: Groundings in the Philosophy of Language (1984). Blackburn operates in the Anglo-American analytic philosophical tradition, as opposed to the existentialist or phenomenological traditions of Europe.

The work is a distinctly personal one, though Blackburn's assessments of philosophical positions and discussions are objective and expository in tone. For example, of Immanuel Kant, he states, "his place as the greatest philosopher of the last 300 years is well assured.. . . [w]hilst his confidence in the a priori and the structure of his idealism have been widely rejected, it is not too much to say that all modern epistemology, metaphysics, and even ethics, is implicitly affected by the architecture he created."

The nearly 3,000 entries cover a wide variety of topics. Biographical entries include Aquinas, Russell, Isaiah Berlin, Michel Foucault, Darwin, and Keynes. While philosophers such as Plato and Nietzsche receive a page or more of treatment, those included for a peripheral contribution to philosophy, such as Keynes or Einstein, receive about half a column. Other entries run from a few lines to a page in length. Topics range back to the beginnings of Western and Eastern philosophy and across fields to discuss philosophical insights or approaches to economics, love, dreams, biology, and so forth. Yet the bulk of the dictionary consists of concise, focused definitions of terms used by analytic philosophers and philosophy students: falsifiability, protocol statements, liar paradox, subjectivism/objectivism, and prisoners' dilemma. Blackburn writes in an interesting and easy-to-follow style. He has made liberal use of cross-references (marked by asterisks within the text) and see and see also references at the end of entries. Some entries include bits of symbolic logic; a two-page appendix defines most of the symbols used.

This book is the most recent dictionary of philosophy. Dagobert Runes edited numerous editions of his Dictionary of Philosophy between 1942 and 1984 (Littlefield). Antony Flew's Dictionary of Philosophy came out in 1979 and 1984 (St. Martin's). Peter Angeles wrote his Dictionary of Philosophy in 1981; a revised edition was published in 1992 as The HarperCollins Dictionary of Philosophy. The Oxford Dictionary is uniquely broad in its coverage. It is accessible to the general reader, while at the same time being useful for the scholar or student. It is recommended for all academic and public libraries.

An Encyclopedia of Claims, Frauds, and Hoaxes of the Occult and Supernatural. By James Randi. St. Martin's, 1995. 284p. bibliog. illus. index. $24.95 (0-312-13066-X).

133'.03 Occultism—Encyclopedias || Parapsychology—Encyclopedias [BKL] 94-6707

RBB has reviewed several books advocating occult views recently, for example, *Encyclopedia of Afterlife Beliefs and Phenomena* [RBB Ap 15 95] and *Divining the Future.* Here is one debunking the occult. Described as "James Randi's decidedly skeptical definitions of alternate realities," it includes an introduction by Arthur C. Clarke. Some entries just define terms (*anima mundi*, *ankh*, and *kachina*), but many of the approximately 700 entries attempt to expose people and movements Randi sees as frauds (e.g., L. Ron Hubbard, Madame Blavatsky, crystals, channeling, pyramid power). Many entries are loaded with sarcasm. For example, the author says that in modern times, witchcraft "is a harmless distraction for otherwise idle persons to embrace." He does, however, point out that many practices erroneously attributed to witchcraft are really related to followers of satanism. Randi goes on to say that "homeopathy . . . falls into the category of magic." He is much kinder to acupuncture, merely describing it and including a diagram of acupuncture points. After describing the chanting practices of Hare Krishnas, he concludes, "It is *very* boring." Appendixes debunk the "Curse of King Tut" and end-of-the-world prophecies. A bibliography lists other skeptical books on the occult. *See also* references and an index make access easy. Illustrations consist of black-and-white photographs and drawings.

Readers who have occult beliefs will be dismayed and annoyed by what they read here, but libraries that want to provide balance in their collections will find this an antidote to the many recent reference books promoting the occult.

Man, Myth & Magic: The Illustrated Encyclopedia of Mythology, Religion and the Unknown. 21v. Rev. ed. Ed. by Richard Cavendish. Marshall Cavendish, 1995. bibliog. charts. illus. index. $549.95 (1-85435-731-X).

133'.03 Occultism—Encyclopedias || Mythology—Encyclopedias || Religion—Encyclopedias [CIP] 94-10784

The new edition of this illustrated encyclopedia, last revised in 1983, has retained the same format and many of the special features. It has returned to the original 20 volumes plus an index (the 1983 edition had 11 volumes plus index), with new and updated articles. Many of the articles are signed; those revised by someone other than the original author are indicated by an asterisk next to the earlier contributor's name. According to the "Reader's Guide" found in volume 1, the set is designed to provide an "unbiased exploration" into the religions and cultures of the world, past and present, and their belief systems. High-school students researching a particular religion, culture, or mythical subject will be able to trace aspects of the topic throughout the work.

Volume 1 contains a list of original contributors with expertise and works mentioned, tables of contents for each volume, and 21 thematic bibliographies with classified subject guides to articles. New works published since 1983 have been added to these bibliographies and to the "Further Reading" lists found at the end of some essays. The encyclopedia is well illustrated, with relevant color and black-and-white photographs and drawings, many of which are full page. The only illustrations new to this edition accompany new articles. Major articles range in length up to 10,000 words and may include cross-references and sidebars with additional information or quoted material.

New entries include *Multiple Personality*, *Afro-American Lore*, *Rastafarians*, *Urban Myths*, and *Hare Krishna*. Some of the revised articles contain new information, but others are only editorial overhauls. The index volume contains a traditional A-Z index and a classified index that lists all the entries under one of 21 headings (*Rites of Passage*, *Eastern Religions*, *Foretelling the Future*, etc.).

High-school and public libraries that field requests for anthropological research of any type will find this encyclopedia valuable. Browsers will also enjoy looking at this set. Institutions owning earlier editions will find the update worth purchasing.

The National Directory of Haunted Places. By Dennis William Hauck. Athanor Press, P.O. Box 22201, Sacramento, CA 95820-4742, 1994. 402p. bibliog. illus. paper $24.95 (0-9637914-1-9).

133.1'0973 Ghosts—U.S. || Parapsychology—U.S. || Haunted houses—U.S. || U.S.—Guidebooks [CIP] 93-90992

This guidebook to supernatural phenomena in the U.S. is arranged alphabetically by state and then city or location name. The more than 2,000 sites are considered "haunted" because events occur there that are beyond our ability to explain. Each entry contains a synopsis of the case along with a precise address and travel directions. Black-and-white photographs are provided for a sampling of sites. Entries are footnoted to a 400-item bibliography presented at the end of the book. The bibliographic entries are complete, including ISBN or LC card number. Most references are to books or periodicals published between 1970 and 1993. Another interesting feature of this directory is a list of organizations (with their addresses) that are mentioned in the text, such as the Ghost Research Society and the Institute of Noetic Sciences.

The work is aimed at individuals searching for new experiences or unusual places to visit. Hauck, an internationally known authority on paranormal phenomena, adds a few words of common sense in his introduction (e.g., "secure the permission of owners or tenants of private residences"; "always confirm and update directions locally"). Small editorial mistakes were noted, misspellings or wrong tenses used for verbs. The editor should apologize to the people of Oshkosh, Wisconsin, for calling it Oshgosh.

Similar works such as *A Ghosthunter's Guide* (Contemporary, 1993) and *Haunted Heartland* (Warner, 1985) are narrower in scope or less thorough in coverage. Readers interested in the supernatural will enjoy this directory and will read it cover to cover. At its reasonable price, buy one for reference and one for the circulating collection.

Divining the Future: Prognostication from Astrology to Zoomancy. By Eva Shaw. Facts On File, 1995. 293p. illus. index. $35 (0-8160-2937-7).

133.3'03 Divination || Fortune-telling [CIP] 94-25586

"A sweeping A-Z reference to fortune-telling practices, past and present" is how the press release introduces this book. The author describes divination practices ranging from tea-leaf reading to reading the placement of holes in Swiss cheese (tironmancy). Unfortunately, overly inclusive selection criteria, sloppy proofreading and copyediting, and poor illustrations make the work an incomplete attempt.

The word *querent*, used for a person seeking information, is misspelled throughout as "querant." Jeane Dixon's name is misspelled within her entry. She is said to have predicted the deaths of astronauts White, Chaffee, and "Grisson." The correct spelling of the latter's name is Grissom. *Prophecies* (the plural noun) is frequently spelled "prophesies" (a singular verb).

The author seems to describe everyone who ever said anything about the future as a psychic or diviner. George Fox, the founder of the Quaker movement, and Mother Ann Lee of the Shakers may have prophesied on the life to come, but they were hardly fortune-tellers or augurs. Describing Jules Verne as a mystic because of his science fiction novels is even more of a stretch. The Chinese practice of feng shui is used to divine suitable locations for buildings, graves, or other constructions, not for divining the future. Verses such as "red skies at night, sailors' delight" are not so much divination formulas as easily transmitted folk knowledge based on observation of the skies by early sailors.

The format is dictionary style with both an index and cross-references. Entries range from a brief paragraph to several pages. Each entry has a brief list of further reading. These lists are a disappointment. Such prolific writers as Helena P. Blavatsky and Aleister Crowley do not have works of their own listed. Skeptic James Randi's fine biography of Nostradamus is not mentioned. Many of the sources given can be located in the occult section of chain bookstores. *The Donning International Encyclopedic Psychic Dictionary* and the Time-Life *Mysteries of the Unknown* series are frequently cited. Illustrations are not good. The line drawings are adequate, but many of the reproductions of woodcuts and photographs are blurry or too dark.

This is not a necessary reference purchase, and the price is a little steep for a circulating copy.

Philosophy, Psychology, Religion

The Complete Vampire Companion. By Rosemary Ellen Guiley. Macmillan, 1994. 258p. bibliog. illus. index. paper $16 (0-671-85024-5).
133.4'23 Vampires [CIP] 94-10737

The Vampire Book: The Encyclopedia of the Undead. By J. Gordon Melton. Gale, 1994. 852p. bibliog. illus. index. $39.95 (0-8103-9553-3).
133.4'23 Vampires—Encyclopedias [BKL]

The current popularity of vampires is attested to by the publication of several reference works on the subject. Guiley and Melton have established reputations as compilers of numerous reference titles. Although similar in information, the approaches of these two books differ. The Vampire Book is an encyclopedia with articles on various subjects pertaining to vampires arranged in alphabetical order. The Companion contains a series of essays.

The Complete Vampire Companion has chapters dealing with the history and folklore of the vampire, the vampire in entertainment, and "real" vampires. It also has four appendixes: a lengthy bibliography, a filmography, a calendar of important dates, and a list of vampire organizations. It concludes with a subject and name index. The work is illustrated with both black-and-white drawings and photographs. The quality of the pictures is good.

The Vampire Book has 375 entries ranging in length from 100 to 5,000 words. The work is illustrated with black-and-white photographs that range from excellent quality to grainy and indistinct, such as those of the new Dark Shadows cast and of Leonard Wolf. Four appendixes list vampire organizations and fanzines; a filmography of 650 feature films; a section on vampire drama, opera, and ballet; and a bibliography of vampire books beginning with Dracula in 1897 up to the present. A special section in the bibliography is devoted to books on Dark Shadows. An index and see references are used to direct the reader to the appropriate headings.

The Vampire Book has some problems. The main one is repetition of information. For example, the work has entries for Barnabas Collins, Jonathan Frid, Ben Cross, Dark Shadows, and Dan Curtis that repeat a great deal of the same information. Some of the repetition is incorrect, such as the reference to Jeremiah as Barnabas' uncle on one page and as his brother on another. (Jeremiah was his brother.) Another problem is the choice of what to make a separate entry and what to subsume within an entry. For example, the cartoon character Count Duckula has a separate entry, but the literary character Bunnicula is just mentioned in three entries, with a longer paragraph in one of them than the separate entry for Count Duckula.

A similar work to the ones under consideration is The Vampire Encyclopedia by Matthew Bunson [RBB O 1 93]. It has 2,000 alphabetically arranged entries that range in length from one line to a page. It covers much of the same information as The Vampire Book and The Vampire Companion. The Vampire Companion might be useful in the circulating collection with The Vampire Book in reference. But if demand is low, libraries that own Bunson's Vampire Encyclopedia will find it adequate.

Alternative Realities: The Paranormal, the Mystic and the Transcendent in Human Experience. By Leonard George. Facts On File, 1995. 360p. bibliog. index. tables. $35 (0-8160-2828-1).
133.8 Parapsychology [CIP] 94-7630

George describes his admirably balanced book as introducing the reader "to the range of the supranormal." While the more than 450 entries cover an impressively broad range of topics, the jacket's claim that Alternative Realities is the first one-volume reference book to deal with virtually every reported type of "unusual experience" seems an overstatement. The breadth of coverage has required selectivity in the choice of entries and, in many instances, lack of depth. The entire entry for Bigfoot, for instance, is the following: "The popular American name for a hairy humanoid occasionally sighted in wooded areas, mostly in the northwest coast region." Cross-references to Cryptic and Humanoids, Anomalous, at one and two pages, respectively, are more helpful.

In an extensive directory of entries, George classifies them under three headings. Those under "General Topics" include Skepticism, Magical Thinking, Delusion, Epilepsy, and Vision of Paul. Entries under "Varieties of Unusual (Supranormal) Experience" include Astral Projection, Doppelganger, Channeling, False Memory, UFO Abduction Experience, and Ghost Light. Entries under "Deliberate Inducement of Unusual Experiences" include Flagellation, Vision Quest, Peyote, Koan, and Glossolalia. Among these latter entries are about 100 associated with Buddhist, Hindu, Islamic, Christian, Judaic, and esoteric traditions. Entries themselves are lucid and range from one sentence to several pages. Most contain see also references and a brief list of further reading. Concluding the book are tables and lists of studies correlating supranormal beliefs and anomalous phenomena, a 20-page bibliography, and an index.

Covering much of the same ground is Rosemary Guiley's Harper's Encyclopedia of Mystical and Paranormal Experience (Harper, 1991). A sampling of 33 entries there revealed that only eight are found in Alternative Realities, while only about half appear in the index. Guiley contains biographies while George does not. George is especially good at presenting the views of both skeptics and believers. Alternative Realities is recommended for academic, public, and high-school libraries.

Encylopedia of Afterlife Beliefs and Phenomena. By James R. Lewis. Gale, 1994. 420p. bibliog. illus. index. $37.95 (0-8103-4879-9).
133.9'03 Future life—Encyclopedias || Death—Encyclopedias || Reincarnation—Encyclopedias || Occultism—Encyclopedias || Spiritualism—Encyclopedias [CIP] 94-29172

A foreward by Raymond A. Moody, author of Life after Life and other works about near-death experiences, makes plain this work's perspective. It is written from the believer's point of view. This is not to say that the skeptic or person with a particular religious view will not find useful information here, provided this is kept in mind.

The approximately 250 articles are in dictionary format. They range from a few lines to several pages, and each has a list of sources. Eliade's Encyclopedia of Religion is used heavily in articles on religious topics. There is an appendix listing related organizations and an index. Within articles, cross-references refer to terms that have their own separate articles.

Some of the articles suffer from their generalizations, such as that on Africa, where the beliefs of all of Sub-Saharan Africa are summed up in nine pages; this cannot do justice to the rich variety of African belief systems. The article on Buddhism suffers from the same problem, although the author does concentrate on the Tibetan tradition, probably the most complex Buddhist death tradition. Topics range from the very broad to the obscure, including the Raelian Movement (a flying-saucer religion). There are biographies of many people in the psychic and near-death-experience fields, including Edgar Cayce, Elisabeth Kubler-Ross, and William Crookes.

Some articles, such as those on Virgil and Dante, seem to be included because an afterlife was mentioned in their works, although their political nature is not mentioned. The reproductions of black-and-white line drawings and photographs illustrating the book are not always good, with some quite fuzzy. There is some confusion of -ise and -ize endings that suggests that more copyediting needed to be done. The question of fraud is not addressed, although the author mentions problems the Spiritualist movement had with frauds in the 1920s. An article on how readers might protect themselves from frauds might have been useful.

This is not a necessary purchase, but if there has been some demand for circulating works on the afterlife, this book can fill reference needs in public libraries.

Encyclopedia of Human Behavior. 4v. Ed. by V. S. Ramachandran. Academic Press, 1994. bibliog. illus. index. $499 (0-12-226920-9).
150'.3 Psychology—Encyclopedias [CIP] 93-34371

Both the bright side (e.g., Altruism, Language Development, Social Support) and the dark side (e.g., Alzheimer's Disease, Suicide, War) of human nature and human experience are described and analyzed in this scholarly encyclopedia's 250 signed articles. A six-member editorial board helped editor Ramachandran select the topics. Ramachandran's academic credentials and appointments resemble the encyclopedia's scope. He has both a medical degree and a doctorate in neurophysiology and holds appointment as a professor in the neurosciences program of the department of psychology at the University of California, San Diego. Like its editor's training, the encyclopedia covers both the physiological and the psychological aspects of human behavior. All entries carry the names and institutional affiliations of their authors. Most are from North America; a few are European.

Article titles and scope tend toward the broad more than the specific. The outline that opens each article, as well as the thorough 15,000-entry index, allows users to locate discussion of specific topics. Each article adheres to a helpful four-part structure of article outline, glossary of key terms, article proper, and bibliography. Through the index this set can double as a makeshift glossary of psychological terms, since glossary entries within the articles are indexed; however,

Philosophy, Psychology, Religion

since nothing in the index differentiates glossary citations from other types of citations, this is not the encyclopedia's strength. Yet the glossary entries signify the editors' concern for clarity and intelligibility.

Entries range from five pages (*Self-Esteem*) to 17 pages (*Schizophrenia*). Topics covered include the senses (*Taste*), various emotions (*Anger, Jealousy*), developmental theory (*Cognitive Development*), medical subjects (*Glial Cells*, *Hypothalamus*), and disorders (*Autism*, *Epilepsy*). The bibliographies at the ends of all entries list scholarly books and journal articles.

Ramachandran has written for popular publications such as *National Geographic* and *Discover*; the encyclopedia shows that he understands what it takes to present complex knowledge to a diverse audience. Although the work displays the accoutrements of scholarship in its bibliographies and its *see also* references within articles, one does not need to be a scholar to reap knowledge from its pages. Even when presenting abstractions such as theories about why individuals make the vocational choices they make, the text is clear and readable. For this reason many users will prefer it to the academic prose, studded with numerous parenthetic references to its extensive bibliography, in Raymond Corsini's *Encyclopedia of Psychology* (also reviewed in this issue). Both sets supplement text with tables, charts, and diagrams; however these are more evident in Ramachandran. Whereas articles in Ramachandran address such broad topics as *Creative and Imaginative Thinking*, *Criminal Behavior*, or *Crowd Psychology*, Corsini favors more specific topics such as *Computerized Adaptive Testing*, *Contamination (Statistical)*, and *Cranial Nerves*. While there is overlap between the two, neither encyclopedia can be considered a substitute for the other. From a collection-development point of view, the question about these encyclopedias is not an either-or proposition. Both serve a useful purpose and complement one another far more than they overlap. The same may be said of Frank Magill's *Survey of Social Science: Psychology Series* (Salem Press, 1993), whose 410 articles, written in a popular style for the benefit of students, address both broad and narrow topics.

Carefully crafted, well written, and thoroughly indexed, the *Encyclopedia of Human Behavior* will help people—whether they are specialists in a branch of psychology or students just beginning formal study of that broad field—understand the field as well as themselves and their fellow humans and how and why we behave as we do.

Encyclopedia of Psychology. 4v. 2d ed. Ed. by Raymond J. Corsini. Wiley, 1994. bibliog. illus. indexes. $475 (0-471-55819-2).
150'.3 Psychology—Encyclopedias [CIP] 93-22638

Kudos to both Corsini and Wiley for bringing this reference set up to date! When the *Encyclopedia of Psychology* was first published in 1984, it quickly became known as the standard source in the multifaceted domain of psychology and a staple in library and professional collections. During the intervening 10 years, the field of psychology has given birth to new theorists, practitioners, and innovators, as well as new tests, measurements, techniques, and applications. While numerous specialized dictionaries and single-volume encyclopedias have appeared in recognition of distinct areas of psychology, they provide only brief definitions and short articles. The encyclopedia is the constant and reliable source for information on the major areas of psychology—applied, clinical, cognitive, developmental, educational, forensic, industrial, measurement, personality, physiological, social, and theoretical.

The second edition features more than 2,000 alphabetized entries by more than 500 expert contributors; contains 800 biographies in the first part of volume 4 (more than 100 of them new); boasts a unified bibliography of 15,000 entries in volume 4; and utilizes cross-references at the end of practically every entry. In comparison, the 1984 edition claimed some 1,500 separate entries. New entries include *Artificial Intelligence*, *Fetal Alcohol Syndrome*, *Managed Mental Health Care*, and *Video Psychology*. Also for comparison, while three volumes of the 1984 edition were devoted to text and the last to indexes and bibliography, volume 4 now also contains text, specifically, 180 pages of biographies.

Strengths of the 1984 edition are carried over to this new one. Articles continue to be authoritative and of high quality. The physical aspects of the set (typeface, binding) continue to be good. Some problems with the 1984 edition have been corrected. Subjects are no longer as scattered, and articles are no longer indexed without relation to the work as a whole. Cross-references appear to be more conscientiously and consistently applied. Other attempts have been made to make finding information as easy as possible. For example, the name and subject indexes and the spines of the four volumes have been designed to make locating the proper volumes and pages convenient for users. While the single bibliography saves space, some users may experience frustration going back and forth from the incomplete "Further References" listed at the end of most articles to the complete bibliography in volume 4. Some of the shortcomings of the 1984 edition have not been corrected. Article headings continue to be almost the same size as the boldface subheadings and cross-references. The arrangement of the subject index is once again not explained.

Students (college and up), professionals, and the general public interested in topics as wide-ranging as *Body Image*, *Brief Therapy*, *Crisis Intervention*, *Loss and Grief*, the *Nature-Nurture Controversy*, *Race Bias in Testing*, *Occultism*, *Ritual Behavior*, and *Sleep Treatment* will find much that is useful in this encyclopedia. Recommended once again for large public and academic libraries.

The Encyclopedia of Memory and Memory Disorders. By Richard Noll and Carol Turkington. Facts On File, 1994. 265p. bibliog. index. $45 (0-8160-2610-6).
153.1'2 Memory—Encyclopedias || Memory disorders—Encyclopedias [CIP] 94-1590

In his foreword, Noll, a postdoctoral fellow at Harvard University's Department of the History of Science, states that "we provide a wealth of complex information about human memory in plain language for the general reader, the journalist, the family member of a person with a memory disorder such as Alzheimer's, and even the medical or mental health professional who is lacking the expertise to understand the highly technical professional literature on human memory." The relative contributions of the coauthor are unclear.

The Encyclopedia of Memory and Memory Disorders provides more than 700 lucid entries ranging in length from a sentence or two (e.g., *Narrative Chaining* and *Pursuit Rotor Task*) to several pages (*Alzheimer's Disease* and *Memory Enhancement*). There are entries for drugs, famous researchers, physical and mental disorders, and psychological terms. *See* and *see also* references abound, and terms used within articles that are themselves main entries are indicated in all capital letters. Many of the longer articles are accompanied by short lists of references. A bibliography of several hundred entries draws somewhat more heavily from scholarly sources (e.g., *Nature*, *Psychopharmacology Bulletin*) than from popular ones (*Newsweek*, the *Philadelphia Inquirer*). Appendixes include lists of scholarly journals that publish research in memory and associations dealing with memory problems.

In its treatment of memory, Macmillan's 678-page *Encyclopedia of Learning and Memory* [RBB Ap 15 93] covers substantially the same ground on a more technical level; its signed articles are, unlike *The Encyclopedia of Memory and Memory Disorders*, often complemented by diagrams or photographs. The current work, though, is recommended for its comprehensiveness and accessibility to a general audience. Recommended for academic, public, high-school, and health/medical libraries.

Encyclopedia of Human Intelligence. 2v. Ed. by Robert J. Sternberg. Macmillan, 1994. 1,235p. bibliog. charts. illus. index. $150 (0-02-897407-7).
153.9'03 Intellect—Encyclopedias || Intelligence levels—Encyclopedias [CIP] 93-46975

Interest in intelligence is shared by a range of scholars. The bestselling book, *The Bell Curve*, by Herrnstein and Murray, has reopened the controversy about the relationship of intelligence, social class, and race. Psychologists and educators continue to debate the determiners of intellectual ability. The subject of intellectual growth and decline challenges gerontologists. Interest in intelligence inevitably trickles down to students.

Examples of some of the subjects covered in the *Encyclopedia of Human Intelligence* are abilities and aptitude, achievement testing, age-to-age changes, the bioecological theory of intellectual development, gender differences in intellectual abilities, imaging techniques, clinical neuropsychology, practical intelligence, and spatial abilities. Editor Sternberg, IBM professor of psychology at Yale University, deserves no less than a platinum apple on his desk for his superlative editing abilities.

The 250 alphabetically arranged, signed articles represent a diverse array of topics. The effects of birth order, parenting, and socioeconomic status on intelligence are treated. There are also entries on important researchers in the field, such as Binet and Thorndike, and on intelligence tests, such as the Wechsler Scales of Intelligence. Some entries are illustrated with drawings, charts, or photographs that are useful in explaining anatomy and function of the brain and nervous system. Bibliographies follow each article, and entries are cross-referenced and indexed. Lists of articles and contributors precede the first volume. A 58-page index concludes the set.

There is surprisingly little direct competition for this work. The Oxford Companion to the Mind (Oxford, 1987) is an A-to-Z of nearly 900 pages, considering all aspects of the mind, from the nervous system to sex, from genius to language. The Encyclopedia of Learning and Memory (Macmillan, 1992) is a compendium of 189 articles prepared by scholars in neuroscience and psychology. Its focus is on the process of acquiring new information and the persistence of learning as stored information.

Reference librarians have long wanted a scholarly overview of intelligence. This set is recommended without hesitation for all academic and large public libraries.

Ethics. 3v. Ed. by John K. Roth. Salem Press, 1994. bibliog. illus. indexes. $270 (0-89356-395-1).
170'.3 Ethics—Encyclopedias [CIP] 94-3995

Ethics becomes increasingly important as reasoning power develops; however, the answers to ethical questions are rarely easy or unambiguous. Ethics is designed for those whose ability to make distinctions between right and wrong has developed beyond a basic level but not yet to the sophisticated level of academicians, philosophers, or theologians. In form, its 819 alphabetically arranged articles combine the features of a dictionary and an encyclopedia. That form, unlike the ethical dilemmas real life poses, follows a set pattern—identification of the category of ethics, the date that the topic became relevant, related topics, a brief definition, a summary statement of the topic's significance, the article proper, and see also references. Articles range in length from 250 words to 3,000. Longer articles are signed and include a bibliography. Time lines are provided for some topics, and there are black-and-white portraits of people treated.

Longer articles cover both theoretical and applied ethics as well as the thinkers who developed the concepts, not only in Western thought, but also in Asian and Islamic cultures. In the theoretical category, representative topics include Altruism, Freedom of Expression, Loyalty, Manichaeanism, Selfishness, and Will. In the applied category, topics include Divorce, Illness, Profit Taking, Racism, and Torture. Ethics further demonstrates its concern for applied ethics by covering such topics of current interest as Ethnic Cleansing, Health Care Allocation, Insider Trading, Gay Rights, Surrogate Motherhood, and Kevorkian, Jack. All of these are accessible through a complete table of contents, a thematic index, an index of persons, and a general subject index.

The writing is suitable for students just grappling with knotty ethical problems. The authors explain the history and foundations of each topic, the relation of one thinker's ideas to his or her predecessors', and the topic's ethical implications. Articles on such volatile questions as abortion or the right to die lay out the various arguments in favor of certain positions but refrain from judgments.

Ethics covers nearly twice as many topics as Lawrence Becker and Charlotte Becker's Encyclopedia of Ethics [RBB O 1 92] and has a much stronger emphasis on applied ethics than does that book. It also has more articles on nonwestern cultures and on individual theoreticians. Given the wide range of topics Ethics touches on and its accessible level, this set will enjoy frequent use in public, high-school, and college libraries. The questions it addresses are timeless, and it will help readers come to informed, but probably not uniform, answers.

Encyclopedia of Bioethics. 5v. Ed. by Warren Thomas Reich. Macmillan, 1995. bibliog. index. $425 (0-02-897355-0).
174'.2'03 Bioethics—Encyclopedias || Medical ethics—Encyclopedias [CIP] 94-38743

In 1978, when the highly acclaimed first edition of this encyclopedia appeared in four volumes, bioethics was a new field. Since then the discipline has undergone tremendous change, which is well reflected in this new edition. More than 450 new and updated signed articles cover such topics as Public Health, Population Ethics, and Animal Welfare and Rights. Movements such as Ecofeminism and abstract concepts such as Compassion and Beneficence are treated. International coverage has been strengthened. Essays on medical ethics in many parts of the world are written by authors from those areas or traditions. In addition to the religions treated in the first edition, African Religion, Native American Religion, and Sikhism have been added. Since the first edition was published, such issues as AIDS, DNA typing and the genome project, female circumcision, organ and tissue transplantation, and assisted suicide have arisen. Reproductive technologies such as in vitro fertilization have been successfully employed. All these subjects are covered at length in this five-volume set. In this edition Interpersonal Abuse replaces child abuse and includes elder and domestic-partner abuse. Substance Abuse is broadened to include alcohol. Some articles from the first edition, such as Talcott Parson's Death in the Western World, have been updated with a postscript article by another author. Of special interest to librarians is the new entry Medical Information Systems.

Reich, a professor of bioethics in the School of Medicine at Georgetown University and senior research scholar at the Kennedy Institute of Bioethics, assembled an editorial advisory board of 57 scholars from around the world. They helped select 437 authors from such disciplines as psychology, philosophy, religion, anthropology, law, and history.

The work is organized alphabetically; topics are often subdivided into subtopics, with each section written by a different author. Lengthy bibliographies of scholarly and popular materials conclude entries. A detailed index of almost 100 pages, see references, and extensive cross-referencing at the ends of articles provide access. These cross-references appear in descending order of relevance, under the headings "directly related to this entry," "for further discussion of topics mentioned in this entry," and "for a discussion of related ideas."

Special features include the section "Additional Resources in Bioethics," which contains directory listings of journals and organizations arranged by country. An appendix, "Codes, Oaths, and Directives Related to Bioethics," has increased from four to six sections; "Ethical Directives Pertaining to the Environment" and ". . . to the Welfare and Use of Animals" are new. Other additions include ethical codes from other countries.

By using a wide range of subject experts, the editors have met the challenge of objectivity. Where inevitable conflict of opinion occurs, different viewpoints are presented. For example, the section on male circumcision outlines varying cultural attitudes toward the practice and the medical and ethical issues involved. Language is generally accessible to the layperson; however, due to the variety of authorship, some presentations are more technical than others. The revision is so extensive as to almost make it a new work. It belongs in any library that serves users interested in the wide array of subjects treated. Health-care practitioners, students from high-school through college, and anyone seeking information on bioethics will find a wealth of material in this outstanding reference work.

The New Interpreter's Bible. v.1 of 12. Ed. by Leander E. Keck. Abingdon, 1994. 1,214p. bibliog. $65 (0-687-27814-7).
220.7'7 Bible—Commentaries || Abingdon Press [CIP] 94-21292

It's been more than 40 years since The Interpreter's Bible (IB) was first published (1951–57). With this volume, Abingdon Press (a division of the United Methodist Publishing House) begins publication of a new edition of the set, scheduled to appear in 12 volumes over the next six years. With an 11-person editorial board chaired by Leander E. Keck (Yale University Divinity School), 14 consultants, and 97 contributors, The New Interpreter's Bible (NIB) "is to bring the best in contemporary biblical scholarship into the service of the church to enhance preaching, teaching, and study of the scriptures."

NIB is an ecumenical work with some 25 religions represented among the contributors, though the majority come from Protestant denominations. Nevertheless, as Keck points out in his introduction, the writers in NIB are a far more theologically diverse group than those in IB, which "inevitably reflected the perspectives of white male liberal Protestants." Keck notes that contributors include 22 women (compared with one in IB) as well as African American, Asian American, Hispanic American, and Native American authors.

This first volume includes general essays on the biblical canon and English versions of the Bible and various essays on biblical interpretation and the Old Testament. These introductory essays alone suggest the increased ecumenism of the work; witness the series of essays with such titles as "Reading the Bible as African Americans" and "Reading the Bible as Asian Americans." The bulk of the volume consists of texts and commentary on the books of Genesis, Exodus, and Leviticus. As in IB, the work features two translations and commentary. Unlike IB, however, the dual translations are the New International Version and the New Revised Standard Version, replacing the Authorized (King James) Version and Revised Standard Version of IB. The translations stand out nicely on a green background. The other significant change is that commentary appears after the various units of scripture (such as Genesis 50:15–21 or Exodus 20:12–17) rather than right in the middle of the translations, as was the case with IB, which printed the exegesis and exposition on the same pages as the translation. This created a somewhat confusing appearance for the novice. Each section of the scripture concludes with a "Commentary" and "Reflections." The introductory essay, "Features of The New Interpreter's Bible," indicates that the "Commentary" is an exegetical analysis while the "Reflections" "are meant to stimulate the thought of preachers and teachers." The work is extensively footnoted, and there are several bibliographies as well.

The Board noticed a few minor problems. The text is often of light type; while certainly not unreadable, differences in darkness can be noted from page to page. Also, many of the main, boldface headings in the essays appear in a difficult-to-read green typeface, though many headings also appear in black. Like IB, maps and illustrations are few and far between. Nevertheless, this volume represents an excellent start to the new series. Although the Board will withhold final judgment until the set is complete, academic and public libraries will almost certainly want to add this reasonably priced volume to their collections.

Who's Who in the Bible: An Illustrated Biographical Dictionary. Ed. by Joseph L. Gardner. Readers' Digest. 480p. illus. indexes. maps. $32 (0-89577-618-9).
220.9'2 Bible—Biography [CIP] 94-17591

Described here are more than 500 men and women from the Bible (Hebrew and Christian Scripture and Apocrypha of the Revised Standard Version) or important to biblical history, but not mentioned by name (Alexander the Great, for example). The individuals are in alphabetical order by Anglicized spelling. Most have a paragraph or two, but several need many pages (Abraham gets 10, Moses 11, Peter 7, Paul 12, and Jesus 17). Each entry includes pronunciation and original name (Hebrew, Greek, Latin) as well as a literal meaning, if there is one. Analysis of the person's importance to Judeo-Christian history is offered in many cases, and chapter and verse from the Bible are cited. Cross-referenced names are in bold print. If a name is used for more than one person, they are entered in chronological order as best as can be determined. The index covers topics as well as people. It is preceded by a complete list of every name (more than 3,500) in the Bible. This section has some interesting facts placed throughout ("Jesus is mentioned 990 times, second only to David at 1,100; Moses is third with 870 citations"). Each name is followed by a reference to the Bible passage in which it first appears.

The color illustrations are taken from classical paintings, illuminations, stained glass, and photographs of objects, plus 50 drawings original to this work. Ten maps show the Middle East in Biblical times, some tracing journeys through the area (e.g., Moses, Jesus, Paul). All the illustrations are sharply reproduced. Sidebars with important information are scattered throughout. They cover such varied topics as the Sermon on the Mount, rabbis, child sacrifice, and the Babylonian Noah.

There are many reference works providing biographies of biblical figures— Who's Who in the Bible (Bonanza, 1980), Harper's Bible Dictionary (1985), etc.—but this new biographical dictionary will be an asset to all public and high-school libraries. It is readable and full of beautiful illustrations that will please the browser and be helpful to the researcher. This should be on libraries' A list for purchase; consider getting a second copy for the circulating collection.

Dictionary of Fundamental Theology. Ed. by René Latourelle and Rino Fisichella. Crossroad, 1994. 1,222p. indexes. $75 (0-8245-1395-9).
230'.03 Apologetics—20th century—Dictionaries [CIP] 93-42818

Fundamental theology is a postwar Roman Catholic term for apologetics, and is not to be confused with Protestant fundamentalism. The main concerns of this work are "Christian revelation; its credibility; the response of faith; relations with other Christian communities and other religions; and the relationship of Christian revelation to history,

Philosophy, Psychology, Religion

philosophy, the sciences, culture and language." This dictionary replaces the Dictionnaire Apologétique de la Foi Catholique by A. d'Alxs begun about a hundred years ago. It is a translation of the 1990 Italian Dizionario di Teologia Fondamentale.

Fundamental theology takes into account and addresses today's religious pluralism, the indifference of many people to Christianity, and science as an element in contemporary thought. Fundamental theology has an attitude of dialogue rather than confrontation. The articles Ecumenism, Anglicanism, Lutheranism, Evangelical Churches, Judaism, Islam, and Marxism demonstrate the dialogical approach. Contemporary concern includes anthropology, communication, feminism, the New Age, and the relation between imagination and theology and between literature and theology. There are articles on the great Catholic apologeticists—Augustine, Pascal, Newman, Teilhard de Chardin, as well as on other important Catholics.

The 223 signed articles are written by 93 contributors, 37 of whom (including the editors) teach at the Pontifical Gregorian University in Rome. Other contributors, whose affiliations are also given, represent 15 countries. Articles are long and thorough. Many are divided into sections, and most provide bibliographies. Although written clearly, articles assume familiarity with the complicated body of thought involved and its specialized vocabulary. Two indexes, analytic and systematic, assist in pulling together related topics.

The book is addressed to students of universities and theology schools, clergy, and the layperson—"all who are eager to reflect on the ultimate meaning of the human condition." Libraries of theology schools and universities with strong religion or philosophy departments would certainly want to consider this landmark work, as would some church libraries.

Dictionary of Christian Art. By Diane Apostolos-Cappadona. Continuum, 1994. 376p. bibliog. illus. index. $39.50 (0-8264-0779-X).
246'.03 Christian art and symbolism—Encyclopedias [CIP] 94-34345

This dictionary is intended to give the reader access to the pictorial tradition that was once the common visual vocabulary of Christians. According to the author, an editor of several books on art and religion, laypersons of the medieval and Renaissance periods understood the symbolic significance of objects or saints' attributes depicted in artwork. This dictionary is a fascinating guide to these symbols for contemporary readers. In her introduction, the author describes how the reader might use the dictionary to decipher the meaning of symbolic elements in a painting of the baptism of Christ by the Master of the Saint Bartholomew Altarpiece.

The 1,100 entries are arranged alphabetically and are of several categories. Entries for symbols such as colors, animals, plants, clothing (e.g., scapular), and architectural elements (e.g., apse) are generally brief, with cross-references to longer entries that provide historical background. Persons selected include saints and biblical figures who were either the subjects of a large array of artworks throughout the history of Christianity or were popular during a particular period. Old Testament figures, mythological figures that prefigure Christian figures (Athena as a foretype of Mary), Christian theologians and artists are included if they influenced the symbolism of Christian art. Entries about persons, events with which symbols are associated, or artists usually provide more background than entries for specific symbols. The entry Barbara, for example, explains that the tower became her attribute because she was imprisoned in one; that Barbara is the patron saint of artillery soldiers, gunsmiths, architects, builders, and miners; and that she was invoked against lightning, thunderstorms, and sudden death. It describes her usual depiction in northern medieval art as a richly dressed young woman seated before a tower, reading a book. When appropriate, citations to the New Revised Standard Version of the Bible are included. Entries do not usually list specific artworks that represent the person, event, or symbol.

Other entries provide concise overviews of broader topics, such as Evangelists and Romanesque Art. Longer entries provide numerous cross-references and an index provides access to terms that are not easily identified within the alphabetical arrangement of the book. The 162 small black-and-white illustrations were selected because they exemplify particular symbols. The illustrations do not provide enough detail for thorough examination of the symbolic images they contain. A list of illustrations provides the name of the artist, title of the work, date, current location, size, and medium. A bibliography lists approximately 70 publications that complement the dictionary.

This book is closest in format and scope to George Ferguson's *Signs and Symbols in Christian Art* (Oxford, 1954; reprinted 1972), which is listed in the bibliography. Many of the topics are defined similarly in both books. Apostolos-Cappadona expands the scope of the older work by including references to classical figures, artists, and art terms. Some of her entries provide more cross-references and more detail. Its combination of appeal to a wide variety of readers, engaging subject, and lack of up-to-date competitors make the *Dictionary of Christian Art* an essential purchase for academic, public, and seminary libraries.

Dictionary of Baptists in America. Ed. by Bill J. Leonard. InterVarsity Press, 1994. 298p. paper $16.99 (0-8308-1447-7).
286'.0973 Baptists—U.S.—Dictionaries [CIP] 94-31573

This dictionary is intended as a guide to the largest Protestant religious tradition in America. Ideas, events, people, movements, traditions, institutions, and denominations are presented in 650 signed articles from more than 100 contributors, specialists in historical studies and related to Baptist institutions. Its primary focus is historical, with concentration on movements in the U.S.

The introductory essay, "The Baptists: A People, a History, and an Identity," provides a perspective on widely divergent Baptist beliefs, origins, and the 80 groups that call themselves Baptist. Twentieth-century issues, education, and future developments are considered. Asterisks throughout the essay refer to related articles, providing a subject approach to the alphabetically arranged material that follows.

The articles range from less than a column to several pages. Many have appended bibliographies. Some represent original research and correctives to previously published information. Articles include not only the prominent, but also the obscure. Scope is broad and detail rich: the long article *Baptist Hymnody*, the shorter one *Sacred Harp*. Contemporary issues are addressed: recent Southern Baptist controversies, emergent groups and institutions, some biographies of contemporaries. Such topics as *Inerrancy Controversy* and *Racial Attitudes, Baptist* are treated in a balanced fashion. Asterisks and *see* and *see also* references enable readers to move easily throughout the volume.

William Henry Brackney's *The Baptists* (Greenwood, 1988) would be a good companion to the dictionary. It consists of six essays on central principles of Baptist thought and a biographical dictionary of Baptist leaders. It is much less comprehensive. The only other encyclopedic reference on Baptists is the *Encyclopedia of Southern Baptists* (4v., Broadman, 1958–82).

The *Dictionary of Baptists in America* is a convenient, well-organized, and thorough reference tool. Any interested audience, clerical or lay, Baptist or non-Baptist, will appreciate it. Recommended.

A Sourcebook for Earth's Community of Religions. Rev. ed. Ed. by Joel Beversluis. Sourcebook Project, P.O. Box 6902, Grand Rapids, MI 49516, 1995. 366p. index. paper $18.95 (0-9637897-1-6).
291 Religions || Religions—Relations [CIP] 94-074622

The second World Parliament of Religions, held in Chicago in 1993, 100 years after the historic first parliament, provides the impetus for this volume. Indeed, the first edition was published by the Council for a Parliament of World's Religions on the eve of that meeting. This book is a collection of documents that illustrate the interests of the parliament. It has actual accounts of the parliament and the documents it produced, some of which were in draft form in the earlier edition.

The opening section contains descriptions of the various religious traditions of the world. The scope is broad, extending beyond the traditional religions to include African and Native American religions, wicca, and anthroposophy; even the nonreligion of humanism is included, as well as the controversial Unification Church. The documents in this section not only outline the beliefs of these various groups, but, in many cases, address how each tradition approaches the concerns of ecumenism, the environment, and economic and social justice that were the focus of the parliament. The second section contains documents on interfaith cooperation, notably "Towards a Global Ethic," authored by Hans Kung and adopted by the parliament. The next section examines various social and environmental problems, with responses by various faiths and by the interfaith community; the fourth section, "Choosing Our Future," looks at such groups as women, children, and dispossessed peoples, and at ways the religious community can help solve the world's problems. The final section, new to this edition, is an annotated resource guide, listing organizations, books, videotapes, and Internet resources.

This is by its nature an eclectic group of documents. Many come out of other organizations with interests similar to the World Parliament, such as the Inter-Religious Federation for World Peace. Prayers and meditations are interspersed with more discursive materials. There is a great deal of value here for patrons seeking information or source material for interfaith cooperation, or for liberal religious perspectives on global problems. Certain material may strike some as overly trendy, such as the "Twelve Steps of Ecological Spirituality." But there is enough significant material that most libraries will want this on their shelves; most will place it in the circulating collection, despite the inclusion of a detailed index in this edition.

The Encyclopedia of Eastern Philosophy and Religion. Ed. by Stephan Schuhmacher and Gert Woerner. Shambhala, 1994. 468p. bibliog. illus. paper $22.50 (0-87773-980-3).
291'.095 Asia—Religion—Dictionaries || Religions—Dictionaries || Philosophy, Oriental—Dictionaries [CIP] 88-15837

This encyclopedia purports to be "a complete survey of the teachers, traditions, and literature of Asian wisdom." With more than 4,000 entries compiled by four experts, one each for Buddhism, Taoism, Zen, and Hinduism, it is certainly as close to complete as any single-volume work covering four religions can be.

The short introduction explains the compiler's intention to give the nonscholar a readable guide to these complicated belief systems. There is a pronunciation guide to the five original languages: Pali, Sanskrit, Tibetan, Chinese, and Japanese. Entries are in alphabetical order in their most common transliteration. Each entry includes a symbol indicating its religion and a literal translation of the term followed by its definition. The numerous cross-references are indicated by an arrow preceding the term. In-depth explanations or biographies are often included in the entries in smaller print. There are many diagrams and photographs to enhance the text. Those terms that are common to two or more disciplines, but have divergent meanings, have separate entries. An extensive bibliography is divided into the four religions and subdivided by primary and secondary sources.

It seems appropriate to compare this title to the recently reviewed *Historical Dictionary of Buddhism* (HDB) [RBB N 1 93], which also covers Zen. The pronunciation guides are similar; the encyclopedia includes a detailed chart of pinyin to Wade-Giles transliteration. The entries in HDB are shorter, and the language is more scholarly, whereas the encyclopedia has more in-depth explanations and is easier to read. For example, in HDB the entry *Shambhala* is 59 words in length with no cross-references; in the encyclopedia it is 250 words with six cross-references. There is no entry in HDB for *Yoga*; the encyclopedia's entry is more than 200 words. The encyclopedia devotes 1 pages to *Zen* and includes a Ch'an/Zen lineage chart, whereas HDB has a 150-word paragraph.

On the whole, the encyclopedia is easier and more interesting to read than HDB (in spite of the smaller type) and includes illustrations. At half the price, it is the better choice for high-school and small public libraries. An academic, religious, or large public library may want both titles.

Larousse Dictionary of Beliefs and Religions. Ed. by Rosemary Goring. Larousse, 1994. 605p. illus. $30 (0-7523-5000-5).
291.03 Faith || Religion || Religions || Theology [OCLC] 93-72903

Jacket copy describes this dictionary as "a comprehensive outline of spiritual concepts from pre-history to the present." Indeed, it covers ideas conceived in caves and "rediscovered" by New Age seekers. In the preface, the editors explain their three main objectives: to give insight into the major tenets of current and historic religions, to point out the similarities and differences in these teachings, and to explain rituals in order to allay some cultural biases.

Most of the alphabetically arranged entries are 100–250 words in length. They cover people, places, ideas, deities, and rituals of 29 religions or groups of religions (e.g., Native American religions, secularism). Cross-references are indicated at the ends of articles by a triangle. Line drawings illustrate some entries. Pronunciation is given for most foreign terms. The writing is to the point and quite readable.

There are three appendixes—population distribution by religion in various countries, festivals by religion using both the Gregorian calendar and that for the particular culture, and a list of entries by religion or concept (e.g., *Study of Religion*). A quick perusal of this list shows that Christianity has more entries than any other religion.

In reading the entries, the Board found some interesting anomalies that reflect the limitations of the scope of the dictionary. The general entry *Festival* is followed by entries for Ancient Near East, Christian, Chinese and Greek festivals, but none for Jewish, Hindu, Buddhist, or Muslim festivals (these are, however, represented in the appendix). There is the entry *Holy War, Jewish*, but none for Muslim or even holy wars in general, and no cross-references to *Jihad*, the entry that describes the Muslim concept of holy war, nor *Crusades*. The entry *Holocaust* speaks only of its use for the genocide of the Jews in World War II, not its biblical meaning, which would explain why it is used in its current context.

This work is similar to *The Facts On File Dictionary of Religions* (1985). In spite of the criticisms above, Larousse has given religion reference collections a title well worth considering, especially by small public and school libraries, for its affordability and usefulness.

Goddesses, Heroes, and Shamans: The Young People's Guide to World Mythology. By David Bellingham and others. Kingfisher, 1994. 159p. illus. index. $19.95 (1-85697-999-7).
291.1'3 Mythology—Juvenile literature || Legends [CIP] 94-1374

This attractively illustrated encyclopedia is intended for children in the upper-elementary grades. Its short entries on more than 500 mythical characters, heroes, and shamans were written by qualified contributors who lecture at universities on the topic of mythology. The work begins with an overview essay about the development and origin of myths. The body of the work is divided by geographic regions: "Northern Lands," "Africa," "Mediterranean," "Eastern Asia," "Central and South America," and "South Pacific Lands." Each of these regional chapters begins with a short essay introducing the different peoples and their mythologies, a map, and a time line. The six geographic chapters are further subdivided into subsections such as North America or Greece. These subsections contain A–Z entries for the mythical characters. Colorful drawings often highlight key deities or heroes. Names in small-capital letters indicate that there is another entry for that character in the encyclopedia; however, no page numbers are given for these *see also* entries. The reader must turn to the index in order to find the additional entry.

The entries, which vary in length from about 25 to 75 words, contain adequate information for the curious young reader, but the arrangement of the information will make it difficult for anyone doing research. Since it is not in a single alphabetical arrangement, the reader must use the index.

The one-page glossary contains useful information about such terms as *shaman*, but it does not have a pronunciation guide, nor is there one in the body of the work. There also seems to be a real bias toward Greek mythology—a full 17 pages are devoted to this system, whereas only three pages are devoted to Roman mythology. The information on Native American mythology is not detailed enough for the North American market.

In school and public libraries that need additional information on mythology, this volume will supplement other titles, such as *Greek and Roman Mythology A to Z: A Young Reader's Companion* (Facts On File, 1992) and *Norse Mythology A to Z* (Facts On File, 1991).

Voyages in Classical Mythology. By Mary Ellen Snodgrass. ABC-Clio, 1994. 478p. bibliog. illus. indexes. $49.50 (0-87436-734-4).
291.1'3 Mythology, Classical || Voyages and travels—Mythology [CIP] 94-21167

This volume retells the stories of the voyages of 44 heroes and dieties from Greek mythology, arranged from *Achilles* to *Theseus*. An introduction explains the importance of these stories to the ancient Greeks. It also explains that they are related here in the purest, least-embellished form, as they existed before the gods were renamed and given different qualities by the Romans. Snodgrass is a prolific author of reference books for young adults and librarians.

Each traveler has a chapter that begins with a black-and-white illustration depicting the god or hero. These illustrations vary in style, and many are not attractive. A phonetic spelling is given after each name, and then the chapter is divided as follows: "Genealogy and Background" ; "Journey," which describes the voyage and what makes the subject's story important; "Alternate Versions," which gives some common variations on the basic tale; and "Symbolism," which explains symbols commonly associated with the subject and what they represent. Each chapter concludes with cross-references to other tales in which this subject appears and a bibliography of ancient writings in which this tale is told. Each also includes a family tree and a map showing where incidents occured. The book includes a glossary, a bibliography, a time line, and both general and geographic indexes.

This book appears to be intended for the high-school student or adult. The illustrations would not attract younger readers, and the information is not presented in an entertaining manner. The book would be an excellent tool for the older student reading *The Odyssey* or *The Illiad* or the plays of Sophocles or for the adult trying to get some facts straight concerning familiar tales.

Encyclopedia of Creation Myths. By David Adams Leeming and Margaret Adams Leeming. ABC-Clio, 1994. 330p. bibliog. illus. index. $60 (0-87436-739-5).
291.2'4 Creation—Comparative studies—Encyclopedias [CIP] 94-7169

This attractively illustrated work is the first to bring together creation myths from a wide variety of cultures in an encyclopedic format, though a number of anthologies of creation myths do exist. The principal author, a professor of English and comparative literature at the University of Connecticut, has written or edited several popular books on mythology. The majority of entries are retellings of various creation myths; for example, *Eskimo Creation* or *Hebrew Creation*. There are also entries for important themes (*Creation from Clay*), gods and other figures (*Prometheus*), bodies of literature (*Bible*), and scientific "myths" (*Big Bang Theory*). Entries range from a single sentence to several pages; a number contain extensive portions of important creation texts. Most contain references to one or more sources listed in the bibliography at the end of the book. Liberal cross-references are both embedded in the text and at the end of entries. The 30 black-and-white illustrations depict creation myths in art and artifact. An extensive, detailed, and generally accurate index concludes the book.

Unfortunately, despite a great deal of useful information contained in this book, it too often falls short of the standards of accuracy and completeness one expects. The entry *Maori Creation*, for example, indicates that the god Io is the "timeless *ex nihilo* creator of the universe," failing to mention that many now believe this conception of Io to be the result of missionaries attempting to reconcile the native religion with Christianity. The entry *Shoshonean (Luiseno) Creation* indicates that the "Shoshonean Indians" and Luiseno people refer to the same group, while in fact the Luiseno are only one small tribe who speak a language from the Shoshonean language group, one that includes the Hopi, Shoshoni, and Comanche languages, among others. *Yahweh* contains the puzzling statement that Yahweh "formed part of the Indo-European invasion into the Fertile Crescent region." The article *Earth-Diver Creation* explains this common form of the creation story as a supreme being who "sends an animal . . . into primal waters," and that the diver animal "can best be seen as the creator's spirit or soul." This is certainly an interpretation of this myth that has been made. Here, however, it is presented as the primary meaning of the myth, with no mention that in many versions the diver is (or is sent by) a cultural hero distinct from and often antagonistic to the supreme being. A check of the *Encyclopedia of Religion* will yield a very different account of this archetype.

There are other problems as well. For a significant number of entries, the only reference given is to Maria Leach's *The Beginnings* (Crowell, 1956), a young adult book. This encyclopedia seems aimed at users in high-school, undergraduate, and public libraries; however, words such as *parthogenic* appear without definitions. The work also lapses into vague and overgeneralized statements; we are told that the Maori "possess a highly sophisticated and complicated religious and mythological system that concerns itself with profound spiritual matter and the nature of Being itself." In short, although this work contains much useful information and fulfills a need, it cannot be recommended.

The Atlas of Sacred Places: Meeting Points of Heaven and Earth. By James Harpur. Holt, 1994. 240p. bibliog. illus. index. $45 (0-8050-2775-0).
291.3'5 Sacred places—Guide-books [CIP] 94-4597

The Atlas of Wild Places: In Search of the Earth's Last Wildernesses. By Roger Few. Facts On File, 1994. 240p. illus. index. $35 (0-8160-3168-1).
508 Natural history || Biotic communities || Wilderness areas [OCLC] 94-11375

Though these books have different U.S. publishers, they were both prepared by the same U.K. packager and are similar in format.

The Atlas of Sacred Places treats 33 places sacred to various religions of the world, ranging from Mount Sinai to Canterbury Cathedral. Each four- to eight-page entry is about half text and half beautiful color photographs. There is a small locator map for each site; simple two-page maps are provided for some entries (e.g., "The Mounds of Ancient North America"). A "gazetteer" giving information for the visitor is followed by a bibliography and index.

The Atlas of Wild Places treats 53 wilderness areas around the world. Again, it has gorgeous pictures and practically no maps. Entries on such places as the Okefenokee Swamp and the Empty Quarter are followed by a gazetteer and index.

These handsome books are not atlases by any stretch of the imagination, but they will be useful additions to circulating geography and travel collections in public libraries. —*Sandy Whiteley*

Junior Judaica: Encyclopaedia Judaica for Youth. 6v. Rev. ed. Ed. by Raphael Posner. Macmillan, 1994. 185p./v. illus. index. $150 (0-02-897172-8).

296.03 Jews—Dictionaries and encyclopedias [OCLC]

This six-volume set is a condensed and updated version of the *Encyclopaedia Judaica*, a 16-volume work published in 1972. Originally published in Israel, this is the first edition of *Junior Judaica* available in the U.S. Designed for students in middle and high school, the 1,200 alphabetically arranged entries (compared with 25,000 in the parent set) cover various aspects of Jewish life, history, and culture. Entries include biblical and historical figures, religious observances, and places or events relevant to Judaism. While the set was compiled in Israel, specifically American institutions are treated. There are the entries, for example, *Galveston Plan, Jewish Theological Seminary of America*, and those on famous American Jews from Abraham Joshua Heschel to Sammy Davis Jr. Most entries in this set appear to be derived from the parent set, but they do not carry the name of the original contributor. Some entries are new (*King David Hotel; Law, Jewish*). All of the 1,500 illustrations are in black and white, and all are captioned with additional information not contained in the relevant article. The visuals consist of maps, photographs, charts, and paintings. Many of the illustrations are from the 1972 set. Although most are of historical events and thus the age doesn't matter, some are dated. Every article about a country includes a small outline map of the world region, with the country highlighted. Some illustrations, though on the same page, are positioned a confusing distance from the relevant article. Asterisks next to words in entries indicate cross-references; many entries end with lists of additional cross-references. There are no bibliographies.

Each volume begins with a transliteration guide to be used with the Hebrew words found in many articles. Volume 6 contains a comprehensive index and a 100-year Jewish calendar with Gregorian equivalents. The index contains cross-references, foreign terms and their definitions, and short sketches of people, places, or items not included elsewhere; illustrations are not indexed.

Coverage is generally current, with separate entries for each of the independent states formerly in the Soviet Union and mention of the Rabin-Arafat handshake. Even though there is no individual article on Arafat, there is one on the PLO. The population figures in *Israel* have been updated, as has the table of Jewish Nobel Prize winners. Famous Jews who do not have an individual article are often listed in the entry for their profession, such as *Theater, Inventors,* or *Sports*. Many contemporary Jews, however, have not been added to these articles. There is no mention of Steven Spielberg, for example. The parent set had excellent coverage of American Jewish writers, including Saul Bellow and Elie Wiesel, but authors are given scant coverage in *Junior Judaica*. The article *United States* discusses important issues for American Jews, but they all date to the 1960s; there is no mention, for example, of intermarriage. Rabbi Stephen Wise, an important American Jewish leader, is not given an entry.

Most of the information here can be found in other encyclopedias, but this work presents the Jewish perspective. The relationships between Judaism and the everyday world can be seen in articles on secular topics such as *Birds* and *Blindness*. The vocabulary is appropriate for students in middle or lower high school. The explanations are easily understood, even by a non-Jew. *Junior Judaica* will be valuable in a multicultural context in school or public libraries.

Body, Mind & Spirit: A Dictionary of New Age Ideas, People, Places, and Terms. By Eileen Campbell and J. H. Brennan. Tuttle, 1994. 250p. bibliog. paper $14.95 (0-8048-3010-X).

299'.93 New Age movement—Dictionaries [CIP] 94-4904

Covering a range of subjects—spiritual and esoteric traditions, paranormal phenomena, and people and places—the authors hope their work "will provide a useful starting point for those embarking on a voyage of self-discovery." Entries range from *Acupuncture* to *Zoroastrianism* and include biographical sketches of the standard people in the field, such as Madame Blavatsky and Edgar Cayce. Such current popular theories as *A Course in Miracles, Crystals,* and *Pyramid Power* are treated. Most entries are a paragraph in length; a few, such as *Hypnosis*, are more than two pages. *See* references are clearly indicated; *see also* references are shown in boldface type. (It would be helpful to have the latter convention explained in the foreword.) The authors attempt to represent a variety of traditions, including Western and Eastern religions, Native American spirituality, and others. The extensive bibliography is a mixture of the scholarly and the popular.

Originally published in Great Britain as *Dictionary of Mind, Body and Spirit*, this book is similar to other popular treatments of this topic, such as *Harper's Encyclopedia of Mystical & Paranormal Experience* (1991). While not an essential purchase, *Body, Mind & Spirit* will be useful in libraries where clients are interested in New Age religions and spiritual movements.

Social Sciences

From Aristotelian to Reaganomics: A Dictionary of Eponyms with Biographies in the Social Sciences. By Richard C. S. Trahair. Greenwood, 1994. 693p. bibliog. index. $110 (0-313-27961-6).

300'.3 Social sciences—Dictionaries || Eponyms—Dictionaries || Biography—Dictionaries [CIP] 93-37503

Eponyms—naming things, events, or social phenomena for persons—are a way of immortalizing those with whom we associate memorable and/or notorious activities. Trahair limits the eponyms here to the social sciences and related disciplines. Eponyms were chosen from general reading and scanning textbooks, dictionaries, professional journals, and newspapers. The final choice of entries was his personal predilection, which accounts for the inclusion of such entries as *Brokaw hazard*, a reference to the TV journalist's style of interviewing. Some entries are recent, for example, *Clinton Republicans, Clintonism, Clinton doctrine*. He includes fictitious characters such as *Fagin*, names of places such as *Masada* and *Jonestown*, and such familiar terms as *Nobel Prize* and *Fulbright Scholarships*. Where this dictionary differs from others is in the often scholarly choice of entries. For example, the pocket-size *Webster's New World Dictionary of Eponyms* (Simon & Schuster, 1990) uses the term *maverick* to refer to anyone who "takes an independent stand." Trahair lists *maverick independent*, a reference to a British political term. There are more than 1,000 entries; almost one-third are from government and politics. With half as many, the nearest competitor is sociology, followed by economics, religion, business, psychology, philosophy, education, anthropology, legal studies, popular culture, language and linguistics, human geography, gender, and journalism. The eponyms are listed under these classifications in an appendix.

The alphabetically arranged entries include a definition, the period when the term was used, a brief biographical sketch of the individual for whom the term was named, and a list of biographical sources that are easily found in most academic libraries. A select bibliography of titles about eponyms is at the end of the volume, followed by an index.

Beeching's *Dictionary of Eponyms* (Library Association, 1989) and *Webster's* are not focused on the social sciences and are more suited for quick reference for familiar eponyms. *Eponyms Dictionaries Index* (Gale, 1977) is much larger but dated. Zusne's *Eponyms in Psychology* (Greenwood, 1987) is an excellent source for that discipline. For eponymous nouns, adjectives, and phrases, *From Aristotelian to Reaganomics* spans centuries of social science and touches important people, places, and events throughout the history of Western civilization. It is a useful purchase for academic libraries, especially those serving political science and upper-level sociology programs.

Fieldwork in the Library: A Guide to Research in Anthropology and Related Area Studies. By R. C. Westerman. ALA, 1994. 357p. indexes. paper $45 (0-8389-0632-X).

016.301 Reference books—Anthropology—Bibliography || Anthropology—Research || Anthropology—Bibliography [CIP] 94-5684

Westerman believes a search should be guided by "a sense of process rather than by a knowledge of forms." In the construction of this guide he abjures "linear arrangements." The result is a veritable cat's cradle of references to library tools in anthropology and related disciplines. According to the author, it is designed to assist librarians and students of anthropology who are without anthropological training; however, *Fieldwork* goes well beyond this. It begins with the introductory chapter "What Every Anthropologist Needs to Know." Throughout this work, the author refers the reader to other guides, such as John Weeks' *Introduction to Library Research in Anthropology* (Westview, 1991), Kibbee's *Cultural Anthropology: A Guide to Reference and Information Sources* (Libraries Unlimited, 1991), and *Guide to Reference Books* (ALA, 1986 and 1992). He avoids repeating their fundamental groundwork and supplements with scholarly works that augment the basic sources. These are often in French or German and represent worldwide scholarly research.

Westerman rejects the traditional method of organization by format. Part 1 covers the theoretical framework of anthropology. He devotes a chapter to a thorough coverage of computer files, including online services and CD-ROMs in related disciplines. Chapters on archaeology and material culture, ethnology/cultural anthropology, anthropological linguistics, and physical and biological anthropology follow. Each entry is fully annotated with copious advice on what to use and where to go next. This is facilitated by the use of an alphanumeric code for each entry. Throughout *Fieldwork* Westerman refers back and forth to other entries by their codes, weaving a process of research. Formats such as bibliographies, handbooks, maps, unpublished materials, and dissertations are repeated as strategic headings. Part 2 of the work is devoted to area studies, which include, in addition to standard regions, "CIS and Europe" and a unique section, "Islamic Influence and Israel."

Westerman is responsible for the chapter on anthropology in Webb's *Sources of Information in the Social Sciences* (ALA, 1986). He retains the same method of coding in *Fieldwork*, drops many of the sources, and adds a tremendous amount of value. This book belongs in every library devoted to anthropological research, especially at the graduate level.

The PDR Family Guide to Women's Health and Prescription Drugs. Medical Economics Data, 1994. 926p. bibliog. illus. indexes. paper $24.95 (1-56363-086-9).
301.15 Women—Health and hygiene || Gynecology—Popular works [OCLC] 94-76809

According to Ehrenreich and English in their book, *For Her Own Good: 150 Years of the Experts' Advice to Women* (Anchor, 1978), "In 1972, a women's health movement—composed of women health workers, community activists, and dissatisfied health care consumers—was taking form as a distinct feminist force." Today, women's health issues are a focal point in medical research, public policy, and the political arena. From the publishers of the nation's leading professional drug reference, *The Physician's Desk Reference*, comes a source that will quickly become a "must have" for libraries. The guide is the second in the publisher's consumer series. It is divided into two major parts. An overview of the diseases and disorders that threaten women constitutes the first part of the book. They are arranged into sections: the reproductive system; general health concerns (heart disease, AIDS, headaches, plastic surgery); fertility and family planning, pregnancy, menopause; emotional problems (stress, depression, eating disorders); and cancer.

The second part provides readers with detailed information on medicines their doctors are most likely to prescribe. Readers will appreciate the presentation of information in an easy-to-read format. Entries for each drug include the reasons why it is prescribed, how the medication should be taken, side effects, possible food and drug interactions, special information for those who are pregnant or breastfeeding, and recommended dosage. A "Drug Identification Guide" in the beginning of the book includes color photographs of pills. Appendixes include a directory of support groups, a glossary of common words in women's health, and information on safe medication use. A disease and disorder index is followed by a general index. Finally, a list of sources rounds out the volume. The guide is heavily illustrated with drawings and useful sidebars, tables, and charts.

Shortcomings of the guide merit attention, although they do not compromise the Board's recommendation of this source. The specific health problems of women of color or HIV-positive women are not adequately covered. Black women would be better served by works that look directly at the health issues that confront them, such as *The Black Women's Health Book* (Seal, 1990). Similarly, HIV-positive women will find the *Gynecological Care Manual for HIV Positive Women* (Essential Medical Information Systems, 1993) a much-needed reference. A second shortcoming is less obvious, yet equally significant. The subject of sexual health is buried in the guide. Readers interested in obtaining the essential facts for a safe, healthful sex life will be frustrated. A final shortcoming is the book's organization. Diseases and disorders in the first part are arranged from a medical perspective, not from a woman's perspective. An alternative arrangement might have been the one used in a recent popular source, *Woman, Your Body, Your Health: The Essential Guide for Well-Being* (Harcourt/Harvest, 1990).

Competition is provided by Facts On File's *A-to-Z of Women's Health*, now in its second edition (1989), which literally goes from *abnormal presentation* to *zygote intrafallopian transfer* with concise, straightforward information. It can often be found on the bookshelf next to the recently updated *Our Bodies, Our Selves* (Simon & Schuster, 1992). By and for women, this tome covers relationships and sexuality, fertility, childbearing, growing older, common and uncommon health and medical problems, and women and the medical system.

None of these books bills itself as a substitute for a clinical examination. Each serves to raise facts and questions that merit further discussion. *The PDR Family Guide to Women's Health* joins these standard works in encouraging women to take responsibility for their health by becoming aware of available care and treatment. All librarians (high school and up) will want to make room for this title in their reference collections.

The Continuum Encyclopedia of Symbols. By Udo Becker. Continuum, 1994. 345p. bibliog. illus. $39.50 (0-8264-0644-0).
302.2'2203 Signs and symbols—Dictionaries [CIP] 94-11000

Becker, an authority on semiotics (the theory of signs and symbols), has produced a scholarly compendium of symbols. Translated from the original German, more than 1,500 entries are arranged alphabetically, along with 800 illustrations, most of them in black and white, with an insert of colorplates. As he states in the foreword, the selection from the inestimable number of symbolic signs is always a personal one by the editor. Readers will find symbolic meanings for common objects, such as the rose, cross, and numbers, as well as the Greek god Tyche, valerian weed, and ancient mythical giant Ymir. Exploring a wealth of objects and concepts, this encyclopedia traces symbols to their cultural, religious, or mythological origins in 50–100 words. A short bibliography provides additional references.

Dictionaries of symbols abound, and each covers some different symbols. *Dictionary of Symbols* [RBB Ja 1 92] has 1,500 symbols arranged by shape and is more strictly limited to graphic symbols. This new book gives the symbolic meaning of such things as *hair*, *the desert*, and *sneezing*, which are not written symbols. It would be appropriate for academic libraries that need additional sources in this area.

Marching to a Different Drummer: Unrecognized Heroes of American History. By Robin Kadison Berson. Greenwood, 1994. 368p. bibliog. illus. indexes. $45 (0-313-28802-X).
303.48'4 Social reformers—U.S.—Biography || Dissenters—U.S.—Biography [CIP] 93-49533

Profiling 35 reformers and activists prominent in American history from the eighteenth to the twentieth century, the author says her work is "a celebration of the maladjustment that has, small increments at a time, moved American society closer to the ideals we are proud to profess." Many of these individuals are familiar only to students of the discipline. They include such figures as Sara Josephine Baker, George Washington Cable, Florence Kelley, and Rose Schneiderman. Berson says her selection of subjects was based "not on material success or achievements (of the subjects), but on the breadth and quality of the vision that animated these lives."

To emphasize the scope and balance of her selection of reformers, the book begins with four subject lists: social reformers by date of birth, by gender, by ethnicity, and by major focus of activity. The gender breakdown includes 20 women and 16 men, while in terms of ethnicity, the book includes eight African Americans, two Asian Americans, two Native Americans, two Hispanics, and 23 European Americans. The major focuses include six abolitionists, 20 civil or minority rights activists, nine labor rights activists, seven social reformers, nine women's rights activists, and 11 "freedom of conscience" activists. Some of the reformers appear in more than one category.

The profiles are arranged alphabetically by surname (William Apess

Social Sciences

to Minoru Yasui). The birth and death dates for each activist are given, as well as a brief abstract summarizing the significance of the reformer's life and activities. A photo or illustration of each individual follows. A lengthy essay puts the reformer's life in perspective, discusses and analyzes his or her activities and puts them in the context of the times, and assesses the individual's place in American history. The essays are followed by a list of references used by the author in compiling the profile.

Marching to a Different Drummer will be a valuable addition to academic, public, and high school libraries interested in building their resources on some of the unsung heroes of American history.

American Population Change Annual: A Between-the-Census-Years Guide to Local Area Population Data and Trends. Toucan Valley, 142 Milpitas Blvd., Ste. 260, Milpitas, CA 95035, 1994. charts. paper $42 (1-884925-01-4; ISSN 1078-0033).
304.6'2 U.S.—Population—Statistics—Periodicals || Cities and towns—U.S.—Statistics—Periodicals [OCLC] 94-643181

Private enterprise continues to publish government information in a more timely manner than the government itself. Toucan Valley Publications has taken statistics issued by the Census Bureau in April 1994 and packaged them in a volume designed to supplement the 1990 census. The introduction to this first edition of *American Population Change Annual* says that the population estimates are the most current. The Board could find no reason to dispute this statement.

Provided in tabular form are the 1990 official population and 1992 percent change, number of births and deaths, and net domestic and foreign migration for all counties or county-equivalents. These statistics, which are arranged by state, then metropolitan areas, and then counties, are ranked by the percent change 1990–92. Preceding each state table are three or four paragraphs of text that discuss the salient points of the statistics. A map of each state shows population change: a loss, 0-2 percent gain, 2.1-4 percent gain, and greater than 4 percent gain. Metropolitan areas are identified on the maps, but unfortunately the counties are not.

The last third of the book is an alphabetical list of counties, cities, and incorporated places giving their 1992 estimated population and the percent change from 1990. There are two appendixes—one with a list of states ranked by population growth (these are not numbered, so it is necessary to count to discover that New York is forty-fifth) and the other listing metropolitan areas, also ranked by growth. It is ironic that the largest net population decrease (-3.6 percent) occurred in our nation's capital, the District of Columbia.

Responding to the great interest in and concern about domestic migration to the South and West and immigration to the country as a whole, this book provides a clear, concise, up-to-date look at these statistics. Recommended for public, high-school, and academic libraries.

The Penguin Atlas of Diasporas. By Gerard Chailand and Jean-Pierre Rageau. Viking, 1995. 184p. charts. illus. maps. $34.95 (0-670-85439-5).
304.8 Man—Migrations—Atlases || Migrations of nations—Atlases [CIP] 94-20640

The diaspora or dispersion of a people from their native land has been a phenomenon since the beginning of recorded history. In their introduction to this beautifully illustrated survey of major dispersions, two French historians establish their criteria for a diaspora: the forced dispersion of a religious and/or ethnic group, the memory of the group in transmitting historical facts and cultural heritage, the will to survive through transmission of this heritage, and dispersion over a long time period.

The diasporas described in separate chapters are Jewish (one-third of the book), Armenian, Gypsy, African, Chinese, Indian, Irish, Greek, Lebanese, Palestinian, and Vietnamese and Korean. Each dispersion is described objectively from the beginnings of the group's movement to the situation today. Clearly drawn colored and coded maps trace each group's movement across continents and over oceans and show the areas where they settled. Scale is not noted on maps, but this is unnecessary in conveying the sense of the dispersion. When appropriate, chronologically arranged tables, population charts, pictorial illustrations, or pertinent quotations are included. Some of the chapters have only one to two pages of text, but the maps and illustrations complete our understanding. Some facts are footnoted, and sources of quotations are cited.

The Penguin Atlas of Diasporas will be a welcome addition to school, public, and undergraduate libraries. More detailed information on each group is available in other works, but this attractive atlas will provide a clear and accurate overview for students and general users.

Older Americans Almanac. Ed. by Ronald J. Manheimer. Gale, 1994. 881p. bibliog. charts. illus. index. $99.50 (0-8103-8348-9).
305.26'0973 Old age—U.S.—Encyclopedias || Aged—U.S.—Encyclopedias || Aging—U.S.—Encyclopedias || Gerontology—U.S.—Encyclopedias [CIP] 94-9305

If there is any doubt that the population is aging, the number of recent books dealing with all aspects of aging will certainly convince the skeptics.

This title is similar in concept to such other Gale sources as *African American Almanac* and *Hispanic American Almanac* [RBB Ap 15 93]. It incorporates some of the statistical information from the *Statistical Record of Older Americans* [RBB Je 1 & 15 94]. Eleven major topics are organized into 38 chapters. The focus is on aging-related topics, facts, statistics, and interpretation of research. Self-help and how-to materials are included only in the bibliography. Sections include aging processes, employment and retirement, finance, relationships, health, elder care, and lifestyle. Chapters in the demographics section, for example, cover the history of aging, population growth, and gender and ethnic diversity among the older population. The technology section includes chapters on the attitudes of older adults toward technology and a discussion of medical technology and assistive technology available to this group.

Statistical tables, charts, and graphs illustrate the points made. Where appropriate, directory information is given for agencies, organizations, and businesses. Throughout the book, profiles of outstanding, innovative older people are featured in highlighted boxes. Black-and-white photographs add interest. Access to the information is provided through the detailed table of contents and the subject index.

This is a serious overview of the aging population, which expands on the statistical information. For example, demographic terms are explained, and factors that influence the aging of a population are explored. Aging legislation and national policy are reviewed as are the attitudes and policies of organized religion toward the elderly.

Colleges, universities, and professional schools with gerontology programs will find this title a useful purchase. Public libraries may also want to consider it.

Statistical Record of Children. Ed. by Linda Schmittroth. Gale, 1994. 800p. index. tables. $99 (0-8103-9196-1; ISSN 1075-5063).
305'.23 Children—Statistics [BKL] 94-4882

This compendium of statistical data reflects practically every aspect of childhood. Information has been gathered from government documents and databases, surveys from private associations and organizations, magazine polls and periodical articles, and other references to present a statistical portrait of contemporary American children. More than 150 original sources have been consulted to provide numbers on topics ranging from how many children live in poverty (21.8 percent, according to the Bureau of Census) and how many children are injured in sledding accidents (1,574 in 1991, as quoted in the *Detroit Free Press*) to favorite sports (basketball is first, followed by baseball, football, swimming, soccer, softball, biking, horseback riding, and roller skating, as rated in a *Sports Illustrated for Kids* survey). All sources are listed with complete bibliographic and ordering information in a separate appendix.

As with similar titles from Gale, such as *Statistical Record of Older Americans* [RBB Je 1 & 15 94], data are presented almost exclusively in tables, although a few bar graphs and pie charts are included. A minimum number of entries appear in text format: brief newspaper articles, excerpts from annual reports, etc. Explanatory commentaries that appeared with original documents are sometimes included. Print is large, and the tables are laid out in a readable format. The 929 tables are arranged in 10 broad subject areas, such as education; nutrition, health and medical care; child care; domestic life; and international comparisons. Like topics are grouped together; in the chapter on crime, individual tables regarding cognitive, emotional, interpersonal, physical, and psychological adult implications of childhood sexual abuse follow each other. In the keyword index, both general and specific terms are used.

Of particular interest to educators and child-care providers, and containing a wealth of information for researchers, this tool will be of use in public, high-school, and academic collections. While some of the information is taken from such standard titles as the *Statistical Abstract of the United States* and *American Demographics*, much of the data have been drawn from unpublished or less widely accessible sources.

500 Great Books By Women: A Reader's Guide. By Erica Bauermeister and others. Viking/Penguin, 1994. 426p. indexes. hardcover $27.95 (0-670-84829-8); paper $12.95 (0-14-017590-3).
016.3054 Women—Bibliography || Literature—Women authors—Bibliography [OCLC] 94-15989

Representing diverse voices and cultures ranging from the thirteenth century to the contemporary period, the 500 works by women recommended in this guide are those that the compilers "found to be thought-provoking, beautiful, and satisfying." Among the selections are works by Aphra Behn, Jane Austen, Marguerite Duras, Barbara Tuchman, Gail Godwin, and Amy Tan.

To be considered for inclusion, books had to be written in prose, available in English, and in print. Although approximately half were published in the U.S., the selections also represent 70 other countries. The compilers note that they made a particular effort to include works by women of color and those originally written in languages other than English.

The bibliography is divided into 21 sections according to broad themes, among them "Growing Old," "Mothers and Mothering," and "Power." Each section is preceded by a brief introduction and a list of the titles and authors of the works treated in that section. The entries, which are arranged alphabetically by title, include rather skimpy bibliographic information: author, year of publication, country of book content, and translation information (when appropriate). Each work is also identified by genre (e.g., essays, novel, autobiography). The lively and captivating annotations of 225–250 words were written by the compilers or one of the 30 other women who served as contributors. Skillfully written and unabashedly enthusiastic, the descriptions, which are frequently interspersed with carefully chosen excerpts, succeed in enticing the reader.

Five indexes provide access by title, author, date of publication, genre, and region and country, while two additional indexes identify books about people of color in the U.S. and those with lesbian or gay themes.

Although this work is a welcome addition to the numerous bibliographies pertaining to women, it is not without flaws. First, the compilers' decision to include only in-print works results in a distorted picture of good books by women. Only 51 of the titles included were published before 1900, while more than half were published between 1980 and 1993. Because the status of being in print is ever-changing, it would have been better to list works based on their merits and let users rely on their libraries for copies of out-of-print works. Secondly, the compilers themselves note that they make "no claim to objectivity," and this seems particularly evident in their nonfiction selections, which appear to have been chosen with a bias toward works about women or women's issues. For instance, all of the biographies listed are about women, which could leave the false impression that women have not written good biographies of men. In addition, specific inclusions and omissions are questionable. How, for instance, can Sue Grafton's " G" Is for Gumshoe be included but no works by either P. D. James or Dorothy Sayers? And how could Jane Goodall's acclaimed *In the Shadow of Man* not be selected?

In spite of its limitations, this reasonably priced guide will be a useful acquisition for public and academic libraries, where it can serve as a readers' advisory aid and as a selection tool for women's studies collections.

Chronology of Women's History. By Kirstin Olsen. Greenwood, 1994. 506p. bibliog. index. $39.95 (0-313-28803-8).
305.4'09 Women—History—Chronology [CIP] 93-50542

While this chronology spanning 20,000 B.C. to 1993 is not an exhaustive list of female accomplishments, it makes an effort to be inclusive, profiling nearly 5,000 women from 114 countries. It begins with the Cro-Magnon era and ends with Janet Reno and the Tailhook scandal. Entries are arranged by year or span of years and subdivided into 10 categories, such as "General Status and Daily Life," "Literature and the Visual Arts," "Performing Arts and Entertainment," "Athletics and Exploration," and "Business and Industry." Text is arranged two columns on a page, not in tabular form, so information is not easy to scan. Some information is provided consistently each year (e.g., award winners, women elected to office). Other facts seem random:

under 1978, "The average Dutch woman has 1.6 children" and, under 1986, "In Italy, 12% more rapes are reported than last year." A detailed index of more than 100 pages provides access, but references are only to page numbers, so readers will have to examine the whole page. Browsing is the best way to unearth all the hidden jewels contained in this volume.

Readers looking for a specific piece of information will do better to consult one of the many topically arranged reference books on women. However, students wanting to know events in women's history during a particular year or broader time period will find this chronology useful.

Great Lives from History: American Women Series. 5v. Ed. by Frank N. Magill. Salem, 1995. bibliog. index. $365 (0-89356-892-9).
305.4'0973 Women—U.S.—Biography || Women—Canada—Biography [BKL] 94-38308

This is the sixth set in an ongoing series providing coverage of the lives, careers, and achievements of individuals from antiquity to the present. It is the first to focus specifically on women. It includes people who have achieved international recognition for their accomplishments, as well as lesser-known figures who are deserving of attention. Featured are 409 women whose lives have had an impact on American society and culture, including 45 African Americans, 11 Asian Americans, 8 Hispanic Americans, 8 Native Americans, and 7 Canadians. The range of figures covered varies from colonial poet Ann Bradstreet and Sacagawea of the Lewis and Clark Expedition to such contemporary women as Nobel Prize–winner Toni Morrison and comedian Carol Burnett.

Articles begin with general facts about each individual. The remainder of the article is divided into four parts. The "Early Life" section covers the subject's life up to the point at which her major work began. "Life's Work" covers the period during which her most significant achievements were made. The "Summary" section constitutes an evaluation of the woman, providing an analysis of her achievements in the larger context of American culture and women's history. Closing the entry is an annotated bibliography for further research. Featured in volume 5 are indexes by name and occupation and a time line that places each woman in chronological order based on date of birth.

Thirty-three of these women are also covered in other titles in this series (American series and Twentieth Century series), though the essays here are new. Also, information on most of these women is available elsewhere. Most of the deceased women can be found in *Notable American Women*; living ones are in *Current Biography*. High-school and public libraries needing coverage in this area should consider purchase.

Her Heritage: A Biographical Encyclopedia of Famous American Women. CD-ROM. Ed. by Robert McHenry. Pilgrim New Media, 955 Massachusetts Ave., Cambridge, MA 02139, 1994. $49.95 (1-88521-302-6).
305.4'092 Women—U.S.—Biography [BKL]

Readable biographies of more than 1,100 women, both living and deceased, are found on this CD-ROM. Both Mac and Windows versions are on the same disc. We looked at the Windows version, which requires a 486 IBM-compatible PC, 4MB of RAM, a VGA color monitor, a sound card, DOS 6.0 or higher, and Windows 3.1. To run the multimedia applications (i.e., video) one needs 8MB of RAM and a double-speed CD-ROM drive. *Her Heritage* includes QuickTime for Windows 2.0 on the disc, which must be installed in order to show video. Otherwise, the video is shown as a series of stills over the audio track. Installation is simple, and an on-screen tutorial takes one through the basic steps. The manual gives only installation instructions, but there is context-sensitive help. The text was prepared by McHenry, editor of *Encyclopaedia Britannica*.

The two main ways to search are by name or vocation/avocation. The latter method presents 11 broad categories (e.g., *Athletes*, *Teachers and Librarians*); clicking on one brings up subcategories. Clicking again gets a list of names. Some women are listed under more than one vocation. However, more women need to be cross-referenced. For example, Hanna Gray is listed under *Educator* but not *Historian*; she was a history professor for many years before becoming a university administrator. Each entry is approximately 400 words in length and many are accompanied by a small photo in the left-hand corner of the screen, some in black and white, others in color. The photographs can be enlarged by clicking on them. There are no por-

Social Sciences

traits for some women for whom photographs are widely available. Some photographs have a strip of film as an icon indicating the presence of a video clip. These are usually under a minute in length and in black and white. Most clips are of athletes or entertainers. For example, those of Marian Anderson and Ethel Merman contain a few bars of a song; one of Lucille Ball is taken from a scene in her TV program; one of Grace Kelly is from a newsreel of her wedding; another newsreel clip shows Wilma Rudolph winning gold medals at the Olympics. Within the text of entries, hypertext links to the names of other women for whom there are biographies are noted in red, but there are no other links. A Find button can be used to do a keyword search of all the biographies. We looked for all entries that mentioned Evanston, Illinois, and found 13 women, but the search took more than three minutes. There are cross-references from pseudonyms in both the name lists and vocation lists and also a separate section that lists pseudonyms. Clicking on *Awards, Prizes* brings up a list of 14 awards; clicking on one results in a list of the American women who won that award. It is possible to jump from this list directly to a biography. "In Their Own Words" is a list of autobiographies giving only the title. It is usually not clear whose autobiographies they are, but clicking on a title leads to the entry for the appropriate woman. It is difficult to see the usefulness of this section and the pseudonym section.

Coverage ranges from colonial times to the present. Many African American and Native American women are found, but few Asian Americans or Hispanics. Even with coverage as broad as this product's, one can question some of the choices of subjects. For example, why an entry on the Everleigh sisters, who ran a brothel in Chicago, but none on Congresswoman Pat Schroeder? Why a film clip of Gypsy Rose Lee but none of Martha Graham?

The product has standard features found on many CD-ROMs: the ability to bookmark, copy to a word processor, and print. It is also possible to make the type size larger. Screens are attractive, but why does every CD-ROM developer have to come up with its own set of icons, buttons, etc? If some of these were standardized it would help make CD-ROMs easier to use.

The student who needs a quick biography on a specific woman will find it just as fast to use a printed source, but browsing in this interesting product will introduce students to an array of women, many of them unknown to them. The photographs and video make the women come alive, but more examples would make this a richer experience. Middle-and high-school libraries should preview. —*Sandy Whiteley*

The Information Please Women's Sourcebook. Ed. by Lisa DiMona and Constance Herndon. Houghton, 1994. annual. 568p. charts. index. paper $13.95 (0-395-70067-1; ISSN 1077-5994).
305.4'0973 Women—U.S.—Handbooks, manuals, etc. [BKL] 94-1313

This book uses an almanac format familiar to librarians, similar to *The Information Please Environmental Almanac* [RBB Ag 92]. It provides an overview of the major issues facing women and is a guide to finding sources women need to make informed decisions about their lives. It will also be used by anyone doing a report on women's issues. The editors maintain that it is the result of a survey of more than 1,000 organizations and resources. The editors also performed two additional informal surveys: the first of elementary-school-age girls and a second nationwide survey of women of all ages. Neither of these surveys were statistically significant, but the editors use the results in sidebars that add interest to the text.

The book itself is divided into 12 major headings, including *Education, Work, Child Care, Health, Well-being, Politics, Violence,* and *Activism*. Each of these headings is further subdivided for ease of use. The sections are packed with the full-text of short speeches by prominent women, statistics, bibliographies, graphs, tables, charts, and lists of sources for additional information.

The book contains six appendixes: a list of judicial and legal decisions, addresses of federal government agencies concerned with women's issues, addresses of newsletters and periodicals, a national women's hall of fame, a list of lesbian/gay archives and libraries, and a section listing resources that were used to compile this book. Two indexes conclude the book: an organization index and an extensive subject index.

There is a wealth of usable information here. This inexpensive book belongs on the ready-reference shelf. It will be useful in every public and academic library and probably in most high-school libraries as well.

Second to None: A Documentary History of American Women. 2v. Ed. by Ruth Barnes Moynihan and others. Univ. of Nebraska, 1994. 775p. illus. hardcover $45/vol. (0-8032-3167-9); paper $20/vol. (0-8032-8205-2).
305.4'0973 Women—U.S.—History—Sources [CIP] 93-14347

Women's Rights in the United States: A Documentary History. Ed. by Winston E. Langley and and Vivian C. Fox. Greenwood, Nov. 1994. 349p. bibliog. index. $49.95 (0-313-28755-4; ISSN 1069-5606).
305.41'0973 Women's rights—U.S.–History—Sources || Women—U.S.—History—Sources || Women—Law and legislation—U.S.—History—Sources [CIP] 94-7429

These two collections reprint documents by and about American women.

Second to None is a fascinating documentary history reflecting the experiences of American women through their own words. In the tradition of collections of readings such as Gary B. Nash's *The Private Side of American History: Readings in Everyday Life* (4th ed., Harcourt, 1987) and Thomas B. Frazier's *The Underside of American History* (Harcourt, 1987), these two volumes illuminate areas of American history seldom covered in textbooks. The 275 documents were chosen to illustrate the experiences of women of all ages, classes, sexual orientations, races, and geographic and ethnic origins. The voices of farmers, grandmothers, warriors, housewives, doctors, prostitutes, and pacifists are heard throughout these pages.

The editors, college professors of history, selected passages that had worked in their own classrooms. The documents are arranged chronologically from sixteenth century Native American myths through the 1990s. A brief introduction explains the context of each document. Source notes are provided for each excerpt; for unpublished works, the location of the manuscript collection is provided. The excerpts include letters, diaries, autobiographies, poems, legal documents, sermons, speeches, and magazine articles. Interesting black-and-white illustrations have explanatory captions. The detailed table of contents is the only means of access. Subject and author indexes would have improved this work's reference usefulness.

The women represented include the famous—Abigail Adams, Elizabeth Cady Stanton, Phyllis Schlafly—and the obscure. Detailed descriptions of how to make linen, how to dress deerskins, and other accounts of daily life are included. The work traces the hardships of colonial life, the hopes of the American Revolution, the cult of domesticity, the rigors of the Depression, and the pain of racial integration.

As a supplementary text for American history or women's history, these volumes provide an outlet for voices too seldom heard in traditional courses. They are a worthy purchase for all public, high-school, and academic libraries, though they may get more use in the circulating collection.

Women's Rights in the United States has a narrower focus. Edited by professors of political science and history, the 125 documents include letters, diaries, policy statements, laws, and court decisions. There is virtually no overlap in documents with *Second to None*. Some of the documents are by men, for example, "Should Women Throw Away Their Privileges?" by Edward C. Lukens (1925) and the U.S. Roman Catholic Bishops' Letter on Women (1992). The documents are arranged chronologically from the seventeenth century to the present. Brief introductions give the context. The source of each document is noted; all of them appear to have been previously published. A glossary, a directory of women's organizations, and an extensive bibliography are followed by an index.

Women's Rights contains more legal documents and policy statements and not as many personal accounts by women as *Second to None*. For this reason, it is not as interesting to read. However, because of the many important documents it contains (The Family and Medical Leave Act of 1993, U.S. *v. Susan B. Anthony*, Socialist Statement on Women's Rights) and the light they cast on women's fight for equal rights in America, it will be a useful addition to reference collections in public and academic libraries.

The Timetables of Women's History: A Chronology of the Most Important People and Events in Women's History. By Karen Greenspan. Simon & Schuster, 1995. 459p. illus. index. $35 (0-671-67150-2).
305.4'09 Women—History—Chronology [CIP] 94-41762

This latest in Simon & Schuster's Timetables series (*Timetables of History, Timetables of American History, Timetables of Jewish History, Timetables of*

Science) lists thousands of entries in parallel columns. In the introduction, Greenspan defines the 10 categories under which women's activities are listed: *Daily Life/Customs/Practices, Humanities/Fine Arts, Reform, Science/Technology/Discovery, Statecraft/Military,* etc.

Short essays that focus on key individuals and events or provide overviews of issues and trends in women's history distinguish this title from the other chronologies, *Chronology of Women's History* [RBB S 15 94] and *The Women's Chronology* [RBB O 15 94]. Essays cover such topics as "The Italian Women's Movement" and "The Feminization of Poverty and Homelessness." Black-and-white photographs throughout the book add interest. The detailed index cites year and category.

This chronology begins in approximately 4000 B.C., discussing deities in the Sumerian religion. It ends in 1992, including such events as Katherine Dunham's hunger strike, the designation of 1992 as the "Year of the Woman," and the UN conference in Geneva dealing with poor rural women.

Not as comprehensive as the *Chronology of Women's History*, this attractive book is similar to *The Women's Chronology*. It is a recommended purchase for public and school libraries that don't own one of the other chronologies.

The Women's Atlas of the United States. Rev. Ed. By Timothy H. Fast and Cathy Carroll Fast. Facts On File, 1995. 246p. bibliog. charts. illus. index. $75 (0-8160-2970-9).

305.4'0973 Women—U.S.—Maps || Women—U.S.—Economic conditions || Women—U.S.—Social conditions || Sex distribution (Demography)—U.S.—Maps [CIP] 94-29084

Two developments since the publication of the first edition in 1986 have made for significant differences in this thorough revision of the *Women's Atlas of the United States*. The first is changes in the condition of American women as a result of shifts in political power. These changes ripple through the atlas' text and maps. The second is rapid advances in computer technology as dramatically illustrated by the fact that all of the maps in the first edition were prepared by hand, and all of them in this edition have been prepared on a computer.

The same seven broad categories (i.e., demographics, education, employment, family, health, crime, and politics) used to organize information in the first edition prevail here. However, most of the flippant titles used within those categories have been replaced by more sober, informative titles. Unfortunate exceptions remain, such as "The Birds and the Bees" to introduce a section focusing on abortion, or "Up the River" for a section on women criminals.

The compilers have made good use of the new technology available to them. Their introduction continues to provide lucid explanations of the types of maps used and how to interpret each. They have judiciously matched map types (choropleth, symbol and graduated symbol, pie chart, and dot maps and cartograms) to the nature of the data depicted. Text has been updated to reflect changes in society and to interpret the information provided by newer sources. Those sources are cited in notes at the end of the book, just as a bibliography cites the data source for each map. Updating and revision of maps has been done with an eye on improved clarity. For example, whereas the first edition combined in a single map state-by-state data on women's smoking and drinking, this edition treats each of those behaviors in a separate map. New maps treat homelessness and AIDS, phenomena whose impact on women has increased in the past decade.

When the first edition was published, it merited close comparison with the *Atlas of American Women* (Macmillan, 1987). However, the passage of nearly a decade has blunted the value of such a comparison; the up-to-date revision of *Women's Atlas of the United States* is unquestionably today's preferred source. Even though it uses a sophisticated array of cartographic techniques, it is readily intelligible for a broad audience from high-school students up.

The Guide to National Professional Certification Programs. By Phillip Barnhart. Human Resource Development Press, 22 Amherst Rd., Amherst, MA 01002, 1994. 650p. indexes. paper $99.95 (0-87425-965-7).

305.553 Professional employees—Certification [BKL]

Here's the perfect complement to Gale's *Professional and Occupational Licensing Directory* [RBB D 15 93], which describes state and federal licensing, registration, and certification requirements. This new *Guide to National Professional Certification Programs* provides information about voluntary certification in various occupations.

In times when mobility makes it difficult for employers to observe a person's development or expertise, certification by an impartial, third party using objective measures can be useful. Technological change requires continued growth and development in many occupations; different levels of certification allow equitable rankings within a field and provide incentive for further progress.

This guide is arranged first by industry (such as *Hospitality and Travel*) and then by job title (*catering executive, culinary educator, hotel supplier,* etc.). Each entry includes the sponsoring organization, program data (number of members, number certified, approximate cost of certification), program description (experience, courses, points system, etc.), examinations required, and recertification information. The first appendix indexes certifications by designations (i.e., the letters that certified people can put after their names). The second appendix is arranged by sponsoring organization.

Broad fields include *Business and Management, Insurance and Personal Finance, Real Estate and Property, Engineering and Science, Trade and Technical,* and *Medical and Fitness*. The latter encompasses aerobics instructor, laboratory equipment specialist, and nursing home administrator—but no information is provided in the fields of mental health or alternative medical practice, and physician certification boards are not included. This is not an oversight. Some certification programs did not respond to the questionnaire, while other areas were either "too specialized" or "lacked agreement within the community."

Most certification programs exist where there is no governmental regulation. They are guilds with a new twist, quality control rather than numbers control. Individuals seeking portable credentials that will be recognized wherever they go and employers searching for relatively objective criteria for developing job descriptions and for evaluating potential hires should find this directory useful.

Ethnic Relations: A Cross-Cultural Encyclopedia. By David Levinson. ABC-Clio, 1994. 293p. bibliog. illus. index. $49.50 (0-87436-735-2).

305.8 Ethnic relations—Cross-cultural studies—Encyclopedias [CIP] 94-40253

Timely and authoritative information on a crucial world problem is found in this work, a volume in ABC-Clio's new series, Encyclopedias of the Human Experience. It covers two kinds of topics: definitions of terms pertinent to the study of ethnic relations (e.g., *ethnocentrism, genocide, irredentism*) and descriptive profiles of 38 contemporary ethnic conflicts. A specialist on global ethnicity and social relations, as well as vice president of Human Relations Area Files, Levinson recently edited the 10-volume *Encyclopedia of World Cultures* [RBB Jl 91].

The alphabetically arranged work under review covers *Ethnic Cleansing* and other expected topics, but also such lesser-known issues as internal colonialism and Third World colonialism (in the entry *Colonialism*). The entry *Kurds* is an example of the interweaving of statistics with background information on a conflict to present a clear portrait. The articles are succinct but lengthy enough (seven pages on *Indigenous Rights*) to convey a full understanding of the material and will be accessible to high-school students as well as adults.

Cross-references are noted at the end of articles, and *see* references are sometimes provided, though use of the index is still necessary. For example, there is no *see* reference from *Tutsi* to *Hutu and Tutsi*, but *Tutsi* is listed in the index. Assistance in pronunciation would have been helpful at various entries. Information is current; for example, the April 1994 South African election and the June 1994 French presence in Rwanda are noted. Black-and-white photographs and tables illustrate and clarify the text. After each entry, bibliographic references, including both classic and current titles, direct the user to further sources. Following the entries is a 17-item annotated "Directory of International Organizations Concerned with Ethnic Relations," which includes such lesser-known groups as Cultural Survival. A bibliography of works cited and an accurate index complete the work.

Medium-size to large public libraries, high-school libraries, and academic libraries will find *Ethnic Relations: A Cross-Cultural Encyclopedia* useful and fascinating reading.

Hispanic American Almanac. Ed. by Bryan Ryan and Nicolas Kanellos. Gale/UXL, 1995. 213p. illus. index. $29 (0-8103-9823-0).

305.8'68 Hispanic Americans [BKL]

This source, another entry in Gale's UXL list aimed at middle-school students, provides information about "the heritage, the communities

Social Sciences

and the growing influence of Hispanics on U.S. culture." It is based on the adult title, The Hispanic-American Almanac [RBB Ap 15 93], also edited by Kanellos. Fourteen chapters cover Spanish exploration; immigration to the U.S. from Mexico, Puerto Rico, and Cuba; family structure and the role of religion; the workplace and education; and contributions in the arts and sports. Each chapter is an easy-to-read essay on the topic, beginning with a boxed "Fact Focus" that highlights key concepts, events, and the like presented in the chapter. Boxed "Words to Know" and other facts are in sidebars. Black-and-white illustrations, some of which appear blurred, are scattered throughout. Further reading and an index complete the book.

The editors try to give all sides of the picture, and discrimination and enslavement are discussed. The emphasis is on Mexican, Cuban, and Puerto Rican influences with a brief mention of Central Americans. In each case, a history of a country or area and its subsequent U.S. involvement is related, followed by a discussion of the reasons these people immigrated to the U.S. No sources are cited for the chapters. The further-reading list includes adult rather than young-adult books. The index does not include all names mentioned. For example, Gary Soto rates an illustration and mention for his poetry, but no index entry. Also, the index entry for Hatuey lists an incorrect page number.

All in all, this volume provides a much-needed point of access for middle-school students and their teachers—and older, reluctant readers or those with limited English proficiency—to Hispanic American history and culture. The essay format and fairly simple index do not lend themselves to ready reference. Libraries may find this volume better suited to the circulating collection.

Kaleidoscope: A Multicultural Booklist for Grades K–8. Ed. by Rudine Sims Bishop. National Council of Teachers of English, 1994. 168p. illus. indexes. paper $14.95 (0-8141-2543-3).
016.3058'00973 Minorities—U.S.—Juvenile literature—Bibliography || Afro-Americans—Juvenile literature—Bibliography || Asian Americans—Juvenile literature—Bibliography [CIP] 94-22268

This book from NCTE is another impressive addition to its Booklist series. It annotates approximately 400 books published between 1990 and 1992 for children in grades K–8 about African Americans, Asian Americans, Hispanic Americans/Latinos, and Native Americans. Some books set in countries other than the U.S. are also included. The chapters are arranged according to specific themes rather than cultural or racial groups. The nonfiction topics include "The Arts," "Ceremonies and Celebrations," "History: The Way We Were," and "People to Know and Places to Go." In some instances, a fiction book is included in a theme section: for example, "Ceremonies and Celebrations" lists An Island Christmas. The fiction listings are divided into four sections by age, from the very young to older readers. The book concludes with a chapter listing anthologies and "A Potpourri of Resources," a list of print materials and organizations to assist the teacher in furthering the study of the diversity of American society. Each entry notes author, title, illustrator, and age level ascertained by the publisher or assigned by the reviewers. Annotations summarize the story or content, refer to the illustrations, and mention honors or awards. References to related books, books by the same author, and books on similar subjects are also noted. Following the annotations are indexes of award-winning books, a directory of publishers, and indexes of authors, illustrators, subjects, and titles. The subject index gives access by racial or ethnic group.

Kaleidoscope, although already two years out of date, is an affordable resource for the classroom teacher, parent, or librarian for recent books about other cultures. It will update Our Family, Our Friends, Our World: An Annotated Guide to Significant Multicultural Books for Children and Teenagers [RBB My 1 92], which lists more than 1,000 books published between 1970 and 1990. This Land Is Our Land [RBB Ja 15 95] annotates 570 multicultural books published between 1985 and 1993 for grades K–12 but doesn't include nonfiction.

The Peopling of America: A Timeline of Events that Helped Shape Our Nation. 3d ed. Comp. by Allan S. Kullen. Americans All, 5760 Sunnyside Ave., Beltsville, MD 20705, 1994. 363p. paper $15.95 (1-56192-021-5).
305.8'0973 Ethnology—U.S.—History—Chronology || Chronology, Historical [BKL] 91-91027

Produced by Americans All, whose teaching materials promote multiculturalism and diversity for students ages kindergarten to college, this book of time lines is useful for readers from fifth grade to adult, for the instructor, or for the history buff. It provides comparative parallel chronologies for major ethnic groups (Native, African, Asian, European, and Hispanic Americans) along with more general events in the Americas and in the rest of the world.

Covering the period from pre-1500 to 1976, columns are provided for each of the ethnic groups, the Americas, and the world. For example, in 1776, in addition to familiar events in the colonial U.S., the explorations of Captain Cook, and the invention of the steam engine, we can see that George Washington was being aided by a gift from the Oneida Chief Shenandoah and African Americans were serving in the Revolutionary army. At the same time, Japanese sailing vessels made contact with the Pacific Coast, Jews in New York were granted equal treatment under the law, and Mission Delores in San Francisco was established. Dates in parentheses indicate cross-references, and definitions are provided for difficult words. This one-volume work is also published in a two-volume format, which divides during the Civil War period; volumes are $9.95 each.

The Peopling of America offers a rich view of our heritage not found in any other timetable or encyclopedia of dates. While there are chronologies for specific ethnic groups (e.g., The African American Chronology [RBB F 15 95]), this one is unique in covering all major groups in one volume. Its price, relevance, and coverage make it highly recommended for any school, academic, or public library that collects U.S. history material.

Who's Who among Asian Americans. Ed. by Amy Unterburger. Gale, 1994. 780p. indexes. $75 (0-8103-9433-2; ISSN 1075-7104).
305.85'073 Asian Americans—Biography—Dictionaries [BKL] 94-244

Compiling a biographical directory of notable Asian American contemporaries is another first for Unterburger, who also edited Who's Who among Hispanic Americans and Who's Who in Technology. Criteria for selection include "positions held through election or appointment to office, notable career achievements, or significant community service." Reference value is stated as the determining factor. "Asian Americans" refers to U.S. citizens or residents whose ethnic background is Asia or the Pacific Islands. Most candidates completed the publisher's form to submit biographical facts. The editors wrote entries based on other sources for notables who did not supply information directly.

Entries are easy to read and comfortably spaced. The layout using boldface type for names and headings allows quick location of facts within entries. Entries include occupation, ethnic and cultural heritage, personal data, educational background, career information, organizational affiliations, honors and awards, special achievements, military service, biographical sources, and address. A "Geographical Index" is arranged alphabetically by state and then by city of residence in the U.S. The "Occupational Index" lists more than 200 categories. The largest, Education, College/University, has 20 percent of the entries; engineering, management, and medicine each list about 10 percent. The "Ethnic/Cultural Heritage Index" is alphabetical by Asian country of background. More than 30 percent of the entries are under China, almost 20 percent under India, and more than 10 percent from Japan. The remaining entries are from 18 other backgrounds, including Cambodia, the Philippines, and Sri Lanka.

Fewer than 10 percent of the people in this book are also in Who's Who in America. What seems to be recognized in this publication is middle class professional achievement. Sports, music, and art seem underrepresented, excluding Cleveland Browns defensive lineman Pio Sagapolutele and martial artist Ernie Reyes, star of the Sidekick TV series. Dith Pran is out, but the doctor who played him in The Killing Fields, Haing Ngor, is in. Illustrators of children's books, Gyo Fujikawa (dozens of preschool books) and Jose Aruego (Leo the Late Bloomer), are out, but authors Lawrence Yep and Allen Say are in. Toshiko Akiyoshi, jazz musician, is out; Midori, classical violinist, is in. Sammy Lee, Olympic gold medalist, physician, and coach to Greg Louganis, is out, but Louganis, Olympic gold medal diver, is in.

Quibbles aside, this shakedown edition will allow readers to suggest additions for future editions. It deserves an A for effort. An important new specialized source, this will be used in academic or public libraries serving Asian American communities.

From Afar to Zulu: A Dictionary of African Cultures. By Jim Haskins and Joann Biondi. Walker, 1995. 205p. bibliog. illus. maps. $16.95 (0-8027-8290-6); lib. ed. $17.85 (0-8027-8291-4).
306'.096 Ethnology—Africa—Dictionaries || Africa—Social life and customs—Dictionaries [CIP] 94-11545

This handbook of African peoples for young readers ages 10 and up treats the continent's 32 most populous and well-known cultures, such as the Maasai and the Yoruba. It is not inclusive, for example, omitting Egyptians, whose culture reflects the Arab Mediterranean area. Haskins is an award-winning children's author, and Biondi is a former professor of geography.

The book's arrangement is alphabetical by culture, with each entry similar in format and 5–8 pages in length. Each begins with a map locating the country (or countries) where the people live and notes their population, language, and primary foods. Clearly and concisely, the articles cover history (including oral traditions or legends), geography, interaction with other cultures, white colonization and settlement, changes in economy through the years, living patterns and gender roles, rites and traditions, food patterns and art forms, religion and cultural change, and the prominence of this group in government today.

The information is current, for example, noting the warfare between Tutsi and Hutu in 1994. Each entry also includes a few black-and-white photographs that reflect the culture and drawings of designs found in the group's artistic creations. After the 32 entries, five of the most well-known lost cultures (e.g., Kush) are briefly described. An appendix lists additional cultures and the nations where they are located. A helpful glossary and a current bibliography of books for children and adults complete the work.

Peoples of the World: Africans South of the Sahara by Joyce Moss and George Wilson (Gale, 1991) covers culture, geographic setting, and historical background of 34 African peoples for middle- and high-school students. *From Afar to Zulu* fulfills its intent as a concise, clear source of information on the peoples of Africa for upper-elementary and middle-school students. It will be useful in public and school libraries.

The Rating Guide to Life in America's 50 States. By G. Scott Thomas. Prometheus, 1994. 325p. $39.95 (0-87975-938-0); paper $19.95 (0-87975-939-9).
306'.0973 Quality of life—U.S.—States [CIP] 94-22550

Thomas, the author of *The Rating Guide to Life in America's Small Cities* (Prometheus, 1990), uses statistics from a variety of sources to rank the 50 states. H. L. Mencken rated them, based on approximately 100 statistics, in the September 1931 issue of *American Mercury*. His objective was to find "the worst American State"; he proclaimed Mississippi the "winner." (Massachusetts placed first in his quality-of-life index.) John Gunther traveled to all 48 states in preparation for writing *Inside U.S.A.* (1947). His objective was to determine what made each state different from the others. While he used statistics, he also relied on firsthand observations to grade the states.

Thomas has combined Mencken's and Gunther's views: statistics can pinpoint the best—and worst—states (Mencken), and numbers can identify what makes each state unique (Gunther). His 24 categories include the expected ones: natural resources, such as crude oil reserves and timberland; health, showing major causes of death and number of doctors; racial equality, demonstrating minority college graduates and minority businesses; housing, displaying housing costs and housing size; and education, with high-school dropouts and education spending. Other categories include sports, public safety, politics, and international relations (foreign employers, export-related jobs, foreign-born populations). For each section, Thomas asks a "big question": for example, in history, "Which state has had the richest past, both in terms of historic events and famous people?" In each category, he discusses how he arrived at the figures, which was the best state and which was the worst, the regional winners in the category, the biggest surprise, and the bottom line. He concludes by ranking the states and devising a report card for each state, examining strengths and weaknesses. Thomas provides a list of sources and a brief glossary. His cutoff date was May 1, 1993.

The Rating Guide to Life in America's 50 States will not replace such tools as *Places Rated Almanac* or others that rank *cities* by quality of life; its scope is broader than those books. It can provide guidance for people seeking information about a state either with a view to moving there or for school assignments. A topical index would be useful; however, the lack of one is not cause for rejecting the book. It will be useful in school, public, and academic libraries.

Dr. Ruth's Encyclopedia of Sex on CD-ROM. Ed. by Ruth K. Westheimer. Creative Multimedia, 513 NW 13th Ave., Ste. 400, Portland, OR 97209, 1994. $29.99 (1-880428-47-4).
306.7'03 Sex—Dictionaries || Sex—Dictionaries [BKL]

Based on the book of the same name [RBB S 1 94], this interactive CD utilizes animation, film clips, slides, and sound to provide biological facts and explanations of psychological, cultural, legal, and moral questions about sex. In addition to the book's 250-plus entries, which were written by Dr. Ruth and more than 50 other researchers and practitioners, the CD features a three-dimensional tour of the human reproductive system. A textless slide show ranges through a wide array of sex-related images: movie stills, biological slides, gay rights parades, a tampon, AIDS-related posters, erotic art from the *Kama Sutra*, and an old leather wallet with a condom ring showing, to name a few.

The "tour" begins in an animated version of Dr. Ruth's office, which houses an old radio, a television set, a dictionary, an encyclopedia, a telephone directory, an anatomy chart, a diploma, and a clipboard. Clicking a mouse on any of these objects leads into some segment of the product. The diploma provides a biography of Dr. Ruth herself, featuring various phases of her interesting life. Clicking on the television brings up a menu of animated or filmed topics, such as impotence, putting on a condom, masturbation, and virginity. The visuals are high quality and feature cutaways and zooms. The dictionary and the encyclopedia allow access to alphabetically arranged entries from the book; searching by keyword points to multiple entries that discuss that term. The radio and the telephone lead to recordings from Dr. Ruth's nationally syndicated radio show. The clipboard offers an interactive sex quiz that is informative and fun: Dr. Ruth rewards correct answers with encouraging comments, and incorrect answers result in her typically nonjudgmental "I wouldn't have said that."

The CD arrived with no directions other than installation instructions. Using the MPC for Windows version was easy, once the reviewer played around with the mouse and uncovered the hidden clues linked with the objects on the desk and around the office. After that, everything was menu driven. System requirements for this version are a 486SX/25 running Windows 3.1 or later, 4MB of RAM, 5MB hard-drive space available, a double-speed CD-ROM drive, a 256 color Super VGA monitor, and a SoundBlaster or compatible sound card with Windows drivers. Technical support by phone is available Monday through Friday, 8:00 a.m.–5:00 p.m. Pacific Time; there is 24-hour BBS support via CompuServ or Internet.

Adults and young people who enjoy Dr. Ruth's books and shows will have fun and learn with this product. Others will find it informative but might not appreciate Dr. Ruth's mannerisms and opinions. Schools, for example, will want to be aware that she advocates contraception, and some might find her flippancy possibly misleading for young people. For example, encouraging the user to take the fertility tour, she says, "Click around. That you can do without a condom!"

Another caution: while the visual effects enhance this item, the sound effects might be annoying. "Burps" accompany moves from question to question in the sequential portions, and the slide show is accompanied by upbeat, but intrusive and incredibly repetitive, music.

A Research Guide to Human Sexuality. By Kara Ellynn Lichtenberg. Garland, 1994. 497p. bibliog. indexes. $75 (0-8153-0867-1).
016.3067 Sex—Reference books || Reference books—Sex || Sex—Library resources || Sex—Bibliography [CIP] 93-37236

This guide to the literature of sex is comprehensive and up-to-date. It describes more than 1,000 print and electronic resources, lists 400 organizations, and tells how to locate experts. The book is arranged by format, including specialized libraries, reference tools, library catalogs (including online ones), sexual-behavior surveys, and media resources. Formats with many listings, such as indexes and abstracts, periodicals, and organizations, are subdivided under such headings as AIDS, *Alternative Lifestyles*, *Homosexuality*, and *Nudism*. "How to Find" boxes explain how to search for additional information. About the only thing missing is detailed instructions on finding sex information on the Internet. Appendixes include a list of LC subject headings relevant to the topic and abridged LC classification schedules for appropriate subjects. There are title and institutional-name indexes. Readers will need to use the detailed table of contents in lieu of a subject index.

Sources range from the scholarly to the pornographic, and Lichtenberg's annotations make clear which is which. A useful addition to academic and large public library collections. —*Sandy Whiteley*

Dr. Ruth's Encyclopedia of Sex. Ed. by Ruth K. Westheimer. Continuum, 1994. 319p. bibliog. illus. index. $29.50 (0-8264-0625-4).
306.7'03 Sex—Dictionaries [CIP] 94-5009

High-school and public libraries will want to consider Dr. Ruth's lat-

Social Sciences

est book even if they already have other dictionaries and encyclopedias of sex. It will be popular because its editor has a large following and because it will be marketed to teens, as well as adults. Her introduction restates her desire to help eliminate "sexual illiteracy" among "the many people out there, especially young people, who need to know more." While professionals were asked to write the articles, the encyclopedia was prepared for the general reader, "especially for high school and college students."

Dr. Ruth writes the way she talks—enthusiastically, nonjudgmentally, and informatively—and her style is evident throughout the book, regardless of the actual authors of the unsigned articles. The contributors come from a variety of fields: law, psychology, sociology, and the expected medical specialties (adolescent medicine, epidemiology, obstetrics and gynecology, pediatrics, psychiatry, rehabilitative medicine, and urology).

Arranged in A–Z format, the articles cover diverse topics: *Abortion*, *Abstinence*, *Brothel*, *Impotence*, *Lesbian Sexual Techniques*, *Sexual Response Cycle*, *Virginity*, etc. These often include brief historical surveys, as well as overviews of current thought. Many articles address health aspects of sex, such as *Arthritis and Sex*, *Cervical Cancer*, *Handicapped Persons and Sex*, and *Yeast Vaginitis*. There are a few entries that describe individuals: Magnus Hirschfeld, Helen Singer Kaplan, and, of course, Kinsey and Masters and Johnson. There are numerous cross-references throughout the book and within the detailed index. The glossary is followed a "Glossary of Sexual Slang"; both will assist in communication, neither is as complete as *The Sexual Dictionary: Terms & Expressions for Teens & Parents* (Larksdale, 1993) or *The Language of Sex: An A-to-Z Guide* [RBB Je 15 92].

The articles that describe sexual techniques (*Coital Positions*, *Fellatio*, *Homosexuality*, etc.) are straightforward and objective, and they will answer most individuals' questions. It is unfortunate that the illustrations sometimes do not measure up to the text. They are a mix of black-and-white photographs and drawings. Some are crudely drawn ("Development of the Adolescent's Sex Organs," "Breast Feeding," etc.). Other illustrations are quite helpful, such as those showing penile implants and self-injection therapy used in treating impotence and those showing the stages of labor. The topically arranged bibliography includes some dated items. For example, the category "Cancer" lists only three sources, dated 1983, 1977, and 1984. "Prostitution" has five citations, all from the 1970s.

Although there are other good books on this subject aimed at a similar audience, including Bullough's *Human Sexuality: An Encyclopedia* [RBB My 1 94], Dr. Ruth's will be requested by many and will be useful for those comfortable with her earlier works.

Gale City & Metro Rankings Reporter. Ed. by Helen S. Fisher. Gale, 1994. 1,324p. indexes. $129 (0-8103-9875-3; ISSN 1077-9132).
307'.0973 Cities and towns—U.S.—Ratings || Metropolitan areas—U.S.—Statistics [BKL]

Similar in concept to *Gale State Rankings Reporter* [RBB O 1 94], this new work contains 3,000 tables ranking cities or Metropolitan Statistical Areas (MSAs) on a wide variety of factors. Most tables list the top 50, 25, or 10 cities in rank order, though a few rank more than 280. Sources are given for all tables so that readers can find additional cities, if desired. In most cases, sources are census publications, but data were also taken from other government publications, trade-association publications, and newspapers and magazines. Most figures are from the late 1980s or 1990s. Browsing through this book one can find the city with the highest average percentage of sunny weather (Phoenix), where the most Hmong live (Merced, California), the city with highest rate of active TB (Atlanta), the city where the highest percentage of workers commute by motorcycle (Bryan-College Station, Texas), where the largest number of persons gave Finnish as their first ancestry (Duluth, Minnesota), the city with the most households with incomes of $150,000 or more (Naples, Florida), where consumers spend the most on tobacco products (Chicago), the place with the most establishments making synthetic rubber (Beaumont-Port Arthur, Texas), and the city with the largest percentage of felony arrests resulting in a trial (Portland).

There are indexes by city and by subject. Users will need to know the cities that make up a MSA to use the city index effectively. For example, the Appleton-Oshkosh-Neenah, Wisconsin, MSA is listed only under Appleton; there are no cross-references from the other two cities. All tables are also listed in the lengthy table of contents. Market researchers, city planners, government officials, college students and professors, and others will find this compilation of data useful. Academic and large public libraries should consider purchase. —*Sandy Whiteley*

Health and Environment in America's Top-Rated Cities: A Statistical Profile. Ed. by Rhoda Garoogian. Universal Reference Publications, 1355 W. Palmetto Park Rd., Ste. 315, Boca Raton, FL 33486, 1994. 666p. charts. paper $65 (1-881220-12-5).
307'.76 Cities and towns—U.S.—Ratings || Quality of life—U.S. || Public health—U.S.—Statistics [BKL]

The health care, public safety, and climate information on 71 cities that appeared in *America's Top Rated Cities* [RBB S 1 92] has been expanded here.

The cities are listed alphabetically; each entry contains statistical tables covering such topics as infant mortality, substance abuse programs, municipal budget expenditures for health services, alcohol and vehicle safety laws, and crime statistics. Explanatory comments follow some tables, and sources are cited for each. A useful feature of some tables is the comparison of a city's figures with the U.S. average, enabling the user to see if health-care costs, for example, are higher or lower than the national average.

Statistics are from a variety of sources—government agencies, magazine articles, and professional directories. Most figures are current (1990–94), with only a few from the late eighties. The death and death-rate table uses the 1989 figure of 360 for death by homicide in the District of Columbia from *Vital Statistics of the United States*, but the figure in the crime and crime-rate table, taken from the 1992 FBI *Uniform Crime Report*, gives the number of murders as 443.

Other relocation sources cover some of this information but not in as much depth. *100 Best Small Towns in America* (Prentice Hall, 1993), *50 Fabulous Places to Raise Your Family* (Career Press, 1992), and *Places Rated Almanac* (Prentice Hall, 1993) all include the number of health-care providers and facilities in the areas they rate, and all include climate information. The strength of this new title lies in the environmental statistics provided. While other sources comment on water and air quality, this one ranks air quality of the 71 cities, provides an environmental-stress index, municipal budget figures for environmental services, the amount of toxic chemical releases, a pollen calendar, and a detailed table of air pollutants that compares monitored levels to the acceptable level.

While it does not cover as many cities as *Places Rated Almanac*, *Health and Environment in America's Top-Rated Cities* is a valuable addition to collections having frequent requests for relocation or health information.

Gale State Rankings Reporter. Ed. by Gary Alampi. Gale, 1994. 1,657p. indexes. tables. $95 (0-8103-9190-2; ISSN 1074-8792).
317 Social Sciences—Statistics—U.S. [OCLC] 94-48690

This massive work provides 5,200 rankings, arranged in more than 3,000 tables, for the 50 states and the District of Columbia. Among the areas covered are the physical characteristics of each state, as well as various aspects of culture and education, economics, government, jobs and income, leisure, and social structure.

The majority of the information for the rankings, based on data primarily from the late 1980s, is drawn from federal government sources. Where available, information is also taken from associations, state agencies, and various reports and periodicals. The format of the tables is simple. Each table presents the raw numbers for the states as well as the rankings. Sometimes a total is given for the U.S. as well. Source information and any footnote information complete the table. States are listed alphabetically, not by rank, which enables users to easily find a particular state, but those needing states in rank order will have to rearrange the tables themselves.

The table of contents gives a complete listing of the tables. Two indexes are supplied, a location index and a keyword index. In the first, the states are presented alphabetically, and under each is listed the tables in which it appears. Not all tables include all 50 states; those on rice production, for example, rank only the five rice-producing states.

Whether one is looking for information on the number of trees planted in each state, the number of shoe retailers, or the number of motion picture drive-in theaters still in existence, it will be found in this book. It will be useful to librarians, educators, professional analysts, students, and anyone interested in finding out how a state ranks on a particular issue. Morgan Quitno's *State Rankings: A Statistical View* of the 50 States [RBB Je 15 90] consists of only 274 tables taken from government publications.

Datapedia of the United States 1790–2000: America Year by Year. By George Thomas Kurian. Bernan Press, 1994. 466p. charts. index. tables. $90 (0-89059-012-5).
317.3 U.S.—Statistics ‖ Power resources—U.S.—Statistics ‖ Electricity—U.S.—Statistics [OCLC]

This valuable source updates the indispensable government publication, Historical Statistics of the United States, Colonial Times to 1970. Combining data tables and text, it provides a foundation for examining our "nation's growth-revealing historical patterns and principal changes" for 23 selected areas, including health, agriculture, housing, energy, finance, and government. "Except in cases where a reader is seeking highly specialized data, Datapedia will serve as a convenient and complete statistical profile of the U.S."

Wisely, the author has followed the pattern established in Historical Statistics, maintaining the chapter divisions and table numbers. Each data set has a unique letter and number, and these access points are consistent between Datapedia and its predecessor. With this feature, researchers will find it easy to cross-reference and compare data. For example, if one sees in Datapedia that in 1921 there were 55,260 miles of oil pipeline in operation, one need only carry the chapter letter and set number into Historical Statistics to verify the figure in the earlier source. This consistency of arrangement adds tremendously to Datapedia's value. Anyone who is familiar with its venerable cousin will be able to use it efficiently right from the start.

For the period up to 1970, Datapedia is based entirely on Historical Statistics. For 1970–90, it is based on the annual Statistical Abstract of the United States. Where possible, as with demographics, projections are extended to the year 2010. The author has included a five-page list that groups sources by the chapters they support. Readers may assume that all sources are from the U.S. government unless otherwise indicated (e.g., National Catholic Education Association, American Medical Association, Metropolitan Life Insurance Company).

With large type and cranberry-colored lines to define the charts, the publisher has produced a work that is much easier on the eyes than Historical Statistics. Also, each chapter begins with a "Highlights" section that lists succinctly points of information relevant to the chapter topic. For example, highlights for the "Forestry and Fisheries" chapter include summary statements about the growth of the aquaculture industry and the number of people employed in the timber industry.

As with many statistical sources, this compilation would be great to have on disk. However, there is no indication that a disk version is forthcoming, and the print version is fairly priced at $90. Datapedia is a highly recommended purchase for all medium to large public libraries and for all academic libraries.

CQ's Desk Reference on American Government. By Bruce Wetterau. Congressional Quarterly, 1995. 349p. bibliog. index. $49.95 (0-87187-956-5).
320.473 U.S.—Politics and government—Handbooks, manuals, etc. ‖ Federal government—U.S.—Handbooks, manuals, etc. [CIP] 94-44948

This quick-reference source touches on all aspects of the federal government. Using a question-and-answer format, author Wetterau provides information on the government in general, the presidency (including sections on first ladies, vice presidents, presidents' personal lives, and the cabinet), Congress, campaigns and elections, and the Supreme Court. At the end of each answer is an abbreviation for its source, often, but not always, another CQ publication. The list of abbreviations at the end of the book includes complete information on the cited works; this is followed by a bibliography of the sources arranged by author. A detailed subject index provides access to the more than 600 questions. The text of the Constitution, including Amendment XXVII, forms an appendix.

Almost anything anyone would want to know about the U.S. government can be found here: scandals, from Abscam to the Whiskey Ring; cabinet members convicted of crimes; lists of governors who became president; members of Congress serving in both houses; Supreme Court Justices who served in the cabinet; and summaries of some landmark court decisions. There are some minor criticisms: it would be helpful to have the bibliographic abbreviations listed in the front of the book, and there are no illustrations or maps. These are minor shortcomings; Congressional Quarterly's Desk Reference on American Government is recommended as a useful resource, particularly for middle, high-school, and public libraries.

New Encyclopedia of Zionism and Israel. 2v. Ed. by Geoffrey Wigoder. Herzl Press/dist. by Associated Univ. Presses, 1994. 1,521p. bibliog. illus. tables. $185 (0-8386-3433-8).
320.5'4 Zionism—Encyclopedias ‖ Israel—Encyclopedias [CIP] 91-11828

The first edition of this work was published as the Encyclopedia of Zionism and Israel in 1971 and favorably reviewed by the Board. Wigoder has been the director of the oral history department, Institute of Contemporary Jewry, Hebrew University, and previously edited the Encyclopedia of Judaism and the multivolume Encyclopedia Judaica. He did not edit the first edition of the current work.

The list of contributors includes their affiliation and the articles they wrote. Nearly all of the articles are signed. A helpful glossary defines many Hebrew words used in the text. Cross-references (noted by an asterisk) and see references only partially compensate for the lack of an index. Since many of the articles are lengthy, the lack of an index is a hindrance.

The foreword notes that the new edition was prepared in Israel with the participation of many scholars from abroad, and 30 percent of the material is new. The length of the alphabetically arranged entries ranges from a paragraph to 8 pages on Agriculture and 13 pages on Zionism, History of. The clear illustrations consist of black-and-white photographs, statistical charts, and maps (wars and partitions, flora and vegetation).

The articles are readable and, for the most part, current. They include entries for people, locations, topics, movements, and groups. Users will learn about Zionism in Chile and Ireland, Palestinian Jewish parachutists in Europe during World War II, Israel's relations with many foreign countries, ethnic groups in contemporary Israel, and the various waves of immigration. There are entries on many institutions in contemporary Israel: architecture, banking, education, libraries, music, police, and theater. Biographical entries note the location where the person was born (and died), but only the birth and death years are listed. Moshe Arens was not in the earlier edition but is in the current work as defense minister in 1992. Writer Yehuda Amichai, also not in the first edition, is now shown as being awarded the Israel Prize for literature in 1982. Winners of the Israel Prize for outstanding achievement in a variety of fields are listed through 1993. The academic position of writer Amos Oz in 1993 is noted. The entry on Yassir Arafat contains 1991 information, but the article on the Palestine Liberation Organization does not include the Oslo Peace Agreement in 1993. The article Arabs in Israel describes the beginning of the Palestinian uprising but is current only through August 1988.

An eight-page topical bibliography lists a 1969 guidebook to the country, and the most recent books on the Arab-Israeli conflict are 1987. More recent publications in both areas should have been included. Not listed as a reference source is the Israel Yearbook and Almanac, which has been available for many years. A 34-page table of Israel localities lists the name, affiliation, region, founding year, governing council, 1988 population, basis of founding, and settlement.

This new edition continues to fulfill its purpose as a comprehensive reference source on the history of Zionism and Israel and on contemporary Israel. Academic libraries, medium- to large-size public libraries, and others where there is interest in modern Israel and Zionism will find the work helpful.

Real Life Dictionary of American Politics: What They're Saying and What It Really Means. By Kathleen Thompson Hill and Gerald N. Hill. General Publishing Group, 1994. 414p. illus. $19.99 (1-881649-41-5).
320.973'03 U.S.—Politics and government—Dictionaries ‖ Political science—Dictionaries [CIP] 94-9307

The Hills have defined more than 1,300 terms that they deem important in the world of U.S. politics. The subtitle notwithstanding, the definitions are short and to the point with a minimum of anecdotes and history. Words or phrases included are the expected political terms (muckraker, by-election, spoils system); numerous associations, agencies, and acts (AARP, OAS, Civil Rights Acts); newspapers (LA Times, Chicago Tribune); books (The Other America, Rights of Man); and words of the nineties (Generation X, outerclass, Packwood diaries). Addresses and phone numbers are provided for organizations. Interspersed throughout the text are sketches, photographs, and cartoons. Appendixes include important American documents, election returns for all presidential elections through 1992, brief biographies of the presidents, addresses and phone numbers for the president and members of Congress, Democratic and Republican state party chairs, and governors.

Although the majority of the information is current and correct, the 1970 membership of the National Rifle Association, 1.1 million, is given rather than the 1993 figure of 2.5 million. Also, the *Times* is distinguished as the oldest New York City newspaper rather than the *Post*.

Safires' New Political Dictionary (4th ed. [RBB Ja 15 94]) will continue to be the standard, comprehensive dictionary in this field. The *Real Life Dictionary* may be considered as a supplementary source for public and academic libraries.

Gay and Lesbian Rights: A Reference Handbook. By David E. Newton. ABC-Clio, 1994. 214p. bibliog. index. $39.50 (0-87436-745-X).
323.3'264 Gays—Civil rights—U.S.—Handbooks, manuals, etc. || Gay liberation movement—U.S.—Handbooks, manuals, etc. [CIP] 94-28365

A retired teacher and now full-time writer, Newton provides readers with a handbook touching on all aspects of the gay and lesbian rights movement. It follows the general format of other titles in the Contemporary World Issues series. A 30-page overview of the dispute over gay and lesbian rights is followed by a chronology of events relating to the gay rights movement over the past century. A third section contains biographical sketches of some of the leading figures in the gay and lesbian rights movement, as well as some opposed to the movement. Pat Robertson, an outspoken critic, is profiled alongside Craig Rodwell, the founder of the Oscar Wilde Memorial Bookstore in New York City. Barney Frank, Barbara Gittings, Harry Hay, Jesse Helms, and Magnus Hirschfeld are examples of others treated. These sketches are followed by "statements and documents," a mixed bag of opinions of individuals and organizations that have appeared in the popular and scholarly press; summaries of existing legislation, regulations, and executive orders dealing with gay rights as well as examples of these laws and regulations; samples of documents dealing with legal and corporate provisions for domestic partnerships; documents from and discussion of some important court cases; and Clinton's proposed plan for modification of military policy dealing with gay men and lesbians. The directory of organizations is also selective, and no criteria are provided for inclusion. Annotations are helpful; while phone and fax numbers are provided for most organizations, no E-mail addresses are given. Three of the best-known organizations opposed to gay and lesbian rights are listed after those in support of gay and lesbian rights. The list of print resources includes bibliographies, general books, and periodicals; annotations are provided for the former two categories. As in other parts of the book, a mixture of pro- and anti-gay titles are listed. Films and videos that are appropriate for high school through adult ages are listed next. A six-page glossary concludes the work. Finally, access provided by the 15-page author-title-subject index is not sufficient.

Other titles that provide more detailed information on some aspects of this topic include *The Alyson Almanac* (Alyson, 1989), a chronology of the major events during the last 4,000 years that have affected gay people, and Jonathan N. Katz' *Gay/Lesbian Almanac: A New Documentary* (Harper, 1983). Readers will certainly want to consult Wayne R. Dynes' *Encyclopedia of Homosexuality* (Garland, 1990) as backup. But as an overview, this handbook will help reference staff aid readers who wish to either do further research or better understand this critical issue. The Board recommends this title for high-school libraries and for public or academic libraries that have little in their collections on gay and lesbian rights.

Government Affairs Yellow Book: Who's Who in Government Affairs. Ed. by Sanja Klima. Leadership Directories, 104 Fifth Ave., 2nd Fl., New York, NY 10011, 1995. semiannual. 1,024p. indexes. paper $180 (ISSN 1078-9812).
324.4'025 Lobbyists—Directories [BKL]

This is the eleventh in the Yellow Book series published by Leadership Directories, formerly Monitor Publishing. The directory illustrates the magnitude of governmental affairs (i.e., lobbying) by supplying in directory format information about personnel in more than 900 corporations, 500 financial institutions, 900 trade associations, 500 lobbying firms, and a significant number of offices in the federal, state, county, and municipal governments involved in this area. The people identified in the directory from the private sector either deal with legislators or research and analyze legislative proposals. Those working for the government are responsible for intergovernmental affairs or act as spokespersons for the government.

The volume is arranged by type of organization and supplies address, phone number, concise information about the institution, and names of the CEO or president, general counsel, and other people involved in governmental affairs. Education background and career history is provided for some of the individuals, and political action committees of organizations are listed. For the major lobbying firms, clients and legislative issues are included. The six indexes (issues, industry, government subject, geographic, personnel, master) would help a user find that the president of Boeing received an MBA from Harvard, that airline bankruptcy is a legislative issue for the company, and that the vice president for congressional affairs is Emory W. Baragar.

As with other Leadership Directories, *Government Affairs* will be issued semiannually in paper form, and Chadwyck-Healey has announced that it will be issuing all the directories on CD-ROM. Some of the information in this volume may be found in other sources, such as the *Washington Information Directory* or *S & P's Register of Corporations*. However, for libraries with a clientele interested in who is lobbying whom, this book will have the answer.

Congressional Quarterly's Guide to U.S. Elections. 3d ed. Ed. by John L. Moore. Congressional Quarterly, 1994. 1,543p. charts. indexes. maps. $220 (0-87187-996-4).
324.973 Elections—U.S.—History—Statistics || Political conventions—U.S.—History || Political parties—U.S.—History [CIP] 94-19015

One wonders why the publisher didn't delay publication of this third edition of the *Guide to U.S. Elections* until after the 1994 election. However, since the new edition has 200 pages more than the second, a wait might have necessitated two volumes.

The third edition updates the second edition (1985), including information and statistics from two more presidential and four congressional elections, a full-page box on voter turnout for the 1992 presidential election (78 percent of registered voters voted), and a revised section on redistricting and reapportionment. A new 50-page essay covers the politics and issues of gubernatorial and congressional elections from 1945 to 1992. Other new material includes a discussion of term limits and a list of officers and keynote speakers at the national conventions of the Democratic and Republican parties. Different photographs have been substituted, including those for Reagan, Carter, Mondale, and Ford, and some tables have been changed.

The beginning page for House popular vote returns is dated 1824–1985 rather than 1824–1993, the period covered. The correct heading is on the previous page and in the table of contents. As with many of CQ's publications, the indexing is not exceptional. To find information on term limits one must look under *Congress*, subheading *sessions and terms*, and then *term limit*. The variety of indexes remains the same: separate indexes for presidential candidates, senate candidates, etc.

This is a standard source for political science collections in colleges and universities. Libraries that have the second edition will want to consider purchasing the 1994 edition for the new and updated material.

The ABC-Clio Companion to the American Peace Movement in the Twentieth Century. By Christine A. Lunardini. ABC-Clio, 1994. 269p. bibliog. illus. index. $55 (0-87436-714-X).
327.1'72 Peace movements—U.S.—History—20th century [CIP] 94-10405

"There has never been a monolithic peace movement in the U.S. with a simple goal and with all participants agreeing on the means of reaching that goal." Recognizing the diverse nature of this movement, the author of this alphabetically arranged reference source has wisely chosen to include only those individuals and groups who were "truly advocates of peace and not merely objectors to a particular conflict."

Her research is based largely on four of the more than 150 sources listed in the unannotated bibliography at the end of the book. (Each entry in the book is followed by a list of two to three resources used to research the entry.) For the entries on mainstream individuals who contributed to the peace movement in this century (such as Wayne Morse, A. J. Muste, and Jeanette Rankin), she most often uses Harold Josephson's *Biographical Dictionary of Modern Peace Leaders* (1985); for more obscure figures, she utilizes the *National Cyclopedia of American Biography*. For organizations that have been important in the peace movement (such as War Resisters League and the American Friends Service Committee), she depends on Robert Meyer's *Peace Organizations: Past and Present* (1988); and for her research into the movement's influence during the Vietnam

War era, she relies on *Who Spoke Up? American Protest against the War in Vietnam 1963–1975* by Gerald Sullivan (1984). Lunardini covers the full political spectrum in her selection of people and organizations devoted to peace. She includes William Jennings Bryan and Henry Ford's Peace Ship (with a cautionary note about Ford's anti-Semitism) and Socialists Eugene Debs and Norman Thomas. Likewise, both the isolationist America First Committee and the internationalist American League against War and Fascism are covered.

There are a few factual errors. In the entry on the *Children's Crusade*, which led to the downfall of LBJ, Eugene McCarthy is identified as a senator from Oregon rather than Minnesota. The entry on William Sloane Coffin says he studied with Reinhold Niebuhr's son Richard; H. Richard Niebuhr was Reinhold Niebuhr's brother. Following the main body of the book is a chronology that begins with the founding of the American Peace Society in 1828 and ends in 1983. An index successfully brings together people whose lives crossed paths; it also connects such broad subjects as education and socialism and specific organizations with individuals mentioned in the book's entries.

This ABC-Clio companion provides an overview of the American peace movement for academic and public libraries.

The Congressional Yearbook, 1993: 103rd Congress, 1st Session. Congressional Quarterly, 1994. annual. 352p. illus. index. $29.95 (1-56802-011-2); paper $21.95 (1-56802-009-0) (ISSN 1079-8129).
328 U.S. Congress—Periodicals || U.S.—Politics and government—1993—Periodicals [OCLC] 94-6059

Following the success of its *Supreme Court Yearbook* [RBB Ag 91], CQ has launched a new annual that reviews what Congress accomplished during a session. For example, in the first session of the 103d Congress, NAFTA was passed and the economic-stimulus package defeated. Legislation is discussed here in essays arranged by broad topic: economic and trade policy, environment and energy, education policy, law and justice, etc. Coverage ranges from three pages on Somalia to a paragraph on the resolution against China as the site for the 2000 Olympics. When specific laws are mentioned, bill numbers, committee report numbers, and public-law numbers are provided for further research. Each chapter concludes with a section that discusses Senate confirmations of presidential appointees. The final chapter deals with Congress itself, including its membership, operations, and ethics investigations. Black-and-white photographs and boxed information add interest. Appendixes include a glossary and lists of members of the House and Senate; a detailed index follows.

Not as detailed as *Congressional Quarterly Almanac*, which gives complete voting records, *The Congressional Yearbook* is a reasonably priced overview for libraries that don't own the *Almanac* or that would like to have an annual report on Congress to put in the circulating collection. —*Sandy Whiteley*

Congressional Voting Guide: A Ten Year Compilation. 5th ed. Comp. by Victor W. Bosnich. CVG Press, P.O. Box 180956, Dallas, TX 75218-0956, 1994. 621p. indexes. $39.95 (0-9618958-5-3).
328.73077 U.S. Congress—Voting || U.S.—Politics and government [CIP] 94-94050

Even as the recent Congress stumbled to its rancorous conclusion before the 1994 midterm elections, the *Congressional Voting Guide* smoothly rolled on to its fifth edition. Like its predecessors, this edition drops off two years of coverage (1982–83) and adds two (1992–93), reporting the votes on key measures for each member of both houses of the 103d Congress. This edition "covers 154 major bills from the House of Representatives, 156 major bills from the U.S. Senate, including nominations, amendments and veto overrides." It records votes on 55 new House bills and 58 new Senate bills. Among these are a bill to extend unemployment benefits, a bill to permit voter registration when applying for a driver's license, the "Brady" bill for a waiting period before purchase of a handgun, NAFTA passage, and family medical leave.

Separate sections for the House and the Senate, each organized by state delegation, are introduced by an annotated list of bills in reverse chronological order. The annotations explain the bill's purpose, report the cumulative vote in that house, break that vote out by party (and, among Democrats, by northern and southern representatives), and report whether a "nay" or a "yea" vote supported the position of the president. The vote record for each member follows the same chronological order as the list of bills. Each member's vote record concludes with two "presidential support scores," each expressed as the percentage of the recorded votes that supported the position taken by the president. Even though this book extends back into Ronald Reagan's second term, presidential support scores are reported only for members' support of Bush and Clinton. Name and subject indexes conclude the compilation, allowing one to find either bills on a particular subject or a specific representative's record on 150-plus key issues.

Congressional Voting Guide provides a fuller picture of a representative's voting behavior and its patterns than the two-year selection of key votes reported in the biennial *Almanac of American Politics* (National Journal) or the three-year selection of key votes in the biennial *Politics in America* (Congressional Quarterly). It is a useful analytical tool for examining individual representatives, party cohesion, and presidential influence over Congress.

The Encyclopedia of the United States Congress. 4v. Ed. by Donald C. Bacon and others. Simon & Schuster, 1995. bibliog. charts. illus. index. tables. $355 (0-13-276361-3).
328.73'003 U.S. Congress—Encyclopedias [CIP] 94-21203

This substantial work aims to present a coherent and comprehensive overview of the history and workings of one of the most important and most maligned of American institutions. For the most part, it succeeds admirably. The three editors have each published extensively on Congress, one as a journalist, one as a political scientist, and the third as a historian. The more than 500 contributors are drawn from these fields as well as from the ranks of public officials, giving this work a notable breadth of viewpoint, though on occasion resulting in some unevenness of treatment and tone in articles.

The encyclopedia consists of 1,056 signed articles, which range from less than a page (*C-Span*) to 10 pages or more (*Committees*). All save one contain brief annotated bibliographies. In addition, the entry *Congress: Bibliographical Guide* is an annotated bibliography of print and electronic reference sources. Articles cover various aspects of congressional institutions, procedures, polity, and traditions, as well as various issues dealt with by Congress, from *Abortion* to *World War II*. There are articles on more than 200 members of Congress, as well as such survey articles as *Hispanic Members* and *Women in Congress*. All presidents receive separate entries, focusing on each's relationship with Congress. Articles on each state concentrate, for the most part, on the history of the state's congressional delegation, though at least one, *New Jersey*, chooses to focus on the role of that state's delegation at the Constitutional Conventions. Other articles deal with major pieces of legislation, important events in the history of Congress, constitutional amendments, and significant court cases.

Views of Congress in the wider culture are presented in *Movies on Congress*, *Humor and Satire: About Congress*, and *Literature on Congress*, which discusses fiction. The work is generously illustrated with photographs and political cartoons, some of the latter reproduced for the first time since their original publication. Tables accompany many articles, often with hard-to-find information, such as the names, dates of service, and religious affiliations of all the chaplains of Congress, or all significant legislation concerning veterans benefits. A glossary of terms and a synoptic outline of contents are included, in addition to a detailed index. A few errors did make their way into this work; the text of the article *Library of Congress* misidentifies the librarian who succeeded Ainsworth Rand Spofford as John Russell Long, though the accompanying table correctly lists him as John Russell Young. A table in the article *Political Parties* identifies John Anderson and Ross Perot as candidates of the American Independent Party, along with George Wallace.

There is little competition to this work; a number of single-volume reference works on Congress exist, but these do not challenge its breadth and depth. *The Encyclopedia of the American Legislative System* [RBB Jl 94] is a serious work with considerable information on the U.S. Congress. However, it consists entirely of long thematic articles on the history and political processes of various legislative institutions at the local and state, as well as federal, level and is less useful for documenting the personalities and the life of Congress and the issues that body has dealt with. Similar in scope and treatment to S&S's Dartmouth Medal-winning *Encyclopedia of the American Presidency* [RBB Ja 15 94], this new encyclopedia is an impressive achievement and an essential purchase for most large public and academic libraries.

The United States Congress: An Annotated Bibliography, 1980-1993. By Robert U. Goehlert and Fenton S. Martin. Congressional Quarterly, 1995. 640p. indexes. $185 (0-87187-810-0).
016.32873'07 U.S. Congress—Bibliography [CIP] 94-47925

Goehlert and Martin complete their series of bibliographies of the

Business, Economics

three branches of the federal government with this volume on Congress. Previous volumes were *The U.S. Supreme Court: A Bibliography* (1990), *The American Presidency: A Bibliography* (1987), and *American Presidents: A Bibliography* (1987). The major difference between this new volume and the earlier bibliographies is the paragraph-length annotations provided for each citation.

More than 25 indexes were used in compiling this source, including PAIS, *Social Sciences Index, Index to Legal Periodicals,* and *Dissertation Abstracts.* Books, essays, reports, and government documents are cited as well as journal articles. Government documents are limited to CRS studies and briefs. Congressional hearings or prints were excluded because of the overwhelming number. The annotations that accompany the citations were either written by the authors or taken from the indexes or journals, in some cases modified for editorial consistency. The volume is arranged by broad topic, beginning with the history of Congress and continuing with powers, reform, investigations, committee structure, leadership, members, etc. The subject index would be more useful with more headings and fewer subheadings.

This is an excellent source for college students researching this venerable institution. It is recommended for academic libraries with a strong political science collection or libraries that have Goehlert's *The United States Congress: A Bibliography* (Free Press, 1982), which this updates.

Business, Economics

China Business: The Portable Encyclopedia for Doing Business with China. World Trade Press, 1505 Fifth Ave., San Rafael, CA 94901, 1994. 418p. bibliog. charts. index. maps. tables. paper $24.95 (0-9631864-3-4).
330.951 China—Economic conditions—1976– || China—Economic policy—1976– || Investments, Foreign—Government policy—China || International business enterprises—China [CIP] 93-45977

Mexico Business: The Portable Encyclopedia for Doing Business with Mexico. World Trade Press, 1994. 496p. bibliog. charts. index. maps. tables. paper $24.95 (0-9631864-0-X).
658.8'48 Mexico—Economic conditions—1982– || Mexico—Economic policy—1970 || Investments, Foreign—Government policy—Mexico || International business enterprises—Mexico [CIP] 94-15696

A team of experienced international businesspeople, professional researchers and writers, a lawyer, translators, and a cartographer have produced an outstanding series of Country Business Guides. In addition to the titles listed above, there are volumes for five Pacific Rim countries: Hong Kong (0-9631864-7-7), Korea (0-9631864-4-2), Japan (0-9631864-2-6), Singapore (0-9631864-6-9), and Taiwan (0-9631864-5-0). Each volume is $24.95.

Each volume includes current coverage of 25 key topics (e.g., current issues, importing and exporting opportunities, business culture, taxation, marketing, economic conditions, and trade fairs). Charts, tables, cartoons, and other previously published material add to the wealth of information here. Each book also contains more than 800 addresses for government agencies, financial institutions, publications, etc.; a business dictionary in the local language with transliteration, when necessary; and a set of country, regional, and city maps in color. The series editor, Edward G. Hinkelman, is an international trade consultant.

This type of "doing business in" book is becoming very popular as the U.S. becomes more a part of the global economy. For 20 years, Price Waterhouse has been putting together a Doing Business . . . series for Korea, Japan, Mexico, etc. These new Country Business Guides from World Trade Press add more addresses, a business dictionary, and wonderful maps. Both series are reasonably priced, and both are useful to importers as well as exporters and foreign investors.

Great Events from History II: Business and Commerce Series. 5v. Ed. by Frank N. Magill. Salem Press, 1994. 2,076p. bibliog. indexes. $375 (0-89356-813-9).
330.9 Economic history—20th century—Chronology || Business—History—20th century—Chronology [BKL] 94-27299

Notable Corporate Chronologies. 2v. Ed. by Susan B. Martin. Gale, 1995. 800p./v. bibliog. indexes. $375 (1-8103-9217-8; ISSN 1078-3865).
338.74 Corporations—History—Chronology [BKL] 95-657052

This new title in the Great Events from History II series describes major developments in the worldwide evolution of business and commerce from 1897 to 1994. Arranged chronologically in five volumes, 374 articles describe the events: for example, 18 articles discuss consumer affairs, 32 touch on finance and financial operations, and 64 focus on how government has interacted with the business community through laws and court cases. Some articles treat specific companies, usually the introduction of a new product: "Kodak Introduces the Brownie Camera," "Sony Introduces the Walkman."

Each article of approximately 2,500 words notes a category for the event discussed, from advertising to transportation; the time the event occurred and the locale; a brief summary of the event's significance in the history of business and commerce; and descriptions of persons who were key players in the event. The following text is divided into "Summary of Event" and "Impact of Event." Concluding each entry is a bibliography with annotations indicating the focus and usefulness of each source and cross-references to other articles in the set. Among the six indexes are a chronological list of the entries, an alphabetical list of entries by title, and a subject-keyword index. The category index lists the articles by the categories at the beginning of each article, the geographic index identifies events by region or country where they occurred, and the principal-personages index lists the names of all individuals.

Notable Corporate Chronologies (NCC) chronicles historic milestones for more than 1,150 corporations worldwide. Coverage is a balance between long-established giants such as General Electric, Nestle, IBM, and Wells-Fargo and up-and-comers such as AutoZone, Blockbuster Entertainment, and Microsoft. Arranged alphabetically by company, each entry is a time line listing and briefly describing 30 to 40 major events in that corporation's life. Examples of key dates are the founding, major product introductions, scandals, mergers, strikes, and stock offerings. Each entry also includes the corporate headquarters address and phone and fax numbers. Following each time line, a further-reading section provides other sources relevant to the firm's history.

Four separate indexes facilitate access. The master chronology, beginning with the 1700s, is a selection of key corporate events for companies listed. The geographic index lists companies according to the country of their headquarters. The alphabetic index provides a comprehensive list of all companies listed as well as former names, major acquisitions, product names cited, key executive officers, and other appropriate keywords from the descriptions. The forthcoming anniversary index lists companies celebrating significant anniversaries from 1995 to 2005.

While some duplication can be found between the two sets, especially concerning huge corporations and major events, each approaches the topic differently. *Great Events from History* covers fewer events in much greater detail and emphasizes business history and its impact on world history. NCC will be used more by job seekers and researchers interested in specific company histories. Academic libraries, especially with MBA programs, will want both.

Ferguson's Guide to Apprenticeship Programs. 2v. Ed. by C. J. Summerfield and Holli Cosgrove. Ferguson, 1994. 806p. illus. indexes. $89.95 (0-89434-154-5).
331.25'922 Apprenticeship programs—U.S.—Directories || Occupational training—U.S.—Directories [CIP] 94-36764

Opportunities for Vocational Study: A Directory of Learning Programs Sponsored by North American Non-Profit Associations. By Phillip C. Wright and others. Univ. of Toronto, 340 Nagel Dr., Buffalo, NY 14225, 1994. 409p. index. paper $35 (0-8020-7776-5).
374'.013 Occupational training—Canada—Directories || Occupational training—U.S.—Directories || Corporations, Nonprofit—Canada—Directories || Corporations, Nonprofit—U.S.—Directories [CIP] 94-931021

School-to-Work Programs: A State-by-State Guide. Conway Greene, 1994. 356p. loose-leaf $50 (1-884669-04-2).
373.0113783 National service—U.S.—Finance || Volunteers—Legal status, laws, etc.—U.S. || National service—Law and legislation—U.S. || Industry and education—U.S. [OCLC]

The abundance of college selection guides makes it easy to forget that great numbers of students fail to graduate from high school, choose not to attend college, or are otherwise in need of information about vocational opportunities and training. Welcome, then, is this trio of guides to apprenticeship programs, vocational study, and school-to-work programs. Adults facing layoffs or career changes might benefit equally from their use.

Ferguson's Guide to Apprenticeship Programs provides information on more than 1,500 programs in some 76 job categories. Entries were compiled from the responses to questionnaires sent to more than 22,000 national, intermediate, and local labor unions. *Ferguson's* is arranged in four parts. Part 1 contains an overview of apprenticeship programs, a guide to choosing the right program, and an explanation of the organization and use of the book. Part 2 contains directory listings for traditional apprenticeships such as boilermakers, carpenters, machinists, theater workers, and welders. Part 3 covers such nontraditional apprenticeships as cosmetologists, firefighters, gunsmiths, funeral directors, and preschool workers. Typically included for each entry in parts 2 and 3 are address, telephone number, contact, hours of classroom instruction and on-the-job training required, starting and ending wage, how many generally apply for how many positions, admission requirements, and application documents needed. Introducing each apprenticeship occupation is an *Occupational Outlook Handbook*-style overview of the field and its employment projections. Part 4 includes a glossary, a listing of Bureau of Apprenticeship Training offices and state apprenticeship councils, and indexes by state and job title.

Opportunities for Vocational Study claims to be "the first attempt to list and to describe" the many learning opportunities sponsored by nonprofit associations of the U.S. and Canada. The focus "is on qualifications for use in business/commerce/industry and, to a lesser extent, in technical occupations." Data were gathered by questionnaire and from promotional material. Typically included in each entry are address, contact, telephone and fax numbers, general information, certification program, delivery method, qualifications for completion of program, and recertification requirements. Of the nearly 300 programs, more than 80 are Canadian or Canadian-American. When an organization sponsors more than one type of certification (e.g., engineering designer, design drafter, and drafter by the American Design Drafting Association), the requirements for each are given. The lengthy table of contents is a complete list of the associations and the learning programs each offers. The index arranges these associations and programs by profession, craft, or trade. Opportunities range from certified kennel operator and elevator inspector to registered dietitian and CPA.

School-to-Work Programs quotes President Clinton on the occasion of his signing into law the School-to-Work Opportunities Act of 1994, the implementation of which appears to be the reason for this book, Volume 2 in the Career Dollars series. (Volume 1 is *National Service Corps: A State-by-State Guide* [RBB N 1 94].) Part 1 reprints the act, the Senate Report for School-to-Work Opportunities Act, and the National Skill Standards Act. Part 2 provides details for the award of federal grants to statewide systems and local partnerships for school-to-work programs. Part 3 is a state-by-state school-to-work directory. Typically included under each state are one or more contacts with addresses and telephone and fax numbers; the 1994 planning grant budget, fiscal agent, and project team; the school-to-work plan overview; and details on the current environment. Programs include apprenticeships, high-school co-op programs, and partnerships with local businesses. Part 4 contains a reprint of the Bureau of Labor Statistics' 1992 *Career Guide to Industries*, sources of local and state job-outlook information, and an index.

Each of these three titles warrants a place on the shelves of high-school counselors as well as in the reference sections of high-school and public libraries. Academic libraries may want a copy of *Opportunities for Vocational Study*.

Encyclopedia of Careers and Vocational Guidance. CD-ROM. Ferguson, 1994. $199.95; network version available. (0-89434-153-7).
331.7'02 Vocational guidance—Handbooks, manuals, etc.—Software || Occupations—Handbooks, manuals, etc.—Software [OCLC]

The ninth edition of this standard four-volume reference set [RBB Ja 15 94] is now available in electronic form. Hardware requirements for Windows version: IBM PC 386 or higher, DOS 5.0 or higher, 4MB of RAM, Microsoft Windows 3.1.; for Macintosh: System 7.0 or higher, 8MB of RAM.

This review is of the Mac version. Fears about working in a non-IBM environment lasted maybe 60 seconds—the amount of time it took to load, double click, and begin using the program. Once the double click of the mouse is mastered, even the instruction booklet is barely needed to plunge right in and retrieve information, the program is that simple to use.

A tool bar at the top of the screen provides quick access to important functions: New Search, Custom Search, Graphics, Prior Step, Print, Information, and Exit. New Search displays the main index window. Custom Search provides a window to implement a Boolean search (AND, OR, NOT commands to be clicked on and off) by education, industries, and occupation. Terms may be entered by clicking on the desired word in the list provided or by typing in a word. A search asking for careers that require a bachelor's degree (education) in broadcasting (industries) with a professional slant (occupation) led to actors, cartoonists and animators, meteorologists, musicians, radio and TV announcers and newscasters, reporters and correspondents, and writers. The Graphics button provides color bar graphs of the fastest-growing occupations requiring a high-school diploma or less, requiring a four-year degree, requiring some training beyond high school, and those requiring the largest number of new people. Prior Step goes back a window at a time. Information provides a brief overview of the program.

The main index offers five ways to explore: job title, industry profile, occupational category, personal interests, and school subjects. Job title leads to an alphabetic browser of titles. Once a job title is selected, a window with a split screen appears. To the left is a list of information categories from which to choose: definition, history, requirements, opportunities for experience, methods of entering, advancement, employment outlook, earnings, conditions of work, requesting information by mail, and related careers. To the right, the text of that part of the entry appears. Unfortunately, the text is somewhat squeezed due to the limits of half a window. The industry-profile index leads to a similar setup with such choices as industry structure, careers, education, outlook, and related articles. The occupational category leads to a menu featuring categories ranging from agricultural, forestry, and conservation to services occupations. A selection from this menu then leads to a list of careers in that category. Personal interests leads to lists of careers based upon interests in, for example, airplanes, drawing, or plants. School subjects reads like a master schedule. Next to each subject is the number of related careers. Religion is low with only 6; anthropology has 12; education, 66; art, 93; and English, a whopping 340. The wait for the English-related careers to be listed seemed long but was actually quite fast when the length of the list is considered. With any of these last four entry points into the database, once a career is identified, the appropriate split screen pops up.

Its ease of use, general layout, and customized searches clearly recommend this CD-ROM program to secondary-school and public libraries with heavy demands for career information. As with any CD-ROM program based upon an existing print source, librarians must decide whether the improved access makes purchase of the product a necessity. The ability to customize and print out career searches with this version of the encyclopedia certainly enhances patron access to information and will probably increase library usage of the print version of this classic reference work as well.

Free and Inexpensive Career Materials: A Resource Directory. Ed. by Cheryl S. Hecht. Garrett Park Press, 1995. n.p. bibliog. paper $19.95 (1-880774-09-7).
016.3317'02 Vocational guidance—U.S.—Information services—Directories [CIP] 94-44945

This work, designed to help librarians develop vertical files, lists 821 organizations that provide career information in the form of pamphlets, reading lists, college financial-aid resource sheets, and the like for $5 or under. The organizations include trade and professional associations, federal and state agencies, academic departments, foundations, and publishers.

An index of more than 250 occupations and subjects precedes the main body of the work. Some subjects, such as *auctioneering* or *blind*, refer to just one entry. *Library Science* refers to eight, and such subjects as *Financial Aid* or *Occupational Outlook* refer to 35 or more entries. Arrangement within the main section is alphabetical by organization. (A subsection, "United States Government," includes 76 entries for various agencies). Entries themselves include address, telephone number, the titles of the materials offered, type of item, any cost (including a small envelope symbol if an SASE is required), and a brief description of many items.

Free and Inexpensive Career Materials suffers from inadequate subject indexing. For example, Kraft General Foods publishes *Choosing to Succeed*, a directory of 97 historically black colleges. Kraft is indexed along with 27 other organizations under *College Admissions and Testing* and with one other organization under *Minority-Oriented: African American*. Other headings, such as *Black Colleges* or *African American Colleges*, would have

Business, Economics

been useful. The Board recommends this work, with this reservation, to libraries serving career planners and to high-school media centers.

Specialty Occupational Outlook: Professions. Ed. by Joyce Jakubiak. Gale, 1994. 254p. index. $49.95 (0-8103-9644-0; ISSN 1077-3851).
331.7'12 Professions—Supply and demand || Occupations—Directories || Vocational guidance [BKL] 94-2701

Specialty Occupational Outlook: Professions (SOOP) covers 150 professional jobs not included in the Occupational Outlook Handbook (OOH). These include financial planners, animal breeders, geophysicists, broadcast engineers, and coaches. The format is almost exactly that of OOH: entries include "Nature of the Work" ; "Working Conditions" ; "Employment" ; "Training, Other Qualifications, and Advancement" ; "Job Outlook" ; "Earnings" ; "Related Occupations" ; and "Sources of Additional Information." An added "At a Glance" table lists one or more Dictionary of Occupational Titles (DOT) classification numbers, preferred education level, average salary, and a "Did You Know?" fact. An example of the latter is "Several years of management experience are generally required to become a public transportation coordinator."

There are two indexes: one by DOT number, the other by job title. The job-title index includes all the jobs in OOH plus SOOP job titles in bold type. Gale plans to publish another supplement to OOH covering vocational jobs in the Fall of 1995. These books will be published biennially, as is OOH.

The work under review is a helpful supplement to OOH. The most comparable title is the loose-leaf service Chronicle Occupational Briefs, which includes more jobs and more information on each job. There is some overlap in job coverage between these works, but both provide valuable information. SOOP is recommended for all libraries with career resource material.

World Market Share Reporter. Ed. by Marlita A. Reddy and Robert S. Lazich. Gale, 1994. 602p. charts. indexes. $295 (0-8103-9641-6; ISSN 1078-6783).
332 Marketing—Analysis—Statistics || Marketing research—Statistics [OCLC]

Modeled on Market Share Reporter [RBB Ja 1 91], this collection of global market-share data was compiled from periodicals and government publications. Some tables are limited to one country (e.g., "Top R & D Firms—Japan"). Others list brands or companies for a region or the entire world (e.g., "Color Television Brand Leaders" or "Global Media Companies"). The largest number of tables rank countries on a topic (e.g., "Man-Made Fiber Production Worldwide"). A few tables seem anomolous: "Destinations of Emigrating U.K. Scientists." Some entries include bar or pie charts. Each table notes its source; many are foreign publications. Tables also note SIC number, International SIC number, and Harmonized Commodity code. Arranged by SIC number, the 1,632 tables are indexed by source, place-name, product or service, company, brand, and SIC codes. These indexes list not only the subjects of tables but also the brands, companies, or countries on the tables. The place index shows that European countries and Japan are most heavily represented, but more than 100 nations are listed on tables. Toshiba is the most frequently cited company; Renault, the most frequently cited brand. Lists of International Standard Classification coverage and Harmonized Commodity code coverage are in an appendix.

For libraries serving international business, this is an essential purchase. Researchers in economics and political science will also find it useful. But browsers will also be fascinated by some of the tables here: cellular phones in Europe by country, top-10 grocery brands in Europe, leading toiletries producers in India, leading restaurant chains in France (McDonald's is second on the list). —*Sandy Whiteley*

Dictionary of Banking: Over 4,000 Terms Defined and Explained. By Charles J. Woelfel. Probus, 1994. 256p. $24.95 (1-55738-728-1).
332.1'03 Banks and banking—Dictionaries [BKL]

The Language of Banking: Terms and Phrases Used in the Financial Industry. By Michael Gordon Hales. McFarland, 1994. 169p. $24.50 (0-89950-919-3).
332'.03 Finance—Dictionaries [CIP] 94-3646

The banking profession and the financial services industry in general have developed a language of their own. Both the Dictionary of Banking (DOB) and The Language of Banking (LOB) provide understandable and reliable definitions of banking terminology.

DOB aims to be a practical desktop tool for bankers and financial professionals, as well as students and general readers. More than 4,000 alphabetical entries define terms in clear, concise, and accurate language. Also included are illustrations and charts to clarify meanings. Examples include "Statement of Cash Flow" and "Break-even Analysis Chart." A much-needed glossary of acronyms concludes the dictionary; only the military and aerospace industries employ more acronyms.

Author Woelfel is a retired professor of accounting from the University of North Carolina at Greensboro, the editor of the Encyclopedia of Banking and Finance, tenth edition, and the author of The Handbook of Bank Accounting. Woelfel recognizes banking's relationships to the professions of law, accounting, and government, making his dictionary an ideal training guide for bankers and banking students.

LOB is a a guidebook for consumers and business owners, limiting itself to understandable explanations of 850 terms and phrases used in everyday financial transactions, such as deposits and withdrawals, borrowing money, etc. LOB has many one- or two-sentence entries but also includes in-depth two- to three-page entries explaining complex banking transactions, such as *bank holding companies*, *Fair Debt Collection Practices Act* (FDCPA), and *Joint Policy Statement of Basic Financial Services*. First-time home buyers who don't know what an amortization schedule or an ARM is will find help here.

These two current titles on banking terms will appeal to different clientele: DOB, to academics and professionals, LOB, to the general public. Academic and large public libraries will want to purchase both, especially at these reasonable prices.

International Business Information: How to Find It, How to Use It. By Ruth A. Pagell and Michael Halperin. Oryx, 1994. 371p. illus. indexes. tables. $74.95 (0-89774-736-4).
332.1'753 Business information services—Handbooks, manuals, etc. || Business—Bibliography—Handbooks, manuals, etc. [CIP] 93-49000

According to the authors, the emerging global economy requires "librarians and business researchers to learn about new sources of information and expand their understanding of international business subjects." With its own sources, language, and coding, mastering this field may seem a formidable undertaking. Thankfully, Pagell and Halperin, both business librarians, have modeled International Business Information (IBI) on a similarly titled, proven source, Michael Lavin's Business Information: How to Find It, How to Use It. Reviewed favorably by the Board [RBB Jl 92], Lavin established a model closely followed in IBI, which combines in-depth descriptions of major business publications with basic concepts essential to using them effectively.

IBI is highly selective, focusing on authoritative, affordable, and generally available English-language sources, both print and electronic. A practical guide for the researcher and librarian, it covers sources used in the core of business research, companies, industries, markets, and finance. The 16 chapters are arranged into five major areas, such as company information, marketing, and international transactions. Each chapter begins with a list of topics and a list of 6–10 major sources discussed in the chapter. (In total, IBI covers more than 600 sources.) Following is a succinct subject overview and in-depth treatment of each major source. Chapter 4, "Company Information: Directory Sources," is typical. It is generously sprinkled with signposts, making it simple to quickly find critical information. A checklist for selecting international directories (e.g., "If the book contains sales data, is the date for those figures given?") is followed by sections on basic company directories (international, regional, Eastern Europe/former Soviet Union), industry directories, product directories, and company histories. Principal International Businesses, D&B Europa, and Kompass International Editions are three of the sources given detailed coverage. Automated sources, while treated in each chapter, are allotted extra coverage in chapter 6, "Company Information: Electronic Sources." Given heavy coverage here are Dialog, Data-Star, Lexis/Nexis, and Dow Jones. IBI will not help with Internet use.

A major strength of IBI is its liberal use of exhibits (more than 150) and tables (more than 100). The exhibits are high-quality facsimile copies of entries from sources. For example, when discussing Dialog's International Dun's Market Identifiers file, the editors provide a reproduction of an IDMI record. Similarly, the researcher trying to decipher an entry from Business Directory for the Soviet Union is presented with a sample entry accompanied by explanatory notes. IBI ends with

10 appendixes (e.g., synthesis of accounting standards in 48 countries, disclosure requirements of major stock exchanges, checklist for selecting an international database) and two indexes, subject and title.

IBI is a highly recommended purchase for any library— public, special, or academic—that provides international business information. The editors have done a skillful job of explaining major sources and the business concepts involved in their use. IBI will serve as both a teaching and a ready-reference tool.

The Fitzroy Dearborn Directory of Venture Capital Funds. By A. David Silver. Fitzroy Dearborn, 1994. 470p. index. $65 (1-884964-09-5).
332.6'712 Venture capital—.S.—Directories || Small business—U.S.—Finance—Directories [BKL]

This directory of 420 venture-capital investors and strategic partners that "collectively have more than $16 billion in venture capital available to invest in the *right* companies" is intended to assist the entrepreneur in search of potential sources of capital for his or her business. In the brief introductory chapters, author Silver offers an overview of the entrepreneurial process and some practical advice to the businessperson attempting a venture. The author has published numerous books and articles on entrepreneurship and venture-capital and has himself worked in venture capital investing and merchant banking.

The directory is divided into five categories, each alphabetically arranged. The largest is the broad category of "Generic Venture Funds," followed by "Medical/Biotech/High Technology Venture Funds," "SSBIC/Minority Venture Funds," "Socially Useful Venture Funds," and "Strategic Partners." Individual entries offer address, telephone and fax numbers, brief information about the size of the fund, investment criteria ("start-up only," "Ohio only"), companies in which the fund has invested, industry preference, and names of officers, with some background on these individuals where available. The directory lacks a master list of companies, so any search for a known company must be conducted in all five categories. Although specific industry preferences are given in the entries, there is no efficient way to find funds with an interest in, for example, communications or entertainment. The book's index covers only the introductory chapters. Foreign venture-capital firms are integrated into the existing lists, so it is not possible to readily determine how many are present.

Comparison must be made to the annual *Pratt's Guide to Venture Capital Sources* (Oryx, $195). *Pratt's* is arranged by state, with a complete master index of companies, as well as a detailed index of industry preferences and individual's names. Selected foreign venture-capital firms are listed separately. However, *Pratt's* does not list minority firms separately, so a user seeking such a listing would be better served by Fitzroy. *Pratt's* contains nearly twice the number of entries found in Fitzroy, so there is inevitably some overlap in entries between them, but there are a surprising number of unique entries in Fitzroy. Of the listing of 33 SSBIC/minority venture funds in Fitzroy, only 10 appeared in the master company list of *Pratt's*.

The Fitzroy Dearborn Directory of Venture Capital Funds is recommended for business collections serving the entrepreneurial community. The price of *Pratt's* has climbed steadily in recent years, which may make Fitzroy an attractive alternative for collections on a limited budget. But collections currently receiving *Pratt's* should continue to do so (funds permitting), adding Fitzroy as a useful complement. Smaller collections that can afford only one such directory may confidently choose either, understanding the limitations of each as described above.

American Military History: A Guide to Reference and Information Sources. By Daniel K. Blewett. Libraries Unlimited, 1995. 295p. indexes. $52 (1-56308-035-4).
016.335'00973 Reference books—U.S.—History, Military—Bibliography || U.S.—History, Military—Bibliography [CIP] 94-21436

Blewett is bibliographer for history and political science at Loyola University, Chicago, and has written numerous articles on the bibliography of military history. This guide covers all branches of the military services from the colonial period through the Persian Gulf War. Coverage is restricted to books in English. The 1,284 entries for such works as atlases, biographical sources, chronologies, encyclopedias, government publications, and statistics are divided into 23 chapters. After a general section, chapters are arranged chronologically by war or period. In addition, nine chapters are devoted to specialized topics (e.g., arms control, terrorism, electronic sources, organizations and associations, journals).

A typical entry includes full bibliographic information, including price. Approximately 60 percent of the entries are annotated. Included within annotations are many citations to similar works, all of which also have full bibliographic information. Annotations vary in length from a couple of sentences to half a page. Unannotated entries are usually grouped under the category "Other Related Titles" toward the end of chapters. An appendix showing the Dewey Decimal, LC, and Superintendent of Documents Classification systems is followed by a 52-page author-title index and a 10-page subject index. One inconsistency is that books mentioned within annotations are indexed only by title in the author-title index.

There are a plethora of bibliographies on U.S. military history. The most comprehensive is A *Guide to the Sources of United States Military History* by Higham (Archon, 1975-93). This excellent book and its three supplements have bibliographic essays written by experts citing hundreds of monographic and periodical references in each volume. Similar is the *Reference Guide to United States Military History* by Shrader (Facts On File, 1991-95). This five-volume work has outstanding essays, biographical information, illustrations, and citations to many monographs. In contrast, *American Military History* is more limited in scope, covering only reference tools. However, it is current, with entries for many electronic sources and new reference books. It should be considered for acquisition by all academic and public libraries with an interest in military history.

Companies International. CD-ROM. World Trade Centers Association; dist. by Gale, 1994. $1,995 (0-8103-9973-3).
338 Business enterprises—Directories [BKL]

The two titles on this CD-ROM, *Ward's Business Directory* [RBB Ag 91] and *World Business Directory* [RBB Ja 1 93], can be searched independently or combined into one massive database of 275,000 companies in the U.S. and 190 foreign countries. Each record may include address, telephone number(s), type of business, revenue and revenue type, number of employees, export/import designation if applicable, sales per employee, founding date, if traded, stock exchange and symbol, SIC codes, fiscal year, a short description, and chief officers. Depending on the size of the company (and, in particular, for international companies), some or most of this information may be lacking.

The license includes a clause recognizing library use. (The fine print in a number of business CD-ROMs restricts use to employees of the purchasing organization, frequently mentioning penalties for releasing the information to nonemployees. Obviously, this causes problems for libraries.) The manual, an 80-page plus index paperback, is well written and should be adequate for even unsophisticated users. Hardware and software requirements are not unusual: a 386DX or faster processor is recommended with at least 1MB of hard-disk space, DOS 3.1 or higher, and MSCDEX 2.0 or better.

Installation, run from the CD-ROM, is uncomplicated. Options to disable the ability to save text to hard disk and/or prevent printing of text are part of the installation routine. One can also chose to require a password to exit to DOS. I would not recommend that libraries rely on this to prevent the public getting to DOS. I found that simply pressing CTRL-BREAK after entering an incorrect password will drop the user out to DOS. A nice feature of the installation is the option for automatic deletion of user-created notes upon exiting from the program. This should avoid a routine problem that occurs with some programs when patrons create files on the hard disk and eventually it fills up with unwanted files.

There are six main search options to find company information: Company Name, Industry, Location, Products, Word or Phrase, or Screening Mode. The latter choice puts the user into Expert Mode, which allows for a customized search strategy involving some or all of the elements of a company profile. Since the profile includes so many different elements, I was prepared to be impressed with the power of the search engine. After some experimentation, I found the searching capabilities good, but with some strange quirks. Users need to be relatively sophisticated to retrieve complete returns when searching by industry or product because of the linkage to SIC codes. For example, in one search I ran, the program could identify only one computer software company in Redmond, Washington, and it wasn't Microsoft! After some experimentation, a refined search yielded 12 companies, including the giant.

There seem to be gaps in the coverage of the database. For example, searching for *tea* as a product and *United States* as a location produced

Business, Economics

a list of 12 companies. Redco Foods, which makes Red Rose tea—supposedly rated the best regular black tea in America by a leading consumer magazine—was not on the list. This company just isn't in the database. Gale Research is included, but Fulcrum Technologies, which created the technology for this CD-ROM product, is not. There are only two companies included from the state of Washington involved in the multimedia software business—a serious undercounting. I also noticed that, although the disc reviewed had a June 1994 date, the revenue year reported for Microsoft is 1992 (whose fiscal year ends June 30). I would have thought that the 1993 data would have been available by the time of pressing this CD-ROM. The revenue year for another Redmond firm, Apex Computer, is even older: April 30, 1991.

I tried to determine through a search in Expert Mode how many reports were filed for 1993 or 1994. This mode method of searching is completely command driven. The user is presented with a nearly blank screen and must remember different search terms (which fortunately do mimic somewhat Z39.50 standards, albeit with extra characters added: FI for FIND turns into FIN, and DI for DISPLAY appears as DIS). To search successfully, it's also necessary to remember field descriptors that aren't always intuitive. The alternative is to continually access the Help Screen or the documentation. The latter claims all fields are searchable, but there was no field descriptor given for "revenue year." There was one for the year of founding, but this didn't help in my quest. Randomly looking at companies did not produce any with revenue years later than 1992.

On the other hand, as a directory, there are clear and significant advantages to the search capabilities in Expert Mode for producing lists of companies tailored to individual user needs. For example, entering FIN STA IL AND IMP EXPORT will find companies in the state of Illinois that export. FIN CTY DETROIT OR REV 1000 TO 5000 will locate companies in Detroit or those that report revenues between $1 and $5 million. FIN ACD 212 finds companies within the 212 area code; FIN CTY NEW YORK AND ADR HOUSTON finds companies in New York City that are on Houston street.

Other search features include truncation, lookup tables (alphanumeric lists in each category accessible by pressing the F4 key), and the ability to save and recall search strategies. There is a Convert Currency feature that will change any currency displayed in a record to any other currency. According to the documentation, exchange rates used are from approximately three months before the disc was released.

Finally, there are some useful features for downloading information. Selected records may be exported to a floppy or hard disk, either in full format, selected fields only, as mailing labels, as telemarketing cards, or in comma-delimited format for use in another database program. The telemarketing format, for example, produces this kind of list:

Access West Inc.
3950 Industrial Blvd.
West Sacramento, CA 95691
Voice: (916)371-7226
Mark Cedarloff - President
Ray Ryan - Vice President

There are definite advantages to using these directories in electronic format, especially the capability of producing customized lists of companies and exporting the information in a mailing list or other format. Libraries will have to decide whether these advantages outweigh the hefty price, the questionable currency of financial data, and possible omissions of relevant companies. —*Charles Anderson*

Small Business Profiles: A Guide to Today's Top Opportunities for Entrepreneurs. v.1. Ed. by Suzanne M. Bourgoin. Gale, 1994-. 277p. bibliog. charts. index. $90 (0-8103-9178-3).
338 Small business—Entrepreneurship [BKL] 94-2644

Gale's *Small Business Sourcebook* (SBS), now in its eighth edition, is well known as a vital source of information for small business owners. This new companion work will be useful, too—especially for those who are considering starting a business or beginning to explore opportunities in a variety of fields.

Projected to be an annual compilation on current practices and trends in each of 60 "hot" businesses, *Small Business Profiles* (SBP) will enable a student or potential entrepreneur to evaluate options, to estimate startup costs and profits, to produce a marketing plan, and to contact useful sources of information and financing. The straightforward language, easily read layout, and thorough indexing (including keyword cross-references and a franchise index) make this a logical place to begin researching small businesses. The sources cited at the end of each essay direct the reader to more information as do the recommended reading lists in some chapters.

The authors of the articles are not identified by credentials. Members of the advisory board seem to be practitioners in business, government, and libraries. Although there is some redundancy (SBA information, in one form or another, is in every essay), this allows each entry to stand alone—a plus for those with limited time or funds for photocopying.

Persons wanting more, or more scholarly, information will still want to consult *Small Business Sourcebook*. In addition to the profiles of small businesses, startup information, primary and secondary associations, statistical sources and trade periodicals included in SBP, SBS lists educational programs, sources of supply, computer databases and software, and libraries and research centers relevant to each business described. SBS also includes a glossary of business terms and state-by-state (and provincial for Canada) listings of SCORE agencies, Small Business Development Centers, and SBA regional offices. And of vital interest to entrepreneurs wanting to develop or distribute new products is the list titled "Incubators/Research & Technical Parks."

Small Business Profiles is a useful addition to the wealth of information on small businesses and an excellent introduction to the specifics of the businesses profiled and to the intricacies of business startup.

Encyclopedia of American Industries, v.1: Manufacturing Industries. Ed. by Kevin Hillstrom. Gale, 1994. 1,637p. charts indexes. $250 (0-8103-8998-3).
338.0973 Industries—U.S.—Encyclopedias [OCLC] 94-34720
Encyclopedia of American Industries, v.2: Service & Non-Manufacturing Industries. Ed. by Kevin Hillstrom. Gale, 1994. 1,794p. indexes. $250 (0-8103-8999-1).
338.0973 Industries—U.S.—Encyclopedias [OCLC] 94-34720

This comprehensive work treats every U.S. industry that has a four-digit SIC code: volume 1 covers 460 manufacturing industries and volume 2 covers 544 service and other nonmanufacturing industries. Each volume is arranged by SIC number—volume 1 begins with *Meat Packing Plants* and ends with *Linoleum*; volume 2 begins with *Wheat* and ends with *International Affairs*. The format of this encyclopedia is similar to that of the U.S. *Industrial Outlook*, which emphasizes the current and long-term prospects for an industry.

Each major industry receives a five-page essay with an overview of the industry in the 1990s, its organization and structure, its history, current conditions, companies that dominate the industry, the size of the work force, the industry's place in the global marketplace, technological advances, and a bibliography. The bibliographies include company annual reports, government and other Gale publications, current newspaper and business periodical articles, and books published in the last five years. Fewer pages are devoted to smaller industries (*Schiffli Machine Embroideries* and *House Slippers* each rate less than a page). All entries are signed, with notes on the contributors at the back of each volume. Most are identified only as freelance writers, with a few having credentials such as the editor of *Textile World*. Even with numerous contributors, the writing style is consistent.

Hundreds of graphs are interspersed throughout the text, including one on canned-fish consumption (tuna is on top with an average of three pounds per person per year from 1975 to 1992). Another graph depicts the decline of the farm population as a percentage of the total U.S. population from 40 percent in 1900 to less than 5 percent in 1990. The preface and indexes (general and industry) are repeated in both volumes. The general index includes companies, associations, and government agencies.

The U.S. *Industrial Outlook* groups industries in 51 broad categories, such as *Textiles* and *Chemicals*. Even counting subcategories, only a little more than 200 industries are covered. It emphasizes forecasting more than this encyclopedia. With coverage of more than 1,000 industries, the *Encyclopedia of American Industries* offers a unique description of what makes the U.S. a world leader in the global economy. It may become a standard reference for business collections in academic and public libraries.

The Travel Dictionary. By Claudine Dervaes. Solitaire Publishing, P.O. Box 14508, Tampa, FL 33690-4508, 1994. 326p. maps. paper $14.95 (0-933143-45-1).

338.4'79103 Tourist trade—Dictionaries [OCLC] 94-65011

While it carries no edition statement, this book has been published since at least 1990. The author's intent was to compile a quick-reference handbook for use by travel industry personnel. As a former travel agent, tour company representative, and travel industry instructor, Dervaes relied upon her experience as the gauge for determining the style and content of this work. The idea is excellent; unfortunately, the book misses its mark. It contains a concise specialized dictionary, with brief definitions of travel terms and abbreviations. For example, *pool route* is defined as "When two carriers share equally their facilities, total revenues, and borrow planes and crews from each other." STCR is a code for "stretcher passenger." Many of the 6,000 terms defined are common words that could be found in a standard dictionary: *brothel, cavern, harbor*. Appendixes contain time zone and metric conversion charts, international clothing sizes, a smattering of geographic world facts (major rivers, deserts, ship canals, islands, continents), all of which can be found readily in commonly used reference sources. The numerous lists of specialized codes appears to be the most important information this guide has to offer. Here are codes for airlines, airports around the world, cities, countries, currencies, car rentals, hotels, credit cards, airfares, and special meals.

The Travel Dictionary is best left to travel and tourism personnel. Libraries will be wise to continue to rely on standard sources such as *Travel Industry Personnel Directory* and the *Official Airlines Guide* for this information.

Hoover's Guide to Private Companies: Profiles of 500 Major U.S. Private Enterprises, 1994–1995. Reference Press, 1994. 328p. indexes. $79.95 (1-878753-55-X; ISSN 1073-6433).

338.7 Business enterprises—Directories || Corporations—Directories [CIP]

The reasonably priced *Hoover's Handbook of American Business* has proven to be popular in libraries. It contains some privately held companies, but this new title treats 500 of these firms. *Hoover's Guide to Private Companies* has full-page entries for 125 leading companies; 65 of these entries are reprinted from *Hoover's Handbook*. Information is in standard Hoover format: a brief history; executives; key competitors; a list of products, brands, or retail outlets; and sales and net income figures shown on a table and a bar chart. For nonprofits, other statistics are substituted: Harvard University (revenues and tuition), Ford Foundation (revenues), United Way (revenues and amount raised). For the remaining companies, brief entries are limited to mostly directory information, with no tables or charts.

Some of America's best-known companies are in this book: L. L. Bean, Del Monte, Ocean Spray Cranberries. Librarians will be interested in reading about Baker & Taylor and Ingram. The 45 largest universities in terms of revenues are included, most of them with brief entries. There are indexes by industry, by headquarters location, and by brands, companies, and people in entries.

Ward's Business Directory (Gale, 1994) includes more than 100,000 private companies. However, entries are limited to directory-type information and the set costs more than $1,000. This new title in the Hoover's series will prove popular in public and academic libraries and is highly recommended. It is also available online with many services, including America Online, CompuServe, and LEXIS/NEXIS and on CD-ROM as part of *Hoover's Company and Industry Database*. —Sandy Whiteley

Law, Public Administration, Social Problems and Services

National Directory of State Business Licensing and Regulation: A Descriptive Guide to State and Federal Licensing Requirements and Regulations for Specific Businesses. Ed. by David P. Bianco. Gale, 1994. 1,139p. index. $89.50 (0-8103-9141-4; ISSN 1077-8063).

343.07 Licenses—U.S.—States [BKL] 95-657532

This book (NDSBLR) brings together detailed information on more than 100 specific lines of business that are licensed and/or regulated by state and federal agencies. The directory also indicates if a business type is *not* licensed by a particular state (acupuncturists do not require licensing in South Carolina, for example). Gathered from state and federal agencies, this information will be useful to individuals starting a small business, government regulatory and enforcement officials, consumers concerned about business regulation, trade and business associations, and small business development centers.

NDSBLR has separate chapters for each line of business, arranged alphabetically, with corresponding SIC codes noted after each chapter heading. A "Master List of Businesses" guides users from variant terms to those used in the book (e.g., "*Doctor's Office*, see Physician's Office"). An "SIC Thesaurus and Geographic Index" provides additional access points. Each chapter contains an alphabetical listing of states that require licensing for that particular business. For businesses where federal regulations apply, these are given first, with state requirements following. For example, aerial pest-control services are subject to EPA regulations covering use of restricted pesticides, and pilots flying for these services must be licensed by the FAA. For all requirements, statutory authority is given, along with the address and phone number of the licensing body. Editor Bianco also served as editor for the *Professional and Occupational Licensing Directory* [RBB D 15 93], which this book complements.

Users of this book must verify information, as regulations (and fees) are subject to change. NDSBLR reports that tattoo parlors are governed by regulation in only two states (Hawaii and Iowa), but as of January 1, 1995, proprietors of tattoo parlors in North Carolina must apply to the state health department for a permit, submit to an inspection, and pay a fee. Also, this compilation reports that in North Carolina and Pennsylvania alcoholic beverages are to be sold only in state owned stores. While it is true of hard liquor, it is not the case with the vast majority of table wines, which are sold in privately-owned establishments.

Small inaccuracies notwithstanding, NDSBLR fills a niche. Recommended for general business collections in medium-size or large public and academic libraries.

Divorce Help Sourcebook: A Guide to Organizations, Agencies, & Publications, with Expert Advice on Legal, Financial, & Personal Matters. By Margorie L. Engel. Gale, 1994. 419p. index. $44.95 (0-8103-9622-X; ISSN 1075-3494).

346.0166 Divorce—Law and legislation—U.S. || Divorce—Law and legislation—U.S.—States || Divorced people—Counseling of—U.S.—Directories || Divorced people—Counseling of—U.S.—States—Directories [OCLC]

This work combines in one volume information that otherwise would have to be pulled from many works. It is designed to help those going through divorce by simplifying the search for information that might be needed. Each of the five main chapters ("Legal Matters," "Financial Matters," "Practical Matters," "Parenting," "Health and Well-Being") begins with an essay by a recognized expert in an area of divorce. Following this, the chapter lists organizations and publications that can be consulted for further information. These resource listings of books, periodical articles, and videos are broken down into various subjects. The entries are well annotated, and sources are current.

Special areas of concern in each chapter are highlighted with a gray background. These inserts provide a summary of things to be aware of. The final section of the book, organized alphabetically by state, provides summaries of key laws related to divorce as well as listing contacts that may be useful, such as child-support enforcement offices, self-help clearinghouses, and bureaus of vital statistics. The index is detailed, listing subjects, organizations, and publications.

This is an excellent reference tool that may also be considered as a circulating book, due to the wealth of information it contains for those who are in some way touched by divorce. Recommended for college and university libraries as well as all public libraries.

The Supreme Court Justices: A Biographical Dictionary. Ed. by Melvin I. Urofsky. Garland, 1994. 570p. illus. indexes. $75 (0-8153-1176-1).

347.73'2634 Judges—U.S.—Biography—Dictionaries || U.S. Supreme Court—Officials and employees—Biography—Dictionaries [CIP] 94-10028

For evidence of the continued importance of the Supreme Court in American society, one has to look no further than the number of reference works published in recent years on this topic. The latest work, edited by legal historian Urofsky, offers a series of signed essays on the 107 men and women who have served on this bench, from John Jay to Ruth Bader Ginsburg, each written by a historian or legal scholar. Arrangement is alphabetical, and each essay is prefaced with a header that gives birth and death dates, and dates of service on the Court. Essays vary from one to nine pages. Brief annotated bibliographies are included for each justice, and there is a subject index and index of cases. Portraits are included for about half of the justices.

The particular strength of this work is the focus the essays maintain on the judicial contribution and legal philosophy of each justice. Biographical details are provided, but they are not the emphasis of the essays, which are intended to be interpretive. A great deal of the focus is on the justices' written opinions and other evidence of their roles on the court. Thus, such justices as John Rutledge and James Francis Byrnes, who had important careers outside the court but whose contributions as justices were minimal, receive rather brief treatment. Each essay is careful to present varying viewpoints on its subject, as appropriate, and the authors do a generally good job of making clear the legal issues involved. One minor blemish is some carelessness in editing the chapter header information; Joseph Story was nominated in 1811 (not 1832), a retirement date is lacking for Harry Blackmun, and the headers are inconsistent about indicating whether an individual served as chief justice. In all these cases correct information is supplied in the text.

This work most closely resembles *Supreme Court Justices: Illustrated Biographies, 1789–1993* (Congressional Quarterly, 1993). That work, however, offers unsigned entries that concentrate more on the lives and characters of the justices and gives a more cursory treatment of their judicial opinions. It is more profusely illustrated than the work under review. The most extensive treatment of the various justices is still the five-volume *Justices of the United States Supreme Court* (Chelsea House, 1969–78), frequently cited in the bibliographies of Urofsky's work. Biographical sketches of the justices can also be found in A *Reference Guide to the United States Supreme Court* (Facts On File, 1986), *Congressional Quarterly's Guide to the U.S. Supreme Court* (2d. ed., Congressional Quarterly, 1990), *The Oxford Companion to the Supreme Court of the United States* (Oxford, 1992), and *The Supreme Court A to Z* (Congressional Quarterly, 1993). However, *The Supreme Court Justices* is unique in providing substantial treatments of the justices' legal contributions in a convenient and current manner, and thus should find a place in all but the smallest reference collections in academic and public libraries.

Legal Problem Solver: A Quick-and-Easy Action Guide to the Law. Reader's Digest, 1994. 639p. indexes. $32.95 (0-89577-550-6).
349.73 Law—U.S.—Popular works [CIP] 93-27340

Reader's Digest publications are popular and useful; this one is no exception. Most people become involved in legal situations at various points in their lives and need help in identifying which problems require a lawyer's services, comprehending the terminology involved, and communicating with professionals. This volume is not intended to serve as a substitute for a lawyer, but to create a better-informed client who knows when to hire a lawyer and how to select, utilize, and evaluate legal counsel.

Nearly 700 alphabetically arranged entries cover the legal issues that an average American is likely to encounter, both at home and at work. Included are home buying, estate planning, accidents (at work, in the home, in public places, on government property, and on public transportation), consumer rights, divorce, child custody, and home schooling, to name a few. One can learn how to spot counterfeit money, remove one's name from unwanted mailing lists, and discover how each state defines the rights of adoptees to obtain information about their birth parents.

Definitions utilize lay terms and are bolstered by easily understood examples. In addition, there are checklists, sample legal forms, and sidebars that clearly indicate steps to take with or without a lawyer in order to dispose of a legal problem. Cross-references and a comprehensive index lead readers to relevant information. While the information appears reliable, the credentials of the listed consultants and contributors are not provided.

Individuals and public libraries will find *Legal Problem Solver* a good place to begin research on a legal issue but will certainly want to supplement it with other sources, such as one or more law dictionaries and the numerous topic-specific law books for laypersons that are available.

The Librarian's Guide to Public Records. BRB Publications, 4653 S. Lakeshore #3, Tempe, AZ 85282, 1995. 299p. paper $39 (1-879792-23-0).
350.714 Public records—U.S.—Directories || U.S.—Genealogy—Directories [OCLC]

The locations of public records in this guide have been compiled and condensed from the publisher's database and four of its nine sourcebooks (e.g., *The Sourcebook of County Court Records; The Sourcebook of Federal Courts, U.S. District and Bankruptcy* [RBB De 15 93]). The more than 11,500 listings are its core, with introductory matter serving as a concise guide to access.

The guide is arranged in three levels: county courts and recorders offices (white pages), state agencies (yellow pages), and federal courts (blue pages). Summaries for each level provide overviews of records organization and searching hints. The listings are essentially name, address, and telephone numbers, with time zones and office hours for county and state offices. Editor's notes point researchers to relevant sourcebooks that provide particulars about courts and cases.

In the county-records section the real estate recording office is listed first, followed by court listings noting the kinds of records found at that location (felony, misdemeanor, etc). If vital records are a county function, they are listed also The state section's opening article surveys search strategies for business records, lien and security interest records, and individual records. A real convenience is topical indexing: locations for DMV, legislation, and vital statistics, for instance, can be quickly found. A state public-records restriction chart indicates to whom these records are available.

The federal-records section lists more than 600 court locations in U.S. District Courts, Bankruptcy Courts, Courts of Appeals, and Federal Records Centers. Addresses include division and district offices. A chart cross-references each state to its corresponding circuit court, appeals court, and Federal Records Center.

Reference librarians and other researchers will find this volume a clear and efficient introduction to public-records organization and searching. The editors have produced a practical reference that will be welcome in public libraries, especially those that haven't been able to purchase the more specialized titles from this publisher.

Bibliographic Checklist of African American Newspapers. By Barbara K. Henritze. Genealogical Publishing, 1995. 206p. bibliog. index. $35 (0-8063-1457-5).
011.35'08996 Afro-American newspapers—Bibliography [BKL] 94-79984

If ever a reference work could be described as a labor of love, this one is it. What began as an article-length list of African American newspapers in the Cleveland area grew into a book-length publication with more than 5,000 entries. More than 100 resources were searched to compile this list, including annual editions of the *Ayer* and *Rowell's* directories and *Editor and Publisher Year Book*. Many of these resources are local newspaper lists that are not widely held or are unpublished; in addition, a number of repositories were consulted directly. Titles are listed by state and city, along with their frequency and dates of publication, as that information is available. References are then given to the source lists in the back of the book. An extensive bibliography is provided in addition to the source list, as is a title index and a table showing the number of entries by state.

Henritze's introduction indicates her working method in some detail and is quite direct about what she sees as the shortcomings of the work. Nonetheless, some of these shortcomings do make this a less useful work than it might have been. Newspapers are often listed under more than one title, without cross-references, so that one publication may appear to be two or more separate items. Dates of publication are often at variance with those stated in such standard sources as *Newspapers in Microform*. In many cases, the author has inferred the continued existence of a publication from its listing in a particular directory, though she acknowledges that such directories often list publications for years after they have ceased. In all fairness, however, definitive information about dates of publications for these items is often difficult to establish. The checklist also makes no attempt to exclude periodicals, which appear with some frequency. Several titles that are quite far afield, such as the *Alternative Press Index*, make their way into the list. Finally, while it would perhaps not be reasonable to expect the author to list every source for each publication, it is regretted that references to widely held lists such as *Newspapers in Microform* or the *United States Newspaper National Union List*, so useful for locating files of these newspapers, are sometimes omitted.

Nevertheless, this list brings together a great deal of information not readily accessible except by laborious searching of many disparate sources, identifies many titles missing from standard newspaper lists, and points researchers to sources of information for these titles. This is the first attempt to compile a comprehensive, historical list of African American newspapers since Warren Brown's *Check List of Negro Newspapers in the United States* (Lincoln University, 1946) and is many times the size of that list. It is certain to receive heavy use where there is active interest in African American history or genealogy, particularly until the union list of African American newspapers currently being compiled by the State Historical Society of Wisconsin is completed. It is recommended for large academic and public libraries and for other libraries supporting work in these areas.

National Service Corps: A State-by-State Guide. Conway Greene, 11000 Cedar Ave., Cleveland, OH 44106, 1994. 309p. loose-leaf $50 (1-884669-03-4).

351.4'0973 Americorps (U.S.)—Directories || National service—U.S.—States—Directories [BKL]

The National Community Service Act, passed by Congress in 1993, provides opportunities for students to perform community service and earn money for college. This guide could not have come at a better time as the program, known as AmeriCorps, was just launched this fall.

The guide begins with an informative introduction that covers such areas as what national service is, how it is organized, who is eligible, and the application procedure. The work is divided into four sections. Section 1 reprints laws and regulations relevant to the program that list and define the various types of service programs. Subsequent chapters in section 1 deal with participants and how they are chosen, how educational awards are made, and so on. The section ends with information on the various appropriations for the program. Section 2 concerns itself with the administration of the program, dealing with issues of training, selection criteria, and applications, with emphasis on the subject areas of various programs. This information was reprinted from *Principles of High Quality National Service Programs: The Corporation for National and Community Service* (January 1994).

Section 3 is a useful directory of state contacts and programs, which includes the name of the lead contact for the state and information about the funding and number of programs being run in each state. Section 4 begins with a listing of examples of service activities and skills, followed by a detailed index to the laws and regulations. The guide comes in loose-leaf format so that it can be amended as laws and regulations are amended and as new programs are approved by the states.

This volume will be useful in high-school and college libraries as well as public libraries.

The Presidents Speak: The Inaugural Addresses of the American Presidents, from Washington to Clinton. By David Newton Lott. Holt, 1994. 419p. illus. $35 (0-8050-3305-X).

353.03'54 Presidents—U.S.—Inaugural addresses [CIP] 94-9616

The president's inaugural addresses have been published in several places over the years. The GPO's *Public Papers of the Presidents* has always included them. *Speeches of the American Presidents* (Wilson, 1988) reprints "significant" speeches through Ronald Reagan's presidency and includes some, but not all, of the inaugural addresses. In 1989 the GPO produced a bicentennial collection of inaugural addresses (101st Congress, 1st Session, Senate Document 101–10, *Inaugural Addresses of the Presidents of the United States from George Washington 1789 to George Bush* 1989). In that attractive compilation, each president's contribution is accompanied by a portrait and a brief description of the inauguration. Other books attempt to "flesh out" these speeches. Fred Israel's *Chief Executive: Inaugural Addresses of the Presidents of the United States, from George Washington to Lyndon B. Johnson* (Crown, 1965) included an introductory essay on the history of the presidency by Arthur Schlesinger and featured Israel's commentaries on each president and his time.

Now comes a new edition of *The Presidents Speak: The Inaugural Addresses of the American Presidents*, first published in 1961. More than a simple compilation, it provides its users with a capsule biography of each president, an overview of what was happening in the U.S. and the world at the time of the election and the inauguration, statistical insight into the election results, and a portrait of each president at the time he took office. Most important, however, and what makes this book special, are the annotations of the speeches. Lott's analytical comments are set apart in the wide margins and are interesting reading. He comments on Washington's blunt request to put party animosities aside, as well as his eloquence in "the sacred fire of liberty" passage. He compares John Adams' eulogy of Washington with his private thoughts (learned from a letter to Mrs. Adams). He explains James Buchanan's special concern for exiles from foreign shores; his father was an Irish immigrant. He identifies sources of quotes and literary allusions, such as President Carter's reference to "a timeless admonition from the ancient prophet Micah." He explains the symbolism of using the West Front of the Capitol for Ronald Reagan's inaugural ceremony. His opinions on the president's abilities, accomplishments, rhetoric, and character make interesting reading, whether one agrees with them or not.

Appendixes include chronological charts of the presidents and brief entries on presidents not inaugurated. A detailed index aids access. Lott is a retired Navy officer and a "longtime collector of material on presidents and their inaugural addresses." This new edition of *The President's Speak* will be appreciated by anyone doing ready reference, in-depth research, or browsing.

A Dictionary of Military History and the Art of War. Ed. by And Corvisier. Blackwell, 1994. 916p. bibliog. illus. index. $64.95 (0-631-16848-6).

355'.003 Military art and science—Encyclopedias || Military history—Encyclopedias [CIP] 92-46136

Translated from the French edition (1988) by Chris Turner and revised and expanded by John Childs, this dictionary complements R. E. and T. N. Dupuy's *Encyclopedia of Military History* (4th ed., HarperCollins, 1993). Corvisier's interesting introduction reviews the reasons for our disaffection with military matters and the school of event-based history. His purpose is to integrate military history into general history, striking the right balance between precise historical facts and general ideas. Ranging in time from the ancient Middle East to the Gulf War, this dictionary is a complete success and deserves a place in all library collections.

All entries are signed by their authors and promote interest and understanding. Brief bibliographies follow most entries. The text includes cross-references, tables, and rather pale black-and-white illustrations. A major contribution and the reason for this new work earning shelf space beside Dupuy is the essay-length articles on such topics as *Glory, Nationalism, Pacifism, Popular Warfare, Military Symbolism*. These essays promote understanding of ideas associated with war. Discussions of battles and military leaders point to their significance to military history and the advancement of military tactics. For example, the entry for U. S. Grant points out how his methods foreshadowed twentieth-century war and served as a model for "specifically American approaches to the conduct of war." There are also entries for countries, weapons, such concepts as *Deterrence*, and institutions associated with the military, such as *Medical Services* and *Museums*.

The indexing is complete, including all entries, illustrations, proper names mentioned in entries, and cross-references. Highly recommended for academic and public libraries.

Dictionary of Military Abbreviations. By Norman Polmar and others. Naval Institute Press, 1994. 307p. $23.95 (1-55750-680-9).

355'.00148 Military art and science—Abbreviations [CIP] 93-34566

This is a new listing of military abbreviations, acronyms, and initialisms compiled by staff associated with the U.S. Naval Institute. Most of the abbreviations are in current use. The listing is divided into six sections: "Military Abbreviations" (which takes up more than three-quarters of the book), "Aircraft Designations," "Aviation Unit Designations," "Military Ranks," "Missile and Rocket Designations," and "Ship Designations." This organization helps those associated with one service to more easily identify terms used by other services. Chapters concerned with designations include brief explanations for letter designation schemes, most often associated with weapons. Tables are included that outline the designation systems. The stated purpose of the dictionary is to assist U.S. military officers to better communicate and coordinate military activities with other branches of the armed services.

This selective dictionary of abbreviations complements a more comprehensive work, *Dictionary of Military, Defense Contractor and Troop Slang Acronyms* (ABC-Clio, 1990), by Philip C. Gutzman. Gutzman contains 32,000 entries; this new dictionary, an estimated 6,000. Gutzman is intended for military contractors, the new dictionary for military officers. The Naval Institute Press promises updated editions of the dictionary, an important consideration for libraries that do not have ready access to government publications that include these terms.

Encyclopedia of the American Military: Studies of the History, Traditions, Policies, Institutions, and Roles of the Armed Forces in War and Peace. 3v. Ed. by Joseph E. Jessup. Scribner, 1994. bibliog. charts. indexes. maps. $300 through 12/31/94; $320 thereafter (0-684-19255-1).

355'.00973 U.S.—Defenses—History || U.S.—History, Military || Military art and science—U.S.—History [CIP] 93-49621

Over the course of the last two decades, Scribner's has published a series of outstanding multivolume encyclopedias that discuss various aspects of American civilization. Previous sets have examined foreign policy (1978), economic history (1980), political history (1984), the judicial system (1987), religion (1988), social history (1993), the North American colonies (1993), and the legislative system (1994). The objective of this encyclopedia is to assess the American military by describing the American view of war and the nature, development, and attainment of American national military objectives through history.

The editors are well qualified for such a vast undertaking. Jessup is dean of the American Military University and coauthor of A *Guide to the Study and Use of Military History.* The 66 contributors are a distinguished group, including Senator Daniel K. Inoue of Hawaii, three retired brigadier generals, plus a scattering of retired colonels and captains. Academic contributors include Frank Vandiver, former president of Texas A & M University; Harold Langley, curator of naval history at the Smithsonian; and Robin Higham, professor of military history at Kansas State University.

The 69 articles, averaging 30 pages and including lengthy bibliographies, examine many aspects of the American military experience. They are arranged topically in six parts. The text is preceded by an 80-page chronology, which contrasts general American history with American military history. For example, the period 1837–45 lists the key cabinet officials of the Van Buren and Harrison administrations on far left-hand pages, chronicles general American history in the center, and lists American military highlights on the far right-hand page. While this arrangement makes it easy to follow particular periods, it also wastes a great deal of paper, since some pages include only a few lines of text.

Part 1, "War in the American Experience," has excellent essays that serve as an introduction to the set. Notable among these is Robin Higham's discussion of "War and the Military in American Society." Jacob Kipp closes this section by reviewing the development of American military history from a suspect field to a topic of serious inquiry. Part 2 includes five chapters that review the formulation of American military policy by looking at the changing relationships between the presidency, Congress, the judiciary, and the military. The longest essay, "Congress and the Military," by Senator Inoue, notes that the military has evolved from the "hollow armed forces" of the 1970s with large numbers of poorly equipped units to the small armed forces of the 1990s with higher standards of training and readiness.

The third part looks at the evolution of the various components of the American military, with separate chapters on the army, navy, marine corps, coast guard, and air force. Part 4 reviews the performance of the American military from the colonial period to the post-Vietnam era.

One of the most intriguing sections is part 5, "Military Arts and Sciences." Essays explore 14 topics, ranging from decision making to military law. Ray Cline's discussion of "Intelligence" includes a cameo look at its role in the Persian Gulf crisis. He argues that a combination of high-technology intelligence complemented by battlefield reconnaissance contributed to the relatively casualty-free victory.

The last part deals with most of the controversial issues of our times, ranging from the military-industrial complex, women in the armed forces, and the military and minorities to sexual orientation and the military. The section concludes with an interesting essay on the changing relationship between the news media and the military up through the Gulf War. Perhaps the best essay in this section is by Jeanne Holm, who traces the role of women in the armed forces from the spies and nurses of the Civil War to the Tailhook scandal of 1991. In her discussion of this year's hot topic, "Sexual Orientation and the American Military," Judith Stiehm charts the frequently changing regulations concerning homosexuality, noting that the army changed its regulations 24 times between 1945 and 1950. Two final chapters discuss the dispersed nature of military archives and the plenitude of military museums.

The set has only 27 maps and few other illustrations. All in black and white, the maps range in quality from helpful to several with such small print that they are virtually impossible to read without a magnifying glass (e.g., one on the War of 1812 and one on the European Theater in World War II). There is an alphabetical list of essays, a list of contributors, and a very detailed 86-page index.

Taken as a whole, this encyclopedia makes a major contribution to our understanding of the American military and represents the coming-of-age of American military history as a field of study by historians. It should have broad appeal at all levels, ranging from inquisitive term-paper writers in high school and college classes to serious academics.

On the Trail of the Buffalo Soldier: Biographies of African Americans in the U.S. Army, 1866–1917. Ed. by Frank N. Schubert. Scholarly Resources, 1994. 519p. bibliog. $125 (0-8420-2482-4).

355'.0092 Afro-American soldiers—Biography || U.S. Army—Biography || U.S. Army—Afro-Americans—History—20th century || U.S. Army—Afro-Americans—History—19th century [CIP] 93-46408

Four African American army regiments served through almost the entire period of the segregated army, the Ninth and Tenth until 1944 and the Twenty-fourth and Twenty-fifth until 1951 and 1949, respectively. In the course of the Tenth Cavalry's early clashes with the tribes of the southern plains, the men of the regiment came to be called "buffalo soliders." The name apparently originated with the Indians, who may have seen a similarity between the hair and skin of the soldiers and the buffalo. Most writers on the subject contend that the name reflected the respect that the Indian warriors had for the African American soldiers. The buffalo became a prominent element of the Tenth's regimental crest and, before long, the Ninth's troopers also became known as buffalo soldiers and ultimately infantrymen as well.

This book provides biographical information on about 8,000 African American soldiers who served in the army in the 50 years between the Civil War and World War I, a little-known group that contributed significantly to the nation's development. The entries, arranged in alphabetical order, range from virtually complete life histories to fragments of data, depending on how much information researchers were able to find. Entries include a wide range of personal information, as well as details of military service, while illuminating the range of sources available to historians and genealogists. A bibliography of sources consulted is followed by a number of appendixes that list the number of blacks in the four regiments from 1867 to 1916, the number of soldiers killed in action, those that received the Medal of Honor, and the locations of regimental headquarters.

This is a special resource for all major historical collections that support African American studies programs. It is recommended for universities, colleges, and large public libraries.

Women and the Military: Over 100 Notable Contributors, Historic to Contemporary. By John P. Dever and Maria C. Dever. McFarland, 1995. 163p. bibliog. index. $24.95 (0-89950-976-2).

355.2'2 Women soldiers—Biography || Women and the military [CIP] 94-30910

This book contains 100 biographies of military women from around the world. John Dever has been a faculty member at the U.S. Army Area Intelligence School at Fort Bragg, North Carolina. The preface describes controversies revolving around women as officers, pilots, and combat troops. The authors' inclusion criteria are pioneer status, unusual experience involving bravery, an exemplary life, or a victim of extraordinary prejudice.

Divided into three sections—"Major Biographies," "Women in Military Service," and "Women Who Aided the Military"—the book presents 55 Americans (18 out of the 21 major biographies), with the rest from such diverse countries as Hungary, Lithuania, and Zimbabwe. Entries within each section are presented alphabetically. The book closes with a lengthy bibliography and an index.

This book has some valuable strengths, for example, brief paragraphs about women who aided the military such as Pearl Buck, Julia Child, and Mary Roberts Rinehart. There also is a balance of different ethnic groups. Paula Couglin, who took a stand in the Tailhook affair is profiled. There are, however, a number of difficulties with this book. Its scope is overly ambitious in that the authors try to sample a wide range of eras from Joan of Arc to the present day. Some of the brief notes in the third section, "Women Who Aided the Military," fail to give birth dates or clearly identify the conflict in which the biographees were involved.

Some notes in this section are only a single sentence. Buried in "Women Who Aided the Military" is "Molly Pitcher," known to most young people from biographies such as Augusta Stephenson's. She is obscured because only her real name, Mary Ludwig Hays McCauley, is given in the table of contents. The excellent work, *The Book of Women's Firsts*, by Phyllis J. Read and Bernard L. Witlieb, is missing from the otherwise extensive bibliography.

The writing style seems to be intended for junior-high and high-school students. It is difficult to recommend this book as other than a lightweight introduction to the topic. The entries might inspire interested students to do more research, and possibly the book might inspire some young women to consider a military career.

Directory of U.S. Military Bases Worldwide. Ed. by William R. Evinger. Oryx, 1995. 412p. indexes. $125 (0-89774-822-0).
355.7'0973 Military bases, American—Directories || U.S.—Armed Forces—Facilities—Directories [CIP] 94-38709

In 1991, when the *Directory of Military Bases in the U.S.* made its debut, it was described as the most complete guide available on the topic. Four years later, the same can be said about the greatly enlarged and appropriately renamed second edition. The title says it all—*Directory of U.S. Military Bases Worldwide*. While the format remains unchanged, the 700-plus listings have been expanded to more than 1,100 listings of active military bases and installations within the continental U.S. and abroad. Military branches now include the National Guard, the reserves, Joint Services Installations, Department of Defense Agencies, military camps, stations, recruiting offices, and command headquarters. All information was supplied by the installations themselves in the form of printed information (pamphlets, surveys). As expected, domestic sites comprise the bulk of the directory's main sections. Arrangement is alphabetical—by state, city, and name. All branches of the armed forces are interfiled, as in the first edition. The most important addition to each affected entry is information on anticipated and future base closings. This information had been only in the appendix of the first edition. The second edition also includes two appendixes that pertain to the closures and realignments outlined in the 1993 Defense Base Closure and Realignment Commission report and the July 1994 report update. There are indexes by official base name, by branch of service, and by state or country. An alphabetical unit index lists major units and their home bases.

Libraries owning the first edition will want to update their collections with the second. Those libraries that missed purchasing the original edition will find the second edition an invaluable reference tool, ideally suited for ready reference.

Encyclopedia of Social Work. 19th ed. 3v. Ed. by Richard L. Edwards. National Association of Social Workers, 1995. 3,000p. bibliog. charts. index. $150 (0-87101-255-3); paper $120 (0-87101-256-1); CD-ROM $275 (0-87101-258-8).
361'.003 Social service—Encyclopedias [CIP] 30-30948

Most encyclopedia publishers build on earlier editions to reduce costs and save time. That editorial tradition has little hold on the successive editors of the *Encyclopedia of Social Work*. The eighteenth edition (1987) represented a radical departure from its predecessors. The nineteenth edition follows its example.

Of the topics addressed by the 290 articles, approximately 55 percent are new to this edition. Only about 40 topics have been dropped, resulting in a greatly expanded encyclopedia that now fills three volumes rather than two. (It is also available, for the first time, on CD-ROM.) Even in the 135 topics covered in both this edition and its predecessor, differences are significant, since in most cases a new author has been commissioned. Only about 40 articles by the same authors repeat from the eighteenth to the nineteenth edition; these have been revised and updated to reflect changes since the mid-1980s. In short, this edition should be considered an all-new reference work.

The only section that strongly resembles its older counterpart is the biographical chapter, and even it has been expanded from 99 to 142 subjects. Selection of subjects was guided by a decision "to include more entries on women and people of color who had a significant impact on social work and social welfare." The preface clearly explains the editors' interest in diversifying not just the biographical section, but also the encyclopedia's authorship. Whereas the majority of contributors to the last edition were men, the majority of authors in this edition are women. Representation of individuals belonging to minority groups has risen from 16 percent to 24 percent. The preface also explains the editors' interest in using language that identifies groups in a neutral manner. However, it does not explain why, in a tool designed to explain the present state of social work practice, articles were dropped on such topics as divorce and separation, parent training, sex discrimination and inequality, and infertility services. Since these topics continue to be of interest, libraries should not discard the eighteenth edition.

Articles new to the nineteenth edition address both enduring topics (e.g., children's rights, family therapy, marriage/partners, professional conduct) as well as newer ones (e.g., bisexuality, the deaf community, HIV/AIDS, women and health care). Most of the 344 contributors are academics or social work practitioners. They have taken seriously the editors' guidelines to incorporate more statistical data into their articles; some use tables, graphs, or charts to present quantitative information graphically. The authors base their writing on literature published through the early 1990s and cite these up-to-date sources in the end-of-article bibliographies.

Several devices provide ready access to the encyclopedia's contents. *See* references guide users from variant forms of a topic to its entry title, and articles conclude with copious *see also* references. A box lists up to five keywords supplied by the author to describe the major concepts of the article. These are intended for use with the CD-ROM version but can also be used as entry points in the printed version's comprehensive index. Each volume opens with a table of contents covering the entire set. "Reader's Guides" list titles of articles in the encyclopedia related to 80 broad topics such as *Aging*, *Employment*, *Sexuality*, or *Welfare*.

This new edition explains current thinking and practice, as well as the foundation for current theories and practices, for the benefit of practitioners, students preparing for practice, and professionals in allied fields. It succeeds, without wholly superseding, the eighteenth edition.

Rather than incorporate a relatively ephemeral statistical section in the encyclopedia, the editors asked Leon Ginsburg to produce a second edition of his *Social Work Almanac* ($34.95, 0-87101-248-0), "a separate volume of statistical tables, charts, and graphs." It is being published simultaneously with this edition of the encyclopedia (and is also on the CD-ROM version, along with the third edition of *The Social Work Dictionary*) and should be considered an essential companion.

Dictionary of Counseling. By Donald A. Biggs. Greenwood, 1994. 229p. bibliog. index. $59.95 (0-313-28367-2).
361.3'23 Counseling—Miscellanea [CIP] 93-39352

Biggs is professor of counseling psychology at SUNY–Albany. His lengthy introduction explains the term *counseling*; a discussion is also included on the roles of counselor and client.

The dictionary itself is comprised of more than 250 alphabetically arranged entries. These include terms and phrases such as *Confidentiality* and *Oedipus Complex* in addition to important names in the field like *Jung, Carl (1875–1961)*. Various types of counseling, such as *Career Counseling*, *Marriage Counseling*, and *School Counseling*, are treated, as well as such therapies as *Developmental Counseling* and *Milieu Therapy*. Each entry is divided into four sections: general definition of the term, narrative definition, cross-references, and references to the scholarly counseling and psychotherapy literature. Each term is carefully and completely described for the layperson. The typical entry is one-half page in length, but some, such as *Black Racial Identity Development*, are more than two pages. The index is complete and proved to be accurate.

This dictionary will be useful for students in any of the counseling fields and for other persons about to become involved in some aspect of counseling.

The Best Hospitals in America. 2d ed. Ed. by John W. Wright and Linda Sunshine. Gale, 1995. 609p. indexes. $34.95 (0-8103-9874-5); Visible Ink, paper $18.95 (0-8103-9887-7).
362.1'025 Hospitals—U.S.—Directories || Hospitals—Canada—Directories [BKL] 94-37062

Choosing a hospital for treatment of a serious medical problem is an important decision. Although insurance providers may dictate hospitals, those in need of the advanced, specialized care provided by major teaching hospitals will find the new edition of *The Best Hospitals in America*, last published in 1987 by Holt, helpful in choosing the most appropriate facility.

The book is organized alphabetically by state or Canadian province and then by hospital name. Each entry includes a narrative section on the history, special facilities, programs, and research done at the institution. There is also information on medical specialties available, well-known physicians on the staff, the admissions policy (including care of uninsured patients), and patient satisfaction. The "At-a-Glance" statistical profiles include number of beds, occupancy rate, average patient stay and count, annual admissions, clinic and emergency room visits, number and type of personnel, room charges, address, and telephone number. Appendixes list hospitals commended by the Joint Committee on Accreditation of Healthcare Organizations, federally funded cancer centers, and the U.S *News and World Report Survey of Best Hospitals*, 1994. A general index and specialists index complete the work.

Although this book does not provide information about local community hospitals, it is valuable as a directory of specialized research and advanced-treatment facilities. It also tells patients what to look for in a hospital and how to judge the care given. It is a useful addition to consumer-health collections.

The Consumer's Medical Desk Reference. By Charles B. Inlander and others. Hyperion, 1995. 656p. charts. index. $24.95 (0-7868-6056-1).
362.1 Medicine, Popular—Handbooks, manuals, etc. [CIP] 94-22256

Practical information about obtaining health care is especially welcome at a time when this issue is under national scrutiny. *The Consumer's Medical Desk Reference* is a different type of general medical source. Prepared by the People's Medical Society, a leading consumer health-care advocacy group, it offers sound advice on dealing with the bureaucratic and technical aspects of the system.

The book is divided into 11 sections covering various aspects of the health-care system. These sections include basic information on anatomy and physiology, diseases and conditions, health-care practitioners, hospitals, medical schools, government agencies, professional associations and certifying boards, referral agencies, and a bibliography of books and periodicals. What sets this book apart from other general lay reference books is its emphasis on the patient's participation in all aspects of health care. Discussions of diseases and conditions consider all treatment options and suggest questions to ask before deciding on a care plan. Various types of traditional and alternative practitioners are listed along with criteria for choosing care. Sections on malpractice, evaluating care, patient's legal rights, insurance providers and how to choose and deal with them, health maintenance, and basic family health supplies and health while traveling are very useful. Lists are a unique feature of this book. Among them are the most common surgical procedures and tests and the risks associated with them, top toll-free health-information lines, and rankings of states by health.

Although *The Consumer's Medical Desk Reference* covers diseases and drugs in less depth than such encyclopedias as *The Mayo Clinic Family Health Book* (Morrow, 1990) and *The Complete Drug Reference* (Consumer Reports, annual), it provides valuable practical information about a broad range of health-care issues. The many lists and the coverage of insurance and legal issues are especially useful. At $24.95, it is affordable for both reference and circulating collections and is an excellent addition for public and patient-education libraries.

HIV/AIDS Resources: The National Directory of Resources on HIV Infection/AIDS. By Marion L. Peterson. National Directory of Children, Youth & Family Services. P.O. Box 1837, Longmont, CO 80502-1837, 1994. index. paper $110.
362.1'969792 AIDS (Disease)—U.S.—States—Directories [BKL]

This is the latest resource directory on AIDS. Other titles are similar, though each provides some unique entries. This new book was compared with the *National Directory of AIDS Care* (NDAC) published by Helenmae Hammrich and the *AIDS Directory* (AD) [RBB My 15 93]. NDAC is a state-by-state listing of facilities that offer AIDS and HIV services. AD is an alphabetical listing of facilities and organizations that provide such services. AD provides complete descriptions of each facility while NDAC has only address and telephone number. HIV/AIDS *Resources* (HAR) is a state-by-state listing of facilities, further subdivided by county and then by five types of services: health and human, mental, medical, community, and education. Each entry provides address, telephone number, key personnel, and a very brief statement of type of service offered. The format is similar to the yellow pages of a telephone directory. There is no index to facilities, so the user must know the city and county to locate an entry. NDAC does not have an index either, but AD has eight separate indexes.

There is no indication of how the information was obtained for inclusion in HAR, but it is assumed that a questionnaire was used. Some major facilities have been omitted. In Chicago, the Howard Brown Memorial Clinic is a major AIDS service provider with more than $500,000 in federal aid, but it is not included in this directory. On the other hand, HAR appears to be comprehensive in providing information about city and county health departments as well as state agencies.

There can never be too many directories for an extensive AIDS collection, and this directory is recommended for comprehensive collections in academic, medical, and large public libraries. Although the AIDS *Directory* is more expensive, it provides much more information than HIV/AIDS *Resources* and is therefore recommended for libraries that can buy only one directory.

Multicultural Clients: A Professional Handbook for Health Care Providers and Social Workers. By Sybil M. Lassiter. Greenwood, 1995. 197p. bibliog. index. $65 (0-313-29140-3).
362.1'0973 Transcultural medical care—U.S. || Social work with minorities—U.S. [CIP] 94-30927

The author of this important work teaches adult and family/community nursing at East Tennessee State University and has written articles in professional journals. The introduction notes that people should be viewed as individuals who may subscribe to the standards of their culture in varying degrees and situations, or not at all. Information on a group does not apply to all individuals in the culture, and there are more differences in beliefs and practices within than between cultures.

Each cultural background is given a separate chapter: African, Arab, Chinese, Cuban, East Indian, Filipino, German, Haitian, Irish, Italian, Japanese, Jewish, Korean, Mexican, and Vietnamese. The groups were selected on the basis of high population estimates plus recent immigrant groups about whom knowledge of health beliefs and practices may be limited. As a result, Native Americans are not included. It is questionable if the groups with roots deeps in the U.S., such as Germans, approach health care or social work from the national origin of their forebears. The arrangement of each chapter usually includes descriptions of the U.S. population, communication patterns, socioeconomic status in the U.S., chief complaint, traditional and modern family patterns, regard of the elderly, maternal and child-rearing practices, morbidity and mortality, socialization patterns, religious beliefs about death and dying, and physical assessment such as body size and hair.

For eight of the groups, vocabulary lists are provided that will be useful in treatment, for example, "hello," "pain," and "cold." An explanation of pertinent terms is presented in other chapters, such as restraint or reserve in the culture. Some comparison of cultures is made, but professionals can use the chapters independently. References are found at the end of each chapter, many from public health studies or medical journals. A brief list of periodicals and associations and an index are provided.

This is a valuable work for postsecondary training and academic institutions with health-care and social work programs. It will also be useful for public libraries working with health and social agencies serving the cultural groups included.

Homelessness: A Sourcebook. By Maurice Isserman and Rick Fantasia. Facts On File, 1994. 320p. bibliog. index. $45 (0-8160-2571-1).
362.5'0973 Homelessness—U.S.—Encyclopedias || Homeless persons—U.S.—Encyclopedias [CIP] 92-37762

Homelessness in America, 1893–1992: An Annotated Bibliography. Comp. by Rod Van Whitlock and others. Greenwood, 1994. 215p. indexes. $55 (0-313-27623-4; ISSN 0742-6895).
016.3625'0973 Homelessness—U.S.—History—Bibliography || Homeless persons—U.S.—History—Bibliography [CIP] 93-11876

These two new reference works will be helpful in answering questions and directing customers to further research on this continuing national social problem.

The 1,700 numbered sources (books, articles, dissertations, and unpublished papers) in *Homelessness in America* provide a comprehensive national picture. The authors are psychology professionals; the items in the bibliography are from the scholarly literature of the social sciences. The arrangement of the 11 chapters is topical, such as "Mental Health," "Alcohol and Drug Abuse," "Families and Children," and "Special Populations: Elderly, Minorities, and Veterans." The sources are then listed alphabetically by title, with 700 of the entries annotated. These descriptions will be valuable to users. Author and subject indexes are accurate, although users will locate additional references through browsing the entire work. While there are many other bibliographies in this area, *Homelessness in America* will be useful in public and academic libraries.

An extended introductory essay in *Homelessness: A Sourcebook* provides a perspective on the topic, while the bulk of the work consists of alphabetically arranged entries on agencies, issues, people, places, and programs. The articles range from a brief explanation, such as the problem of homelessness and the response to it in Minneapolis, to several pages, as in the entry *Mental Illness*. The entries provide a historical context (for example, Coxey's Army of the Unemployed in 1893) and some international perspective. The emphasis, however, is on problems in U.S. cities over the past three decades, with examples and data often drawn from New York City.

The compilers recognize the problems with statistics in this area and draw from many sources, in particular the annual Status Report on Hunger and Homelessness issued by the U.S. Conference of Mayors. Three appendixes are helpful: a national list of groups and resources with addresses and telephone numbers, data from the 1990 Shelter and Street Night Enumeration by the U.S. Bureau of the Census, and an extensive, unannotated bibliography, with separate sections for books, articles, U.S. government documents, reports (local and state), and bibliographies.

Homelessness: A Sourcebook will be useful to a wide range of users. As an encyclopedia that includes a fine bibliography, it will be more immediately valuable for student assignments than *Homelessness in America*.

Encyclopedia of Home Care for the Elderly. Ed. by Ada Romaine-Davis and others. Greenwood, 1995. 387p. bibliog. $85 (0-313-28532-2).
362.6 Aged—Home care—U.S. || Aged—U.S. [CIP] 94-17989

This work focuses on trends, issues, and facts relating to one of the fastest-growing sectors of the health-care field, home health care. The encyclopedia contains 88 alphabetically arranged articles that provide an interdisciplinary perspective on its many facets. The signed articles cover such fields as medicine, nursing, social work, administration, policy analysis, and physical therapy.

Entries include such practical topics as *Abuse of the Elderly, Alzheimer's Disease, Pet Therapy,* and *Cancer Patient Care,* as well as such policy and ethical issues as economic support for caregivers, decisions caregivers face, and legislation that has impacted the development of home health care. Many articles are in-depth discussions of the needs of patients being cared for at home. For example, the article on accidents in the home provides a detailed description of how to adapt a home to prevent accidents. Alzheimer's articles cover case management of eating disorders and wandering behavior. On the other hand, the articles on such broad issues as specific ethnic groups and AIDS and the elderly, while informative, are not specific to home health-care issues. There are two appendixes, one a list of public and private organizations related to home care. These entries give a service description, address, and telephone number of the organization. Appendix B groups encyclopedia entries by topic.

This work will be of greatest interest to health-care and social work professionals and students as well as policy makers in the home care field. It does not take the place of home health-care manuals designed for primary caregivers but is intended to provide a broad spectrum of information about an important issue in our aging society.

Historical Dictionary of Refugee and Disaster Relief Organizations. By Robert F. Gorman. Scarecrow, 1994. 283p. bibliog. tables. $32.50 (0-8108-2876-6).
362.87'8 Refugees—Services for—Directories || Disaster relief—Directories [CIP] 94-8247

With the Rwandan refugee crisis in the headlines of the world's newspapers, this new guide is particularly timely. Gorman (professor of political science, Southwest Texas State) has written extensively on refugees in Africa and Southeast Asia and is a former fellow in the State Department's Bureau for Refugee Programs.

His aim in preparing this book was twofold. First, he sought to chronicle twentieth-century events that produced refugees, displaced persons, or emergency victims, such as the Spanish Civil War, World War II, and civil war in the Sudan. Second, he sought to document how the international community responded to these events. Examples cited include the Mariel boatlift from Cuba and emergency food relief in Somalia.

The elements of the book include a time line of important refugee and disaster relief events from 1912 to the present; a glossary describing key terms related to refugees and disasters; profiles of intergovernmental and nongovernmental agencies involved in refugee work; legal instruments, conferences, and peace-keeping forces; discussions of humanitarian relief events; and an annotated bibliography. All of these sections are organized alphabetically. He notes that the United Nations Disaster Relief Organization (UNDRO) began operations in 1972 and was charged with coordinating relief activities of the UNHCR, WFP, FAO, UNDP, UNEP, WHO, WMO, and UNESCO. He profiles each of the above organizations and thus brings some light to the confusing array of interlocking agencies involved in this work. Similarly, he describes the role of an array of nongovernmental agencies ranging from the American Friends Service Committee to World Vision. For each he provides addresses. Finally, he outlines the major relief efforts of this century, from the Afghanistan civil war to that in Yugoslavia.

The bibliography is well constructed with a table of contents and ranges in scope from classic works to reference works. Various appendixes list important people in international assistance, provide global refugee statistics, and list NGOs by country. There are even a series of flow charts describing the operation of various agencies and organizations.

Overall, this is a superbly well-crafted book that provides important information on a timeless topic. It goes far in helping us sort out the agencies and organizations responding to perennial refugee and disaster relief crises.

Choose to Reuse: An Encyclopedia of Services, Products, Programs & Charitable Organizations that Foster Reuse. By Nikki Goldbeck and David Goldbeck. Ceres Press, P.O. Box 87, Woodstock, NY 12498, 1995. 455p. paper $15.95 (0-9606138-6-2).
363.7'23 Salvage (Waste, etc.)—Sources || Waste minimization—Sources [BKL] 95-067960

Well-known authors Nikki and David Goldbeck have turned their attention from food (*The Supermarket Handbook*) to a timely new topic. In their introduction, they explain that there are two types of "reuse." The first involves the reutilization of an item for the same purpose as it was originally intended; the second involves using the item for a new purpose. Recycling, on the other hand, is reprocessing of an item into raw material to create another new product.

Choose to Reuse is an alphabetical directory of more than 2,000 products, services, and organizations that facilitate the reusing of goods. Entries usually include a brief overview of the item and its impact on the environment. The entry is subdivided into various topics relevant to reuse: resources (where to find the materials); maintenance (how to keep an item in good working condition); repair (how to decide if it is worth fixing); rental sources; remanufacture; used marketplace; when not to reuse; surplus (where to find good items that industry no longer uses); donation; and finally disposal. The book also offers suggestions on what to do with such old items as eyeglasses and offers tips on where to find classroom craft supplies. There is a list of charitable and volunteer organizations that reuse materials. Peppered throughout the book are "choice stories," fascinating accounts of people and businesses that have implemented reuse projects.

This readable, unique guide contains a list of publishers and a short bibliography. A brief topic index and the table of contents provide access. At this price, public and academic libraries of all sizes will want two copies—one to circulate and one for reference.

The Encyclopedia of the Environment. Ed. by Ruth A. Eblen and William R. Eblen. Houghton, 1994. 846p. index. $49.95 (0-395-55041-6).
363.7 Environmental sciences—Encyclopedias [OCLC] 94-13669

Think Globally, Act Locally is the motto of the Center for Human Environments, founded by the scientist René Dubos. In 1990 the center launched the Decade of Environmental Literacy in cooperation with the United Nations Environment Programme. *The Encyclopedia of the Environment,* which grew out of that initiative, is based on Dubos' humanistic approach to environmental issues. The editors, officers of the center, report the purpose of the work is to help individuals, consumers, and voters make informed choices and to understand basic terms and concepts. Articles signed by more than 350 experts in the field provide nontechnical information. Essays from *Acid Rain* to *Zoning and Other Land Use Laws* reflect the center's emphasis on the relationship between humans and their environment. *Ecological Stability* traces the concept of human effects on nature and the effect of nature on humans back to the prescientific beliefs of the Greeks and Romans. A limited number of short biographies are included, among them Frederick Law Olmsted, Arne Naess, and Dubos. Organizations are treated under the umbrella article

Environmental Organizations. Articles on major legislation, such as the *Clean Air Act, Federal Insecticide, Fungicide and Rodenticide Act,* and *Clean Water Act,* offer concise, historical overviews. Issues awaiting further legislation are treated, such as protection of groundwater and wetlands and promotion of water conservation. There are unique essays on major religions and their activities concerning environmental issues. References for further reading accompany most articles.

Entries vary in length from one or two paragraphs to more than two pages. There are cross-references from some inverted forms (e.g., from E*cology,* H*uman* to H*uman Ecology*), but others, such as E*cology,* D*eep* and E*cology,* M*arine*, are used as entries. *See* references from terms not used often lead to several entries: "A*gent Orange* see Herbicides; War and Military Activities: Environmental Effects; Environmental Disasters." Entries are current. U*nited Nations System* mentions the Russian Federation and refers to Boutros Boutros-Ghali. Also included are a few tables and figures, a general index, and an index of contributors.

The Green Encyclopedia (Prentice Hall, 1992) is similar in focus to *The Encyclopedia of the Environment* but offers fewer encyclopedic entries and more directory information, including addresses of environmental organizations and lists of Superfund sites, toxic chemicals, and endangered species. Since they complement one another, both books are excellent purchases for most libraries.

Crime: An Encyclopedia. By Oliver Cyriax. Trafalgar Square, 1994. 468p. bibliog. illus. index. $29.95 (0-233-98821-1).
364'.03 Crime—Encyclopedias [BKL]

This addition to the reference literature of true crime provides fascinating and often new information and interpretations about some of history's most controversial crime cases. Written in an engaging style, the encyclopedia covers the entire gamut of crime, from assassinations to kidnappings to serial killers to art forgeries.

In his introduction, Cyriax states that in researching the encyclopedia, he has attempted to shed light on some of crime's biggest enigmas. He asks, How did America come to pass legislation banning alcohol? What is the best way to crack a safe? How do lethal injections work? Does a head survive decapitation? It's the author's painstaking attempt to answer such questions that helps put this encyclopedia a notch above many others.

The entries for crime cases and subjects are arranged alphabetically. The information provided for each varies from a few paragraphs to a page or more. Many entries make for a good read. Under *Kidnapping*, for example, we learn that the first reported case dates from 1874, when four-year-old Charles Ross from Philadelphia was not returned and the ransom of $20,000 was not collected. The author provides what he says is new information on crimes he considers unsolved, including the famous deaths of Marilyn Monroe and Pope John Paul I, but some of it is dated or has been discredited. With regard to evidence of a conspiracy in JFK's death, for example, he relies too heavily on lawyer Jim Garrison, while not mentioning Gerald Posner's book *Case Closed*.

The book has a few errors (the former president of Colombia is Virgilio Barco, not Barca) and omissions (there is no entry for Colombia's powerful drug Mafia). But the book's strengths far outweigh any drawbacks. Illustrations, both black-and-white photographs and pen sketches, enhance the book's readability. The index, however, could be improved upon. Pope John Paul I, for example, does not appear under any of the elements in his name.

Overall, *Crime* offers a wealth of material on a fascinating subject in an attractive format. It is recommended for purchase by all types of libraries wanting to build their true-crime reference collections.

The MVR Book Motor Services Guide. 5th ed. Ed. by Michael Sankey. BRB Publications, 4653 S. Lakeshore Dr., Ste. 3, Tempe, AZ 85282, 1994. 255p. tables. paper $17 (1-879792-14-1).
364.147 Automobile driver's records—U.S.—States—Information services—Directories || Automobile driver's licenses—U.S.—States—Information services—Directories [BKL]

The Sourcebook of Public Record Providers. 2d ed. Ed. by Carl R. Ernst. BRB Publications, 1994. 281p. indexes. paper $29 (1-879792-13-3).
350.714 Public records—U.S.—Information services—Directories || Information services industries—U.S.—Directories [BKL] 94-70823

The Sourcebook of State Public Records. Ed. by Carl R. Ernst. BRB Publications, 1994. 296p. paper $29 (1-879792-12-5).
350.7146 Public records—U.S.—States—Directories [BKL]

These volumes are part of a growing series of reference works titled the Public Record Research Library. There are 10 in print at this time to guide researchers through the maze of public records.

The MVR Book is a state-by-state guide to motor vehicle records for both drivers and vehicles. Information includes a directory of important telephone numbers, driver's license facts, driver-related record information (e.g., privacy restrictions, dial-up access to records), financial responsibility, inspection and plate facts, and vehicle-related records. These sections provide information about state laws on suspension and revocation of driver's licenses, state reciprocity of records, convictions that do not appear on driver history records, as well as commercial access to vehicle ownership records. The volume ends with a helpful glossary of programs and networks. The work is well arranged and will be useful to employers who need to check the driving records of potential employees.

The Sourcebook of Public Record Providers is a national guide to companies that either furnish automated public record information or provide search or investigation services. The volume is divided into five sections, one a short reference guide to public record retrieval. Section 2 indexes all profiled companies alphabetically, geographically, and by content or media (e.g., credit, criminal, educational records). Section 3 gives details on 305 search firms that furnish public record search and document retrieval services, section 4 describes 187 private investigation firms, while section 5 lists and profiles agency and trade groups.

This volume will be useful to individuals or companies seeking national or regional public record search firms, providers of proprietary database and CD-ROM products, background screening firms, or investigative firms utilizing online methodologies.

The Sourcebook of State Public Records is BRB's newest addition to this series. It serves as a guide for researchers needing public information available at the state level. It lists and details state by state more than 5,000 locations where 19 different types of information may be obtained, for example, criminal records, vital statistics, accident reports, worker's compensation histories, corporate records, trademark and trade-name records, and hunting and fishing licensure.

Within each category of every chapter, the following information is provided: location, including mail and courier adresses, as well as hours of operation; general indexing and search information, including search requirements and years of accessibility; restrictions on who can retrieve or limitations of access; accessing modes, including phone, fax, and computer numbers; and a cost schedule of any applicable fees. This volume should be purchased with BRB's *Sourcebook of County Court Records* [RBB D 15 93], since many states divide record keeping responsibilites with their counties.

All three volumes are written in a straightforward and succinct manner. Researchers, businesses, and libraries requiring public record retrieval information will find these reference works invaluable.

Education, Communication, Customs

The Encyclopedia of Education Information: For Elementary and Secondary School Professionals. Ed. by Leslie Mackenzie. Grey House, 1994. 563p. indexes. paper $125 (0-939300-59-1).
370 Education—Directories || Education—Societies, etc. || Education—Bibliography [BKL]

This comprehensive volume lists 5,387 resources for teachers, ranging from A *Better Chance* (organization) to *WoodKrafter Kits*. The entries are divided into the following categories: *Associations, Organizations & Government Agencies; Conferences & Trade Shows; Databases, Directories & Centers; Employment Resources; Grants & Fundraising; Publications; Education Publishers;* and *Suppliers*. Most entries include a sentence or two of explanation. For example, entry number 3198 in the *Resources for Grants* section (arranged by state) is the Herrick Foundation, which "offers grants to colleges and universities, health agencies and social service organizations." It is notoriously difficult to find the correct contact person in two areas: submissions to publications and application for teaching abroad. Both of these areas are well covered in this encyclopedia, although the list of Department of Defense schools has some private schools included in error. Education professionals will be able to use this source for employment, publishing, and conference opportunities. Merely browsing the topics will most likely cause readers to discover new avenues they had not previously considered. The *Professional Development/Books* section has descriptions of books for sale, including prices. The volume ends with state-by-state statistics from the U.S. Department of Education and National Center for Education Statistics and indexes by title, publisher, and subject to further help readers find what they're looking for.

This one volume has the capacity to save literally hours of valuable research time. While most of the information can be found scattered in other sources, this book will be a useful addition to a school system, public library, or academic library that offers degrees in education.

Youth Exchanges: The Complete Guide to the Homestay Experience Abroad. By John Hawks. Facts On File, 1994. 240p. bibliog. index. $22.95 (0-8160-2922-9).
370.19'62 Student exchange programs—U.S. || American students—Foreign countries || Student exchange programs—U.S.—Directories [CIP] 93-14178

A guide to more than 50 foreign exchange programs for high-school students, this book also provides extensive information on the homestay experience. Eight essays answer such questions as, How do I choose a program? and What will I do when I get there? A final essay discusses hosting foreign students in this country. The directory entries note contacts, profit or nonprofit status, country destinations, number of participating students, length of stay, ages served, fees, language and grade-point requirements, selection process, and support services (orientation and counseling overseas). An index by country served shows a wide range of destinations from Argentina to Zimbabwe. Other appendixes include lists of passport offices and services that expedite passports and visas for a fee, foreign embassies in the U.S., other organizations involved in youth exchange, and a bibliography.

The High School Student's Guide to Study, Travel and Adventure Abroad (5th ed., St. Martin's, 1995) describes organized tours, work or volunteer activities, and camping vacations as well as homestays. *Youth Exchanges*, while narrower in scope, describes more homestay options. For example, it lists nine programs in Turkey while *Going Places* lists two, neither of them homestays. High-school and public libraries will want a copy of *Youth Exchanges*. —*Sandy Whiteley*

The NASDTEC Manual, 1994-1995: Manual on Certification and Preparation of Educational Personnel in the United States. Ed. by Theodore E. Andrews. National Association of State Directors of Teacher Education & Certification; dist. by Kendall/Hunt, 1995. n.p. tables. paper $74.95 (0-8403-9235-4).
370.7 Teachers—Certification [BKL]

"The 1984, 1988, and 1991 editions of the Manual," claims the introduction, "have become recognized as the most comprehensive printed source of information pertaining to the preparation and certification of teachers and other school personnel." It is to be updated every other year.

The heart of the text describes certification requirements for teachers, administrators, and support service personnel (e.g., counselors, school psychologists, library media specialists) for the 50 U.S. states and 10 Canadian provinces, the District of Columbia, and Department of Defense Dependents Schools. The volume provides for each state (and in less detail for provinces) standards for the initial teaching certificate and for the second stage of teacher certification, certification fees, standards for professional development, special education certification requirements, examinations and assessments, reciprocity agreements for teachers moving across state lines, teacher training institutions and approved programs, background clearance and discipline of certification holders, support systems for beginning teachers, and emerging trends. Fifty tables covering more than 150 pages are of equal importance to the text, often supplying information not found in the text.

The annually updated *Requirements for Certification of Teachers, Counselors, Librarians, Administrators* (Univ. of Chicago) is comparable in scope to the opening section of *The NASDTEC Manual*, describing each state's certification requirements. The former, however, neglects the Canadian provinces and in some cases (such as the entry for Texas in the 1994-95 edition, which omits counselors, librarians, and administrators entirely) provides less information than *The NASDTEC Manual*. If a comprehensive source is desired, *The NASDTEC Manual* is preferred.

Education Career Directory. Ed. by Bradley J. Morgan and Joseph M. Palmisano. Gale, 1994. bibliog. index. 337p. $17.95 (0-8103-9158-9; ISSN 1074-2867).
371'.0023 Education—Vocational guidance || Teaching—Vocational guidance [BKL]

Film and Video Career Directory. Ed. by Bradley J. Morgan and Joseph M. Palmisano. Gale, 1994. bibliog. index. 264p. $17.95 (0-8103-9159-7).
791.45'023 Motion picture industry—Vocational guidance || Video recordings—Production and direction—Vocational guidance || Acting for television—Vocational guidance || Motion picture industry—U.S.—Directories [BKL]

Performing Arts Career Directory. Ed. by Bradley J. Morgan and Joseph M. Palmisano. Gale, 1994. bibliog. index. 306p. $17.95 (0-8103-9160-0; ISSN 1074-2840).
791'.023 Performing arts—Vocational guidance [BKL]

Physical Sciences Career Directory. Ed. by Bradley J. Morgan and Joseph M. Palmisano. Gale, 1994. bibliog. index. 296p. $17.95 (0-8103-9157-0; ISSN 1074-2824).
500.2'023 Physical sciences—Vocational guidance || Science—Vocational guidance [BKL]

Public Administration Career Directory. Ed. by Bradley J. Morgan and Joseph M. Palmisano. Gale, 1994. bibliog. index. 315p. $17.95 (0-8130-9161-9; ISSN 1074-2832).
350'.00023 Public administration—Vocational guidance [BKL]

These are career-guidance directories that patrons will actually want to sit down and read. Each volume covers several related occupations and provides standard career information: desirable skills, required education, typical career paths, and salary scales. Volumes also offer practical job-hunting techniques: targeting companies, networking, résumé preparation, cover letters, interviews, and so on. Also included is a "Job Opportunities Databank," a listing of companies and organizations that offer entry-level positions or internships. Along with basic corporate data (address, telephone and fax numbers, business description, corporate officers), information of special interest to new job seekers is given: benefits, human resources contacts, and application procedures. Every volume also has a chapter, "Career Resources," that specifies places to begin a job or career search: help-wanted ads (online services, placement bulletins, etc.), professional associations, employment agencies and search firms, professional and trade periodicals, and basic reference guides.

The unique feature of this series is the inclusion of a section called "Advice from the Pro's," essays by practicing professionals. Seasoned workers share their personal experiences: how they made their career choice, what training they had, what their typical day is like, what the rewards and heartaches are. *Performing Arts* includes contributions from actors, agents, comedians, choreographers, a set designer, a ballet dancer, an opera director, a composer, and a cruise ship entertainer. The field of education is represented by teachers from high school, middle school, and early childhood, Montessori, special, music, speech, physical, environmental, bilingual, and adult education; a school counselor; a library media specialist; a superintendent; and university-level instructors. These essays make for entertaining and enlightening reading. For example, Clair E. Villano, director of the Consumer Fraud Division of the Denver District Attorney's Office, has obvious enthusiasm for her job; analytical chemist Peter O. Warner points out the contribution his profession has made to the literature of detective stories.

This Career Advisor series, which now consists of 20 volumes, is aimed at high-school and college students, recent graduates, or those seeking to begin in a new field. The *Career Information Center* (5th ed., Macmillan, 1993) is designed for individuals at any stage of their career or professional development; it tracks ongoing changes in the job market due to technological advances or economic conditions. Several publishers offer lower-reading-level monograph series that consider one occupation at a time: VGM *Career Books*, Peterson's *Careers without College*, Franklin Watts *Concise Career Guides*. This Gale series provides unique insights and should be considered by high school, academic, and public libraries, as well as guidance departments and career resource centers.

Handbook of Alternative Education. Ed. by Jerry Mintz. Macmillan, 1994. 432p. bibliog. index. $75 through December, 1994; $90 thereafter (0-02-897303-8).
371'.04'0973 Non-formal education—U.S.—Handbooks, manuals, etc. || Educational innovations—U.S.—Handbooks, manuals, etc. [CIP] 94-13903

Alternatives to mainstream education vary widely, but most are more experiential, offer more respect for student and teacher, and

Education, Communication, Customs

have greater emphasis on the individual learner, according to editor Mintz in the first part this directory, which covers options for preschool through adult students. Creation of this handbook was supported by the Alternative Education Resource Organization, and directory information was gathered from state and provincial education departments and alternative education associations, foundations, and publishers. Short essays in part 2, "Alternative Education Viewpoints," review the research on educational alternatives and describe public alternatives, Montessori and Waldorf schools, home schooling, and the challenges that alternatives bring to our assumptions about schooling.

The directory, part 3, is the largest section of the book and contains nearly 7,500 entries that are arranged by zip code within alphabetically ordered state listings. These are followed by Canadian and international alternatives and a resource section of associations, publishers, and home-based and Montessori resources. Many entries provide name and address only, but fuller entries may include district or county, contact person, telephone and fax numbers, boarding and nonprofit status, tuition figures, numbers of teachers and students, age range, grade levels, entrance requirements, affiliations and accreditation, governance, teacher qualifications, and special features. Such terms as *choice*, *at-risk*, and *gifted* are defined, and a glossary of abbreviations and acronyms is provided. Independent alternatives such as Montessori and Waldorf schools are included, as are public-choice programs (Colorado's Jefferson County Open School), magnet schools (Miami's New World School of the Arts), public at-risk schools (Maine's Penobscot Job Corps), colleges (Naropa Institute), and home-based groups.

In part 4, vignettes portray a day in the life of a student in seven alternative education settings. Part 5 contains a bibliography, a list of colleges that have accepted students from alternative schools, and lists of Quaker and Waldorf schools, alternative colleges, other independent schools, home-based education groups, and boarding schools. Part 6 is an index of institutions and associations.

This handbook will be especially useful for parents seeking alternatives for their children and educators looking for nontraditional positions. Although the directory is not comprehensive, omitting many Montessori schools and magnet schools in particular, there is no similar reference work, and it will fill a gap in the field of education directories.

Art & Design Scholarships: A Complete Guide. Conway Greene, 1995. 324p. indexes. paper $20.95 (1-884669-06-9).
371.22 Art—Scholarships, fellowships, etc.—U.S.—Directories || Universities and colleges—U.S.—Directories [OCLC]

Music, Dance & Theater Scholarships: A Complete Guide. Conway Greene, 1995. 493p. indexes. paper $20.95 (1-884669-07-7).
792.07973 Music—Scholarships, fellowships, etc.—U.S.—Directories || Dance—Scholarships, fellowships, etc.—U.S.—Directories || Theater—Scholarships, fellowships, etc.—U.S.—Directories [OCLC]

Standard scholarship guides cover funds available from organizations, foundations, corporations, and governmental agencies that can be used at any school. These two guides attempt to provide information regading talent scholarships available from colleges, professional schools, conservatories, professional dance or theater companies, museum schools, and craft centers for study at those institutions. "A Note from the Publisher" in each book states that "we have included all available information regarding amounts (often presented as a range), the decision process and criteria, special stipulations (such as for entering students or majors only), portfolio requirements, and contact information." The covers tell us the books were "compiled from hundreds of personal interviews" and provide "everything you need to know to receive" a scholarship from 900 art and design programs or 1,800 performing arts programs.

Even a cursory examination reveals that the books do not deliver. Countless entries provide only the institution's address and department telephone and state "Contact school for financial aid information" or "Contact department for more information." When data are provided (e.g., student-faculty ratio, acceptance rate), they duplicate information found in standard college guides. Neither tuition nor housing costs are included.

A closer look at *Art & Design Scholarships* reveals other weaknesses. The entry for Pratt Institute, the lengthiest in the volume, lists 112 named scholarships, most described only as "awarded on the basis of academic achievement and/or financial need" and, for all but two, "amount available varies." The entry for Cooper Union states "Contact school for financial aid information" but fails to explain that tuition is free.

The directories are alphabetical with "Concentration and Scholarship Locators" and a "State-City Locator." *Art & Design Scholarships*, in addition to specific headings such as *Ceramics*, *Graphic arts*, and *Photography*, uses the generic term *Art* for more than 800 institutions. *Music, Dance, & Theater Scholarships* has three "Concentration and Scholarship Locators," each with the same flaw, using broad headings. The Board questions the placement of the American Academy in Rome under New York City in the "State-City Locator" as well as its inclusion in the guide, because its fellowships require a professional degree or three years professional experience. Students interested in studying in New York City may be surprised to find the Skowhegan School of Painting and Sculpture, a nine-week program in rural Maine, administered in the city.

Both volumes share the same staff, the same flaws, and the "not-recommended" judgment of the Board.

The Internet Resource Directory for K–12 Teachers and Librarians: 94/95 Edition. By Elizabeth B. Miller. Libraries Unlimited, 1994. 194p. bibliog. index. paper $25 (1-56308-337-X).
371.3'34574 Internet (computer network)—Directories || Database—U.S.—Directories || Education, elementary—U.S.—Information services—Directories || Education, secondary—U.S.—Information services—Directories [CIP] 94-36550

Among the 35 recent Internet users' guides and directories annotated in RBB May 15, 1994 ("Getting on the Information Superhighway: Books about the Internet"), only one—Eric Persson's *NetPower: Resource Guide to Online Computer Services*—appears to be aimed primarily at K–12 educators. As of early 1994, it was estimated that some 350,000 K–12 teachers had Internet accounts. The Internet Resource Directory for K–12 Teachers and Librarians is a welcome addition to the small body of Internet resources for a large and potentially much larger body of users.

Miller offers her book as "a starting point for teachers and school library media specialists to use in designing individual directories of Internet resources." It provides details on accessing more than 400 discussion groups, electronic books and newspapers, lesson plans, and a variety of other teaching resources by E-mail, gopher, telnet, and FTP. If a resource is accessible by more than one of these methods, access by each is described. An important proviso, noted in the introduction, is that this directory "does not provide step-by-step instructions" on how to use the Internet; that is not the purpose of a directory. Nevertheless, a brief overview of these methods is contained in the introduction. Following the directory itself are an up-to-date bibliography, a brief history of the Internet, and an index.

The directory proper is arranged under broad curricular areas plus resources for educators, reference, and school library media applications. Each of these is further divided by narrower disciplines (e.g., biology, chemistry, physics) and/or type of resource (e.g., discussion groups, newsletters and journals, graphics and multimedia). Length of entries varies considerably but always includes access method (e.g., E-mail, gopher) and address. Depending upon the resource and how it is accessed, an entry may also include login and password, path, instructions, and an annotation giving details about the resource.

Resources were chosen because they support and enrich the K–12 curriculum, supplement school library core collections due to uniqueness or searchable features, are free, are current and regularly updated, and are "specifically designed to help educators develop professionally, collaborate with peers, and share information and ideas." Persson's aforementioned *NetPower*, although lengthier and broader in scope, is not as up-to-date as *The Internet Resource Directory*. Such subject directories to Internet resources as *New Rider's Official Internet Yellow Pages* (New Riders, 1994) and *The Internet Yellow Pages* (Osborne, 1994), although quite user-friendly, will not be as useful to K–12 educators for their curriculum needs. Recommended for all school library media centers.

The Special Education Sourcebook: A Teacher's Guide to Programs, Materials, and Information Sources. By Michael S. Rosenberg and Irene Edmond-Rosenberg. Woodbine House, 1994. 325p. indexes. paper $21.95 (0-933149-52-2).
371.9'0973 Special education—U.S.—Handbooks, manuals, etc. || Special education—U.S.—Directories [CIP] 94-21554

This sourcebook lists special education materials for both the resource specialist and mainstream teacher and the interested parent.

The authors developed their lists from publishers and producers and relevant organizations. Most materials were reviewed, although annotations are not evaluative. Emphasis was placed on current sources (a few classic titles were kept for reference). Resources include textbooks, general books, multimedia, periodicals, and organizations (clearinghouses, government agencies, advocacy groups). Rather than include computer software, the authors list technology vendors.

Sections include general special education, specific disabilities (LD, behavior, sensory, physical, mental, multiple, autism), early childhood special education, assessment, specific academic skills, and lifelong partnerships (transitions to work and post-secondary education; support teams). A separate subsection covers technology in special education. A list of publishers and producers with addresses and phone numbers is followed by title, author, organization, and subject indexes. Writing is clear and succinct, and annotations are useful. Emphasis is on teaching and otherwise facilitating the growth of youth with special needs, particularly in terms of early intervention. The strongest lists are those for books, periodicals, and organizations.

A complementary work, *The Complete Directory for People with Learning Disabilities* [RBB D 15 93], lists more specific titles and groups but lacks the broad-based perspective of this book. As a first-stop bibliography, particularly for educators, this inexpensive *Special Education Sourcebook* should prove valuable.

Hooray for Heroes! Books and Activities Kids Want to Share with Their Parents and Teachers. By Dennis Denenberg and Lorraine Roscoe. Scarecrow, 1994. 243p. indexes. $27.50 (0-8108-2846-4).

372.83 Education—Biographical methods || Education, Preschool—Activity programs || Education, Primary—Activity programs || Children—Books and reading [CIP] 93-48983

This bibliography of biographies is designed to be used by children ages 3–14 and their parents or teachers. It is enhanced by activities that are generalized enough to be used in conjunction with any of the books.

The book lists are divided by age group: preschool (ages 3–5), primary (ages 6–8), intermediate (ages 9–11), and young people (ages 12–14). The preschool list contains only 14 books. Within each age group, the titles are divided into two categories, "Ordinary People in Extraordinary Situations" and "Biographies" (everyone else). These categories do not seem to be used consistently. Books about Joni Eareckson Tada, a quadriplegic who paints holding the brush in her mouth, are listed under extraordinary situations, while those about Jim Abbott, the one-armed major league pitcher, are in the biographies section. The activities are described separately in two sections, preschool and primary, then intermediate and young people, and include crafts, food, music, drama, and reading and writing. The activities are nonspecific, with little mention of adult cooperation.

Most books in the bibliography are still in print, the majority published in the 1980s and 1990s. The entries, arranged by biographee (with a descriptor of claim to fame) and then by author, include title, publisher, year, number of pages, and illustrations. Some have a short annotation prefaced by an asterisk, which indicates favorable reviews. Boxed entries with longer annotations are provided for books on the Notable Children's Trade Books list from the National Council for the Social Studies. Readers are left to wonder if the bulk of the unannotated titles, which include *Diary of a Young Girl* and *Rosa Parks: My Story*, have not received favorable reviews.

The volume has a separate list of six collective biographies recommended by the National Council for the Social Studies. These entries have extensive annotations that list the people included in each title. A list of the 1993 notables from the NCSS and indexes of series, subjects, and biographees complete the work.

Librarians will find the biography sections of the bibliographies published by the National Council of Teachers of English more useful for collection development or patron support. Students, parents, and teachers (including librarians) might find some interesting activities in *Hooray for Heroes!* but will find other sources of biographies more helpful.

The National Directory of Internships. Ed. by Garrett D. Martin and Barbara E. Baker. National Society for Experiential Education, 3509 Haworth Dr., Ste. 207, Raleigh, NC 27609, 1994. 594p. indexes. paper $24 (0-937883-11-5; ISSN 1044-9841).

373.27 Internships—Directories || Occupational training—U.S.—Directories [BKL] 90-640948

Internships offer on-the-job training opportunities in a wide variety of career areas. Increasingly, internships make a difference in competing for top-notch jobs. *The National Directory of Internships* (NDI) lists opportunities in nonprofit organizations, government, and business in 85 different fields for high school and college students, adults, and young people not in school. Opportunities are listed by 10 broad areas (e.g., business and industry, communications, environmental affairs and the outdoors). Additional sections are devoted to clearinghouses and resources for international internships. Access is facilitated by 204 pages of alphabetical, geographic, and field-of-interest indexes. In general, the organization of this source is similar to its rival, *Internships 1994: On-the-Job Training Opportunities for Today's Job Market*, published since 1981 by Peterson's. Peterson's lists internship opportunities in eight broad sections (27 career areas); separate sections cover internship referral and placement services and international opportunities. Peterson's has a geographic and employer index.

In NDI, entries contain a brief profile of the organization, a description of the internship, eligibility requirements, and application facts. Entries in Peterson's profiles include general information, internships available, benefits, eligibility, and contact. What gives NDI the leading edge? First, it is published under the auspices of the National Society for Experiential Education, since 1971 a national resource center that supports the use of learning through experience. It benefits from an index by field of interest, particularly useful because organizations may have opportunities in several fields. Nonetheless, NDI's profiles are less detailed than those in Peterson's. This is true across all categories of information within each entry, but most frustrating in the descriptions of internships. Unfortunately, it is next to impossible to ascertain overlap in coverage. Neither source indicates the total number of internships listed.

Peterson loyalists will no doubt be reluctant to break tradition, and their runs of this guide, to commit to NDI. Academic, public, and school libraries will find NDI provides another option in the pursuit of internship information. Students and others who want to make the most of internships will benefit by checking both sources.

DistanceLearn. [databases]. Regents College, 7 Columbia Cir., Albany, NY 12203-5159, 1994. Biennial. diskettes $99.

374 Distance education—Directories || Correspondence schools and courses—Directories || Regents College—Curricula [BKL]

The *DistanceLearn* database provides information on courses that can be completed for college credit without classroom attendance. Developed with adult learners in mind, it is a product of Regents College, which offers more than two dozen accredited associate and bachelor external degrees based on courses offered by other institutions. Videotape, audiotape, computer, and correspondence/print materials are included as delivery modes. Those "courses that use technology but have site-based requirements (such as telecourses with . . . on-campus final exams, or courses delivered by satellite to remote classrooms) *are not* included," excepting credit by examination and external graduate degree programs, which usually require on-site testing. *The Electronic University*, *The Adult Learner's Guide to Alternative and External Degree Programs* [RBB Mr 1 94], and *The Oryx Guide to Distance Learning* [RBB N 1 94] do contain information on televised courses, possibly the fastest-growing area of distance education.

Easy to install and use, *DistanceLearn* may be searched by type of entry (course, proficiency exam, or external degree program), DANTES-approved courses, organization name, subject area, reception system (videotape, correspondence, etc.), course level, or keyword. Boolean searches may be performed, but instructions for doing this are not made explicit. Eighty-four external graduate programs from 18 institutions, as well as more than 500 proficiency exams and nearly 7,000 courses from more than 100 institutions, are described. Each detailed entry lists address and telephone contacts, enrollment information, DANTES affiliation, course or program description, semester hours, reception options, cost, and Regents College codes for elective and core credits. Many of the course descriptions are the same as those appearing in the titles listed above. Some abbreviations such as DANTES (a military educational organization) and OLFSP are not defined. Regents College information can be partially hidden but always displays or prints at the course entry level.

Neither the database nor its manual indicates how data were gathered. Is the primary emphasis upon courses that have been reviewed and deemed acceptable for Regents College credit? Since the data are presented in a manner emphasizing the Regents College program,

Education, Communication, Customs

librarians should use it with caution, employing some of the other sources listed above.

The Oryx Guide to Distance Learning. By William E. Burgess. Oryx, 1994. 423p. paper $98.50 (0-89774-823-9).
378'.03 Distance education—U.S.—Directories ‖ University extension—U.S.—Directories ‖ Distance education—U.S.—Curricula ‖ University extension—U.S.—Curricula [CIP] 94-10004

The distance-learning movement is expanding, as educational institutions develop more courses that can be delivered via television, computer conferencing, satellite, and audio or videocassette. The Oryx Guide to Distance Learning covers 116 universities, consortiums, and public broadcasting stations that offer such media-assisted courses for academic credit.

Arranged alphabetically by state, institutional entries give address, telephone, geographic access (local, nationwide, international), delivery systems, brief institution description, and details regarding accreditation, admission, tuition, credit, grading, and library. The bulk of each entry consists of individual course descriptions, similar to those found in a college catalog. Back matter includes a glossary of delivery systems and indexes by subject, delivery system, and institution name.

Although OGDL and The Electronic University [RBB Mr 1 94] cover similar territory, OGDL's emphasis is on individual courses, rather than on degree programs. In fact, it is difficult to determine from OGDL's listings whether all or most of a degree is available through distance learning; this is clearer in EU and in Oryx's Adult Learner's Guide to Alternative and External Degree Programs [RBB Mr 1 94], both of which include institutions that offer at least one degree or certificate through off-campus means. (Many of ALG's degrees are based on correspondence study rather than media-assisted courses.) Entries for the same school also vary: OGDL lists 11 education courses for Portland State University, but EU and ALG describe its degree program in business administration, and EU notes that individual for-credit courses are offered in geography, social work, and teacher education. Since there are other similar discrepancies, and more than half of the entries in OGDL and EU are unique, libraries with a demand for distance-education information will need both directories.

Athletic Scholarships: A Complete Guide. Conway Greene, 11000 Cedar Ave., Cleveland, OH 44106, 1994. 561p. index. paper $20.95 (1-884669-05-5).
378.34 Scholarships—Directories ‖ College athletes—Scholarships, fellowships, etc. [BKL]

Young athletes will find information in this guide to help them identify and apply for scholarships in all major varsity sports plus activities as diverse as golf-course management, cheerleading, and wheelchair basketball. With information compiled from "over 1,000 personal interviews with athletic directors and coaches," Athletic Scholarships covers both two- and four-year colleges.

An introductory page explains the two main approaches for using this source. First, students can use a "sports locator" to identify colleges by sport. There are locator sections for men and women. Second, players for whom location is the important consideration may begin with a "state/city locator," then check to see which programs are offered by the colleges in the city of their choice.

The bulk of Athletic Scholarships consists of alphabetically arranged entries for colleges. The authors include up to 18 types of information for each: address; main conference affiliation; name of the athletic director; who the student should contact first (e.g., head coach); the cost of tuition, room, and board; and whether work study is available. A scholarship summary describes the scholarship opportunities for each sport. Entries for most colleges give graduation rates for athletes versus nonathletes and the average number of years it takes students to graduate. Athletic directors were asked to provide the single most-important piece of advice they would give to applicants (e.g., "Athletic scholarships are not the be all and end all of academic process. Don't lose sight of what college is all about").

A special section provides eligibility checklists (e.g., test scores, residency, credit hours) for the NCAA and similar organizations. A second special section lists intercollegiate athletic conferences with contact people, affiliations, restrictions, and recruiting.

There are a number of other directories of athletic scholarships, including College Athletic Scholarships: A Complete Guide (McFarland, 1988), Athletic Scholarships (Facts On File, 1993), Peterson's Sports Scholarships and College Athletic Programs (1993), and Athletic Scholarships: Making Your Sports Pay (Firefly, 1992). All secondary school and public libraries will want to own at least one of them. Because of its currency, readable style, and moderate price, Athletic Scholarships is a recommended buy. However, definitely plan to spend money on a new binding. The original one will not survive handling by more than a few teens.

America's Black & Tribal Colleges. By J. Wilson Bowman. Sandcastle, 1994. 307p. bibliog. index. maps. paper $19.95 (1-883995-02-7).
378.73 Afro-American universities and colleges—Guide-books ‖ Afro-American universities and colleges—History—Guide-books ‖ American Indian universities and colleges—Guide-books ‖ American Indian universities and colleges—History—Guide-books ‖ Universities and colleges—U.S. [CIP] 94-66573

Black American Colleges & Universities: Profiles of Two-year, Four-year, & Professional Schools. Ed. by Levirn Hill. Gale, 1994. 796p. bibliog. illus. index. $55 (0-8103-9166-X).
378.73'08996073 Afro-American universities and colleges—Directories [CIP] 94-3898

America's Black & Tribal Colleges (ABTC) is an expanded version of America's Black Colleges [RBB Je 15 92]. It now includes listings of American Indian colleges, as well as historically or predominantly black colleges, for a total of 124. The colleges are arranged by state. The profile of each institution gives pertinent information on academic programs offered, fees, and distinguished alumni. Appendixes have separate lists of black and tribal colleges by state and alphabetically, a list of colleges affiliated with the United Negro College Fund, and church-related black colleges.

Black American Colleges & Universities (BACU) contains detailed profiles of 118 two-year, four-year, and professional schools that are historically, traditionally, or predominantly attended by African Americans. Arranged by state, the thorough entries range from three to seven pages and contain such data as degree of competitiveness for admission. Useful for quick browsing is the "Schools-at-a-Glance" section that gives data on total enrollment, type of school, coed or single sex, estimated cost per year, average GPA of freshmen, student-teacher ratio, and level of selectivity. The individual school profiles list more than 20 attributes for each, including degrees available, financial and admissions information, athletics and special programs, student-life information, and notable alumni. Appendixes include lists of land-grant schools, state-supported schools, two-year schools, professional schools, and Thurgood Marshall Scholarship Fund member schools.

America's Black & Tribal College's introduction states that students from these institutions are more likely to complete a degree than those at nonminority schools, so a selection of these college guides is essential for high school and public libraries serving this population. Black American Colleges & Universities has the most comprehensive data and is the first choice for reference collections. ABTC is enhanced by its attention to tribal colleges. Libraries needing an inexpensive book for the circulating collection will want to consider ABTC. Two other titles, The Black Students Guide to College Success and The Multicultural Student's Guide to Colleges [RBB N 15 93] are not restricted in focus to traditionally black schools.

The Millennium Whole Earth Catalog: Access to Tools and Ideas for the Twenty-First Century. Ed. by Howard Rheingold. HarperSanFrancisco, 1994. 381p. illus. index. $50 (0-06-251141-6); paper $30 (0-06-251059-2).
380.1'029 Manufacturers—Catalogs ‖ Handicrafts—Equipments and supplies—Catalogs ‖ Appropriate technology—Catalogs [CIP] 94-1125

The Whole Earth Catalog and its progeny have been part of American life since the countercultural movements of the sixties. First published in 1968, supplements came out until March 1971's "last supplement." Later in 1971, there was The Last Whole Earth Catalog, and 1974 ushered in The Updated Last Whole Earth Catalog and The Whole Earth Epilog. The 1980s brought several editions of The Next Whole Earth Catalog and The Whole Earth Software Catalog. The Essential Whole Earth Catalog gleaned some of the best of its "tools and ideas" and seemed to end it all. But then 1990 brought Whole Earth Ecolog: The Best of Environmental Tools and Ideas. All along, Whole Earth Review, Coevolution Quarterly, or Whole Earth Software Review have kept the alternative vision in print.

And now, The Millennium Whole Earth Catalog, "committed to helping people think and act independently." While earlier versions promoted practical information for those going "back to the land," this newest edition includes information for dealing with the world of computers and the virtual community. Editor Rheingold wrote Virtual Reality (Simon & Schuster, 1992) and The Virtual Community (Addison-Wesley, 1993).

In this catalog reviewers evaluate "books, magazines, tools, software, video and audiotapes, organizations, services, and wild ideas." The work's contents are arranged in "domains," such as biodiversity, community, health, sex, political tools, and learning. Each domain covers from a few to 50 or so topics. The communications domain, for example, has pages on writing, language, "zines" (both printed and electronic), desktop audio and video, bulletin board systems, the Internet, and investigative reporting. The Internet section's five pages include a helpful introduction, descriptions of features from E-mail to the World Wide Web, access nodes, and recommended background resources.

The Millennium Whole Earth Catalog is formatted in the same effective style as its forebears. It provides meaty excerpts and commentaries, phone and fax numbers, E-mail and "snail mail" addresses, photos of book covers and computer screens, diagrams, and drawings on its oversize pages. Book reviews, which make up a good bit of the work, usually include an annotation, three or four paragraph-length excerpts, and a picture. Often "other great resources" are noted. While this work includes an eight-page index, many users will browse and follow the frequent cross-references.

The Millennium Whole Earth Catalog will be a welcome addition to the shelves of most public, academic, and high-school libraries. Circulating copies are a must.

The Exhibit Review. Phoenix Communications, P.O. Box 5808, Beaverton, OR 97006-0808, 1995. annual. 400p. indexes. $59.95 (1-886497-00-1; ISSN 1046-2872).
381.1'0294 Exhibitions—Directories [BKL]

More than 8,000 trade and consumer shows worldwide are arranged here by industry, from *Aerospace/Aviation* to *Travel/Tourism*. Within each subject, shows are listed by state, followed by foreign shows arranged by country. For each show are provided future dates (sometimes through 1999), location, frequency, show contact, number of attendees and if open to the public, number of booths available, and a brief description. For example, the ALA Annual Conference is listed under *Printing/Publishing* with the description "Exhibits include library supplies, equipment, audiovisual materials and database services." There are indexes by show name, keyword, and place. Prefatory material includes addresses for convention and visitors bureaus and convention centers.

Trade Shows Worldwide (Gale, annual) and two titles from Bowker—*Tradeshow Week Data Book: The Annual Statistical Directory of U.S. and Canadian Tradeshows and Public Shows* and *Tradeshow Week Data Book International Edition*provide additional information on shows, such as cost of booth space, profile of attendees, and an index by date. However, these directories cost more than $200. Libraries needing a reasonably priced guide to trade shows should consider *The Exhibit Review*. —*Sandy Whiteley*

USA Unzipped. CD-ROM. CD Light, 8861 Silverstone Way, Sandy, UT 84093-1679, 1995. $49.95.
383.1'45 Zip code—U.S.—Directories [BKL]

This disc provides nine-digit zip codes (i.e., "ZIP 4") for 30,000,000 residential and business addresses. This is the same information found in the 35-volume zip code directory that costs $500 from the Postal Service. The product runs under Windows. There is no manual, but instructions can be printed out from the disc and there is online help.

Searching is easy. A template provides space to type in a city name, resulting in a list of cities. After clicking on the appropriate one, if the community is small, the zip is immediately provided. For larger cities with more than one zip code, the user is prompted to type in the street address or the names of various institutions—post office boxes, apartment buildings, banks, public library, doctors' offices, etc. The record is then verified and put in standard Postal Service format. The clipboard is used to transfer the address to one's database or word processing software. Programs such as Wordperfect and Microsoft Word will also print the Postnet barcode on a label or envelope if the address includes ZIP 4. An updated version of the CD-ROM is issued twice a year.

Most libraries depend on the two-volume *National Five-Digit Zip Code & Post Office Directory*, which does not provide the four-digit extensions. The 1995 edition of *Microsoft Bookshelf* has an address finder that provides zip codes, but only the five-digit versions. Libraries that want to update their mailing lists to nine-digit zip codes to take advantage of preferential postal rates and faster delivery times will find this product useful. —*Sandy Whiteley*

Education, Communication, Customs

Jones Cable Television and Information Infrastructure Dictionary. 4th ed. By Glenn R. Jones. Jones Interactive, 9697 E. Mineral Ave., Englewood, CO 80112, 1994. 216p. $24.95; book and CD-ROM $49.95 (1-885400-00-4).
384 Cable television—Dictionaries || Information technology—Dictionaries [BKL]

In this fourth edition of Jones' dictionary, the number of entries has increased from 1,600 (in 1988) to 2,900. This edition is also available in diskette or CD-ROM formats. The author is CEO of several cable television and telecommunications companies.

The terms are derived from a variety of electronic information technologies, including cable television, cellular technology, computers, and multimedia; government agencies and awards are also included. The definitions, which range in length from one to several sentences, are written in simple terms and provide for the needs of the newcomer to the information superhighway. The terminology used in the meanings places the entries in related applications, including the field of education. Words in definitions that would not be familiar to the layperson are defined elsewhere in the dictionary. Acronyms are cross-referenced to their spelled-out versions. Terms included range from the well known, such as *Internet*, *interlibrary loan*, *cable drop*, and *C-Span*, to the more technical, such as *plesiochronous*, *phased-array antenna*, and *sync generator*.

This easy-to-use volume is excellent for the neophyte befuddled by acronyms or the more experienced looking for a greater understanding of emerging technologies. It will be of great value for school libraries entering the age of technology and for reference librarians answering patrons' questions in public and academic libraries.

Gale Guide to Internet Databases. Ed. by Joanna Zakalik. Gale, 1995. 477p. bibliog. indexes. paper $95 (0-7876-0198-5; ISSN 1081-2385).
384'.3 Internet (Computer network)—Databases—Directories [BKL]

The Internet Compendium: Subject Guides to Social Sciences, Business and Law Resources. By Louis Rosenfeld and others. Neal-Schuman, 1995. 424p. indexes. paper $75 (1-55570-220-1); 3v. set $175 (1-55570-188-4).
300'.467 Social sciences—Computer network resources || Business—Computer network resources || Law—Computer network resources || Internet (Computer network) [CIP] 95-2183

There's money to be made in books about the Internet, as Gale and Neal-Schuman clearly recognize. Thanks to the terabytes of information on the Net and its general lack of organization, guides to tools and resources are big business. With reference shelves in this area already bulging, we approached these two new guides with caution. They overlap slightly in coverage but are organized completely differently.

The *Gale Guide to Internet Databases* provides full descriptions of 2,000 databases available via the Internet. It does not include bulletin boards, i.e., listservs and newsgroups. Entries feature content descriptions and complete access information. An entry in the alphabetically arranged "Descriptive Listings" section may contain up to 24 items of information, including files available, updating frequency, time span, fees (if any), searchable elements, host and contact information. A few sources have special limitations. For example, the entry for the *Oxford English Dictionary* notes that it is only available to students and faculty of the University of Virginia. The guide also boasts a bibliography listing Internet instructional and reference publications; a "Specialized Home Pages" listing; a glossary of Internet terms; and five indexes (host/provider, alternate format such as print or CD-ROM, white pages of contacts for individual databases, subject, and a keyword master index). The Board applauds the inclusion of the directory of specialized home pages. This section lists WWW sites that function as directories to many other sites on topics such as agriculture, arts and humanities, environment and conservation, music and entertainment, and transportation.

If you are wondering whether a particular kind of information is on the Internet, this is a useful directory. It also promises to be helpful in finding that source that you know is out there, but you can't recollect where. Purchase is recommended for public, high-school, and academic libraries of all sizes.

The Internet Compendium is a print version of a selection of the Internet subject guides available online from the Clearinghouse for Subject-Oriented Internet Resource Guides at the University of Michigan (http://www.lib.umich.edu/chhome.html). These guides list databases and bulletin boards on such topics as German history, international trade, operations research/management, personal finance, Latinos, Asian Americans, and women. Each guide was compiled by a different person so their coverage and arrangement are not uniform. Neal-Schuman released two more volumes of The Internet Compendium in June: *Subject Guide to Health and Science Resources* and *Subject Guide to Humanities Resources*.

The Board found this source disappointing because of its flawed index. For example, a citation to some GAO Reports appears on page 83; the index listing GAO has five listings, but does not include page 83. Further down, with no cross-reference, the heading *Government Accounting Office* appears; the only page listed is page 83. A reference to the Federal Reserve Bank of Boston is located on page 143. The index posting *Federal Reserve* refers the reader to two other pages, but not this one. Little care appears to have been used in selecting index terms or in cross-referencing, for example, the listings for *research*, *Latino* (page 183 cited) and *Latino research* (pages 173, 175 cited.) Browsing a guide will be useful for the person interested in that topic but this is not the place to look for a specific source.

The key question is, "Do we need these guides which are available online in print?" In some measure, their packaging in print is antithetical to the spirit of the Internet. However, there are still many Internet users who prefer a book at arm's reach. Additionally, Neal-Schuman has provided some useful sections on Internet basics (Archie, Veronica, WAIS, for example) and a tantalizing section on building your own subject-oriented resource guide. If any of these reasons apply to your library, consider purchase.

Internet Access Providers: An International Resource Directory. By Greg R. Notess. Mecklermedia, 1994. 309p. paper $30 (0-88736-933-2).
384.3'3 Internet (Computer network)—Directories [CIP] 94-12259

Today, for-profit and not-for-profit companies, universities, cooperatives, and telephone companies all offer Internet connections. Those in the position of choosing a provider must consider such factors as reliability, restrictions, user support, security, and cost. And, to complicate matters, many different connection levels are available, ranging from E-mail only on up to fast dedicated-line connections.

For those shopping for an access provider, this book is the first step to unraveling the many options available. Until this directory, users had three, not altogether satisfactory, means to obtain this information: hunting for relevant sections in Internet guides, searching online lists that cover dial-up connections, and requesting lists of member networks from organizations that network providers join. Thanks to Montana State University Libraries' Notess for providing a more satisfactory solution.

Internet Access Providers features dial-up accounts, but SLIP, PPP, and dedicated-line connections are included as well. Two sections, the first covering dial-up access providers in the U.S. and Canada, and the second, providers on the international scene, include more than 100 providers. Entries include contact information, type of connections, rates, services, and system information. Services noted are the availability of such features as mailers, editors, open FTP archive, menu front-end option, menu access to library catalog or other services, USENET news feed, newsreaders, outgoing and incoming finger, and compression, decompression, encryption programs. Appendixes cover dedicated-line providers and E-mail gateways to the Internet. There are geographic indexes listing providers that offer service in only one state, province, or country, as well as a phone-number index, indexes to SLIP and PPP providers, and cost indexes for local access and for nationwide access (U.S. only). One cautionary note: the author observes that providers "continue to appear at about the rate of one a week." As a result, he includes an addendum listing the newest providers, with information in abbreviated form.

Move those Internet reference resources over and make room for this important directory, which merits a front-and-center position in collections in academic and public libraries.

Net Money: Your Guide to the Personal Finance Revolution on the Information Highway. Ed. by Kelly Maloni and others. Random, 1995. 288p. illus. index. paper $19 (0-679-75808-9).
384.3 Internet (Computer network)—Directories || Finance, Personal [OCLC]

From the editors of *Net Guide* and *Net Games* [RBB N 1 94] comes a guide to online sources of personal financial information. Like the other titles in this series, this paperback describes Internet sources; sources on commercial services such as Dow Jones/News Retrieval, eWorld, and Prodigy; and freestanding BBSs. Sources are arranged under such topics as financial software, banking, taxes, buying a car, paying for college, shopping, investments, job search, and running a small business. They range from the technical (the Federal Reserve Bulletin Board) to the silly (the Last Will and Testament of Jacqueline Kennedy Onassis), but most will prove very useful for laypeople who want to read annual reports and 10Ks, track their Visa Gold Card account, or find a job at Microsoft. A list of Internet providers, a glossary, and an index conclude this book, a must purchase for public libraries with patrons who need directions on the information superhighway. —*Sandy Whiteley*

The Facts On File Dictionary of Television, Cable, and Video. By Robert M. Reed and Maxine K. Reed. Facts On File, 1994. 226p. $24.95 (0-8160-2947-4).
384.55'03 Television broadcasting—Dictionaries || Cable television—Dictionaries || Video recordings—Dictionaries [CIP] 94-1221

The premise of this dictionary is, on the surface, a simple one: to define terms from three overlapping fields of electronic media. What complicates the authors' work, however, is the invasion of terms from allied fields of communication. The authors include words and phrases from advertising; agencies, associations, companies, and unions; broadcasting and cablecasting; education and corporate communications; engineering; government and law; home video; production; and programming. They specifically exclude terms relating only to film; as they point out, "film practitioners have different perspectives and vocabularies. This is a dictionary of the electronic media."

Entries are arranged word by word. Words are defined in clear, easy-to-understand English. For example, *letterboxing is defined as "a method of showing widescreen motion pictures in their original dimensions on television, and, with increasing frequency, on home video. Letterboxing is necessary because most theatrical motion pictures are shot in a format that is incompatible with television."* See references are liberally provided (e.g., *access* has a *see* reference to *prime-time access*), and *see also* references are shown in small caps.

The Facts On File Dictionary of Television, Cable, and Video will be useful not only in libraries serving its intended audience of students and communications professionals, but—because of its clear definitions—in medium-size to large public libraries as well. Highly recommended.

The Used Car Reliability & Safety Guide. By Adam Berliant. Betterway Books, 1507 Dana Ave., Cincinnati, OH 45207, 1994. n.p. $12.99 (1-55870-371-3).
388.342 Used cars—Guide-books || Automobiles—Performance—Guide-books [BKL]

Berliant, a reporter for *News-Tribune* (Tacoma), offers a compilation and interpretation of the most common complaints filed with the National Highway Traffic Safety Administration on cars made between 1983 and 1992. Complaints about tires are not included.

The volume is divided into three sections. Section 1, "Troubleshooter's Guide," is organized alphabetically by make and model and year. A typical listing includes the following: a summary of complaints and suggestions to prospective buyers, such as "Test the steering for noises and turning difficulty, give the brakes a thorough test, listen for odd noises" (1988 Dodge Dynasty); a five-star accident-rating system as determined by the percentage of complaints to NHTSA that were associated with accidents; "recall alert" (with a reference to see the "Recall Index," section 3); and "Hot Spots," which excerpts complaints by category (automatic transmission, brakes, etc.). A theft-alert rating is given for the 100 most frequently stolen automobiles in 1993 (as determined by a Chicago firm that provides information to insurance companies). Section 2, "Safety Comparisons," is a ranking of the top-100 vehicles with the worst accident-to-complaint ratio and the major causes of accidents for each vehicle, with the same two breakdowns arranged by automobile class (compact cars, large cars, etc.). The "Recall Index" (section 3), listing NHTSA-mandated recalls, describes defects, consequence of the defects, and corrective action. A brief glossary of technical terms used in the guide concludes the volume.

Besides Berliant, three other guides—with established reputations for providing reliable information—are available: Jack Gillis' *Used Car Book* (HarperPerennial), *Used Car Buying Guide* (Consumer Reports Books), and *Best Used Car Buys*, the August 1994 issue of *Consumer Guide Magazine's Auto Series*. Each adds much additional information, such as miles per gallon, average price and price range, buying tires, insurance, warranties, and specifications. *Used Car Reliability & Safety Guide* supplements but does not supplant the Gillis, Consumer Reports,

The Macmillan Dictionary of Measurement. By Mike Darton and John Clark. Macmillan, 1994. 538p. illus. index. $27.50 (0-02-525750-1).
389.1'03 Weights and measures—Dictionaries [CIP] 93-47005

The term *measurement* is used broadly here. Neither mathematics nor engineering are neglected, but some 33 other categories are covered, such as music, sports, geological time, and military rank.

The alphabetically arranged entries range from a few words to a page or more. The subject field from which the term is taken is given, and frequently its origin as well. Charts and graphs are used when helpful. Definitions are understandable, even when the term defined is technical. Not only are terms defined directly under their own name, but they are frequently grouped under broader terms. Sports measurements, for example, are found under the name of the sport. The ranges of musical instruments are found under the category of instrument: brass, string, woodwinds, etc. Under *Coins and Currencies of the World* monetary terms and their values are listed alphabetically by the name of the country that uses them. More detailed definitions of monetary terms are found directly under the terms themselves.

The *Macmillan Dictionary of Measurement* is rich in obsolete, rarely used, and non-English terms. The British background of the authors is demonstrated by especially thorough treatment of the cultures of the British Commonwealth. The format here is excellent. Cross-references, which are numerous, are in small capitals. A topical index is arranged by the subject fields that appear in every entry.

Although the information in this book is already in commonly held dictionaries, encyclopedias, and handbooks, the convenience of having it in one volume justifies the modest price.

Encyclopedia of American Indian Costume. By Josephine Paterek. ABC-Clio, 1994. 516p. bibliog. illus. index. $75 (0-87436-685-2).
391'.0089 Indians of North America—Costume—Encyclopedias [CIP] 93-39337

Many nations share the North American continent; the diversities of clothing styles of Native Americans are documented in this book. Offering complete descriptions and the cultural context of the dress and ornamentation of these Americans, this authoritative book is accessible to everyone from the upper elementary student to adults.

The book is divided into 10 cultural regions north of Mexico. Each region is described in a general manner. The tribes that inhabited the area are listed in a table at the beginning of the chapter, and those that are further described are followed by a page number. The description of the costume of each specific tribe is given in a consistent order, including men's basic, women's basic, footwear, outer wear, hairstyles, headgear, accessories, jewelry, armor, special costumes, garment decoration, face and body embellishment, and masks. A final paragraph on transitional dress refers to how clothing changed after involvement with Europeans. Beyond the basic description, the author includes insight into the culture, natural materials, and societal influences that led to the diversity of costumes. More than 400 large black-and-white photographs, some of them by famous photographers such as Edward Curtis, and drawings and paintings by noted artists, such as Karl Bodmer and George Catlin, illustrate the entries. A list of key sources for the information follows each entry. Appendixes include a glossary and descriptions of the materials used in clothing and the techniques of their production, with line drawings of many articles. An extensive bibliography, divided by cultural region, is followed by a detailed index. The index lists not only tribes and pieces of clothing, but also such subjects as puberty customs and looms.

Although technically a book on clothing, the *Encyclopedia of American Indian Costume* would serve well in the college, public, or school library for broader research on the many tribes listed.

Holidays and Festivals Index. Ed. by Helene Henderson and Barry Puckett. Omnigraphics, 1995. 782p. bibliog. indexes. $65 (0-7808-0012-5).
394.2'69 Holidays—Indexes || Festivals—Indexes [CIP] 94-39351

This volume indexes 27 reference books that provide information on more than 3,000 holidays, festivals, celebrations, commemorative days, feasts, and fasts in more than 150 countries. The criteria used for inclusion were that the holiday holds some cultural significance, is observed on a regular basis, and appears in the standard reference sources used.

The volume begins with a list of legal holidays by state and country; a dictionary of words relating to periods of time (e.g., *hebdomadal*—*weekly*), brief descriptions of calendar systems around the world, a comparative table of calendar systems, an annotated bibliography of the sources indexed, and a list of additional sources.

The entries are arranged alphabetically by English name with alternate forms or foreign names of the holiday in parentheses (e.g., *Epiphany* [*Trettondag Jul*]). Entries provide the location of the event, the ethnic or religious groups who celebrate it, the year the holiday was established, the date observed, and a list of the reference sources in which further information can be found. There are four additional indexes. The "Ethnic and Geographical Index" lists events by the places where they are celebrated or the ethnic groups that celebrate them (e.g., *Warsaw, Poland*—Theatre meetings, December). The name index lists people with whom the holidays and festivals are associated (e.g., *Houston, Sam*-Independence Day, Texas, March 2). The religion index lists holidays and festivals by religion, and the chronological indexes list fixed events by date under the Gregorian calendar and various movable Chinese, Christian, Jewish, and Muslim holidays.

This volume is a worthwhile purchase for public and university libraries that have access to the sources indexed. Gale's *Folklore of American Holidays* (2d ed., 1991), *Folklore of World Holidays* [RBB Ap 15 92], and Omnigraphics' *Holidays, Festivals, and Celebrations of the World Dictionary* [RBB Ag 94], for example, are indexed here.

International Holidays: 204 Countries from 1994 through 2015. By Robert S. Weaver. McFarland, 1995. 361p. index. tables. $45 (0-89950-953-3).
394.2'6 Holidays—Calendars || Special days—Calendars [CIP] 94-19445

This book of lists enables readers to determine where and when particular holidays are celebrated. "Holiday" seems to mean "official holiday;" bank holidays are included, festivals are not. Some arbitrarily selected "soft holidays" are included for convenience, including Mother's Day and Valentine's Day. An introduction surveys various calendars, including the Gregorian, into which all dates for this book are translated. Also discussed are complications of dating and observance caused by movable religious holidays.

Approximately half the book breaks down the years 1994–2015 into monthly listings. Daily entries list country and holidays celebrated. Four appendixes and an index follow. Appendix A is an alphabetical list of fixed multinational holidays, such as Labor Day and Christmas Day, with the countries that celebrate them. Appendix B is a listing of algorithmic holidays (a term appearing in the tables, undefined, referring to dates arrived at by computation—Easter, for example). Within Asian, Christian, Orthodox, Hindu, and Islamic categories, countries are listed that celebrate holidays of these faiths. Method of reckoning is given, with reference to tables and calendar for exact dates. Appendix C is a table of dates for selected algorithmic holidays from 1900 to 2100. These include dates for Chinese New Year (with the associated animal), and Christian, Orthodox, Hindu, Islamic, Jewish, and Theravada Buddhist holidays. The Jewish holiday Shavuot is listed as Pentecost; while technically this is not incorrect, this is not the term used by Jews. Appendix D is an alphabetical list of countries, the holidays they celebrate, and whether the holidays are fixed or algorithmic, multinational or unique to that country. An index and holiday register guides readers to all nations celebrating a particular holiday.

Because holidays are listed without description, readers will welcome a companion volume such as *Folklore of World Holidays* [RBB Ap 15 92], which describes holidays and festivals, as well as official holidays of 150 countries. *Holidays, Festivals, and Celebrations of the World Dictionary* [RBB Ag 94] describes 1,400 celebrations in 100 countries. *International Holidays* is clearly most useful in determining dates. Aside from the lack of definitions, it is easy to use. Anyone needing to plan for holiday crowds or closed businesses will find it practical, as will librarians working ready reference.

Forms of Address: A Guide for Business and Social Use. Comp. by Andrea Holberg. Rice Univ. Press, 1994. 217p. index. $27.50 (0-89263-333-6); paper $12.95 (0-89263-334-4).
395'.52'0973 Letter writing || English language—Address, Forms of || Commercial correspondance || Etiquette [CIP] 94-17521

When it comes to questions pertaining to formal etiquette and of-

Education, Communication, Customs

ficial protocol, it is always best to consult the experts—Emily Post (*Emily Post's Etiquette*), Letitia Baldridge (*Complete Guide to New Manners for the '90's* and *Complete Guide to Executive Manners*), and Mary Jane McCaffree and Pauline Innis (*Protocol: The Complete Handbook of Diplomatic and Social Usage*). These guides, especially when used together, will provide the answers to etiquette for levels of formal entertaining—from friends and business associates to the diplomatic corps and foreign heads of state.

In the event that these experts are not readily available, and the etiquette question pertains solely to forms of address—invitations, correspondence, introductions, place cards, name tags—Houston International Protocol Alliance's *Forms of Address* is the source to consult. It contains the same information (only differing in presentation format) as the sections on titles and forms of address and addressing people properly in the McCaffree and Baldridge guides. It is more comprehensive than the related section in *Emily Post*. *Forms of Address* is a straightforward, down-to-earth, clearly illustrated handbook. It is ideal for quick or at-a-glance reference. Using the theory of one item to a page, each title or position examined takes up an entire page of illustrated examples. There is no guesswork when it comes to letter, envelope, or place-card layout. Men and women holding high positions are treated equally. Each example explains the format to be used, regardless of the gender of the VIP or VIP and spouse/guest. All bases are covered, be it "Dr. and Dr.," "Dr. and Mrs.," "Dr. and Mr.," "Mrs. Clinton" or "Hillary Rodham Clinton," and more. "Her Highness," "Their Highnesses," "His/Her/Your Excellency," apostolic delegates, all faiths, sects, nations, commoners, collegians, and others are included. Nothing is left to chance. Users of this handbook will have no excuse for ignorance. A must purchase for most libraries.

Atlas of the Mysterious in North America. By Rosemary Ellen Guiley. Facts On File, 1995. 178p. bibliog. index. tables. $27.95 (0-8160-2876-1).
398.2'097 Folklore—North America—Maps || Folklore—U.S.—Maps [CIP] 93-41985

John Keel, author of *The Mothman Prophecies*, writes a complimentary foreword to this book, which suggests that it was written by a believer in the paranormal. Guiley is the author of numerous reference works, including *The Encyclopedia of Ghosts and Spirits* and *The Encyclopedia of Witches and Witchcraft*.

The book is in eight sections including "Haunted Places," "Phantom and Mystery Ships," and "Curious Creatures." "Power Points" includes Native American holy places and New Age sites. Wyoming's Devil's Tower is noted both for its Native American significance and for being in *Close Encounters of the Third Kind*. "Earthworks" covers earth constructions and burial mounds built by Native American cultures. "Stoneworks" lists stone circles, petroglyphs, and pictographs. "Ghost Lights" lists "major sites of recurring activity," including the Marfa Lights of Texas. "Water Monsters" includes sites where strange things washed ashore or from which creatures like Champ, Lake Champlain's answer to the Loch Ness Monster, can be seen.

Sections are broken down by state and Canadian province and then alphabetically by site. For states or regions with heavy concentrations of sites, there is a detailed map. Each chapter has a brief description of the sites listed. Notes on sites vary from a line or two to several paragraphs. The index is detailed, and there is a bibliography arranged under the headings used for sections. Unfortunately, there are no footnotes in the body of the book, so there is no way to determine if a statement is from a mainstream or scholarly work or one of the many paranormal works listed. The black-and-white line drawings and maps are clear, and the quality of the photography is good, if occasionally a little dark. There is no indication of the accessibility of sites. The citation for ghost lights in Oviedo, Florida, for instance, mentions State Road 13, but not where lights have been seen on it.

This is not a necessary purchase, but where there is an interest in the paranormal, it is a good value.

Companion to Literary Myths, Heroes and Archetypes. Ed. by Pierre Brunel. Routledge, 1993. 1,223p. index. $125 (0-415-06460-0).
398.2'03 Mythology—Dictionaries || Mythology in literature [OCLC] 92-28204

First published in France in 1988 as *Dictionnaire des Mythes Littéraires*, this work is a compilation of scholarly essays written by members of a research group at the University of Paris. The majority of the 124 articles focus on an eclectic assortment of biblical, historical, and mythical figures (e.g., Apollo, Daphne, Joan of Arc, Job, Louis XIV, Moses, Prometheus) and mythical themes (e.g., doubles and counterparts, heroism, the wandering Jew, virile women). In addition, eight essays treat myths pertaining to a particular nationality or group, such as African, Hindu, Japanese, and Scandinavian. Several articles, including "Historical and Mythical Figures" and "Literary and Mythological Narratives," provide a general overview and analysis that is valuable for understanding the more specific entries. Regardless of their focus, all articles appear in a single alphabetical sequence.

Individual essays vary considerably in length: the shortest is three pages, while the longest is 35. The organization and scope of the articles are also highly individual, but, in general, each explores the historical background of the original myth and then traces its treatment in works of literature through the ensuing centuries. Greater emphasis is placed on European writings based on myths rather than on British or American works. Although bibliographies are not provided at the end of each essay, a substantial list of sources for further reading appears at the end of the text. An index covers themes, mythical figures, and topics but, unfortunately, does not include references to authors and titles of literary works that have drawn upon mythical themes.

Approximately one-fifth of the topics treated in this work are also explored in Horst and Ingrid Daemmrich's *Themes & Motifs in Western Literature* (Francke, 1987). Surprisingly, there is relatively little overlap with Jean-Charles Seigneuret's two-volume *Dictionary of Literary Themes and Motifs* (Greenwood, 1988). *Encyclopedia of Traditional Epics* [RBB N 1 94] has some overlap (e.g., *The Cid*, *The Flood*, *The Grail*), but its 1,500 entries are much briefer. Although less approachable for undergraduates than any of the aforementioned works, this scholarly tome is an appropriate and useful addition to academic and research libraries.

Encyclopedia of Traditional Epics. By Guida M. Jackson. ABC-Clio, 1994. 640p. bibliog. illus. index. $65 (0-87436-724-7).
398.22 Epic literature—History and criticism || Epic literature—Encyclopedias [OCLC] 94-9303

This is the most comprehensive reference work published on epics from cultures worldwide. Jackson is a lecturer in the English Foundations Department at the University of Houston. She defines *epic* as "a long narrative poem of grand scope, style, and theme that recounts the fantastic exploits of a legendary or historical figure or figures endowed with superhuman might and . . . epitomizes the character or ideals of a certain race, tribe, or nationality." The scope of *Traditional Epics* includes both oral or folk epics and epics in literary form evolved from oral tradition.

Traditional Epics consists of approximately 1,500 entries on specific epics and epic cycles (*Fenian Cycle*, *Beowulf*), names of individuals (*Hiawatha*, *Sinbad the Sailor*), places (*Asgard*, *Valhalla*), and objects (*Trojan Horse*, *Grail*). The length of entries ranges from a few lines identifying a character (e.g., *Minerva*—"*the Roman Goddess of handicrafts*") to several pages devoted to major epics and concepts. Longer articles on the most important epics typically include the origin of the legend, when and where it was collected (including definitive collections), principal figures, analysis of the poetic pattern, relationship to historical characters and events, means of transmission, and a summary of the epic's content, often listed by chapter. Articles include parenthetical references to sources listed in a bibliography at the end of the encyclopedia.

An examination of the geographic origins of the epics reveals the multicultural approach for which the work is valuable. Readers would expect to find entries for the best-known epics from the ancient world (*Aeneid*, *Gilgamesh*) and medieval Europe (*Arthurian Legend*); they will not be disappointed. They will also find entries for less familiar, but no less fascinating, epics from the Philippines (*Hudhud*), Hawaii (*Pele*), Vietnam (*Lac Long Quang and Au Co*), and American Indian groups such as the Brule Sioux (*Uncegila's Seventh Spot*). Appendixes list epics chronologically and geographically. Seventy black-and-white illustrations include photographs of art objects, pages from illustrated manuscripts, and contemporary depictions of epics.

One of the most useful features of the *Encyclopedia of Traditional Epics* is its discussion of motifs that appear in epics worldwide, such as *Flood*, *Hubris*, and *Abduction*. These articles discuss the concept before proceeding to examples from different cultures. For example, *Abandonment* discusses Sargon I, Moses, Siegfried of the Norse legends, a Seneca myth, and the hero twins of the Maya Popol Vuh. Despite Jackson's attention to detail, the entries are written lucidly enough to be understood and enjoyed by the nonspecialist.

The *Encyclopedia of Traditional Epics* is an essential purchase for academic and large public libraries. Libraries of secondary schools that address epics in their language or social studies curricula may also want to consider purchase.

Index to Fairy Tales, 1987–1992: Including 310 Collections of Fairy Tales, Folktales, Myths, and Legends with Significant Pre-1987 Titles Not Previously Indexed. Comp. by Joseph W. Sprug. Scarecrow, 1994. 602p. $59.50 (0-8108-2750-6).

016.3982 Fairy tales—Indexes || Mythology—Indexes || Folklore—Indexes || Folk literature—Indexes [CIP]
93-29709

In this seventh supplement to a popular series begun by Mary Eastman in 1915 and continued by Norma Olin Ireland, author and subject, as well as title, entries note the book where a tale may be found. (In earlier volumes, this information was noted only under title entries.) Though the purpose of the book remains the same—providing access to collections of fairy tales with coverage "comprehensive for the children's area"—about 50 percent of the 310 titles indexed are aimed at the librarian, researcher, teacher, or student of folklore. Sprug, a librarian, compiled *Ireland's Index to Inspiration* (1990) and the previous volume (1989) of the work reviewed here.

The detailed introduction notes the distribution of books indexed by date (only 46 percent were published between the years cited in the title) and includes an explanation of indexing level, reading level, and other information noted in entries.

There are some reservations about this work. For example, entries for at least 43 professional reference tools, such as Betsy Hearne's *Choosing Books for Children: A Commonsense Guide* (1990), are interspersed with entries for tales. The previous volumes in this series indexed strictly collections of folk and fairy tales rather than critical material for researchers. It is confusing to find reference works intermingled with collections of tales. This often means that the user has to consult more than one source to locate the story desired. Why not create two categories in this work: (1) collections of fairy tales, and (2) reference and critical tools? This book, moreover, includes poetry, such as *Halloween ABC* (1990) by Eve Merriam, and folklore, such as Simon Bronner's *Piled Higher and Deeper: The Folklore of Campus Life* (1990). It is strange that Jane Yolen's masterful *Favorite Folktales from around the World* (1986), with its excellent bibliographies, is missing from the list of indexed sources. The increasing number of modern retellings and spoofs on older tales such as were done so well by James Marshall are also not indexed. Turning to the index itself, there is ambiguity about the headings used for Native Americans, with this term used as well as *American Indians* and *Indians*, followed by geographic location or tribe. On the plus side, there seems to be a balance of tales from different ethnic groups.

Since this seems to be a tool for the professional, with a heavy emphasis on research, libraries should purchase based on their use of earlier volumes in the series

Language

The American Sign Language Dictionary on CD-ROM. By Martin L. A. Sternberg. HarperCollins Interactive, 1994. Windows version, $69.95 (0-06-279015-3), with paperback dictionary, $79.95 (0-06-279017-X); Macintosh version, $69.95 (0-06-279014-5, with paperback dictionary, $79.95 (0-06-279016-1).

419 Sign language—Dictionaries [BKL]

American Sign Language is the third most commonly used language in the U.S., with its own distinct grammar. Based on the American Sign Language dictionary series by Sternberg, also published by HarperCollins, this CD-ROM provides signs for 2,200 words and phrases using text, audio, and video. Sternberg, deaf since age seven, has spent most of his career working with deaf people.

Hardware requirements for the Windows version are a 386-based computer (486 recommended), Windows 3.1 or higher, 4MB RAM (8MB recommended), 256-color monitor, a mouse, and a sound card. For the Macintosh, a 25-MHz 68030 processor running System 7, 4MB RAM (8MB recommended), and 256-color monitor are required. A double-speed CD-ROM drive is recommended for both versions.

The product is easy to install. The instruction manual is brief; the excellent online tutorial is a better way to learn to use the system. The initial screen gives a choice of five areas to search: Dictionary, Skills, Fingerspelling, ASL Overview, and Guided Tour (the tutorial).

Words in the dictionary can be accessed by typing in a few letters, by browsing A–Z, or by browsing categories. The latter consists of such topics as animals, family life, and thoughts and feelings or parts of speech. After selecting a word, the text on the screen provides pronunciation in standard dictionary format, the part of speech, a description of how the sign is made, a line drawing of the sign, and a hint to help remember the sign. Also, a voice says the word and describes how to make the sign. This sound option can be turned off. On the right-hand side of the screen is a video box where a person makes the sign. It is possible to slow down or speed up the video and increase the size of the box. The signers don't always say the word in such a way that it is possible to lipread. Since some signs are used for more than one word, a cross-reference box lists other words using that sign. It is also possible in this section to type in a common word in French, German, Italian, or Spanish and get the entry for the English equivalent.

The skills section provides ways to test skills by reviewing or playing a game. The fingerspelling section teaches the manual alphabet to be used for words, such as proper names, that must be spelled out, and also has a game to test fingerspelling skills. The ASL Overview section gives a history of the language and some hints for learning it. It also has an extensive bibliography and lists of services and devices for the hearing impaired with addresses. A help icon in the lower right-hand corner of every screen leads to a table of contents listing various explanatory messages.

This disc has a relatively small vocabulary, with only half as many words as Sternberg's *American Sign Language Dictionary* (rev. ed., 1994). Such common words as *table*, *river*, and *forest* were not found. However, this CD-ROM is much more complete than the floppy-disk product, *Interactive Sign Language Fingerspelling & Numbers* [BKL D 1 94]. There is limited information on the CD-ROM about grammar (in the Guided Tour we are told that adjectives usually follow nouns), so students of ASL will have to consult other tools to learn to construct sentences. In the entries for the words *big* and *large*, the sign as shown in the video is slightly different from the written and audio description of the sign.

The convergence of various media here on one disc results in a product that is more valuable than the sum of its parts. Since signing is not static, it is a natural for this medium. Being able to see facial expressions and motion of the hands and body is far superior to viewing the simple drawings provided in print ASL dictionaries. The interface is simple enough to be used by upper-elementary-school children. This innovative CD-ROM is highly recommended for academic libraries and schools where ASL is taught and for public libraries. —*Sandy Whiteley*

The Cambridge Encyclopedia of the English Language. By David Crystal. Cambridge, 1995. 489p. charts. illus. indexes. $49.95 (0-521-40179-8).

420 English language—Handbooks, manuals, etc. [CIP] 94-23918

This attractive resource is organized thematically in segments covering the history of the English language (Old English, Middle English, Modern English, English in different parts of the world); English vocabulary (its nature, structure, sources, etymology, and the dimensions of the lexicon); English grammar (structure of words and sentences, definitions of the main branches of grammar); spoken and written English; English usage (varieties of discourse and regional, social, and personal usage variations); and how people learn English and new ways to study English. Appendixes include a glossary, a list of symbols and abbreviations, references and addresses, further readings, and indexes of names, items, and topics. Crystal, a linguist, is the compiler of many reference books published by Cambridge, for example, *The Cambridge Encyclopedia of Language* (1987).

Throughout the book (which focuses on British English, not American English), readers will find liberal use of color in the many charts, illustrations, reprints of pages from historically significant works, maps, and photographs. The author does not shrink from exploring and delivering opinions on controversial topics such as the "opaque inspecific, or empty" language of politics and the dangers of "political correctness."

Each segment can be read as if it were the only section of the book, or, the work can be read cover to cover so that a cumulative effect is achieved. The only comparable resource that provides the same type of broad-ranging coverage in one volume is *The Oxford Companion to the English Language* [RBB O 15 92]. That work is arranged alphabetically within 22 themes (e.g., geography, history, media) and provides "an interim report on the nature and use of the English language" in all nations that speak English. The two works complement each other;

Cambridge provides historical perspective and *Oxford* a snapshot of current English. *The Cambridge Encyclopedia of the English Language* lives up to the reputation of other resources published under the Cambridge imprint and will make an excellent addition to the collections of large public libraries and all academic libraries.

The American Heritage Talking Dictionary. CD-ROM. SoftKey, 201 Broadway, Cambridge, MA 02139, 1994. $59.95 (1-56434-380-4); disc bundled with the print *American Heritage Dictionary of the English Language*, 3d ed., Houghton, $75 (0-395-71146-0).
423 English language—Dictionaries [BKL]

The *American Heritage Dictionary* has been converted to numerous electronic formats, most recently as a competently executed component of *Microsoft Bookshelf* '94 [RBB O 1 94]. This new CD-ROM version of the third edition comes as a stand-alone package with both IBM PC–compatible and Macintosh retrieval software included. The PC version requires at least a 386/25-based PC with 4MB RAM, at least 2MB of hard-drive space, an 8-bit sound card, and Windows version 3.1. The Macintosh version requires 1MB RAM with System 6.X or 2MB RAM with System 7, and at least 500K hard-drive space. The Board tested the PC version of the software.

The *American Heritage Talking Dictionary* (AHTD) comes with only a four-page insert in the CD-ROM jewel case, which covers installation; all other documentation is on the disc, though a 15-page manual may be printed from the Windows Write program. Technical support is available from SoftKey via a toll-free number from 9:00 a.m. to 8:00 p.m. weekdays. The publisher also has a 24-hour automated service (including fax on demand) and a 24-hour BBS, along with a forum on CompuServe. Fortunately, installation is straightforward and one can choose from a variety of options. "Partial" installation uses only about 2MB of hard-drive space, since only program files and word processor macros are installed on the hard drive; the dictionary and thesaurus files remain on the CD-ROM. "Full" installation requires 15MB of hard-drive space since all files except the pronunciation files reside on the hard drive. This quickens response time but still requires the presence of the CD-ROM and will not run without it.

The AHTD retrieval software offers straightforward dictionary lookup, a WordHunter feature that will find words within definitions, an Anagram feature, as well a thesaurus based on *Roget's II: The New Thesaurus*. All methods of retrieval may be invoked by clicking clearly labeled buttons. The screen may be split in two so the dictionary information appears on top and the thesaurus information (when available) on the bottom. After viewing an entry, the user may click the Browse icon to retrieve a list of other dictionary entries surrounding the selected term in an alphabetical list, or simply click a forward arrow key to move to the next alphabetic entry. Spoken pronunciation of the word may be selected by the user to be automatically invoked every time an entry appears or suppressed until the Pronunciation icon is clicked. The audio pronunciation of approximately 75,000 words is provided by a variety of male and female voices. Double-clicking a word within an entry will retrieve the entry for that word. Like many Windows programs, AHTD may be accessed from within a Windows word processing program. In this case, the user may highlight a word in a document and have the dictionary look up the highlighted word. In WordPerfect for Windows 6.0a, for example, the user chooses Tools, then Macro, then clicks the appropriate macro number. Instructions for installing AHTD as a macro for various Windows word processors comes in Write files with the program. Entries from the dictionary may be copied and pasted into other Windows programs, which is also—unfortunately—the only way entries may be printed.

The dictionary offers as full an entry as the printed work [RBB O 1 92], including "Usage Panel" notes and synonym studies. Unlike the *Bookshelf* version, AHTD includes information on Indo-European roots, both as separate entries as well as appended to entries for other words. The entry *cainotophobia*, for example, includes the Indo-European root *ken-*, which in the printed work is in an appendix. This makes AHTD particularly valuable for users wishing to learn more about word origins. (This is also a part of the program where an apparent bug was discovered. If, after viewing an entry with an Indo-European root, the user wishes to use the Browse feature to look at other nearby entries, the Indo-European appendix on the original entry will *not* appear if that entry is looked at again.)

The WordHunter feature includes some powerful retrieval capabilities, though with some inconsistencies. In addition to Boolean searching (AND, OR, NOT), the user also may restrict a search by a specific usage label (a scrolling list including such terms as *Astronomy*, *Regional*, and *Vulgar*), search by an exact phrase, and search for partial words—the latter effectively serving as right- and left-handed truncation. Thus, a user may search on the word *phobi* after clicking the box for searching partial words and retrieve 52 hits. (This search, incidentally, took close to five minutes to execute on a double-speed CD-ROM drive, which is much quicker than doing a similar search in *Bookshelf*. *Bookshelf*, however, is generally quicker on keyword searches since the retrieval software automatically truncates entries at the end. A Find search on the word *endanger* in *Bookshelf* retrieves 17 entries almost immediately; a partial-word search on *endanger* in AHTD takes more than 7 minutes to retrieve the same 17 entries.) Most parts of an entry are searched for in a WordHunter search, including synonyms and words within usage notes and etymologies. However, when using the WordHunter search, any diacritical marks must be included when typing in a query. *Bookshelf* is not so exacting in its Find search, which ignores diacritical marks. Run-on entries are also retrieved inconsistently. A search on *gaiting* and *rabbiting*, for example, will retrieve the entries *gait* and *rabbit*, but a search on *nabber* and *pathetically* does not retrieve *nab* or *pathetic*. The main drawback to WordHunter, however, is that the selected word is not highlighted within the entry, making it difficult to spot in longer entries.

Oddly, truncation is not allowed in the WordHunter search, but is allowed in the Dictionary search, with a * serving for unlimited truncation and a ? serving for one letter. Entering *phobi* in the Dictionary search retrieves 135 hits in well under a minute. The extraordinarily large number of entries is accounted for by the fact that the Dictionary search also retrieves variant forms of the word such as plurals and possessive forms. Thus, there are listings for *sitophobia*, *sitophobia's*, *sitophobias*, and *sitophobias'*—all leading to the same main entry.

Despite the inconsistencies in retrieval—a characteristic that also appears in *Bookshelf*—AHTD is generally a reliable work. The inclusion of Indo-European roots, the partial word search, and the ability to limit specifically by label makes for some nice retrieval capabilities. On the other hand, the lack of illustrations may be considered a drawback to some. *Bookshelf*, of course, offers six reference works in addition to *The American Heritage Dictionary*, along with illustrations for some entries, though at a considerably higher cost. *The Random House Unabridged Dictionary* on CD-ROM [RBB F 1 94] contains more words but does not provide audio pronunciation. Libraries and home users wanting a low-cost, fairly comprehensive dictionary with powerful retrieval capabilities will not be disappointed by AHTD.

The Chambers Dictionary. Ed. by Catherine Schwarz. Chambers, 1994. 2,062p. $35 (0-550-10255-8).
423 English language—Dictionaries [BKL]

Completely revised and updated, and designed to be used more for finding the meaning, rather than the spelling, of a word, *The Chambers Dictionary* is the official dictionary for U.K. Scrabble tournaments and succeeds *The Chambers Twentieth Century Dictionary of the English language* (1952) and *The Chambers English Dictionary* (1988). It was published in the U.K. in 1993.

Changes from the 1988 edition include the front matter, which no longer provides a justification for Americans using a British dictionary, but rather a commentary on the importance of grammar and standard English. Other changes include a revised list of abbreviations, which reflects modern usage (e.g., labels for American Indian and West African have been added, the label for ablative has been deleted), and addition of a list of rules for English spelling. Main entries include derivatives, compounds, and phrases within a headword's etymological family (a signature characteristic of the Chambers dictionaries), cross-references (215,000), pronunciation keys, alternative forms of headwords, inflections, and part-of-speech and classification labels. Definitions (300,000) are generally ordered from the most common to least common, and abbreviations are alphabetized within the main A–Z text; there are no biographical entries. Appendixes include a list (with meanings) of first names; five pages of phrases and quotations from Latin, Greek, and modern foreign languages; the Greek and Russian alphabet; Roman numerals; books of the Bible; plays of Shakespeare; the chemical elements; temperature and measurement conversions; and international paper sizes.

The 25,000 new entries reflect modern usage (AIDS is now defined under its acronym rather than within the definitions for *acquire*), science and technology (added words include *virtual reality*, CD-ROM), current societal concerns (*ecotourism, sexual harassment*), and even American slang (*rad, yo*). In the Chambers tradition, definitions are clear, print is small but readable, boldface is effectively used to help find words, and an international focus is evident.

This is a superior dictionary that belongs on the shelves of academic and public libraries, alongside the various American Webster's.

The Dorling Kindersley Children's Illustrated Dictionary. By John McIlwain. Dorling Kindersley, 1994. 255p. illus. $19.95 (1-56458-625-1).
423 English language—Dictionaries, Juvenile [CIP] 94-9561

The Kingfisher Illustrated Children's Dictionary. Ed. by John Grisewood. Kingfisher, 1994. 480p. illus. $19.95 (1-85697-841-9).
423 English language—Dictionaries, Juvenile [CIP] 93-45414

These two attractive dictionaries have similar titles but different audiences. The DK dictionary is aimed at children five and up who are gaining independence in reading. Kingfisher, on the other hand, is for upper- elementary-school children.

The author of the DK dictionary is a teacher turned education writer. The 5,000 entries combine "a core of common vocabulary with words that have a high interest level for children of this age group." A double-page spread introduces parts of speech ("Prepositions . . . show how one person or thing relates to another"). The next spread explains dictionary usage, followed by dictionary games.

Each page has four columns of definitions, typically five words to a column. The headword appears in large, bold print, followed by plurals or tenses, the part of speech, and the definition(s). Definitions are brief but effective (e.g., "*gulp*: to swallow something quickly or in large amounts"). Some entries have example sentences. Pronunciations are given occasionally with simple respelling (e.g., "say zoe-dee-ak"). Appendix materials include abbreviations, a spelling guide, prefixes and suffixes, a miscellany of facts and figures, and a list of countries with capital, the name for residents, and currency. Twenty-six full-page spreads scattered throughout the book picture a variety of members of a category (e.g., musical instruments, fruits). This book has the colorful, clean Dorling Kindersley look. The majority of entries are illustrated, usually by photographs, always in color. The choice of words goes well beyond those likely to be of interest to five-year olds (e.g., *parallel*, *individual*, *ambition*), but the look of this dictionary may put off users old enough to be interested in many of the words.

This is an attractive but low-priority item for libraries. It is probably most useful for browsing in a classroom or home. A good purchase for curriculum materials centers in school districts and academic libraries.

Described as a dictionary with encyclopedic aspects for children nine and up, *The Kingfisher Illustrated Children's Dictionary* contains more than 12,000 dictionary entries and 1,000 encyclopedic entries. Prefatory material consists of pages on dictionary usage and on the evolution of the English language. Entries include pronunciation (using standard symbols such as the schwa), part of speech (abbreviated), and one or more definitions. Words are divided into syllables. Also given, although not for every entry, are cross-references, example sentences, and other forms of the entry word. The supplement lists information on countries, states, and presidents; U.S. and world chronologies; and rulers of Great Britain and Canadian prime ministers. The basic page layout consists of two columns of definitions, plus a wide outside margin. The latter is used for pronunciation symbols, introductions to a new letter, illustrations, etymology, and other information. There is roughly one illustration (mostly drawings) per column. Encyclopedic entries are boxed. There is no indication of method of word choice. Entries include places (e.g., *Westminster Abbey*, *Osaka*) events (*Boston Tea Party*), and people (*Sophocles*, *Ramses*). Indeed, the proper names—and the encyclopedic entries—imply a slightly older audience than one would expect from the words selected.

The Kingfisher Illustrated Children's Dictionary has a reasonable choice of words, definitions that are clear and simple, and an attractive appearance. Browsers will enjoy it. Although some definitions are labeled as British, there is no obvious British slant. With the proliferation of children's dictionaries, it is increasingly difficult to recommend purchase priority. This is a must purchase only for curriculum-materials centers and a solid purchase for elementary and public libraries.

The Harcourt Brace Student Thesaurus. Ed. by Christopher Morris. Harcourt, 1994. 320p. illus. index. $14.95 (0-15-200186-7).
423 English language—Synonyms and antonyms—Juvenile literature [CIP] 94-15603

The Kingfisher Illustrated Thesaurus. By George Beal. Kingfisher, 1994. 144p. illus. $14.95 (1-85697-520-7).
423'.1 English language—Synonyms and antonyms—Juvenile literature [CIP] 93-50709

These two children's thesauruses illustrate the old adage that you can't tell a book by its cover.

Although it looks a bit forbidding in size and design, once *The Harcourt Brace Student Thesaurus* is opened, the student of almost any reading level should feel at ease. It consists of 800 main entries, plus an index of synonyms and antonyms. There are 3,500 synonyms, 500 antonyms, and 150 color illustrations. The illustrations are bright, done in various styles, and include multicultural characters. Approximately three entries appear on a page, each followed by four or five synonyms. Antonyms are not always given but are clearly labeled when they are included. Each synonym is then used in a sentence, which seems a bit unnecessary.

One entry is a bit disturbing: "*Woman*: lady, female. NOUN: an adult person who is not a male." The entry for *man*, however, is "*Man*: male, fellow, guy. NOUN: a male person who is no longer a boy." In summary, this thesaurus is extremely elementary, in contrast to the scholarly looking cover.

Initially, *The Kingfisher Illustrated Thesaurus* is appealing, with a bright-red illustrated cover that will appeal to young readers. However, the actual thesaurus is not as simple or entertaining. The number of entries on each page (approximately 40) and the size of type will be intimidating for beginning readers. Fewer than half the pages have illustrations of an unattractive mixture of light blue, black, and white. They do not always appear where they should in the alphabetical sequence. For example, in a blue box is a partial list of dog breeds from Afghan hound to whippet. The entries on the page go from *devour* to *discord*; *dog* would belong on the next page. Also, chances are, if the reader wanted some other words for *dog*, he or she would most likely want something like *mutt* or *canine*, not a list of breeds.

There are more than 4,000 entries in this volume, with three to eight synonyms for each. Antonyms are bolded and starred immediately after the list of homonyms; this will confuse the reader who didn't read the introduction to the book. Only some of the entries have example sentences. There are scattered blocks of trivia, such as "Borrowed Words," which lists words currently in use in the English language and the countries where they originated. This is a nice touch, but this information would not be found unless the reader had time to browse, since it is not in any particular order. There are some sophisticated entries such as *morose* and *purloin*. There is also a decidedly British flavor illustrated by the following amusing sentence for the word *futile*: "I shall go in for the race, but it's a forlorn hope I shall win."

All in all, this book is a good effort, but the degree of difficulty hinted at by the cover and what is found in the actual contents are quite different.

NTC's Dictionary of Acronyms and Abbreviations. Comp. by Steven R. Kleinedler. NTC, 1995. 311p. paper $12.95 (0-8442-5376-6).
423 Acronyms—Dictionaries || Abbreviations, English—Dictionaries [OCLC] 93-188151

This handy guide to approximately 2,100 acronyms, initialisms, blends, clippings, and abbreviations was originally published in 1993. The differences among these terms are defined in a brief introduction. This work provides a selection of "shortened forms" one is most likely to encounter in newspapers, directions, instructions, and on packaging, as well as acronyms for major governmental organizations.

Entries include the shortened form in boldface type; the word or words for which the entry stands; usually, one of the words *initialism*, *acronym*, *blend*, or *clipping* (to indicate whether the entry is pronounced by sounding out its letters one by one, for an initialism, or as a whole word, for the others); a definition or explanation of the entry; and a usage example. Some entries include cross-references and/or derivations.

This work is quite manageable and helpful. It will not identify thousands of terms like Gale's *Acronyms, Initialisms, and Abbreviations Dictionary*, nor is it meant to. What it does well is to clarify meanings of common shortened forms through examples and alternate forms

Language

(e.g., FT can mean free throw or full-time). It will prove a useful and practical addition to most libraries.

Random House Unabridged Electronic Dictionary on CD-ROM. Version 1.7. Random, 1994. hardcover & CD-ROM $100 (0-679-75748-1); CD-ROM only $79 (0-679-44045-3).

423 English language—Dictionaries || CD-ROM books [BKL]

It took awhile, but Random House has finally produced an electronic version of its unabridged dictionary of which it can be justifiably proud. When first reviewed by the Board [RBB F 1 94], it was criticized as having several indexing errors, a buggy Anagram search, and slow retrieval time.

Version 1.7 fixes most of these problems and adds a new feature, audio pronunciations, though it has higher hardware requirements than its predecessors. Minimum requirements are at least an 80386 IBM or compatible PC, 2MB of RAM, a hard drive with at least 1.5MB free, MS-DOS version 3.1 or later, Windows version 3.1, and a Windows-compatible sound card with speakers to access the pronunciations. Whereas previous versions included DOS, Windows, and Macintosh software on one CD, the current version runs only through Windows. The program may be invoked by clicking the proper program group or via a "hot key" combination within another Windows-based word processing program. With *WordPerfect for Windows 6.0*, the dictionary is automatically installed as an option in the Tools pull-down menu. Like previous versions, there is no direct printing capability—an entry must be pasted into a word processor. Unlike previous versions, an eight-page manual is included in the jewel case rather than merely in a READ.ME file.

Although the basic ways of retrieving entries remain the same in this new version, the retrieval time, particularly for Boolean searches, is much quicker. Furthermore, DefSearch now allows the use of wildcards, which is a noteworthy enhancement. In addition to the standard Boolean operators that were allowed before, Def-Search also has a More Options button, which allows one to limit a search to within a single definition of an entry or limit a search within a certain range of words. There are also boxes to check to specify case sensitivity, limit a search only to definitions with illustrations, and to turn Exact Match on or off; turning it off will include inflected forms of a word in a search. Finally, all words searched with DefSearch are highlighted in the entry, making the selected words easier to spot.

Other major enhancements include more than 115,000 spoken pronunciations and more than 2,200 line drawings. This makes *Random House* far and away the superior CD-ROM dictionary in number of pronunciations—surpassing the 80,000 in *The American Heritage Dictionary* in *Microsoft Bookshelf '94* [RBB O 1 94]. Words with pronunciation available are shown with a speaker icon. A particularly nice touch is that often first names as well as the last names of individuals are pronounced. Thus, such names as *Horthy, Miklos von Nagybanya* are pronounced in their entirety—unlike *Bookshelf '94*, which has pronunciations for only the last names. The illustrations included precisely match the line drawings that appear in the print version of the work and are noted by a camera icon.

Problems noted in the previous review have been corrected, including the Anagram search and inconsistency in retrieving words that appear as synonyms within entries. In fact, a few surprises in retrieval capability were discovered. Although a Help screen specifies that one cannot search the etymologies with DefSearch, actual sample searches suggest otherwise. An undocumented feature is that phrases may be searched by including the phrase within quotation marks. With this capability, users may search idioms by exact wording.

Indeed, this dictionary is everything it should have been the first time it was released. The retrieval capabilities are more than adequate for most users, and the number of spoken pronunciations is unexcelled. However, we strongly urge Random House to consider replacing the heavily promoted previous versions with the newest version—or at least provide version 1.7 to libraries for a moderate upgrade fee. With this version, users should not be disappointed. Highly recommended.

The Language of Small Business: A Complete Dictionary of Small Business Terms. By Carl O. Trautmann. Upstart, 1994. 396p. bibliog. index. paper $19.95 (0-936894-59-8).

423'.02465 English language—Business English—Dictionaries || English language—Terms and phrases || Small business—Dictionaries [CIP] 94-808

Designed by the author, a member of the Service Corps of Retired Executives, as a glossary and self-help resource for small businesspeople, start-up entrepreneurs, and students of business theory, this book defines 2,500 commonly used business terms and practices. The second half of the book contains 13 self-help guides, including writing a business plan; filling out a personal financial statement; getting a business loan; preparing balance sheets and income statements; agencies, organizations, and people who provide help for small businesses; and start-up checklists to determine whether a potential entrepreneur has the temperament and wherewithal to start a business.

The small business focus is evident in the definitions, which are written in less specialized language than general business dictionaries. They include small business applications as examples (e.g., *net* is defined in terms of sales discounts, as well as in terms of net income; both *inventory* and *take inventory* are defined). Missing from this dictionary are many specialized terms from the fields of investing, economics, and business law, but it includes terms from the small business environment that more specialized dictionaries often leave out (e.g., *Publication #583, unaudited*). The self-help guides are helpful, but users will have to follow up with more detailed information such as the financial report information in the *Irwin Business and Investment Almanac* or the start-up information in Fallek's *How to Set Up Your Own Small Business* (1993).

Overall, this will be a useful first stop for people considering establishment of a business and for new business owners. It is recommended to public libraries and academic libraries that serve local business communities.

Dorling Kindersley Ultimate Visual Dictionary. Ed. by Jo Evans. Dorling Kindersley, 1994. 637p. illus. index. $39.95 (1-56458-648-0).

423'.1 Picture dictionaries [CIP] 94-11173

The Macmillan Visual Dictionary: Multilingual Edition. Ed. by Jean-Claude Corbeil and Ariane Archambault. Macmillan, 1994. 959p. illus. indexes. $60 (0-02-578115-4).

413'.1 Picture dictionaries || Dictionaries, Polyglot [CIP] 94-15016

Here are are two dazzlingly illustrated visual dictionaries for young people and adults alike. Each is an outgrowth of a previous title. *The Macmillan Visual Dictionary: Multilingual Edition* is exactly the same as the English-language edition [RBB D 1 92], with the addition of French, Spanish, and German labels as well as indexes for these languages. It costs $60 compared with $45 for the English-language edition. A press release from the publisher describes the dictionary as "timely," so it is strange to see in its bibliography encyclopedias with copyright dates from the 1980s. The only addition to the bibliography in the multilingual edition seems to be four French and English dictionaries; no corresponding German or Spanish resources are cited.

The Dorling Kindersley Ultimate Visual Dictionary is not unlike the publisher's earlier single-concept books such as *The Visual Dictionary of Dinosaurs* [RBB D 1 93]. It integrates some of the single-concept books into a multiconcept volume. While it contains the same exciting graphics and cutaways as the single-concept books, one wonders if this single volume is needed when the smaller single-concept books, which often circulate in libraries, are available.

In comparing the two visual dictionaries, moreover, there are some omissions in both. Dorling Kindersley has omitted such measuring instruments as telescopes, microscopes, and the universal symbols found in navigation and science. Also, subways and overall views of airports or space stations are conspicuously absent. On the other hand, Macmillan has some curious omissions, such as all too brief mention of the Solar System, prehistoric periods, minerals, photosynthesis, and the like. Additionally, the Macmillan dictionary sidesteps the development of a baby found in DK, a feature that forever fascinates young people. The "Vegetable Kingdom" in Macmillan begins with mushrooms, omitting mosses and other familiar plants.

These books complement each other, and each has different features. It is enjoyable to see telescopes in detail in the Macmillan dictionary, and prehistoric life and technology in the Dorling Kindersley volume. Depending on whether the earlier volumes on which they are based are already owned, both can be recommended for school and public libraries and for academic libraries that need images for students of advertising and graphic design. The addition of foreign languages to the Macmillan dictionary may motivate young people in their vocabulary building or help students speaking these languages find equivalents in English.

My Big Dictionary. Houghton, 1994. 40p. illus. paper, $18.95 (0-395-66377-6).
423.1 Picture dictionaries, English—Juvenile literature [OCLC] 93-33756

The American Heritage Picture Dictionary. Houghton, 1994. 138p. illus. $10.95 (0-395-69585-6).
423.1 Picture dictionaries, English [OCLC] 94-75431

The American Heritage First Dictionary. Houghton, 1994. 362p. illus. $13.95 (0-395-67289-9).
423 English language—Dictionaries, Juvenile [CIP] 93-24530

The American Heritage Children's Dictionary. Houghton, 1994. 842p. illus. $15.95 (0-395-69191-5).
423 English language—Dictionaries, Juvenile [CIP] 93-24531

The American Heritage Student Dictionary. Houghton, 1994. 1,094p. illus. $16.95 (0-395-55857-3).
423 English language—Dictionaries, Juvenile [CIP] 93-32433

These dictionaries for young people are reviewed—and listed above—in the order of their intended audience's age, with the youngest first. Two of the *American Heritage* titles are essentially reprintings of earlier editions reviewed here [RBB Je 15 91]. Two are complete revisions of 1986 editions; *My Big Dictionary* is a new title.

My Big Dictionary is a giant (16 by 19 inches) wordbook most suited for use with groups. The publisher intends it as an introduction to letters, words, and alphabetical order for preschoolers. Lined pages generally contain six words, each accompanied by a simple colorful drawing. Some pages feature a lively scene full of objects beginning with a given letter; the pictures are unlabeled. The inside front cover suggests activities in which adults can engage children; the back cover indexes the contents, including those terms only pictured.

The American Heritage Picture Dictionary is a reprint of the 1986 and 1989 editions. It is intended for preschool and lower-grade children; the 600 entries were chosen from various counts of words frequently used by this age group. The aim is to serve as a kind of dictionary primer. Pages have five or six entries. Sometimes there is only the entry word, as in *sky*, illustrated by trees against a blue sky. Other entries have an example sentence. The dictionary concludes with nine spreads on such themes as the body, the supermarket, and dinosaurs. The colorful illustrations are pleasant, and the words chosen seem appropriate for younger children. AHPD suffers from the problem of all picture dictionaries: the difficulty in providing meaning. Examples: "Maria gets a FREE kitten" (which could mean "cute," "white," or "lonely"). "Here is Ben's LEFT hand" (The raised hand is on the viewer's right). The most successful entries are concrete words that can be defined visually.

The American Heritage First Dictionary is totally revised from the 1986 edition. All the text and illustrations are new. It comes closer to being a true dictionary. The suggested audience is grades 1 and 2 (ages 6–8). An introduction, aimed at the child, explains dictionary uses, alphabetizing, variants, and homonyms. The entry word is typically followed by a one-sentence definition and an example sentence. Variant forms of a word may be noted in a single definition. Guide words are provided, and superscripts are used for homonyms. Each page has one or more color illustrations, mainly photographs but some drawings. Word choice appears appropriate, text is simple but effective, and the layout is appealing.

The publisher's blurb describes the above sources as "training shoes" for *The American Heritage Children's Dictionary*, which has eight- to 12-year-olds in mind. The text in this printing is the same as in the 1986 edition; some drawings have been replaced with photographs, and the map and facts about the states have been dropped. A 17-page introduction shows a sample page with labels, then discusses dictionary features (e.g., synonyms, word histories, homophones). There are said to be 37,000 entries. Entries give part of speech, one or more definitions, example sentences, pronunciation, comparatives, and superlatives. Pages have an average of one color illustration; special features (e.g., word history, synonym list, vocabulary builders) are in boxes. A brief thesaurus with index completes the work.

The American Heritage Student Dictionary is a complete revision of the 1986 edition and is aimed at sixth- to ninth-graders. New words include *genome*, *pixel*, and *triathlon*. The 24-page preface includes some elements of a style manual. The outside margin of each page is used for the pronunciation guide, small black-and-white illustrations, and enrichment (e.g., word histories, usage). All entries include pronunciation, part of speech, and definition. Featured in some entries are example sentences, syllabication, etymology, synonyms, cross-references, inflected forms, homophones, homographs, abbreviations, usage, variants, principal parts of verbs, irregular plurals, and comparatives and superlatives. The publisher states that there are 68,500 entries, chosen from materials used by middle-schoolers. Biographies are included in the main alphabetic sequence. Definitions are clear, and the use of the margins for special features adds browsing appeal.

This is a solid series, worth considering for all collections serving children, and a must for curriculum-materials centers. The *Student Dictionary* could be included in the adult reference section for adults poorly served by other dictionaries. Only *The American Heritage Children's Dictionary* and *The American Heritage Student Dictionary* are likely to find use in the reference collection; copies of the other titles should be most useful in the circulating collection or in classrooms.

Proper Names Master Index: A Comprehensive Index of More Than 200,000 Proper Names That Appear as Entries in Standard Reference Works. 2v. Ed. by Frank R. Abate. Omnigraphics, 1994. 1,915p. bibliog. $125 (1-55888-837-3).
423'.1 English language—Etymology—Names—Indexes ‖ Names, English—Indexes [OCLC] 94-22479

Obviously modeled on Gale's *Biography and Genealogy Master Index*, this set indexes entries for proper names, other than personal names, that appear in 68 English-language reference works. Because of the wide variety of subjects represented by the works chosen for inclusion (among them literature, politics, medicine, science, music, history, and religion), the more than 200,000 index entries range from song titles to battles, from geographic entities to mythical figures, from television programs to court cases.

Sources indexed in *Proper Names Master Index* (PNMI) were selected on the basis of two criteria: that they "provide authoritative information on names," and that they "be widely held by public and academic libraries." Among the titles indexed are such general works as the *Harper Dictionary of Modern Thought* and the *New Century Cyclopedia of Names* and an eclectic assortment of more specialized sources, including 12 of the Oxford companions, *Benét's Reader's Encyclopedia*, *Halliwell's Film Guide*, *Popular Names of U.S. Government Reports*, and *Dictionary of Wines and Spirits*. In a surprising number of instances, the editor has not indexed the most recent edition of a source. For example, the fifth edition (1979) of *Black's Law Dictionary* is indexed rather than the sixth edition (1990), and the fourth edition (1988) of the *Complete Directory to Prime Time Network TV Shows, 1946–Present* is listed instead of the fifth (1992).

Entries appear alphabetically except for a numerically arranged section for names beginning with numbers (e.g., 60 *Minutes*, 1812 *Overture*), which precedes the alphabetized entries. Following each entry are codes representing the sources in which the name appears. These source codes and their corresponding titles are listed on the inside covers of each volume and again following the introductory material. A particularly useful feature is the provision of an encircled P after a code to indicate when a source provides pronunciation of the name. In addition, when a source is not arranged alphabetically or when the name indexed does not appear under the same heading in the original source, the appropriate page number, section number, or other information designating the location of the entry is provided.

Both volumes contain a foreward that provides historic and linguistic background on proper names, a guide to the use of the index, and a descriptive bibliography. The latter includes complete bibliographic information for each source indexed, an annotation describing its coverage and organization, and an explanation of which and approximately how many entries from the source were selected for indexing. This list also includes the complete Library of Congress classification number and the Dewey classification for each work and provides space for local call numbers to be added. The publisher is to be commended for having designed the covers of these volumes in such a way that none of the information on the spines will be obliterated by the addition of a call number.

Only six of the sources indexed in this work are also indexed by Joe Ryan's *First Stop: The Master Index to Subject Encyclopedias* (Oryx, 1989). Since that source excluded articles of fewer than 250 words as well as those not accompanied by a bibliography, the amount of overlap between the two works is inconsequential.

Most experienced and knowledgeable reference librarians will not need to consult PNMI very often since they will be able to take their users directly to a source that is suitable for their needs. Moreover, indiscriminate and uncritical use of this index could lead a user to inappropriate sources. For example, someone seeking historical information on the Illustrated London News will not be well served by the eight word entry in Webster's Dictionary of Proper Names, the only source cited for that publication. However, for those elusive allusions or when patrons cannot place a name in its context (e.g., when they do not know whether a title is a song, painting, novel, etc.), this may come in handy in public and academic libraries.

The Barnhart New-Words Concordance. Comp. by David K. Barnhart. Lexik House, Box 247, Cold Spring, NY 10516, 1994. 704p. loose-leaf $65; $52 to academic and public libraries (0-936368-07-1).
427'.09 Encyclopedias and dictionaries—Concordances [BKL] 93-80483

This is an index to words appearing in eight publications, including The Oxford Dictionary of New Words, 12,000 Words: A Supplement to Webster's Third New International Dictionary, The Third Barnhart Dictionary of New English, and a quarterly published by the compiler, The Barnhart Dictionary Companion. While the indexed sources have varying definitions of new, generally they list words that have entered the language since 1961. Entries here are straightforward. Each word is followed by abbreviations for the dictionaries that contain it. Many words list only one source; some list five or six. When a word has more than one meaning, a brief definition is given in parentheses with each listing. Among the more than 28,000 words and phrases included are emoticon, ethnic cleansing, flame mail, and Zoë Baird standard. While libraries will find the loose-leaf format a problem, this work will be a time-saver in academic and large public libraries owning the indexed sources. —Sandy Whiteley

The Thesaurus of Slang. Rev. ed. By Esther Lewin and Albert E. Lewin. Facts On File, 1994. 456p. bibliog. $50 (0-8160-2898-2).
427'.09 English language—Slang—Dictionaries || English language—Synonyms and antonyms [CIP] 93-42890

The 165,000 entries in the second edition of this thesaurus include 15,000 additions. The work retains the function and organization of the original edition published in 1988. Slang terms are arranged under the "formal English word . . . most likely to occur to the reader searching for a slang synonym" (e.g., chomp, dig in, munch, pig out, wolf down, nosh, and put away are among the many slang words listed under eat.) If there is no formal equivalent for the slang word (e.g., shark as slang for a sea lawyer), an entry is made under the slang term itself. A brief definition may be included when needed to clarify the meaning of an obscure slang term.

The largest number of new terms is found among the slang words relating to the drug culture. "There are more new terms for marijuana than in any other category: 98 new words amounting to a 46 percent increase." Drunk continues to be the largest single category with more than 800 slang terms, although the new entries in this category amounted to only 7 percent. Other categories showing a significant increase were sex, guns, and racial words and phrases, most of which are derogatory. A revised bibliography of sources used in compiling the thesaurus is included.

High school, public, and academic libraries that did not purchase the original edition should consider acquiring the newer version. Libraries owning the earlier edition may wish to replace it with the revised and expanded volume.

War Slang: Fighting Words and Phrase of Americans from the Civil War to the Gulf War. By Paul Dickson. Pocket, 1994. 402p. bibliog. index. $25 (0-671-75022-4).
427'.09 Soldiers—U.S.—Language (New words, slang, etc.)—Dictionaries || Military art and science—U.S.—Slang—Dictionaries || U.S.—History, Military—Slang—Dictionaries || English language—U.S.—Slang—Dictionaries || Americanisms—Dictionaries [CIP] 93-16264

Dickson's popular dictionaries include The Congress Dictionary [RBB D 1 93], The Ways and Meanings of Capitol Hill (Wiley, 1993), and Dickson's Word Treasury (Wiley, 1992). This latest work is organized by conflict, beginning with the Civil War and including the Spanish American War, World Wars I and II, Korea, Vietnam, and the Gulf War. The work ends with a "Doomsday's Dictionary: Verbal Fallout from Nukes, the Cold War and the Puzzle Palace." The latter term is defined in this section as "(1) The Pentagon. (2) The National Security Agency." This brief explanation is typical of too many other definitions in this dictionary. Like most slang dictionaries, grammatical labels, etymological notes, usage notes, and example sentences are scarce. Such phrases as no-man's-land, brush-off club, topside from the top receive fuller treatment with definitions of 50 to 70 words and including quotations with works cited. Sources are listed at the end of each section; they will lead users to other war dictionaries, memoirs, and major secondary works. The author's brief but carefully thought-out informal introductions to each section help define the flavor of the period. The chronological arrangement of the dictionary leads users from a more romantic and, perhaps, patriotic time through the hardened and grim Korean and Vietnam conflicts. An index lists all the entries.

Elting's Dictionary of Soldier Talk (Scribner, 1984) is a comprehensive work, arranged in one alphabet, but it doesn't cover the most recent wars. The following works provide more extensive coverage of specific wars: Colby's classic work completed early in World War I, Army Talk: A Familiar Dictionary of Soldier Speech (Princeton, 1942); Reinberg's In the Field: The Language of the Vietnam War (Facts On File, 1991); and Clark's Words of the Vietnam War (McFarland, 1990). Librarians looking for a popular dictionary that will appeal to laypersons will want to consider War Slang; its arrangement helps users understand one aspect of our history.

Black Talk: Words and Phrases from the Hood to the Amen Corner. By Geneva Smitherman. Houghton, 1994. 242p. hardcover $17.95 (0-395-67410-7); paper $10.95 (0-395-69992-4).
427'.973 English language—U.S.—Glossaries, vocabularies, etc. || English language—U.S.—Slang—Dictionaries || Afro-American—Language—Dictionaries || Black English—Dictionaries || Americanisms—Dictionaries [CIP] 94-591

This is a somewhat less formal work than Juba to Jive [RBB Mr 1 94], and the language covered is more contemporary, with a strong emphasis on hip-hop culture. Smitherman's long introduction is as polemic as it is introductory. She buys into a number of stereotypes of European-descended American culture: it is monolithic, bland, without oral tradition, and without passion. The section entitled "They Done Took My Blues and Gone: Black Talk Crosses Over" suggests that whites use black language partly to spice up their dreary lives and partly as an act of cultural oppression. "What is Africa to Me?" is a useful brief discussion of grammar, pronunciation, and context of black speech. A phonetic key to pronunciation would have been helpful. Smitherman mentions some scholarly works but does not provide complete bibliographic information for them. In her "Explanatory Notes" she describes her sources for definitions and pronunciation as primarily oral.

In the dictionary, definitions and example sentences illustrating use are given for words and phrases. Some regional or special group uses are noted, but not consistently. There are extensive, helpful cross-references. Every area of life from church to gangs is covered. Many of the phrases speak with a painful poetry of violence, sex, and drugs. Others show an ironic wit—the term chicken for a preacher suggests that children have more imagination than adults suspect. There are plenty of terms to shock both liberal and conservative sensibilities.

As in Juba to Jive, claims for the exclusivity of some terms to the black speech community are debatable. Crib as a term for one's home is cited in OED as far back as 1812 in Flash Dictionary, a book of English street talk.

Smitherman has pulled together words and phrases and their meanings through the early 1990s. Black Talk will be a useful purchase for medium-size to large public libraries and most academic libraries with interest in black speech and American slang.

Happy Trails: A Dictionary of Western Expressions. By Robert Hendrickson. Facts On File, 1994. 274p. index. $24.95 (0-8160-2112-0).
427'.978 English language—Dialects—West (U.S.)—Dictionaries || West (U.S.)—Social life and customs—Dictionaries || Americanisms—West (U.S.)—Dictionaries || Figures of speech—Dictionaries [CIP] 93-42888

This is the second volume in Facts On File's Dictionary of American Regionalisms. The first, also by Hendrickson, was Whistlin' Dixie [RBB D 15 92]. The introduction indicates that the work "represents a lone writer's attempt to corral a good representative selection of Western speech."

In 1993 Facts On File published a similar work, Blevins' Dictionary of the American West [RBB Ap 1 93]. It is not listed among the sources Hendrickson used. He seems to have relied mostly on his own voracious reading of Western novels, biographies, short stories, movies, and television. Even so, since the two works are about the same length (approximately 3,500 entries in each), some comparisons are in order. The letter O was chosen at random for comparison; Hendrickson has 64 entries to Blevins' 42. Comparing them, 27 of Hendrickson's entries are not in Blevins, while 25 of Blevins' are not in Hendrickson.

Hendrickson frequently gives quoted examples of the usage of a word, usually with the source of the quote. Neither work places accents on non-English words, though Blevins gives the phonetic pronunciation of many Spanish words. He lists 10 words beginning with *gu-*, and the pronunciation of each is given. Hendrickson lists only one of these, *guayave*, and gives no pronunciation.

Some of Hendrickson's definitions are rather naive. He defines *alkali dust* as "dust of the alkaline deserts of the Southwest." His entry *gringo*, on the other hand, disparages the traditional meaning, "gibberish," derived from the Spanish word *griego*, as if to say, "it's Greek to me," and suggests a derivation from the name of Major Samuel Ringgold, a great fighter against Mexicans up to 1846. Blevins accepts the traditional derivation, while admitting that "the etymology remains uncertain." There is no bibliography in Hendrickson, while Blevins has four pages of further reading.

Should a library with a Western-oriented clientele buy Blevins or Hendrickson, or both? One or the other of these works should suffice for all but the true aficionado of Western words.

Random House Historical Dictionary of American Slang. v.1, A–G. Ed. by J. E. Lighter. Random, 1994. 1,006p. bibliog. $50 (0-394-54427-7).
427'.973 English language—U.S.—Slang—Dictionaries || English language—U.S.—Obsolete words—Dictionaries || Americanisms—Dictionaries [CIP] 94-9721

A fascinating mixture of the clever, the colorful, the crude, and the coarse, this first historical dictionary to be devoted exclusively to American slang has been in progress for more than two decades. Volume 1 of the projected three-volume set covers A–G; volumes 2 (H–R) and 3 (S–Z) are scheduled for publication in 1996 and 1997, respectively. In his excellent 27-page introduction, Lighter, a research associate in the English department of the University of Tennessee at Knoxville, traces the historical development of slang in the English language and discusses its sociological and cultural aspects. Following the introduction, Lighter provides a useful, annotated bibliography of significant books and articles dealing with American slang and an admirably thorough guide to the dictionary.

Defining slang as "an informal, nonstandard, nontechnical vocabulary composed chiefly of novel-sounding synonyms for standard words and phrases," Lighter notes that his intent in this compilation is to treat words and phrases that can be considered American slang, either presently or in the past. Therefore, some of the entries are for terms now considered colloquial or even Standard English (e.g., *bamboozle, cliffhanger, dandy, flapper, fluke*), but which were at one time viewed as slang. Other entries range from informal, inoffensive words and phrases that make our language more lively and interesting (e.g., *can of worms, circular file, foodaholic, goof off, grungy*) to terms that are generally considered offensive or vulgar, such as racial and ethnic epithets and expressions pertaining to sexual relations and body functions.

Entry headwords are arranged letter by letter (e.g., *bassackwards* precedes *bass fiddle*), with phrases usually appearing within the entry for the main word of the phrase. Abbreviated field labels indicating that a particular group of people uses the word (e.g., military, underground) precede the definition when appropriate. Usage and status labels are used to indicate other aspects of a term, for instance, whether it is usually considered vulgar or offensive or whether it is generally used jocularly or derisively.

The approximately 20,000 definitions included in this volume are models of succinctness. Following each definition are illustrative quotations, which are arranged chronologically, beginning with the earliest documented use. These quotations, which are the true heart of each entry, serve not only to document a word's usage at a particular time but also to further elucidate its meaning. Culled from a wide variety of written and oral sources, including literary works, popular novels, other dictionaries, magazines, newspapers, motion pictures, television programs, and anonymous conversations, the more than 90,000 quotations in this volume range from the seventeenth century to the 1990s. The degree of currency is particularly impressive since a number of 1993 sources, and at least one 1994 publication, are represented. A complete list of the approximately 8,000 sources cited throughout the dictionary will not appear until volume 3. This delay may prove problematic for users trying to locate the source of a quotation because titles are provided in abbreviated form. For example Nathan McCall's *Makes Me Wanna Holler* is referred to as "N. McCall, *Wanna Holler.*"

While there is no denying that perusing the pages of this volume can rattle one's sensibilities, the increasing permissiveness regarding language in today's society cannot be ignored. Only a decade or so ago, many of the words in this work were considered taboo, not just in polite society but also in the mass media. Today the infamous *f* word and words and phrases of similar ilk are cropping up in song lyrics, films, television programs, literary works, and mainstream magazines. The increasing usage and heightened awareness of such terms are not only reflected in this volume, but also make its publication even more timely and appropriate.

When completed, Lighter's dictionary will be, without a doubt, the most definitive and scholarly treatment of American slang ever published. Most academic and large public libraries will want to add this work, since its historical treatment complements the coverage of slang terms in the *Dictionary of American Regional English* and *The Oxford English Dictionary*. Getting down to the nitty-gritty, Lighter evidently is cooking with gas because he has done a bang-up job in compiling this tome. In short, it's awesome, fantabulous, rad, the cat's meow!

Usage and Abusage: A Guide to Good English. By Eric Partridge; ed. by Janet Whitcut. Norton, 1995. 389p. $27.50 (0-393-03761-4).
428 English language—Grammar || English language—Errors of usage [BKL] 94-98672

First published in 1942, this classic work by noted British lexicographer Partridge, who died in 1979, has been updated by Whitcut. Recent editions had included American usage, but more has been added here, for example, the difference in use of *specialty* and *speciality*. The list of *vogue words* is almost totally new; Whitcut added *born-again* and *ethnic* and dropped *Bolshevism* and *ego and id*. The entry *Muhammad* notes that *Muslim* is the correct form for believers, not *Muhammadan*, as in previous editions (but the entry *Mecca* still says it "is a place of religious pilgrimage for Muhammadans"). The entry *Jew* is an improvement over the offensive *Semitic*; *Hebraic*, *Hebrew*; *Jewish*. The entry *black* replaces *Negro*, and a racist example has been removed from the list of similes. But most of the book is still pure Partridge; witness the witty entries *Johnsonese* and *wooliness*, for example, which have not been changed. Most entries have not been updated; many still quote examples from newspapers and magazines of the 1930s and 1940s. Libraries with an earlier edition of Partridge on their shelves will be happy to replace it with this new one, and language mavens will still find it interesting reading. For public and high-school libraries, though, it is still too British and too dated to be the first choice for a usage guide. *Webster's Dictionary of English Usage* (Merriam-Webster, 1989) is a better alternative. —*Sandy Whiteley*

Encyclopedia of English Studies and Language Arts. 2v. Ed. by Alan C. Purves. Scholastic, 1994. 1,338p. bibliog. index. $150 (0-590-49268-3).
428'.007 English philology—Study and teaching—Encyclopedias || Language arts—Encyclopedias [CIP] 93-33627

A project of the National Council of Teachers of English, this work focuses on the multifaceted issues related to the study and teaching of English at all levels of education. Its entries explore topics pertaining to 10 major areas: language, literature, composition, reading, drama, media, technology, curriculum, teaching and learning, and assessment. Purves, director of the Center for the Study of Writing and Literacy at the State University of New York, Albany, indicates in his introduction that the encyclopedia intends to "explain English teaching to the world at large, particularly to administrators of schools, community colleges, and universities."

Ranging in length from 300 to 3,000 words, the approximately 700 signed entries were written by almost 600 contributors representing a wide range of academic institutions in the U.S. and Canada. Most articles are followed by a brief bibliography, and many provide cross-references to related entries. Articles are arranged alphabetically by title, but an inconsistent practice of ignoring prepositions, conjunctions, and articles within titles in determining alphabetical sequence can be confusing. For example, *Writing Curricula* comes before *Writing across the Curriculum*, but *Writing in the Disciplines* follows *Writing Evaluation*.

Entries cover a broad range of topics, including specific programs or projects (*America 2000*, *Plowden Report*), practical aspects of teaching (*Marking and Grading*, *Writing Conferences*), concepts and issues (*Deconstruction*, *Multicultural Education*), and computer applications (*Artificial Intelligence*, *Hypertext/Hypermedia*). In addition, a number of articles provide useful overviews of literature by a specific group or for a particular audience (e.g., *Canadian Literature in English*, *Young Adult Literature*). In general, the articles are well written and accessible to the nonspecialist. When NCTE has adopted a policy relevant to a topic, that policy is noted in the entry. Occasionally, tables, diagrams, or other black-and-white graphics are used to supplement the text.

Unfortunately, this set lacks several important features necessary for effective access. Most significantly, it does not have a detailed subject index or an overall table of contents. The only index is a topical one that simply groups article titles under 11 broad categories, such as *Learning and Reading*. Moreover, the index cites only a page number, not the volume number, and neither the spines nor the title pages of the volumes indicate the part of the alphabet covered or the inclusive pagination within each volume. Without adequate indexing, the wording of article titles is particularly crucial since this becomes the principal finding point. Therefore, one wonders how many users interested in the history of the teaching of writing will locate the entry *Nineteenth-Century Writing Instruction*, and if anyone will ever find the extremely useful annotated bibliography of relevant journals under the entry *Professional Publications in the English Language Arts*. The editor himself indirectly acknowledges these shortcomings by encouraging users to skim the article titles, the topical index, and the texts of articles in order to locate the information or terms they are seeking.

Additionally, the set bears evidence of careless editing. A number of blind *see also* references occur (e.g., *Adult Literacy Testing* refers to the nonexistent *Concepts of Literacy*, and *Dialect in Literature* refers to the nonexistent *American English*). Moreover, *see also* references sometimes lead only to a *see* reference. For example, a user referred to *Standardized Tests* from the entry *Test Score Decline* will not find an article but a *see* reference to other entries. In addition, some page headers are incorrect, and an initially confusing mishmash of incomplete articles on pages 884–87, upon further examination, turns out to be caused by a reversal of page numbers: the text for page 885 is on page 886 and vice versa. Furthermore, the volumes are not bound to withstand heavy use. Early in the review process the cover of one of the volumes came loose from the spine.

Many of the articles in this set (e.g., *Ethnic Studies*, *Television and Children*, *Test Bias*) address concerns that have relevance to the entire field of education, not just the teaching of English language and literature. Thus, this work could be used to supplement related entries in the now-dated *Encyclopedia of Education* (Macmillan, 1971) as well as to complement the material in *Handbook of Research on Teaching the English Language Arts* (Macmillan, 1991).

Although the information in this encyclopedia will be valuable for teachers, librarians, and educational administrators at all levels and for college students who are training to be teachers, potential users will almost assuredly be hampered by the lack of a well-conceived subject index and the other inadequacies mentioned above.

The Oxford Dictionary of English Grammar. Ed. by Sylvia Chalker and Edmund Weiner. Oxford, 1994. 448p. bibliog. illus. $25 (0-19-861242-7).
428'.003 English language—Grammar—Dictionaries [OCLC] 94-19818

Defined here are 1,000 terms used within the current mainstream of grammar, as well as within the related fields of phonetics and semantics, generative grammar, and linguistics. Examples of terms include *fricative*, *linking verb*, *participial adjective*, and *plupluperfect*.

Entries provide cross-references to synonyms (with the definition placed following the preferred term), indications of terms that enjoy a contrastive relationship, and cross-references to related and overlapping words. Entries include part-of-speech labels and illustrative quotations (sometimes with an indication of a phrase's earliest recorded appearance). The definitions constitute an interesting combination of telegraphic writing style (for the formal definition of a word) and narrative writing style (for explanations of the formal definition). Where British and American English differ, explanations for both are provided. For example, the definition for *present perfect* explains that American English often uses simple past, while British English prefers present perfect.

This is a remarkable resource. It is not a usage dictionary, but its definitions of grammar terms include usage information. The illustrative quotations are superb at facilitating understanding of complicated concepts; the format is unusually clear; and everything seems to be included, from A ("adverbial as an element of clause structure") to Z ("any of the functional parts into which clause and sentence structure is analysed"). This book will be used often by teachers, students (high school through college), writers, and of course, students of grammar. It is highly recommended for purchase by public and academic libraries; school librarians will want to preview before making a purchasing decision.

Science

Reference Sources in Science, Engineering, Medicine, and Agriculture. By H. Robert Malinowsky. Oryx, 1994. 355p. indexes. $49.95 (0-89774-742-9); paper $39.95 (0-89774-745-3).
026.6 Reference books—Science ‖ Science—Bibliography ‖ Engineering—Bibliography ‖ Medicine—Bibliography ‖ Agriculture—Bibliography [CIP] 94-16133

Malinowsky is principal bibliographer for science and engineering at the University of Illinois, Chicago. He has written extensively on collection development in scientific and technical fields. The intended audience for this annotated guide to the literature are collection development and reference librarians, library science students, and students and researchers in these disciplines.

The book is in nine chapters. The first four are short essays (two contributed by other experts) regarding serial prices, scientific communication, sources of scientific and technical information, and types of reference works. Chapter 5 is a guide to multidisciplinary materials; the remaining four chapters cover science, engineering and technology, medicine, and agriculture. Within each chapter are four to ten subchapters (e.g., chapter 8, "Medicine," has "General Medicine," "Nursing," "Pharmacy/Pharmacology," and "Special Areas").

Each subchapter is subdivided into as many as 16 categories by type of work (e.g., abstracts, atlases, handbooks, standards). Each entry has full bibliographic information, including distributor, price, and ISBN or ISSN. Most titles listed are in English, but important foreign-language materials are also included. Annotations mention whether a source is available online or on CD-ROM. It would have been helpful to note when the title of the electronic version is different from the print version (e.g., that *Metadex* is the online version of *Metals Abstracts and Index*). Frequently, an annotation refers to alternative works that are not listed separately. At the end of each subchapter is an unannotated list of periodicals. Almost one-third of the book is composed of detailed author, title, and subject indexes. The subject index is especially useful for locating cross-disciplinary materials.

Another good guide to the literature of science and technology is *Information Sources in Science and Technology* [RBB O 1 94] by Hurt. It has 2,068 numbered entries compared with Malinowsky's 2,459. However, Hurt lists a substantial number of unnumbered Internet sources; Malinowsky doesn't mention the Internet. Malinowsky covers agriculture and has a separate section on nursing; Hurt does not. Malinowsky lists more 1992 and 1993 titles. A random comparison shows that there is a fair amount of duplication between the two guides. However, sometimes there are differences of emphasis or preferences for titles that would be of interest to collection-development librarians. Libraries on a tight budget may wish to purchase only one of these books. *Reference Sources* is an excellent guide and will be useful in academic, public, and high-school libraries.

Wilson Applied Science & Technology Abstracts. CD-ROM. Wilson, 1994– . monthly. $2,495 annually.
016.6 Engineering—Periodicals—Indexes ‖ Technology—Periodicals—Indexes ‖ Industrial arts—Periodicals—Indexes [BKL]

Wilson General Science Abstracts. CD-ROM. Wilson, 1994– . monthly. $1,995 annually.
016.5 Sciences—Periodicals—Indexes [BKL]

These CD-ROM versions of the well-known print indexes have been enhanced with article abstracts of 50–150 words written by Wilson staff; some author abstracts are included. These abstracts are also available online, updated twice weekly, from Wilson, on OCLC's FirstSearch, and from BRS. They can also be leased on magnetic tape to be mounted on a library's own computer. CD-ROM versions of the indexes without abstracts have been available for the last five years. The CD-ROM versions with abstracts cost $700–$1,000 per year more than those without.

With both CD-ROM versions, users with modems and a telephone line can go online and search Wilsonline to identify entries added to the database since the date of the compact disc. Records on the discs can be annotated to show if the library owns a particular journal.

Hardware requirements are an IBM PC or fully compatible computer, DOS 3.1 or higher, 640K with 475K RAM, hard disk with at least

3MB of free disk space, and a Hayes or fully compatible modem. The software comes on a separate floppy disk.

While the print version of *Applied Science & Technology Abstracts* dates back to 1957, indexing on the CD-ROM begins in October 1983 and abstracting dates from March 1993; there are 672,852 abstracts on the July 1994 disc. Coverage ranges from journals that can be used by the high-school student to those aimed at the academic researcher. *Applied Science & Technology Abstracts* is updated with approximately 5,100 records monthly with references to articles that appear in 400 periodicals. Only seven of them are also indexed in the *Readers' Guide*.

The print version of *General Science Abstracts* dates back to 1978; on the CD-ROM indexing dates from May 1984 and abstracting begins with March 1993 and includes 389,725 records. It provides access to popular science literature just as *Readers' Guide* indexes popular non-scientific literature. *General Science Abstracts* is updated with approximately 3,500 records monthly from 150 periodicals plus the science section of *The New York Times*. Twenty-nine of the periodicals are also indexed in *Readers' Guide*. Five periodicals indexed in *General Science Abstracts* are also indexed in *Applied Science & Technology Abstracts*.

Users familiar with Wilson's other CD-ROM products will find these databases easy to use. Wilson products offer three levels of searching; these search modes give users progressively greater levels of access to individual data elements. Each search term is highlighted when the search results are displayed.

The single-subject search (BROWSE) mode is for the beginning user and for the two titles under review offers only controlled-vocabulary searching of subject headings, including corporate and personal names as subjects. (Note: Selected Wilson databases offer BROWSE mode access to other data elements.) Terms are searched, and the closest match is highlighted in the controlled-vocabulary listing. This is the same kind of search that can be done in the print index.

The next level of searching is the multiple-subject search (WILSEARCH). In this mode, multiple search terms can be typed into boxes and searched free-text; the Boolean operator AND will be performed by default. Personal names, titles, subject headings, journal names, organizations, and words in abstracts can be searched. Searching the abstracts is optional.

Command-language disc search (WILSONLINE) is the mode for the advanced searcher. The search commands and strategy are those used by BRS. The user is presented with a blank line on which to construct a search statement. Boolean operators, neighboring, expanding, truncation functions, and search qualifiers can be used.

The ability to search abstracts does lead to better results. Searching *Applied Science & Technology Abstracts* for the concept *clean air act* in the BROWSE mode resulted in 357 hits. When searching in the WILSEARCH mode without abstracts, there were 371 hits and, with abstracts, 515 hits. Using the WILSONLINE mode produced 515 hits, too. In *General Science Abstracts*, searching on *dinosaurs and argentina* resulted in 11 hits. From those entries that had abstracts it was possible to learn that the name of the new dinosaur found in Argentina is Eoraptor. Searching on *northwestern and university* led to entries where the abstracts noted that the researchers were affiliated with Northwestern. However, because the keywords were searched individually in the database, one irrelevant hit was retrieved, where the abstract stated that a University of Chicago professor was working in northwestern Argentina.

Both these indexes are useful for the novice and the expert user. Even those with no prior Wilson or CD-ROM experience can follow the instructions. The ability to search by author is another enhancement of the CD-ROM version over the print version. In libraries where funds are limited and access to popular or applied science information is important, these products should be considered. Library patrons and librarians will find them valuable reference sources.

H. W. Wilson has announced the upcoming release of four more Wilson Abstracts products. In September 1995, *Wilson Art Abstracts* and *Wilson Education Abstracts* will be available. *Wilson Humanities Abstracts* and *Wilson Social Sciences Abstracts* will be released in March 1995. —*Lillian Lewis*

Handbooks and Tables in Science and Technology. 3d ed. By Russell H. Powell. Oryx, 1994. 359p. index. $95 (0-89774-534-5).
016.5 Science—Handbooks, manuals, etc.—Bibliography || Technology—Handbooks, manuals, etc.—Bibliography [CIP] 94-16149

This third edition of a well-known bibliography last published in 1983 contains 3,662 handbooks and tables in the fields of science, technology, and medicine. As in previous editions, coverage is limited to books containing hard data that can be used to answer reference questions. Many government publications and research reports that would be hard to find elsewhere are listed. Popular works are excluded. Almost 400 outdated titles have been dropped from this edition and 650 new ones added. Powell is head librarian of the University of Kentucky Engineering Library. He is a scientific-literature subject specialist and has written several books on the subject.

The bibliography is arranged alphabetically by title. All entries have a complete bibliographic citation. In addition, most include the Library of Congress card number and price. The majority of entries have annotations that vary in length from one line to a paragraph. Within the annotations are frequent references to other titles in the book. No books published later than 1992 appear to be listed, and superseded editions of some titles are included. For example, the CRC *Handbook of Chemistry and Physics* is published annually, yet the 1991 edition is listed. The fourth edition (1973) of the *Merck Veterinary Manual* is listed; the most recent one available is the seventh edition (1991). Assisting users are two indexes, author-editor and subject.

This unique publication can be a useful collection- development tool, although users will need to check the availability of later editions. Academic, public, and special libraries with interests in this subject should give consideration to this new edition.

Information Sources in Science and Technology. 2d ed. By C. D. Hurt. Libraries Unlimited, 1994. 412p. indexes. hardcover $55 (1-56308-034-6); paper $32 (1-56308-180-6).
016.5 Reference books—Science—Bibliography || Reference books—Technology—Bibliography || Science—Bibliography || Technology—Bibliography [CIP] 93-43934

Hurt, director of the Graduate Library School at the University of Arizona, is a well-known expert on the literature of the sciences. The second edition of his guide to the literature of science and technology, originally published in 1988, has undergone substantial change. The history chapter has been dropped and this material incorporated within each subject chapter. The number of chapters has been expanded from 17 to 20 with an additional 50 pages added to the text. Although the number of numbered entries has increased by only 41, this is somewhat misleading. Some chapters have slight increases in their numbered entries; for example, "Astronomy" from 83 to 89. But an "Electronic Sources" section has been added at the end of all but four of the chapters, listing more than 700 unnumbered citations to the Internet.

This book is organized in five sections: "Multidisciplinary Sources of Information," "The Biological Sciences," "The Physical Sciences and Mathematics," "Engineering," and "Health and Veterinary Sciences." Within sections, chapters are arranged alphabetically (e.g., "Biology," "Botany," "Zoology"). Typically, a chapter will list such sources as guides to the literature, abstracts and indexes, dictionaries, and handbooks. Each entry has full bibliographic information, including ISBN. The critical annotations vary in length from one sentence to a paragraph. Emphasis is upon English-language materials, but some French, German, and Russian sources are also examined. The online versions of sources are noted (e.g., *CA Search*, *CAS Online*) but usually not the CD-ROM version. Author-title and subject indexes assist users in locating entries. The Internet sources are not indexed.

A comparable title is *Scientific and Technical Information Sources* by Chen (MIT, 1987), which covers 5,300 titles and provides one-sentence annotations. In contrast, Hurt has 2,052 entries with lengthier annotations plus citations to the Internet. While Hurt is more current, this book is not as current as its publication date would indicate. Many important 1992 titles are not included, for example, *Academic Press Dictionary of Science and Technology*, *Who's Who in Science and Engineering*, and the seventh edition of the *McGraw Hill Encyclopedia of Science and Technology* (the sixth edition from 1987 is listed). *Grzimek's Encyclopedia of Mammals* (1990) is also not listed. There are few 1993 books.

Despite some problems with currency, this guide will be useful in academic and public libraries, especially for its list of Internet sources. It is also available on floppy disk from the publisher.

McGraw-Hill Multimedia Encyclopedia of Science & Technology. CD-ROM. McGraw-Hill, 1994. $1,300; annual update $325 (0-07-046759-5).
500 Science—Encyclopedias || Science—Dictionaries || Technology—Encyclopedias || Technology—Dictionaries [BKL]

The *McGraw-Hill Multimedia Encyclopedia of Science & Technology* (MEST) incorporates the text and graphics of the 20-volume, seventh edition (1992) of the print encyclopedia and the text of the *McGraw-Hill Dictionary of Scientific and Technical Terms* (1994). It is to be updated annually, a clear advantage over the print set, a new edition of which is published every five years. According to press information, in addition to the text there are 550 photos, drawings, maps, and charts, 39 animation sequences, and nearly 40 minutes of audio. Hardware and software requirements include a 386 or better PC with 4MB RAM and a hard disk, Windows 3.1, and a VGA or SVGA color monitor (the pictures will not display without an SVGA driver set for 256 colors, although this is not mentioned in the manual). A mouse and sound board are also necessary to use multimedia features. Networked versions are available.

Installation is uncomplicated through Windows, although one will probably get a "Fatal Error" message as I did when one tries to install this with any other Windows program open—something else not mentioned in the documentation. The documentation is only eight pages in length; McGraw-Hill evidently feels that its on-line help, described as "detailed" in the manual, is the best way to provide instructions. However, none of the help screens I accessed were particularly detailed. For example, the explanation of "photo command" says, "Use this command to view photographs associated with an Encyclopedia article." On this particular help screen, further information is offered under "Related Topics," for example, "View a photograph." The "detailed instructions" under this related topic consisted of "Select Photo from the Document Menu or press Alt, D and P." These particular screens seemed a bit tautological to me. They did not help explain why the actual photo command was dimmed out and unworkable. Tech Support could only suggest that I make sure my display driver was set for 256 colors and reinstall MEST. This advice did not solve the problem, so I was unable to view any photos.

MEST offers several ways to search for subjects, beginning with a choice of databases: Encyclopedia, Dictionary, Animations, Biographies, etc. Clicking on the Search button offers two options, "simple" or "advanced." Simple search allows users to enter a term, while advanced search allows one to use the Boolean connectors AND, NOT or OR with up to four terms. One can also restrict the search by a topic or discipline (Engineering, Physics, etc.) and/or by proximity.

The search engine is very fast and easy to use. The users sees a window of "search results," with the number of articles and number of occurrences of the search term. One can also use the index button to browse or skip directly to an alphabetic list of all terms. The only weakness I found in this part of the program was the sometimes confusing way that I had to enter a search to locate a reference. For example, to find information on "circuit elements" one must use a phrase search in the simple search mode; a Boolean search for these terms doesn't retrieve the same article.

All of the power of Windows is available through MEST, including the ability to display multiple windows on one screen. Printing text is easy. Photographs, animation stills, and illustrations that appear in separate boxes cannot be printed. The 39 animation sequences seem quite primitive, although the audio explanations are clear. I could see no particular rationale for why these specific examples were included and wished for more.

There are clear advantages to a multimedia approach for an encyclopedia like MEST. The ability to bring to life concepts and explanations, including pronunciations, certainly makes a good teaching tool. Although the publisher claims that all of the text from the print version is included on the CD-ROM, I found that some diagrams and figures are not included. When a figure is dropped, the text reference to it, quite naturally, also is dropped. However, in some cases, entire explanatory paragraphs that include the reference to a figure number are also dropped. For example, in the print version there is a clear illustration of magnetic induction including an illustration of the field pattern around power lines. On the CD-ROM this "Figure 1" reference is dropped as well as approximately 75 additional words of text explanation.

It would be helpful if future versions contained more extensive help screens including explanations for such items as a second Find button that appears on text information screens and does nothing that I could find other than display the message, "Text could not be found."

In its printed form, *McGraw-Hill Encyclopedia of Science & Technology* is an important reference tool; in the present incarnation, I would give it a limited recommendation for high-school and college libraries. Having watched the difficulties public library reference staff can have in explaining CD-ROMs to the public, MEST might be a bit difficult to use in the latter environment. —*Charles Anderson*

McGraw-Hill Concise Encyclopedia of Science & Technology. 3d ed. Ed. by Sybil P. Parker. McGraw-Hill, 1994. 2,241p. illus. index. tables. $115.50 (0-07-045560-0).
503 Science—Encyclopedias || Technology—Encyclopedias [CIP] 94-16592

As with its first two editions, this is based on the multivolume *McGraw-Hill Encyclopedia of Science and Technology*, in this case the seventh edition published in 1992 (favorably reviewed here [RBB S 1 92]). That review holds for the concise encyclopedia as well, since the articles are just abbreviated versions of the original. The *Concise Encyclopedia* contains some 7,900 alphabetically arranged articles (300 new to this edition), with more than 1,600 photographs and line drawings. An analytical index aids in locating information for topics that do not have their own entries. There are also 15 appendixes covering such topics as the Greek alphabet, conversion tables, the periodic table of elements, mathematical notations, a geological time scale, and biographical listings.

This is an excellent, affordable one-volume encyclopedia that is highly recommended for all libraries that do not own the multivolume set. It is easy to use, has an excellent format, is highly reputable, and is up-to-date as of 1992. It may be time, however, to divide this work into two volumes. The weight of this one-volume edition is such that it may become a safety hazard. Being dropped a few times will quickly destroy its binding, not to mention injuring a toe or two.

Science Navigator. CD-ROM. Release 3.0. McGraw-Hill, 1995. $149.95; Network version $295 for up to 10 users.
503 Science—Encyclopedias—Databases || Engineering—Encyclopedias—Databases [BKL]

A new version of the *McGraw-Hill Science and Technical Reference Set* [RBB Jl 92], *Science Navigator* provides on one disc DOS, Windows, and Macintosh versions of two reference works: *McGraw-Hill Concise Encyclopedia of Science & Technology*, Third edition [RBB N 15 94], and *McGraw-Hill Dictionary of Scientific and Technical Terms*, Fifth edition [RBB Je 1 94]. The DOS version has been completely overhauled with this release, and the Windows and Macintosh versions are new. The Macintosh version was not reviewed by the Board. Documentation for all three versions is provided in a 29-page booklet. A toll-free technical support number is provided, though there is no indication of the hours this support is available.

The DOS version features a Windows-like retrieval interface, right down to the ability to use a mouse. Commands are invoked through a series of pull-down menus. The user may choose, using the Books pull-down menu, to search the Encyclopedia, Dictionary, or Biographies (which are pulled from the Dictionary). Depending on the book searched, the user may retrieve entries by searching the main entry, words in the text, categories (such as mathematics or telecommunications), countries (for the biographical entries), or contributors. Only individual words may be searched—there is no Boolean searching. Words within entries may be double-clicked to go to an entry for the selected word or, if no entry exists, to call up a pull-down menu of the closest words alphabetically. Entries may be printed out, though not downloaded. Unfortunately, the print setup offers a series of cryptic abbreviations in a pull-down menu (hpdskcvh, for example, is for a Hewlett-Packard DeskJet 500C printer). We never could get an entry to print on our Epson inkjet printer.

Most libraries will likely opt for the Windows version of the program, hardware permitting. Searches may be carried out using pull-down menus or icons on a button bar. The same types of searches are available as in the DOS version, but Boolean searching is allowed, and truncation and proximity operators also may be used. In addition, more than one book at a time may be searched. The minimum requirement of a 386-based processor should be taken seriously; a proximity search of *solar* #20 *eclipse* (*solar* within 20 characters of *eclipse*) took more than one minute, 15 seconds on a 386/33 with a double-speed CD drive. There were also the occasional noticeable lags in simply navigating from article to article. The illustrations are very crisp, however, and will print out with the accompanying article. Articles also may be copied onto the Windows clipboard, and a separate icon will load an article directly into Microsoft Word.

Science Navigator offers a significant price reduction when compared with previous versions and costs some $80 less than the purchase of its printed counterparts. Libraries already owning the print volumes will have to consider if full-text searching capability is a necessity in what are basically ready-reference works. On the other hand, libraries needing to beef up their science reference collection will want to consider this modestly priced CD-ROM.

Science Dictionary. By Seymour Simon. HarperCollins, 1994. 256p. charts. illus. tables. $29.95 (0-06-025630-3).
503 Science—Dictionaries, Juvenile [CIP] 94-9962

The author, an award-winning writer of science books for children, states in his brief introduction that "like any foreign language, science can be translated into ideas and concepts that use simple English words," and that is what he does here.

More than 2,000 up-to-date entries cover all branches of science, from astronomy to zoology. For words that have both a scientific and an everyday meaning, only the scientific meaning is included. In many instances the origin of the word is provided: for example, *marble* comes from a Greek word meaning "to sparkle"; *placer* from the Spanish American word meaning "sandbank." Definitions are clear and adequate for intended use, ranging from two to about twenty lines. The author indicates that every definition in the book was checked by Sheldon Aronson, professor of biology, Queens College, CUNY, or Alfred B. Bartz, physicist at the College of Education, Duquesne University. There are no pronunciation guides. Also included are brief biographies of about 85 important scientists.

The 250 simple line drawings that illustrate the volume are either in black and white or highlighted with blue. A final section includes classification of living things, maps of constellations, common weights and measures, weather-map symbols, a geological time scale, the periodic table, and eight other charts and tables.

The Kids' Science Dictionary by Q. L. Pearce (Checkerboard, 1989) has more than 500 very briefly defined terms with phonetic pronunciations. Many entries are accompanied by color illustrations. Several one-volume works are more encyclopedic than strictly dictionaries: *The Dorling Kindersley Science Encyclopedia* [RBB D 1 93] has 400 major entries organized into 12 thematic sections. The entries cover one or two pages; illustrations are attractive photography and art. Use is mainly for middle school. *The Kingfisher Science Encyclopedia* [RBB D 1 93] is geared for elementary and middle school. The arrangement of its 1,000 entries is alphabetical, with information ranging from a paragraph to several pages.

Science Dictionary is a useful, accurate, comparatively inexpensive science wordbook for upper-elementary and middle-school grades. Even older students will find it helpful.

Van Nostrand's Scientific Encyclopedia. 2v. 8th ed. Ed. by Douglas M. Considine. Van Nostrand, 1995. 3,455p. charts. illus. index. tables. $199.95 (0-442-01864-9).
503 Science—Encyclopedias || Engineering—Encyclopedias [CIP] 94-29100

First published in 1938, this desktop science encyclopedia has been published in two volumes beginning with the sixth edition. It is edited by Douglas Considine and Glenn Considine. Distinguished in their respective fields of engineering and information management, they are also the editors of several other well-known technical reference books (e.g., *Van Nostrand Reinhold Encyclopedia of Chemistry*). Approximately 250 scientists, engineers, and educators from eight different countries contributed to this new edition.

Van Nostrand's covers the six general areas of earth and space sciences, life sciences, energy and environmental science, materials science, physics and chemistry, and mathematics and information sciences. Where appropriate, entries have an identifying tag (e.g., *Bond* [Chemical]). The length of entries varies from one sentence (*Aeolian Tones*) to 11 pages (*Climate*). Only the longer entries are signed by their authors and have appended reading lists. The entries appear to be current. For example, *Jupiter* mentions the *Ulysses* satellite flyby of the planet in 1992, and 13 new readings have been added to its bibliography. *Telescope* has been expanded from 8 to 12 pages, has several new illustrations, and its bibliography is twice as long. This entry mentions the 1993 corrections to the *Hubble Space Telescope*. Similarly, the coverage under *Television* has been expanded to include a discussion of high-definition television, with mention of developments as recent as 1994. This work does not contain any biographies. Information on symbols and mathematical conversions is found under *Units and Standards*.

This encyclopedia has a good history of revision. A comparison with the previous edition shows that about 200 new pages have been added to the text. There are approximately 7,300 entries, an increase of several hundred. Throughout the text are many appropriately placed black-and-white photographs, line drawings, tables, charts, and diagrams. In the past this work has been criticized for the quality of its illustrations. There are several instances in this new edition of attempts to improve the contrast and size of photographs.

The index now appears at the end of each volume so the volumes can be used independently. A sampling determined that there are approximately 12,600 index entries and more than 5,300 cross-references in the text. This dual system of cross-references and indexing is barely adequate.

The only comparable work is the *McGraw-Hill Concise Encyclopedia of Science & Technology* [RBB N 15 94]. It has 7,700 alphabetically arranged entries, 1,700 illustrations, and an outstanding index of 30,000 citations. More than 3,000 authors contributed to the work, and all articles are signed. There is a bibliography of databases and appendixes of conversion units, symbols and abbreviations, and a classification of living organisms. In addition, there is a list of important scientists. McGraw-Hill is clearly superior in illustration quality and indexing. In contrast, *Van Nostrand's* has almost twice the number of pages and longer entries than McGraw-Hill. Academic, public, and high-school libraries should consider *Van Nostrand's Scientific Encyclopedia* for their collections.

Science Experiments & Projects Index. Ed. by Lisa Holonitch. Highsmith, 1994. 324p. bibliog. $40 (0-917846-31-1).
016.5078 Science—Experiments—Juvenile literature—Bibliography—Indexes || Science projects—Juvenile literature—Bibliography—Indexes || Science—Juvenile literature—Bibliography—Indexes [CIP] 94-6327

This index, compiled by the staff of the children's division at the Columbus (Ohio) Metropolitan Library, lists 8,400 science experiments and projects in more than 400 books published between 1980 and 1993. It is designed for use by students in grades K–12. It is similar to *Science Fair Project Index* (Scarecrow, 1992) and *Science Experiments Index for Young People* (Libraries Unlimited, 1988).

The volume is arranged alphabetically by subjects, most of which are similar to those found in nationally recognized subject heading lists, so finding needed entries is not a problem. Entries include a single-sentence description of the experiment, source title, author, and page number. Cross-references are provided, and more general topics, such as plants and electricity, are subdivided. Bibliographic information on the 400 books is found in the back of the book and includes space for a library to indicate call numbers for those titles it owns. Grade-level designations are not included in the index itself or the bibliography. The lack of this information precludes its use for collection development and hinders teachers and parents from using the book effectively with a particular-age student.

Libraries with large science collections that include many of the titles found in the bibliography will find use for this index. Otherwise, patrons will find appropriate projects just as easily by consulting the library's catalog or the librarian.

Great Scientific Achievements. 10v. Salem Press, 1994. 110p./vol. illus. indexes. $250 (0-89356-860-0).
509'.04 Science—History—20th century—Encyclopedias || Technology—History—20th century—Encyclopedias [CIP] 94-1829

This is the third set in the Salem Press/Magill Twentieth Century series that gave us *Great Athletes* [RBB Jl 92] and *Great Events* [RBB Ap 15 93]. Like its predecessors, it is geared for middle-schoolers and up. This time the focus is on "important scientific and technological achievements that have influenced the way in which people live and work." The set covers 21 disciplines, including agriculture, astronomy, biology, computer science, food science, transportation, and weapons technology. As with any attempt to single out the "greatest," cries of "Why wasn't X included?" can be expected. For example, why wasn't the Golden Gate Bridge included? What about videophones?

Arranged chronologically, the volumes span 1880–1994, with each volume covering 8 to 25 years of history. The only 1994 event is the Hubble Space Telescope's transmission of images to Earth, an endeavor actually begun with its deployment in April 1990. Interestingly, the volumes covering the fewest years are those for 1950–58 and 1958–64. Apparently, these were years of great scientific achievements.

The 367 articles have a format similar to the previous sets in the series: large type, a black-and-white illustration, plenty of white space. Each entry runs three pages and includes a half- or full-page illustration. A boxed synopsis of the event appears below the entry title. Close by is a boxed list highlighting what (i.e., a discipline such as medicine), when, where, and who. The articles are divided into three parts. The first two discuss the achievement and pertinent background; the last, its impact. Definitions for difficult scientific terms (e.g., *empiricism, chlorofluorocarbons*) are unobtrusively given in parenthesis in the text.

Pagination is continuous throughout the set. Each volume includes four cumulative indexes: chronological, alphabetical keyword, discipline, and personages. Volume 10 also includes a subject index and a time line. Unlike the chronological list, which gives date, event, volume, and page number, the time line provides date, event, country, and region. Unfortunately, no footnotes, bibliography, or other references to further reading appear anywhere in the set. Thus there is no way to track down such stories as the yellow fever epidemic in Santo Domingo, which killed 29,000 of Napoleon I's 33,000 troops there. This caused him to change his plans to send troops up the Mississippi; instead he sold the Louisiana Purchase to the U.S.

All in all, this source meets the standards set for the series. Middle-school and junior-high report writers will find it useful. The layout will appeal to older reluctant readers and ESL students as well. Browsers will also enjoy dipping into its pages.

American Women in Science: A Biographical Dictionary. By Martha J. Bailey. ABC-Clio, 1994. 440p. bibliog. illus. index. $60 (0-87436-740-9).
509.2'273 [B] Women scientists—U.S.—Biography—Dictionaries [CIP] 94-10096

Against the odds, women have made contributions in every field of scientific endeavor. *American Women in Science* is a biographical treatment of more than 400 women in the social, physical, and medical sciences and technology who began their careers before 1950. Coverage ranges from early female scientists with no formal training, such as Elizabeth Agassiz, founder of Radcliffe College, to Nobel Prize winners Rosalyn Yalow and Barbara McClintock. Many women had to study in Europe, such as Gerty Theresa Cori at the University of Prague. Some were the first women to graduate from their institutions, such as Nora Barney, a civil engineer from Cornell University, or Florence Bascom, the first female doctorate from Johns Hopkins University. Contributors to home economics, such as Fannie Farmer, are treated as are popular nature writers. Minority women are included: Sophie Aberle, a Native American, and Katherine Dunham and Zora Neale Hurston, African Americans, all of whom were anthropologists.

The introduction is a historical overview of the professional opportunities that were open to female scientists in the nineteenth and first half of the twentieth centuries. For many, government agencies offered employment. Each entry includes the birth and (when appropriate) death dates of the subject, as well as educational background and employment history. The accompanying essay of several paragraphs to a page describes achievements and major contributions to her particular field. Closing each entry is a bibliography of other sources in which the subject can be found. Black-and-white photographs are provided for about 45 of the women.

When this work was compared with other sources, such as *Women in Science* (MIT Press, 1986) or *Women in Chemistry and Physics* [RBB Ap 15 94], there was not much duplication. *Women in Chemistry and Physics*, for example, treats only 75 women and they are not all Americans. *American Women in Science* is a unique reference source that highlights many women who have been neglected in other biographical sources. It is highly recommended for academic, public, and secondary school libraries.

Larousse Dictionary of Scientists. Ed. by Hazel Muir. Larousse, 1994. 595p. index. $35 (0-7523-0002-4).
509.22 Scientists—Biography [OCLC] 94-75739

Notable Twentieth-Century Scientists. 4v. Ed. by Emily J. McMurray. Gale, 1994. bibliog. illus. indexes. $295 (0-8103-9181-3).
509.2'2 [B] Scientists—Biography—Dictionaries || Engineers—Biography—Dictionaries [CIP] 94-5263

Attention librarians inundated by the request, "I have to write a biography of a scientist!" Here are two sources that might help more than two aspirin.

The *Larousse Dictionary of Scientists*, an inexpensive one-volume source, focuses on "scientists who have made their mark in the traditional sciences (physics, chemistry, biology, astronomy, earth sciences) and their applications, and includes an extensive selection of mathematicians." It includes Nobel Prize winners in physics, chemistry, and physiology or medicine from 1901 to 1993. "Most entries have been expanded and updated from the database of *Chambers Biographical Dictionary*." Five hundred new entries were added to bring the total to more than 2,200. The entries span the centuries from the ancients to the present.

Each entry gives the scientist's years (birth and death), nationality, field of study, and main achievements. Don't look here for family life, hobbies, and similar background information. Cross-references in bold print link entries. Included is a special list of Nobel Prize winners chronologically by category and an index by field of study. Scientists such as Eduard Suess, Jean Martin Charcot, and John Couch Adams, who were not found in general encyclopedias or in such sources as *The Great Scientists*, were found here.

Notable Twentieth-Century Scientists, in contrast, focuses on approximately 1,250 scientists of this century. Aimed at high-school students, researchers, and general readers, the set covers applied and physical sciences, including astronomy, botany, chemistry, computer science, ecology, engineering, medical science, and technology. Special attention was paid to the coverage of women, minorities, and non-Western scientists. The result: approximately 225 female scientists; 150 Asian, African, Hispanic, and Native American scientists; and 75 from outside North America and Western Europe (e.g., Algeria, Columbia, India). Due to the scarcity of published information on many of these scientsts, interviews with the scientists, their families, and organizations were used to augment the entries.

Four criteria determined inclusion: (1) whether the discovery, invention, and/or overall contribution impacted twentieth-century scientific progress; (2) whether a major science award was received; (3) whether the scientist is involved in "education, organizational leadership, or public policy"; (4) whether there was a notable "first" achievement (e.g., first space flights).

Each entry includes birth and death dates, nationality, and field of specialization. The 400–2,500 word essays cover parents' occupations, spouse and children, educational background, career positions, awards and honors earned, scientific endeavors and achievements, selected writings, and sources of additional information. Cross-references to other entries are in bold print. Black-and-white portraits are provided for almost 400 entries. Biographees include Bill Gates, Robert Jarvik, Mae Jemison, Dian Fossey, Stephen Hawking, and Miriam Rothschild.

Each volume includes a table of contents and a "Chronology of Scientific Achievement, 1895-1993." The indexes in volume 4 include field of specialization, gender, nationality or ethnicity, and subject. These will be useful when planning multicultural displays or events. Volume 4 also has a bibliography of biographical sources with subdivisions for autobiographical collections, historical collections, dictionaries and encyclopedias, and directories.

Both titles are suitable for middle school/junior high and up and will appeal to general researchers as well. *Larousse*'s low price and greater historical scope is offset by the comparative brevity of its entries. The *Notable* set offers longer entries but is limited to the twentieth century. Both sources deserve a place in reference collections. *Larousse* will supplement and update such sources as *Asimov's Biographical Encyclopedia of Science and Technology* (2d ed., Doubleday, 1982). *Notable Twentieth-Century Scientists* will update such sources as *McGraw-Hill Modern Scientists and Engineers* (3v., 1980).

The Universe Explained: The Earth-Dweller's Guide to the Mysteries of Space. By Colin A. Ronan. Holt, 1994. 191p. bibliog. illus. index. $35 (0-8050-3488-9).
523 Astronomy—Popular works || Cosmology—Popular works [CIP] 94-16294

Drawing on telescopes, satellites, computer imagery, and intriguing current theories, this book examines the interlinked relationships of the cosmos. Ronan, a noted astronomy writer, has written a book that explains the marvel and mystery of the universe for all ages.

Five major sections concentrate on the universe from our observatory Earth, the planets, the sun and stars, nebulae and galaxies, and how it all works. An introductory page to each section is followed by double-page spreads on specific topics. Such topics as "Clouds That Never Rain," "Mapping the Sky," and "Wormholes in Space" intrigue and lead the reader to a fresh view of the macrocosm we inhabit. Each topic is highlighted by readable, stimulating text, spectacular art and photography, colorful diagrams, informative captions, and a sidebar that leads the reader to connections with related ideas. Feature boxes that relate to science or scientists add historical or technological interest. The extensive use of analogies allows the reader to make associations with familiar items or experiences such as likening geysers on a moon of Neptune to a coffee percolator or the colors of the stars to the heated metal in a foundry.

A welcome addition to any collection for budding scientist or curious information seeker, *The Universe Explained* is recommended for all school or public libraries. Reading any topic in this book is like taking an excursion to an astronomy exhibition or space museum.

Encyclopedia of Time. Ed. by Samuel L. Macey. Garland, 1994. 699p. bibliog. illus. index. $95 (0-8153-0615-6).
529'.03 Time—Encyclopedias [CIP] 93-43355

Time has many facets and dimensions, and all are explored by experts in the *Encyclopedia of Time*. Macey, author of several previous books about time, is a professor at the University of Victoria (Canada) and immediate past president of the International Society for the Study of Time. Gathered together here are articles by some 200 scholars, primarily U.S., Canadian, and British, but also from around the world, including Japan and Turkey. Their specialties range from philosophy, psychology, and astrophysics to geology, music, and medicine. This is the first encyclopedic volume to document the whole interdisciplinary field of time studies that has emerged in recent years. While time is readily apparent in some entries, such as those on clocks and calendars, it is implicit in all entries, as contributors stress aspects of their subject that are related to time.

Entries begin with *Age of the Oldest Stars and the Milky Way* and end with *X-Ray Universe* and vary in length from less than a page to more than nine pages. All are signed, have brief lists of further readings, and frequently have *see also* references to other entries. An amazing array of topics is found, from persons (Foucault, Emerson, Dickens, Petrarch, and F. W. Taylor) to medical (*Cardiovascular Chronopharmacology*), religious (*Judeo-Christian Traditions on Time*), literary (*Clock Metaphor, Stream of Consciousness*), astronomical (*Anasazi Archaeoastronomy, Star and Galaxy Formation*), sports (*Racing Sports and the Stopwatch*) to such entries as *Time for the Family, Mathematics of Musical Time*, and *Tidal Rhythms in Marine Organisms*. Because many topics are discussed in specific entries, a list of articles by major disciplines allows one to find related entries quickly. For example, *Horology* lists *Clocks: America and Mass Production, 1770–1890; French Clocks and Watches, 1660–1830*; and *Precision Timekeeping, 1790–1830* among its 14 entries. *Time's Measurements and Divisions* includes *Aztec Calendar; Calendar: Chinese and Japanese*; and *Standard Time: Time Zones and Daylight Saving Time* among its eight entries. Neither the sundial nor flextime has its own entry, but an index provides quite detailed access and both of these topics are found there. Illustrations include formulas, tables, diagrams, drawings, and black-and-white photographs.

The *Encyclopedia of Time* is a fascinating volume for browsing that also supplies readable scholarly information concerning all facets of this topic. Not just science libraries, but all academic and large public libraries, even some high-school libraries, may find it a valuable addition to their collections.

Concise Encyclopedia Chemistry. 2d ed. Ed. by Hans-Dieter Jakubke and Hans Jeschkeit. Trans. by Mary Eagleson. Walter de Gruyter, 1994. 1,201p. charts. illus. tables. $69.95 (3-11-011451-8).
540'.3 Chemistry—Encyclopedias [CIP]

This is more of an encyclopedic dictionary, with many entries having only a one-sentence definition. There is no index. Instead, a *see* reference is made for a term covered in a longer article. For example, under *shoe polish* is the reference "see Leather care products." This method works quite well, providing an easy way to locate discussions. The text of each longer entry is well written and understandable to the educated layperson. This book is smaller than the *McGraw-Hill Encyclopedia of Chemistry*, a true encyclopedia with few dictionary entries. The number of terms covered in the *Concise Encyclopedia*, however, is just as extensive, with shorter discussions of each. The *Concise Encyclopedia* is well illustrated, with many line drawings, tables, and charts.

A couple of minor points indicate de Gruyter's publishing standards may have been relaxed. The *Concise Encyclopedia Chemistry* is referred to in the preface as the *Concise Encyclopedia of Chemistry*. It is described as a translation of *ABC Chemie*, with no publication date. OCLC reveals that the real title is *Brockhaus ABC Chemie*; according to the publisher it was last published in 1987. These discrepancies do not, however, take away from the usefulness of the encyclopedia; they are only irritating for catalogers. This is a good, reasonably priced chemistry dictionary and is recommended for academic and public libraries.

Data Sources for Business and Market Analysis. 4th Ed. By John Ganly. Scarecrow, 1994. 473p. bibliog. index. $55 (0-8108-2758-1).
016.56588'3973 Marketing—U.S.—Information services || U.S.—Commerce—Information services || Marketing—Bibliography || Commerce—Bibliography [CIP] 93-23453

Originally issued under the title *Market Analysis: A Handbook of Current Data Sources*, the second and third editions of this book were published in 1969 and 1983 under the current title. This fourth edition has the same scope as earlier ones, which is to provide for the business researcher a guide to business information sources "primarily but not exclusively" related to statistics in all formats on a global scale. Coverage has been expanded to take into account the revolution in publishing of statistical sources on CD-ROM; the important global marketplace and changes in Eastern Europe and the former Soviet republics, as well as East Asian business markets; and the move by federal and state governments to reduce costs by shifting to private publishers or by ending informational programs altogether.

According to the editor, sources were selected on the basis of their usefulness in researching economic conditions, business trends, and consumer and industrial markets. The cutoff date for inclusion was January 1992. The first of half of the volume covers federal statistical publications (Bureau of the Census, Congress, the various executive branches, boards, committees, and commissions). Federal government databases are listed as well. Entries include Sudoc number and addresses and phone numbers for agencies. Foreign sources are divided into national, intergovernmental, and multinational organizations. The basic statistical abstract for each country is given under the country listing. Inclusion is limited to accessible sources that give official statistics. Numerous United Nations publications are listed.

The second half of the book concentrates on private sources, such as university programs, research institutes, professional and trade associations, advertising media, directories and mailing lists, and periodicals.

Each section begins with a scope note on the type of information sources covered and an annotated list of the sources. Electronic formats are noted where appropriate. The fourth edition has eliminated the complex alphanumeric numbering scheme of the previous edition but continues its "source type" arrangement for entries, which the editor feels will aid the researcher in identifying the major suppliers of information. The sections on directories and mailing lists have been greatly expanded because of the new CD-ROM products in this area. The index lists titles of sources as well as subjects, report headings, organization headings, and country and state headings

More than 11 years have passed since the last edition of *Data Sources*. There have been great technological changes in the way statistical sources are accessed. The processes by which governmental bodies disseminate information have been modified, too. Libraries owning the previous edition will want to update with this new one. Large public libraries not owning the original work should invest in the fourth edition, an up-to-date global guide to business statistical sources.

Encyclopedia of Endangered Species. Ed. by Mary Emanoil. Gale, 1994. 1,230p. bibliog. illus. indexes. $95 (0-8103-8857-X; ISSN 1077-1352).
574.529 Endangered species—Encyclopedias || Endangered species—Encyclopedias [OCLC]

This guide to endangered species worldwide is highly selective, describing 700 animals and plants of the many thousands that are threatened with extinction. The species have been selected from lists compiled by the U.S. Fish and Wildlife Service, the Convention on International Trade in Endangered Species (CITES), and IUCN-the World Conservation Union. Animal entries are arranged by species and then by family and genus; there is a separate section for plants. Entries are listed by common name, followed by scientific name. A shaded box contains phylum, class, order, and family; the status of the animal or plant on the lists of any of the three organizations; and geographic range. Essays provide a physical description, breeding and habitat information, and conservation efforts and survival outlook for the species. These entries are one to two pages in length. A small black-and-white photograph is provided for about half the entries; some of these photographs have been too tightly cropped, cutting off the animal's horns or its tail. Supplementary material consists of lists of extinct species and of wildlife and conservation organizations, a bibliography arranged by species, and a series of simple black-and-white maps of regions of the world. The geographic index shows that there is good representation of animals from all parts of the world. American species are listed both under U.S.A. and specific states. The index lists both popular and scientific names.

Several other reference tools cover more endangered species. For example, the encyclopedia under review includes only 133 species from the U.S.; *The Official World Wildlife Fund Guide to Endangered Species* (4v., Beacham, 1990-94), with coverage limited to the U.S., lists more than 800 plants and animals. The Beacham set also cites bibliographic references for each species. The 11-volume *Endangered Wildlife of the World* from Marshall Cavendish [RBB My 1 93] does not cover plants but includes 1,200 species and subspecies of animals. The 10-volume *Grolier World Encyclopedia of Endangered Species* [RBB S 1 93] covers more than 600 animal species. These three titles all have color as well as black-and-white photographs; the Marshall Cavendish and Grolier titles are especially well illustrated. These titles also have locator maps for each species.

The *Encyclopedia of Endangered Species* is recommended as a good overview and as a less expensive alternative for public and high-school libraries that don't own one of the titles listed above. — *Sandy Whiteley*

Amazing Animals of the World. 24v. Ed. by Lawrence T. Lorimer. Grolier, 1995. 50p./v. illus. index. maps. $279 (0-7172-7396-2).
591 Animals—Juvenile literature || Animals [OCLC]

This elementary-grade-level set covers more than 900 animals arranged from *Aardwolf* to *Zebrafish*. Animals are listed as a student would look them up. For example, *Yellow-Eyed Penguin* is found in the Y section, not under *Penguin, Yellow-Eyed*. Coverage includes simple animals, such as sponges and corals, and extinct ones, such as dinosaurs. Each one-page-per-animal entry includes a sidebar listing the animal's common and scientific names and classification; data such as length, weight, diet, number of young, and home; a map showing the animal's range; and symbols indicating natural biome, class, and endangered or extinct status. A color photograph and a 250-word profile highlighting how the animal lives and reproduces fill the rest of the page. These profiles also note environmental threats to the animal. Each volume includes a list of animals covered in that volume, an identical glossary, and an explanation of environments and how animals are classified. Volume 24 includes the easy-to-use set index. Here animals are gathered together by class, for example, all the entries for birds.

This attractive set will be helpful in grades 2–5 at animal-report time. The writing style and clear layout also make the set appropriate for ESL/sheltered English students.

A Guide to the Zoological Literature: The Animal Kingdom. By George H. Bell and Diane B. Rhodes. Libraries Unlimited, 1994. 504p. indexes. $85 (1-56308-082-6).
016.591 Zoology—Bibliography [CIP] 94-12694

Finally, an up-to-date guide to reference sources that pertain to zoology. There has been nothing available since *Smith's Guide to the Literature of the Life Sciences* by Roger C. Smith (9th ed., Burgess, 1980), which has served as the source for zoological literature for many years. This book will surely take up where Smith left off and become another classic that we hope will pass through many editions.

Bell and Rhodes have developed a book that is pleasing to look at and easy to use to serve as a collection development tool and a text or guide for students and researchers in the zoological sciences. The book consists of eight sections: "General Reference Sources," "Invertebrates," "Arthropods," "Vertebrates," "Fishes," "Amphibians and Reptiles," "Birds," and "Mammals." Each section is further divided by type of reference source: dictionaries, bibliographies, indexes and abstracts, field guides, journals, taxonomic keys, checklists and classification schemes, biographies, style manuals, etc. This selective guide has 1,655 entries with full bibliographic information, including price. Entries, including those for journals, are fully annotated; the only ones not annotated are those for associations. The lengthy annotations note electronic sources, when appropriate. A useful appendix of Internet information sources on the animal kingdom includes listservs, news groups, databases, library catalogs, electronic journals, directories, and gophers. The author-title index is followed by a detailed subject index.

As with any bibliographic work of this magnitude, some errors can be found. In this case, the ninth edition of *Smith's Guide to the Literature of the Life Sciences* is listed in "References," but in the chapter "General Reference Sources" the seventh edition is listed under the original title of *Guide to the Literature of the Zoological Sciences*. This does not detract from the authoritativeness of this guide. It is well compiled and a necessary purchase for any academic or large public library. There is no comparable guide to the literature.

The Kingfisher First Encyclopedia of Animals. By David Burnie and Linda Gamlin. Kingfisher, 1994. 141p. illus. index. $16.95 (1-85697-994-6).
591'.03 Animals—Encyclopedias, Juvenile [CIP] 93-46611

This encyclopedia for children ages 7–11 provides the young reader with more than 450 entries encompassing individual animal species, animal groups, and topics relating to the lives of animals (e.g., *Animal Partnerships, Behavior, Migration,* and *Parental care*). The animal entries are arranged from *Aardvark* to *Zebra*. Each entry has a short descriptive paragraph easily understood by the young researcher. Full-color illustrations are found on every page. In the main alphabetical sequence ten major habitats (e.g., coniferous forests, deserts) are discussed and illustrated on two-page spreads. Following the entries, an index references text pages, as well as illustrations (numbers in italics).

This encyclopedia is similar in format to *The Kingfisher Illustrated Encyclopedia of Animals* [RBB O 15 92], which describes more than 2,000 animals for upper elementary school children. *The Kingfisher First Encyclopedia* is a good, simple encyclopedia on animals for the young researcher.

The Grolier Student Encyclopedia of Endangered Species. 10v. Ed. by Diane Chando Frenick. Grolier, 1995. 90p./v. illus. index. maps. $279 (0-7172-7385-7).
591.529 Endangered species—Encyclopedias, Juvenile || Wildlife conservation—Encyclopedias, Juvenile [BKL]

This set states that it was designed as a user-friendly guide to endangered animals of the world, and it makes good on its claim. It was designed with students in the upper-elementary and middle-school grades in mind. (*The Grolier World Encyclopedia of Endangered Species* [RBB S 1 93] covers more animals for a high-school and adult audience.) The 400 entries are organized alphabetically by common name (*Bat*) rather than by specific name (Marianas flying fox) or scientific name (*Pteropus mariannus*). This means that all the animals of the same family are grouped together for easy research. This also means that the curious can easily find out the extent to which a type of animal is endangered.

Each attractive green volume contains the same introductory information about how to decode the entries. In addition, the introduction explains the different categories of endangerment and says that the term *endangered* may be applied to animals that exist in large numbers if certain factors in their environments are working against them. These data were gathered from the 1994 IUCN Red List of Threatened Animals. Volume 1 includes detailed information about the composition of the IUCN and its World Conservation Monitoring Center. There are also essays on different habitats: polar or tundra, coniferous forests, deserts, etc. A section entitled "The Pathway of Endangerment" discusses the effects of nature (volcanic eruptions) and the impact of humans (hunting or poaching, agriculture, use of pesticides and poisons, capture of live animals). Other sections discuss the part humans play in conservation, the reasons for creating reserves and restoring lands, and protective laws. The last section suggests things people can do to support the environment. Volume 10 contains short essays on the four animal classes covered in this set. This volume also contains a name index, a 10-page glossary with no pronunciation guides, addresses and phone numbers for 26 environmental organizations, and a list of 16 unannotated recommended readings.

The real strength of this set is the individual entries. Each begins with a colorful graphic that serves as a summary of the animal's vital statistics: common name, Latin name, endangerment code, a small map with the animal's habitat marked in red, and a color code that identifies the animal as a mammal, bird, reptile, or amphibian. The entry contains a description of the animal, its size, habitat, diet, breeding habits, young, and interesting facts. It also notes the estimated remaining populations, the reasons for endangerment, and whether any conservation measures are being employed. Each entry is about a page in length. The best part of each entry is the large color photo of the animal in its natural habitat. The sharp-focus photos often cover a full page or a double-page spreads.

This is a set that will get a lot of use in school and public libraries. The easy-to-use format coupled with the beautifully reproduced photographs mean that it will be used for more than just reports. Students and teachers will love it.

Swallowtail Butterflies of the Americas: A Study in Biological Dynamics, Ecological Diversity, Biosystematics, and Conservation. By Hamilton A. Tyler and others. Scientific Publishers, 1994. 376p. bibliog. illus. indexes. maps. $49.50 (0-945417-90-X); paper $24.50 (0-945417-91-8).

595.78'9 Papilionidae—America || Papilionidae—America—Pictorial works || Conservation—Insects [CIP] 92-25090

Swallowtail butterflies, a major family of insects, are threatened with extinction around the world. In the Americas alone, 40 of the 143 species are on the critical list of the World Conservation Union. This meticulously prepared book was obviously a labor of love by Tyler, its primary author, and those who took up the challenge of completing it after his death.

The first two-thirds of the book are organized thematically on subjects of general interest, including butterflies in nature and culture, ecology and behavior, population biology of adults, host plants, mimicry, biogeography, classification techniques, and diversity. Text is usually on the right-hand page, with tables, graphs, maps, and illustrations on the left-hand page. The text itself is delightful to read, the author having a deft command of the English language ("a very particular kind of leaf tissue must be chewed up by an intermediary food processor called a caterpillar"). At the same time it is highly technical, using scientific terminology that may stymie the casual reader ("Graphiine larvae have in the first instar bifurcate setae on the dorsum, and very rarely retain any setose tubercles in later instars"). The typeface of the text is of average size, but that in the charts, graphs, tables, and maps is small and often so crowded as to be difficult to decipher. Words included in the glossary at the back of the book are indicated by a superscript butterfly. Illustrations include both black-and-white and color photographs, electron microscope views, and drawings. Each chapter ends with a section of do-it-yourself exercises. The instructions are complete enough for the novice, but younger students may need guidance from a science teacher or experienced naturalist. The last third of the book gives a synopsis of American swallowtails, with 94 pages of colorplates. Plate data include scientific name, gender, area where found, and owner/collector of specimen.

The bibliography is 10 double-columned pages. A gazetteer of locations mentioned in the book gives latitude and longitude. Also included is a summary of name changes for swallowtails. There is a systematic index to plants and animals and a separate subject index.

The lay reader may be confounded by this work because of its scientific focus. This should not, however, deter those who enjoy reading popular science. The text is so well written that those who read authors such as Gould or Sagan will find this book fascinating, too. It may be too cumbersome to use for ready reference but will have a readership in academic libraries that support zoological and ecological programs and in high schools with AP science curricula. It will also make an excellent textbook.

Aquariums of North America: A Guide Book to Appreciating North America's Aquatic Treasures. By James M. Hillard. Scarecrow, 1995. 199p. $27.50 (0-8108-2923-1).

597'.0074 Aquariums, Public—North America—Guidebooks [CIP] 94-18440

Aquariums are not as plentiful as zoos, but their numbers are increasing along with their popularity as we become aware of dwindling marine resources. This book has information on 67 aquariums in the U.S. and Canada, plus a list of national and state fish hatcheries.

Arranged by state and then alphabetically by city of location, each entry includes directions to the aquarium by car or public transportation and its hours of operation. Although admission and parking fees are included, they may not be as accurate because of the time delay between information gathering and publication. Other amenities are listed (gift shops, cafeterias, etc.) as well as accessibility for the physically disabled. A history of the aquarium and its major aquatic displays and programs are given; most feature the resources of the local region. An address, telephone number, and person to contact for further information completes each entry, and an index to aquarium names concludes the book.

This slim volume is recommended for public libraries where people are seeking travel information or for collections that focus on aquatic treasures.

The Birds of North America. v.2. Ed. by Alan F. Poole and Frank B. Gill. American Ornithologists' Union and the Academy of Natural Sciences of Philadelphia, 1900 Ben Franklin Pkwy., Philadelphia, PA 19103-1195, 1993. n.p. bibliog. illus. index. maps. $195/volume; $2,995/set. (ISSN 1061-5466).

598 Birds—North America—Behavior [BKL]

The Birds of South America. v.2: The Suboscine Passerines. By Robert S. Ridgely and Guy Tudor. Univ. of Texas, 1994. 814p. bibliog. illus. indexes. maps. $85 (0-292-77063-4).

598.298 Birds—South America [CIP] 88-20899

Handbook of the Birds of the World. v.1: Ostrich to Ducks. By Josep del Hoyo and others. American Lynx Editions, 2305 Beach Blvd., Ste. 102, Jacksonville, FL 32250, 1992. 696p. bibliog. illus. index. maps. $165 (84-87334-10-5).

598 Birds—Identification [OCLC]

The publishing of bird books has exploded in recent years. Prices vary from under $20 to well over $1,000 for such multivolume sets as Oxford University Press' nine-volume *Handbook of the Birds of Europe, the Middle East, and North Africa* (1977–94). With this wide selection of titles, deciding which to purchase becomes a challenge. Libraries serving serious ornithologists need to decide among several sets.

The three titles in this review each have their own merits. The first, *The Birds of North America*, is a massive project that will take 10 years to complete. It is being published in parts, with one species in each part. There are 40 parts to a volume; there will eventually be 18 volumes covering 720 birds. The species profiles are published in the order in which they are received, so there is no scientific logic to the grouping of the accounts in volumes. A cumulative index accompanies each volume, listing both common and scientific names. The Board saw volume 2, parts 41–80. Volumes 1–3 are currently available; volume 4 will be published later this year. Entries provide comprehensive and authoritative summaries, including distinguishing characteristics, distribution, systematics, migration, habitat, food habits, sounds, behavior, breeding, demography and population, conservation and management, appearance, measurements, and references. The text devotes much attention to breeding aspects of the species. For each bird, there is a detailed distribution map and one color photograph. Although a slipcase to hold the parts comes with each volume, the one with the review volume was already broken. Most librarians will probably want to have the volumes bound, each in two parts so they are manageable. The descriptions are detailed, but providing only one illustration is a disadvantage in an otherwise monumental effort to document all of the birds of North America.

Complementing that set is *The Birds of South America*, which will cover some 3,000 species in four hefty volumes, and which is also being done in association with the Academy of Natural Sciences of Philadelphia. Volume 1, *The Oscine Passerines*, was published in 1989 ($70, 0-292-70756-8); volume 2 was seen by the Board. Each family is given a brief description, followed by more detailed discussions of individual species, providing descriptions, similar species, habitat, behavior, and range, plus a fairly clear distribution map. The colorplates with one illustration per species are all grouped together at the beginning of each volume with the text keyed to the plates. These color paintings are excellent, but having to refer to a separate section for an illustration is somewhat cumbersome. A bibliography is followed by indexes to common and scientific names. Like the other titles here, this is a research source for the professional, not the amateur.

The third series, *Handbook of the Birds of the World*, when finished, will be in 10 large volumes approaching folio size. This project began in 1982 when data about the world's approximately 9,000 bird species were computerized with the help of the International Council for Bird Preservation. Its involvement was intended to bring to the world's attention that some 1,000 of these species are threatened with extinction and another 5,000 are declining in numbers at an alarming rate. One of the main purposes of this set is to analyze the status and conservation of bird species, including those known to be extinct. The set is being compiled in Barcelona, Spain, but all text is in English.

Each chapter is dedicated to a family, with the first part giving a general overview with numerous species examples, including beautiful, crisp, clear photographs of adult birds as they appear in natural habitats. The text covers systematics, morphological aspects, general habits, voice, food and feeding, breeding, relationships with humans, movements, status and conservation, and bibliography. Following this, each species is described, providing vernacular and scientific names, plus other common names, full taxonomic data, subspecies and distribution, habitat, food and feeding, breeding, and movements. Also included is the status of the species: endangered, vulnerable, rare, or indeterminate. Distribution maps and a bibliography are provided as well as a beautiful painted rendition of the adult male. There is an index for each volume. This a magnificent work that, when finished, will be a standard in any major reference collection. Volume 2, *New World Vultures to Guinea Fowl*, is now available ($165, 84-87334-15-6).

Of the three sets, the last has the most beautiful illustrations, and its discussion of the status and conservation of each species is unique. The other two series have excellent species descriptions, and those in *The Birds of North America* are the most detailed, but the relative lack of illustrations may make some hesitate in purchasing them if they are going to buy the *Handbook of the Birds of the World*. Obviously, there are unique pieces of information in each set.

Bird's Eggs. By Michael Walters. Dorling Kindersley, 1994. 256p. illus. index. $29.95 (1-56458-178-0); paper $17.95 (1-56458-175-6).
598.233 Birds—Eggs [CIP] 92-53468

Whales, Dolphins and Porpoises. By Mark Carwardine. Dorling Kindersley, 1995. 256p. illus. index. $29.95 (1-56458-621-9); paper $17.95 (1-56458-620-0).
599.5 Cetacea || Cetacea—Pictorial works || Cetacea—Identification [CIP] 94-33301

Here are the two latest titles in DK's attractive Eyewitness Handbooks series. Other volumes treat rocks and minerals, shells, butterflies and moths, trees, fossils, gemstones, herbs, and various animals.

Bird's Eggs describes the eggs of 500 species. For each bird, one or more eggs are shown in actual size and color. Each entry has a small drawing of the bird and egg in correct proportion. Notes beside the pictures point out specific features, and information is also given about nest building or other breeding activity and the geographic range in which the bird is found. Arrangement is by species, further subdivided by order and family. Both popular and scientific names are given.

Forematter includes essays about the characteristics of eggs, such as shape and color. A cross-section of an egg shows the developing embryo. A list of bird families describes egg characteristic of each. Because the gathering of eggs to satisfy science, or curiosity, is a factor working against the survival of many species, the authors state that no eggs were gathered in the writing of this book and discourage its use as a field guide. Since many widely held general reference books on birds have little information about eggs, many academic and public libraries will find this book a useful supplement.

Whales, Dolphins and Porpoises is also arranged by species. Each entry has a drawing of the animal; drawings of body parts, such as teeth and fins; and a map showing the distribution of the species. Information is given on status, population size, threats to survival, birth and adult weight, and diet. The introduction discusses cetacean behavior and where and how to observe the animals. An identification key helps in distinguishing among various cetaceans. Cetaceans are popular with children, so this volume should be considered by school as well as public and academic libraries.

Foxes, Wolves and Wild Dogs of the World. By David Alderton. Facts On File, 1994. 192p. bibliog. illus. index. $25.95 (0-8160-2954-7).
599.74'442 Foxes || Wolves [CIP] 92-46595

The latest in the Of the World series (*Whales of the World*, etc.), this book's first five chapters describe the physiology, reproduction, and evolution of the Canid family, which includes wolves, foxes, and dogs. The narrative is scholarly but understandable. Each time an animal is mentioned by its popular name, the scientific name follows in parentheses. Measurements are given first in metric, then in British Imperial units. Chapters 6–9 describe individual species by area of territory: Holarctic, including North America and Europe; Africa and the Middle East; Southern Asia and Australia; and South America. The range of a species is illustrated on a map. The narrative then describes the animal's distribution and habits. The text is beautifully illustrated with color photographs, often two on a two-page spread. They are placed appropriately and captioned.

The small type and scientific vocabulary mean this book is not suitable for elementary school children. The photographs represent only half of the species mentioned in the text. There should have been one photograph of each species described. A few of the pictures are blurry. This American edition keeps the original British spelling. There are no charts. Since the authors mention endangered species, conservation, and the CITES Treaty, charts of populations and changes would have been useful. But on the whole, this is an excellent volume and should be considered for purchase by most libraries, though for the circulating collection, rather than reference.

The Quintessential Cat. By Roberta Altman. Macmillan, 1994. 288p. illus. index. $27.50 (0-671-85008-3).
599.74'428 Cats—Encyclopedias [CIP] 94-14095

"After looking through countless cat books on countless shelves, I could find none that was what my fantasy cat book would be. I wanted a cat book that would have it all—from proverbs, superstitions, and fables, to cats in movies, music, and literature, to cat breeds and behavior, and so on." This is not a how-to book of cat care or a work of feline scholarship, but an idiosyncratic and literate collection by an intelligent catlover.

In dictionary format, the book includes short pieces on various professions, including writers and artists. Baker & Taylor appear in the entry *Library Cat Society*, and there is an entry for Switzerland's Katzen Museum. Individuals who have strong cat interests get brief paragraphs that concentrate on their cat relationships. Kingsley Amis' wish to put a cat door into his study is discussed, not his literary reputation. Sidebars are scattered liberally throughout the book. Some are brief quotations: "How neatly a cat sleeps" (Pablo Neruda). Others are longer pieces, full short stories such as Kipling's "The Cat That Walked by Himself." T. S. Eliot's cats are represented, as is Don Marquis' Mehitabel. Felix the Cat, Garfield, and Fritz the Cat are given paragraphs, as is First Cat Socks. The Cat in the Hat doesn't have one, but he is mentioned in essays on children's books and on Dr. Seuss. Cat legend and lore is not confined to the West. Japanese, Chinese, and Native American cat tales, among others, are included.

The book is lavishly illustrated with photographs, line drawings, and reproductions of works of art from ancient Egypt to Andy Warhol. There are appendixes of resources (stores, humane societies, medical assistance, cat-fancy groups, etc.), a bibliography, and lists of artists and authors whose works appear.

Some omissions are noted (e.g., *The Cat Who Went to Paris*), and a few errors (Garfield's unduly cute nemesis is Nermal, not Nermel). Quotations are usually sourced no further than the author, but that is enough for a browsing book. While not an imperative purchase, this book will be useful for casual reference in a public library

Medicine, Health, Technology, Management

Historical First Patents: The First United States Patent for Many Everyday Things. By Travis Brown. Scarecrow, 1994. 224p. illus. $39.50 (0-8108-2898-7).
608.773 Patents—U.S.—History || Inventions—U.S.—History [CIP] 94-14814

Brown, a retired patent examiner from the U.S. Patent and Trademark Office, has compiled an interesting new work on patents. The entries for 84 inventions are arranged alphabetically (e.g., *Frozen Food*, *Glass Bottles*, *Zipper*). A three-page table of contents will assist users in quickly locating a topic. The work begins with a fascinating introduction providing a history of patents, U.S. patent laws, and the U.S. Patent and Trademark Office. Entries range from two to four pages in length and are illustrated with a black-and-white drawing or the specification for the original patent application. Entries give biographical information about the inventor and a history of the invention. Many patent firsts are found within the book, for example, the first colonial American patent, U.S. patent number one, and the first presidential patent (awarded to Abraham Lincoln). A bibliography cites approximately 300 books and articles. A 10-page index includes the names of many famous inventors—Birdseye, Borden, Goodyear, Otis, Tesla, Westinghouse.

A plethora of reference books deal with inventions and patents, but most are massive lists or descriptive essays on hundreds or thousands of inventions. In contrast, this selective book provides unique coverage of topics that should prove useful to students. Because of its organization and unique perspective, Historical First Patents should be considered for acquisition by public and junior and senior high-school libraries.

Historical Inventions on File. By the Diagram Group. Facts On File, 1994. 288p. illus. index. loose-leaf $155 (0-8160-2911-3).

609 Inventions—History || Inventions—Experiments [CIP] 94-7098

The renowned Diagram Group has compiled an interesting new source utilizing the popular On File format (i.e., three-ring binder with heavy bond paper suitable for reproduction), with 65 experiments re-creating famous inventions. The purpose of these re-creations is to assist students in understanding important concepts and innovations in science. Intended for grades 6–12, the work is multidisciplinary in approach, making use of history, science, mathematics, and abstract and applied thinking. It is also multicultural, noting discoveries from Asia and the Middle East. All the experiments have been classroom tested for effectiveness. The experiments are designed to be completed inexpensively by one or two students at home or school. A check determined that approximately 60 percent of the projects require or recommend adult supervision.

The beginning pages on safety procedures are followed by 11 sections. Section 1 is a 15- page chronology of key inventions from 9,000 B.C. to 1991. Inventions are highlighted and a citation number noted if they are included within the text. Sections 2 through 9 cover experiments in various subject fields (e.g., "Construction," "Transportation," "Electricity"). Experiments within these fields are arranged chronologically (e.g., under "Observation": compound microscope, refracting telescope, reflecting telescope). Each subject section has a two-page chronology of inventions in that field from ancient times to the present. Section 10, "Our Findings," is a list of the concepts discovered in each experiment. Section 11 consists of an appendix and index. The appendix lists the experiments by grade levels, the need for adult supervision, home or school setting, numbers of participants, and the amount of time to do the project.

There is a standard format for each experiment. Each has a one-sentence objective; a half-page introduction provides the historical background of the invention and describes key concepts. Next is a statement of time needed to accomplish the project and a list of the materials required. The procedures and analysis sections then go through each step of the project. These sections are well illustrated with line drawings. Also, whenever necessary, formulas needed to calculate results are provided along with examples. A few sections even have data tables to allow the recording of information. Within each project is a safety-procedures box that refers the user to the list of safety procedures in the front of the work and notes hazards (e.g., "be careful with the sharp knife").

Libraries owning similar volumes (e.g., Nature Projects On File [1992], Science Experiments On File [1989], and More Science Experiments On File [1991]) will want to consider acquiring Historical Inventions on File. A check determined approximately 30 percent of the experiments were suitable for grades 6–8 and 70 percent for grades 9–12. This will be a useful source for middle- and high-school students and teachers doing science projects and experiments.

Handbook of Current Health & Medicine. By Bryan Bunch. Gale, 1994. 632p. charts. index. $50 (0-8103-9551-7; ISSN 1078-9707).

610 Medicine, Popular—Handbooks, manuals, etc. || Health—Handbooks, manuals, etc. || Medical care—Handbooks, manuals, etc. [BKL]

This basic overview of major developments in health and medicine during the early 1990s is easy to use and accessible to the layperson. It is similar to a collection of magazine articles that can be browsed. Specific topics can also be located via the index. A convenient source for health care professionals, students, teachers, medical writers, and general readers, the handbook covers 11 broad subjects: "Genetics" ; "Conception, Development and Birth" ; "Childhood Health and Diseases" ; "Wellness" ; "Differing Health Problems for Women and Men" ; "Environment and Health" ; "Mind and Body" ; "Viruses, Bacteria, and Other Parasites" ; "Heart Disease, Cancer, Auto-Immunity, and Other Chronic Conditions" ; "Treatment, from Diagnosis to Surgery and Drugs" ; and "Old Age and Death." Each subject section begins with an article on the state of the field. Background material may be given when necessary to an understanding of the current situation. Articles on topics recently in the news include, "The Return of Tuberculosis," "The Gay Gene," "Cell Transplantation: Fetal Tissue and More," and "Is EMF a Cause of Disease?" Each section has a time line of important events in that field. Statistics and charts help with the presentation of information, as do appendixes listing the elements in the human body, human hormones, Nobel Prize winners for physiology or medicine, Albert Lasker Medical Award winners, and obituaries 1990–93.

The overall picture of health and medicine today given in this book will make it a dependable source. Recommended for public, academic, and high-school libraries. Gale plans biennial volumes.

Statistical Record of Health and Medicine. Ed. by Charity Anne Dorgan. Gale, 1995. 1,218p. charts. index. tables. $99 (0-8103-9745-5; ISSN 1078-6961).

407.3 Health status indicators—U.S. || Public health—U.S.—Statistics || U.S.—Statistics, Medical [OCLC]

More than 900 tables, charts, and graphs from more than 300 government and private sources are provided in this useful reference work. Eleven chapters cover summary indicators, the health status of Americans, lifestyles, health expenditures, health-care programs, workplace health issues, medical professions, the medical establishment, and the health-care industry. There is a chapter on politics, public opinion, and law and also one comparing U.S. health care to that in other countries.

A broad spectrum of information is covered, including statistics on such topics as aging, dental health, alternative medical treatment, biotechnology, telemedicine, medical advertising, and state and local government health expenditures. Under these topics are more specific data such as the comparative costs of different types of dental filling materials, death from bee stings, and organ donors by race and ethnicity. Tables rank the top-10 hospitals in 16 medical specialties.

Format is similar to other titles in the Gale Statistical Record series (e.g., Statistical Record of Children [S 15 94]). Each chapter begins with a headnote explaining its contents. Some data are presented on bar and pie charts. The source of the data is given for each table and chart. The table of contents lists each individual table title. The keyword index can be searched by broad subject area, specialized terms, names, organizations, and facilities. All sources are cited in a bibliographic appendix, and there is a list of abbreviations and acronyms.

Students, health-care practitioners and consumers, and job seekers will find this statistical compilation a useful and accessible information source.

Health Industry QuickSource: A Complete Descriptive Reference to Health Care Information Resources. Ed. by Mary Jeanne Cilurzo. QuickSource Press, 10 Pelham Ave., Nanuet, NY 10954, 1995. 1,023p. paper $225; $180 for libraries in nonprofit institutions (1-886515-08-5; ISSN 1077-9469).

610 Medical care—Bibliography || Public health—Bibliography [BKL] 94-74627

Finding material on the many subjects in the health sciences and related industries can be a formidable task. Trying to choose the appropriate periodicals and databases is not always easy. Health Industry QuickSource is an annual directory of CD-ROMs, online databases, and print periodicals that covers 75 health fields. It includes basic sciences (e.g., cytology and histology, virology); clinical specialties (e.g., internal medicine, podiatry); business (hospital administration, manufacturing); law (regulatory and legal affairs, patents and trademarks); and general reference (statistics, funding sources).

The book is divided into three major sections: CD-ROMs, online databases, and printed periodicals. Each section has two parts: a list of sources and a directory of vendors. There is a detailed subject index subdivided by type of source at the beginning of the book. Entries for databases include vendors, time period covered, frequency of update, hardware requirements for CD-ROMs, features and utilities, contents descriptions, and subject categories. No price information is provided. Entries for periodicals include publisher, address, telephone

Medicine, Health, Technology, Management

and fax numbers, ISSN, subscription prices, frequency of publication, circulation size, advertising contacts, features, description, and subject categories.

Health Industry QuickSource has a broader scope than volume 2 of Gale's *Medical and Health Information Directory* because it includes resources in business and technology as well as health and medicine. Gale includes newsletters, directories, audiovisual materials, and libraries, which are not in *QuickSource*. The two complement each other. Academic and health-science libraries will probably want both directories for full coverage. Public and business libraries will be able to manage with *QuickSource*.

The Oxford Medical Companion. Ed. by John Walton and others. Oxford, 1995. bibliog. illus. $50 (0-19-262355-9).
610'.3 Medicine—Encyclopedias || Dictionaries, Medical [OCLC] 94-30681

Don't expect this medical companion to be a list of diseases and their treatments. It can best be described as a combination medical dictionary and encyclopedia covering the social as well as the clinical aspects of medicine. The first edition, published in 1986 as *The Oxford Companion to Medicine*, appeared in two volumes. This edition is in one, containing more than 8,000 alphabetically arranged entries.

Entries range in length from one-sentence definitions of medical terms to 182 lengthy articles on broad medical and medically related topics. Articles appear on such subjects as *Doctors in Literature*, *Art and Medicine* (accompanied by a chart of congenital malformations and genetic disorders depicted in paintings), *Medical Education*, *Medicine and Stamp Collecting*, *Aerospace Medicine*, and *Patients, Notable*. These articles are signed and include bibliographies of medical literature.

There are also overviews of areas of medical specialty, such as *Opthamology* and *Neurology*. These summary articles describe the field, trace its history and development, and give a synopsis of the types of conditions the specialist treats. Several articles describe the practice of medicine in the U.S., Europe, Canada, Africa, and Southeast Asia. Line drawings and charts accompany some entries. Nobel prizes for physiology and medicine are given in a useful chart. Appendixes list medical and professional abbreviations.

The British origin of the book is evident in the list of contributors, the British spelling of words, and the focus on British medicine and medical practice. This focus is balanced somewhat by comparisons with the U.S. in many of the articles. The long articles are readable and easily understood by the layperson, but the definitions of medical terms use clinical language that demands specialized knowledge. For example, the definition of *Bowman's capsule* reads "the glomerular capsule compromising a dilatation of each renal tubule at its commencement surrounding the glomerulus."

Definitions are cross-referenced using *see* and *see also*. Asterisks before a word indicate internal cross-references. This placement of the asterisk can be disconcerting to the reader's eye, especially in a five-line definition with five asterisks.

There is much that is of interest here for the browsing reader, students, and medical practitioners, but this work in no way should be viewed as a replacement for standard medical dictionaries and encyclopedias.

Introduction to Reference Sources in the Health Sciences. 3d ed. By Fred W. Roper and Jo Anne Boorkman. Medical Library Association and Scarecrow, 1994. 301p. bibliog. index. $35 (0-8108-2889-8).
610'.72 Reference books—Medicine—Bibliography || Medicine—Bibliography || Medicine—Information services [CIP] 94-10707

It has been 10 years since the publication of the last edition of this work. While this edition follows the format of the first two, it brings health-science reference work into the age of technology. New users of this guide will find more than the title indicates. Basic tools are listed and described, but in addition, instruction in reference delivery and collection development is provided. The book is divided into three parts: reference collection, bibliographic sources, and information sources.

The reference-collection section is an in-depth discussion of the organization and management of a health-science reference collection. Topics covered include categories of reference tools, their selection and evaluation, collection development, and weeding policies. Part 2 is a guide to bibliographic sources. The six chapters cover monographs, periodicals, indexing and abstracting services, electronic bibliographic databases, government documents and technical reports, and conferences, reviews, and translations. The features of each electronic database are described as well as how it relates to print sources and how each functions in the reference setting. In addition, the databases are compared with one another in terms of scope, coverage, indexing, and search protocol.

The information-sources section is composed of chapters covering drug information sources; terminology; statistical, biographical, and historical sources; and tools for accessing grant information. A chapter on audiovisual material has been expanded to include microcomputer and multimedia sources.

This work is an excellent comprehensive introduction to health-sciences reference sources and their use. The description of sources, how they are used, and how they compare with one another provide valuable information to library-school students and health-sciences librarians. Librarians in public and academic libraries should also consider purchase for use in collection development and reference training.

Peterson's Guide to Nursing Programs: Baccalaureate and Graduate Nursing Education in the U.S. and Canada. Peterson's Guides, 1994. 675p. illus. indexes. tables. paper $21.95 (1-56079-355-4; ISSN 1073-7820).
610.73 Nursing—Directories || Nursing schools [OCLC]

Compiled with the cooperation of the American Association of Colleges of Nursing, this guide includes an array of information, starting with a series of essays on the future of the profession, selecting a nursing program, the international nursing student, and paying for nursing school. The major part of the work is a profile of nursing programs, arranged geographically by state or province. In typical Peterson's format, each profile has information on the school, programs offered, contacts, expenses, financial aid, and enrollment. More than 1,500 bachelor's, master's, doctoral, and continuing-education programs at more than 600 colleges are covered. The second half of the book contains in-depth profiles submitted by some of the institutions.

Three indexes aid access. The first, "Concentrations within Master's Degree Programs," lists schools by specific areas of study available. The second is an index of programs by degree level. The last is an index by institution name.

Peterson has a long history of compiling useful directories for higher education, and this volume meets its standard. It will be an asset in libraries of community colleges, secondary schools, and counseling centers, as well as public libraries. Libraries will continue to rely on other directories for information on associate-degree-level nursing training.

The Body Atlas. Rev. ed. By Mark Crocker. Oxford, 1994. 64p. charts. illus. index. $16.95 (0-19-520963-X).
612 Human physiology—Atlases—Juvenile literature [CIP] 92-11313

The Children's Atlas of the Human Body: Actual Size Bones, Muscles, and Organs in Full Color. By Richard Walker. Millbrook, 1994. 63p. illus. index. $18.90 (1-56294-496-7).
611 Human anatomy—Atlases—Juvenile literature [CIP] 93-41527

The Body Atlas uses color drawings to show the various systems of the human body. It uses a country as a metaphor for the body; *The Children's Atlas* (below) uses a town. Chapters in *The Body Atlas* are organized by systems: digestive, transport (circulatory, respiratory, and immune), musculoskeletal, nervous, and reproductive. Inserts and sidebar articles add interest; for example, one shows the relative lifetimes of various types of cells. "Body Facts" answers such common questions of children as What are freckles? Not to be confused with Steve Parker's *Body Atlas: A Pictorial Guide to the Human Body* (Dorling Kindersley, 1993), this is the first edition of this work to be published in the U.S. It is appropriate for collections supporting upper-elementary-school students and up.

The Children's Atlas of the Human Body features color photographs and drawings (some of them life-size) of the major components of the human body. Six sections consider bones, muscles, and organs that are involved in supporting and moving, circulation and breathing, food processing and waste disposal, and sensing and understanding. A final chapter, called "Lifeline," deals with reproduction.

The text is straightforward and nontechnical and includes basic biological information as well as more trivial details. For example, the two-page spread on blood first describes the basic functions and components of blood; a sidebar states that the average adult body contains a blood volume that would fill 15 soft drink cans. The text is

Medicine, Health, Technology, Management

basic enough that this atlas could be used with lower elementary students, who could access it independently beginning in grade 4. A life-size anatomy chart of an adult is included in a pocket at the back of the book; it should be laminated to be used as a teaching resource. This atlas is especially suited to elementary- and middle-school collections, but will appeal to older students and adults as well. Its attractive photographs and (often) life-size drawings of organs make it a first choice.

Both these books have glossaries and indexes to aid research. They join other juvenile reference works such as *The Human Body* (Viking, 1983) and *The Book of the Body: The Way Things Work* (Simon & Schuster, 1973) that intrigue children and adults who wonder about the basic workings of our bodies.

The Human Body: An Illustrated Guide to Its Structure, Function, and Disorders. Ed. by Charles Clayman. Dorling Kindersley, 1995. 240p. charts. illus. index. $29.95 (1-56458-992-7).

612 Human physiology—Popular works || Human anatomy—Popular works [BKL] 94-37165

This body atlas uses current medical illustration techniques to provide unique views of human anatomical features. Color-enhanced microscope photographs and computer-generated images accompany detailed drawings to illustrate various organs, demonstrate body functions, and depict problems or complications. The introduction explains various types of medical illustration such as computerized tomography, ultrasound, and magnetic resonance imaging. These and other techniques are used throughout the next 12 chapters. The first chapter deals with cells, skin, and epithelium (the outer surface of the body). One page features a six-inch cross-sectional view of one layer of skin next to a greatly magnified photograph of a couple of strands of scalp hair. The next 10 chapters look at various systems (e.g., skeletal, muscular, reproductive). The last chapter, "The Human Life Cycle," considers fetal development, childbirth, growth, aging, and inheritance.

Each section is introduced by a one-page essay and a double-page full-body map showing the location or layout of each system. The rest of the chapter contains a series of pertinent illustrations, accompanied by captions and text. Boxed inserts, charts, and photographs highlight special features ("How Muscles Contract," "Types of Neurons," etc.). Diseases and disorders are also pictured. Treatment options, including more than 30 surgical procedures (hysterectomy, coronary bypass, mastectomy) are depicted, as are some standard medical tests.

The illustrations are clear and easy to comprehend, but the text often employs technical language (a glossary is provided). Although essentially a picture book, this is intended for an adult audience. Both *The Children's Atlas of the Human Body* (Millbrook, 1994) and *The Body Atlas* (Oxford, 1994) are designed to be accessible to children. The array of photographic techniques used to create high-quality illustrations make *The Human Body* a unique visual guide. For both reference and circulating collections in public libraries. Libraries may also be interested in an unrelated CD-ROM from DK, *The Ultimate Human Body: A Multimedia Guide to the Body and How It Works* [BKL F 1 95]. With audio and animation, it is available in Windows and Mac versions for $79.95.

Great Health Hints & Handy Tips: More Than 4,000 Ideas to Help You Look and Feel Your Best. Ed. by Alma E. Guinness. Reader's Digest, 1994. 445p. illus. $28 (0-89577-619-7).

613 Health || Family—Health and hygiene [CIP] 94-10839

This compendium of brief facts on health, safety, and fitness is divided into chapters covering broad subject areas: diet and nutrition, looking your best, your family's well-being, and more. One-to four-page articles within each chapter discuss specific subjects such as stress management, skin care, childproofing the home, and choosing an HMO. The information is presented in list format, recommending specific steps for achieving a goal (e.g., putting nonskid mats both inside and outside bathtubs and showers to reduce falls). Emphasis is on simple, practical information. Charts and color illustrations supplement the text.

The information is current, but the book lacks focus, covering many subjects on a superficial level. One can find first aid tips, advice on composting, step-parenting techniques, and house-cleaning hints. Patrons using the reference collection require more depth than this book provides. Lay medical encyclopedias such as *The Mayo Clinic Family Health Book* (Morrow, 1990) offer better coverage of health topics, while Charles B. Inlander's *Consumer's Medical Desk Reference* (Hyperion, 1995) provides superior information about insurance and medicolegal issues. *Great Health Hints & Handy Tips* is best suited to home libraries or circulating collections. It is not a necessary purchase for reference collections.

Health On File. Facts On File, 1995. n.p. charts. illus. index. loose-leaf $155 (0-8160-2993-8).

613 Health—Charts, diagrams, etc. [CIP] 94-7097

This three-ring binder contains loose-leaf sheets covering a wide variety of health-related topics. The 10 sections, separated by tabbed and labeled dividers, cover physical, mental, social, and environmental health; growth and development; food and nutrition; diseases; substance abuse; consumer health; and accidents and safety. Diseases and disorders and food and nutrition receive the most coverage. While the information in each section is topically related, each entry stands alone as a discrete entity. For example, the mental and emotional health section contains a stress rating scale, an illustrated list of the signs of depression, and a chart describing types of phobias. Other sections give statistics on family size, accidents, cigarette smoking, and HIV cases. There are also illustrations of poisonous plants and the life cycle of the deer tick. The majority of the entries are presented graphically through the use of charts, graphs, drawings, and cartoons. The purpose of the visual format is to provide reproducible materials for use by classroom teachers.

Students looking for an illustration to supplement a research report will find this work useful, but with a price tag of $155, libraries will find it of limited value since most of the information can be found elsewhere.

Encyclopedia of Plague and Pestilence. Ed. by George C. Kohn. Facts On File, 1995. 408p. bibliog. index. $40 (0-8160-2758-7).

614.4'9 Epidemics—History—Encyclopedias [CIP] 94-23135

Disease has decimated populations, defeated armies, and caused great suffering all over the world. The *Encyclopedia of Plague and Pestilence* offers an introduction to the role of disease in world history, with information on major epidemics and their effects on civilization.

The book is arranged alphabetically by the location of the epidemic, e.g., *Afghan Influenza Epidemic of 1918*, *Zanzibar Cholera Epidemic of 1916*. Multiple entries are listed chronologically: *Asiatic Cholera Pandemic of 1846–63*, *Asiatic Cholera Pandemic of 1865–75*. There are some inconsistencies in titles, such as *Plague of Athens*, *Great and Plague of Florence (Black Vomit)*. With the exception of *Black Death*, there are no general entries for diseases. General and geographic indexes facilitate access, and *see also* references direct readers to related articles.

Entries range in length from one paragraph to two pages. They present basic facts about location, date, how and why the epidemic started and spread, the people affected, and its outcome or significance. Clinical and epidemiological information is minimal. The cause, mode of transmission, and symptoms are mentioned in some entries, but not repeated in every article about the same disease. The focus of the book is historical. More than 700 epidemics, ranging from various outbreaks of cholera, smallpox, and typhus to *English Sweating Disease* and the *French Army Syphilis Epidemic of 1494*, are covered. A time line of epidemics supplements the text. Most entries have references for further reading, and there is an extensive bibliography of both classic and contemporary literature.

Although this book lacks the depth of *The Cambridge World History of Human Disease* (1993), it provides a fine introduction to a fascinating subject. The *Encyclopedia of Plague and Pestilence* is a good source for high-school and public libraries.

Physicians GenRx/Merck Manual. CD-ROM. Physicians GenRx, 1111 E. Putnam Ave., Ste. 303, Riverside, CT 06878, 1994– . quarterly. Single user $295; network (5 concurrent) $900, site license (unlimited users) $7,000.

615 Pharmacology—Databases || Symptomatology—Databases [BKL]

This product will be extremely useful for medical and public libraries as well as physicians' offices and clinics. By combining clinical and diagnostic information with pharmacological data, users can discover treatment options for most diseases and conditions.

GenRx/Merck Manual is available for both Macintosh and IBM-compatible computers. It requires a Macintosh running system 6.0.7 or later, 2MB RAM—4MB RAM recommended and required with System 7 operating system—and a hard drive with at least 1 MB free space.

93

IBM or compatible computers must have a 386SX/25Hz or higher processor with MS-DOS 5.0 or higher, 4MB RAM, Windows 3.0 or 3.1 in enhanced mode, a hard disk with at least 2MB free space, and a mouse.

As the name implies, this disc contains the complete text of the 1995 *Physicians GenRx*, a drug guide last reviewed here [RBB Jl 92], and the sixteenth edition of the *Merck Manual*. Other texts are available through the Stat!Ref service for additional fees. Among them are Stein's *Internal Medicine*, William's *Obstetrics*, the *Current Diagnosis and Treatment* series from Appleton & Lange, and the last 10 years of Medline citations. The basic disc includes samples of these so that users can preview the service. It also contains a search tutorial for new users. There is a toll-free helpline available during business hours.

Searching the database is easy. The center of the search screen displays the list of books in the Stat!Ref library. By clicking the mouse, one can select a title or titles to use in a search. After choosing these, one types in the subjects to be searched and clicks on the Search For box. One can refine the search by using the Match Summary, Smart Match, and Precision Control options. Match Summary is similar to a table of contents. It scans the text to find every occurrence of the search statement and lists the number of matches found. Smart Match is similar to an index. A Smart Match search produces a list of specific citations ranked by relevance with the exact chapter and section of the text. Precision Control functions as a combination of Boolean and proximity operators. The scale at the bottom of the screen has five settings. Dragging the mouse to the desired point and clicking will set the control. Low is equivalent to using OR in a search, while the next step up is equivalent to AND. Further steps up the scale require both terms to be within ten words, five words, or adjacent to each other. Once a list of citations is produced, clicking on a specific title will display the full text.

The help screens, accessed by clicking on the ? icon, are easy to understand and quite useful. Other features available from icons include printing, creating bookmarks to highlight selected texts, attaching notes to text sections, viewing the table of contents of a book, and displaying the history of the last 50 searches executed.

The Stat!Ref system is very efficient. One can retrieve the most relevant information on a subject with ease. To quickly obtain drug information, typing in either a generic or brand name will lead to all the information about the product. Clicking on the contents icon will then display the topics available, allowing the searcher to select dosage, interactions, adverse effects, or even "How Supplied—Rated Equivalents" for generic substitution. One can also type in the term *adverse* plus a list of side effects and retrieve a list of drugs that may cause them. Typing *indications* plus a term will locate drugs that might cure a particular symptom. Cost, manufacturer, and HMO formulary information are also available.

Although the CD-ROM *GenRx/Merck Manual* is more expensive than the print sources that it contains, the quarterly updates and flexible search options make it a powerful reference tool. Academic, medical, and hospital/clinic libraries will certainly want to add it to their collections. Large public libraries with sufficient funds and hardware will want to consider it also.

The Handbook of Over-the-Counter Drugs and Pharmacy Products. By Max Leber and others. Celestial Arts, 1994. 464p. bibliog. indexes. paper $14.95 (0-89087-733-5).
615'.1 Drugs, Nonprescription—Popular works || Health products || Consumer education [OCLC] 94-23405

With more drugs becoming available without prescription and more people treating themselves for minor ailments, accurate information about over-the-counter medication is a necessity. This handbook, written by two pharmacists and a physician, offers an overview of this subject.

The book is organized alphabetically by broad topics: diet aides and stimulants, foot care, pain and soreness relievers, etc. Each section contains an introduction explaining the types of drugs available to treat the symptoms in question and instructions for using them safely and effectively. This is followed by discussions of each type of drug and its ingredients. Drugs are listed by generic names with trade names mentioned in the articles. The index lists both trade and generic names. A separate symptom index refers users to appropriate areas within the book. In addition to drug information, the authors cover such devices as blood pressure cuffs, glucometers, and infant home health care products. They also offer brief advice about alcohol interactions with other drugs, drugs and pregnancy, first aid, and poisoning. There is even a section on pet care.

This book offers less detail than *The Complete Drug Reference* (Consumer Reports, annual), but it covers a wider variety of products. It also lacks the color identification section present in *The Complete Drug Reference* and *The Physicians Desk Reference for Non-Prescription Drugs* (Medical Economics, annual). Some of the items in the bibliography are a bit dated, too. Despite these shortcomings, *The Handbook of Over-the-Counter Drugs and Pharmacy Products* is a useful, reasonably priced source that will serve as a good companion to *The Complete Drug Reference*.

The Alternative Health & Medicine Encyclopedia. By James Marti and Andrea Hine. Gale, 1995. 376p. bibliog. index. $49.95 (0-8103-9580-0).
615.5'3 Holistic medicine [CIP] 94-34460

An article in the *New England Journal of Medicine* reported that more than one-third of the American population preferred alternative medical treatments over conventional methods. There is now an Office of Alternative Medicine at the National Institutes of Health. This widespread interest in nontraditional health care has created a need for objective information about disciplines in this field. *The Alternative Health & Medicine Encyclopedia* provides a good introduction to this subject.

With a medical advisory board of well-known experts, including Dana Ullman, Andrew T. Weil, Gary Lindsey, and Yan-Chi Lin, the authors present material on alternative therapies, nutrition, botanical medicines, stress, exercise, and treatments for common ailments. They also discuss alternative treatments for cancer, heart disease, mental illness, and substance abuse. They emphasize patient participation in choosing practitioners and therapies and using alternative methods in conjunction with traditional medicine in the treatment of serious diseases.

Each chapter contains an overview of the subject followed by sections offering more detailed information on the major points. Fact boxes highlight key ideas. Chapters conclude with a summary, bibliography, and referral list of organizations. The last chapter is an interesting discussion of the future of alternative medicine by members of the advisory board. A glossary, general bibliography, and index complete the book.

Although it is less detailed then *Alternative Medicine: The Definitive Guide* [RBB Ap 15 94] and libraries owning that book do not need to purchase this new one, *The Alternative Health & Medicine Encyclopedia* provides current, objective information that will help people make decisions about their health. It is a good choice for most collections.

Consumer Health USA: Essential Information from the Federal Health Network. Ed. by Alan M. Rees. Oryx, 1995. 543p. index. tables. $49.50 (0-89774-889-1).
616 Medicine, Popular || Consumer education [CIP] 94-37594

It is often difficult to locate the vast amount of health information available from federal government agencies. Most of the publications of the National Institutes of Health and the Public Health Service are not indexed in the *Monthly Catalog*. The *NIH Publications List* is not always current, accurate, or complete. Since these valuable sources are useful for patrons seeking medical information, making them accessible is important. *Consumer Health USA* does this.

This new source compiles 151 consumer health-information documents produced by various departments of NIH, the Food and Drug Administration, the Centers for Disease Control, and the Public Health Service. The full text is provided, but space considerations have limited illustrations to only those essential to understanding the text. The documents are arranged in chapters by subject (e.g., AIDS and sexually transmitted diseases, genetic disorders, women's health). Topics include various cancers, unstable angina, depression, and anabolic steroids. The source of the document is listed at the end of the text. Agency addresses and publication numbers are provided for some of the items. *See also* references offer access to related material. Subject and title indexes are followed by appendixes explaining the Physicians Data Query (PDQ) cancer information system and providing directories of health hotlines and state agencies on aging.

Consumer Health USA is an extremely useful source because it offers a great deal of accessible information in one place. The subjects covered are encountered daily in reference work. Small libraries and those without access to depository collections will definitely want to add this book. Patient-education and public library collections will appreciate it too.

Allergies A–Z. By Myron A. Lipkowitz and Tova Navarra. Facts On File, 1994. 352p. bibliog. charts. index. $40 (0-8160-2824-9).
616.97'003 Allergy—Encyclopedias [CIP] 93-33379

Allergies to food, medications, plants, or other environmental agents are very common. Allergies A–Z, written by a physician-pharmacist and a nurse, will answer many questions posed at reference desks about these conditions and the function of the immune system. It is an excellent introduction to a complex subject.

The book begins with a brief chronology of the history of allergy and immunology, noting that the Egyptian pharaoh Menes died from an anaphylactic reaction to a wasp sting in 2640 B.C. The main body of the text is an alphabetical list of entries ranging in length from several lines to several pages. Topics include medical and biological terms (antibody, expectorant); conditions (grocer's itch, polymer fume fever); allergens (ragweed, citrus fruit); treatments and tests (postural drainage, challenge); drugs (diphenhydramine); and important contributors to the field. Major topics such as asthma are covered in a series of entries. Drugs are listed by their generic names with see references from their brand names. Other immunological diseases such as AIDS, diabetes, and lupus are also included. Numerous tables offer diverse information such as lists of trees and weeds that cause hay fever, drugs to avoid if one is sensitive to aspirin, measures for reducing exposure to cat allergens, and the incidence of asthma on the 1984 U.S. Olympic team. Several appendixes list pollens in the U.S. and Canada by region, available radioallergoabsorbant (RAST) allergy tests, professional and lay organizations, and guidelines for camps for children with asthma. A bibliography of medical and lay literature from the 1980s and 1990s and a detailed index complete the text.

Easy to use, reasonably priced, and current, Allergies A–Z is a fine introduction to allergy and immunology. It is a good ready-reference source as well as a starting point for research and will be a good addition to public and consumer-health library collections.

The National Directory of AIDS Care 1994–95: The Authoritative Reference for Health Care Providers, Community Support Systems and Consumers. 5th ed. Ed. by Lori Hullfish and Kathy Wolden. NC Directories; dist. by Gale, 1994. 362p. $125 (0-925133-34-5).
616.979 Acquired Immunodeficiency Syndrome—U.S.—Directories [OCLC]

Now in its fifth edition, The National Directory of AIDS Care has come of age. It is a compact, easy-to-use directory providing information that is most often asked for, although it does not include the many local smaller private agencies. The first section covers national organizations and hotlines, while the second and largest section covers state, county, and local services (listed by state). Section 3 lists federal agencies and programs, and the last section covers clinical trials and research sites. For each entry, the following information may be listed: address, telephone and fax number, contact, and services provided.

For each state a map is included noting cities and towns. However, even with a magnifying glass one can hardly read the names. The layout of entries, however, is pleasing with three columns to a page. Within each state, entries are listed under counties. Within counties, agencies are further broken down by community services, home-health-care, county health departments, medical services, and testing sites. The most useful aspect of this directory is its comprehensive coverage of state, county, and city health departments. The information for these agencies rarely changes from year to year. Unfortunately, many private agencies are omitted. For example, the prominent Howard Brown Health Center in Chicago is listed only in the home-health-care section for Cook County. It does not appear under testing sites, even though it is a major site for HIV testing.

All in all, this is a useful directory that will provide reference departments, health-care centers, and other libraries the referrals that patrons may be looking for. It is not exhaustive in the information provided, but no directory is. Other directories that complement this one include The AIDS Directory [RBB My 15 93] and AIDS Information Sourcebook (3d ed. Oryx, 1991).

The Encyclopedia of Advanced Materials 4v. Ed. by David Bloor and others. Pergamon, 1994. illus. index. $1,600 (0-08-040606-8).
620.1'1 Materials [CIP] 94-18013

Advanced materials are artificially produced materials that have been "fabricated by the use of skill" and "tailored to endow specific properties to meet the requirements of particular applications." Researchers have learned how to manipulate the microstructure of known materials to produce advanced materials that possess unique properties.

Many will wonder why it is necessary to have another expensive encyclopedia on materials when there is the well-respected, comprehensive Encyclopedia of Materials Science and Engineering (MIT, 1986) (EMSE), which is periodically supplemented with new material. Before saying no to a new encyclopedia on this topic, it should be understood that the field of materials science is a fast-developing one. New products and processes are being developed throughout the world. Thus the Encyclopedia of Advanced Materials (EAM), which provides definitions and discussions of the vocabulary of advanced materials. Some of this information can be found in EMSE but in a broader context; EAM provides the more in-depth information needed by the researcher.

The 518 signed articles in the encyclopedia cover such topics as Aerogel Catalysts, Biomedical Polymers, Color in Ceramics, Fast Ion Conduction in Ceramics, Hydrogels, Metal Matrix Composites, Oligomers, Polymer Blends, and Thin-Film Batteries. These well-researched, comprehensive articles are written for those who understand this highly technical field, not for laypersons. There is ample use of photographs, charts, diagrams, and other illustrative matter as well as bibliographies. An extensive cross-referencing system provides both in-text and end-of-text references. To further aid the user, a classified list groups articles under broad subject headings that reflect the structure and hierarchy of the materials field (e.g., Metals Processing and Fabrication, Fundamental Physical Metallurgy, Films and Coatings, etc.). The subject index is an excellent aid, containing some 30,000 indexed terms. An alphabetical list of contributors notes their affiliations and the titles of the articles they wrote.

EAM is an important reference source that will be used in technical, research, and engineering libraries and laboratories, as well as in large academic libraries where the latest information on advanced materials and new technologies in this field is needed. However, if need for this information is marginal, and the Encyclopedia of Materials Science and Engineering is already on the shelf, the Encyclopedia of Advanced Materials may not be a necessary purchase.

Encyclopedic Dictionary of Gears and Gearing. By David W. South and Richard H. Ewert. McGraw-Hill, 1994. 414p. bibliog. illus. tables. $54.50 (0-07-059796-0).
621.8'33 Gearing—Dictionaries [CIP] 94-10985

This highly specialized dictionary is intended for those working in the gearing industry, manufacturing, or engineering design facilities so that standardization in terminology can be maintained. Presented are definitions for materials (copolymer), tools (chuck), and processes (martempering). Computer applications in machine tooling are defined. In addition to gearing terms, acronyms, association names, and personal names are identified. Six appendixes cover the nomenclature for grinding, gaging, hob, gear shaving cutter, milling-cutter, and broaching. Since these are all gear-related, they could just as well have been included in the main part of the dictionary. Also, the Board questions why such terms as time study, combined work, and access time found their way into the dictionary when they have little to do with gears and gearing. All in all, however, this unique dictionary is quite readable, with definitions that are easy to understand and clear drawings as illustrations. It is recommended for engineering and manufacturing libraries as well as university and large public libraries.

The McGraw-Hill Illustrated Encyclopedia of Robotics & Artificial Intelligence. Ed. by Stan Gibilisco. McGraw-Hill, 1994. 420p. illus. index. $40 (0-07-023613-5); paper $24.95 (0-07-023614-3).
629.892'03 Robotics—Encyclopedias || Artificial intelligence—Encyclopedias [CIP] 94-14309

To create computers that exhibit human intelligence and learn and adapt through experience is a goal of those in the field of artificial intelligence, or AI. Conversely, on parallel tracks, scientists have been developing robots that will use this artificial intelligence. From the tests devised by Alan Turing in the 1940s, to today's robots, voice-recognition personal computers, and expert systems, the fields of AI and robotics have become an integral part of our everyday existence.

This encyclopedia attempts to connect these two fields with concise, easy-to-read definitions and illustrations. More than 500 terms, concepts, and important people and corporations in AI and robotics are arranged alphabetically. Each is clearly defined in entries ranging in length from one or two paragraphs to more than two pages. Such terms as Prototype, Nanotechnology, and Joint-Force Sensor are defined in one or two sentences. Broader concepts such as Language, Memory,

Medicine, Health, Technology, Management

Problem Reduction, and *Speech Recognition* have entries of several paragraphs to more than a page.

Some of the other topics covered include *Binocular Robot Vision, Computer Consciousness, Police Robots,* and *Speech Synthesis.* People and corporations discussed include Forrest Carter, Microsoft Corporation, and George Lucas of *Star Wars* fame. Hundreds of black-and-white illustrations help visualize such difficult concepts as *Artificial Stimulus, Biased Search,* and *Dynamic Transducer.* The editor makes liberal use of cross-references to link concepts together. An index provides additional access.

In an attempt to give a broad overview of the fields of AI and robotics, this encyclopedia lacks the detail of larger publications. The *Concise International Encyclopedia of Robotics* (Wiley, 1990) and the two-volume *Encyclopedia of Artificial Intelligence* (2d. ed., Wiley, 1992) offer readers more in-depth scholarly treatment of these topics, but they can be complicated and confusing for the novice. Therefore, libraries not owning these other two works, or those desiring a good overview of two difficult subjects, will want to purchase *The McGraw-Hill Illustrated Encyclopedia.*

Encyclopedia of Agricultural Science. 4v. Ed. by Charles J. Arntzen and Ellen Ritter. Academic, 1994. bibliog. charts. illus. index. maps. tables. $595 (0-12-226670-6).

630'.3 Agriculture—Encyclopedias [CIP] 94-3143

This book fills a niche vacant since the last comprehensive work on this subject, *Bailey's Cyclopedia of American Agriculture,* was published at the beginning of the century. The most recent comparable work is the 1992 McGraw-Hill *Encyclopedia of Science and Technology,* which provides only brief coverage of the field. In format, the work under review is similar to the *Encyclopedia of Earth System Science* (1992) and the *Encyclopedia of Microbiology* (1992), also published by Academic Press.

The editorial advisory board numbers one Nobel laureate (Norman Borlaug) and seven members of the U.S. Academy of Sciences among its 15 members. Both the subjects of the articles and their authors were nominated by this board and other specialists. All completed articles were subject to peer review. The result of this effort is 210 articles averaging 10 pages in length, arranged alphabetically in four volumes. Topics cover animal, plant, range, and soil science; food processing, storage, and distribution; agricultural education and policy; agricultural engineering; biotechnology; pest management; rural sociology; and water resources. A complete table of contents is found at the beginning of each volume. Individual articles contain an outline, a glossary of terms, cross-references, and a bibliography. About 450 tables and 650 black-and-white illustrations are provided. The fourth volume contains a complete list of contributors followed by a detailed subject index (138 pages) and an index that groups together related entries. Appendix A is a list of U.S. colleges and universities offering academic programs in agriculture, while appendix B covers United Nations agriculture and related organizations.

This new encyclopedia was compared with the McGraw-Hill *Encyclopedia of Science and Technology.* For randomly selected articles, 48 percent had either no coverage in McGraw-Hill or coverage was extremely limited. For the remaining 52 percent, McGraw-Hill contained only about one-third the amount of information in the *Encyclopedia of Agricultural Science.* The strength of the *Encyclopedia* rests in its much greater depth. Also, it offers articles of a nature not included in McGraw-Hill, such as *World Hunger and Food Security.* Information in articles and bibliographies tends to be more current, even allowing for differences in date of publication. Entire articles are devoted to such topics of current interest as *Food Irradiation* and *Transgenic Animals.* Minor problems do exist with the set. Searching the subject index for *tea* under its scientific name will produce no result, although searching for *sugarcane* will. Also, the length of articles makes searching the subject index for specific topics a sound strategy. In spite of minor indexing problems, the *Encyclopedia of Agricultural Science* is highly recommended for colleges and universities with agricultural programs as well as large agencies needing agricultural information. Libraries with extensive science reference collections should also consider this set for purchase. Its price will probably make high schools and libraries with minor interest in agriculture continue to refer to McGraw-Hill for brief information.

Agricultural Entomology. By Dennis S. Hill. Timber, 1994. 635p. illus. indexes. $89.95 (0-88192-223-4).

632'.7 Insect pests || Beneficial insects || Plant mites || Agricultural pests [CIP] 91-39244

This new text presents "a global view of the insect groups that are of major significance to human resources." Many other volumes on insects restrict coverage to a single country or region or to the tropics or temperate zones. Adopting a global approach, Hill emphasizes the similarities and important differences among pests of the major continents, thus "bringing attention to insect species that might spread as pests to new geographical areas." The objective of the book is "to look at the Class Insecta (and some Arachnida) systematically and to indicate which are pest species and which are beneficial." The major emphasis is on crop pests, but some veterinary, forestry, ornamental plant, and selected medical pests are included.

Hill brings extensive professional experience to this effort. He has served as professor of crop protection at Alemaya University of Agriculture in Ethiopia and as senior lecturer in entomology at the University of Hong Kong. He is the author of numerous works on insects, including *Agricultural Insect Pests of the Tropics and Their Control* (Cambridge, 1983) and *Pests of Stored Products and Their Control* (CRC, 1990).

Part A includes extensive introductory material on insect distributions, beneficial insects, and insect and mite pests. The main body of the work is part B, an examination of insect groups, life history, and important pest species. Entries describe the insects and note their distribution and the plants they attack. For example, the larvae of *Hydrelli tritici* (wheat leaf miner) mine leaves of wheat in temperate Australia. The user is assisted by a glossary, a lengthy bibliography, indexes of common and scientific names, and a subject index.

Agricultural Entomology is intended for use as a college text for specialized courses and assumes a basic knowledge of entomology. Particular care has been taken to provide detailed drawings and clear photographs in recognition that few students will have the experience of seeing these insects in the field. But *Agricultural Entomology* has reference value beyond classroom use. It is recommended for science collections supporting agricultural practice and research.

Succulents: The Illustrated Dictionary. By Maurizio Sajeva and Mariangela Costanzo. Timber, 1994. 240p. bibliog. illus. $39.95 (0-88192-289-7).

635.955'.03 Succulent plants—Dictionaries [BKL]

Succulents are plants that are able to withstand drought because of their ability to store water. This book is essentially a catalog illustrating varieties from 195 genera. Designed as an identification tool, it should fill the needs of growers and collectors.

The core of the work is the "Illustrated A–Z of Species," which consists of 1,200 sharp, close-up color photographs. Six two-by-three-inch photos per page enable accurate identification and easy searching. The photo captions include descriptions of growth and flowering habits, size, place of origin, alternate name, and CITES (Convention on International Trade in Endangered Species) status.

A brief overview of succulent families and genera opens the work. Appendixes include a bibliography, CITES codes, and the code of conduct for the International Organization for Succulent Plants Study. The checklist of alternate plant names does not include popular names. The elephant foot palm/ponytail palm will need to be located by browsing the photos, as will jade trees and living rocks. Also not included are lists of societies, journals, or suppliers. *Succulents* is descriptive only; it does not provide growing information. As an identification tool, it is superb. For collectors who have encountered dealer's lists that consist primarily of species and varietal names, this catalog will be invaluable in making selections. The collector can leaf through, for example, lithops (16 species), aloe (25 species), or crassula (14 species).

There is no comparable work. *The Wonderful World of Succulents* by Werner Rauh (Smithsonian, 1984, o.p.) describes many species, but most are not pictured. Gordon Rowley's *Illustrated Encyclopedia of Succulents* (Crown, 1978, o.p) has fine photographs but does not approach this illustrated dictionary in scope.

Succulents are a widely collected, diverse group of plants. The appearance of this work will be welcomed by houseplant gardeners and succulent specialists.

Taylor's Master Guide to Gardening. Ed. by Frances Tenenbaum. Houghton, 1994. 611p. bibliog. illus. index. $60 (0-396-64995-1).

635.9 Landscape gardening || Gardening || Landscape plants [CIP] 93-48865

Colorful books on gardening are a joy to browse in addition to being useful sources of information. *Taylor's Master Guide to Gardening* is no exception. With colorful photographs of 1,000 plants and entries for

Medicine, Health, Technology, Management

3,000 species for American gardens, gardeners from novices to professionals will find plenty to interest them. The editors and contributors are well versed in their areas of speciality. The late Norman Taylor was the author of *Encyclopedia of Gardening* (Houghton, 1961) and a series of *Taylor's Guides* on types of plants.

The guide is divided into such sections as "Creating a Garden," "Gallery of Plants," "Encyclopedia of Plants," and "Growing Healthy Plants," ending with "Hardiness Zone Map," "Glossary," and "Further Reading." Information on all aspects of gardening, such as planning, soil evaluation, watering, and fertilizing, are covered in detail with special attention given to regions and conditions that will effect the results. The index is essential in tying the information together. Here the editors matched common names with scientific names to make locating information easier. For example, in the index under *camellia* are listed the varieties by scientific and common name with page numbers referring to the encyclopedia section and photo gallery.

The greatest strength of this work is the attention paid to the six distinct gardening regions of the U.S. Nothing is more disappointing to the beginning gardener than falling in love with a certain type of plant only to find it will not grow in a particular region or in conditions that are dry, shady, sandy, etc. An example of this type of information is a boxed list of "Recommended Hostas." The size, growth patterns, and conditions are outlined for each of the 15 varieties listed.

A number of gardening encyclopedias of different sizes and price ranges are currently available. T*he American Horticultural Society Encyclopedia of Gardening*, edited by Christopher Brickell and Elvin McDonald [RBB N 1 93], is similar in price, size, and content. If gardening is a high-demand area, both works will be useful. *Taylor's Master Guide to Gardening* is a beautiful and informative reference work. It is highly recommended for purchase for public libraries.

The Encyclopedia of the Horse. By Elwyn Hartley Edwards. Dorling Kindersley, 1994. 400p. illus. index. $39.95 (1-56458-614-6).
636.1 Horses—Encyclopedias || Horse breeds—Encyclopedias || Horsemanship—Encyclopedias [CIP] 94-644

Edwards is a noted authority on horses and horsemanship with three other books on this subject to his credit. This beautifully illustrated encyclopedia covers 150 different breeds. More than 1,000 full-color illustrations, maps, photographs, and portraits are included.

The work is divided into 10 parts: the evolution of the horse, domestication, Eastern influences, classical riding, stud farms, ponies, American influences, work horses, war horses, and sporting horses. A glossary with brief explanations of terms used and an index round out the work. The index is a guide to breeds (in italics), people, equipment, geographic locations, etc., within articles and picture captions. Entries are dominated by color portraits of the breed with brief text on development, uses, confirmation, and temperament. Map inserts show the locations where the breed developed. Scattered among the entries for horse breeds are such topical entries as *Police Horses* and *The American Cowboy*.

The work does have some curious omissions. For example, Man o' War is listed, but not Secretariat. Famous pairings such as Alexander the Great and Bucephalus, Napoleon and Marengo, and Wellington and Copenhagen are mentioned, but not Robert E. Lee and Traveler.

Several other horse encyclopedias are still in print, such as the *International Encyclopedia of Horse Breeds* by Jane Kidd (HP, 1986); *The Horse: A Complete Encyclopedia* by Pam Cary (Octopus, 1987); and Hartley's own *Horses* (Dorling Kindersley, 1993). Unless demand is high for information on horses, one of these titles will answer most basic questions. *The Encyclopedia of the Horse* is a beautiful work with outstanding pictures and interesting text. The author's knowledge of horses is apparent in all of the articles. It would be a good purchase for school and public libraries that do not have an illustrated horse encyclopedia.

The Reader's Digest Illustrated Book of Dogs. 2d ed. Ed. by Patricia Sylvester. Reader's Digest, 1994. 384p. illus. index. $27 (0-88850-205-2).
636.7 Dog breeds || Dogs [CIP] 93-9088

Based on a book first published in France, this publication is divided into six major sections. The first considers the history of the domestic dog and its ancestors. Then there is a portion on dog identification by physical characteristics and on classifying breeds. The central section of the volume follows—an alphabetically arranged, well-illustrated catalog of more than 150 dog breeds from affenpinscher to Yorkshire terrier that are recognized by kennel clubs in the U.K., Canada, Australia, South Africa, and Europe. Entries consider each breed's background, development, and physical and temperamental characteristics. This section also includes a discussion of unofficial breeds and consideration of mongrels. The section entitled "You and Your Dog" considers choosing a dog, hygiene, canine psychology, and training. The fifth area discusses a dog's anatomy, physiology, and medical care. The final section has information on international kennel clubs and show criteria and competition. The book concludes with a glossary and an index.

Compared with the 1989 revised edition, the jagdterrier has been dropped and the Jack Russell terrier and shar-pei have been added; the information on the Shetland sheepdog has been shortened. The Jack Russell terrier and shar-pei were listed in the 1989 edition under "Unofficial Breeds"; the former is still not recognized by the American Kennel Club. British spelling continues to be used. Measurements are in metric and imperial. The format and the color drawings and photographs of dogs are attractive.

This easy-to-use reference will be helpful to those deciding on a dog and to dog owners, although those who want to show dogs will need to consult the American Kennel Club's *Complete Dog Book* [RBB O 15 92].

The Book of Food: A Cook's Guide to Over 1,000 Exotic and Everyday Ingredients. By Frances Bissell. Holt, 1994. 275p. illus. index. $40 (0-8050-3006-9).
641 Food || Cookery [CIP] 93-80835

The Great Food Almanac: A Feast of Facts from A–Z. By Irena Chalmers. HarperCollins, 1994. 366p. illus. index. paper $25 (0-00-255233-7).
641.3'00973 Food || Diet || Cookery [CIP] 94-13950

Since Eve Ate Apples: Quotations on Feasting, Fasting & Food from the Beginning. Ed. by March Egerton. Tsunami Press, P.O. Box 80151, Portland, OR 97280-1151, 1994. 319p. index. paper $17.95 (0-9637709-1-8).
641'.013 Food habits—Quotations, maxims, etc. || Gastronomy—Quotations, maxims, etc. || Quotations [BKL]

Of these three fine sources, *The Book of Food* and *Since Eve Ate Apples* are appropriate for reference; *The Great Food Almanac* is a good choice for circulation, but with so much trivia, it will also be useful for reference.

The Book of Food was first published in England in 1989 as *Sainsbury's Book of Food*. Famous chef Alice Waters writes in the introduction that the variety of fresh food has drastically diminished in this country since colonial times. From thousands of varieties of apples 100 years ago, less than 10 are usually available today. This book goes far to illustrate the range of foods we have. Within broad topic areas (eggs, fruits, oils, cheese, etc.), foods are listed alphabetically. The description of each of the more than 1,000 food items is usually a paragraph or two with origin, suggestions for preparation, and often a personal comment. The majority of foods are pictured in color, and entries note the page number for photos. Sidebars and tables include instructions on how to prepare a pomegranate, how to skin and fillet a flat fish, and how to handle meat. A selection of more than 70 pasta shapes has a reminder that the list is not exhaustive, since there are probably more than 200 shapes of pasta with 600 names.

There are very few specifically British references in this American edition. In addition to standard American food, foreign items are included—andouille (French sausage), gjetost (Norwegian goat cheese), matasutake (Japanese mushroom). This book will be an excellent addition to food reference collections. *The Wellness Encyclopedia of Food and Nutrition* [RBB Ja 1 94] is similar but has more nutritional information.

Chalmers, a prolific cookbook author, has compiled an unbelievable number of facts into a coffee-table-size paperback. Each page is an eye-catching delight. Information is arranged alphabetically by topic and covers all aspects of food from *Advertising* to *Zzz-Bedtime Food*, with *Herring*, *Labeling*, *Popcorn*, and *Table Manners* in between. An example of a typical page is the one for *Butter*—three short reprinted articles, a cartoon, three "Did you know?" questions, definitions of butter sauces, two addresses for more information, a hotline number, and a Dutch proverb.

Some recipes are indexed individually and also under the heading *recipes*. Many are from well-known cookbooks or famous people—James

Beard's French-style bread and Hilary Rodham Clinton's cookies. The author suggests that the book should not be read from cover to cover but instead opened to any page and begun. Whatever way this volume is approached, the result will be entertaining, enjoyable, and informative reading. Highly recommended for cookbook collections.

The quotations in *Since Eve Ate Apples* are arranged by subject, which include *Aroma, Cheese, Exercise, Junk Food, Never Eat, Soul Food, Water,* and *Yeast*. Within a subject, quotations are arranged chronologically, with the exception of proverbs, which come last. The author, source, and date are listed for those that are known, and there is an author index. The sources of quotations range from the Bible ("Man doth not live by bread only") to Byron ("Since Eve ate apples, much depends on dinner!") to Sophia Loren ("Everything you see I owe to spaghetti").

There are other books of food quotations, but for cooking collections lacking one, Egerton will fill the bill.

Larousse Encyclopedia of Wine. Ed. by Christopher Foulkes. Larousse, 1994. 607p. charts. illus. index. maps. $40 (2-03-507022-8).
641.2'2 Wine and wine making [BKL] 94-77220

The Oxford Companion to Wine. Ed. by Jancis Robinson. Oxford, 1994. 1,087p. illus. maps. $45 (0-19-866159-2).
641.2'2 Wine and wine making [OCLC] 94-26509

Since the proverb says *in vino veritas*, the least one should expect in reference books treating wine is truth. Both of these references, each with its own strengths, live up to that sober standard.

The *Larousse Encyclopedia of Wine* notes that there are no rules for either making or enjoying wine; however, there are guidelines, developed through centuries of experience and increasingly validated by modern science. Even though more than 100 experts from around the world contributed to the work, they followed editorial guidelines to produce a product that, like a good vintage, offers consistency at the same time it delivers delightful surprises. The main guideline they adhered to is a strong sense of an audience composed of curious but not expert enjoyers of wine. The encyclopedia's first section, covering approximately 100 pages, provides information on choosing wines, keeping wines, mating wines with foods, and serving wine. It also explains the process of turning soil, grapes, and sun into still, sparkling, and fortified wines. Clear color illustrations show how to use a corkscrew, how to decant a wine, how to open a sparkling wine, choosing and caring for glassware, and the processes of wine making. The extensive second section surveys the world's wine-growing regions, from the fabled vineyards of France and other European countries to the Americas, Australia, and smaller industries developing in South Africa, England and Wales, India, China, and Japan. Country profiles describe national wine traditions and laws and describe specific regions. Descriptions of regions note local regulations, identify châteaus' main labels as well as the labels of their "second wines," and briefly describe specific vineyards and characterize their principal products. Coverage of producers is necessarily selective.

A final "reference section" of approximately 20 pages precedes the detailed index. Through comparative checklist tables accompanied by defining annotations, this section explains the information various countries require on bottle labels, growing and production methods, and quality levels. Its vintage charts also make broad recommendations regarding the quality and best regions. The *Larousse Encyclopedia* provides basic information that will enrich any culinary collection.

Although it also covers countries and wine-producing regions, *The Oxford Companion to Wine* is much broader in scope and much different in organization. In customary A-*to*-Z Oxford companion fashion, its 3,000 entries also cover the chemistry of wine making, specific varieties of grapes, agricultural practices, laws, major appellations, descriptive tasting terminology, characteristics of wine, people, customs, commerce, equipment, and even the role of wine in lyric poetry. An international team of experts contributed the articles; those not signed were written by the editor, a knowledgeable columnist for the *Wine Spectator*. Scholarly in tone and depth, many articles conclude with one or more bibliographic references. Country articles survey the national history of viticulture and discuss the effects of geography and climate, contemporary wine-making practices, and the organization of trade. Cross-references to articles on regions, terms, and other topics—either embedded in the text or listed at the end of a section of these country articles—lead to related topics and additional detail. And that is the most significant difference between this and *Larousse*: *Oxford* provides much more detail as it treats wine, not just as an enjoyable drink, but also as an industry, a science, and the subject of a rich and unique history. Even at that, *Oxford* inevitably covers many of the same practical topics (e.g., matching food and wine, corkscrews, decanting) as *Larousse*. However, *Oxford*'s much more sparing use of illustrations and its dispersal of practical information through its alphabetical arrangement make it better suited as a reference source for those with some knowledge than as an introductory how-to guide or aid for selecting wine. *Oxford* provides much more information than the other significant wine dictionary, *The New Frank Schoonmaker Encyclopedia of Wine* (Morrow, 1988). Different in depth and approach to their subject but comparable in quality, *Larousse* and *Oxford* complement one another and provide both enologists and occasional wine drinkers with copious useful information.

The Parents' Resource Almanac: Where to Write, Who to Call, What to Buy, and How to Find Out Everything You Need to Know. By Beth DeFrancis. Bob Adams, 1994. 779p. index. hardcover $39.95 (1-55850-396-X); paper $15 (1-55850-394-3).
649'.1 Parenting—U.S.—Handbooks, manuals, etc. || Parenting—U.S.—Bibliography || Children—Services for—U.S.—Directories || Child rearing—U.S.—Handbooks, manuals, etc. [CIP] 94-15476

This handy reference will be used often by parents and educators to locate products and services related to children. Unlike Starer's *Who to Call* (Morrow, 1992), which includes a great deal of information about specialized topics of childhood, such as special diseases, alternative parenting arrangements, and loss of a child, *The Parents' Resource Almanac* focuses on more mainstream topics, including child development, parenting and grandparenting, children's physical and mental health, leisure and recreation for children, and books and videos for children.

Each chapter lists free and inexpensive materials, books, periodicals, associations, businesses, computer software, radio programs, videotapes, and mail-order catalogs related to the chapter topic. Appendixes provide informative annotations and addresses for companies and publishers mentioned in the main text, and list U.S. government bookstores, youth orchestras, children's museums and science and technology centers, zoos and aquariums, and national forests and parks. A detailed name index concludes the volume; subjects can be found through the table of contents.

This book is mainly a guide to resources; although sidebars provide information on such topics as determining when a child is ready to be left alone or selecting a restaurant for children, this type of information is better found in a book such as Franck and Brownstone's *Parent's Desk Reference* (Prentice Hall, 1991).

Written with the help of many contributors whose professional backgrounds match the chapter subjects, *The Parents' Resource Almanac* will be heavily used in all public libraries and in academic libraries supporting education programs, even those owning the other two titles cited here. It will also be useful as a circulating item.

Sourcebook on Parenting and Child Care. By Kathryn Hammell Carpenter. Oryx, 1995. 269p. bibliog. indexes. tables. paper $35 (0-89774-780-1).
016.649'1 Parenting—Bibliography || Child care—Bibliography [CIP] 94-39012

Aimed at those who require practical information on modern-day parenting, this bibliography provides evaluative annotations of approximately 940 books, journals, and agencies dealing with the topic, published or in existence between 1990 and 1993. Also included are approximately 90 videotapes and tables of statistical data. Separate author, title, and subject indexes conclude the volume.

The book is arranged in seven parts that list general publications on parenting, parenting concerns related to family characteristics (e.g., adoptive families, homosexual parents), parenting for children at specific ages, how children grow and develop, parental responsibilities (e.g., discipline, education), crises (child abuse and substance abuse), and reference tools (including Internet listservs and discussion groups). Within each chapter, resources are listed under the categories of books (popular and professional), journals (popular and professional), and national agencies. Highly recommended resources are indicated with an asterisk.

Carpenter, an academic medical librarian, has put together a helpful first stop for parents seeking information, collection-development librarians working on core collections in the area of parenting, and childcare professionals looking for resources to recommend to clients. The listed resources are on target, except for the occasional odd lapse (e.g., in the chapter on religious training, the only agency listed is the Association of Jewish Family and Children's Agencies), and coverage seems to be even. It should be noted that the videotape listings are not critically evaluated (most of the annotations were taken from publisher's blurbs). This resource will be most helpful in public libraries, alongside such related resources as Starer's *Who to Call* [RBB Je 1 92] and Franck and Brownstone's *Parent's Desk Reference* [RBB Ag 91]. It will also be useful in academic libraries supporting curricula such as education and social services.

American Jobs Abroad. Ed. by Victoria Harlow and Edward W. Knappman. Gale, 1994. 882p. index. $55 (0-8103-8899-5).
650.14 Americans—Employment—Foreign countries || Employment in foreign countries—Handbooks, manuals, etc. [OCLC]

Here is a good source of information for requests from job hunters about overseas opportunites. It lists 814 U.S. firms and government agencies that employ significant numbers of Americans in their out-of-country offices. The preface outlines the process used to survey the employers—American companies, government departments and agencies, and not-for-profit organizations—that provide long-term positions at wages and working conditions comparable to their domestic situations.

The work is divided into seven sections. The first three outline job-hunting strategies and information on moving and living abroad. The core of the book is the listings for companies and organizations and the 110 countries where they have positions. Entries for each company may provide address of head office, CEO, international recruiter, type of business, number of employees in total and overseas, location of overseas offices, job categories, requirements, language requirements, training, benefits, and average overseas posting periods. The country information includes population, number of American residents (if known), language, currency, climate, economy, cost of living, visa information, health care, schools, crime, pros and cons of living there, addresses of embassies in the U.S., and companies/organizations with offices there. The health care paragraph lists such useful information as pollen counts in Toronto (the highest in North America), the safety of drinking water in India, and precautions about fruits and vegetables in Russia. The pros and cons of living in a country are helpful.

The last section of the book is an index by type of occupation using such broad categories as accountants, customer service, finance, marketing, and sales, which refer to specific companies. There are no entries for librarians or information specialists.

This is a good attempt to put together practical information for adventurous job hunters and will be the place to start if one is interested in working in a major Fortune 500–type firm. Recommended for public and academic libraries where job hunters congregate.

Job Hunter's Yellow Pages: The National Directory of Employment Services, 1994–95 Edition. Career Communications, P.O. Box 169, Harleysville, PA 19438, 1994. 624p. paper $59 (1-881587-05-3).
650.14'025 Job hunting—U.S.—Telephone directories || Business enterprises—U.S.—Telephone directories [BKL]

The first half of this directory of more than 15,000 employment-service organizations is an alphabetical listing; the second half, a listing by state.

All entries consist of company or organization name, address, and phone number. About 95 percent of the entries include a contact name; about 5 percent, a fax number. For each entry, one of the following industry classifications is assigned: career and vocational service, employee-leasing service, employment agency, employment-training service, executive-search consultant, outplacement consultant, résumé service, or temporary-help contractor.

How does this work compare with the phone company's yellow pages? First of all, having the contact name can be a real boon. Also, readers interested in jobs in another city can check listings nationwide. On the down side, state listings are not subarranged by city. Thus, for example, to find the one service listed for Westminster, Maryland, one must scan the 219 entries under Maryland. A local phone book will provide a much more comprehensive list, under various headings beginning with the word *Employment*, as well as under the headings *Career & Vocational Counseling*, *Résumé Service*, and (for major cities) *Executive Search Consultants*. Again using the Westminster, Maryland comparison, there are 17 different employment services in the phone company's yellow pages, but the one listing from *Job Hunter's Yellow Pages* does not appear.

For the contact names alone, this work has some value. However, given the shortcomings noted above, it is a secondary purchase for libraries serving job hunters.

The Job Seeker's Guide to Socially Responsible Companies. Ed. by Katherine Jankowski. Gale, 1995. 927p. indexes. tables. $59.95 (0-8103-2294-3).
650.14 Job hunting—U.S.—Directories || Social responsibility of business—U.S.—Directories [OCLC] 95-137447

This book brings together information on more than 1,000 successful public and private companies from more than 700 industries, selected on the basis of "social responsibility." The editors have judged the success of a company not only on the basis of financial gains, but also on whether the company has had a positive impact on employees, customers, and the community at large.

The guide contains a geographic index, industry index (organized by four-digit SIC), and a master index of companies. However, what sets this directory apart is the "Socially Responsible Indicator Index"—designed to identify companies by the criteria or social "screen" that qualified them for inclusion (e.g., community involvement, employee relations, product safety, minority hiring/promotion, concern for the environment). These broader categories are broken down into such specific ones as *Employee Matching Gift Program*, *Recycling Program in Place*, and *Smoke-Free Environment*. Additional information is drawn from the Domini Social 400 Index, which monitors the performance of 400 corporations that pass multiple, broad-based social screens. Each entry includes a brief description of the firm and its history, the number of employees, very brief financial information, the company's mission statement (where available), a paragraph describing "socially responsible activities," benefits of employment, job application procedures, names of officers, and other significant contacts with addresses and telephone numbers.

This book appears at a timely moment. *Rating America's Corporate Conscience*, published by the Council on Economic Profiles (Addison-Wesley, 1986), evaluates only 130 corporations and has not been updated. *Companies That Care* (Simon & Schuster, 1991) concentrate on 124 companies that are "family-friendly" to employees. *Companies with a Conscience* (Birch Lane, 1992) contains information on only 12 firms. No directory of this nature is comprehensive and accurate to the minute. Names of human resource contacts may change, and it is likely that some readers may disagree with how the editors have defined social responsibility. Nonetheless, the *Job-Seekers Guide to Socially Responsible Companies* brings together a significant amount of information that would otherwise be difficult and time-consuming to assemble. It will prove useful for both job seekers and interested investors. Recommended for academic and public libraries.

Peterson's Internships 1995: Over 35,000 Opportunities to Get an Edge in Today's Competitive Job Market. 15th ed. Peterson's, 1994. 432p. $29.95 (1-56079-406-2; ISSN 0272-5460).
658.3'1243 Internship programs—U.S.—Directories || Employees, Training of—U.S.—Directories [BKL]

Looking for an internship in public television in Kansas? Perhaps interning with an organization that promotes hiking in the Green Mountains is more in line with your career goals. At one time or another, all reference librarians have assisted patrons in their navigation of the "internship path."

The fifteenth edition of this directory promises to help students in many fields of endeavor broaden their base of experience. More than 35,000 internship opportunities across the U.S. and abroad are listed by such broad subjects as business and technology; communications; environmental organizations and parks; and research organizations. Each of these areas is then further divided into more specific fields-of-interest—under human services, for example, internships are listed under education, health services, and social services. Profiles contain the following information: internships available, benefits, eligibility, and contact. A field-of-interest index, geographic index, and employer index complete the book. The field-of-interest index is new to this edition. The geographic index contains entries for only the U.S.; however, some of the internships are based overseas.

The competition includes *The National Directory of Internships* (NDI) [RBB O 15 94], published under the auspices of the National Society for Internships and Experiential Education. One of the reasons the

Business Plans Handbook: A Compilation of Actual Business Plans Developed by Small Businesses Throughout North America. Ed. by Kristin Kahrs. Gale, 1995. 649p. bibliog. $99 (0-8103-9222-4).
658.4'012 Small business—Planning || Business planning [OCLC] 94-36046

The lack of good, real-life examples of business plans was the motivation for this book. The business plan is the first document that the individual wishing to start or expand a business must do in order to convince potential investors that the venture is worth financing. This book provides 33 business plans arranged in 25 industry groupings. Industries covered include traditional ones, such as aerospace supplier, car wash, and elder care. There are also a few high-tech companies, such as online consulting and virtual reality. Each is an actual business plan for a company that has succeeded, although names, products, etc., have been changed to protect confidentiality. A typical plan includes statement of purpose, business and industry trends, identification of the market (demographics, demand, competition), marketing strategy (pricing, promotion, growth potential), product and production (process, patents, trademarks, suppliers, equipment needs), personnel (required training, salaries, benefits), and financials (sources of funding, capital-equipment lists, balance sheet, income projections). All of the businesses except two are retail or service companies. A nonprofit venture is also profiled. Each plan differs in length and detail. For instance, the plan for an import shop is six pages, while the one for a retail tobacco and news business runs to 50 pages.

The strength of *Business Plans Handbook* is that it gives real-life examples of business plans; its weakness is that it gives no instructions on the research process involved in writing one. It does provide a state-by-state listing of Small Business Development Centers throughout the U.S., which would prove helpful in the researching and resource phase. Also included is a 150-item bibliography on business planning.

This new source is a worthwhile purchase for public and academic libraries. To increase its usefulness, though, it should be cataloged to reside in the circulating collection near the how-to books on business plans.

Marketing Information: A Professional Reference Guide. 3d ed. By Hiram C. Barksdale and Jack L. Goldstucker. Georgia State Univ., 1995. 473p. indexes. $149.95 (0-88406-260-0; ISSN 0732-7331).
658.8 Marketing—Information services—U.S. || Marketing research—U.S.—Directories || Marketing—Bibliography [OCLC]

Marketing professors Barksdale and Goldstucker of Georgia State University have authored numerous monographs and articles. Originally published in 1982, the first edition of this work was selected in 1984 as an RASD Outstanding Reference Source. As in previous editions, the authors have been assisted by a panel of marketing experts from 21 corporations and universities. A comparison of the first and third editions shows that the book has grown by 102 pages.

This book is divided into two parts. The first is a "Guide to Associations and Organizations" arranged in seven subject areas (e.g., marketing associations, research centers, special libraries). Entries are arranged alphabetically and provide information on staff size, address, telephone and fax numbers, names of key persons, date founded, and a description of the organization. Following are subject and geographic indexes.

Part 2 is a bibliography of more than 4,000 books, periodicals, software, and audiovisual materials organized into 27 subject areas. New to this edition are the sections "Consumer/Buyer Behavior," "Health Care Marketing," "Nonprofit Marketing," and "Services Marketing." A typical section is arranged in the order of bibliographies, directories, general texts, handbooks, magazines and periodicals, and newsletters. Entries include frequency, price, and a descriptive annotation. Following this section is a directory of publishers and a title index divided into sections for books and periodicals. A detailed table of contents at the beginning of the work assists users; within each part and section are also detailed contents pages.

This unique specialized reference will be useful to businesspersons, students, and business librarians. It should be considered for acquisition by academic and public libraries.

CD's, Super Glue, and Salsa: How Everyday Products Are Made. 2v. Ed. by Sharon Rose and Neil Schlager. Gale/UXL, 1995. 288p. illus. index. $34.95 (0-8103-9791-9).
670 Manufacturers—Juvenile literature [CIP] 94-35243

This two-volume set offers information on the manufacturing of 30 common products that are found in the home or part of our popular culture. It is a version of *How Products Are Made* [RBB My 1 94], also edited by Schlager, rewritten for middle schools. The purpose of these essays is to acquaint readers with the complex processes required to manufacture these objects we take for granted. Short paragraphs with simple explanations make this set appropriate for its intended audience. In addition to material about the manufacture and assembly process, background information is offered about the product's development or related products, such as an explanation of bar codes in the *Bar Code Scanner* article.

Entries are arranged alphabetically and contain sections on raw materials, product design and features, byproducts, quality control, and possible future products. A current bibliography for each 1,500-to 2,500-word essay includes titles with copyright dates from the 1980s and 1990s. The material is up-to-date with references to the 1994 California earthquake in the *Seismograph* article. Text is enhanced with black-and-white photographs and line drawings. The well-labeled drawings, with explanatory captions, depict the manufacturing process. The photos, also captioned, are used to illustrate the product's use or history. Some are unnecessary, such as the photo of several tubes of super glue or a woman applying lipstick, while others are fascinating, such as the use of super glue in surgery. In some cases the use of color would have improved the presentation. Some essays are also enriched by the inclusion of boxed and margin notes that provide special-interest facts or statistics about a product. Each volume contains the entire table of contents and subject index for the set.

This work is similar in coverage to such books as Macaulay's *The Way Things Work* (Houghton, 1988). Approximately half of the products covered in this work can also be found in Macaulay, who is cited in the bibliographies. The scope of this new work differs slightly in that it focuses on the manufacturing process. Therefore, school and public libraries will find that the two complement each other.

Fine Arts, Decorative Arts, Music

Adventure Heroes: Legendary Characters from Odysseus to James Bond. By Jeff Rovin. Facts On File, 1994. 314p. bibliog. illus. index. $40 (0-8160-2881-8).
700 Heroes in mass media—Dictionaries [CIP] 93-46603

This guide to fictional characters presents the exploits of individuals who provide inspiration through their examples of courage and determination. Characters endowed with supernatural or superscientific powers are not included, nor are legendary historical figures. This volume features such diverse personalities as *Peer Gynt*, *Sky King*, and the *Mod Squad*.

The approximately 570 entries are arranged alphabetically, either according to the character's first or last name (both Dick Tracy and Dorothy Gale are found in the Ds or by their title (Dr. Richard Kimble, Sergeant Preston). An index is provided and will need to be consulted on a regular basis. The entries range from one paragraph to a couple of pages; some feature black-and-white photographs. Codes indicate various media that have featured each character: comic book, folklore, literature, mythology, motion picture, opera, radio, stage, toy, trading card, television, and video or computer game. Each entry includes the character's first appearance, a biography, and a section of commentary—background information on the evolution of characters, actors who have portrayed them, and related articles.

Several obscure characters not usually found in other sources are included: Ilya Murometz from Russian folklore, cartoon-character Thundarr the Barbarian, and Admiral Fudge, whose comic strip first appeared in 1908. Family histories span various media formats, such as the article on the Cartwrights of Virginia City or the selection on the Hardy Boys. Characters who play supporting roles can be found in main entries: the essay on Captain Jean-Luc Picard includes the entire cast of Star Trek, The New Generation; Huck Finn appears in the entry on Tom Sawyer. Some entries need to be updated. Prince Valiant's biography states that he and Aleta have four children, but the family has grown: Arn, and the twins, Galen and Nathan.

This latest offering joins Rovin's other unique guides, such as The Encyclopedia of Superheroes (Facts On File, 1985), The Encyclopedia of Monsters (Facts On File, 1990), and The Illustrated Encyclopedia of Cartoon Animals (Prentice-Hall, 1991). All of these titles feature easy-to-read text and attractive formats and appeal to researchers and browsers from upper elementary school through adults. Not comprehensive (the Virginian is included, but not Shane; Tin Tin, but not Mr. Magoo; the A-Team, but not the Rat Patrol) but thoroughly entertaining, this book will be welcome in libraries where there is an audience for his earlier works.

Peterson's Professional Degree Programs in the Visual and Performing Arts, 1995. Peterson's, 1994. 555p. index. tables. paper $21.95 (1-56079-281-7; ISSN 1073-2020).
700'.0711 Performing arts—Study and teaching (Higher)—U.S.—Directories || Art—Study and teaching (Higher)—U.S.—Directories [BKL]

This new directory from Peterson's will be a welcome addition to college-guide collections. Organized in four main sections—art, music, theater, and dance—it profiles more than 900 accredited U.S. and Canadian colleges and universities, music conservatories, and art/design schools that offer performance-oriented undergraduate professional degrees. Entries begin with factual data: enrollment, degrees offered and majors, student and faculty profiles, student groups, special housing, tuition and fees, financial aid restricted to arts students, and application and contact information. Following many entries is a lengthy "More about the School." Content varies, but the aim appears to be to give prospective students the kind of detail they would gain from a campus visit—philosophy, history, distinguished alumni, descriptions of facilities (practice rooms, individual studios, computer labs), student performance and exhibition opportunities, etc. Each of the four sections is introduced by an admissions officer or administrator of one of the professional schools who provides cogent advice on how students can determine which program is right for them.

Access is enhanced by a "Quick Reference Chart of Programs" arranged by state that displays for each school degrees granted, enrollment, tuition and fees, and page number. An appendix lists "all U.S. and Canadian four-year colleges and universities that offer the Bachelor of Arts or Bachelor of Science degree in addition to or instead of the professional degree programs profiled" in the guide. The list is alphabetical and supplies majors, addresses, phone numbers, and names of contact persons.

Even libraries that provide the Index to Majors, standard college guides, and specialized directories such as those published by the College Art Association should consider adding the inexpensive, readable, and informative Peterson's Professional Degree Programs in the Visual and Performing Arts.

Atlas of Western Art History: Artists, Sites, and Movements from Ancient Greece to the Modern Age. By John Steer and Antony White. Facts On File, 1994. 334p. illus. index. maps. $59.95 (0-8160-2457-X).
700'.22 Art—History—Maps [CIP] 92-11226

Overlapping and backtracking pathways of artistic influence can be confusing to even the most astute art history student. The Atlas of Western Art History introduces a "cartographic approach to western art history" in which "maps explain the historical context of artistic developments, the rise of particular styles, the locations where individual artists worked, and the sites of thousands of important works of art." It is designed to be a "visual companion to narrative histories of art" rather than competing with such standard surveys as H. W. Janson's History of Art. Although the atlas has some shortcomings, it is a visually appealing publication that generally accomplishes its goals. Steer is professor emeritus of art history at London University, and White is professor of art history at the University of Calgary and Columbia University.

The atlas consists of about 150 two-page spreads on specific aspects of art history. Text appears on the left-hand page, with one or more thematic maps on the right. The essays were written by contributors who are listed, without credentials, in the front of the book. They are intended to "provide a general introduction to someone approaching each subject for the first time." Chapters are arranged chronologically from "The Greek World and its Colonies" (from the eighth to the fourth century B.C) to "American Art 1900–1950." They are distributed among five major sections corresponding to the traditional divisions of western art history. Each section begins with an introduction, one or more large colorplates, and several maps establishing the political context of the artistic developments of the period. For example, the three maps in the section "The Medieval World" depict "Byzantine Europe," "The Europe of Charlemagne," and "Europe in the Fourteenth Century." Most of the thematic maps fall into several categories: maps with symbols indicating types of artistic activity, site, or style (e.g., ivory carving, printing press, monastery); maps of cities or regions with locations of individual artists or monuments indicated; and maps with arrows tracing artistic exchange ("Art and Architecture in the Holy Land and its Influence on the West") or routes of materials ("Italian Art: Sources of Stone"). Small locator maps appear at the tops of the pages. The excellent illustrations—200 color and 100 black and white—often present less-familiar monuments rather than the best-known examples of the style or period.

Some chapters are more successful than others. The best are lucid overviews of complex subjects for the nonspecialist. "Cistercian Architecture," for example, provides an excellent introduction to this austere monastic style. The map indicates mother houses, affiliated houses, and outposts far from the order's French origins. Symbols on the map are easy to read, and the color photo of the Abbey Church of Senanque across a field of lavender is striking. The article will make nonspecialists want to learn more about Cistercian architecture. Unfortunately, readers will find no suggestions for further reading. The most successful maps present information that is not easily available graphically and with easily distinguishable colors and symbols. Most city maps ("Trecento Siena," "Venetian Architecture") fit this description, as do those tracing movements of artistic styles. In "Artists' Travels in the 17th Century," for example, an arrow from Naples to Malta represents Caravaggio's journey of 1607–08.

Other chapters will be less clear to the nonspecialist. "Art and Architecture from Constantine to Theodoric" refers to artworks as though the reader should already be familiar with them and without placing them geographically. The article "Early Medieval Ravenna" refers to a "peristyle courtyard," and the article "Viking Art" to "dendochronological studies," without explaining the terms. The use of colors and symbols is also problematic. Many maps use small symbols filled with subtle colors to indicate monuments, dates, or styles. "North Italian Architecture and Sculpture in the 15th and 16th Centuries," for example, uses numbered squares filled with pale yellow and green to indicate major architectural sites. Unfortunately, it is difficult to distinguish the colors. In "Medieval Secular Architecture," so many symbols for dates and types of architecture are clustered around Paris and London that it is difficult to tell which dates go with which types of architecture.

The atlas ends with an index to place names, artists, styles, and movements. Names of artworks are generally not included (e.g., Bear Run, Pennsylvania, is listed in the index, but not Frank Lloyd Wright's Fallingwater, although it is shown on the map and in a photograph). Text references are in regular type, maps in boldface, and illustrations in bold italic type.

The value of this innovative geographic approach to art history and the quality of most of the chapters more than compensate for the awkwardness of some maps and essays. The Atlas of Western Art History is recommended for academic and public libraries.

Timeline of the Arts and Literature. By David Brownstone and Irene Franck. HarperCollins, 1994. 711p. index. $30 (0-06-270069-3).
700'.2 Arts—Chronology [CIP] 93-11603

This chronology includes areas such as painting, fiction, classical and popular music, film, theater, television, sculpture, belles lettres, photography, dance, and architecture. It ranges from prehistory (100,000–5000 B.C.) through 1992. From 1500 A.D. on, information is presented year by year. Coverage is international, with good coverage of Asia and the Middle East.

The basic arrangement of the entries is by date under six main categories: "Literature," "Visual Arts," "Theater and Variety," "Music and Dance," "Film and Broadcasting" (in later years), and "World Events." Entries are concentrated in literature, with approximately equal space provided for the other categories. There are approximately 20,000 entries, running to 50 words at most, with most entries only a brief phrase. For example, entries for Alessandro Manzoni are found on three pages: the first notes the publication of a book of poems; the second the publication of his most significant novel, I *Promessi Sposi*, and the third his death.

A 56-page index helps in locating an entry when the searcher does not know the date. The index is by personal name only; subjects or minor disciplines in the arts do not appear.

Because it focuses only on arts and literature in an international context, *Timelines* is unique in its field. Unfortunately, the lack of a subject index limits the locating of events or places. Wonderful for browsing, this source will find users in both the reference and circulating collections. Recommended for libraries wanting a chronology specifically on the arts.

Dictionary of the Arts. Facts On File, 1994. 564p. tables. $29.95 (0-8160-3205-X).
700'.3 Arts—Dictionaries || Artists—Biography—Dictionaries [CIP] 94-16276

This glossary of terms and personal names for the general reader treats literature and the visual and performing arts, including fashion, design, architecture, and photography. The concisely written entries provide sufficient detail to satisfy most generalist inquirers.

Approximately 6,000 entries range in time from ancient Egypt to the 1990s. Heavily Western in coverage, the slight British emphasis will cause no difficulty. Symbols within entries indicate topics and persons having their own entries. There are no entries for individual works of art, although biographical entries may mention works by title. Approximately 100 biographical entries include a one-or two-sentence quotation by the subject in a sidebar. Probably more useful are the chronological tables listing major developments in various fields (dance, pottery and porcelain, works of Thomas Hardy, Academy Award winners, etc.).

Reminiscent of the Oxford companions in style and format, the *Dictionary of the Arts* is a comprehensive, straightforward reference book that will receive steady use in public, academic, and high-school libraries.

The Art Book: An A–Z of Artists. Phaidon, dist. by Chronicle, 1994. illus. $35 (0-7148-3032-1).
700.92 Artists—Biography—Dictionaries || Art—Dictionaries [OCLC]

Believe it or not—there is a gorgeous art book on the market that is a bargain. Thirty-five dollars brings your library a massive 9 by 11 inches 8 pound tome containing 500 full-page colorplates of typical works of 500 painters and sculptors from medieval to modern times. A line of small type at the bottom of each page provides the artist's name, place and date of birth and death, and documentation on the pictured work: title, date, media, dimensions (in inches and centimeters), and location. In a bar across the top of each page is a discussion of 150–175 words as one would hear from a docent in a gallery. Themes, symbolism, and movements are explained, and the artist is placed in the history of art. These succeed in making art history accessible to neophytes, but there is no tone of condescension. Terms are always defined, and a small icon of a pointing hand refers to contemporaries and artists with similar styles. For example, the Hokusai text explains that he belonged to the "Ukiyo-e (or floating world) school, which concentrated on ordinary things of everyday life . . ." and that he greatly influenced European artists, particularly Edouard Manet and his circle." The entry on Alberto Burri explains his use of ugly material in *Sacco*, and the one on Pieter Claesz explains the theme and symbolism of items in his pictured still life.

The colorplates are supplemented by two spare glossaries of artistic movements (32 of them) and technical terms (18). These helpful features explain terms used in the text; for example, Dada "with its cult of the irrational, was important in preparing the ground for the advent of *Surrealism* in the 1920s." Nothing is taken for granted—the definition of *illumination* reads "the manuscripts made from parchment or vellum (treated animal skin)." The final appendix is a directory of museums and galleries that own the works, organized by country.

In a strict evaluation as a reference work one could fault the lack of criteria for selection. There is no list of artists included except on the dust jacket flaps. But this feast for the eyes with its accessible text can be recommended for most libraries. The striking dust-jacket will attract young people, and the illustrations should interest them.

Adults can consult it to place an artist chronologically and to get an idea of his or her style.

Performing Artists. 3v. Ed. by Molly Severson. Gale/UXL, 1995. 710p. illus. index. $57 (0-8103-9868-0).
700.92 Entertainers—Biography—Juvenile literature [OCLC]

This set in Gale's middle-school imprint is a handy biographical dictionary of performing artists of interest to teens. Each volume begins with an alphabetical list of entries in the set and lists individuals by type of performance: comedy, dance, film and television, and music (some names appear in more than one list). A readers' guide at the front of each volume explains the contents and format, but there is no explanation for the artists chosen or omitted. Each volume ends with an index to the set, which includes references to groups and organizations, titles of works, and other important names that appear in entries but are not entries themselves.

The entries are arranged alphabetically from *Abdul, Paula* to *Winfrey, Oprah*. Birth dates and places and death dates, where applicable, begin the three-to nine-page entries. Most entries include a black-and-white photograph and a quotation from the entertainer. The biographical information focuses on the youth of and early motivational influences on the subjects. Successes and failures are described with an emphasis on rebounding from adversity. Writing is easy to read, and information is current to early 1995. Each entry ends with a bibliography of popular sources.

The personalities profiled represent a wide range of cultures: African American (Queen Latifah, Bobby McFerrin); Asian American (Midori, Yo-Yo Ma); Hispanic (Gloria Estefan, Los Lobos); and a variety of music types: country (Dolly Parton, k.d. Lang); rock (10,000 Maniacs, Beatles); rap (Snoop Doggy Dogg, NWA); pop (Bette Midler, Madonna); and opera (Jessye Norman, Luciano Pavarotti). Old-timers as well as newcomers are profiled: Gene Kelly, Laurence Olivier, Katharine Hepburn, Jim Carrey, Rosanne, Amy Grant.

A quick comparison with *Current Biography* shows 72 percent coverage in CB of the individuals treated here. Small libraries without CB will want to purchase *Performing Artists*.

The Book of Art: A Pictorial Encyclopedia of Painting, Drawing, and Sculpture. 10v. Ed. by Herbert Read and others. Grolier, 1994. illus. $339 (0-7172-7356-3).
709 Art—Dictionaries [OCLC]

This is essentially a reprinting of a standard work first published in 1965. Volume 8, *Modern Art*, has a dozen new biographies of artists of the 1970s and 1980s with reproductions of their works. But most of the set remains unchanged, with biographies of more than 650 European, American, and Asian artists and essays on historical periods and schools of art. The only coverage of African art is in a discussion of its influence on modern sculpture. The more than 4,000 photographs, many of them beautiful colorplates, are the set's best feature. A three-volume version of this title published in 1976 contained all the colorplates but very little text and none of the black-and-white photographs.

Public and high-school libraries that need a heavily illustrated history of art and that don't own an earlier printing of this set will want to consider investing in it. Libraries with a worn copy of *The Book of Art* may want to replace it, but the amount of revision doesn't merit purchase by libraries with a set in good condition. —*Sandy Whiteley*

Dictionary of Contemporary American Artists. 6th ed. By Paul Cummings. St. Martin's, 1994. 786p. bibliog. illus. $85 (0-312-08440-4).
709'.2 [B] Artists—U.S.—Biography || Art, Modern—20th century—U.S. [CIP] 93-46372

Since 1966 the works of artists have been chronicled in this dictionary. More than 900 artists are detailed in this new edition.

The bulk of the volume is composed of the biographies. A new addition is the inclusion of cross-references to earlier editions for artists who have been dropped from this edition. Entry lengths vary from three pages for Jasper Johns to not quite a column for Ben Kamihira. Forty-one artists have been added to this edition and 65 dropped. Of those added, eight were born since 1950. The essays include birth and death dates, education, teaching experience, awards, commissions, exhibitions, and collections holding the artist's works; some include bibliographies. The medium in which the artist works is noted specifically only in the index of artists. About 150 black-and-white illustrations are provided. The dictionary opens with a list of illustrations followed by the index of artists, pronunciation guide, and a key to symbols used in the essays to represent schools and museums. The book closes with a 55-page bibliography, stemming in part from the citations in the essays.

For those libraries owning *Who's Who in American Art* (Bowker, biennial) there is considerable overlap, although that book is limited to living artists and Cummings includes deceased artists as well. His entries for artists like Johns, Guston, and Warhol are considerably longer than any entries in *Who's Who*. *Who's Who in American Art*, while twice as expensive as the dictionary, includes 11,824 artists versus the dictionary's 900. The dictionary is recommended for active public and academic library art collections.

Women Artists: An Historical, Contemporary and Feminist Bibliography. 2d ed. By Sherry Piland. Scarecrow, 1994. 454p. illus. $59.50 (0-8108-2559-7).
016.7'092 Women artists—Bibliography || Feminism and art—Bibliography [CIP] 93-27248

Compiled by one of the compilers of the first edition (1978), the second edition is an expansion of its predecessor. The materials cited remain almost all in English, but the number of artists has been increased from 161 to 185, and additional biographical references are provided for artists carried over from the earlier edition. The chronological range is from late Middle Ages through twentieth-century artists born before 1930, including painters, sculptors, photographers, printmakers, and craftswomen. Architects have been dropped from this edition. In all, 29 artists appear for the first time.

The arrangement is the same as the first edition. Preceding the artist entries is a section on general works (biographical dictionaries, bibliographies, dissertations, etc.) grouped as books (including microfilm and slide sets), periodicals, and catalogs. A majority of the entries have brief descriptive annotations. The main part of the book, which contains entries for individual artists, is divided by century. Under the appropriate century, artists are entered alphabetically, each with a brief biographical sketch preceding the citations of information sources. Most entries list public collections where the artist's work can be seen. A six-page bibliography of books and periodicals on needlepoint follows the entries for individual artists. An insert of black-and-white art reproductions contains some new works.

The second edition of *Women Artists* merits the same comment the Board made about the first edition. It "will be useful in libraries where readers are deeply interested in art history or in feminist studies." Small libraries owning the first edition will have to decide whether acquisition of the second edition is vital to their users.

Encyclopedia of American Architecture. 2d ed. Ed. by Robert T. Packard. McGraw-Hill, 1995. 724p. bibliog. illus. index. $89.95 (0-07-048010-9).
720'.973 Architecture—U.S.—Dictionaries [CIP] 94-13941

Editor Packard was a colleague of the late William Dudley Hunt, editor of the original 1980 edition of this work. The basic format has been retained, a mix of several types of articles: biographies of architects of major historical importance, articles on periods in American architectural history, and survey articles on aspects of architectural practice, building types and elements, kinds of materials, and such related topics as climate and real estate. A major enhancement is the replacement of the black-and-white photographs in the first edition by a superb selection of color photographs by illustration editor Balthazar Korab, a celebrated architectural photographer.

More than 20 new biographies have been added, covering figures who have come to prominence in recent decades (I. M. Pei, Frank Gehry, Richard Meier, Robert Venturi) and historically significant architects such as Alexander Jackson Davis and Julia Morgan, who were missed in the original edition. Other new articles cover such topics as *Health-Care Facilities*; *Lead*; *Patron, Architectural*; and *Building, Vernacular*. A few of the original articles have been renamed as well as updated; *Earthquake Protection*, for instance, has become *Seismic Design*. The article *Environmental Protection* has been carried over unchanged from the 1980 edition, with only the short "Further Reading" list updated. *Computer* is also unchanged except for a new concluding section on recent developments; here, as in some other cases, the "Further Reading" list has been dropped. *Contemporary Architecture* is now defined in the updated and slightly expanded article on the topic as "American work produced after 1970." The article on the history of architecture has been carried over unchanged and remains a superficial overview amounting to little more than lists of noteworthy structures from various periods.

The strength of this encyclopedia continues to be its combination of coverage of American architectural history and styles with attention to practice and to the links with the construction industry, all in nontechnical language aimed at the general reader.

The Illustrated Encyclopedia of Victoriana: A Comprehensive Guide to the Designs, Customs, and Inventions of the Victorian Era. By Nancy Ruhling and John Crosby Freeman. Running Press, 1994. 208p. bibliog. illus. index. $24.95 (1-56138-405-4).
724'.5 Victoriana in interior decoration—Victoriana [OCLC] 93-87457

Described in the introduction as "comprehensive, but by no means complete," this encyclopedia provides an introduction into the social history of an era. Ruhling is a freelance writer for various publications, including *Victorian Homes*, specializing in antiques and historical preservation. Freeman is the author of *Victorian Entertaining* (Running Press, 1989) and a contributing editor for *Victorian Homes*.

The Victorian era's passion for color and exuberant decorating are showcased in more than 210 color photographs of nineteenth-century homes, household objects, and period ephemera along with brief descriptions, discussions of historical perspective, and notes on cultural attitudes. Alphabetically arranged, approximately two to four entries appear on each page. Illustrations do not accompany each entry; none exist for *Lambrequin*, *Bog Oak Jewelry*, *Sewing Bird*, *Chiffonier*, or many others. However, the entry *Tender Bulbs and Tubers* is illustrated by a full page of gladiolus, *Books* by a full-page photograph of two books and some dried flowers, and *Hardy Bulbs* and *Roses* with lovely photographs accompanying each. A three-page bibliography and an index that brings together related entries complete the work.

In *The Encyclopedia of Victoriana*, edited by Harriet Bridgeman and Elizabeth Drury (Macmillan, 1975), noted authorities contributed chapters on categories of antiques from the era. That more comprehensive and scholarly treatment provides a history of the decorative arts in Britain and America with mostly black-and-white illustrations. *The Illustrated Encyclopedia of Victoriana* is colorful and manages to give beginners to Victoriana a peek into the past, but it is more appropriate for the circulating collection.

The Visual Dictionary of American Domestic Architecture. By Rachel Carley. Holt, 1994. 272p. bibliog. illus. index. $40 (0-8050-2646-0).
728'.0973 Architecture, Domestic—U.S.—Dictionaries || Architecture—U.S.—Dictionaries [CIP] 94-20071

This collection of detailed black-and-white drawings of houses and other domestic buildings (barns, garages, gazebos) is presented in 12 chapters arranged chronologically, from Native American dwellings to contemporary trends. Each chapter is introduced by one page of text, and additional comments accompany the illustrations. Each drawing is labeled with the names of various architectural details.

Several examples are provided for each time period. For example, seven drawings reflect Federal-style homes in the chapter on neoclassical styles. The section on prefab housing in the postwar chapter includes traditional kit structures as well as Quonset huts and mobile homes. Some drawings highlight special interior or exterior features: fireplaces, staircases, gates, and so on. A series of inserts called "anatomies" look at basic construction methods: trusses, double-hung sashes, log notching. Floor plans are often provided. One helpful feature is that common usage is included in parenthesis next to technical terms that accompany illustrations; for example, split-wood shingles are also defined as *shakes*, a thatched sun shelter is also identified as a *ramada*.

Intended for architecture students and design professionals, this book could also be used as a resource for secondary school American history units. The first chapter covers Native American dwellings such as Algonquin wigwams, Apache wikiups, Navaho hogans, and Tlingit plank houses, and chapter 8 deals with folk and frontier houses. The index includes all the terms used as labels.

A better choice for public and school collections is the *Eyewitness Visual Dictionary of Buildings* (Dorling Kindersley, 1992), which uses photographs as well as illustrations and spans all sorts of structures from ancient through modern times. Other visual dictionaries, such as the *Macmillan Visual Desk Reference* (1993) and *What's What: A Visual Glossary of the Physical World* (Hammond, 1981), also include sections on architecture that satisfy many browsing and general reference needs. However, as a specialized resource, Carley's unique graphic guide will be a welcome addition to architecture and design collections.

The Bulfinch Illustrated Encyclopedia of Antiques. Ed. by Paul Atterbury and Lars Tharp. Little, Brown/Bulfinch, 1994. 330p. illus. index. $50 (0-8212-2077-2).
745.1 Antiques—Dictionaries [OCLC] 94-75734

Good color photographs of carefully selected items, helpful introductions, a good index, and a pleasing format separate this book from most single-volume guides to antiques. Since most of the photographs are taken from two of the world's premiere auction houses (Christie's and Sotheby's) and contributors are associated with these houses or museums, only antiques of the better sort are pictured and discussed. The encyclopedia includes pottery, porcelain, glass, silver, furniture, oriental wares (carvings, netsuke, cloisonne, etc.), and clocks and watches. All photographs are in color, and single items are displayed so that form and surface features stand out. A most useful feature of the work is provided by three well-thought-out tables. One table enables users to associate geographic areas with periods (colonial, Georgian, federal, neoclassical, art nouveau, etc.) and styles (gothic, baroque, rococo, neoclassical, arts and crafts, art nouveau, and art deco). Geographic areas included are Great Britain and Ireland, U.S., France, northern Europe, China, and Japan. A table of pottery and porcelain illustrates the development of glazes, firing techniques, color, and body. Cabinetmakers and designers are featured in a table associated with the largest section in the book, furniture. There is a helpful glossary.

Users of the pottery section might well reach the erroneous conclusion that most of the creamware produced in the U.K. was ornamented with handcolored illustrations. Transitional furniture is not easily identified in the section devoted to furniture. Pressed glass—America's major contribution to the history of glass manufacturing—receives little attention. However, these are minor problems in a work attempting to introduce readers to the array of quality antiques presently in the marketplace. Unfortunately, the contributors have not included suggestions for further reading. Books and journal articles, as carefully selected as the photographs of quality antiques, would have added to the reference value of this attractive new encyclopedia.

The Oxford Dictionary of Music. 2d ed. By Michael Kennedy. Oxford, 1995. $39.95 (0-19-869162-9).
780'.3 Music—Dictionaries || Music—Bio-bibliography [CIP] 94-4539

Kennedy, a longtime British music critic and author, has updated and expanded his 1985 Oxford Dictionary of Music with more than 1,000 new entries plus revisions (in many cases major) to about four-fifths of the original 11,000 entries. Entries define and identify all facets of music from titles of individual works to performers, orchestras, musical forms, instruments, and composers. Identifications can be as short as one line (*moll*) or as long as four pages (*Mozart*). Much mention is made of debuts in various places and of first performances; almost no note is made of personal lives apart from music. Among new entries are those for performers Cecilia Bartoli, Evelyn Glennie, Hakan Hardenberger, and Bryn Terfel; composers Robert Moran, Andrew Toovey, and Ellen Taaffe Zwilich; and conductor Esa-Pekka Salonen. Many composer entries have added compositions, including such operas and musicals as William Bolcom's 1992 *McTeague*, John Corigliano's *Ghosts of Versailles* (which also has its own entry), and Andrew Lloyd-Webber's *Sunset Boulevard*. *Death of Klinghoffer* and *Einstein on the Beach* also have their own entries. An update to the entry for Paul McCartney includes his 1991 *Liverpool Oratorio*. Many 1990s dates of new compositions, debuts, first performances, and deaths are noted, including those of Copland and Bernstein. Entries for Carreras, Domingo, and Pavarotti are all updated, but no mention is made of the "Three Tenors" concert(s). A few people not included: Nadia Salerno-Sonnenberg, Ofra Harnoy, neither Wynton nor Branford Marsalis, nor Ida or Ani Kavafian. The Beaux Arts Trio entry still includes the names Pressler, Cohen, and Greenhouse even though they have left the group; the Juilliard Quartet entry mentions Robert Mann as the sole original member left while not naming others.

The first edition of this title received an unequivocal endorsement in RBB stating that it was "indispensable to all types of libraries"; this new edition merits the same recommendation.

The Chronicle of Classical Music: An Intimate Diary of the Lives and Music of the Great Composers. By Alan Kendall. Thames and Hudson, 1994. 288p. bibliog. illus. index. $39.95 (0-500-01627-5).
780.922 Composers—Biography || Music—Chronology [OCLC] 94-90046

Classical Music: An Introduction to Classical Music through the Great Composers and Their Masterworks. By John Stanley. Reader's Digest, 1994. 264p. illus. indexes. $35 (0-89577-606-5).
780'.9 Music—History and criticism || Music appreciation [CIP] 94-1931

The Chronicle of Classical Music is a profusely illustrated chronology of Western composers from 1600 to 1994. The year-by-year summary is subdivided into musical "year clusters," which give form to the events. For instance, baroque musical history has 15 clusters of three to ten years each, for example, "1600-04, The Birth of Opera in Italy"; "1605-16, Venice: Musical Capital of the World"; and "1617-23, The Early German Baroque." Each of the clusters includes sidebars giving the reader a context for other world events. The 300 illustrations are in color and black and white. There is no index, but cross-references are provided through the use of four symbols representing key people and key works; documents (letters, diaries, and articles); key places; and issues, events, and themes. Other special features include a glossary of technical musical terms; biographies of star performers of the twentieth century and of composers; and a bibliography.

Another recent sourcebook on this topic is *Classical Music*. Although its arrangement is chronological beginning with the Middle Ages and continuing to the late twentieth century, the book is a classical music listener's companion. Each chapter includes a lengthy introduction to the events and music of the period, but the meat of the text is biographical sketches of the important composers of the age. Each composer's biography notes a recording of a representative piece of music, with the publisher, order number, cast, and summary critique from a *Gramophone* review. (*Gramophone* is a British magazine that for more than 70 years has reviewed classical music recordings.) The selected work is also discussed in the text. The book covers more than 800 years of music and 150 composers. It, too, is heavily illustrated with 400 full-color and black-and-white photographs and artworks. There are two indexes to *Classical Music*: one of composers and the other of subject terms, illustrations, and musical works mentioned.

These chronologies are similar to Charles H. Hall's *Twentieth-Century Musical Chronicle: Events 1900-1988* [RBB D 15 89], a detailed chronicle of music history that is limited to the twentieth century. There are several music dictionaries that are more thorough than these two new titles. However, there is always a need for beautifully illustrated, well-written sources in music history and biography for the circulating collection, which is where these two books belong.

Richard Baker's Companion to Music: A Personal A–Z Guide to Classical Music. By Richard Baker. BBC/Parkwest, 1994. 208p. illus. $26.95 (0-563-36414-9).
780.9034 Music—History [OCLC] 94-16525

Baker's Companion is a straightforward, alphabetically arranged handbook dealing with (mostly) classical music of the Western world. Compiled by a veteran presenter of radio and television programs for the British Broadcasting Company, the content reflects its British origin and the interests of the compiler.

Intended for the layperson interested in classical music, the clearly written brief entries, which cover from Palestrina to the 1990s, include composers, soloists, orchestras, concert halls, famous compositions, musical forms, and instruments. Most entries are 6–10 lines in length, although broad subjects (*Choral Music*, *Jazz*, the *Proms*) receive a two-page spread. Not surprisingly, British names (Elgar, Simon Rattle) are often granted double spreads. There seems to be inconsistency in space allocations. Kiri Te Kanawa rates a two-page spread, while Birgit Nilsson is dismissed with four lines and Joan Sutherland with 28. The two-page spreads are not in exact alphabetical order, and an inexperienced reader may not find the topic sought.

Scattered throughout the text are 16 full-page color photographs as well as approximately 75 small, clear black-and-white illustrations, each adjacent to the appropriate entry. A time chart of the life span of 62 composers concludes the handbook.

Baker's Companion is a reference book for the musical beginner or the concert goer who has little background. More personal in tone and less scholarly than *The New Harvard Dictionary of Music* (1986), *The Norton/*

Grove Concise Encyclopedia of Music (1988), and others, it will be useful in high-school and public library reference departments.

World Music: The Rough Guide. Ed. by Simon Broughton and others. Penguin, 1994. 697p. illus. index. paper $19.95 (1-85828-017-6).
781.62 Music—Dictionaries || Folk music—Dictionaries [OCLC] 94-90549

Popular music is drawing inspiration from literally the four corners of the earth, in turn creating a pool of listeners for the artists of those countries. The *Virgin Directory of World Music* [RBB Ja 1 93] began introducing listeners to them, and now authors of the Rough Guide travel series have expanded on the theme.

Divided into regional chapters and then subregions, the text explores the history of indigenous or traditional music and its current status and permutations. Individual bands and performers are described within the text, and such performers as Mari Boine, a Sami performer, and King Sunny Ad of Nigeria are highlighted in sidebars. Other sidebars cover special instruments such as the Uillean pipes, genres such as Taarab, glossaries of important terms, or lists of festivals. Annotated discographies end each subsection. Some countries not included in the narrative are given space in the discographies (e.g., Denmark).

The text has a breezy conversational flow. Topics covered range from India's movie-music industry to Hungarian and Gypsy music to Klezmer's comeback. Black-and-white photographs, both historic and contemporary, dot the book. The guide's closing information includes a list of the credentials of contributors and an index. There isn't a bibliography, because much of the information was gathered while the contributors traveled, which also accounts for the personal flavor of the entries.

World Music works well to update the smaller *Virgin Directory*, the author of which is also a contributor to the new work. This highly readable book will prove popular in high-school, public, and undergraduate libraries.

Television Theme Recordings: An Illustrated Discography, 1951–1994. By Steve Gelfand. Popular Culture, 1994. 332p. illus. indexes. $55 (1-56075-021-9).
781.5016 Television music—Discography [BKL] 91-61882

While this book will not help the reference librarian who encounters someone humming a few bars of a theme and asking that it be identified, it will prove useful for answering such questions as, What's the title of the theme from *Quick Draw McGraw*? or Did anyone ever record the theme from *Dark Shadows*?

Arranged alphabetically by program title, each entry notes whether the theme was used in other media (radio or film); dates; theme title; composers; performer of the theme; recording format; record title, label, and number; release date; and whether it is instrumental or vocal. Gelfand includes a list of abbreviations in the introduction; it would be useful to have them as running footers. "TV Theme Trivia" and "TV Theme Quizzes" are scattered throughout the book. The introduction includes a brief bibliography of books that "contain information on various aspects of television, music, and recordings supplemental to the material in this volume."

Appendixes list the top-10 most-recorded TV themes; composers of the most number of different recorded themes; themes that have reached the popular-music charts, beginning with "Woody Woodpecker Song" in 1948; original soundtracks and original cast recordings; recordings that have the same title as a theme or program, but that are not from TV shows (for example, the Rodgers and Hart standard "Bewitched"); a list of soundtrack LPs that do not contain the program's themes; themes recorded by a regular cast member; and themes used for spinoffs, revivals, and sequels. Gelfand also offers a basic LP collection for those wishing to begin collecting TV theme recordings. Finally, there is a list of Grammy award winners.

Indexes by composer and by recording artist refer users to the program titles. The recording-artist index contains cross-references; for example, under *Boston Pops Orch* are citations to Arthur Fiedler and John Williams. A third index lists the title of themes and cites the program. For example, the entry "When You Wish upon a Star" cites both *Disneyland* and *The Wonderful World of Disney*.

There are some minor errors. Although an album cover showing a recording of "Hawaiian Eye" is pictured, there is no listing for the program. There is no entry for "Cover Up." However, these are slight problems. *Television Theme Recordings* will be useful in public libraries and academic libraries supporting performing-arts curricula.

The All Music Book of Hit Singles. By Dave McAleer. Miller Freeman, 1994. 431p. charts. illus. indexes. paper $22.95 (0-87930-330-1).
781.64'0973 Popular music—U.S.—Discography || Popular music—Great Britain—Discography || Popular music—U.S.—Chronology || Popular music—Great Britain—Chronology [CIP] 94-11272

In the middle of the night, Slim Whitman's TV ads claim number-one hit songs no one has heard of. With this new book you can check out his sales and see that for the U.K. his claims are true.

The bulk of the book is made up of top-20 charts from 1954 through 1993. Each section opens with an overview of the decade before presenting the charts year by year. U.K. and U.S. monthly charts are given on facing pages for easy comparison. Each listing gives that month's and the previous month's position, title, artist, record label, weeks in the top 20, position in the other country's chart, and initials indicating gold or platinum sales or first or last appearance on the charts. Alongside the charts are sidebars with music trivia, illustrated with black-and-white photographs.

Two indexes allow access by artist and song title. The artist index gives song title and first month it appeared on the charts. Notation is given for shared hits and reissued songs. The title index cross-references the user to the artist index.

The All Music Book of Hit Singles complements rather than competes with Whitburn's *Billboard Book of Top 40 Hits* (5th ed., Watson-Guptill, 1992). McAleer allows easy access by date and covers the hits in the U.K. as well as the U.S. Whitburn covers recordings weekly rather than monthly and looks at the top 40, not just the top 20. At this price, public libraries will want to own both.

All Music Guide to Jazz: The Best CDs, Albums & Tapes. Ed. by Ron Wynn and others. Miller Freeman, 1994. 727p. bibliog. index. paper $22.95 (0-87930-308-5).
781.65'0266 Jazz—Discography || Sound recordings—Reviews [CIP] 94-11273

The *All Music Guide* is "an ongoing database project" consisting of substantive reviews of different kinds of music. The first volume in the series, *The All-Music Guide: The Best CD's, Albums and Tapes* [RBB F 1 93], covered a wide variety of music genres. A second edition of that work will be published in February ($24.95, 0-87930-331-X). This new title focuses on 26 styles of jazz—from boogie woogie and bebop to soul jazz and big band. It consists of biographical sketches of about 1,150 jazz artists and groups and reviews and ratings of their best recordings (more than 9,000 records, tapes, and CDs). The book is edited by Ron Wynn, a well-known jazz freelance writer who wrote many of the entries in the book.

The organization of this volume is very similar to that of the first in the series. Introductory material summarizes the 26 styles of jazz covered in the book and defines important jazz terms. The main body of the book consists of entries arranged by musician. Each contains birth and death dates (if applicable), type(s) of jazz played, a biocritical statement, a chronological list of recordings with record label and number and date, and a signed review written by one of the many jazz critics who contributed to this volume. A symbol before each recording indicates the editor's opinion about its importance: "landmark recording," "essential collection recording," and "first-purchase recording."

"Music maps" that mark the chronological development and use of various jazz instruments are interspersed throughout the book. At the end of the volume, there are several appendixes: a directory of record labels with annotations describing the history and development of each, a listing of producers accompanied by biocritical notes, a descriptive list of clubs where jazz musicians regularly performed, an annotated list of jazz periodicals, a list of mail-order sources for jazz recordings, and an unannotated bibliography. The name index includes musicians who are mentioned within entries for other musicians.

The two weaknesses of the series' first volume are also present here—small print and the lack of detailed discographic information for each recording. Nonetheless, this volume is even more valuable than the first because it exclusively focuses on jazz and because the quality of writing and the intelligence of its criticism are uniformly high. It is, as the editor claims, the "most comprehensive reference on jazz recordings and its performers" in print. The *All Music Guide to Jazz* can be used as a source list to develop a personal collection of recordings or as a beginning resource for research into this intriguing genre of music. It is highly recommended for academic and public libraries.

Fine Arts, Decorative Arts, Music

Building a Classical Music Library. 3d ed. By Bill Parker. Jormax Publications, 407 E. 100th St., Bloomington, MN 55420, 1994. 286p. index. paper $14.95 (0-9641332-0-2).
016.78'0266 Music—Discography ‖ Music appreciation [CIP] 94-36266

Classical Music on CD: The Rough Guide. Ed. by Jonathan Buckley. Rough Guides; dist. by Penguin, 1994. 465p. illus. indexes. paper $19.95 (1-85828-113-X).
781.680266 Compact discs ‖ Music—Discography [BKL]

In this third edition of his *Building a Classical Music Library*, Parker continues to strive to "make the composers come to life as real humans . . . and to recommend recordings that have wide consensus as to their merits." He points out that new recordings come out every year but that "the acknowledged greatest recordings tend to stay in print and to retain their status as classics over a period of many years." Parker lists only compact discs, reasoning that other formats are "nearly extinct or have not yet become widely accepted."

The book contains entries for more than 100 composers, arranged by stylistic period (Middle Ages and Renaissance, baroque, early romantic, mainstream romantic, late romantic, modern), then alphabetically within these categories. Entries begin with a brief assessment of the composer's life and place in music history, followed by selected representative works and recommended recordings of these works. Specialized terms are usually explained in the text as they are used. A listing of public radio stations arranged by state is inserted between the main body of the book and its index. Parker is a former announcer, producer, and commentator for Minnesota Public Radio.

Building a Classical Music Library is one of several similar, unabashedly personal volumes published recently by authors affiliated with public radio. *The NPR Guide to Building a Classical CD Collection* by Ted Libbey (Workman, 1994) features the author's choices arranged by genre. Libbey hosts the "Basic Record Library" segment of National Public Radio's *Performance Today*. Jim Svejda's *The Record Shelf: Guide to Classical CDs and Audiocassettes* (Prima, 1995) is arranged by composer. Svejda hosts "The Record Shelf," a Public Radio International program out of Los Angeles.

Classical Music on CD: The Rough Guide represents a group effort. Written by a team of 12 contributors, it contains listings for more than 400 composers, arranged alphabetically. Following a biographical entry for each composer is a discussion of selected works arranged by genre, with annotated recommendations of recordings. The book includes illustrations, an index by title and genre, and a selective glossary.

These reasonably priced volumes are not intended for the serious collector, who might be better served by a volume such as *Penguin Guide to Compact Discs and Cassettes* by Ivan March (Penguin, 1994), which concentrates in detail upon the various recorded versions of a particular piece and the finer points of performance and audio quality. Rather, they are intended for readers who wish to broaden their knowledge and appreciation of classical music. Libraries that can afford only one may wish to choose *The Rough Guide* for its additional reference value (greater number of entries, chronology of composers, brief biographies of selected artists, a variety of indexes). However, collections that can justify more than one will not regret the purchase of both.

Cash Box Pop Singles Charts, 1950-1993. By Pat Downey and others. Libraries Unlimited, 1994. 526p. index. $55 (1-56308-316-7).
016.78164'0973 Popular music—U.S.—Discography [CIP] 94-30806

Joel Whitburn's Top Pop Singles, 1955-1993. By Joel Whitburn. Record Research, P.O. Box 200, Menomonee Falls, WI 53052-0200, 1994. 892p. $74.95 (0-89820-104-7); paper $64.95 (0-89820-105-5).
016.788912 Popular music—U.S.—Discography ‖ Popular music—U.S.—Statistics [OCLC]

Your Hit Parade & American Top Ten Hits: A Week-by-Week Guide to the Nation's Favorite Music, 1935-1994. 4th ed. By Bruce C. Elrod. Popular Culture, 1994. 655p. illus. indexes. $80 (1-56075-037-5).
782.42164 Popular music—U.S.—Chronology [BKL] 94-68618

The public is fascinated by music charts, and publishers are providing more compilations to choose from. Three new U.S. chart titles join the recent *All Music Book of Hit Singles* [RBB D 1 94], which covers U.S. and British charts.

Cash Box and *Top Pop* (based on *Billboard* charts) are similar in many respects, although based on different charts, so ratings vary. Arranged alphabetically by artist, both give debut and peak position, number of weeks on the chart, and label and record number. Both have title indexes. *Top Pop* includes black-and-white photos, the value of the single as a collectible, gold status, a brief description of the band, and the position in the "Top 500 Artist" list. *Top Pop* closes with a variety of "top" lists. *Top Pop* is different from Whitburn's *Billboard Book of Top 40 Hits* (Watson-Guptil, 1992), but many artists appear in both books, although charting may vary. *Cash Box* goes five years further back in time than *Top Pop*. Neither has date as an access point.

Your Hit Parade is arranged by date and has both name and title indexes. The lists go back to 1935 and end in May 1994. The number of hits given for each week varies from 15 to 7. When *Your Hit Parade* ceases as a chart, the charts are filled in with American Top 10 Hits. The listings for each song do not give peak position or number of weeks on the chart, although a reader could simply follow the chronology to figure those out. Black-and-white photos are scattered throughout, and sidebars include biographical sketches and trivia questions. The performer and title indexes cover the first half of the book with the chart dates as an identification number. The second half of the volume is composed of a variety of charts, including year-by-year charts for top-20 country singles, R & B, rap, alternative, etc. There are gold, platinum, and multiplatinum artist lists. Top-20 albums are listed for pop, classical, gospel, jazz, metal, etc. Lists are also given for such special categories as novelty records and holiday songs.

In prioritizing among these books, *Cash Box* is the least expensive but also offers less information and is based on a charting system less seen by the public. *Top Pop* is similar to Whitburn's *Top 40*, so libraries may not need both. Libraries could also access Billboard data from the *All Music Book* less expensively and with date access. *Your Hit Parade* offers the longest span of time, charts on more varieties of music, and has date access. However, its charts prior to 1958 are less familiar to the public than *Billboard*'s. Any of these books will be helpful in high-school, public, or academic libraries, depending on which will best complement what is already in the collection.

The Comprehensive Country Music Encyclopedia. By the editors of Country Music Magazine. Times, 1994. 688p. illus. $25 (0-8129-2247-6).
781.642'03 Country music—Dictionaries ‖ Country musicians—U.S.—Biography [OCLC] 94-34561

As the song says, "I was country when country wasn't cool." The editors of *Country Music Magazine* have taken the surge in the music's popularity as an opportunity to compile a replacement for their 1974 *Country Music Encyclopedia*. The 680 entries are mainly biographical, but some cover key features of country music history.

The encyclopedia spans country's history from John Carson (born 1868) to such newcomers as Trisha Yearwood. The biographical entries open with birth and death dates and birthplace. The signed profiles discuss some personal details but focus mainly on careers, hit-song albums, influences, etc. They range in length from three-quarters of a column for Tim McGraw to two pages for Buck Owens. Nonsinging performers such as comedian Rod Brasfield and disk jockey Captain Midnight are also covered. There are no cross-references or discographies. Black-and-white photos accent many entries. Some established artists such as Loretta Lynn are given "now" and "then" shots.

Nonbiographical listings run the gamut from places (*Branson, Missouri*) to companies (*Gibson—the instrument maker*), to genres (*Bluegrass*), to radio shows (*Louisiana Hayride*). The encyclopedia does not include a bibliography or an index.

The Comprehensive Country Music Encyclopedia, with its greater breadth of music history, acts as a complement to the recent *New Country Music Encyclopedia* (RBB Mr 15 94), which emphasizes active performers. A good purchase for public, academic, and music libraries.

A Guide to Native American Music Recordings. Comp. by Greg Gombert. Multi Culture Publishing, P.O. Box 2132, Fort Collins, CO 80522, 1994. 134p. index. paper $12.95 (0-9644454-3-3).
781.6'97 Indians of North America—Music—Discography [BKL]

Ever since the invention of the phonograph by Thomas Edison in 1877, anthropologists have been recording Native American music. Advances in technology from the cylinder to the record to the magnetic tape have changed the quality of reproduction and the availability of Indian music. Political activism and social change in the 1970s coupled with the introduction of new instruments and the blending of music from other cultures have changed the sound of some contemporary Native American music.

This nonevaluative, unannotated compilation is the result of two years of graduate work in ethnomusicology by the author and is an attempt to provide access to the rich and diverse field of commercially available music by U.S. and Canadian Native American composers and performers. It is divided into three sections: "Traditional Tribal Music," "Intertribal Music," and "Crossover Music Styles." Each section is arranged by recording company; sometimes the list of recordings under a company is arranged by title (if there are various artists) and sometimes by performer. At any rate, each entry indicates the catalog or order number and format and the date of release, if known. "Crossover Music Styles" divides the recordings into 20 broad categories—adult acoustic, blues, children's, etc.—and then uses the same arrangement as the other two sections, by recording-company name. Most of the recordings seem to be from the late 1960s through 1994, although many entries do not note the date.

The main body of the book is followed by a list of record companies and distributors with addresses and phone numbers. There is also an index to performers, titles, tribal groups, recording companies, and the 20 categories from section 3. The index is helpful, but unfortunately it doesn't ignore articles at the beginning of titles, so if a recording title begins with *the*, it is indexed under that word.

This useful compilation will provide public and academic libraries with collections of Native American materials access to music in cassette or CD formats.

The Guide to Classic Recorded Jazz. By Tom Piazza. Univ. of Iowa, 1995. 391p. index. paper $22.95 (0-87745-489-2).
016.78165'0266 Jazz—Discography || Sound recordings—Reviews [CIP] 94-36373

More than 800 recordings are discussed here "in stylistic and chronological context" in what Piazza claims is "the only book of its scope and purpose to have been written entirely by one author." In that sense it is different from *The Blackwell Guide to Recorded Jazz* [RBB Ja 15 92] and *All Music Guide to Jazz* [RBB D 15 94], both of which have many contributors. By "classic" Piazza means those "recordings that have formed or that exemplify the definitive elements of the jazz style, in as undiluted a form as possible." Thus the vast majority of recordings discussed here date from the 1920s until about 1970, or not long after Miles Davis' *Bitches Brew*, which signalled a new direction for many jazz musicians.

The guide is organized into two main sections—one highlighting ensembles, the other soloists. The ensemble section covers dozens of bands including those of King Oliver, Jelly Roll Morton, Duke Ellington, Benny Goodman, Art Blakey, and Charles Mingus. Players in the soloist section are arranged by instrument—trumpet, reeds, tenor saxophone, and piano. Within each category, one to two dozen instrumentalists are discussed in roughly chronological order. Obviously there is much overlap here, as well as between the ensembles and soloists sections. Vocalists, guitarists, bassists, and other musicians are covered, but access to them must come through the index rather than the detailed table of contents. Compact disc numbers are cited in the text for all but the very few recordings still available only on LP.

Piazza's jazz knowledge seems encyclopedic, and his writing is both informative and lively. Covering roughly the same time period as Leonard Feather's *Encyclopedia of Jazz* (Horizon, 1960), *The Guide to Classic Recorded Jazz* covers fewer artists but in more depth. It is recommended for academic, public, and large high-school libraries. For treatment of jazz fusion and jazz-influenced world music, one should look elsewhere.

A Guide to the Blues: History, Who's Who, Research Sources. By Austin Sonnier. Greenwood, 1994. 268p. bibliog. illus. index. $50 (0-313-28724-4).
781.643'09 Blues (Music)—History and criticism || Blues musicians—Biography [CIP] 93-30773

Combining the history of the blues and information about those who created that history into one volume is the aim of this latest blues entry.

The first six chapters outline the history of the blues. Of particular interest is the explanation of the similarities and differences in the musical scales used in European and African music and the blues. Other chapters focus on such issues as the influence of slavery on the blues, the geography of blues evolution, the classic blues belters, voodoo and New Orleans blues, and the blues from the 1950s on.

Almost 400 performers are profiled in the biographical dictionary, which comprises the second section. Entries range from a few sentences to a full page. They include, when possible, a brief discography, filmography, and bibliography. The essays cover the performer's important works, influences, collaborations, style, and importance. Performers represent a variety of time periods and styles. They include Big Maceo, Alberta Hunter, Albert Collins, Clifton Chenier, Johnny Winter, Etta James, and Bonnie Raitt. A section of black-and-white photos closes out the biographies. A select filmography, bibliography, and discography (arranged by record label) append the book. The book has a good index, although there are also *see* references in both sections.

With so many good blues books published recently, such as Herzhaft's *Encyclopedia of the Blues* [RBB Ja 1 93], which also includes some historical and geographic entries, or Santelli's *Big Book of Blues* [RBB Mr 15 94], Sonnier has some strong competition for the library dollar. His is a well-written book that will be an attractive choice, if a library needs additional material on the blues.

The Literature of Rock III: 1984-1990. 2v. By Frank Hoffmann and B. Lee Cooper. Scarecrow, 1995. 1,021p. index. $99.50 (0-8108-2762-X).
016.78166 Rock music—History and criticism—Bibliography [CIP] 93-36263

Rock Stars/Pop Stars: A Comprehensive Bibliography, 1955-1994. Comp. by Brady J. Leyser. Greenwood, 1994. 302p. indexes. $59.95 (0-313-29422-4).
016.78166'092 Rock musicians—Bibliography || Rock music—Bibliography || Popular music—Bibliography [CIP] 94-28691

Trying to track down an interview with Snooky Larson or find a discography on David Bowie? These two titles are designed to meet just those needs. *Rock Stars* has a focused scope on performers, while *The Literature of Rock* ranges far afield. Neither bibliography is annotated.

The Literature of Rock III updates volumes published in 1981 and 1986. It presents a potpourri of subjects arranged by time period and genre. Included are citations for historic topics, people (both performers and those behind the scenes), record labels, musical genres, etc. The citations are to both books and articles, with the emphasis on articles. Entries range from *Altamont* to *Digital Audio Tape* to *Holly, Buddy* to *Motown*, which means the reader has more to choose from than in *Rock Stars*, with its strictly biographical focus. The lengthy index includes cross-references (e.g., between *Holly, Buddy* and *Crickets, The*). The table of contents is very detailed, but with the odd arrangement of entries, the index is the best point of access.

The more than 3,700 entries in *Rock Stars* are arranged by artist. Artists can appear under individual or band names (e.g., *Bono* and *U2*). There isn't repetition of citations under related entries; *see* references are in the subject index. The compiler provides for each performer a variety of books: biographies, discographies, chronologies, criticism, interviews, and more, arranged under those headings. To have books in all the categories, it helps to be a supergroup like the Beatles. British titles are abundant, and along with some of the older and small-press titles, may be difficult for patrons to locate. Titles range from works for adult audiences to teeny-bopper bios. The number of entries for each group varies widely (e.g., the Beatles—264, the Eagles—1). Besides newer artists, this book gives space to such earlier performers as Muddy Waters, Johnnie Ray, and even Pat Boone. It covers some nonrock performers such as Arlo Guthrie, Holly Near, and Garth Brooks. There are subject, author, and title indexes.

Rock Stars is a good work, particularly for smaller groups and "shooting stars." *The Literature of Rock* III is a diverse collection which could prove especially useful for tracking down articles not indexed elsewhere. The ability to locate some of the titles for patrons will be the only drawback of both books. They should be considered by public libraries with strong contemporary music collections and by music libraries.

Classical Singers of the Opera and Recital Stages: A Bibliography of Biographical Materials. By Robert H. Cowden. Greenwood, 1994. 509p. index. $75 (0-313-29332-5).
016.7821'092 Singers—Biography—Bibliography [CIP] 94-6329

Nearly a decade has passed since the appearance of Cowden's *Concert and Opera Singers: A Bibliography of Biographical Materials* (Greenwood, 1985). Since then, more than 150 additional collective works and related titles have appeared. In this new work, Cowden has heavily reworked and expanded the earlier effort to account for these new titles and, in the process, has once again produced a superb reference tool.

Classical Singers is divided into three major sections. Section 1, "Collective Titles: Books on Singers," lists 157 books devoted entirely or primarily to classical vocalists. Section 2, "Collective Titles: Related Books," includes 283 books with additional material on many of the singers. The main body of the volume is section 3, "Individual Singers," in which bibliographic entries are listed under the names of the singers, who are arranged alphabetically. Here, too, will be found brief factual data about each artist. Appendix 1 ("Additional Artists") includes material uncovered too late in the process to include in the original entry. Appendix 2 is a listing of singers who are accorded an entry in *The New Grove Dictionary of Opera* (Grove Dictionaries, 1992). A master index of authors, compilers, and editors completes the work.

Any discussion of biographical bibliographies of classical vocalists must also note Andrew Farkas' *Opera and Concert Singers: An Annotated International Bibliography of Books and Pamphlets* (Garland, 1985). Farkas provides entries for only 796 singers compared with 1,532 in Cowden. However, Farkas does provide some unique material (lengthy annotations for many of the works he has included, citations to unpublished manuscripts, and an entry for Mme. Blanche Arral, for example). Farkas is still in print, but at the current price ($65) only comprehensive collections need to consider the purchase of Farkas in addition to Cowden.

Cowden's *Classical Singers of the Opera and Recital Stages* is highly recommended for academic libraries and any collections serving music scholars and aficionados of serious vocal music.

The Encyclopedia of the Musical Theatre. 2v. By Kurt Gänzl. Schirmer, 1994. 1,603p. bibliog. illus. $150 (0-02-871445-8).
782.1'4 Musicals—Encyclopedias [CIP] 93-48237

The author of *The British Musical Theatre* (Oxford, 1987) and *Gänzl's Book of the Musical Theatre* (Schirmer, 1989) shares his passion in this international compendium. Here are approximately 2,700 entries for performers, composers, writers, and shows; some producers, directors, choreographers, and designers are included as well. The scope is the text-based musical (no opera, pantomines, or revues) as performed in Britain, Europe, the U.S., Australia, and New Zealand in the nineteenth and twentieth centuries. While the choice of entries is ultimately idiosyncratic, Gänzl sought subjects most widely known internationally. This means there are no entries for such well-known American performers as Stubby Kaye and Robert Alda while many obscure nineteenth-century European performers are covered.

Entries are generally at least two paragraphs in length and can be as long as three pages (e.g., for Richard Rogers, Franz von Suppé) and start with a brief identifier (e.g., "Musical comedy in 2 acts by Harold Atteridge"). For people, basic biographical information is given with lists of the musicals in which they were involved. When available, biographies or autobiographies are listed. Plot summaries and international performance history are given for musicals. Film adaptations are described, and some recordings and books are cited. The 315 black-and-white illustrations include cast shots and covers of playbills and sheet music. The arrangement is alphabetical; cross-references and an index are lacking.

Gänzl's introduction indicates that he collects everything he can find on musicals but also does library and archive research to verify his facts. The writing here is informal and slangy, often in a British vein. For example, the article on Casanova comments "on those allegedly rare occasions when he was not out putting it about."

Other reference books on musical theater are more narrow in scope (Bordman's *American Musical Theater*, 2d ed. [RBB Jl 92]; Stanley Green's *Encyclopedia of the Musical Theater* [Da Capo, 1980]; Swain's *The Broadway Musical* [Oxford, 1990]) and may suffice in many public libraries. *Gänzl's Book of the Musical Theatre* covers 300 shows from seven countries in much greater detail than this encyclopedia. The coverage in this new set is wide, and articles are readable and informative. Although seemingly adequately researched, it is not written in a scholarly style. An index and/or cross-references would have greatly increased access to the information. This is a must for music collections and is worth considering for academic and large public libraries.

Hollywood Song: The Complete Film and Musical Companion. 3v. By Ken Bloom. Facts On File, 1995. 1,504p. indexes. $195 (0-8160-2002-7).
016.7821'4 Motion picture music—Bibliography || Songs, English—U.S.—Indexes [CIP] 90-22261

This comprehensive guide describes 7,000 Hollywood movies for which songs or scores were especially written. It cover all genres, including rock musicals. Many of the films are not musicals but are listed because a theme song was written for them. Some films listed include no songs; for example, a song was written for *Psycho* but the movie was released without it. Not included are most concert films, which do not usually have original music written especially for them. A notable exception is *Woodstock*. Bloom is also the author of a similar book on musical theater, *American Song: The Complete Musical Theatre Companion* (Facts On File, 1985).

Volumes 1 and 2 of this 3-volume work list the films alphabetically by title. Included in each entry is the studio that released the film, year of release, composer, lyricist, choreographer, producer, screenwriter, director, original source on which the film is based, cast (all stars are listed as well as selected character actors and supporting players), and songs. A notes section contains various other information of interest, such as alternative titles, songs that were cut from the picture, songs used instrumentally only, Academy Award winners, etc. Volume 3 lists the films chronologically from 1922 to 1989 (with three titles listed for 1990). It also includes a name index, which notes if the person was a cast member, choreographer, composer, lyricist, etc. A song index enables the reader to find the films for which songs such as "Moon River" (*Breakfast at Tiffany's*) or "The Power of Love" (*Back to the Future*) were written.

Several books cover movie musicals. Parish and Pitts' *Great Hollywood Musical Pictures* [RBB N 1 92], for example, has lengthy descriptions of 340 musicals. The authors note which cast members performed each song, but the book has no song index. *Hollywood Song*, however, has a much broader scope, covering thousands of films that contain at least one song. This valuable and extensive work will be a good purchase for large film and music collections.

Opera Companies and Houses of the United States: A Comprehensive Illustrated Reference. By Karyl Lynn Zietz. McFarland, 1994. 336p. bibliog. illus. index. $49.95 (0-89950-955-X).
782.1'06 Opera companies—U.S.—Directories || Theaters—U.S.—Directories [BKL] 94-943

As interest in opera grows, the number of performing companies and houses has increased throughout the U.S. Fledgling companies in small cities and established giants in major metropolitan areas are among the more than 90 opera houses and companies profiled here.

The work is arranged by state, city, and company name. Entries include a brief history of opera in the city, with information on the inaugural performance; company staff and its repertory with a list of world or American premieres; and practical information on obtaining tickets and suggestions for lodging in the city. The length of entries varies with the size and age of the company. Opera Roanoke, which began in 1976, is covered in a page, while the New Orleans Opera, which can trace its roots to the eighteenth century, has a longer entry. Illustrations of the interior or exterior of the opera house complement many of the entries. The index lists the titles of major operas, composers, and artistic directors, as well as the companies themselves. A bibliography completes the volume.

This work is useful in that it highlights many small opera companies. *Opera Companies of the World* [RBB My 1 92] covers many of the same companies, especially those in major cities, but includes companies in other parts of the world as well. For many collections, that work may be sufficient. For libraries with a strong emphasis on opera, *Opera Companies and Houses of the United States* will supplement existing works by providing information on little-known American companies.

The Viking Opera Guide. Ed. by Amanda Holden and others. Viking, 1993. illus. indexes. $69.95 (0-670-81292-7).
782.1'3 Opera—Stories, plots, etc. [BKL]

The Viking Opera Guide on CD-ROM. Ed. by Amanda Holden. Viking, 1993. $99.95 with the print version (0-14-088319-3).
782.1'3 Opera—Stories, plots, etc. [BKL]

The *Viking Opera Guide* (VOG) is billed as the "most comprehensive single-volume reference work on opera." It contains more than 800 articles on opera composers and descriptions of 1,500 operas, compared with about 100 composers and 300 operas in *The Definitive Kobbé's Opera Book* (1987). First published in 1919, *Kobbé* has been considered the standard collection of opera plots. It is arranged by period, then country, and then chronologically by composer and opera. The articles in VOG are arranged alphabetically by composer and then chronologically by opera.

The entries in VOG begin with a paragraph or two on the composer's life and work. Entries for the major operas of each composer note genre, duration, librettist, source of libretto, and premiere dates (world, British, and U.S. premiere), followed by a plot summary. For major operas, editions, casting, and orchestration are given. At the end of the entry, recordings (the best at press time) and videos (if available) are listed. Lesser-known operas do not have a summary and are listed chronologically at the end of the composer's entry. The initials of the contributor end the entry; a short biography of each is at the back of the book. The contributors' list is impressive, including conductor David Lloyd-Jones; Peter Jonas, the director of the Bavarian State Opera; Nicholas Kenyon, a former music critic of *The New Yorker*; and Patricia Brauner of the Center for Italian Opera Studies at the University of Chicago. There are a number of black-and-white illustrations, including the act one finale from Sondheim's *Sunday in the Park with George*, the title page of the libretto of *Hippolyte et Aricie* by Rameau, and a 1893 *Vanity Fair* cartoon of Mascagni conducting *Cavalleria Rusticana*.

Composers range from Jacopo Peri, born in 1561 and often considered the inventor of opera, to John C. Eaton, a current American composer. Light opera and musical theater composers are also included— W. S. Sullivan, Richard Rogers, and Andrew Lloyd Webber. Excluded is the contemporary American, David Carlson, who wrote *The Midnight Angel*.

Although the title index is comprehensive, it is frustrating to look for an opera in the composer entry without knowing when the opera was written, especially with such prolific composers as Verdi (29 operas listed) or Rossini (39 operas). This is a minor criticism for a comprehensive and well-written and edited volume. *The Viking Opera Guide* is highly recommended as a supplement or replacement for *Kobbé*.

Penguin USA has taken the VOG and produced its first electronic product, *The Viking Opera Guide on* CD-ROM. The system requirements are an IBM-compatible 386SX computer with an SVGA monitor, 2MB of RAM (4MB is recommended), 4MB of hard-disk space, a mouse, Windows Version 3.1 or above with Multimedia extensions, and ideally a 16-bit MPC-compatible sound card and speakers or headphones. The installation instructions on a stand-alone PC are simple. The CD-ROM also may be used on a network.

The 36-page user manual gives relatively clear instructions on use, with help available on the menu screen as well as on every individual screen. A tutorial also allows users to learn about the features of the CD-ROM. The introduction is shorter than in the printed version but contains color photographs and has Nicholas Kenyon reading the text with operatic excerpts in the background.

The menu options consist of separate indexes for composers, operas, librettists, places (where composers were born and died and where operas were given their world premieres), and audio excerpts. In addition there is a time line, glossary, pronunciation, atlas, and search and full-search options. The advantage of CD-ROM over the print version is the ability to skip quickly from one topic to a related subject. For example, a person browsing through the index of places finds *Worcester, Massachusetts*; with a click the list of composers born in this city appears (John Adams), then a double click takes the user to the page view on Adams. From the page view, there is a summary box with a list of options. Pronunciation, a map, a glossary, or a time line may also be available. In the Adams example, there is a picture from *Nixon in China*, and the map highlights New York as the nearest city. (Boston is really the nearest city. In another entry, *Somerville, Massachusetts* also highlights New York as the closest city. Somerville is five miles from Boston.)

The best route for introductory searching is through the composer index, since that will also list his or her operas on the index screen. If a search is done by opera, to find additional information on the composer or other operas by that composer, it is necessary to return to the index. To find more detailed information, such as where an opera has been mentioned in other entries, the search or full-search feature should be used. For example, a search on *Tosca* will refer to *La fanciulla del West* and its relation to *Tosca*. The full-search option allows Boolean searching by combining different types of information, such as German operas written by composers between 1800 and 1850.

The audio excerpts are under five minutes, and the majority are popular selections from well-known operas, usually with notable performers. Many of the excerpts are truly that—stopping in the middle of a phrase. The audio and place indexes are marred by problems with alphabetization. For example, the audio index lists *The Bartered Bride* only under *The*.

With snippets of opera being used for commercials and famous operatic tenors becoming as popular as rock stars, interest in this art form is increasing. *The Viking Opera Guide on* CD-ROM allows the user to hear an excerpt from an opera or the pronunciation of an unfamiliar term, look at a time line placing a composer in context with others, and search the entire text for a word or phrase. This makes it an exciting introduction for the uninitiated, as well as a possible reference tool for librarians, critics, and opera lovers. Unfortunately, the fact that there is no ability to print text is a drawback to its use in a library setting.

The Green Book of Songs by Subject: The Thematic Guide to Popular Music. 4th ed. By Jeff Green. Professional Desk References, 4815 Trousdale Dr., Ste. 576, Nashville, TN 37220, 1994. 725p. index. $64.95 (0-939735-05-9); paper $49.95 (0-939735-04-0).
016.78242164'0266 Popular music—Discography [CIP] 94-69175

" You know that song. The one about . . . It goes like . . ." Questions like this frustrate library patrons and staff. One solution is *The Green Book*, which indexes 21,000 twentieth-century songs by assigning one or more of 800 subject headings, based on keywords in the title or the subject of the song. Most songs are from the 1950s on. Johnny Cash's "Boy Named Sue" is found, for example, under *Fight* and *Men's Names*. The subjects vary widely from UFOs to *Colors*, *Drugs*, *Marriage*, *Police*, and *States*. Songs under the subject *Door*, for example, include "Crazy Little Mamma," "Let My Love Open the Door," "My Baby Done Changed the Lock," and "One Less Bell to Answer," among 81 songs. *Love* is not a subject, but there are pages of songs under *Sex*. *See* references lead from one subject heading to another. Song titles are listed alphabetically under a subject. For each song, performer, album, and label are given to help track recordings. Most are albums and are in print; a few 45s are included. The book closes with a list translating the abbreviations used for record labels and an index to subjects used.

The Green Book of Songs by Subject is an unusual but useful title. The only drawback is that it is hard to put down. Recommended for medium-size and large public libraries.

American Choral Music since 1920: An Annotated Guide. By David P. DeVenney. Fallen Leaf Press, P.O. Box 10034, Berkeley, CA 94709, 1993. 278p. bibliog. indexes. $49.50 (0-914913-28-X).
016.7825'0973 Choral music—U.S.—20th century—Bibliography [CIP] 93-21428

This catalog lists "original choral music written by composers active in the U.S. from roughly 1920 to the present." Works included are intended to be sung by a choral ensemble, rather than by an ensemble of solo voices. Excluded are most hymns, arrangements of other composers' works, arrangements of folk songs and spirituals, and works written specifically for the stage. Seventy-six composers and nearly 2,000 works are listed (3,000 if specific movements are counted).

Works are arranged alphabetically by composer and then by title. Entry elements used are opus number; date of composition or copyright; performing forces required (SATB, piano, etc.); author or source of text; duration; publisher; location of composer's manuscript; source of annotation, if not seen during compilation of book; reviews; references to works in the bibliography; and notes.

In his introduction, DeVenney, a college music educator, discusses various styles of choral music popular since 1920 and places important composers in the overall music scene. The main catalog is followed by a 229-item annotated bibliography with its own index. The bibliography facilitates locating information on the composers and specific aspects of their work, as well as on other topics (African American composers, mass settings, etc.). Indexes to the main catalog are title, authors and sources of texts, performing forces (children's voices, men's chorus, etc.), and durations.

For choral directors planning programs and for music students and scholars, this book offers a wealth of information. It is a good companion to *A Singer's Guide to the American Art Song, 1870–1980* [RBB My 1 94], which catalogs only music for solo voice. Thirty-six composers are found in both works. *American Choral Music* will be valuable to music libraries, academic and large public libraries, and others as interest dictates.

Twentieth-Century Brass Soloists. By Michael Meckna. Greenwood, 1994. 291p. bibliog. illus. index. $75 (0-313-26468-6; ISSN 1069-5230).
788.9'092 Brass instrument players—Biography [CIP] 93-23943

Professor Harold Hill may have had 76 *Trombones*, but Meckna goes one better with 99 brass instruments.

In entries of at least two pages, each soloist's career is described, including education, associates and influences, various bands or orchestras performed with, important works, and analysis of style. The essays don't include information on the performer's personal life outside childhood influences on music. Following the essay is a select discography and bibliography. The instrumentalists range from such popular performers as Doc Severinsen and jazz greats like J. J. Johnson to such classical performers as Dennis Brain and such multifield artists as Wynton Marsalis. Cross-references to other entries are marked with an asterisk. Concluding information includes an appendix that lists the soloists by instrument, a select bibliography, and an index. The index doesn't include titles of famous works.

Twentieth-Century Brass Soloists fills a gap in musical biography, particularly for classical instrumentalists, who receive scant attention in traditional sources. This is a must for music libraries. The descriptions of technique and recommendations for practice and teaching contained in the analysis section will be useful to brass students.

Performing Arts, Recreation

Favorite Hobbies and Pastimes: A Sourcebook of Leisure Pursuits. By Robert S. Munson. ALA, 1994. 366p. bibliog. illus. index. paper $55 (0-8389-0638-9).

790.1'3 Hobbies—Handbooks, manuals, etc. || Handicraft—Handbooks, manuals, etc. || Leisure—U.S.—Handbooks, manuals, etc. [CIP] 94-21907

Seventy percent of American households have a member with a hobby. Munson has assembled 94 of today's most frequently pursued leisure-time activities in one volume to give those in search of a hobby ample information to make an informed choice.

Arranged from *Antiques and Collectibles* to *Writing*, the format is the same—a concise history detailing the hobby's origin and development followed by a variety of unique descriptive information. For example, each sport entry discusses rules, equipment, playing strategies, scoring, and game variations. Similarly, animal hobbies (*Dogs, Cats, Horses*, etc.) are given uniform treatment. A description of general characteristics of the animal is followed by specific breeds and breeding techniques, training methods, and uses, such as work, house pets, breeding/show, service (to blind and deaf humans), and sport. The *Aviation* chapter delves into the technical aspects of aircraft maintenance, flight planning, and navigational systems and then briefly mentions spectator events and museums. *Cooking* includes directions for specific methods (frying, broiling, roasting, etc.), and a word about cookbooks. A brief list of related materials—books, periodicals, and associations—for the hobby closes each chapter.

Favorite Hobbies and Pastimes is best used as a complementary volume to the *Hobbyist Sourcebook* (Gale, 1990), which treats the same subject entirely differently. The Gale book directs the hobbyist to sources of information—books, periodicals, organizations, associations, libraries, museums, suppliers, databases, and more—on 43 hobbies. Munson focuses on describing the hobby. Public libraries will want both publications in order to provide a well-rounded treatment of this popular subject.

American Film Comedy. By Scott Siegel and Barbara Siegel. Prentice Hall, 1994. 316p. bibliog. illus. index. paper $18 (0-671-89203-7).

791.43'617 Comedy films—Encyclopedias [CIP] 93-48087

Intended to be "as comprehensive and as thorough a volume on American film comedy as reasonably possible," this work comes close, but not quite to, the mark. More than 300 alphabetically arranged entries describe writers, actors, directors, and film terms in concise form. There are no entries on specific film titles. When appropriate, filmographies are added at the ends of entries. Black-and-white photographs, many of them stills, add to browsing interest. Also appended are a selected bibliography and lists of Oscars won for comedies (acting, writing, directing, and best-picture awards) and the author's picks for the best comedy of the year from 1927 to 1993. The index supplements the A–Z arrangement of the entries. The time period covered is wide, from the silent film era to today. Although years of birth (and death) are included in the articles on individuals, nowhere are complete birth and death dates provided: this is one feature that movie fans often expect. One of the work's strengths is the inclusion of many contemporary comedic figures not likely to be found in other film reference works, for example, Rick Moranis, Martin Short, and Mike Meyers. The articles on film terms offer overviews of comedy genres, (e.g., musical comedy, screwball comedy, and series comedy) in essays that include film titles as examples.

A comparable work is Larry Langman's *Encyclopedia of American Film Comedy* (Garland, 1988), which is still in print. However, the film titles cited in that work stop at 1984, while many 1992 and 1993 films are referred to in the work under review. *American Film Comedy* will function as a supplement to the earlier work in collections that own it and a modestly priced choice for collections that don't and need a current comedy reference source.

Animals on Screen and Radio: An Annotated Sourcebook. By Ann C. Paietta and Jean L. Kauppila. Scarecrow, 1994. 383p. bibliog. indexes. $42.50 (0-8108-2939-8).

016.79143'66 Animals in mass media—Film catalogs || Animals in mass media—Discography [CIP]

Devoted to film, TV, and radio animals from Rin-Tin-Tin to Mister Ed, this annotated sourcebook covers from the beginnings of animals in media through 1993. The 1,515 entries include films from other countries as well as the U.S. The book is meant for researchers and animal lovers as well as for buyers for video stores or other collections.

Organized in three sections, the bulk of the entries cover theatrical and television films, followed by additional entries for television and radio series. Each entry is alphabetized by title and notes producer, actors (including animals), country, date, length in minutes, animal trainers, whether black and white or color, and a descriptive annotation of the film's content. If the film is available on videotape, this is indicated. The introduction describes the criteria for inclusion. For example, documentaries are not listed, nor are insect or dinosaur films. Animals are classified as either central to the plot, supportive, or unnamed but still with an impact on the film or radio show. A bibliography and subject and animal-name indexes conclude the book.

This accessible reference source could easily be carried into a film library or video store as an on-the-spot selector. However, many of the entries are for films released between 1905 and 1950. Additionally, materials are not identified for intended audiences. The omission of some children's favorites such as *The Amazing Bone*, a film made from a popular book by William Steig, is striking. Finally, while this book claims to be for animal lovers, some titles seem inappropriate. For example, the annotation for *How Father Killed the Cat* reads "A father attempts to kill a cat by drowning and mangling it but fails. He finally ends up killing it with a violin."

Invaluable for film researchers as well as public library patrons who are fascinated by this subject, students of filmmaking and artists specializing in animal drawings might also find a use for this work. School library media specialists would be better served by the growing number of books and professional journals that review educational media.

A Biographical Dictionary of Film. 3d ed. By David Thomson. Knopf, 1994. 898p. $40 (0-394-58165-2); paper $25 (0-679-75564-0).

791.43'092 Motion picture actors and actresses—Biography—Dictionaries || Motion pictures—Dictionaries

Leonard Maltin's Movie Encyclopedia. Ed. by Leonard Maltin. Dutton, 1994. 976p. $34.95 (0-525-93635-1).

791.63'092 Motion picture actors and actresses—Biography—Encyclopedias [OCLC] 94-30126

These two biographical dictionaries overlap a lot in coverage but reflect the unique styles and interests of their authors.

The third edition of *A Biographical Dictionary of Film* has 200 entries more than the second (1981), for a total of 1,000. The book covers major actors, directors, producers, and cinematographers. Thomson combines an encyclopedic knowledge of international cinema with opinionated views and a lively, witty writing style. Organized by name, each entry contains birthplace, year of birth (and death), and an extended discussion of the person's artistic strengths and weaknesses. A list of films associated with the subject and their dates of release appear at either the outset of the discussion or are interspersed throughout the short interpretive analysis.

Among the entries added to this edition are Don Ameche (as a late bloomer), Tom Hanks (as an overrated actor), Rob Reiner (as a promising director who hasn't yet delivered), and Wayne Wang (as an uneven, unfocused, and uncertain director). Thomson has also thoroughly revised numerous entries. He amends his article on Steven Spielberg by singing praises for *Schindler's List* and severely castigating *Jurassic Park*. In the last edition of this book, he wrote that Warren Beatty "could become one of the most powerful men in Hollywood," but in this edition he criticizes him for lack of direction and unevenness. Like the previous two editions, there is no index. In a more conventional reference source, this would be a weakness, but the primary reference value of this book is in Thomson's trenchant criticism rather than in the filmographic information.

Maltin is well known as the author of *Leonard Maltin's Movie and Video Guide*. His new book contains brief biographies of 2,000 actors and filmmakers. He notes birthplace and date at the beginning of each entry. Films and release dates are usually interspersed throughout the biography, but occasionally additional films are listed at the end of an entry. Maltin differs from Thomson in including many more popular contemporary actors and supporting actors. Billy Crystal, Dan Aykroyd, William Bendix, John Belushi, Zero Mostel, Lily Tomlin, and Lynn Redgrave are all in Maltin but not in Thomson. Thomson, on the other hand, has generally longer entries and includes more foreign filmmakers.

Ideally, libraries will buy both these books, but if only one can be purchased, institutions supporting serious film study should opt for Thomson; popular collections in public and high school libraries will find Maltin useful.

Children's Television, 1947-1990: Over 200 Series, Game and Variety Shows, Cartoons, Educational Programs and Specials. By Jeffery Davis. McFarland, 1995. 285p. illus. index. $42.50 (0-89950-911-8).
791.45'75 Television programs for children—U.S.—Encyclopedias [CIP] 94-10808

Davis discusses TV shows for children arranged by category, from "Action-Adventure" series such as *Robin Hood* to "Specials" such as *Charlie Brown*. The originators of the programs, how long the shows were viewed on television, character portrayals, and brief critiques are included within the entries. Programs that can fit in more than one category are cross-referenced. For example, *Fury* is discussed in "Action-Adventure" with a *see* reference under "Westerns." Appendixes lists awards and citations, series appearing in prime time, and programs originating in radio or movies. A chronology of landmarks in children's programing lists important debuts. The index includes program titles, program originators, and performers' names. Black-and-white photos are provided for a few shows.

This well-researched book spanning 43 years provides the researcher with a comprehensive view of TV for children. For example, *The Kukla, Fran and Ollie* show, which began in 1947, ultimately led the way for such related puppet programs as *Sesame Street*. The work will also be nostalgic reading for those who remember Buffalo Bob or the Mickey Mouse Club. A worthwhile purchase for public and academic libraries.

Dictionary of Film Terms: The Aesthetic Companion to Film Analysis. Rev. ed. By Frank E. Beaver. Twayne, 1994. 363p. illus. indexes. $29.95 (0-8057-9333-X); paper $15.95 (0-8057-9334-8).
791.43'03 Cinematography—Dictionaries [CIP] 94-6350

As the subtitle implies, the entries in the *Dictionary of Film Terms* focus on "aesthetic" terminology dealing with "techniques, concepts, genres, and styles that have evolved as a part of cinematic expression and analysis." First published in 1984, this updated edition covers the cinema from its inception to the present. Entries range from *absolute film* (a term used to describe the abstract experimental European film movement of the 1920s) and *camera obscura* (which describes the principle of photographic reproduction developed by Leonardo da Vinci) to *digital sound*. Many of the definitions refer to specific films as examples. When definitions contain words or terms that are themselves entries in the book, these are boldfaced. *See* references appear at the end of some definitions. This new edition is more than 50 pages longer with new terms (e.g., *computer-generated imaging*, *cult film*) and illustrations. Some entries from the first edition have been updated with current films added as examples. Two indexes list film titles mentioned in the entries and group entries topically under such headings as *Editing*, *Cinematography*, and *Lighting*. The chronology from the previous edition has been dropped.

Ira Konigsberg's *Complete Film Dictionary* (New American Library, 1987) defines 3,500 terms—many more than the *Dictionary of Film Terms*. Konigsberg's entries are more technical than Beaver's, but both books are generally understandable to the layperson. Although the *Dictionary of Film Terms* includes a few terms not included in Konigsberg (such as *introvision*, *last minute rescues*, and *Hitchcockian*), there are many terms defined in the latter book that are not in *Dictionary of Film Terms*. Both books are illustrated with small black-and-white photographs, but *The Complete Film Dictionary* also contains instructive line drawings. In a few cases *The Complete Film Dictionary* goes into more technical detail than the *Dictionary of Film Terms*. (Beaver defines the term *optical printer* in a paragraph, while Konigsberg has a 2-page description of the equipment.)

Most libraries that already own *The Complete Film Dictionary* do not need to add the *Dictionary of Film Terms*; however, large academic and research libraries and specialized film libraries with Konigsberg's book should purchase the *Dictionary of Film Terms* because of its aesthetic emphasis. Public libraries and smaller academic libraries without an adequate film dictionary should consider *The Complete Film Dictionary* instead of the *Dictionary of Film Terms* because of its more comprehensive coverage.

The Film Anthologies Index. By Stephen E. Bowles. Scarecrow, 1994. 468p. index. $52.50 (0-8108-2896-0).
086.79143'75 Motion pictures—Bibliography || Anthologies—Indexes [CIP] 94-13541

More than 600 English-language anthologies published through 1991 containing more than 10,000 essays on film and filmmakers are indexed in this reference source. Excluded are anthologies of exclusively film reviews (unless they center around a "defined theme"), reference books containing "capsule summaries" of films and filmmakers, and single-author monographs on specific filmmakers. No qualitative criteria have been imposed on the selection of essays for this index.

The main body of the book consists of 6,563 author entries (arranged alphabetically) that identify anthologies where particular essays appear and that tie together anthologies containing the same essay. (Essays whose titles have changed or whose contents have been altered are listed separately under the author's entry.) Following this is a useful 156-page index allowing readers to access indexed essays by title of film and names and keywords that appear in the titles of the essays. Unfortunately, there is no general subject index, so that someone looking for information on films that deal with Irish Americans, for example, will be unable to find anything except three essays where the word *Irish* appears in the title.

The index is useful for research libraries, specialized film libraries, and large public libraries with comprehensive film book collections. Most other libraries will find it sufficient to rely on *Essay and General Literature Index* to access essays on film and filmmakers in anthologies.

The Film Encyclopedia. 2d ed. By Ephraim Katz. HarperPerennial, 1994. 1,496p. paper $25 (0-06-273089-4).
791.43'03 Motion pictures—Encyclopedias [CIP] 93-43318

For the last 15 years, the first edition of this title has served as a dependable source of brief film biographies, definitions of terms, explanations of technical film processes, and more. This second edition continues to provide the same comprehensive coverage, now increased by about 18 percent. Its claim to being an encyclopedia of *world* cinema is well founded, as there are entries for Zakes Mokae (South Africa), Pedro Almodóvar (Spain), Hector Babenco (Brazil), Zhang Yimou (China), Daniel Auteuil (France), and Juzo Itami (Japan), along with Ed Harris and Julia Roberts. As in the first edition, there are no entries for individual film titles. Filmographies are included for major actors and directors, and the biographical sketches include not only those two job titles but also composers, producers, screenwriters, art directors, cinematographers, etc. Of particular interest are the overviews of the film industry in individual countries, which provide the names of notable actors and directors and the titles of their films. Coverage of the U.S. film scene is up-to-date, biographical entries are provided for the likes of Linda Hamilton, Kirstie Alley, Sean Young, Tim Robbins, Debbie Allen, and Kyle MacLachlan. Indeed, the biographical entries are the mainstay of this work, which notes even 1993 and 1994 deaths of film notables.

Katz, author of the first edition, lived only long enough to complete about three-fourths of this new one. Those who followed him have fulfilled his original aim to produce "the most comprehensive one-volume encyclopedia of world cinema ever published in the English language." This is one instance where the content is accurately depicted by the cover blurb. Recommended for any reference collection in need of a world view of film.

Film Quotations: 11,000 Lines Spoken on Screen, Arranged by Subject, and Indexed. By Robert A. Nowlan and Gwendolyn W. Nowlan. McFarland, 1994. 745p. indexes. $75 (0-89950-786-7).
791.43 Motion pictures—Quotations, maxims, etc. [CIP] 92-56673

Until now, the only sourcebook of movie lines in print has been *The*

Movie Quote Book by Harry Haun (HarperCollins, 1980). With some 4,000 quotations organized under nearly 400 subject headings, it is dwarfed by *Film Quotations*' 11,000 quotations under more than 900 headings. Clearly, this new work is worth its space on the shelf—not only because it includes more quotations, but also so many more points of access to them. Since neither book has a keyword index, the number of subject headings is crucial. Another welcome feature is the number of cross-references within the subject headings: nearly every subject includes at least two alternative headings for the reader to check.

The pages of this book offer an immense variety of memorable movie lines under headings from Abilities and Capabilities to Youth. Under each subject heading, quotations are entered chronologically by the year of the film's release. If a section quotes more than once from a single film, the quotations appear in the order in which they occurred in the film. Each entry notes the name of the performer who spoke the lines, the film and its studio and release date, and a sentence or two explaining the context. In addition to this panoply of screen gems, there is an index of performers and one of movie titles, which also contains the names of each movie's director and writer.

Films considered classics and B movies are both represented in this compendium. The chronological coverage is broad, from the 1930s to the 1990s. As a source for some of the most common quotations we encounter every day, this book is a solid reference. Recommended for all film and general-reference collections.

First Century of Film. By Martin S. Quigley and others. Quigley, 159 W. 53rd St., New York, NY 10019, 1995. 319p. illus. $49.50 (0-900610-54-9).

791.4309 Motion pictures—Biography—Dictionaries [BKL]

Included here are concise career profiles of important figures in the American film industry who died prior to August 31, 1994. Most entries originally appeared in Quigley's *International Motion Picture Almanac* from 1929 to 1994 and have been updated for currency. Entry elements include profession, real and other names, date and place of birth, parents, education, marriage(s), professional affiliations, summary of career including work in TV and theater, a list of films with which the person was associated, and date of death. Entries note if the list of a biographee's films is complete or partial and tell which pictures won or were nominated for Academy Awards. Liberal use of abbreviations controls the length of entries. A detailed essay on the history of film and a section of 147 black-and-white photographs spanning from Thomas Edison to Jim Henson add interest. Entries are keyed to photographs. The author has written several other books on film.

Many reference books provide information on people in the film industry. *Who's Who in Hollywood* [RBB Ap 15 92] provides biographies for 35,000 actors, both living and deceased, going back to 1893. Katz's *Film Encyclopedia* [RBB O 15 94] has biographies of actors, directors, cinematographers, etc., both living and deceased. A dependable source for retrospective biographical information on those in the film industry, *First Century of Film* is appropriate for public libraries and for libraries from high school through graduate school that need additional coverage in this area.

Hispanics in Hollywood: An Encyclopedia of Film and Television. By Luis Reyes and Peter Rubie. Garland, 1994. 596p. bibliog. illus. index. $95 (0-8153-0827-2).

791.43'08968 Hispanic Americans in motion pictures—Encyclopedias || Hispanic Americans in television—Encyclopedias [BKL] 93-40607

Although Hispanic Americans have been involved in many aspects of the American film industry, there has been little note taken of this fact in standard film-reference works. In addition to the biographical sketches and descriptions of films and television programs that make up the bulk of this work, there are also essays on the role of the Hispanic American in American film and television. The book begins with an essay on movies, followed by alphabeticallly arranged entries on films that had a Hispanic character, setting, or subject or in which a Hispanic actor starred. Each entry includes producer, director, writer, cast, and a brief summary of the plot. Individuals whose names appear in boldface type are the subject of biographical sketches later in the book. The next section begins with an essay on television followed by entries on individual programs, which include network, cast, and a brief plot summary. Again, boldface type is used to indicate persons who are the subject of biographies. This section is followed by brief essays on Zorro and the Cisco Kid, with complete chronologies of their movie and television incarnations. Finally, there is the biographical section, which lists Hispanic American performers and behind-the-scenes personnel. The authors indicate that they have "also included . . . a number of non-Hispanic individuals who are nevertheless identified in the public mind as Hispanic, on the basis of the roles they played or their Hispanic-sounding names." There is a separate section of "profiles of selected non-Hispanic filmmakers who have contributed substantially to shaping the cinematic image of Hispanic Americans through classic films they made." These include such directors as John Ford and John Huston. An index completes the work; a selected bibliography precedes the front matter.

There are throughout the book black-and-white photographs of very good quality. Studio portraits, movie posters, and stills of many familiar (and some unfamiliar) faces and scenes complement the text. Since there is currently little on this increasingly popular subject, it is recommended for film and Hispanic-culture collections alike.

Images in the Dark: An Encyclopedia of Gay and Lesbian Film and Video. By Raymond Murray. TLA Publications, 1520 Locust St., Philadelphia, PA 19102, 1994. 561p. bibliog. illus. index. paper $19.95 (1-880707-01-2).

791.43'08664 Homosexuality in motion pictures [BKL] 94-60358

Broad-ranging, informative, and entertainingly written, this reference source covers 200 gay, bisexual, and lesbian actors and directors as well as more than 3,000 films and videos with gay themes. The book's scope also extends to such straight people as Marilyn Monroe, Judy Garland, and Barbra Streisand who are popular in gay culture. Murray's emphasis is on American and English films, although he does have selective coverage of European and Asian cinema. Films included in the book must be at least 60 minutes in length and have "a gay theme that is relatively evident."

Images in the Dark is organized into nine chapters, the first three of which consist of entries dealing with directors, actors, and writers, artists, dancers, and composers. Each entry summarizes in several paragraphs the person's contributions to film and discusses his or her private life. Following this, the person's films are listed chronologically, noting the year released, running time, and country of origin; each film is also annotated briefly with evaluative comments. The remainder of the book covers films with gay themes. Four chapters are organized by audience: of interest to both gays and lesbians; to gays alone; to lesbians alone; and to "transsexuals, transvestites and drag queens . . . and their fans." The following chapter deals with "cheesy films that feature gay, lesbian or transgendered characters." The last chapter covers "films with lesbian, gay, bisexual or transgender characters in secondary or bit roles and/or films which make references to homosexuality." In the chapters focusing on films, entries contain information on year released, running time, country of origin, and director. The annotations for these films are somewhat longer than those for films appearing in the biographical chapters.

Detailed indexes of film titles, directors, personalities, and themes conclude the book. The themes index lists films by ethnic group, country, genre, and such themes as homophobia, cross-dressing, and vampires. Many black-and-white clips of film scenes and photos of directors and stars complement the entries. Readers may question why some stars appear in the book. Lindsay Anderson's inclusion in the directors chapter is a mystery, since there is no mention of his connection to gay themes except a passing reference to one scene in the movie *If*.

Murray includes both Hollywood and underground films in his book. James Robert Parish's *Gays and Lesbians in Mainstream Cinema* [RBB Mr 1 94] covers 272 films in greater detail. It has full cast credits and quotes reviews. *Facets Gay & Lesbian Video Guide* [RBB Mr 1 94] lists documentaries, foreign films, and offbeat films that have homosexuality as the main subject. Libraries owning these two books may find their coverage adequate. But Murray's coverage of persons as well as films makes *Images in the Dark* a necessary purchase for libraries with major film collections; academic and public libraries should consider purchase, too.

International Dictionary of Theatre, v. 2: Playwrights. Ed. by Mark Hawkins-Dady. St. James, 1994. 1,218p. bibliog. illus. index. $125 (1-55862-096-6).

792'.03 Theater—Encyclopedias [OCLC]

The second volume in a three-volume set, *Playwrights* covers 485 writers for the stage. Volume 1 (1992) of the *International Dictionary of Theatre* covers plays, and volume 3, covering actors, directors, and designers, will be published in December. The scope of the directory is both international, as its name suggests, and historical, ranging from ancient Greece to the present day. *Playwrights* is selective rather than comprehensive, the entrants having been chosen by advisers, whose names are listed following the introduction.

Writers are listed alphabetically, beginning with the medieval French writer and musician Adam de la Halle and ending with Carl Zuckmayer, a twentieth-century German dramatist whose works were banned by the Nazis. Aeschylus and Sophocles are included, as are Neil Simon, Beth Henley, and David Mamet. Each entry contains a brief biographical summary; a list of works, including collections, stage works, screenplays, television and radio plays, fiction and verse, memoirs, letters, and other genres; and a list of secondary works, including bibliographies, books, and articles. These sections are followed by a critical overview. These essays are approximately 1,000 words and are written by more than 200 individual contributors, most of whom are academicians. Finally, each entry has cross-references to plays discussed in volume 1. A number of the entries are illustrated with photographs, portraits, engravings, or designs. Following the alphabetical directory is an index to all stage works, published screenplays, and radio, and television plays listed in the entries. The volume concludes with notes on the advisers and contributors.

Playwrights is an authoritative, attractive, well-organized volume that contains much useful information. Many, though not all, of the writers covered in *Playwrights* can be found in the six-volume sets, *Critical Survey of Drama: English Language Series* and *Critical Survey of Drama: Foreign Language Series*, published by Salem Press/Magill. These sets, also arranged alphabetically by author, cover considerably more people than does *Playwrights*. The Magill sets provide biographical information and critical essays that are generally more than twice as long as those in *Playwrights*. However, the bibliographic information in the Magill sets is much less current and comprehensive, focusing on drama to the exclusion of other genres, and offering highly selective lists of secondary works. Libraries already owning the Magill sets will have to decide whether the advantage of *Playwrights* in terms of currency and bibliographic coverage make it worth adding to their collections. Libraries not owning the Magill sets may wish to consider *Playwrights* as a more convenient and economical alternative.

The Tony Award: A Complete Listing with a History of the American Theatre Wing. Ed. by Isabelle Stevenson. Heinemann, 1995. 176p. index. paper $14.95 (0-435-08658-8).
792'.079 Tony awards || American Theatre Wing [CIP] 94-36644

This slender volume is a new edition of a tribute to the winners of the Tony Award, presented each year to honor distinguished achievement in the theater. Several previous editions were published in the 1980s by Crown; Stevenson continues as editor. There are few changes in this new edition: the awards are still arranged by decade and year, and nominees for each award are listed, with the winner designated by a star. The categories remain the same, and actors and actresses are listed separately for plays and musicals. Other categories are the plays and musicals themselves; director; book; score; scenic, costume, and lighting design; choreographer; revival; and special awards. A brief chapter on Antoinette Perry and an interesting history of the American Theatre Wing remain unchanged.

The body of the work includes awards from 1947 through 1994 (the Tony Award is presented in January). A new section, "Reflections from 1994 Tony Award Winners," features brief remarks by a few recipients. "Rules and Regulations of the American Theatre Wing's Tony Awards 1993–94 Season" is a total revision of a more general section in previous editions. It spells out, in great detail, membership on the decision-making bodies. An index lists personal names and play titles.

Libraries that serve strong performing arts programs will find this work affordable and a handy reference. Those owning the *Tony Award Book: Four Decades of Great American Theater* by Lee Alan Morrow (Abbeville, 1987) will find the latter lavishly illustrated with photographs and much of the same factual information through 1987. The works can be used effectively together.

The World Encyclopedia of Contemporary Theatre. v.1: Europe. By Don Rubin. Routledge, 1994. 1,052p. bibliog. illus. index. $149.95 (0-415-05928-3).
792'.03 Theater—Encyclopedias [BKL]

This projected 6-volume encyclopedia covering theatrical arts throughout the world since 1945 will focus on more than 150 countries. Its purpose is to present the nations' self-view through the eyes of theatrical scholars and artists writing within each country. TV and radio drama are not included. The editorial board includes international regional editors; for volume 1, covering 47 countries, they are from Budapest, Bordeaux, and Moscow. Future volumes will cover the Americas, Africa, the Arab World, and Asia and Oceana; the sixth volume will contain a comprehensive index and a world-theater bibliography.

The introductory essays for volume 1 include a general overview of theatrical activity in Europe, music and dance, theater for young audiences, and puppet theater. The main entries, arranged alphabetically from *Albania* to *Yugoslavia*, are structured alike in 12 sections. A brief section containing historical, sociopolitical, and geographic information is followed by a section on the structure of the national theater community, which includes professional theatrical groups, variety, opera and ballet, the circus, and puppet theater; an artistic profile, which includes companies, dramaturgy, directing, and production; design; space and architecture; training (including schools); criticism; scholarship and publishing; and a short bibliography. The latter tends to contain works in the national language. Within the essays, titles are also given in the national language, with English translations in parentheses. The work is structured so that one may read straight through each essay or do a cross-cultural study of one or more of the 12 aspects of each entry. The index serves as the access point for individual names, titles, and topics. For example, *Waiting for Godot* leads to articles on France, Greece, Ireland, Israel, the Netherlands, Poland, Serbia-Montenegro, the U.K., and Yugoslavia. Black-and-white photos of theaters and productions are found in every chapter. Israel, because of its "cultural links with Europe in the modern period," is treated in this volume as part of the European mainstream. Articles on Yugoslavia, Czechoslovakia, and the USSR give historical overviews; authors were recruited to write individual essays on the new republics.

The 5-volume *McGraw-Hill Encyclopedia of World Drama* (2d ed., McGraw-Hill, 1984) continues to serve secondary-school students, undergraduates, and the general public as an excellent overview of theater topics throughout history. *The World Encyclopedia*, according to its editors, is designed to meet the needs of the "sophisticated professional from abroad," the nonnative researcher who wants to learn about recent theater activity in a country in the context of its sociopolitical culture. This set will be a refreshing journey into unfamiliar territory for researchers and a welcome addition to scholarly theater collections.

Games & Entertainment on CD-ROM: The Ultimate Guide to Home CD-ROM Entertainment. Ed. by Regina Rega and Matthew Finlay. Mecklermedia, 1994. 250p. indexes. paper $29.95 (0-88736-967-7; ISSN 1076-4534).
794.8 Computer games—Directories || CD-ROM—Directories [BKL]

Net Games: Your Guide to the Games People Play on the Electronic Highway. By Kelly Maloni and others. Random, 1994. 272p. illus. index. paper $19 (0-679-75592-6).
794.8 Computer games—Directories || Internet (Computer network)—Directories [BKL]

Move over Parker Brothers and Nintendo—games are now available on CD-ROM and online.

Games & Entertainment, a spin-off of Mecklermedia's *CD-ROMs in Print*, describes more than 1,300 game and home entertainment titles. It's hard to see how some of them, such as *Newspaper Abstracts on Disc*, qualify as entertainment, but libraries that don't own the parent work will want to consider purchasing this version for patrons wishing to find out about games like *Myst* and *Dragon Lore*, cookbooks, children's books, and gardening and sports titles on CD-ROM.

At any hour of the day, millions of people are online playing games. *Net Games*, from the same packagers as *Net Guide* (Random, 1994), is a directory to more than 1,500 games on the Internet and such commercial services as Delphi, GEnie, CompuServe, America Online, and bulletin boards. Games are arranged by type (e.g., shoot-em-ups, role playing and adventure, classic games like chess and Scrabble). Entries note difficulty, number of players, style of competition, if the game is played only at scheduled times, and if there is any extra fee to play. There is something here for everyone from crossword-puzzle addicts to Dungeons and Dragons fans. —*Sandy Whiteley*

Peforming Arts, Recreation

Professional Sports Team Histories. 4v. Ed. by Michael L. LaBlanc. Gale, 1994. bibliog. illus. index. $129.95 (0-8103-8858-8).
796.09 Professional sports—U.S.—History || Baseball—Clubs—U.S. || Basketball—Clubs—U.S. || Football—Clubs—U.S. || Hockey—Clubs—U.S. [BKL]

This set profiles team histories for the top professional sports in North America: baseball, basketball, football, and hockey, with a volume devoted to each. Where other books provide bare-bones statistics or year-by-year summaries of a sport, this set fills a niche by providing narrative histories through the 1992–93 season for each team currently in existence.

Edited by LaBlanc (*World Encyclopedia of Soccer* [RBB Ap 15 94]) with a staff of more than 50, each volume begins with a general history of the professional sport, its beginning, growth and expansion, and thoughtful comments on the state of the sport today. Then the individual team histories follow, arranged alphabetically by division. The major personalities of each team—coaches, players, owners, and managers—come alive. The teams secure their places in the context of the league with facts that provide the background for the reputations and rivalries that make these sports what they are today. The formula for each history includes highlights, major accomplishments, and controversies. Each is written in a compelling style that entertains while it informs. Brief bibliographies of books and periodical articles conclude each entry. An index of personal names, "Team Information at a Glance" boxes, a sizable logo, boxed profiles of outstanding personalities or unique facts, and black-and-white photographs enliven each volume. Entries range from two pages for such new teams as hockey's Anaheim Mighty Ducks and basketball's Miami Heat to more than 30 pages for baseball's St. Louis Cardinals, hockey's Pittsburgh Penguins, and football's Chicago Bears. The baseball volume has a special essay on the Negro Leagues, and the hockey volume, one on the Stanley Cup.

The currency of the volumes is such that the general essay on hockey concludes with the October 1993 appointment of Brian Burke as the NHL director of hockey operations. Baseball's newest franchises, the Colorado Rockies and the Florida Marlins, which started competition in 1993, are mentioned, and Cleveland's and Arlington's new stadiums are included.

Once you start reading these volumes, you wonder why this hadn't been done before. In fact, for baseball it has, by two other publishers. In the two-volume *Encyclopedia of Major League Baseball Team Histories* [RBB O 15 91], each team rates at least 30 pages plus brief statistics and a bibliography. Members of the Society for Baseball Research wrote most of the essays. Paperback editions from Carroll & Graf are updated through the 1992 season. A lively one-volume *Encyclopedia of Major League Baseball Teams* by Donald Dewey and Nicholas Acocella (HarperCollins, 1993) covers "121 teams that have comprised the six leagues officially recognized by Major League Baseball" and includes facts through early 1993.

This set is suitable for general collections in high-school, college, and public libraries, especially those that cannot afford individual team histories. Volumes are also available individually for $39.95 each.

Sports Stars. 2v. By Michael Paré. Gale, 1994. 622p. illus. index. $38 (0-8103-9861-3).
796'.092 Athletes—Biography—Juvenile literature [CIP] 94-21835

The immense popularity of sports in America has at least this consolation for harried teachers: it offers their students a high-interest avenue for reading, writing, and research. But to the young, yesterday's stars may be has-beens. Paré profiles 80 athletes (only 15 of them women) who meet one or more of the following criteria: still active or recently retired from professional or amateur sports, a top performer in the sport, or a role model who has hurdled physical or societal constraints to reach the top. Although athletes from 17 sports are featured, 43 of the 80 represent the big-three American spectator sports: baseball, basketball, and football. Auto racing, bicycle racing, golf, gymnastics, horse racing, skiing, soccer, speed skating, and swimming are represented by only one or two athletes each; boxing, figure skating, hockey, tennis, and track and field are represented by three to nine athletes each. Arthur Ashe is the only deceased athlete profiled. This highly selective work, then, focuses on those who are still sports newsmakers.

Each alphabetically arranged entry has two main sections: one "focusing on the athlete's early life and motivations," followed by one highlighting the career. The writing style of this and other Gale/UXL imprints is clear, lively, and geared to "advanced elementary, middle school and lower achieving high school students." Each entry also features a quick-reference "Scoreboard" box, high-interest sidebar boxes, one or more black-and-white photographs, and (in most cases) an address where the athlete can be contacted. The set begins with a table of contents organized both alphabetically and by sport; it ends with a bibliography of further reading for each star and an index.

The 14-volume *Lincoln Library of Sports Stars* (6th ed., Frontier, 1993), also geared to middle-schoolers, has several times the number of entries and covers athletes from far more sports; its coverage extends throughout the twentieth century. The 23-volume *Great Athletes: The Twentieth Century* (Salem, 1992-94) covers more than 800 athletes in the U.S. and abroad. *Sports Stars*, however, is recommended for school libraries as an inexpensive and readable source on contemporary athletes.

A Who's Who of Sports Champions: Their Stories and Records. By Ralph Hickok. Houghton, 1995. 873p. $22.95 (0-395-68195-2); paper $19.95 (0-395-73312-X).
796'.092 Athletes—North America—Biography—Dictionaries [BKL] 94-49144

Claiming to be the first single-volume biographical reference source for sports in more than 60 years, *A Who's Who of Sports Champions* lists in a single alphabet U.S. and Canadian champion athletes, plus foreign athletes who have won a major championship in North America. The 2,200 entries cover more than 50 different sports at all levels, including professional, college, and Olympic play. Each entry runs from approximately 60 to more than 1,000 words. Who's included? All players, coaches, and managers in the major team-sports halls of fame, winners of major sports awards, and athletes who have led a league in a major statistical category or who are high on all-time career statistics. All Olympians who have won two or more gold medals are included. Unlike most books with *who's who* in the title, this one includes such deceased persons as Babe Ruth and Lou Gehrig. Each entry is accompanied by an icon identifying the sport played. Entries give birth and death dates; statistics are included in the narrative. An index by sport enables the reader to find the champions in a particular sport.

This book is fun to read since many of the entries contain anecdotal material in addition to the statistical. Since it is issued in paperback at $19.95, a library could acquire it for the circulating collection, especially if the six-volume *Biographical Dictionary of American Sports* (Greenwood, 1987-95) is already owned. *A Who's Who of Sports Champions* is highly recommended as an addition to both the reference and circulating collections.

Encyclopedia of College Basketball. Ed. by Michael Douchant. Gale, 1994. 615p. illus. index. maps. tables. $42.95 (0-8103-9640-8); Visible Ink, paper $19.95 (0-8103-9483-9).
796.323'0973 Basketball—U.S.—History || College sports—U.S.—History [CIP] 94-35209

From the introduction written by basketball nut Dick Vitale to the comprehensive index, this encyclopedia covers the world of college basketball from the beginnings by Naismith to Arkansas' defeat of Duke in the NCAA tournament in March 1994. Extensive sections cover the history of college basketball, the NCAA tournaments, the National Invitation Tournament, players, coaches, women's basketball, small colleges, the Olympic games, plus a conference directory, school directory, NCAA awards and records, and statistical trivia. About 200 black-and-white photographs of players and coaches round out the coverage,

This work functions on a number of levels as an encyclopedia, a directory, a statistical compendium, a chronology, and a history of the sport. The excellent chapter on women's basketball is a most welcome addition to the work. One of the most interesting sections is on college players who went on to find fame in other sports, politics, business, or entertainment. The index ties it all together by including individuals, associations, leagues, and teams. It does exclude box scores, statistical boxes, long name lists, and general statistics. Photographs are denoted by italics, and boldface type refers to entire sections.

A number of books on college basketball have been published recently. The list includes *Final Four Records 1939–1991: The History of the Division 1 Men's Basketball Tournament* (Triumph, 1992); *Basketball Biographies: 434 U.S. Players, Coaches and Contributions to the Game, 1891–1990* (McFarland, 1991); and *The Encyclopedia of the NCAA Basketball Tournament: *The Complete Independent Guide to College Basketball's Championship Event* (Dell, 1990). Although sections of Douchant overlap these three works, he gives broader coverage in more areas and all in one reasonably priced volume.

The *Encyclopedia of College Basketball* is an excellent reference work. It complements the three titles listed above and is a recommended purchase for any sports and recreation collection at any level from high-school to public and university libraries.

The Official NBA Basketball Encyclopedia. 2d ed. Ed. by Alex Sachare. Villard, 1994. 842p. illus. index. tables. $39.95 (0-679-43293-0).
796.323'64 Basketball—U.S.—History || Basketball—U.S.—Records || National Basketball Association—History [CIP] 94-11858

With an introduction from the current commissioner of basketball, David J. Stern, and a preface by one of the past greats of the game, Julius Erving, the second edition of *The Official NBA Basketball Encyclopedia* is what most fans expect in a sports reference work. First published in 1989, it continues its tradition of providing historical narratives on the game, an "NBA time line," essays on the ABA and the game as its played around the world, coaches, referees, the official rules of the NBA, the hall of fame, and the NBA All Star Weekend (with all-star game statistics). There is also a chapter on the NBA draft lottery, with a year-by-year accounting from 1947 through June 29, 1994. The narratives are interspersed with wonderful black-and-white photographs that capture the movement and personalities of the game. More than half of the book consists of the "All-Time Player Directory" of players, current and past, who participated in the NBA, Basketball Association of America, or American Basketball Association. Each entry provides nickname, birth date, height, weight, college, season, team, and more than 25 individual statistical measures. A handy name-subject index helps to locate material in the narrative sections. The player statistical summaries are not indexed here.

A couple of small criticisms: although the dust jacket claims that one can find which coach lost the most games, the only statistic given along these lines is the winningest coaches. Also, since half of the book is narrative, a bibliography would help to refer the inquisitive to more information. The nearest competitor to this volume is the Sporting News' annual *Official NBA Guide*, which does not include the historical narratives but excels in the statistical summaries, since it gives season-by-season team records, which the *Basketball Encyclopedia* doesn't. It comes in paperback at about half the cost.

Libraries should acquire both titles for the historical narrative perspective, player statistics, and year-by-year team statistics.

World of Tennis. Ed. by John Barrett. Triumph, 1994. 464p. illus. index. $34.95 (1-881041-73-6).
796.342'021 Tennis—Statistics [BKL]

Now in its twenty-sixth year, *World of Tennis* records the main tournaments and team competitions for 1993 as well as reports on the top tennis players of the world. Published by the International Tennis Federation, it is divided into nine main sections: the first consists of such essays as "The Year in Review," "Players of the Year," "The Davis Cup." The following sections are essays on the Grand Slam Championships, IBM/ATP Tour, and the Kraft World Tour; other official pro tournaments, such as the men's satellite circuits and women's future circuits; international team competitions; rankings; a reference section; and information on the International Tennis Federation, with addresses for national tennis associations.

"Grand Slam Tournaments" gives the pairings in the various rounds right up through the finals. From a glance at a chart the reader can see who beat whom in what round. In the essay "Wheelchair Tennis Review," we learn that wheelchair tennis started in 1976 and is now the fastest-growing wheelchair sport. Rankings are given as well as the most recent champions. Biographies of the top-ten men and women players include a small black-and-white photo along with birth dates, residence, parents, siblings, agent, height, weight, and rankings going back to 1982. Career earnings and most recent annual winnings are also given. The entry includes a paragraph on the player's tennis style and a year-by-year summary of significant events in his or her career. Brief biographies for other players include year-by-year summaries as well. "Championship Rolls" lists winners of tournaments around the world, sometimes as far back as the nineteenth century.

The lack of a name index makes this source less useful as a reference tool. However, the breadth of information on individual players and tournaments makes it a recommended purchase for comprehensive sports-reference collections.

The Martial Arts Sourcebook. By John Corcoran. HarperPerennial, 1994. 434p. illus. paper $18 (0-06-273259-5).
796.8 Martials arts [CIP] 93-46842

The author issued a "revision" of his 1983 book, *Martial Arts: Tradition, History, People*, under the title *The Original Martial Arts Encyclopedia* [RBB S 1 93] but it was primarily a reprint of the 1983 edition. With the publication of *The Martial Arts Sourcebook*, the revision is truly complete.

The volume is divided into five parts: part 1 consists of the various styles and practices of the martial arts around the world; part 2 lists famous martial artists, members in the halls of fame and other awards, and birth and death dates of various personalities. Part 3 is the major section of the book and includes the champions of the martial arts, with competition results for kickboxing, karate, tae kwon do, and other martial art championships. Parts 4 and 5 provide information on films and videos on the martial arts and a business directory and sources for martial arts associations, which is worldwide in scope.

While this edition of *The Martial Arts Sourcebook* covers some of the same ground as earlier editions, the information has been updated to 1992 and in some cases to 1993. Checking on several addresses and telephone numbers of associations listed in part 5 with the long-distance operator showed the information provided was accurate. Libraries needing an up-to-date source on this popular topic should purchase *The Martial Arts Sourcebook*.

Jimmy Cornell World Cruising Handbook. By Doina Cornell. International Marine/TAB, 1994. bibliog. illus. index. paper $49.95 (0-07-013324-7).
797.1'246 Yachts and yachting || Ocean travel || Ports of entry [BKL]

This is the kind of book librarians should know about, even if they do not purchase it for their libraries. Aimed primarily at the yachting and cruising community, it gives precise information on ports of entry, regulations, fees, visa or passport requirements, docking and repair facilities, and other items of interest to sailors. The coverage is the entire world, including the U.S.

Preliminary pages cover three topics: formalities, health precautions, and communications, this last dealing with ship-to-shore radio, the use of satellites for long-distance communication, and search-and-rescue operations. The remainder of the book is divided into 12 chapters, parceling out the world in maritime rather than political divisions, such as the North Pacific Islands, or the North Indian Ocean and Red Sea.

Interesting and sometimes important facts are provided for each of the nearly 200 countries or groups of islands. A paragraph summarizes the locale's present condition—rocky, fertile, forested, sparsely or thickly populated, and so on—as well as its history and present political situation, with occasional warnings, as in the case of Libya, that yachts are unwelcome. There is also a box of "Practical Information," which includes currency, business and banking hours, public holidays, local electric current, and addresses of U.S. and other diplomatic representatives in the principal city.

While some of this information about countries of the world may be found elsewhere, it is handy to have it all in one volume alongside information specifically for sailors. In communities on the eastern, southern, and western coasts where boating is common, this book ought to be in public libraries.

Literature

Merriam-Webster's Encyclopedia of Literature. Merriam-Webster, 1995. 1,236p. illus. $39.95 (0-87779-042-6).
803 Literature—Dictionaries [CIP] 94-42741

A joint effort of editorial staffs from Merriam-Webster and Encyclopaedia Britannica, *Merriam-Webster's Encyclopedia of Literature* (MWEL) "contains entries for authors, works, literary landmarks, literary and critical terms, mythological and folkloric figures, fictional characters, literary movements and prizes, and other miscellaneous matters." The book is encyclopedic in coverage but very dictionary-like in its brevity of entries.

The more than 10,000 entries in this volume cover a vast amount of territory. There are biographical entries covering all nationalities and periods (*Cavalcanti, Guido; Futabatei, Shimei; Joyce, James*), brief entries on literary characters (*Bovary, Emma; Hawkins, Jim*), on specific works (*Driving Miss Daisy; Lotus-Eaters, The*), on forms of criticism (*Feminist Criticism, New Criticism*), on movements and events (*Jindyworobak Movement, War of the Theaters*), and on styles (*Eclogue, Guwen*). The only thing lacking is entries on the literary traditions of specific countries.

The average entry is well under 150 words, with the longest under 700 (*Shakespeare, William*, for example), and some as few as seven (*Lineation* is defined simply as "an arrangement of lines [as of verse]"). Pronunciation is provided for most entries (even *Miller, Daisy* has one) and then an etymology for entries that define terminology. For biographical entries, places and dates of birth and death are given. The entry proper includes any cross-references ("used sparingly" according to the prefatory material) in small-capital letters. Titles of works are given in the original language followed by English translation. All entries are unsigned, and there are no bibliographies. Several hundred small black-and-white photographs and illustrations are provided.

By attempting to cover almost everything, some entries are almost uselessly brief (as in the *Lineation* example above). Others, though with a literary connection, almost seem lifted from a Merriam-Webster dictionary. *Epigraph*, for example, has two definitions, the first being "an inscription on a statue, a building, or a coin," and the second, "a quotation set at the beginning of a literary work." An oddity is the inconsistent description of living writers in both the present and past tense. The entry *Drabble, Margaret*, for example begins, "English writer of novels that are skillfully modulated variations on the theme of...." *Proulx, E. Annie*, however, begins, "American writer whose darkly comic yet sad fiction was peopled with quirky, memorable characters." Nevertheless, MWEL admirably covers topics from a wide breadth of literary subjects. The volume also will serve as a valuable supplementary source for literary allusions, with such entries as *Banshee, Jezebel, Kali,* and a variety of other mythological and religious entries.

MWEL perhaps most closely represents the various Oxford Companion titles for depth of coverage, though even in that series one must first find the appropriate country-or genre-related volume. Any number of literary dictionaries and biographical dictionaries contain similar entries, but for sheer ready-reference capabilities, MWEL is in a class of its own. Its low price further justifies a place for this volume on any library's reference shelf.

A Dictionary of Literary Pseudonyms in the English Language. By T. J. Carty. Fitzroy Dearborn, 1995. 624p. $75 (1-884964-13-3).
808 Anonyms and pseudonyms [BKL]

A standard component of most card catalogs was the provision of cross-references between variant forms of an author's name. This useful feature not only assisted patrons who were interested in reading all books by a certain author, regardless of the name used on the title page, but also frequently enabled reference librarians to answer questions regarding pseudonyms more quickly than by consulting printed sources. Although today's online catalogs offer many advantages over card catalogs, many do not yet provide cross-references that link the various names under which an author has chosen to write. Thus, the need for accurate and up-to-date printed guides to pseudonyms is even more important than ever.

Compiled by a secondhand-book dealer in London, this dictionary identifies the real names behind approximately 12,000 pseudonyms used by about 7,500 English-language writers from the seventeenth century to the present. Therefore, it includes pen names for figures ranging chronologically from Daniel Defoe and Henry Fielding to Stephen King and Joyce Carol Oates. The dictionary is divided into two sections, the first of which lists pseudonyms and identifies the writer who used each name. The second section is arranged by the authors' original names. Each entry includes the person's dates and a brief phrase identifying the writer by nationality and genre, for example, "English romantic novelist." Pseudonyms used by the author are then listed alphabetically, with one or two representative titles provided in parentheses following each.

Although Carty makes several factual errors (the most glaring of which is the identification of Harriet Stratemeyer Adams, the American writer who penned most of the Nancy Drew books, as an "English science-fiction writer"), the most disappointing aspect of this work is its incompleteness. Many authors who used pseudonyms (e.g., Ian Fleming, Louis L'Amour, Edgar Lee Masters, John Steinbeck) are not here at all, while the lists of pseudonyms for those who are included are often incomplete. For example, Carty identifies three pseudonyms for T. S. Eliot, twelve for Harlan Ellison, two for Ken Follet, and one for P. G. Wodehouse. *Major 20th-Century Writers* (Gale, 1991) lists six for Eliot, twenty-one for Ellison, four for Follet, and six for Wodehouse.

Comparisons of this work to other guides revealed that it is not as comprehensive as *Pseudonyms and Nicknames Dictionary* (3d ed., Gale, 1987) and Harold S. Sharp's *Handbook of Pseudonyms and Personal Nicknames* (Scarecrow, 1972; suppl., 1975; second suppl., 1982). Although this dictionary cannot stand alone as a reliable source of literary pseudonyms, it does include some unique entries. Therefore, large libraries will want to add it to complement the above mentioned sources.

Guidelines for Bias-Free Writing. By Marilyn Schwartz and others. Indiana Univ., 1995. 100p. bibliog. index. $15 (0-253-35102-2); paper $6.95 (0-253-20941-2).
808'.027 English language—Usage—Handbooks, manuals, etc. || Discrimination—Language—Handbooks, manuals, etc. || Non-sexist language—Handbooks, manuals, etc. [BKL] 94-29281

This guide is a product of the Task Force on Bias-Free Language of the Association of American University Presses. Concepts are presented in separate, numbered paragraphs similar to familiar style guides such as Turabian's *Manual for Writers*. Boxed examples of text, mostly drawn from university-press books and manuscripts, exemplify disparaging, exclusive, or otherwise incorrect usage.

The chapter "Gender" is the longest, comprising nearly half the book. Much attention is devoted to finding elegant and practical alternatives to the generic use of *man*, its compounds, and the generic *he*. The most controversial alternative will probably be the use of *their* in informal communication ("Everyone has to carry their own luggage"). Other gender issues addressed include the trivializing effects of gender-marked terms such as feminine suffixes (*waitress*), idioms and figures of speech that are now considered sexist ("old wives' tale"), and the problem of quoting historical sources that use sexist language.

The ensuing chapters are shorter. The chapter on race and ethnicity includes a glossary listing preferred terms (*Muslim* over *Moslem*), and offers guidelines for negotiating the differences among such terms as *Native American, American Indian, native peoples, native Indian,* and *Metis*. The chapter "Disabilities and Medical Conditions" includes a discussion of the difference between *disability* and *handicap*, the appropriate use of the word "normal," and the necessity of avoiding the use of disability as metaphor in such phrases as "blind to the truth." "Sexual Orientation" tackles heterosexism and appropriate terminology, including terms for partners in a homosexual or heterosexual couple. *Age*, just three pages in length, sets an age limit of 13 or 14 for use of *boy* or *girl* and suggests using *youth* for ages 13 to 19. *Older person* is now preferable to *senior citizen* or *elderly person*.

A bibliography lists guidelines issued by other organizations (AARP, the National Easter Seal Society), citations to sections of standard style manuals that deal with bias-free writing, and dictionaries of problematic terms such as the *Bias-Free Word Finder* (Beacon, 1991). An index leads readers to discussions of specific terms and such concepts as ethnocentricism or quoting.

Writers will appreciate the common sense with which the task force approaches bias-free writing. The authors caution against embracing such popular terms as *differently abled* or *physically challenged* because they may seem euphemistic. Some writers may feel constrained by stylistic directives such as those against "semantic choices attributing agency to men and passivity to women." The errors in some of the sentences illustrating these concepts are so subtle that they may not be immediately apparent. In another sensitive area, the task force cautions authors against acknowledgments that stereotype or trivialize the contributions of women to the finished work, including *diligent typing*.

While *Guidelines for Bias-Free Writing* is entirely satisfactory as a reference that can be consulted for advice about a specific term or situation, it will be most valuable to those who spend the time to read it cover to cover. Fortunately, reading it is a painless exercise. Like Strunk and White's *Elements of Style*, the book is entertaining and enlightening. Recommended for academic and public libraries.

MLA Handbook for Writers of Research Papers. 4th ed. By Joseph Gibaldi. Modern Language Association, 1995. 293p. index. paper $12.50 (0-87352-565-5).
808'.02 Report writing—Handbooks, manuals, etc. || Research—Handbooks, manuals, etc. [CIP] 94-38577

This fourth edition of a publication based on the "MLA Style Sheet," begun more than 40 years ago, includes a great deal of information about using and citing electronic sources. Designed as a "comprehensive picture of how research papers are created," the handbook was last published in 1988. It will be used by researchers from high school and up. It is aimed at students; The MLA Style Manual (1985) is aimed at scholars. The handbook takes readers through the research paper process step by step, and includes information on narrowing the topic, outlining, note taking, etc. Before dealing with such mechanics of writing as spelling, punctuation, and format, the manual covers the use of catalogs (online and paper), indexes, and databases in the library and offers a list of some standard print and electronic reference works. The sections on documentation in text and citations seem to include every type of source and possible variable. The work concludes with abbreviations for terms used in research, reference sources by subject, and some examples of other styles of documentation. Examples within each section are printed in a font different from the explanatory text, a feature that allows the user to easily find the appropriate format. Chapters are divided by subtopics with numeric denotation; an index makes topics easy to find.

Public and academic libraries should update their style manuals with this edition because of the inclusion of electronic sources, portable and online. High schools that use the MLA style should also include it in their library collections.

The New York Public Library Writer's Guide to Style and Usage.
Ed. by Andrea J. Sutcliffe. HarperCollins, 1994. 854p. bibliog. illus. index. $35 (0-06-270064-2).
808'.027 English language—Style || English language—Usage [CIP] 93-33255

The purpose of this guide is to help new and experienced writers and editors navigate today's world of electronic publishing, beginning with the writing of first drafts and ending with the delivery of computer disks or camera-ready copy.

In five parts, the guide covers (1) current English usage, with special attention given to bias-free language and commonly misused or confused words; (2) grammar, with an emphasis on controversial issues and with many illustrated examples; (3) style, including lists of common abbreviations and a chapter on special characters in 19 different languages; (4) assembling and checking the manuscript, including a discussion of copyright and instructions for indexing; and (5) physical preparation of the manuscript. Information regarding computer-aided writing and production is provided in all relevant sections. A topically arranged, annotated bibliography of style manuals and dictionaries (many of which are referred to in appropriate sections of the book) and an index conclude the volume.

Written by the staff of an editorial and production services company and aided by writers, indexers, librarians, copyright attorneys, printers, and bookstore owners, this guide's nonprescriptive approach is unpretentious. Unlike The Chicago Manual of Style, which is geared toward professional and academic writers, the Writer's Guide is aimed at a wide audience, including students and business and technical writers. Through numerous sidebars and illustrative examples, it provides an entertaining context that has universal appeal (e.g., baseball and physics comprise the context for explaining levels of usage, a quote from Norman Mailer illustrates dangling participles).

The Writer's Guide does not take the place of discipline-specific style manuals such as the MLA Style Manual, the CBE Manual for Authors and Editors, or the ACS Style Guide. It is also not meant to take the place of usage dictionaries such as Webster's Dictionary of English Usage. Instead, it will supplement more scholarly writing guides and will be an invaluable resource for writers whose publishers do not require strict adherence to a particular style manual. Its commonsense approach to documentation will help even scholarly writers who cannot find examples of difficult referencing problems in their discipline-specific style manuals, and it will be the first (and often only) stop for other writers. The Writer's Guide will be heavily used in all libraries, it is an excellent purchase for homes in which there are writers, and it will be a reference-desk staple (especially for telephone reference queries).

Scientific Style and Format: The CBE Manual for Authors, Editors, and Publishers. 6th ed. Cambridge, 1994. 784p. bibliog. charts. index. tables. $34.95 (0-521-47154-0).
808'.0666 Technical writing—Handbooks, manuals, etc. [OCLC] 94-22001

It has been 11 years since the fifth edition of this well-known manual was published under the title CBE Style Manual: A Guide for Authors, Editors, and Publishers in the Biological Sciences. Earlier editions focused on style for those publishing in the plant sciences, zoology, microbiology, and the medical sciences. This quite expanded sixth edition covers all scientific disciplines, excluding only a few technological areas that are not experimental or observational. In order to include new disciplines, the sections on how to write and submit papers to scientific journals have been omitted. This was a sensible change, since each journal already publishes its own procedures.

The Style Manual Committee of the Council of Biology Editors had five aims in producing this excellent book: to support convergence in style in an international framework, to simplify formats for citations and references, to simplify style rules, to offer options based on the deeply rooted conventions of some disciplines, and to reduce work at the keyboard. The major parts of the book are "General Style Conventions," "Special Scientific Conventions," "Journals and Books," and "Publishing Process." Of these parts, the first two make up the bulk of the book. "General Style Conventions" covers every possible aspect, including alphabets, symbols, punctuation, capitalization, abbreviations, and geographic descriptions. Most of these conventions are also used outside the scientific community, so this manual can serve as a style reference for all writers, although some conventions are unique to science. For example, this section recommends the use of Arabic numerals instead of spelled-out words for the numbers one to nine. The "Special Scientific Conventions" section is comprehensive, covering the electromagnetic spectrum, subatomic particles, chemical elements, chemical names and formulas, analytical methods, drugs and pharmacokinetics, chromosomes, viruses, bacteria, plants, algae, human and animal life, the earth, and astronomical objects and time systems. The text is thorough and easy to follow, with many examples. Appendixes cover recommended practices for abbreviating journal titles and publishers' names; a bibliography is followed by an index.

There is no other book like this for the scientific and technological community. It should be the major desk reference for anyone writing a scientific article or book. Students should be made aware of the manual early in their educational career so that old habits can be broken and correct procedures adhered to. Highly recommended for all academic libraries; public libraries should consider purchase, too.

Poem Finder on Disc. CD-ROM. Roth, 1994. $395/yr for a subscription updated twice a year; $295 for a one-time purchase.
808.1 Poetry—Indexes [BKL]

Last reviewed here [RBB Mr 1 92], the major change in this version is the retrieval software. Hardware and software requirements remain the same. Roth now uses the OPTI-WARE interface, the same software used for Bowker's Books in Print Plus and related titles.

This new version, according to the promotional material, indexes some 360,000 poems (up from 265,000 in the first release) in 1,600 anthologies (up from 1,322), 2,100 single-author collections (up from 1,326), and more than 3,000 issues of 109 periodical titles (up from 1,263 issues; the coverage of 109 titles remains the same). The previous edition's weakness in coverage of titles from the 1970s has been alleviated somewhat, as the current edition indexes 30 anthologies and 51 single-author collections from the 1970s (up from 10 and 27, respectively, in the previous release). The program takes up just over 300,000 bytes on the hard drive (program files are copied from the CD-ROM). Poem Finder doesn't allow one to change the name of the subdirectory it's copied into.

Every time the program was invoked, an error message indicating that the program "could not locate the word processor" came up, though it started well enough after that. The familiar pull-down menus labeled Search, Browse, Format, Action, and Options appear. The Search menu allows a variety of Boolean searches on various fields, while the Browse menu is more straightforward and provides a lookup from a specific field.

There are, however, a variety of oddities in both types of searches. The help screen in the Search menu (which is some 14 screens in length and is not context sensitive) indicates that with the p search "any word in a poem title" will be found. In fact, pt retrieves only the first word of the title. Typing in ptwoods to retrieve Frost's "Stopping by Woods on a Snowy Evening" retrieves 28 hits—all with woods as the first word in the title. On the other hand, typing in ptstopping, retrieves 27 hits, including the Frost work. From the Browse menu, choosing the Periodical Title search seems to include many more titles than just periodical titles (such as the book New Modern Poetry: British and American Poetry Since World War II) and also lists titles beginning with The under T.

Admittedly, there are many more search criteria than with *Columbia Granger's* on CD-ROM, once one can figure out exactly what part of which fields are indexed. The safest bet of all appears to be a keyword search under either menu. The addition of last-line indexing is nice (though not present for every poem). Another addition is brief author biographies, but apart from name, nationality, and birth and death dates, there is little given. Oddly, although "Religion" is a searchable field, it does not display in an author's biographical entry. "Nationality" is sometimes inconsistent. For example, there are 1,755 hits for *English*, and 303 hits for *British*. Oliver Goldsmith is British; William Shakespeare is English.

The full citations to the poems themselves consist of author name, title, first line, last line, and references (anthologies, etc.) with page number. If the poem is available from Roth, there is also the note "Full text of this poem is available from CoreFiche." The user may download or print. There is no collection-tagging feature for anthologies a library may own, though Roth sells separate software that will do this.

In sheer numbers, *Poem Finder* easily outranks *Columbia Granger's World of Poetry*. The indexing inconsistencies will make this an occasionally frustrating product to use, but the retrieval-interface change is for the better.

Anatomy of Wonder 4: A Critical Guide to Science Fiction. 4th ed. Ed. by Neil Barron. Bowker, 1995. 912p. bibliog. indexes. $52 (0-8352-3288-3).

016.80883'876 Science fiction—Bibliography || Science fiction—History and criticism [CIP] 94-42363

This fourth edition of *Anatomy of Wonder* is a substantial revision of the last one published in 1987. New contributors with fresh insight, updated coverage through November 1994, elimination of non-English titles, dropping of weaker titles, and increased emphasis on scholarly analyses are hallmarks of this new edition. Barron edited the previous three editions.

Approximately 2,100 science fiction titles and 800 nonfiction works are annotated here. The work consists of 15 chapters, with the first four covering science fiction chronologically from its beginnings to 1994. Other chapters treat young adult sf, publishing, general reference works, history and criticism, author studies, sf in television and movies, illustration (including comics), magazines, teaching science fiction, and research-library collections. One of the best explanations of New Wave and cyperpunk is found in chapter 4. The final chapter consists of lists of best books, awards, series, a series index, translations, organizations, and conventions. An author-subject index is followed by a title index. A theme index is invaluable for those who need works that illustrate "end of the world" scenarios or medicine in science fiction.

Citations include publisher of first edition and date; annotations are a paragraph in length. Related titles with similar or contrasting approaches are cross-referenced by chapter and entry number. Each chapter begins with an interesting essay explaining the history, changes, hallmarks, and chief individuals of the time period. All the great names—Asimov, Clarke, Heinlein, and LeGuin—are included along with such new writers as Brin, Bova, and Willis.

This work will fill many needs. It is a superb source for finding information on titles or authors, building a reference collection, or finding Hugo and Nebula winners. It is an excellent guide to collection development, providing a recommended list of "best" titles. The excellent essays and annotations will be invaluable to anyone teaching or studying science fiction. This work is recommended to any library having a previous edition or serving patrons interested in science fiction.

Cultures Outside the United States in Fiction: A Guide to 2,875 Books for Librarians and Teachers, K–9. By Vicki Anderson. McFarland, 1994. 414p. indexes. $35 (0-89950-905-3).

016.80883'0083 Children—Foreign countries—Juvenile fiction—Bibliography || Children's literature—Translations into English—Bibliography [CIP] 94-6272

Immigrants in the United States in Fiction: A Guide to 705 Books for Librarians and Teachers, K–9. By Vicki Anderson. McFarland, 1994. 144p. indexes. $23.50 (0-89950-906-1).

016.813'54080352069 Children—U.S.—Books and reading || Immigrants—U.S.—Juvenile fiction—Bibliography || Children's stories, American—Bibliography [CIP] 94-1231

Native Americans in Fiction: A Guide to 765 Books for Librarians and Teachers, K–9. By Vicki Anderson. McFarland, 1994. 166p. $24.95 (0-89950-907-X).

016.813008'09282 Children's stories, American—Bibliography || Indians in literature—Bibliography [CIP]

Anderson, a retired librarian and author of *Fiction Index for Readers 10–16* [RBB O 15 92], has created three annotated bibliographies of fiction for use with students in grades K–9. They employ basically the same format. Books are included because they were found in one of the libraries used by the author. Each entry includes author, title, publisher, date, grade level, and one to three subject headings. The author does not reveal how she arrived at the grade level and whether it indicates reading level or interest level. There is no indication whether the books are still in print. Publication dates range from the mid-1950s to 1993.

Cultures outside the United States contains entries for 2,875 picture books and fiction works in English. Works are arranged alphabetically by 150 countries or geographic regions. The short annotations are nonevaluative; this means that Bishop's *Five Chinese Brothers* is listed along with Mahy's *Seven Chinese Brothers*, without any indication that Bishop's "classic" work has been questioned as being racist. There are three indexes: author, title, and subject; an appendix lists books by grade level and geographic region.

Immigrants in the United States identifies more than 700 books about the social customs of people who were born outside the U.S. and later emigrated here. Titles are arranged alphabetically by author within 60 nationalities or ethnic groups. The grade-level appendix has designations (K–2, K–3, 1–3, 1–4, 2–4, 2–5, 3–4, etc.) that make it difficult to use. The coverage is limited for some ethnic groups; for example, only one book is listed under the heading African, and that book was published in 1968.

Native Americans in Fiction lists more than 765 books arranged alphabetically by 115 tribes. The appendix has a table with the tribe, subtribe, and geographic area where they live. When the reader chains back from the subtribe Passamaquoddy to the Abnaki tribe and turns to the section for books about the Abnaki, there is no indication which, if any, of the books are about the Passamaquoddy. The author, title, and subject indexes in this book note tribe.

These titles would be important additions to reference collections, but unfortunately they are not authoritative. The lack of evaluative annotations is the most serious handicap. Given the interest in multicultural literature for children, librarians need to know the authenticity of works.

Fantasy Literature for Children and Young Adults: An Annotated Bibliography. 4th ed. By Ruth Nadelman Lynn. Bowker, 1995. 1,092p. indexes. $50 (0-8352-3456-8).

016.80883'8766 Children's literature—Bibliography || Young adult literature—Bibliography || Fantastic literature—Bibliography [CIP] 94-42549

This annotated bibliography of fantasy novels and story collections for children and young adults in grades 3–12 also has a research guide on the authors who write in this genre.

In part 1, the annotated bibliography, the books listed are novels and story collections published in English (including translations) between 1900 and 1994. Almost 1,500 titles have been added since the third edition (1989), making a total of more than 4,800 books. About 3,100 are numbered main titles, with the remainder being sequels or related works by the same author. Sixty titles out of print for 50 years are listed under "Books Deleted from the Fourth Edition." Entries note grade-level designation, reviewing sources, out-of-print status where necessary, and recommendation symbols where applicable (noting outstanding quality or classic status). Each book has a one-sentence annotation.

In part 2, the research guide, almost 4,000 new books, Ph.D. dissertations, and articles have been added to the 6,000 resources from the third edition. These references are divided into four areas: "Bibliographical and Reference Sources," "Critical and Historical Studies," "Educational Resources," and "Fantasy Literature Author Studies." An excellent introduction to fantasy literature covers definitions, classification, use with children and young people, criticism, and historical overview.

Indexed by author and illustrator, by title, and by subject, *Fantasy Literature for Children and Young Adults* is a valuable resource for librarians and teachers who work with young people and for students of children's literature.

Good Reads. Retro Link Associates, 175 N. Freedom Blvd., Provo, UT 84601, 1995. quarterly. 5 diskettes $395; network prices available.
808.83'016 Fiction—Bibliography—Databases [BKL]

NoveList. CARL, 3801 E. Florida Ave., Ste. 300, Denver, CO 80210, 1995. quarterly. 10 diskettes $750; network prices available.
808.83'016 Fiction—Bibliography—Databases [BKL]

These two readers' advisory tools for adult fiction are on diskette and run under Windows. *Good Reads* will also soon be available through Ameritech's Vista service and *NoveList* CARL's Everybody's Catalog.

Based on the fiction readers' advisory database of the County of Los Angeles Public Library, *Good Reads* describes approximately 10,000 novels. It comes on diskettes that are to be copied to the hard drive of an IBM-compatible 386 computer running Windows 3.1 and MS-DOS 5.0, with 8MB of RAM, 25MB of space available on the hard drive, and a VGA monitor. *Good Reads* will run faster with a 486 PC, 60MB of free space on the hard drive, and MS-DOS version 6.2. A mouse is highly recommended. Quarterly updates come as part of the subscription. It is possible to print entries, though libraries can disable printing if they wish. *Good Reads* comes with brief installation instructions, and there is context-sensitive help.

The initial screen displays icons for 15 genres: Western, sf, family saga, classics, romance, etc. Clicking on one of these leads to a split screen. On the left is a list of titles in that genre, and on the right is information about the first novel on the list. The user pages down the list, clicking on likely titles. The entry for each novel includes the author, a one-sentence summary of the plot, the time period in which it is set, one to eight subject headings, awards won (such as the Booker or Pulitzer prizes), and any films based on the book. Publication dates and publishers are not given, which would be useful in choosing a title. Clicking on a button labeled "other searches" leads to another screen where it is possible to search by author, title, locale, time period, subject, series (including important characters in series), awards, and film adaptations. Pop-up boxes are available for each of these selections prompting the user with choices. Once a novel is selected using either method, it is possible to click on another button and get a list of similar books. This is a list of books in the same genre, which can be narrowed down by locale and time period.

NoveList provides access to more than 34,000 fiction titles. The product requires at least an IBM or compatible computer with a 386 processor, 4MB of RAM, at least 65MB of available hard-drive space, and a mouse. A loose-leaf notebook of instructions contains a list of the Hennepin County Public Library fiction subject headings used in the database, and there is context-sensitive help. It is possible to print single entries or to keep a list of titles and print at the end of a session.

There are two main ways to search: Match and Describe. In the first, the patron enters the author or title of a book previously enjoyed, and *NoveList* looks for similar titles based on the subject headings assigned. Related titles are then ranked according to the number of subject headings they share. Entries note the original publication date and publisher, the most recent publication date and publisher, if the book is a translation, and special editions, such as large print. Entries also include ISBNs and 8–10 subject headings. Some of the subject headings are genres, but they are not consistent with the genre terms used in "Explore Fiction Types" below. More than 3,000 of the entries have reviews from *Booklist* appended. The other main means of access, Describe, searches by subject, which may include location, historical period, characters, or genre. Here it is possible to type in a heading or browse a list. For example, typing in *mystery stories* results in a list of subgenres such as Christian mystery stories, feminist mystery stories, etc. Clicking on one retrieves a list of titles.

There are two additional options in *NoveList*. "Explore Fiction Types" searches the fourth edition of *Genreflecting* (to be published in August). An initial screen shows seven main genres; clicking on one leads to several dozen subgenres. Clicking on a subgenre results in a list of authors and titles. (For prolific authors, it may just say "over 50 novels.") This feature is not linked to the *NoveList* database—there are even titles in this section that aren't in the main database. The final feature is "Best Fiction," with lists of winners of seven awards. This section can be customized with lists of current bestsellers or local favorites. Gale's *What Do I Read Next?* is scheduled to be added in the next release this summer.

Each of these attractive products has its strengths. *NoveList* has the advantage of a bigger database of books and reviews for some titles, which give the patron a better sense of what the book is about. On the other hand, searching by genre in *NoveList* is more difficult than in *Good Reads*. *Good Reads* has information about film adapations and is great for the genre fan. For the person who wants novels set in Chicago in the nineteenth century or fiction about adoption or John James Audubon, both these products are effective, but neither is particularly successful in finding books similar to one the user has already read—sometimes the matches are ludicrous. Fans of romance novels will be surprised to find Nabokov's *Ada* mixed in with Catherine Coulter and Charity Blackstock in *Good Reads*. Solzhenitsyn's *Cancer Ward* is listed with adventure/suspense novels, and Joseph Conrad's *Chance* is in the "Glitz 'n Glamour" genre. *NoveList*, on the other hand, matches the subject headings applied to books, some of which are quite literal. Fans of Doris Lessing's *Landlocked* will be surprised to be referred to Jackie Collins' *Hollywood Wives*, just because both books share the subject heading "married women." Faith Baldwin's *District Nurse* and Danielle Steel's *Wanderlust* are supposedly similar to Hemingway's *A Farewell to Arms* because they share the subject heading "love stories, American." Perhaps these suggestions will help genre readers broaden their reading choices, but many will be mystified by these matches because there is no way to distinguish popular from serious fiction. Librarians who read widely and know their clientele's tastes can do a better job of recommending similar books. However, readers' advisory service is a luxury in some public libraries today, and even the best librarian is ignorant of some genres. Some patrons will appreciate the anonymity of using an electronic product, and those who can remember only the subject or setting of a book will find these products useful. Bookstores are now adding kiosks with *TitleTour*, an electronic guide that lets shoppers browse by author, title, and subject and find links to other books by the same author or on the same subject. Obviously, readers are hungry for suggestions about what to read, and these products are a step in the right direction. —Sandy Whiteley

Recreating the Past: A Guide to American and World Historical Fiction for Children and Young Adults. By Lynda G. Adamson. Greenwood, 1994. 494p. index. $55 (0-313-29008-3).
016.80883'81089282 Children's literature—Bibliography || Young adult literature—Bibliography || Historical fiction—Juvenile literature—Bibliography [CIP] 94-14435

Adamson returns to historical fiction, this time with an annotated bibliography for grades 1–10. (Her *Reference Guide to Historical Fiction for Children and Young Adults* [Greenwood, 1987] profiled 80 authors of historical fiction and their works.) "The 970 works selected are insightful, historically accurate, and for the most part, well written. At least 200 are award winners." The first two chapters cover "Prehistory and the Ancient World" and the "Roman Empire to 476 A.D." The remaining chapters switch to a geographic approach: Europe, South and Central America and the Caribbean, Africa, China, etc. Each of these chapters is subdivided by time period and then arranged alphabetically by author. Bibliographic information and an annotation are given for each work. The annotations try to incorporate date; setting; "a description of the protagonist according to age, sex, and situation"; and a statement about the theme. Seven appendixes and an author-illustrator-title index complete the volume. The appendixes include an index of titles by readability and interest levels; a list of works with protagonists of or plots concerning minority groups; famous groups and people in the works; works with sequels, same characters, or in series; and country and date of setting in Europe.

Though she discusses the historical fiction genre in an introductory essay, Adamson never really sets forth her criteria for inclusion. Lacking a clear statement, questions arise about the omission of such titles as Mazer's *The Last Mission*, Lunn's *The Root Cellar*, and Uris' *Mila 18*, as well as classics such as *The Scarlet Pimpernel*. As might be expected, books on the American colonies and the U.S. dominate the guide. While copyright dates from earlier in this century appear, most are from the late 1970s through early 1994.

This book belongs on all professional shelves in elementary through high schools where it will help identify sequels and aid in collection building. As always with a well-done bibliography, there's the joy of meeting old friends as well as the challenge of attempting to identify those books omitted.

Twentieth-Century Children's Writers. 4th ed. Ed. by Laura Standley Berger. St. James, 1995. 1,256p. bibliog. index. $132 (1-558-62177-6).
808.8'92 Young adult literature—Bio-bibliography [BKL]

Twentieth-Century Young Adult Writers. Ed. by Laura Standley Berger. St. James, 1994. 830p. bibliog. index. $132 (1-558-62202-0).
808.8'92 Young adult literature—Bio-bibliography [BKL] 93-42870

By shifting the focus of the fourth edition of *Twentieth-Century Children's Writers* (TCCW), St. James has paved the way for yet another volume in its Twentieth-Century Writers series. Now concentrating on authors for children 10 and under, this edition of TCCW includes 724 entries in its main section, compared with 830 in the third edition. Although 68 writers—among them Graeme Base, Mem Fox, Nikki Giovanni, and Faith Ringgold—have been added to this edition, 176 entries have been dropped.

Most of the authors removed from TCCW (such teenage favorites as Sue Ellen Bridgers, Rosa Guy, S. E. Hinton, Roald Dahl, and Robert Cormier) now appear in *Twentieth-Century Young Adult Writers* (TCYAW). Covering 406 novelists, poets, and dramatists whose works appeal to readers ages 11–19, this new compilation also treats a large number of authors who write for an adult audience but whose works have found a following among younger readers. Thus, its entrants include such figures as Joseph Heller, Stephen King, William Golding, Terry McMillan, and Amy Tan. Thirty writers (among them Lloyd Alexander, Judy Blume, C. S. Lewis, and Mark Twain) continue to appear in both compilations, but in most cases the entries were either written by different contributors or significantly revised.

The fourth edition of TCCW follows the same format as its predecessor. The main portion of the work covers English-language writers whose works were published primarily after 1900. The initial paragraph in each entry provides brief biographical information and lists career highlights, awards, and other significant accomplishments. The next section consists of a bibliography of the author's publications, divided into those for children and those for adults. Some articles also contain a brief list of secondary sources and comments by the author. Concluding each entry is a signed critical essay. Primary bibliographies have been updated to include imprints through 1994, with some even citing 1995 publications. However, most of the accompanying essays have not been revised to reflect these newer works. The appendixes remain the same: one provides similar treatment for 40 nineteenth-century children's writers, and the other includes brief entries on 80 foreign-language writers. A title index provides access to all the publications for children listed in the entries.

The format of TCYAW closely resembles its parent volume. In general, however, the biographical paragraphs are more detailed and the bibliographies of critical and biographical works are fuller. In addition, many of the primary bibliographies include sections that identify young adult publications. Again, works that are appropriate for young adults are listed in the title index.

Many of the writers in these volumes are covered in other sources, such as *Contemporary Authors, Something about the Author, Dictionary of Literary Biography*, or the Wilson series on junior authors. In addition, most of the writers for adults now featured in TCYAW are also treated in other volumes in St. James' Twentieth Century Writers series or in its *Contemporary Novelists, Contemporary Dramatists*, or *Contemporary Poets*. Librarians who have found the previous editions of TCCW useful are now faced with the dilemma of deciding whether the coverage of children's and young adult writers formerly provided in one volume is now worth the price of two.

Wilson Author Biographies. CD-ROM. Wilson, 1995. $299 single users. network prices available. (0-8242-0865-X).
809 Authors—Biography || Authors—Bibliography [BKL]

Until now, the products in Wilson's Wilsondisc line have been electronic versions of the publisher's famous indexes. *Wilson Author Biographies* (WAB) represents its first full-text database, based on five volumes of the Wilson Authors series: *American Authors, 1600–1900* (last published in 1977), *British Authors before 1800* (1952), *British Authors of the Nineteenth Century* (1936), *European Authors, 1000–1900* (1967), and *Greek and Latin Authors, 800 B.C.–A.D. 1000* (1980). In addition, the disc is supplemented with updated bibliographies drawn from other Wilson databases. All told, the database "contains biographies and bibliographies of some 4,300 writers who lived from 800 B.C. to the early 20th century." The disc is text-only. (The print volumes have black-and-white portraits for some authors.)

Like all Wilsondisc programs, this CD-ROM is DOS based. It requires an IBM or compatible computer (any processor), DOS 3.1 or later (DOS 5.0 or later recommended), 640K RAM (484K conventional minimum available), and 4 to 5MB of hard-drive space. The disc has more than ample documentation: a 64-page manual designed for use with all Wilsondisc products as well as a 16-page manual specifically about WAB. Limits on printing and the enabling of various menus can be set. Technical support is available weekdays from 8:30 a.m. until 8:00 p.m. EST. A fax number and E-mail address are also supplied. Printing and downloading onto a floppy are both easily done.

WAB has the same look as all Wilsondisc products. The opening menu displays three searching options: Browse (name and title search), Wilsearch (multiple subjects), and Wilsonline (command language). Context-sensitive help is available in all three modes.

The Browse mode allows the user to type in an author's name or the title of a work. Authors' names, of course, will typically yield but one hit, but titles of works may receive several. *Wuthering Heights*, for example, retrieves five hits, since the work is mentioned in several author essays. A typical record begins by stating which of the five titles the entry was taken from, followed by the author's birth and death dates. The biography is identical to that in the printed work, concluding with the same list of works by the author with original publication dates and a list of works about the author. However, the disc varies from the printed volumes in that an updated bibliography, "Additional Citations about Author," lists articles and books drawn from other Wilson databases such as *Humanities Index* or *Biography Index*. The fact that these were stripped off a database is evident in that the citations are in reverse chronological rather than alphabetical order. For many authors, a note at the end of the entry points out that yet a further list of citations is provided. Unfortunately, getting at these further citations is incredibly circuitous. The screen prompt "For search instructions press the F1 key" leads to such listings as "POE, EDGAR ALLAN/ALLUSIONS" or "POE, EDGAR ALLAN/WORKS/BLACK CAT." The help screen directs the user to press the ESC key to get back to the list of authors and titles, and press the F8 key to view a list of cross-references to that author. Then, the user must scroll down the list to highlight the cross-reference desired. If the user wishes to view additional cross-references, pressing the ESC key brings the user not back to the list of additional author cross-references, but instead all the way back to the original list of authors and titles, where F8 must be pressed again to get the cross-reference list back.

The Browse mode reveals some other problems. Listed right before the title *Wuthering Heights* in the alphabetical list of authors and titles, for example, is *Wutheiring Heights* [sic]. Fortunately, this still leads to Bronte's entry. If the user types in *Huckleberry Finn* as a title, the entry for Twain will be retrieved. Typing in *Adventures of Huckleberry Finn*, however, retrieves two citations: Twain and author Luigi Capuana, whose biography indicates one of his novels is called "a Sicilian Adventures of Huckleberry Finn." Typing in *Dr. Faustus* retrieves Christopher Marlowe but *Doctor Faustus* retrieves an entry for Wilhelm Muller, who translated Marlowe's work, but not for Marlowe himself, as the work is consistently cited in his biography with the abbreviated spelling.

Choosing the second search mode, Wilsearch, alleviates some of these retrieval problems. With this mode, the user is shown a "fill in the blanks" menu, with an implied Boolean AND between entries. There are two lines available for Subject/Keyword, and separate lines for Author, Genre, Nationality, Language, Gender, Century/Period, and Birthday. A Subject/Keyword search on *Huckleberry Finn* retrieves all relevant hits. Pressing F1 while the cursor is at any of the lines provides a list of the possibilities for what should be entered in that field. However, these help screens do not allow the user to scroll through the indexes and select appropriate words. Instead, the user must remember which of the eight genres or 15 subject areas are searchable in the Genre field. Internal and end-of-word truncation may be used with a variety of symbols. For example, a user may search for all nineteenth-century male novelists by typing in *novelists* for Genre, *m* for Gender, and 19$ at Century/Period. The system quickly (under five seconds) indicates 401 entries. Unfortunately, there is no list of entries retrieved; the user must plow through all of the full entries. Even worse, if the user wants to look at the additional cross-references listed at the end of a specific author's biography at this point, pressing the F1 key for help brings up a help screen for conducting a Boolean search in the *Wilsonline* mode—completely irrelevant to what is being viewed. Not all records are indexed the same way. An Author search for *Stephen, Leslie* retrieves but one record—a bibliographic citation. The biographical record is indexed as *Stephen, Sir Leslie* and is therefore not retrieved.

The final search option, Wilsonline, is unlikely to be used by anyone but librarians used to that command mode. In any event, given that the database itself is rather straightforward, the Wilsearch mode is powerful enough for most uses.

Apart from these retrieval difficulties, the fundamental problem with this disc is that the material on which it is based is anywhere from 15 to nearly 60 years old. Notwithstanding the updated bibliographies, the essays do not incorporate any recent research done on these authors. Having a text-only, DOS-based product based on older material with some perfunctory updating at a cost of only about $35 less than the printed works may have been fine in the late 1980s, but at this stage more is expected, particularly from as reputable a publisher as H. W. Wilson. The added citations and search capabilities may be nice, but only libraries just beginning to build a reference collection in literature will be interested in this product.

Encyclopedia Mysteriosa: A Comprehensive Guide to the Art of Detection in Print, Film, Radio, and Television. By William L. DeAndrea. Prentice Hall, 1994. 405p. bibliog. illus. $25 (0-671-85025-3).
809.3'872 Detective and mystery stories—Dictionaries || Detectives in mass media—Dictionaries [CIP]

This volume by Edgar Award winner DeAndrea covers mystery writers, actors, characters, novels, films, and TV and radio shows in a single A-to-Z arrangement. He says there hasn't been a comprehensive study of the entire genre for the general reader since the *Encyclopedia of Mystery and Detection* (1975). Entries vary from a few lines to six pages. Eleven signed inserts of two to three pages each highlight such topics as *Batman*, *Dime Novels*, and *Dick Tracy*. These essays are easily found thanks to their listing in the table of contents. Compleeting the work are lists of mystery bookstores in the U.S., Canada, and England; organizations and awards; mystery magazines; and a mystery-related glossary. Cross-references abound, keeping a mystery fan following the ties between writers and characters. Important characters merit separate entries with a list of the novels in which they appear. An author's nonseries books are listed under the author's entry. Illustrations consist of black-and-white movie stills and portraits of authors.

DeAndrea claims that "it is simply not possible to include every mystery author and mystery movie ever made," yet the subtitle claims this a comprehensive work. Tom Clancy and critic Jacques Barzun rate entries but not John Grisham, Margaret Truman, Elliott Roosevelt, Sharyn McCrumb, Rochelle Majer Krich, Gillian Roberts, or Sarah Shankman to name a few (and so many of them female!). *The A-Team*, *L.A. Law*, and *Batman* appear but not *NYPD Blue*, *Cops*, or *The Green Hornet*. Anne Perry's entry omits her William Monk series. Anthony Award winners are not listed.

On the other hand, since mystery readers usually like to read all the novels featuring their favorite character, the lists after these entries will prove useful in answering reader's advisor queries. Let your mystery readers know it's available for browsing. If you have legions of mystery buffs and your budget allows, consider a circulating copy as well.

Great Women Writers. Ed. by Frank N. Magill. Holt, 1994. 611p. index. $40 (0-8050-2932-X).
809'.89287 Literature—Women authors—Bio-bibliography—Dictionaries || Women authors—Biography—Dictionaries [CIP] 93-47648

This latest literary reference source from Magill covers women writers from antiquity to the present. Poets, playwrights, and fiction authors are included. Of the 135 authors, 71 are American (11 African American) and the majority of the remainder are European.

Entries follow the standard Magill format. The author's birth and (when appropriate) death dates are followed by a list of principal works, a brief summary of achievements, biographical information, and critical analysis of her work. Each author is discussed in the context of her historical period in the "Achievements" section. Critical reception of her work is outlined, and awards are listed. Biographical sketches are adequate and cite events that influenced the writer or are reflected in her body of work. Themes, influences, and literary techniques and devices are thoroughly discussed in the critical analysis. Textual examples are used to illustrate and explicate work.

Of the 135 women included, only five do not appear in at least one other standard literary reference source, and most appear in several. This book is intended for a general audience, and the information is easily accessible by secondary-school students. Public and high-school libraries needing another reference source on women authors should consider purchase.

Modern Black Writers. v.2. Comp. by Steven R. Serafin. Continuum, 1995. 813p. bibliog. index. $95 (0-8264-0688-2).
809'.889 Literature—Black authors—History and criticism || Blacks in literature [CIP] 76-15656

This volume in the Library of Literary Criticism series is the long-awaited supplement to *Modern Black Writers* (1978), which was compiled by Michael Popkin. It provides a collection of excerpts of criticism on 125 authors from 32 countries. Only 27 of the authors were also treated in the first volume. Among the new writers here are Maya Angelou, Alice Childress, Lucille Clifton, Rita Dove, Audre Lorde, Toni Morrison, Wole Soyinka, Derek Walcott, and August Wilson.

Those writing in English or French constitute the majority of the authors in the supplement, but there is some representation of authors writing in Portuguese and Swahili, as well as other African languages and dialects. At the front of the source is an alphabetical list of authors by country. A number of the treated authors are also critics, and there is a list of those who wrote criticism included in the book, followed by a list of the periodicals from which the criticism was excerpted. Closing the work are a list of authors and their works mentioned in the critical selections and an index to the authors of the criticism.

This supplement is a must for libraries holding the 1978 volume. While there are other sources of criticism for black American writers (e.g., Scribner's *African American Writers*), this series is useful for its coverage of writers throughout the black diaspora. Gale's *Black Writers* provides biographies of both American and African writers and references to criticism, but not the criticism itself.

Larousse Dictionary of Literary Characters. Ed. by Rosemary Goring. Larousse, 1994. 849p. index. $35 (0-7523-0001-6).
809.927 Characters and characteristics in literature—Dictionaries [OCLC] 94-75740

Larousse Dictionary of Writers. Ed. by Rosemary Goring. Larousse, 1994. 1,070p. $40 (0-7523-0006-7).
809.003 Authors—Dictionaries || Literature—History and criticism—Dictionaries || Literature—Bio-bibliography—Dictionaries [OCLC] 94-75741

These titles share more than an editor and a publisher: each offers considerable breadth of coverage, whether cataloging characters "from Beowulf to Billy Bathgate" or acknowledging "international authors from Angelou to Xenophon." In both, an attempt has been made to highlight more than the usual English or American canon of authors.

The *Dictionary of Literary Characters* includes more than 6,000 "major characters from novels, poems and plays written in English." While most of the authors represented are indeed of the Anglo or American variety, the number of contemporary writers cited sets this book apart from such other titles as the *Dictionary of Fictional Characters* by Martin Seymour-Smith (Writer, 1992). The RBB review of that work characterized its treatment of contemporary literature as weak. In comparison, the *Dictionary of Literary Characters* includes characters from the works of such contemporary writers as Alan Ayckbourn, A. S. Byatt, Sara Paretzky, Sue Miller, Salman Rushdie, and Scott Turow. Authors from other parts of the world are also represented, including Wole Soyinka, Chinua Achebe, and Anita Desai. Although the contemporary coverage is considerable, too often authors are represented by the characters of only one novel or play. There are also some errors; for example, Lennie Small is identified as a character in Steinbeck's *Tortilla Flat* rather than *Of Mice and Men*.

Entries are arranged by characters' names, followed by the title of the work, its year of publication, and author. A brief sketch of the character, often using the words of the author, completes the entry. These summaries are much briefer than those in *Major Characters in American Fiction* [reviewed in this issue]. Cross-references to entries on other characters in the same work are indicated by the use of bold type. An index lists authors followed by the title of a work and a list of characters.

The *Dictionary of Writers* is a broad survey of more than 6,000 authors "from all periods and all countries." While the editor admits to a British and American bias, a successful attempt has been made to include authors from numerous nations. A quick tally of the nationality of writers in the As and Cs revealed not only the expected American and English wordsmiths, but their counterparts in Iraq, Brazil, Uruguay, Bulgaria, Iceland, Estonia, and elsewhere. Entries are arranged by name, followed by year of birth and death in parentheses and the briefest of biographical sketches. These sketches usually include mention of works that might be considered representative. Cross-references to similar authors are indicated by bold type. One noteworthy feature for such a compact work is the listing at the end of many of the entries of a biography of the entrant. Unfortunately, there is no index of authors by country of origin: this would have highlighted the breadth of geographic coverage. The *Dictionary of Writers* also includes many contemporary authors. The various Oxford Companions cover many of these authors. But for one-volume handbooks, these two titles are solid offerings and would be especially useful in ready-reference situations.

Literature

This Land Is Our Land: A Guide to Multicultural Literature for Children and Young Adults. By Alethea K. Helbig and Agnes Regan Perkins. Greenwood, 1994. 401p. indexes. $49.95 (0-313-28742-2).
016.8108'09282 Children—U.S.—Books and reading || Minorities—U.S.—Juvenile fiction—Bibliography || Folk literature—Bibliography || Children's stories, American—Bibliography || Children's poetry, American—Bibliography [BKL] 94-16124

The fiction, poetry, and oral traditions of African, Asian, Hispanic, and Native Americans are the focus of this annotated bibliography. Authors Helbig and Perkins, both of whom have published extensively in the field of children's literature, note that books were chosen on such literary values as plot, style, and nonstereotyped characterization. Representatives of the four ethnic groups served as consultants.

The books, 570 in all, were published from 1985 through 1993, with more than 60 percent published since 1990; they cover grades K–12, including some titles originally published for adults (e.g., Amy Tan's *Joy Luck Club*). Each cultural group is divided into sections for poetry, oral tradition, and fiction, under which entries are arranged alphabetically by writer. The number of entries for groups and sections varies, reflecting both publishing and cultural trends. For instance, there are more titles listed about African Americans, but the oral tradition section for Native Americans is the largest. Each entry includes ISBNs for hardcover and paperback editions, price, and age and grade levels. Annotations include a description of plot, characters, illustrations, and critical commentary. The titles of books on similar subjects or by the same author are often mentioned, with a cross-reference provided if appropriate. Five indexes—title, author, illustrator, grade level, and subject—provide further access. Abbreviations indicating ethnic groups are used in the grade-level and subject indexes.

Our Family, Our Friends, Our World: An Annotated Guide to Significant Multicultural Books for Children and Teenagers (Bowker, 1992) covers the same cultural groups, but its strength is in its worldwide coverage. It lists some earlier titles (back to 1970) but has fewer entries per U.S. ethnic group and, unlike *This Land Is Our Land*, includes very few poetry collections. *Native Americans in Fiction* [RBB De 15 94] lists many more titles under specific tribes, but the annotations are not as helpful. Libraries and curriculum resource centers will want to consider *This Land is Our Land* for its currency and comprehensive coverage of quality multicultural literature for children.

Dictionary of Literary Biography, v. 137: American Magazine Journalists, 1900–1960. 2d series. Ed. by Sam G. Riley. Gale, 1994. 411p. bibliog. illus. index. $120 (0-8103-5396-2).
810.9 Journalists—U.S.—Biography—Dictionaries || Authors, American—20th century—Biography—Dictionaries || Journalism—U.S.—History—20th century [OCLC] 93-81776

This volume of the *Dictionary of Literary Biography* is the second devoted to American magazine journalists in the period from 1900–1960. (The first was volume 91, published in 1990.) According to the editor, "the shape of the magazine industry in this period was such that an additional volume was required to do justice to its leading editorial figures." In this volume, 36 publishers, editors, and journalists are profiled.

The introduction provides information on the scope of the volume, as well as the evolution of the magazine during the period. The bulk of the book consists of lengthy profiles of journalists, providing information on major professional positions held, a list of their publications, a biographical profile, biographies written about them, references used in compiling the sketch, and an indication of where the subject's papers are housed. The profiles, which are generally engaging and well written, trace the subjects' lives from childhood through the major points in their journalism careers. Of the journalists profiled, only one (Margaret Cousins) is a woman. Cousins is one of eight journalists covered who were alive at the time of this volume's publication. Some (most notably William F. Buckley, Hugh Hefner, and John Johnson) are still active. At least two of the journalists, Theodore Dreiser and H. L. Mencken, have been profiled in other volumes in this series. The profiles are nicely illustrated with photos of the subject and/or of the magazines they were associated with.

An appendix provides a list of magazine editorial statements from the period covered, taken, for the most part, from the magazine's first issue. This is followed by a list of contributors, a checklist of further readings, and a cumulative index to the 137 volumes in the series. No information is provided about the authors of the profiles other than their academic affiliation.

In compiling this volume, the editor has placed the emphasis on quality, not quantity. Such important figures in the field as Harold Ross and the Wallaces (the founders of *Reader's Digest*) are given extensive coverage. This useful reference tool is recommended for purchase by university libraries building comprehensive collections in mass communications; public libraries will want to consider purchase, too.

Jewish American Women Writers: A Bio-Bibliographical and Critical Sourcebook. Ed. by Ann Shapiro. Greenwood, 1994. 557p. index. $86 (0-313-28437-7).
016.8109'8924 American literature—Jewish authors—Bio-bibliography || Jewish authors—U.S.—Biography—Dictionaries || American literature—Women authors—Bio-bibliography || American literature—Jewish authors—Dictionaries || Women authors, American—Biography—Dictionaries [BKL] 93-40618

As the subtitle suggests, this volume focuses on three aspects of each author: her life, her work, and critical analysis of some of those works. Every profile is actually divided into "Biography," "Major Themes," "Survey of Criticism," and "Bibliography," which includes works by and about the writer. The biographical and themes sections show how the author's background is reflected in what she writes. The surveys of criticism are often short. Researchers looking for critical analysis would do better with Gale's *Contemporary Literary Criticism*.

The more than 50 authors profiled include poets, playwrights, and novelists. About a dozen are deceased, including Edna Ferber and Fannie Hurst, but the majority are still writing today, including Erica Jong and Wendy Wasserstein. In addition to the alphabetically arranged entries, the book includes an overview of the field of writing by Jewish American women. In this introduction, the tenets of Judaism that made writing difficult for these women are pointed out, giving the reader a greater appreciation for their accomplishments. There is also a concluding chapter that examines the many autobiographies written by Jewish American women. This discussion of some of the 200 or so works gives readers insight into the ethnic background from which these authors matured.

Each author entry is written by a recognized scholar in Jewish American literature or related fields, and contributors are identified at the end of the book. A glossary of unfamiliar ethnic terms is included, as is a general bibliography. The index includes personal names and titles.

This title would be most appropriate for large public libraries or academic libraries with ethnic or women's studies collections.

Native North American Literature. Ed. by Janet Witalec. Gale, 1994. 706p. illus. indexes. $99 (0-8103-9898-2).
810.9'897 American literature—Indian authors—Bio-bibliography || Canadian literature—Indian authors—Bio-bibliography || Authors, Indian—Biography—Dictionaries || Indians in literature—Dictionaries [CIP] 94-32397

In providing biographical and critical material on writers and orators of Native American heritage, *Native North American Literature* (NNAL) follows the same general format as two earlier Gale compilations of critical excerpts devoted to specific ethnic groups: *Black Literature Criticism* [RBB D 15 91] and *Hispanic Literature Criticism* [RBB Jl 94]. Representing tribal cultures from Canada and the U.S., the 78 individuals included range from well-known historical figures such as Chief Joseph, Sitting Bull, and Tecumseh to such noted contemporary writers as Louise Erdrich, N. Scott Momaday, and James Welch. However, the majority of the figures treated are not as widely recognized since they tend to be published outside the mainstream press.

An excellent introductory essay by the noted scholar Joseph Bruchac (who is himself the subject of an entry) gives an overview of both the written and oral tradition of Native American literature. The entries themselves appear within two major sections, with part 1 devoted to oral literature (subdivided into oral autobiography and oratory) and part 2 focusing on written literature. Each entry consists of a brief overview of the writer's life and career; a list of major writings; lengthy excerpts from book reviews, critical commentary, interviews, etc.; and a bibliography of secondary sources. Frequently, entries include excerpts from the author's work. For example, the article on Chief Seattle not only includes material questioning the authenticity of his famous speech pertaining to the environment, but also reproduces a version of the speech in its entirety. A boxed note at the end of an entry refers the user to other Gale publications in which the individual is treated. Most articles are accompanied by a photograph of the individual, and maps showing the locations of reservations and other Indian groups in the U.S. and Canada are provided near the front of the volume.

Two indexes categorize the writers featured by tribe and by genre, and a third index provides access to the titles discussed in the critical excerpts. Because the entries appear in the three separate alphabetical sequences mentioned above, an index to the writers would have been useful.

Since so many of the individuals in NNAL are relatively unknown, the amount of duplication between the critical excerpts in this volume and titles in Gale's Literary Criticism series is minimal. Only 10 writers are also represented in Contemporary Literary Criticism, and only five are included in Twentieth-Century Literary Criticism. Biographical information on these individuals is more readily available in other Gale publications: 44 are included in the biographical chapter of Native North American Almanac [RBB My 1 94], while 33 appear in Contemporary Authors.

In addition, 39 of the 78 authors treated here are accorded critical and biographical essays in the Dictionary of Native American Literature [RBB Ap 15 95], but those articles tend to be briefer. However, that work also contains a number of thematic essays, such as "Teaching Indian Literature" and "The New Native American Theater."

The heightened emphasis on multicultural studies has created a strong demand for works in this area. This well-conceived volume will be of particular value to small libraries that lack the broad range of sources excerpted in this compilation. However, since only a small percentage of these excerpts appear in other Gale compilations, even larger libraries will probably want to add NNAL for the convenient access it provides to information on Native American writers.

The Oxford Companion to Women's Writing in the United States. Ed. by Cathy N. Davidson and Linda Wagner-Martin. Oxford, 1994. 1,021p. bibliog. index. $45 (0-19-506608-1).
810.9'9287 American literature—Women authors—Dictionaries || American literature—Women authors—Bio-bibliography || Women and literature—U.S.—Dictionaries || Women authors, American—Biography—Dictionaries [CIP] 94-26359

In recent years, there has been a trend among publishers of literary reference sources for books that group authors in ways that reflect how they are increasingly studied. One of the ways to consider writers is by ethnic group. Another is to draw on the tremendous growth in the area of women's studies and examine women's literature as a distinct field. Now, from Oxford comes a new member of its distinguished Companion series. Editor Davidson is professor of English at Duke University; and Wagner-Martin is professor of English at the University of North Carolina, Chapel Hill.

Five hundred scholars contributed to this multidisciplinary work, which is intended "for both general readers and specialized academic critics." All entries are signed, and the contributors are listed in a directory. The editors explain that they chose "writing" rather than "literature" because they wanted the book to reflect women's contributions in a wide range of genres. Chronological coverage ranges over four centuries. Entries are from 15 lines to several pages in length. See references help guide the reader to appropriate entries, and, within the text, asterisks are used to indicate cross-references.

Coverage includes entries that examine periods of time, such as Colonial Era Writing and Progressive Era Writing. Entries are here for ethnic literature, such as Irish American Writing and Southeast Asian-American Writing, as well as for regions such as New England and the South. Essays cover such genres as Humor, Slave Narratives, Poetry, Protest Writing, and Etiquette Books and Columns and also on writing in various academic and professional fields. Other entries examine such issues as Deconstruction and Feminism, Immigration, Pornography, and Whiteness. Th entries Aging, Daughters, and Romantic Love explore these topics as literary themes. There are entries for historical events, such as the Federal Writer's Project, and for various aspects of reading and publishing. Separate entries appear for more than 400 women, from Anne Bradstreet and Phillis Wheatley to Gloria Steinem, Louise Erdrich, and Amy Tan. Many more are mentioned in the various essays; the index lists page references for writers as diverse as Sara Paretsky, Ann Landers, Anna Quindlen, Virginia Hamilton, Marabel Morgan, and LaVyrle Spencer. With a few exceptions, such as Tillie Olsen's Silences, there are no entries for individual titles.

It is not entirely clear how decisions were made to have entries on some writers and not others. Southern writers Ellen Gilchrist and Lee Smith have their own entries, but Dorothy Allison, Jill McCorkle, and Josephine Humphries are covered in the essay Southern Women's Writing. There is no mention anywhere of Mary Lee Settle. There are entries for Jane Smiley and Terry McMillan, but Mona Simpson is discussed under Arab-American Writing, and Barbara Kingsolver is mentioned only as a poet, in the essay Translators.

Following the main body of the text are a "Timeline of U.S. Women's Writing," an extensive bibliography, and the index. The detailed index is crucial because of all of the information embedded in the text.

As the editors state in the preface, there are already "many excellent resources currently available" on women writers. Information about many of the writers covered here can also be found in Contemporary Authors, Modern American Women Writers (Scribner, 1991), and The Feminist Companion to Literature in English (Yale, 1990), to name just a few. What is unique about this volume is that it aims to explore the entire range of women's writing in a multidisciplinary framework. The reader will learn almost as much about current trends and issues in the disciplines of literature and women's studies as about women's writing itself. Recommended for most libraries, as an authoritative source to support inquiries in both fields.

Major Characters in American Fiction. Ed. by Jack Salzman and Pamela Wilkinson. Holt, 1994. 952p. indexes. $60 (0-8050-3060-3).
813.009'27 Characters and characteristics in literature—Dictionaries || American fiction—Dictionaries [CIP] 94-11460

This is a compilation of nearly 1,600 biographical sketches of fictional characters from American novels and short stories. Many are from classic works of fiction (The Scarlet Letter, The Adventures of Huckleberry Finn), but others are drawn from the works of lesser-known writers and their works (Edgar Huntly by Charles Brockden Brown or Beetlecreek by William Demby). The majority of works included were written for adults, but characters from classic children's literature are also included, most notably, Dorothy and other characters from Baum's Wizard of Oz.

Entries are arranged alphabetically by the character's last name. The title of the book, the author, and the date of publication follow. Details and significant events in the character's life are drawn from the novel or novels in which he or she appears. The length of the "biography" varies from character to character, but all include a brief interpretation of the character's life and significance to the work. In most cases, if the volume contains an entry for another character in the same novel, that character's name is listed in all capital letters. The entry for Scarlett O'Hara highlights the names of Rhett Butler, Ashley Wilkes, and Melanie Hamilton (Wilkes). There are, however, some exceptions to this rule. Entries for the members of Mary McCarthy's The Group do not contain such cross-references to the other characters profiled. Following the biographical entries are a complete list of authors with the names of the characters and the title of the work and a list of titles with the name of the characters and the author.

The editors intend the volume to represent a cross-section of American literature, illustrating its depth and diversity. They do not include any criteria for inclusion, other than to say that the characters profiled were chosen for their importance and significance to the staff of the Center for American Culture Studies at Columbia University. All biographical sketches were written by staff members of the center.

This is a readable work that would be accessible to both high-school students and patrons of the public library. Since it contains more detail than a dictionary guide to famous literary characters, it would be useful to reference and reader's advisory librarians. This work will also interest browsers who are sure to find new characters and new titles to read and enjoy. Dictionary of American Literary Characters (Facts On File, 1990) identifies only the title and author of the book in which 11,000 characters appear.

Science Fiction, Fantasy, and Horror Writers. 2v. Ed. by Marie J. MacNee. Gale/UXL, 1995. 432p. bibliog. illus. index. $38 (0-8103-9865-6).
016.813'0876208 Science fiction—Bio-bibliography—Juvenile literature || Fantastic fiction—Bio-bibliography—Juvenile literature || Horror tales—Bio-bibliography—Juvenile literature [BKL] 94-32459

The lives and works of 80 of "the best-known, highest-praised, scariest, funniest, and most-promising authors of tales of future worlds, alternative universes, psychological spine-tinglers, and more" are covered in this two-volume set. These writers of interest to young adults extend from Mary Shelley and Robert Louis Stevenson to

Stephen King and Anne Rice. YA authors such as Natalie Babbitt and Laurence Yep are also covered.

Each author is detailed in an entry written in an inviting manner for a middle-school audience. Vital information and a black-and-white portrait begin each article. A 1,500-word biographical essay follows that gives specifics on early life, education, career, and the unique characteristics of the genre writer. Brief quotes from the authors or their critics are disbursed throughout the entries. Sidebars include short annotated lists of some of the authors' best works, photos of either a book jacket or movie still, and information about movie adaptations. Suggested sources for further reading are found at the end of each entry. Lists of Hugo and Nebula award winners and an author-title-subject index conclude each volume.

Most of the writers covered in *Science Fiction, Fantasy, and Horror Writers* are also found in *Something about the Author*, but this new title will be convenient for children's services in school and public libraries. It is recommended as a stimulating reference, reading-advisory, and browsing tool for students and librarians.

The Shakespeare Dictionary. Ed. by Sandra Clark. NTC, 1994. 291p. bibliog. $20.95 (0-8442-5755-9).
822.3'3 Shakespeare, William—Dictionaries, indexes, etc. [BKL] 94-65121

This book begins with lengthy introductory essays on Shakespeare's life, his poetry, and theater and play production in his time and an extensive bibliography. The main part of the book is made up of more than 1,000 alphabetically arranged entries on his plays and characters. For each play, there is a plot summary, a list of characters, discussion of the historical sources on which Shakespeare drew, and the early publishing history of the play. The entries for characters are briefer. For minor characters, a sentence identifies the play and the character's role in it; for more important characters, such as King Lear, entries are a paragraph in length. There are also entries for early theater companies, actors famous for Shakespeare roles, other playwrights of the period, and such theater terms as *masque*.

Libraries that bought the more detailed *Shakespeare A to Z: The Essential Reference to His Plays, His Poems, His Life and Times, and More* (Facts On File, 1990) will not need *The Shakespeare Dictionary*, but those that couldn't afford that book will want to consider this inexpensive one. —Sandy Whiteley

Cloak and Dagger Fiction: An Annotated Guide to Spy Thrillers. 3d ed. By Myron J. Smith and Terry White. Greenwood, 1995. 849p. bibliog. indexes. $95 (0-313-27700-1; ISSN 0742-6801).
016.823'087209 Spy stories—Bibliography || Spy stories—Stories, plots, etc [BKL] 94-22017

Thriller in the subtitle here refers to any species of fiction revolving around spies. The heart of this volume is a 5,807-entry annotated bibliography arranged by author (compared with 3,435 entries in the second edition, published in 1983). Most of the titles were published since 1940. With the exception of a key work listed at the beginning of some authors' entries along with biographical notes, annotations are descriptive of plot but are not evaluative. Symbols following many annotations indicate if a title exists exclusively in paperback, portrays no graphic sexuality, is suitable for young adults, features humor, or uses a historical plot, setting, or characters. The lack of running heads for authors' names sometimes makes it difficult to ascertain where a particular entry begins.

Front matter includes a brief historical introduction and bibliography (new to this edition) of books, intelligence journals and fanzines, and reference works on espionage. Back matter comprises five appendixes and author and title indexes. Appendixes contain notes on the craft by espionage writers, and guides to pseudonyms, characters in series, intelligence and terrorist organizations, and espionage jargon. The craft notes and guide to jargon are new to this edition.

The wealth of new material in this edition of *Cloak and Dagger Fiction* justifies its purchase by public and academic libraries, even if they already have an earlier one.

Great Women Mystery Writers. Ed. by Kathleen Gregory Klein. Greenwood, 1994. 417p. bibliog. indexes. $49.95 (0-313-28770-8).
823'.0872099287 Detective and mystery stories, American—Women authors—Dictionaries || Detective and mystery stories, English—Women authors—Dictionaries || Women authors, American—Biography—Dictionaries [CIP] 94-16123

One hundred sixteen women mystery writers are described in this guide edited by Klein, who teaches English and women's studies at Southern Connecticut State University and is the author of other books on detective fiction. Chronological coverage ranges from Mary Elizabeth Braddon, whose *Lady Audley's Secret* was published in 1862, to such contemporary writers as Linda Barnes, Patricia Cornwell, and Elizabeth George. In her introduction, Klein traces the history of mystery fiction in general, and mysteries by women in particular, from the beginnings through the golden age of Agatha Christie, Josephine Tey, and Dorothy Sayers to the emergence of the female private eye in the 1980s. Appended to the introduction is a reading list of 26 titles that "include substantial information about women mystery writers."

Writers are listed alphabetically. Each entry begins with an essay giving biographical information and describing the chief features of the writer's work. Generally, the essays conclude with advice to interested readers. For instance, that for Catherine Aird notes that readers "might also enjoy works by others, like Ngaio Marsh, Josephine Tey, and Dorothy Simpson, who write in a similar vein." Lists of each writer's mystery fiction follow the essays. Works in series or written under different names are listed separately. Finally, each entry concludes with a brief bibliography of critical works. Each of the entries is signed, and information about the contributors is provided in an appendix.

Other appendixes include an essay about the Edgar Awards, with a list of women nominees and winners; a list of winners of the Agatha Award and at the annual Malice Domestic conference; and an essay by Sara Paretsky about Sisters in Crime, the group of women who read, write, sell, publish, or review mysteries. "Putting Out the Word: Alternative Activities for Mystery Fans" lists fan-centered conferences, such as Malice Domestic, and academic conferences, such as those of the Popular Culture Association, as well as periodicals. Another appendix describes Dorothy-L, the electronic discussion group for mystery fans. Other appendixes include a list of mystery bookstores in the U.S. and Canada and a list of 14 categories of mystery fiction, such as *Comic/caper*, *Lesbian*, and *Locked Room*, with examples. The only indexes are by author and title.

In *By a Woman's Hand: A Guide to Mystery Fiction* [RBB Je 1 94], coverage begins in 1977 and so excludes all earlier writers. On the other hand, its more than 200 entries include many contemporary writers not found in *Great Women Mystery Writers*, such as Lindsey Davis and Jennie Melville, as well as writers of romantic suspense, such as Mary Stewart and Phyllis Whitney. Eighty-five authors appear in both sources. Despite the fact that it covers fewer writers, the biographies and bibliographies in *Great Women Mystery Writers* make it a much more useful reference tool. In addition, while *By a Woman's Hand* offers the standard geographic and series character indexes found in many sources, several of the appendixes in *Great Women Mystery Writers* are unique. Finally, while both provide "read alike" information, *Great Women Mystery Writers* goes a step further by adding advice on how to read the author being discussed.

By a Woman's Hand filled a void in the literature of mystery fiction because it focused on women, but it is superseded by the more authoritative *Great Women Mystery Writers*, which is highly recommended for public and academic libraries. A circulating copy of the relatively inexpensive *By a Woman's Hand* would make a useful reader's advisory tool.

Historical Figures in Fiction. By Donald K. Hartman and Gregg Sapp. Oryx, 1994. 352p. indexes. $45 (0-89774-718-6).
016.823'081089293 Historical fiction—History and criticism—Bibliography || Young adult fiction—History and criticism—Bibliography || History in literature—Bibliography || Characters and characteristics in literature—Bibliography [CIP] 94-15105

Two librarians compiled this bibliography of 4,200 novels arranged by the 1,500 historical figures who appear as significant characters. A tag identifies each historical personage (e.g., "Akhbar, 1542–1605, Mogul emperor"). Novels are then arranged by author under each figure, noting title, publisher, and date. Reviews in any of more than 100 journals are cited for each book. Symbols note books for children or young adults. The typical historical figure only has a few novels listed after his or her name, but Elizabeth I has 50 and Jesus has 86. Some books are listed under more than one name. E. L. Doctorow's *Ragtime*, for example, is listed under Emma Goldman, Sigmund Freud, and others. The publication dates of the novels range from 1940 to 1993; more than half the books listed were published before 1970. Indexes by author, title, and occupation conclude the book. The occupation index is often subdivided by nationality or other category, for example, Artist, Italian; Author, American; Political Leader, Canadian; Religious Figure, Jewish.

This is the most comprehensive index to characters in historical fiction available and will be useful to researchers and students. However, because so many of the books listed are old, many public and school libraries will probably continue to rely on less-comprehensive subject guides to fiction, such as Dickinson's American Historical Fiction (5th ed., Scarecrow, 1986). —Sandy Whiteley

Now Read On: A Guide to Contemporary Popular Fiction. 2d ed. By Mandy Hicken and Ray Prytherch. Scolar Press; dist. by Ashgate, 1994. 442p. indexes. $46.95 (1-85928-008-0).
823'.91409 English fiction—20th century—Handbooks, manuals, etc. ‖ American fiction—20th century—Handbooks, manuals, etc ‖ English fiction—20th century—Stories, plots, etc. ‖ American fiction—20th century—Bibliography [CIP] 93-47276

For library patrons who thrive on fiction, the search for new (to them) books and authors will never end, or so it seems. Similar to the avid reader looking for another good novel is the librarian hoping to find another good reference source for locating the same. Now Read On makes a contribution to this effort, joining such ongoing publications as H. W. Wilson's Fiction Catalog, Gale's What Do I Read Next?, Genreflecting: A Guide to Reading Interests in Genre Fiction, Olderr's Fiction Index, and many other guides to fiction. This book offers a British viewpoint, and although many of the authors are American novelists popular in Britain, it may introduce the average American patron to quite a few new writers. Author Hicken is a librarian, Prytherch, an information management consultant.

As was the first edition published four years ago, this is "a guide to the work of popular contemporary authors who write in a specific genre." Westerns and light romance are not covered, although gothic romances are. Of the 20 genres listed, some interesting ones are country life, foreign locations, humorous novels, "perceptive" women's novels, sea stories, and war stories. Mysteries are represented by the categories of detective stories, police work, thrillers, and women detectives.

The section on each genre begins with a description of its characteristics, a brief history, and the leading writers identified with it. A short biography is given for each author, including place of birth, education, field of endeavor, places of residence, and honors and prizes. Next is a list of books with British publishers and publication dates, sorted by series, where applicable. The entry finishes with "now read" suggestions for similar authors. In the adventure genre, the entry for Desmond Bagley ends, "Now read Hammond Innes, Geoffrey Jenkins, Alistair MacLean, Duncan Kyle, Ken Follett, Wilbur Smith, Bob Langley." A list of literary prizes and awards, an index of authors, and an index of series and recurring characters complete the book.

Making no claims to be exhaustive, this is nevertheless a solid work, giving access to many authors and titles of worthy novels, presented in a useful and interesting way. Patrons should enjoy using it and may come to rely on it. The short biographies of authors will be popular also. Library staff members doing book selection may find some authors to add to their collections. Recommended for public libraries.

Masterpieces of Latino Literature. Ed. by Frank Magill. HarperReference, 1994. 655p. indexes. $45 (0-06-270106-1).
860.9'98 Latin American literature—History and criticism ‖ American literature—Hispanic authors—History and criticism [CIP] 94-8803

From the seemingly inexhaustible Frank N. Magill comes this new addition to the Masterpieces series, joining Masterpieces of American Literature and Masterpieces of African-American Literature, among others. Masterpieces of Latino Literature covers works by 105 authors of Latino heritage from South, Central, and North America, from the seventeenth century to the present. It was developed "in response to the growing need for reference works capable of presenting information on ethnic literature in an accessible format." A number of faculty members from U.S. colleges contributed to the volume and are acknowledged in the preface. Individual entries are not signed.

Masterpieces covers a variety of works, both classic and newer fiction and nonfiction. No criteria for inclusion are provided in the preface, although some familiarity to a mainstream English-speaking audience seems to be a factor. Nearly all of the works not originally written in English are available in English translations. Experts in the literatures of the various nations of Latin America would probably dispute many of the inclusions and exclusions. The poetry of the colonial nun Sor Juana de la Cruz and the novels of Nobel Prize–winner Gabriel García Márquez are included, as are such recent popular works as Like Water for Chocolate by Laura Esquivel, How the Garcia Girls Lost Their Accents by Julia Alvarez, and Dreaming in Cuban by Cristina Garcia, perhaps not "masterpieces" in the strictest sense of the word. There are entries for such Hispanic American writers as Rudolfo Anaya, Sandra Cisneros, and Oscar Hijuelos, but not for Ron Arias, whose Road to Tamazunchale was nominated for a National Book Award.

Entries are arranged alphabetically, by title for individual works, and by genre in the case of essays covering all the work of a particular type by an author, such as "The Essays of Jorge Luis Borges" and "The Poetry of Gary Soto." There are 140 entries on individual titles, and 33 entries on genres. Each entry follows a standard format. Brief ready-reference capsules give the author's name, the type of work, the type of plot (for example, "magic realism," "family"), the time of plot, the locale, and the dates of first publication and first English translation. This is followed by a description of the principal characters, an approximately 700-word overview of the plot, a 600-word analysis, and a 500-word section of critical context. The genre entries begin with ready-reference data providing a list of principal published work, followed by a 2,500-word essay. Author and title indexes conclude the book.

Information on many of the authors covered in Masterpieces can be found in other reference works, including various volumes of Contemporary Authors, Contemporary Literary Criticism, and Dictionary of Literary Biography. Most of the authors appear in Gale's Hispanic Writers (1990), which compiles sketches from Contemporary Authors. Masterpieces of Latino Literature differs from these in that it takes a title rather than an author approach and provides more information on individual works. Its limitations in terms of the authors it includes and its formulaic approach make it inadequate for serious study. However, Masterpieces of Latino Literature will serve as a good introductory source in high school and public libraries.

Dictionary of Native American Literature. Ed. by Andrew Wiget. Garland, 1994. 598p. bibliog. index. $95 (0-8153-1560-0).
897 Indian literature—U.S.—Encyclopedias ‖ American literature—Indian authors—Encyclopedias [CIP]

In 1969, when N. Scott Momaday received the Pulitzer Prize for his House Made of Dawn, academics searching for new worlds to explore turned their eyes to the virgin territory of Native American literature. Since that time they have struggled to apply Euro-American techniques of literary criticism as they have grappled with issues of authenticity, authorship, and oral versus written literature.

This book, edited by Wiget of New Mexico State University with the help of an advisory board, contains more than 70 essays by 52 members of the Association for the Study of American Indian Literatures. Do not be misled by the title—entries are not alphabetically arranged. Instead, scholarly essays are arranged by historical period: Native American oral literature, Indian writing to 1967, and from 1967 to the present. Each of the sections begins with an introductory essay by an advisory board member. The signed articles that follow, by scholars from the fields of anthropology, folklore, literature, and Native American studies, are readable and well researched. Each contains a helpful bibliography of primary and secondary sources. A single index combines subjects, authors, and titles.

The section on Native American oral literatures contains articles on such topics as the oral literature of specific regions, Native American tricksters, and myth and religion. The section on the emergence of Native American writing to 1967 covers such topics as women's autobiography and humor, followed by articles on specific authors (e.g., Black Elk, C. A Eastman, D'Arcy McNickle). The final section has essays on such topics as teaching Indian literature and critical approaches to Native American literature, followed by articles on such authors as Vine Deloria, Louise Erdrich, N. S. Momaday, Leslie Marmon Silko, and James Welch. A few topical articles on issues such as Indian policy are included in order to provide background material.

This reference work has breath and depth enough to satisfy most users. Each of the introductory essays is a gem. Wiget's essay on oral literature has an accessible explanation of mimetic, genetic, and intertextual poles. Although this work could easily be used as a textbook, academic libraries, many high-school libraries, and all libraries with collections of Native American studies will need a copy.

Geography, Biography

Timelines of War. By David Brownstone and Irene Franck. Little, Brown, 1994. 562p. index. $29.95 (0-316-11403-0).
902'.02 History, Military—Chronology [CIP] 94-203

This is an interesting chronology focusing on battles, important weapons development, and people, including generals, presidents, kings, spies, etc. In the early sections, entries are grouped by centuries, then by decades, and from 1700 on, by year. Information is arranged in four parallel columns. In the early sections to 500 B.C. the column headings are "Europe and Anatolia," "Africa," "Southwest Asia," and "East, Central, and South Asia, the Pacific, and the Americas." From 500 B.C. to 1700 there are two columns for Europe, and Africa is included with Southwest Asia. From 1700 through 1993, the geographic arrangement is "Europe," "Africa and Southwest Asia," "Central, South and East Asia, and the Pacific," and "The Americas." Entries are, perforce, brief. Some examples: "Ottoman Turks conquered Bulgaria (1369–72)," "American Revolution: Spain declared war on England (June 21)," "Arab-Jewish riots in Palestine claimed more than 200 lives." These entries demonstrate a shortcoming—the authors are inconsistent about giving specific dates. For example, for some conferences or military battles specific dates are given, but not all. A 30-page index concludes the volume.

Many entries will raise interest, and users will need to turn to reference works that give more complete explanations; a good example is R. E. Dupuy and T. N. Dupuy's *Harper Encyclopedia of Military History from 3500 B.C. to the Present* (4th ed., 1993), an excellent work that is arranged chronologically. Those wishing to get an idea of what was going on in other parts of society during the period covered by *Timelines* may wish to use similar chronologies, such as *The Timetables of History: A Horizontal Linkage of People and Events* (Simon & Schuster, 1993) and S. H. Steinberg's *Historical Tables 58 B.C.–A.D. 1990* (12th ed., Garland, 1991). *Timelines of War* is recommended to libraries needing to supplement the information found in *The Harper Encyclopedia of Military History.*

Worldmark Encyclopedia of the Nations. 8th ed. 5v. Ed. by Timothy L. Gall. Gale, 1995. 400p/v. bibliog. index. maps. tables. $335 (0-8103-9878-8).
903 Geography—Encyclopedias || History—Encyclopedias || Economics—Encyclopedias || Political science—Encyclopedias || United Nations—Encyclopedias [CIP] 94-38556

Worldmark Encyclopedia of the States. 3d ed. Ed. by Timothy L. Gall. Gale, 1995. 756p. bibliog. maps. tables. $135 (0-8103-9877-X).
973'.03 U.S.—Encyclopedias [CIP] 94-38557

These standard reference tools now have a new publisher, Gale. Their arrangement and format remain the same.

Encyclopedia of the Nations has entries for an additional 25 nations that emerged since the last edition was published in 1988, for a total of 202 countries. One of the five volumes is devoted to the United Nations. All entries have new black-and-white maps and have been updated with new statistics, most of them from the 1990s. Libraries where this set has received heavy use will want to update with this new edition.

Last published in 1986, *Encyclopedia of the States* has also had all its statistics updated. However, some of the narrative information needs revision. For example, the Illinois entry says that the Chicago Public Library "is hampered by an inadequate central library crowded into an old warehouse." Chicago opened a new central library in 1991. The "Armed Forces" section of *Illinois* lists Fort Sheridan and Chanute Air Force Base, both of which were closed in 1993. The sports section for Pennsylvania still lists Penn State as an independent, though it is now part of the Big Ten. The sections that list famous people from a state seem to have minimal updating. Many of the bibliographies don't seem to have been updated either (Illinois' has been cut to just three titles). Libraries with a current encyclopedia and the *Statistical Abstract of the United States* will be able to locate most of the information found in this volume. —*Sandy Whiteley*

World History: A Dictionary of Important People, Places, and Events, from Ancient Times to the Present. By Bruce Wetterau. Holt, 1994. 1,173p. $60 (0-8050-2350-X).
903 History—Dictionaries [CIP] 93-34819

A revision of the *Concise Dictionary of World History* (Macmillan, 1983), this volume includes more than 10,000 entries in a convenient A-to-Z arrangement. There are also 135 historical outlines or chronologies that contain another 7,000 items.

Biographical and event entries average approximately 100 words. The typical entry for larger or "more important" nations may run up to several pages. Most of the space in these entries is taken up by chronologies that are up-to-date through 1992. Smaller nations, such as Burundi and Rwanda, are treated briefly without a chronology.

Although the number of entries is about the same as in the 1983 edition, some 100,000 words were added to this edition. The treatment of the countries of Asia, especially China and Japan, has been expanded. Entries on the former Soviet-block countries of Eastern Europe, the Cold War, and the former Soviet Union have all been revised to reflect new realities. There are new entries for George Bush, Bill Clinton, and the Persian Gulf War. Space has been made for new entries by dropping those on mythological figures and some cities.

Cross-references are used but sparingly. Whenever the first initials and last name of a person appear, this is a cross-reference to the main entry. Event-type entries may be located under the country's historical outline as well. For example, *Rye House Plot* (1683) has its own entry but is also found in the chronology for Great Britain. This feature allows the reader to see the event within its historical context. However, not all events are cross-listed: *Phoenix Plot Murders* (1882) has no entry in the Ireland chronology but is mentioned within the biographical entry *Parnell, Charles Stewart*. All entries were seen by a board of academic review made up of 19 scholars from American universities to ensure that all important points have been covered.

Because of the considerable textual revision and expansion in this 1994 edition, libraries owning the first edition will want to update, and libraries that don't own an up-to-date dictionary of historical events will want to acquire *World History.*

The Dorling Kindersley History of the World. By Plantagenet Somerset Fry. Dorling Kindersley, 1994. 384p. illus. index. maps. $39.95 (1-56458-244-2).
909 World history—Juvenile literature [CIP] 94-4856

The latest endeavor of Dorling Kindersley, the publisher who introduced the popular and much-copied *Eyewitness* series, is this beautifully illustrated history for young readers. This ambitious volume begins 570 million years ago and ends with the 1990s. It is divided into sections of varying increments and includes such major events as wars, political upheavals, and inventions. For example, the section "1000–1200: Monks and Invaders" begins with a world map noting important events during this 200-year period. A table lists important events on all five continents. An asterisk on the table notes that more detailed information on this event follows. A time line running across the bottom of each page is highlighted to show the time period being covered.

Dealing as it does with the entire history of the planet, it stands to reason that each era could not be dealt with at length. However, the stunning photography and art here is enough to pique readers' interest on a variety of topics and hopefully will inspire them to do more reading elsewhere. A final reference section includes a glossary and an index.

This beautifully planned book is an excellent tool for stirring interest in history. There is only one area that could be improved upon: there is no pronunciation key of any type. The format and visuals will attract a wide range of reading abilities (upper primary to middle grades), and children will have no idea how to pronounce such names as *Cleisthenes* or *Menes*. Phonetic spelling following the more difficult terms and names would have been helpful.

Masterworks of Man & Nature. Ed. by Mark Swadling. Facts On File, 1994. 399p. illus. index. $35 (0-8160-3177-0).
909 Historic sites || Cultural property, Protection of || Antiquities || Historic sites—Pictorial works || Antiquities—Pictorial works [OCLC] 94-11374

This beautiful book is like a combination of *The Atlas of Sacred Places* and *The Atlas of Wild Places* [RBB N 15 95], only with more reference value. It covers more than 900 cultural and natural sites in 90 countries that have been placed on UNESCO's World Cultural List as worthy of preservation. Maps on the endpapers serve as an index to the sites. Arranged by region and then alphabetically by country, entries note the location of the site, describe it, and discuss its significance. More than 500 beautiful color photographs accompany the entries and a one-to two-page essay introduces each country. Sites are a mixture of national parks, historical buildings, and archaeological sites. Appendixes include the UNESCO World Heritage Convention and a list of its signatories, a glossary, and an index. With coverage ranging from the rock-hewn churches of Lalibela, Ethiopia, and the temples of Angkor Wat in Cambodia to Chartres Cathedral and Sangay National Park in Ecuador, this book will appeal to conservationists and art lovers alike. For the circulating collection. —*Sandy Whiteley*

The Larousse Dictionary of World History. Ed. by Bruce P. Lenman. Larousse, 1994. 996p. maps. tables. $40 (0-7523-5001-3).
909'.03 World history || History—Dictionaries [BKL] 93-072902

Several one-volume dictionaries of world history have appeared in 1994: *World History: A Dictionary of Important People, Places, and Events from Ancient Times to the Present* [RBB S 1 94], *The Hutchinson Dictionary of World History* (ABC-Clio), and now The *Larousse Dictionary of World History*. The latter two works were compiled in Great Britain.

Larousse is based on the extensive computerized database of various Larousse biographical and encyclopedia entries. The editor culled from these sources information from the political, military, and diplomatic sides of world history to create a 7,500-entry encyclopedia. More than 40 contributors from British universities prepared the text, which consists of 50- to 400-word entries in a strict A–Z format. Cross-references are used extensively to direct the reader to related entries. Although the introduction states that the publisher has tried to avoid a Eurocentric bias and give as much coverage to American as British topics, it is difficult to escape the point of view of its contributors. For instance, the entry *English Civil Wars* is longer than *American Civil War*. *Larousse*'s strength is biography; it has an entry for Adam Clayton Powell while *Hutchinson* and *World History* do not. All entries are current through 1992. More than 30 black-and-white maps supplement the text, as well as 40 boxed panels that list members of dynasties, popes, etc. Unfortunately, there is no means of access to these special features.

Hutchinson contains 5,000 entries, detailed histories of all countries, and a chronology. *World History* contains 10,000 entries and entries for countries that incorporate chronologies. Neither entries for countries nor a chronology are found in *Larousse*.

The *Larousse Dictionary of World History* is clearly written and accessible to junior high and up, but its fewer entries and lack of country entries and historical time lines make it less useful as a ready-reference source than *World History*. However, all three of these titles have much unique information, and libraries may want to select more than one.

The Oxford Encyclopedia of the Modern Islamic World. 4v. Ed. by John L. Esposito. Oxford, 1995. 450p./v. bibliog. illus. index. tables. $395 (0-19-506613-8).
909'.097671 Islamic countries—Encyclopedias || Islam—Encyclopedias [CIP] 94-30758

The West knows little of the world's second-largest religion, too often hearing only of the terrorists who try to exploit it for political ends. Muslims are found in all parts of the world, many of them far from the religion's origins in the Middle East. (Indonesia has the world's largest Muslim population.) This new encyclopedia is worldwide in scope, treating every part of the globe where Muslims are found, and focuses on the last 200 years. Editor Esposito, a faculty member in the School of Foreign Service at Georgetown University, has recruited more than 450 distinguished contributors from the fields of art history, religion, science, anthropology, political science, and other disciplines. Some of them are originally from the Islamic world but teaching at universities in the U.S. and Europe; others are at institutions in 30 countries ranging from King Abdulaziz University in Saudi Arabia to the Indonesian Institute for the Sciences.

The 750 entries include regional overviews (*Islam in Europe*, *Islam in the Americas*) and articles on specific countries (including the predominantly Muslim states of the former Soviet Union). There is coverage of the major branches of Islam, of Islamic sects, and of such related faiths as *Druze*, *Bah'ai*, and *Nation of Islam*. The diversity of Islamic religious belief and practice is discussed in such articles as *Circumcision*, *Funerary Rites*, and *Pillars of Islam*. But because Islam pervades all aspects of believers' lives, there are also entries on politics, law, economics, science and medicine, and the arts. The lengthy article *Cassettes*, for example, describes the impact of this technology on the politics of the Islamic world. *Communism and Islam* discusses the philosophical differences between these two belief systems and the places in the world where they have led to conflict. There are entries for specific organizations and movements (*Ba'th Parties*, *Muslim Brotherhood*, *Hamas*) and on the relationship of Islam to other religions (*Christianity and Islam*). Muslim views on such social issues as *Family Planning* and *Surrogate Motherhood* are examined. There are biographies of people from 24 nations, ranging from *Muhammad* to *Malcolm X*. Coverage seems current; for example, *Balkan States* refers to the "gruesome combat that began in the spring of 1992."

Articles range in length from 500 words to 10,000 words on broad topics (*Islamic State*, *Popular Religion*, *Secularism*, *Women and Islam*) and contain *see also* references. Some entry headings are in Arabic, but *see* references lead from the English equivalent, for example, from *Pilgrimage* to *Hajj* and from *Crusade* to *Jihad*. Entries conclude with bibliographies, some of which are annotated. They list mostly titles in English, though occasionally sources in other languages are included. Black-and-white photographs are provided for a few articles (*Aesthetic Theory*, *Architecture*, *Calligraphy*, *Gardens*), but the reader wishes for more, especially in such articles as *Dress* and *Textiles*. A few entries have tables, for example, data on universities in *Education*. A synoptic outline of contents in volume 4 lists all entries under such headings as *Schools of Thought* and *Culture and Society*. This outline helps the reader with limited knowledge of the topic to find appropriate entries. For example, listed under *Mysticism* are all the Sufi orders for which there are entries. A detailed index follows, with provision of *see* references from English to Arabic terms.

While this set provides a scholarly treatment of the subject, most articles are accessible to the educated layperson. Articles on some controversial topics such as *Mujahidin*, *Rushdie Affair*, and *Terrorism* won't satisfy all readers, but every attempt has been made to provide a balanced approach, and the inclusion of contributors from many parts of the world has helped to avoid what the editor calls the "pitfalls of Orientalism." The *Encyclopedia of Islam* (Brill, 1954–) covers classical and medieval Islam, not its modern contexts. It is less accessible to the lay reader, requiring a knowledge of Arabic. The *Cambridge History of Islam* (1970) is now dated and tends to emphasize the Middle East. Presenting a rounded picture of a subject about which Americans hear only the extremes, The *Oxford Encyclopedia of the Modern Islamic World* is an important purchase for academic and public libraries. —*Sandy Whiteley*

Third World Resource Directory 1994–1995: An Annotated Guide to Print and Audiovisual Resources from and about Africa, Asia and Pacific, Latin America and Caribbean, and the Middle East. Ed. by Thomas P. Fenton and Mary J. Heffron. Orbis, 1994. 785p. indexes. paper $59.95 (0-88344-941-2).
016.909'09724 Developing countries—Bibliography || Developing countries—Audio-visual aids—Catalogs || Developing countries—Directories [CIP] 94-1601

The compilers of this work are codirectors of Third World Resources, a nonprofit information clearinghouse established in 1984. They also edit a quarterly journal, *Third World Resources*, and have published directories of resources on specific regions. The foreword notes that the purpose of the work is to empower us to see the Third World firsthand through material in which Third World peoples themselves describe and analyze their situations. Although the directory contains a significant number of resources that are Third World in origin, more of the resources were produced in the "North," particularly in the U.S., than in Third World countries. Most materials date from 1984 (when this directory was last published) through 1993. Older resources are included either for their historical value or because more current materials are not available.

The book is in four sections: 977 print and audiovisual resources arranged by region and country, 1,473 resources grouped under 39 topics (e.g., *Agriculture*, *Conflicts and Military Intervention*, *Rainforests*, *Women*), a directory of approximately 2,300 international organizations, and separate indexes to organizations, individuals, titles of resources, geographic areas, and subjects. The annotations, ranging from one to three paragraphs, are clearly written and succeed in providing a global perspective. The "Directory of Organizations" includes the addresses of all organizations whose materials appear in the work and other Third World–related organizations. Some fax and E-mail addresses are included. Readers will need to use the several means of access provided. As an example, while there are 10 pages under *Women* in the topics section, still other materials on women under individual countries and regions are noted in the subject index.

This reference source has been prepared with care, commitment, and broad and deep knowledge of the world. Public and academic libraries that add the book to their collections will provide access to peoples and countries that are too little known in the U.S. Updates to the book will be made through the PeaceNet computer information system.

Encyclopedia of the Cold War. By Thomas S. Arms. Facts On File, 1994. 628p. bibliog. illus. index. $65 (0-8160-1975-4).
909.82 Cold War—Encyclopedias ‖ World politics—1945- —Encyclopedias [CIP] 90-26899

Although it is still too recent for a totally reasoned and balanced final report, the ending of the Cold War brings the need to document its ramifications, to bring into one place the people and events that made up its many parts, from its beginning in 1945 or thereabouts to its end with the breakup of the Soviet Union. As the introduction to this volume puts it, "The Cold War ended not with a bang, but with a whimper. . . . its flame was . . . extinguished by the winds of change."

Encyclopedia of the Cold War provides in an alphabetical arrangement the people, places, and events of this period. Major and minor figures on both sides are found; lives are sketched briefly, with the emphasis on their part in the Cold War. Entries range from less than one-half page to more than three pages and include many internal cross-references using small-capital letters. Most entries have reading lists appended for further information. Included are such world-famous names as Tito, Stalin, Francis Gary Powers, Salvador Allende, Churchill, and Margaret Thatcher and such lesser-known persons as Theodore Streibert, first director of the U.S. Information Agency, and Vernon Walters, "soldier, intelligence officer and diplomat." Topics discussed range from Yalta, Bay of Pigs, Pugwash Conference, and Pueblo Incident to Aswan High Dam, Alliance for Progress, Loyalty Review Boards, and Window of Vulnerability. Country entries such as Indonesia, Cambodia, and Ghana discuss their relevance to and activities in the Cold War. More than 60 black-and-white photographs are included. Many, but not all, of the titles from the brief bibliographies appended to the entries are repeated in a final bibliography divided into broad areas, primarily geographic, (e.g., Latin America and the Caribbean, U.S. and Canada) but also topical (Espionage, Nuclear Issues, etc.). While there are a few see references in the text (e.g., Nosenko, Yuri—see Angleton, James Jesus), an index provides access to many more items not found as separate entries.

A recent three-volume work, The Cold War, 1945–1991 [RBB Ag 93], includes only about one-half the total number of articles as this encyclopedia. They are generally longer with more illustrations and similar bibliographies, but as they are divided into two separate volumes of biography, Western and Soviet, and an additional volume by topic, the set is more cumbersome to use and to follow cross-references. It does, however, include a couple of special features not found here: a detailed chronology, a longer narrative history, and a list of archives. Each title has entries not found in the other, so they are to some extent complementary. Encyclopedia of the Cold War has slightly smaller print and less white space but could be used by high school libraries as well as academic and public libraries. Encyclopedia of the Cold War will be a welcome addition to reference collections, especially those that did not purchase The Cold War.

Exegy. CD-ROM. ABC-Clio, 1994-. bimonthly. $650/year; network version $975/year.
[BKL] 909'.829 History, Modern—1945

Called by its publisher a "curriculum-based body of current events information," Exegy is based in part on ABC-Clio's card service, Kaleidoscope: Current World Data, though much of the content is prepared especially for this product.

Minimum hardware requirements are a 386SX/16 computer (486SX/25 recommended) with 2MB RAM (4MB RAM recommended), VGA display with 16 colors (SVGA display with 256 colors recommended), and a mouse. Minimum software requirements are MS-DOS 3.30 or higher, Microsoft Windows 3.1, and MSCDEX version 2.2 or higher. The documentation indicates 1.2MB of files are installed on the hard drive. Installation is straightforward, though the program gives the user no choice as to where the files will be added on the hard drive. Technical support is available via a toll-free number from 9:00 a.m. to 5:00 p.m. Pacific Standard Time Monday through Friday. ABC-Clio also has a fax number, Internet E-mail address, and CompuServe address. Documentation is provided in a 22-page booklet inserted in the jewel case, which is more than ample for this intuitive program.

Promotional material from ABC-Clio states that "the company enlisted the assistance of school librarians, library consultants, media specialists, and teachers for a product advisory board and beta site testing program," and this effort certainly shows. The program is easy to use, and anyone with a minimum of Windows experience will have little difficulty finding his or her way around. After the title screen, the program opens with a "features page" of color photographs depicting some top news stories on the current CD. Users may click on one of these pictures to go to a story or click on one of the four "buttons" at the bottom of the screen that define the four basic ways of searching Exegy: Countries, International, Sports, and Maps. These four category buttons appear throughout the program on every screen. Once a user has selected a specific country, for example, another pull-down menu can be invoked where the user may select from Overview, Events, Facts & Figures, Biographies, Organizations, Documents, or Map. The International category includes "events, biographies, organizations, and documents that transcend national boundaries." It features the same pull-down submenu as Countries. Here one can find information on the International Monetary Fund, Amnesty International, or summaries of the Geneva Conventions and the Maastricht Treaty.

The most powerful searching capabilities, however, appear in the pull-down menus available through a button bar that is always at the top of the screen. The Index button, for example, lists all indexed topics available in Exegy. The Search button allows for full Boolean search capabilities (AND, OR, NOT, and NEAR—with the latter customizable by number of words) on every text field, as well as phrase searching using quotation marks. The Trail button keeps a list of the last 41 entries viewed. There are also Browse buttons to go forward or back through topics. Help is also available, though it is not context-sensitive.

When entries are retrieved, the right two-thirds of the screen is devoted to the article itself, with the country and story category (Elections, Obituaries, etc.) noted at the top of the screen. The left part of the screen displays the four group buttons, the country flag (if the story is related to a specific country) as well as a photograph (if available). The Caption and Enlarge buttons appear under photos. Within the text of the story, there may be several hot spots and hyperlinks, represented by blue type and green type, respectively. A hot spot will bring up a definition of a term, while a hyperlink will invoke the full entry for the underlined word. The article on the Tailhook Scandal, for example, has hyperlinks to articles on the Tailhook Association and the U.S. Navy.

Finally, Exegy has three ways the user may output information. A Print button sends the article to a printer; a Copy button copies the article to the Windows clipboard; a Write button immediately switches to the Windows Write program, where the user can paste the article. There is no direct download command, though either of the latter options offers a roundabout way of doing it. One nice touch is that the program takes the rare step of providing a screen telling how to cite information found in Exegy, thus answering a recurring reference question when dealing with CD-ROM products. Unfortunately, Exegy's own articles do not cite sources. There is only a general list of sources consulted for the entire Exegy database, citing simply Miami Herald or Ms. Magazine.

Overall, Exegy is a solid product with few problems, though some annoyances. Several articles (such as one on the gross national product in the U.S.) include tables or charts that are virtually impossible to see clearly on the screen; even after printing one on an ink-jet printer, numbers in the tables could not be read. Furthermore, such tables do not paste into the clipboard or the Windows Write program. In the Search option, truncation does not work with phrases. A search of prime minister*, for example, retrieved no hits. Also, not every category features all of the same choices. Poland, Singapore, and South Korea, for example, do not have Documents. Two bugs were discovered. Clicking on the Documents choice for Cambodia resulted in the error message, "Viewer topic does not exist," and booted the program back to the title screen. Also, the biographical entry for Subroto (secretary general of OPEC) generated the message, "The picture could not be displayed because it could not be found" in the spot where a picture would normally be. Not surprisingly, the maps show few details—all too common on general CD-ROM products.

Nevertheless, with enough browsing and trying various search strategies, Exegy has a gold mine of information. Currency conversion figures are given for most countries for October 1993 and October 1994. The Facts & Figures sections for most countries include illiteracy rates, consumer price changes, and military statistics. The Documents section in the entry United States includes lists of Academy Award winners in all categories for 1992-1994, O. J. Simpson's letter to the public, and Maya Angelou's "On the Pulse of Morning" (the poem recited at Clinton's inauguration). Documents for France includes winners of the past three Cannes film festivals. Most countries, however, have Documents that consist solely of a synopsis of that country's Constitution. Though the U*nited States* entry features a synopsis of the NAFTA agreement, *Canada* and *Mexico* do not. The Skiing category under Sports lists but two events; to find Olympic Games-related material, one must go to the International Games category.

E*xegy* tends to take a middle-of-the-road approach to news coverage, which is not surprising given it is "curriculum based." Searches on *Amy Fisher* and B*obbitt* retrieved nothing. A search on *Madonna* yielded but one fleeting reference in the article on JoseCanseco. On the other hand, a search on I*nternet* retrieved but two hits (both dealing with stolen passwords), and phrase searches on *information highway* as well as *information superhighway* retrieved nothing.

E*xegy* covers events of the past three years—something that is nowhere explicitly stated in any of the documentation, though it is mentioned in promotional material. In the November-December disc reviewed by the Board, the latest event covered was Aristide's return to Haiti in mid-October 1994; the earliest news stories were generally in August 1991.

The only product somewhat similar to E*xegy* is *Facts On File News Digest* CD-ROM [RBB Ja 1 93]. It, however, has limited illustrations (mostly maps) and is updated quarterly rather than bimonthly. On the other hand, coverage on F*acts On File* extends back to 1980. E*xegy*'s prime market is obviously middle and high schools. While the price may give some librarians pause, E*xegy* offers a great deal of current information using an easy-to-use, visually appealing interface with powerful searching capabilities.

Global Trends: The World Almanac of Development and Peace. Ed. by Ingomar Hauchler and Paul M. Kennedy. Continuum, 1995. 416p. bibliog. charts. illus. index. maps. tables. $39.50 (0-8264-0674-2); paper $19.95 (0-8264-0785-4).
909.82'9 Economic history—1900– || Economic forecasting [CIP] 94-20985

This book is a project of the International Development and Peace Foundation and is jointly edited by German parliament member Hauchler and professor Kennedy, chair of International Security Studies at Yale and the author of numerous works, including *Preparing for the Twenty-First Century* (Random, 1993). The foundation "argues for a policy of global reform geared to the vision of a global community of responsibility . . . to overcome nation-state thinking . . . to prepare the way for a worldwide domestic politics." The volume is arranged in 18 topical chapters within five broader categories of "World Society," "World Peace," "World Economy," "World Ecology," and "World Culture." Topics range widely from living conditions, human rights, arms transfers, and work to atmosphere and climate, energy, religions, and new technologies. Appendixes include selected country statistics, world maps of poverty, a bibliography, and a subject index.

Global Trends contains numerous footnoted charts, graphs, tables, and maps. These items are both a strength and a weakness of the volume. They help the reader to visualize the issues presented, but in some cases following up the footnotes for further elucidation will be a challenge. An interesting chart of "The World's Major Languages, 1980-92" is attributed to an unpublished manuscript by two researchers in Quebec, with no further clues to their affiliation or whereabouts. The chapter "New Technologies" includes a discussion of biotechnology in agriculture that features a chart comparing the "green revolution" with the bio-or "gene revolution." The assertions presented on the chart are controversial, representing an ideological slant rather than an incontrovertible set of facts.

Global Trends is a provocative polemical work that might best serve as a textbook for a college-level class in economics, global development, or peace studies. As a general reference, however, it is recommended only for large research collections.

Atlas of Shipwrecks and Treasure: The History, Location, and Treasures of Ships Lost at Sea. By Nigel Pickford. Dorling Kindersley, 1994. 199p. illus. index. $29.95 (1-56458-599-9).
910.4'5 Treasure-trove || Shipwrecks [CIP] 93-48856

Though the jacket proclaims this as "the first comprehensive guide to ships lost at sea and the treasures they have yielded," Pickford's introduction more modestly and accurately states that, because of the lack of records over the vast ages and areas involved," no book on this subject could pretend to be totally comprehensive." Defining a treasure ship broadly as "any ship used to transport a high-value cargo of precious metals or artifacts that do not lose their value when immersed for long periods in salt water," Pickford, a professional shipwreck researcher, provides illuminating text set in a sea of illustrations. The result is a book that is a fine starting point for shipwreck research as well as a browsable coffee-table book, because of the graphics for which Dorling Kindersley is esteemed.

The atlas is divided into two main parts. The first, "Shipwrecks," examines 40 significant shipwrecks in two-page spreads combining text with profuse use of photographs and other illustrations. These shipwrecks are arranged into 14 groupings including "The Vikings," "Chinese Junks," and "Pirates and Privateers"; each has its own lavish introductory two-page spread. The book's second main part, "Gazetteer," has two sections: maps and shipwreck listings. The 20 double-page maps locate by number more than 1,400 shipwrecks, indicating for each relative sea depths in yards and meters, date of sinking, and whether or not some salvage history is known. The shipwreck listings indicates, where known, the ship's name and location on a map in the atlas, date of sinking, nationality, tonnage, location, route, cargo, and salvage record.

Concluding the book are a glossary and a bibliography of about 100 entries each, as well as an index. That the index refers not at all to the 34 pages of shipwreck listings in part 2 makes it difficult to easily locate specific information, such as the cargo of the *Titanic* or the captain of the *San Juan*, in that section. The *Lusitania*, perhaps failing to meet the author's broad definition of treasure ship, escapes mention anywhere in the book.

Recommended as a seaworthy addition to public, academic, and elementary and secondary school libraries for both reference and browsing.

Pirates! Brigands, Buccaneers, and Privateers in Fact, Fiction, and Legend. By Jan Rogozinski. Facts On File, 1995. 352p. bibliog. illus. index. tables. $45 (0-8160-2761-7).
910.4'5 Pirates [CIP] 94-12717

Pirates and Privateers of the Americas. By David F. Marley. ABC-Clio, 1994. 458p. bibliog. illus. index. $60 (0-87436-751-4).
910'.9163 Pirates—America—History || Privateering—America—History [CIP] 94-31348

These two works on pirates are as different as black and white. *Pirates!* covers pirates of all times, both mythical and real. *Pirates and Privateers of the Americas* has the narrower scope of piracy in the New World, focusing mainly on Caribbean pirates of the 1600s. The title is somewhat misleading. For example, it does not include an article on Blackbeard, who surely is one of the most famous real pirates of the Americas but who was active in the 1700s.

Rogozinski's *Pirates!* has articles on Stevenson's *Treasure Island* and on five motion-picture versions of it, on such ancient pirates as the Illyrians and Ligurians, and on terms such as *boucan* (a meat-smoking grill from which the word *buccaneer* derived) and *Spanish Main*. Typical of *Pirates!* is an article on the treatment of women, in which Rogozinski distinguishes fact from fiction: "Daniel Defoe . . . created the legend of lust-crazed brigands. . . . At least in Blackbeard's case, Defoe's stories are untrue and the real Edward Teach probably was frightened of women."

Marley has articles on people, places, and terms such as *pieces of eight*, *Spanish Main*, and *dubloon*. His articles on pirates consist primarily of factual accounts of raids, campaigns, and battles. For example, an article on Sir Henry Morgan provides brief biographical background, followed by nine pages on raids and conquests and his final years as lieutenant governor of Port Royal.

To illustrate the difference between these two works, consider that Marley includes the artwork of Howard Pyle on the jacket and in several of the 22 illustrations within the book but does not mention Pyle in his text. Rogozinski also includes Pyle's artwork (sometimes noting a scene as "entirely fictitious") and has an entry on Pyle. Rogozinski's 100 black-and-white illustrations include movie stills as well as pictures from books and periodicals. *Pirates!* has about 1,000 entries, compared with about 350 in *Pirates and Privateers*. Selected bibliographies at the end of both works include only 22 references in common out of 132 in Marley and 184 in Rogozinski.

Both authors have written other historical works: Rogozinski, *A Brief History of the Caribbean* and Marley, *Pirates and Engineers: Dutch and Flemish Adventurers in New Spain* and *Sack of Veracruz: The Great Pirate Raid of 1683*. Marley clarifies our understanding of the real world of pirates of the Caribbean. It will be useful in academic libraries with a specialty in

Geography, Biography

Caribbean history. Rogozinski's *Pirates!* will have broad appeal to users of all libraries. Its delineation of fact and fiction will serve to demythologize and deromanticize the worlds of pirates.

Explorers and Discoverers: From Alexander the Great to Sally Ride. 4v. Ed. by Peggy Saari and Daniel B. Baker. Gale/UXL, 1995. 886p. $76 (0-8103-9787-8).
910.92 Explorers—Biography—Juvenile literature || Travelers—Biography—Juvenile literature [BKL]

This readable work profiles 171 explorers and discoverers for middle-school readers. It is based on the 300 entries in *Explorers and Discoverers of the World* [RBB Jl 93]. The geographers, oceanographers, and other assorted travelers are alphabetically arranged by best-known name with an index in each volume covering the whole set. Unfortunately, pagination is not noted on the spines of volumes. There are also indexes by country of origin and area explored.

Each entry begins with birth and death dates, locations, and a sentence describing the subject's achievement ("Anne Royle Taylor, an English missionary, was the first European woman to travel in Tibet, at a time when the country was forbidden to all Westerners"). Entries range from three to five pages, usually accompanied by a drawing or photo of the explorer. Effort has been made to include women and non-Westerners, such as Cheng Ho, Annie Smith Peck, Isabella Bird, and James Chuma, along with the well-known Stanley, Mackenzie, Cabot, and Cousteau. There are even entries for *Hubble*, *Sputnik*, and *Challenger* that discuss their crews collectively. The introduction makes clear that a discoverer was not necessarily "the first human ever to have been there."

World maps are included at the beginning of the book, and area maps are part of a few entries. The text is readable and interesting for upper-elementary through middle-school students. Readers may wonder whether crossing the "Takla Makan" means a mountain range or lake (it's *Taklamakan Desert* on the map), but most information is clearly presented. Unusual in a book for this age level is how frankly rivalries and hostilities are described. The reader gets a feel for how competitive Speke and Burton were and how life-threatening were journeys such as Susie Rijnhart's. Although no sources are listed, this is a worthwhile purchase where students and faculty regularly look for information on explorers.

Atlas of Classical History. 5th ed. By Michael Grant. Oxford, 1994. 93p. index. $16.95 (0-19-521074-3); paper $10.95 (0-19-521078-6).
911'.3 Geography, ancient—Maps [CIP] 93-48331

Atlas of World War I. 2d ed. By Martin Gilbert. Oxford, 1994. 164p. bibliog. index. $19.95 (0-19-521075-1); paper $12.95 (0-19-521077-8).
912.4 World War, 1914–18—Campaigns—Maps || Historical geography—Maps [CIP] 93-48725

One of a series of similar atlases put out by Oxford University Press, *Atlas of Classical History* is now in its fifth edition, an indication of its long popular appeal. It differs greatly from Shepherd's *Historical Atlas*. It depends largely on contrast between black, white, and gray in all its maps, avoiding the shades of coloring and tiny print of Shepherd. While paying homage to some of its predecessors, notably Hammond's *Atlas of the Greek and Roman World in Antiquity*, editor Grant points out in his preface that the Oxford work puts more emphasis on economic, cultural, and religious aspects of the period.

Features that make this work of interest to readers only casually interested in ancient history are the remarkable clarity of the maps, showing only those place-names essential to the topic being illustrated, such as mining or agriculture, or the locations of religious persecutions. There are also detailed city plans, such as that of Alexandria about 330 B.C., showing the location of the famous library, and maps showing areas outside of the Mediterranean—Britain, and the Persian Empire reaching as far as China.

The work is not without some faults, mainly of interpretation. An example of ambiguity is on a map showing "Places of Origin of Roman Emperors." Marcus Aurelius is listed with his "place of origin" as Spain, though with the reservation that "he was born in Rome." Only his grandfather had come from Spain. The *Britannica* more accurately says he was of "Spanish stock."

In summary, this atlas is useful, clear, and a pleasing contrast to the maps of an earlier generation. However, it has only five new maps, so libraries owning the 1989 edition may not want to replace it. Otherwise, the work is recommended for high schools, colleges, and public libraries with a classics-oriented clientele.

The dust jacket of the second edition of *Atlas of World War I* states that it is "fully revised and contains many new maps." This is somewhat of an exaggeration. The preface still contains the words, "the fighting of over 50 years ago," whereas "over 75 years ago" would be more accurate. And the "many new maps" are only five in number. However, the paper on which they are printed has a sharp white color, for better contrast. The excellent 10-page bibliography has not been updated. There are no titles later than 1970.

Even so, this volume of maps of the "war to end all wars" will be appreciated by students, historians, journalists, and others. The remarkable clarity of the maps; the detail of many maps of the trenches and battle lines around such hard-fought places as Ypres, Verdun, or Lys; and those maps treating broader issues, such as shipping losses worldwide or proposed U.S. mandates in what is now Turkey—all these add up to a useful, inexpensive, easy-to-read atlas of World War I.

Libraries that already have the first edition (published as *First World War Atlas*) need not purchase this second one, as the revision is minimal. Those that do not have the earlier publication, or whose copy is worn out, would do well to obtain this second edition.

Atlas of Westward Expansion. By Alan Wexler. Facts On File, 1995. 240p. bibliog. illus. index. $40 (0-8160-2660-2); paper $19.95 (0-8160-3206-8).
911'.73 U.S.—Historical geography—Maps || U.S.—Territorial expansion—Maps [CIP] 94-756

The excellent clarity of the maps in this volume is supplemented by well-written historical text, resulting in an outstanding effort to condense some 150 years of diplomatic, military, racial, and social events into a clear picture of the expansion of our country from the Alleghenies to the Pacific. Told with lucidity, the story is brought forward to the beginning of the twentieth century, the Indian Territory and Oklahoma land openings being the highlight of its first decade.

In addition to nearly 100 part-page and full-page maps throughout, there are several contemporary photographs, such as one of Kit Carson and an 1860 photo of men working in the Comstock Mine. There are also original pen-and-ink drawings of objects that formed a part of everyday life for both Indian and whites, such as a Blackfoot bow and arrow, a gentleman's beaver hat, and a gold-digger's shovel. Side boxes contain interesting information, not necessarily connected with the adjoining text. One box is about the famous Army Camel Brigade, begun by Jefferson Davis, while another covers the misfortunes of the Donner party.

Supplementing the text are two appendixes, a three-page bibliography, and an index of names and subjects. Appendix A is a listing of the states as they entered the Union, either as states or territories. Appendix B is a year-by-year summary of the principal events from 1750 to 1917 that affected westward expansion. There are some minor inaccuracies in this chronology. It was not in 1825, but 1826, that Jedediah Smith made his remarkable journey from northern Utah to California, the first American to enter it overland from the states. And it was in 1827, not 1826-37, that he made his second trip—1837 is obviously a typographical error.

Much of the historical narrative in this volume may also be found in standard texts, but seldom has there been, in our stories of "how the West was won," so happy a combination of fine maps with such clear, easy-to-read text. Recommended for all public and academic libraries.

The Children's Atlas of Civilizations: Trace the Rise and Fall of the World's Great Civilizations. By Antony Mason. Millbrook, 1994. 95p. illus. index. $18.90 (1-56294-494-0).
912 Civilization—Juvenile literature || Civilization—Atlases—Juvenile literature [CIP] 93-23564

Though it provides a small map for each topic, the strength of this work for elementary-school students is its pictures, not its maps. An introduction defines *civilization* and explains briefly how archaeologists work. The body of the work treats some 40 civilizations from prehistory through the Renaissance. Each is accorded a double-page spread consisting of a map, pictures, and brief commentary. In the case of civilizations about which much is known, such as the ancient Greeks, Romans, and Egyptians, the treatment can only scratch the surface. In the case of those about which less is commonly known, such as the Akkadians, the Minoans, or the Etruscans, articles are more informative. Four early civilizations—the Sumerians and Akkadians, Ancient Egypt, the Indus Valley, and ancient China—are grouped together at the beginning of the book. Other civilizations are grouped geographically.

Because of the arrangement—one section chronological and the others geographical—the time chart listing all the civilizations is an especially helpful feature. There is also an index. Antony Mason is widely published in the area of anthropology.

The Children's Atlas of Civilization has limited reference value, except for the pictures and the time line. As an attractive and readable overview of the subject, however, it will find readers in all young people's libraries.

The Complete Atlas of the World. By Keith Lye. Steck-Vaughn, 1995. 160p. index. $21.95 (0-8114-5804-0).
912 Children's atlases [CIP] 94-19316

In this atlas for upper-elementary and middle-school students, more than 150 full-color maps illustrate the world's geography, environment, industry, and agriculture. Charts and graphs show climate, population, government, religions, and languages.

The front matter focuses on changes in the world's physical, political, and environmental conditions. The atlas divides the continents into 23 regions. Some countries are treated by themselves; others are grouped together. The European bias often found in atlases prepared in the U.K. is detected here. Individual European countries are shown on maps with a scale of 1:150; all of South America is on one map with a scale of 1:800. There are six maps (political, physical, environmental, population, agriculture, and industry) for each country or region, plus a locator map. Text introduces the area to the reader; charts give statistics, and flags are pictured. Charts and graphs provide information on climate. Concluding the work are a five-page gazetteer, a glossary, and a one-page index.

Figures are given in both Standard and metric measurements. Information is timely and accurate. This atlas is similar in many ways to The Dorling Kindersley World Reference Atlas [RBB Mr 1 95], which is more detailed and aimed at an older audience. Teachers will find The Complete Atlas of the World useful in classrooms.

The Dorling Kindersley World Reference Atlas. Ed. by Ian Castello-Cortes. Dorling Kindersley, 1994. 732p. charts. illus. indexes. tables. $50 (1-56458-651-0).
912 Atlases [CIP] 94-19376

Encylopedic World Atlas. Comp. by Richard Widdows. Oxford, 1994. 264p. index. $35 (0-19-521090-5).
912 Atlases [CIP] 94-16312

Both of these atlases cover the nations of the world and provide supplementary sections as well. But the presentation is dramatically different.

The Dorling Kindersley World Reference Atlas is smaller than most atlases, at 8 by 10 inches. It uses numerous icons, charts, graphs, and text to describe the various elements of each country, such as climate, politics, economics, media, and world rankings. Clearly marked headings arranged in the same sequence for each country make comparison between countries easy. The use of color, pictures of sites, and photographs of leaders make this an attractive work. The maps, however, are small and have few place-names. A key to icons, map symbols, and abbreviations is on the endpapers.

The main section of the atlas, "The Nations of the World," consists of 191 alphabetically arranged nations followed by 57 more briefly sketched overseas territories and dependencies. For 13 countries, there are regional maps in addition to the national map. "The World Today" consists of double-page physical and historical maps. "Global Issues" is made up of nine double-page world maps on such issues as "Global Communications," "Hunger & Disease," and "The Final Frontiers." The index-gazetteer lists 25,000 place-names.

The Encyclopedic World Atlas is based on Oxford's Concise Atlas of the World, which in turn is based on the Atlas of the World [RBB F 15 93]. Updated to 1994, countries are arranged by continent, starting with Europe, and then generally west to east and north to south. New to this edition is the country-by-country presentation that follows, including text, a map, a climate graph for the capital or selected cities, and a statistical table.

Certain peculiarities were noted in each atlas. In Dorling Kindersley, the regional map of the Great Lakes cuts off the eastern part of Lake Erie and all of Lake Ontario. The index-gazetteer lists all the place names on the national maps but does not refer to places on the regional maps. The one oddity in the Encyclopedic World Atlas is that it does not include Antarctica at all.

For visual clarity and density of information, Dorling Kindersley is superb. Once the key icons are learned, it's like having an almanac's pages on nations of the world spring vividly to life, but its usefulness as a traditional atlas is limited because the maps are so small. The Encyclopedic World Atlas is more traditional in its approach. The country maps are more cluttered, as they overlay political boundaries on finely delineated relief maps and include many cities. Both atlases are useful and recommended for high-school, academic, and public libraries. The Dorling Kindersley World Reference Atlas is more strongly recommended because of its use of graphics.

The Eyewitness Atlas of the World. Ed. by David R. Green. Dorling Kindersley, 1994. 160p. illus. index. $24.95 (1-56458-297-3).
912 Atlases [CIP] 93-18572

Hundreds of small color photographs surround the maps in this attractive atlas. Coverage of the world's nations is well balanced; this means there are maps of regions of the U.S., not separate maps of individual states. Maps are spread across two pages, and occasionally some detail is lost in the gutter. Symbols are used to show crops, natural resources, industries, and tourist sites. Because pages are somewhat cluttered, it is sometimes hard to find standard features, such as the flag and population for each country. A brief glossary is followed by a map index. Fact boxes for countries in the index have data on population density, life expectancy, literacy, etc. A map of the world on the endpapers also serves as an index to countries.

The maps in this atlas are not detailed enough to rival the standard Rand McNally and Hammond atlases, but the additional information provided by the text and photos make it interesting to browse. School and public libraries will want to consider purchase. —Sandy Whiteley

The Kingfisher First Picture Atlas. By Antony Mason. Kingfisher, 1994. 40p. illus. index. $12.95 (1-85697-836-2).
912 Children's atlases [CIP] 93-48655

My First Atlas. By Bill Boyle. Dorling Kindersley, 1994. 45p. illus. index. $14.95 (1-56458-624-3).
912 Children's atlases [BKL] 94-10467

The New Viking Children's World Atlas: An Introductory Atlas for Young People. By Jacqueline Tivers and Michael Day. Viking, 1994. 47p. illus. $11.99 (0-670-85481-6).
912 Children's Atlases [CIP] 93-41434

These three atlases aimed at children in the lower elementary grades originated in the U.K. All of them are up-to-date, reflecting the breakup of Czechoslovakia and the Soviet Union.

My First Atlas is an oversize volume in the typical attractive but busy DK format. There is a European bias with three maps of Europe but only one each for Africa and South America. There are few place-names on the maps, mostly pictures showing natural features, crops, industries, wildlife, or famous buildings. In place of scale, a boxed insert tells how long it would take to travel from one side of the map to the other. So, for example, it takes 20 hours to drive across the Central Europe map from Amsterdam to Budapest and four days to drive the length of the African map. Flags of the world appear on the endpapers; introductory material explains the concept of maps and atlases. There is an index of country names only. The maps in this atlas are probably too cluttered for children in kindergarten and first grade who are being introduced to maps for the first time.

The Kingfisher First Picture Atlas, for ages 6–9, provides the same sort of introductory material. There are two maps for each continent, one a political map showing countries and physical characteristics, the second covering wildlife, plants, products, and industries in a pictorial format. Scale is given in miles and kilometers on the political maps. Each map page has an "Answer That!" box, with questions for students (answers are found before the index). A color display of the flags of the world appears before the index of countries and cities. Following the index is a folded laminated pull-out map of North America, which obviously has been added for the American market. While this oversize atlas has balanced coverage of the world, it also tries to include too much information in too few pages.

The revision of The Viking Children's World Atlas (1985) has smaller pages and maps than the other two atlases, but the world is divided into smaller units and there are more maps—a separate map for Mexico and Central America, for instance. These maps are also cluttered with pictures indicating crops, industries, and vacation spots. The maps have no indication of scale, and there is no index.

The maps in all these atlases are too cluttered for their intended audience, but The Kingfisher First Picture Atlas and The New Viking Children's

Geography, Biography

Atlas both have attractive illustrations and may be useful with older children.

Thematic Atlases for Public, Academic, and High School Libraries. By Diane K. Podell. Scarecrow, 1994. 176p. bibliog. indexes. $27.50 (0-8108-2866-9).
016.912 Atlases—Bibliography || Public libraries—U.S.—Book lists || Academic libraries—U.S.—Book lists || High school libraries—U.S.—Book lists [CIP] 94-4326

Podell, library science professor at Long Island University and reference librarian at Queensborough Community College, intends that her new book assist librarians in selecting thematic atlases. After surveying the atlas holdings of 26 libraries and checking many bibliographic sources, she compiled a list of several hundred atlases. From this, she selected 100 thematic atlases for inclusion. Criteria are that atlases be in English and be intended for use by the nonspecialist. Most of the evaluated sources were published after 1985, but a few are from the early 1980s.

The author provides several chapters of thought-provoking discussion, with observations and opinions regarding the organization and management of atlas collections. The reviews are arranged alphabetically by title, each following a uniform format. They are one to two pages in length and begin by providing complete bibliographic information, including price and ISBN. Also noted are the number and types of maps and information regarding illustrations, bibliographies, time lines, and indexes. A brief section notes the scope and purpose of the atlas. Following this is a listing of the table of contents, sometimes abbreviated to save space. In a section entitled "Noteworthy Qualities," the author provides information on such topics as the reading level of the text, binding quality, references to other titles, and commentary regarding problems, audience, etc. The atlas evaluation concludes with a list of up to six reviews. Interestingly, the author states she read few of the reviews, preferring to make her own judgments regarding the quality of the atlases.

This work concludes with a glossary that defines 19 terms (e.g., *chloropleth*), a bibliography with 21 citations, and an index of titles by publisher; unfortunately, no addresses are provided. Name-title and subject indexes will assist users in locating appropriate entries.

This is a unique source. The classic atlas references, *Atlas Buying Guide* by Kister (Oryx, 1984) and *General World Atlases in Print* by Walsh (Bowker, 1973), are dated and do not cover nearly as many thematic atlases. A highly useful collection-development tool for public, academic, and high school libraries.

The Young Oxford Companion to Maps and Mapmaking. By Rebecca Stefoff. Oxford, 1995. 302p. bibliog. index. $40 (0-19-508042-4).
912 Cartography—Encyclopedias, Juvenile || Discoveries in geography—Encyclopedias, Juvenile [CIP] 94-7900

Maps add to our fascination with exploration and discovery. This encyclopedia of cartography for children ages 12 and up encourages this interest by describing the technical aspects of mapmaking as well as the historical, social, and cultural influences that have shaped its development.

Stefoff, author of Oxford's Extraordinary Explorers series and Chelsea House's World Explorer and Places and Peoples of the World series, covers all aspects of maps in essays that range from several sentences to one or two pages. Some articles provide technical information, such as definitions of cartographic and geographic terms (*isogram, antipodes*), applications of mapmaking techniques (*surveying*), or types of maps (*quadrangle, projection*). Others are biographies of mapmakers and geographers (*Ptolemy, Mercator Family*) or on such broad topics as *Islamic Geographers and Mapmakers*. Explorers are also included: Ibn Battuta, Roald Amundsen. There are articles on major expeditions, geographic and cartographic organizations, and entries that summarize the exploration and mapping of various regions (*Pacific Ocean, Space*).

Several articles deal with maps of particular historical or social significance. Reading about seventh-century Japanese Gyogi maps, which virtually ignore any area outside Japan, or the Hereford Map, a medieval map that places Jerusalem at the center of the world, reveals how religious and social conventions influenced the way people saw the world.

The articles are accompanied by well-chosen illustrations, both black and white and color. One appendix lists important dates in the history of mapmaking. Another provides addresses and brief descriptions of organizations and publications related to maps, and a third provides a guide to map collections all over the world. A bibliography of primarily adult-level resources and a complete index are also provided.

This unique reference will attract researchers and browsers alike. Aimed at middle-and high-school students but equally appealing to adults, this new addition to the Young Oxford Companion series (*The Congress of the United States, The Presidency of the United States, The Supreme Court of the United States*) should prove popular in school and public libraries.

Atlas of Russia and the Independent Republics. By Moshe Brawer. Simon & Schuster, 1995. 144p. bibliog. charts. index. tables. $65(0-13-051996-0).
912.47 Former Soviet republics—Maps || Baltic States—Maps [CIP] 94-21023

The breakup of the Soviet Union has necessitated the updating of old reference sources and the creation of new ones. This new atlas is a useful contribution to that effort. Author Brawer brings considerable authority and experience to the project. He earned his doctorate in geography at the University of London and has been a professor at Tel Aviv University since 1964. He is also the author of *Atlas of the Middle East* and *Atlas of South America*.

The atlas places the territory it covers in its twentieth-century historical context. An "Introductory Survey" describes the territory's abiding natural features, flora and fauna, and climate; territorial expansion of the USSR; population and ethnicity; and communications and transportation networks. Text and maps in this section, and throughout the atlas, complement one another. Subsequent chapters cover each of the 15 independent republics, beginning with the Russian colossus of the north and working south, first from the west and then to the east. These 15 include the 12 republics that belong to the Commonwealth of Independent States and the three Baltic states (i.e., Estonia, Latvia, and Lithuania).

Country-specific chapters describe each republic's natural regions, climate, population, economy, history, government and politics, and national capital. A fact box introducing each chapter cites statistics on area, population, and demographic trends. Maps, charts, and tables illustrate the lucid text. These employ various shades of red, from a faint pink to a full red reminiscent of the Soviet Union's flag. Brawer's text touches only lightly on civil and ethnic strife such as the recent war in Chechnya. The index confines itself to the national political maps and place-names listed on them. A concluding bibliography cites sources within brief topical bibliographic essays.

Brawer has put together a useful atlas with a combination of analytical commentary and maps that provides a good overview of these countries, most of which westerners had little awareness of while they were subsumed by the Soviet Union. Because the *Economist Atlas of the New Europe* [RBB O 1 93] and the *Historical Atlas of East Central Europe* [RBB D 15 93] cover only the western part of the former USSR, this atlas makes a unique contribution.

The Almanac of State Legislatures. By William Lilley and others. Congressional Quarterly, 1994. 333p. charts. maps. $99.95 (0-87187-959-X).
912.73 U.S.—Administrative and political divisions—Maps || Election districts—U.S.—Maps || U.S.—Statistics, Vital—Maps || U.S.—Economic conditions, y 1981—Maps || U.S.—Social conditions,—1980—Maps [CIP] 93-41800

With this atlas Congressional Quarterly extends its coverage of legislative districts, seen in such titles as *Congressional Districts in the 1990's*, from the national to the state legislative level. This work was prepared by a Washington, D.C., information company specializing in political analysis. Sophisticated computing was used to create accurate maps of 6,743 state legislative districts from the myriad methods used by the various states to define those districts. There are a total of 280 maps: of districts for both houses in each state, with more specialized maps for urban areas where necessary. Accompanying charts for each legislative body provide 13 key statistics for each district in the areas of household income, college education, employment type (e.g., farm, manufacturing), age, and ethnic and racial composition. The data are drawn from 1990 census-tract information.

This is certainly an impressive accomplishment, one which, as the authors note, goes a long way to illustrate the division of our country into politically separate groups of rich and poor. However, it has to be noted that the maps, with all their detail, are difficult to use for the purpose of identifying towns or urban neighborhoods that lie within a particular district. Locations and boundaries of cities, towns, and counties are not shown in the maps; only the locations of interstate highways appear in addition to the legislative-district boundaries. Users may need to determine the number of the legislative district(s) they are researching from another source before using this book. Scales are indicated for all of the statewide maps but for only the larger of the urban-areas maps. Also, while the maps are attractively multicolored, the colors serve only to divide the districts into arbitrary groups; thus for Alabama, orange-red is used for districts 1 to 7, light blue for 8 to 14, light yellow for 15 to 21, and so on, in numerically even increments. The only exceptions are the few states, such as Nevada and New Hampshire, that provide their own groupings of districts according to traditional political divisions or regions. Nonetheless, this will be a useful work for political researchers, lobbyists, and public interest groups and should be considered for purchase by larger collections.

Atlas of Contemporary America: A Portrait of the Nation. By Rodger Doyle. Facts On File, 1994. 256p. bibliog. charts. index. $45 (0-8160-2545-2).
912.73 U.S.—Maps || U.S.—Economic conditions—1981– || U.S.—Social conditions—1980– [CIP]

The State of the U.S.A. Atlas: The Changing Face of American Life in Maps and Graphics. By Doug Henwood. Simon & Schuster/Touchstone, 1994. 127p. charts. tables. paper $17 (0-671-79695-X).
912.73 U.S.—Maps || U.S.—Social conditions—Maps || U.S.—Economic conditions—Maps [CIP] 94-14142

These two thematic atlases complement each other nicely. The Facts On File atlas is divided into seven topical sections; over a third of the maps are based on 1990 census data. The largest section (50 pages) contains maps showing the distribution by county of ethnic, linguistic, and religious groups. The sections on environment, politics, and "contentious issues" include maps showing congressional voting patterns on select key issues from the 102d Congress (1991–92); a 27-page appendix lists the votes by state and member's name. A variety of other topics are covered by the maps, such as distribution of various diseases, equal rights provisions in state constitutions, handgun murder rate, teachers' pay, etc. With the many half-page U.S. maps that show county distribution (the page size is 8 by 11 inches), detail for the most densely populated portions of the eastern seaboard is often hard to decipher, even where a slightly larger-scale inset map of Metropolitan New York or Baltimore-Washington is supplied in the margin.

Henwood, editor of the Left Business Observer, utilizes pie charts and a wide variety of other (often entertaining) graphic devices to illustrate aspects of the mapped topics in The State of the U.S.A. Atlas. Unlike Doyle, he relegates his textual commentary to a 32-page "Notes and Sources" section at the back of the atlas. None of his 35 double-page maps show county distributions; the emphasis is on the 50 states, and an eight-page set of state data tables follows the atlas proper. Again, a wide variety of socioeconomic topics are covered: working women, poverty, voting rates, value of Pentagon contracts, percentage not covered by health insurance, etc. Henwood has a detailed table of contents but no subject index; the reverse is true of Doyle.

While both atlases have a certain reference value, they present so much important current information on the state of the Union in such an attractive, readable format that the circulating collection may be the best location for these admirable compilations of socially conscious maps.

Weissmann Travel Planner for Western and Eastern Europe, 1994–1995. Ed. by Arnie Weissmann. Reference Press, 1994. 232p. index. maps. $49.95 (0-945305-13-3).
914.04559 Europe—Guidebooks [OCLC]

Travel agents rely upon many sources of information when planning tours for clients. Generally unavailable for public purchase, The Weissmann Travel Reports is one such source that has provided the travel industry with accurate destination data. Now the compilers of these reports are making this information more easily accessible for the consumer in the form of the Weissmann Travel Planner for Western and Eastern Europe. This is one of the few sources offering current tourist data on the new nations emerging from the reorganization of Eastern Europe. Arranged in alphabetical order, each of the 49 country profiles contains a brief general history, an overview of the major attractions (festivals, specific sports, museums, shopping, architecture, etc.), highlights of primary cities to tour, recommended travel itineraries, health advisories, native dining, modes of transportation, and types of overnight accommodations. Unlike the more popular travel guides, this book does not list or rate specific hotels or restaurants but merely advises the tourist on what to expect. A handy boxed section entitled "Geostats" states the official name and government of the country, required visas and health certificates, the capital, population, area, languages, climate, economy, currency, time-zone location in relation to U.S. Eastern Standard Time, and the status of the country's relationship with the U.S. An index lists city names.

All in all, this is an excellent source for tourists, the travel industry, and libraries. Because of the format of the profiles, libraries will find this more useful as a reference source than as a circulating item. It is ideal for locating pertinent information on those hard-to-find nations such as Bosnia, Croatia, Georgia, Moldova, and others.

American Places Dictionary: A Guide to 45,000 Populated Places, Natural Features, and Other Places in the United States. 4v. Ed. by Frank R. Abate. Omnigraphics, 1994. indexes. maps. $350 (1-55888-747-4); $100/vol. Northeast (1-55888-146-8); South (1-55888-148-4); Midwest (1-55888-149-2); West (1-55888-149-2).
917.3'003 U.S.—Gazetteers [CIP] 93-12306

This gazetteer may easily be confused with the eleven-volume Omni Gazetteer of the U.S., published by Omnigraphics in 1991. The earlier publication, which was well reviewed, listed 1,500,000 names with a single-line entry giving the name of the place or geographic feature, zip code, 1988 population estimate, and latitude and longitude of localities. American Places Dictionary (APD) fits the definition of a gazetteer (a geographic dictionary) more completely than the Omni Gazetteer. In four volumes, APD describes states, counties, cities, towns, Indian reservations, and military bases.

The volumes, which each have the identical 41-page introductory material and bibliography, are divided by region (Northeast, South, Midwest, West) with the District of Columbia appearing in both the Northeast and South volumes. The introductory material is entertaining as well as informative. The foreword by Kelsie Harder, an English professor at SUNY–Potsdam, is a fascinating discussion on the naming of places; it is followed by a clear description of the coverage of the set and good suggestions on how to use it. There is also a detailed description of the hierarchy of government in the U.S., explaining such variations as the use of minor civil divisions. The most entertaining section is the "Editor's Miscellany"—interesting facts or trivia that were discovered in compiling APD. These include a list of the eight cities that have been U.S. capitals, the 12 states with panhandles, and out-of-the ordinary place-names—Correctionville, Iowa, and East Loony, Missouri.

The section for each state begins with the state seal followed by a full-page state map showing only counties. An introductory section provides basic facts, including the 1990 population with projections, square miles of land and water and miles of coastline, highest and lowest point, housing units, ethnic distribution of population, bordering states, and name origin. Also included is additional information such as state rock, insect, or muffin; area code(s); and abbreviation, both postal and traditional. In addition, at least a page or two of text provide history, government, and business information for each state.

Cities, towns, townships, villages, and boroughs are listed by county with an index at the conclusion of each state section. The county information is boxed with facts similar to the state box—population, area, and name origin. The individual cities, towns, and other locales have zip code, latitude, longitude, population (1980 and 1990), population density, and, for some, name origin and a sentence or two about the location, date of incorporation, or important industries. Name origin is not consistently given, even when it is well known. For example, the entry for Audubon, Pennsylvania does not note that is is named after its most famous resident, John James Audubon. Appendixes in volume 4 include information on Indian reservations and military installations and descriptions of such geographic features as Howe Caverns, Pearl Harbor, Camp David, and Mt. Rushmore. The index in this volume to all four volumes cites volume number, state, and county.

This is an important resource for U.S. place-names. The criticisms are few—a map of the U.S. would be useful, some city and town designations would have been helpful on the state maps, and the general index would be easier to use if page numbers were given. Although the number of names listed is less than in the Omni Gazetteer (which

Geography, Biography

lists many more natural features like rivers and hills and man-made entities such as churches, cemeteries, and mines), the amount of information included is immense. One may discover the population density of Walnut Park, California (21031), the name origin of Saronville, Kansas (for a village in Sweden), and the incorporation date of Portland, Oregon (1851). There is no U.S. place-name dictionary to rival APD. The closest, which covers the world and is now out-of-date, is *The Columbia Lipponcott Gazetteer of the World* (1961). Recommended for public and academic libraries; small libraries may want to buy just the volume for their region.

Pop Culture Landmarks. By George Cantor. Gale, 1995. 401p. illus. index $34.95 (0-8103-9399-2).
917.304'929 Historic sites—U.S.—Guidebooks || Popular cultures—U.S.—History—20th century || U.S.—Guidebooks [CIP] 93-29924

One only has to flip through the index of this folksy travel guide to get a flavor of the various American institutions included here. Under *horses* are entries for Man O' War, Tony the Wonder Horse, and Trigger; the list under *houses* begins with Molly Brown and goes through Pearl Buck, Alex Haley, the Ingalls family, and Babe Ruth. *Roadside attractions* offers Carhenge, Dogpatch, Gator Land, and "The Giant Bureau." Historical sites, movie locations, museums, monuments—more than 300 icons significant to twentieth-century American pop culture are described. Some, such as Alcatraz or the New York Stock Exchange, are obvious choices; others, such as the Boom Boom Room or the Tail o' the Pup, are less well known.

One or two pages are devoted to each landmark, and short humorous essays provide background information. Each entry also includes location, hours, admission, and telephone number. The book is divided into five major regions, subdivided by state, with cities listed in alphabetical order. New York has the most selections (17), including the Apollo Theater, Ellis Island, and Macy's. Regional maps are provided, and approximately 100 black-and-white photos of various sites and personalities are scattered throughout the text. A time line is appended of "selected events that are part of or have influenced American popular culture," noting such significant dates as 1872 (the first New Orleans Mardi Gras celebration).

Most of the landmarks can be found in standard travel resources; some of the more unique attractions have been described in *Amazing America* (Random, 1978) or *On the Road with Charles Kurrault* (Fawcett, 1986). However, Cantor's entertaining style makes this a travel guide that will be read and appreciated by a wide audience. Public libraries, especially those that have found his earlier works useful—of which the most recent are *Landmarks of Black America* (Gale, 1991) and *North American Indian Landmarks* (Visible Ink, 1993)—will want to include this new offering.

The Oxford Children's Book of Famous People. Oxford, 1994. 383p. illus. $35 (0-19-910171-X).
920 Biography—Dictionaries—Juvenile literature [CIP] 94-22379

For children ages 9–12, this book contains biographies of 1,000 people from all parts of the world and all time periods. Subjects range in time from Egyptian pharoah Khufu (26,000 B.C.) to such contemporary figures as Benazir Bhutto and Wayne Gretzky. The typical 100-word entry begins with a tag that identifies the person ("*Saint Thomas Aquinas*, Italian religious leader and philosopher"), birth and death dates, and age at death. Handsome illustrations, most of them in color, appear on every page. Some of them are portraits, but many are of something associated with the person, for example, Hadrian's Wall or a painting by Rossetti. Cross-references point to related entries (e.g., from William Randolph Hearst to Orson Welles). At the end of the book, the subjects are indexed by occupation and by date of birth. They represent not only politics but the arts, sports, entertainment, religion, science, and exploration. A nationality index would have been useful. Many nations are represented; there is good coverage of Americans, and no particular bias for Britons. But Oxford wants to sell this book all over the world, so it includes some people who will be of no interest to American children (e.g., cricket players from Commonwealth countries). Many names will be unknown to children but worth investigating (German chemist Fritz Haber and the Lumiere brothers, early filmmakers). It's questionable whether elementary-school children will really be interested in Gide or Hegel, but there are enough pop-culture stars like Madonna and Michael Jackson to keep kids browsing so that they will encounter the important figures from history attractively presented here. —*Sandy Whiteley*

African American Breakthroughs: 500 Years of Black Firsts. Ed. by Jay P. Pederson and Jessie Carney Smith. Gale/UXL, 1995. 280p. bibliog. index. $29 (0-8103-9496-0).
920.009296073 Afro-Americans—Biography || Afro-Americans—Biography—Juvenile literature [OCLC]

This latest title in Gale's UXL series for middle-schoolers highlights firsts in African American history and is derived from *Black Firsts: 2000 Years of Extraordinary Achievement* (Gale, 1994). Organized by subject, events are then listed chronologically. Subjects include *Business and Labor; Justice, Law Enforcement, and Public Safety; Religion;* and *Science, Medicine, and Invention.* A typical section, *Periodicals,* under the larger subject *Media,* lists eight events, ranging from the founding of the *Emancipator* in 1820 to the appointment of *Time's* first black national correspondent in 1963.

Each of the 500 entries consists of three or four sentences on the person or event with the original source or sources cited. These include the *Negro Almanac, Ebony, Crisis, Encyclopedia of Black America,* Bennett's *Before the Mayflower,* and *Who's Who among Black Americans.* Throughout the text are black-and-white photographs of some of the persons listed. *See also* references note when a person's achievements are in more than one subject area, such as Maya Angelou, who is cited under *Literature* as well as *Film and Television.* A bibliography of all sources consulted is followed by an index.

There are several chronologies available on African Americans, but this one is unique in being arranged by subject and limited to firsts. *African American Breakthroughs* will find a place on the shelves of media centers and public libraries and is recommended for purchase.

An African Biographical Dictionary. By Norbert C. Brockman. ABC-Clio, 1994. 440p. bibliog. illus. index. $60 (0-87436-748-4).
920.06 [B] Africa—Biography—Dictionaries [CIP] 94-31361

100 Great Africans. By Alan Rake. Scarecrow, 1994. 430p. index. $59.50 (0-8108-2929-0).
920.06 Africa—Biography [CIP] 94-25934

Providing "sketches for 549 prominent sub-Saharan Africans with an emphasis on the postcolonial period, *An African Biographical Dictionary* includes such non-Africans as Albert Schweitzer and Dian Fossey if "they had an impact on the continent." While a majority of the entries are of political leaders, many cultural figures, scientists, and religious personalities are included. Many contemporary figures such as Jerry Rawlings, Mohammed Aidid, and Sunny Ad are treated.

Alphabetically arranged, the entries are headed by the country of association and dates. Entries vary from several paragraphs to more than a page and are aimed at the general reader. References at the end of each article give the researcher other points to explore. Black-and-white portraits are provided for some entries. The appendixes in this book are helpful. One lists the sub-Saharan states with their capitals and colonial names. Another gives their present name, date of independence, name of former colonial power, and major leaders, noting which ones are the subjects of entries in the book. Other appendixes list the entries by nation and by field of significance. There are several maps and a detailed index.

100 Great Africans has a wider scope, covering from the time of the pharaohs to the present and including North as well as sub-Saharan Africa. Selection was not limited to those born in Africa but includes "those whose major lifetime contribution was in Africa, or those who lived and worked in Africa most of their lives." Most entries are for rulers or leaders. There are no artists included and few current leaders. Sixty-three of the 100 entries are also found in *An African Biographical Dictionary.*

The entries are arranged in 10 chronological sections. The heading for each entrant gives his or her title and dates. Entries are two to four pages in length, giving more detail than those in *An African Biographical Dictionary.* Rake's journalistic style provides a stimulating group of stories for those who wish to broaden their understanding of this continent and its history, but there are no references to further reading. A few maps and an index of the biographees are provided.

The number of people presented and its current coverage make *An African Biographical Dictionary* a first choice for academic and public libraries. It would be appropriate for high-school libraries where world history courses cover Africa. *100 Great Africans* is a supplementary purchase for libraries.

The Cambridge Dictionary of American Biography. Ed. by John S. Bowman. Cambridge, 1995. 903p. indexes. $44.95 (0-521-40258-1).
920.073 U.S.—Biography—Dictionaries [CIP] 94-5057

This massive work of 9,000 entries attempts to bring together in one place all important as well as not quite so important figures in American life. Addressing all periods of American history and all fields of endeavor, it takes care to include a large number of women and members of minority groups.

More than 40 scholars helped select the biographees. In addition to politics and the military, people are included from the fields of science, academia, the arts and humanities, education, sports, popular culture, and even the underworld, such as John Dillinger. While coverage begins in colonial times, more than 25 percent of the biographees are still living. The brief entries are clear and easy to read, beginning with birth and death information. Entries vary in length according to the person's importance. Pianist John Browning gets three lines, FDR gets a half a page. Entries are similar to those in the *Concise Dictionary of American Biography* (4th ed., Scribner, 1990), which covers 18,000 Americans who died by the end of 1970. Like the *Concise DAB*, entries in *Cambridge* are indexed by occupation. A name index in *Cambridge* lists persons mentioned in a biography of someone else. As is always the case with books of this sort, one can question coverage. Why is Louise Erdrich included and not Michael Dorris? Why Barbara Tuchman and not Garry Wills?

An informative introduction provides insight into the overall make-up of the book. Those libraries already owning the *Concise Dictionary of American Biography* will still want to add this work to their collections based on its inclusiveness and currency.

The Concise Dictionary of American Jewish Biography. 2v. Ed. by Jacob Rader Marcus. Carlson, 1994. 711p. $200 (0-926019-74-0).
920'.0092924073 Jews—U.S.—Biography—Dictionaries || U.S.—Biography—Dictionaries [CIP] 94-20231

Before discussing what *The Concise Dictionary of American Jewish Biography* is, it might be well to review what it is not. It is not a biographical work for contemporary Judaism; thus it will not help someone looking for a biography of the rabbi their synagogue is thinking of hiring. The editors sought to include only those people whom they had reason to believe had died by 1985, the cutoff date. What the dictionary does provide are brief biographies of approximately 24,000 American Jews, ranging from Asser Levy, one of the first Jewish settlers in New York, through individuals identified only as "communal worker."

Entries are alphabetical, with copious cross-references; the searcher seeking information on Rabbi David de Sola Pool will find the reference: "*De Sola Pool, David*; see Pool, David De Sola." Each entry includes other names by which the person was known, such as Russian or Polish names changed after coming to the U.S.; birth and death dates and places; date of immigration to the U.S. or to a particular city or state when appropriate; education; identification by occupation or position in the Jewish community; brief biographical notes presented in a telegraphic style; and citations to biographical sources where further information can be found. A helpful feature is the inclusion of the introduction, instructions on use of the work, a list of abbreviations, and a bibliography in both volumes of the set.

The editors consulted a variety of sources in compiling this work, including the *American Jewish Yearbook*, *Encyclopedia Judaica* and other Jewish encyclopedias, *Who Was Who in America*, *New York Times Obituary Index*, and other works that would be likely to identify people by their religion. They limited themselves to information found in these sources and did not do original research. Thus, both Leonard Bernstein and chess prodigy Bobby Fischer are listed without death dates, though that information would have been easy to find in other sources. Marcus, the senior editor, is archivist at Hebrew Union College, where he has built a large collection of materials on American Jewish history.

Libraries needing an index to Jewish biography will find this dictionary helpful. The book would be strengthened by geographic and occupational indexes, particularly since it includes so many people not covered in standard biographical sources. For large Judaica and genealogy collections.

Dictators and Tyrants: Absolute Rulers and Would-Be Rulers in World History. By Alan Axelrod and Charles Phillips. Facts On File, 1995. 340p. illus. index. $45 (0-8160-2866-4).
920.02 Dictators—Biography || Depotism—History [CIP] 94-6200

Great Leaders, Great Tyrants? Contemporary Views of World Rulers Who Made History. Ed. by Arnold Blumberg. Greenwood, 1995. 344p. index. $49.95 (0-313-28751-1).
920.02 Kings and rulers—Biography || Heads of state—Biography [CIP] 94-16066

That certain rulers have abused power to gain control of an empire or state has been a fact of history from ancient times to the present. These two books try to put this phenomenon into historical perspective. They differ in scope and purpose.

Dictators and Tyrants is a biographical dictionary that provides in varying detail the lives of more than 600 tyrants. The editors say they selected the subjects because "to some significant degree and at least some point in their careers, they ruled illegitimately by the terms of the society by which they originally came to power." The book begins with an introduction that discusses the "classical" tyrant and his or her place in history. The biographies, ranging in length from from several paragraphs to more than two pages, cover the high points of the subjects' lives. Tyrants range from Egyptian pharoahs to Jean-Claude Duvalier and Deng Xiaoping. There are brief bibliographies at the end of most entries. Sixty-five black-and-white illustrations add interest, and there is a fairly detailed index.

Great Leaders, Great Tyrants, on the other hand, is a collection of profiles of 52 leaders from the fourteenth century to the present that attempts to answer the question, Is it possible for a ruler to be creative and effective without abusing the civil rights of citizens? The profiles are arranged alphabetically by surname. According to the editor, the subjects were selected because "on balance, they left a legacy of ideas, attitudes, or physical accomplishments that benefited society." Some readers may find that statement less than credible, given the inclusion of such unredeemed despots as Robespierre, revolutionary leader of France, and Joseph Stalin. Some of history's most famous despots are excluded. According to the editors, "we have deliberately excluded those tyrannical leaders who, like Adolph Hitler or Benito Mussolini, destroyed their creativity through the excesses of their tyranny. Joseph Stalin, on the other hand, has been included because his contributions to history are still much in evidence, even though the Soviet Union has ceased to exist." Fifteen of the people profiled here are not included in *Dictators and Tyrants*, perhaps because of differing definitions of these terms. *Great Leaders* includes, for example, Charles DeGaulle, Indira Gandhi, and Mikhail Gorbachev; *Dictators and Tyrants* does not.

The biographies were written by 36 scholars and include offices held and birth and death dates. They are six to seven pages in length and begin with a brief biographical sketch telling how the person became a leader. Next comes the assessment of the subject as a great leader and as a tyrant; a brief bibliography concludes the biographies. Some biographies are more analytical than others and will stimulate some discussion about the tyrant. Others, such as that for Cuban leader Fidel Castro, are little more than a rehash of existing information and do not shed new light on the leader. A detailed index aids access.

These two reference books complement each other and used together will provide researchers and students with keen insights into the beliefs and actions of history's despots. If forced to choose, academic libraries will prefer *Great Leaders, Great Tyrants*? Public libraries will prefer *Dictators and Tyrants*.

Heads of States and Governments: A Worldwide Encyclopedia of over 2,300 Leaders, 1945 through 1992. By Harris M. Lentz. McFarland, 1994. 912p. index. $95 (0-89950-926-6).
920.02 Heads of state—Biography || Statesmen—Biography || History, Modern—20th century—Biography [CIP] 94-13310

Lentz has compiled a comprehensive study of the postwar leaders of all countries of the world. His definition of a country is based on its membership in the U.N. Thus colonies are not included, but the independent homelands carved from South Africa (Ciskei, Transkei, Venda) are.

The book is arranged alphabetically by the name of the country; then the heads of state (presidents or kings or queens) and government (prime ministers) are listed chronologically with a biography of less than a column covering their time in office. It is interesting to see the number of leaders for a particular country. The top five seem to be Switzerland with 48; Greece, 46; Jordan, 45; Cambodia, 41; and France, 38.

Perhaps to emphasize the great amount of time spent on this book, the bibliography precedes the text. Both it and the statement in the preface that each fact was verified in two sources indicate that this is a carefully researched work. The index is complete, indexing references to countries or such subjects as World War II or the Mongoose Gang, a parapolice squad of Eric Gairy, prime minister of Grenada in the 1970s.

There is no apparent similiar source, so this is a recommended purchase for academic or research libraries with users who want to

Geography, Biography

know the presidents of Bolivia or another of the 200 nations included and what happened to them. Because coverage extends only through 1992, it does not list the current leaders of some countries. George Bush, for example, is the most recent head of state listed for the U.S.

Legends in Their Own Time. By Coral Amende. Prentice Hall, 1994. 384p. bibliog. index. hardcover $24 (0-671-88052-7); paper $14 (0-671-88053-5).
920'.003 [B] Celebrities—Biography—Dictionaries [OCLC] 93-47630

This ready-reference tool contains very brief biographical descriptions of more than 10,000 celebrities. The editor, a copywriter and crossword-puzzle creator, has assembled a collection of well-known people from around the globe, from earliest recorded time to the present day. These luminaries can be accessed four separate ways. The most extensive information is found in the listing by last name, which provides birth and death dates, pen or nickname, familial relationships to others included in this work, nationality, field of specialization, and major awards. The three indexes are by first name, nickname, and famous marriages.

Coverage ranges from Yahoo Serious to Mother Seton. Information seems to be accurate; however, Anne Boleyn is misidentified as a "French queen." Many familial relationships are identified, such as that between father Martin Sheen and sons Emilio Estevez and Charlie Sheen, and the family lines connecting the nine members of the Kennedy clan included here. However, the 18 Ford entries fail to identify the connection between Henry and Edsel. Some personalities who would seem to be eligible for inclusion based on other entries have been omitted, e.g., boxer Thomas Hearns, and actress Vera Ellen.

The second section is useful when only the first name is known, or when a list of, say, "famous Woodys" is needed (Allen, Guthrie, Harrelson, Hayes, and Herman). The last two sections, "Nicknames" and "Famous Marriages," answer equally specialized questions. Some stage names, such as "Baby Snooks" or "Weary Willie," are found in the "Nicknames" section, while others, such as "Pee Wee Herman," are found in the first section only, with no entry for Paul Reubens. "Famous Marriages" includes a preponderance of twentieth-century liaisons, with asterisks noting those couples who were still together at press time.

This work seems well suited to its identified audience: "student, writer, trivia buff, or crossword puzzle aficionado." While not an essential reference selection, libraries may want to consider purchase.

World Leaders: People Who Shaped the World. 3v. By Rob Nagel and Anne Commire. Gale, 1994. 160p./vol. illus. index. $57 (0-8103-9768-4).
920.02 Kings and rulers—Biography || Heads of state—Biography || Revolutionaries—Biography || Statesmen—Biography [CIP] 94-20544

This set for middle-schoolers in Gale's UXL line seems to be modeled on its *Historic World Leaders* [RBB Jl 94], also edited by Commire. That set has biographies for 620 leaders in five volumes; this set covers 120 people in three volumes (*Africa & Asia, Europe*, and *North & South America*). The people selected seem to be a good cross-section of cultures and time periods. The entries include black-and-white portraits and other illustrations, quotations by or about the leader, birth and death dates, and a three- to five-page biography written for this age group. The chronology of events in the leader's life and the sources for further reading from *Historic World Leaders* have been dropped. The volumes are sequentially paginated, with a cumulative index in each volume. The volumes are not numbered, so students may have to look at all three to find the biography they are looking for. The same index of leaders by country and a time line appear in all three volumes.

This wide-ranging collection of biographies will be useful in middle school and public libraries. —*Sandy Whiteley*

European Immigrant Women in the United States: A Biographical Dictionary. Ed. by Judy Barrett Litoff and Judith McDonnell. Garland, 1994. 357p. bibliog. illus. index. $55 (0-8240-5306-0).
920.72'08 Immigrant women—U.S.—Biography—Dictionaries || European Americans—Biography—Dictionaries [CIP] 94-29001

With the controversy surrounding immigrants to the U.S., this work is a timely look at the accomplishments of a particular group of them. A book of this type helps illustrate the important contributions that immigrants have made to the U.S.

Arranged alphabetically by last name, the book features 239 women. A summary of the life and career of each subject, 200 to 500 words in length, is followed by an annotated bibliography of published and unpublished source materials for further research. Black-and-white portraits are included for 31 women. The 96 contributors of the signed entries are professors and graduate students. An appendix arranges the women by career. The index includes names, titles, and subjects.

The women selected for inclusion are deceased and made their contributions after the American Revolution. Not all of them became American citizens or resided in the U.S. for a long time. The selection process attempted to provide a cross-section of women immigrants. Famous women, such as Emma Goldman, Helena Rubinstein, Hannah Arendt, and Greta Garbo, are found along with mathematician Charlotte Scott, labor-activist Rose Pesotta, and midwife Hanna Porn. One can learn about the original "Tugboat Annie," the inventor of packaged crackers, and the female producer of *Our American Cousin* for Ford's Theater.

Information on many of these women can be found in *Notable American Women* and other standard reference works. But there are some unique biographies, and bringing these women together based on their immigrant status is a useful idea. Recommended for women's studies collections and for immigrant studies.

African American Genealogical Sourcebook. Ed. by Paula K. Byers. Gale, 1995. 244p. bibliog. indexes. tables. $69 (0-8103-9226-7).
929.1'08996073 Afro Americans—Genealogy—Handbooks, manuals, etc. || Afro Americans—Genealogy—Bibliography [CIP] 95-2263

Hispanic American Genealogical Sourcebook. Ed. by Paula K. Byers. Gale, 1995. 224p. bibliog. indexes. tables. $69 (0-8103-9227-5).
929'.1 Hispanic Americans—Genealogy—Handbooks, manuals, etc. || Hispanic Americans—Genealogy—Bibliography [OCLC] 94-37509

Gale has launched another new project—Genealogical Sourcebook series—and the first volumes look promising. The remaining volumes on Asian Americans and Native Americans will be published this summer. Libraries can order all four volumes for $239 (0-8103-8541-4).

Part 1 of each volume consists of informative essays on immigration and migration, basic genealogical methods and resources, and problems specific to ethnic genealogy—such as naming practices, the reuse of graves where families could not afford perpetual sites, and reasons for deliberate falsification of records. Explanations and tips on accessing records specific to these groups, such as those of the Freedmen's Bureau and the Inquisition, records of religious orders, and an overview of newspaper ads and Hispanic heraldry are instructive and pragmatic. Tables, examples, and an extensive bibliography are included.

Part 2, "Directory of Genealogical Information," lists libraries and archives, public and private organizations, print resources, and other media that "hold materials relevant to genealogists whether their focus is on genealogy in general or on a specific ethnic group." Libraries and archives are listed geographically; those outside the U.S. are in Canada for African Americans, and in Guatemala, Spain, Mexico, Argentina, Peru, Uruguay, Venezuela, Cuba, Chile, Colombia, Ecuador, and Canada for Hispanic Americans. There are surprisingly few listings for Florida, which has a substantial Hispanic population. Private and public organizations include commercial ventures (publishers, researchers for a fee, bookstores) and nonprofits (genealogical societies, the American Antiquarian Society, etc.). The section entitled "Print Resources" lists many sources from the 1980s, but there are also current publications.

The author and title-organization indexes access only the products and sources listed in part 2. The subject index accesses the essays in part 1. Libraries that hold books such as George R. Ryskamp's *Tracing Your Hispanic Heritage* (1984) will want to keep them for their scholarly thoroughness. They will want to add these new books for their relative currency and for their simpler explanations of complicated facets of black and Hispanic culture.

The Genealogist's Handbook: Modern Methods for Researching Family History. By Raymond S. Wright. ALA, 1995. 190p. charts. illus. index. $40 (0-8389-0625-7).
929'.1 Genealogy [CIP] 93-29750

The Genealogist's Handbook takes its users beyond the straight facts of who their ancestors were and when and where they lived to the sources and skills needed to comprehend what those lives were like and how they influenced their own and future generations. The author describes himself as "historian, librarian, genealogist" in that order and his work as "not simply a handbook on genealogical and family history research methods . . . but a guide to discovering as much as resources can reveal about who the ancestors were and how they lived." Wright's nearly 20 years' experience at the Family History Library in Salt Lake City, his subsequent service on the American Library Association's Genealogy Committee, and his teaching of family history, genealogy, and paleography at Brigham Young University make him well qualified to prepare this guide, which can be used either as a textbook or as a reference tool.

Beginning with a chapter that compares genealogy and family history, the book progresses logically through basic methodology (group records and pedigree charts, etc.), advice on evaluating sources and tools (including computer programs), locating records (family, neighborhood, town, state, country), learning about ethnic origins, and writing a family history. Sample charts and examples from records illustrate many chapters. The bibliography includes solid classics as well as publications as recent as 1994. The index seems thorough and includes cross-references. The author acknowledges that the appendixes are not exhaustive: "Genealogical Research Centers" covers selected sources in the U.S. and Canada, while "Ethnic and Immigration Research Centers" lists centers in 20 states and 5 foreign countries.

All of this information can be found in other good genealogical sourcebooks, and true beginners will probably still want to start with Angus Baxter's how-to books. But what makes this one special—and working with its practitioners a joy—is its emphasis on fleshing out the images of the ancestors identified and on comprehending how their existence influenced present lives.

In Search of Your Canadian Roots. 2d ed. By Angus Baxter. Genealogical Publishing, 1994. 350p. bibliog. index. paper $16.95 (0-8063-1448-6).

929'.1 Canada—Genealogy—Handbooks, manuals, etc. || Genealogy [CIP] 94-76789

In Search of Your European Roots: A Complete Guide to Tracing Your Ancestors in Every Country in Europe. 2d ed. By Angus Baxter. Genealogical Publishing, 1994. 292p. bibliog. index. paper $16.95 (0-8063-1446-X).

929'.1 Europe—Genealogy—Handbooks, manuals, etc. || European Americans—Genealogy—Handbooks, manuals, etc. [OCLC] 94-76791

In Search of Your German Roots: A Complete Guide to Tracing Your Ancestors in the Germanic Areas of Europe. 3d ed. By Angus Baxter. Genealogical Publishing, 1994. 114p. bibliog. index. paper $11.95 (0-8063-1447-8).

929'.1 Germany—Genealogy—Handbooks, manuals, etc. || Germans—Europe—Genealogy—Handbooks, manuals, etc. [OCLC] 94-76790

Baxter published his first book on genealogical research in 1978, and family historians and professional researchers have been guided since then by his orderly approach (place-by-place listings of sources), commonsense wisdom ("Most of us are not descended from royalty"), and helpful tips ("Send return postage if you expect to get a reply"). These new editions of earlier works are similar in format, and all provide welcome updates regarding the existence and accessibility of records. New sources of data have been found or reconstructed, and political changes such as the reunification of Germany and the breakup of the former Soviet Union have changed the availability of some materials.

Each book assumes some knowledge of genealogical research but offers fundamental advice and guidelines about finding, verifying, and organizing facts. Chapters 1, 2, and 21 of *Canadian Roots* should be required reading for anyone just starting a family history project. Baxter creates an imaginary family and shows how to begin to trace its history by talking to family members, looking at family Bibles and old photographs, writing letters to archives and libraries, and then visiting the actual sites. He tackles problems of faulty memory, name changes, and family resistance and discusses the pros and cons of hiring professional researchers. His examples show the novice how to organize the information and, ultimately, how to write a family history that shows more than cold facts.

Each volume has its own character. *European Roots*, because it covers every country from Albania to Yugoslavia (including Germany), is arranged like a dictionary except for the introductory chapters on genealogical research in general and the contributions of the Mormons in particular. Each entry provides a brief history of the country, followed by a list of the locations and contents of various archives and other sources. There is a separate chapter on European Jewish records with a country-by-country list of sources. The selected bibliography includes tips for finding additional sources and is followed by a list of ethnic genealogical organizations within the U.S.

German Roots focuses on sources in Germany, Austria, and countries with German-speaking settlements. Some information is provided about records in Pennsylvania, the Midwest, and the Kitchener area of Canada. The reunification of Germany, the transfer of the Berlin Document Center (which is the most complete collection of Nazi files) from U.S. administration to German control, and changes in the Lutheran Church make this new edition a must for anyone interested in this aspect of genealogy. Problems of deciphering German script and of locating Jewish records are addressed, and helpful bits of information are included (such as the fact that upside down or sideways entries in church records usually indicated illegitimacy, and that Switzerland did not require the use of surnames until 1863). While there is some overlap with *European Roots*, most of the information here is unique.

The first edition of *Canadian Roots* focused on sources outside Canada. The recent surge of interest in genealogy in Canada has impacted libraries, archives, and genealogical societies sufficiently to require an update that identifies the many sources within Canada. The expected records regarding family histories, census returns, quarantines, land, military service, and school attendance are here, as well as Russian consular records, métis land claims, and other specialized collections. Although church records and registers are neither centralized nor systematically preserved, they are available in the provinces. These and other sources are listed locality by locality.

Baxter's appreciation for research and his love of history are evident in all his books. His identification of sources and practical suggestions for accessing and using them should be helpful to all researchers, regardless of their level of expertise.

Genealogy in the Computer Age: Understanding FamilySearch. Rev. ed. By Elizabeth L. Nichols. Family History Educators, P.O. Box 510606, Salt Lake City, UT 84151-0606, 1994. 56p. illus. index. paper $9.95 (1-880473-07-0).

929'.3 FamilySearch (Computer file)—Handbooks, manuals, etc. || Genealogy—Software [BKL]

Genealogy Online: Researching Your Roots. By Elizabeth Powell Crowe. McGraw-Hill, 1994. 280p. illus. index. paper $29.95 (0-07-014749-3).

929'.1'0285 Genealogy—Data processing [CIP] 94-10208

Computers have made researching family histories much easier. These books address two different aspects of computer-assisted research.

Genealogy in the Computer Age is a guide to the FamilySearch CD-ROM indexes produced by the Mormon church. They are available in the church's 1,000 Family History Centers around the country and can also be purchased by libraries. Using sample screens, the author shows how to navigate through the Ancestral File, the International Genealogical Index, the Social Security Death Index, and other genealogy resources on CD-ROM.

Genealogy Online shows how to do research on the Internet, bulletin boards, and commercial online services such as CompuServe and Prodigy. There is also a chapter on Mormon computerized resources, even though they are not yet available online, only on CD-ROM. Sample screens and step-by-step instructions will be helpful for the online novice. A final chapter discusses dial-up OPACs. Appendixes include a list of genealogy bulletin boards and information about genealogies at the Library of Congress. A floppy disk with genealogy shareware is included with the book. —*Sandy Whiteley*

The Sanders Price Guide to Autographs. 3d ed. By George Sanders and others. Alexander Books, 65 Macedonia Rd., Alexander, NC 28701, 1994. 462p. bibliog. illus. $29.95 (1-57090-001-9); paper $21.95 (1-57090-003-5).

929.88 Autographs—Prices [OCLC] 94-70942

The world of autograph collecting is enormous. In the three years since the publication of the last edition of this book, the popularity of this hobby and the multitude of available autographs have lead the authors to publish specialized subject guides to be used in conjunction with this general guide. The first is *The Sanders Price Guide to Sports Autographs*. Consequently, all sports-related names and prices were omitted from the general guide. In the same format as the previous editions, it is two books in one. The first half is a historical overview and introduction to the field, with valuable advice on attending auctions, handling dealers, various ways of acquiring autographs, and preservation. Additional information about manuscripts, collectors clubs, and a bibliography of related resources conclude the first half of the guide.

The second half is the actual price guide to signatures. International in scope, the listing is alphabetical by the person's name. Each name is accompanied by an identifying category (author, military, entertainment) and further identification (film star, Union general, humorous columnist). Values stated are for signature only, signed letter or document, signed handwritten letter, and signed photograph or art.

Although not touted as the definitive work on the topic, *The Sanders Price Guide to Autographs* ranks among the top works in this field. For the last three years it was selected as the best reference source of the year by the CompuServ Autograph Collectors Club. Libraries owning the previous editions will want to update their collections with this one. Libraries needing material on autograph collecting will want this excellent resource in their collections.

State Names, Seals, Flags, and Symbols: A Historical Guide. 2d ed. By Benjamin F. Shearer and Barbara S. Shearer. Greenwood, 1994. 438p. bibliog. illus. index. $49.95 (0-313-28862-3).

929.9'2 Names, Geographical—U.S.—States || Seals (Numismatics)—U.S.—States || Flags—U.S.—States || Capitols || Mottoes—U.S. [CIP] 93-49552

The title hardly indicates the full scope of this greatly expanded second edition. New chapters cover legal holidays and observances, automobile license plates, festivals and fairs, and U.S. postage stamps issued in honor of states and territories. Chapters from the 1987 edition on names and nicknames, mottoes, seals, flags, capitols, flowers, and other topics have in many cases been revised or expanded. The result is a book nearly double the length of the first edition (but still shorter than George Shankle's 1951 *State Names, Flags, Seals, Songs, Birds, Flowers, and Other Symbols*, upon which the first edition was based). U.S. Territories and the District of Columbia are now covered in addition to the 50 states. In most cases, not merely listings, but useful explanations are provided; the 30-page chapter on birds, for instance, provides information on size, range, physical description, and behavior comparable in coverage to that found in the standard field guides.

Other features make this a valuable reference. A 32-page four-color insert has illustrations of all state and territory symbols, seals, flags, flowers, trees, birds, automobile licenses plates, and selected commemorative stamps. The previous edition contained a 20-page color insert showing seals, flags, flowers, trees, and birds. Ample source notes at the end of chapters and a selected bibliography of state and territory histories provide excellent documentation. A detailed index follows.

Upper elementary and secondary school students would probably constitute the greatest audience for this work, but due to the difficulty of finding so much information on these topics in any other single source, public and academic libraries will be interested, too

History

The American Historical Association's Guide to Historical Literature. 2v. 3d ed. Ed. by Mary Beth Norton. Oxford, 1995. 2,027p. indexes. $150 (0-19-505727-9).

016.9 History—Bibliography || Bibliography—Best books—History [CIP] 94-36720

It has been 34 years since the last *Guide to Historical Literature* appeared, years that have seen significant developments in the field of history. The old guide, long a standard bibliography, has joined the ranks of those works rarely consulted because they are too dated for the purpose for which they were created. In this case the purpose was to guide the beginning researcher to the most significant literature on any historical topic. This new edition has been 10 years in the making, and it is worth the wait.

The new guide's 48 sections, covering the different areas of history, are each edited by a senior scholar in the field, with the assistance of additional scholars. In all, more than 400 historians were involved in the making of this work. Each section has an introduction that briefly summarizes developments and issues in that field. Then follow the bibliographic entries, nearly 27,000 in all by the publisher's count, each with brief signed annotations that vary between the purely descriptive and the evaluative. The entries are grouped into classification schemes within each section, often beginning with a list of reference works. In some cases this scheme is very detailed, while in other sections the editors have opted to use a small number of broad categories. An effort was made to avoid listing an item more than once, though there are a number of cross-references. Consequently, items of interest to a particular user may be listed in several places, and users will often need to browse the classification schemes, which are given at the head of each section, or use the remarkably detailed subject index, in itself nearly 300 pages in length. An author index and list of historical periodicals by field are also included.

Even with 27,000 entries, this is a selective bibliography and consequently aimed not at the advanced researcher, but at someone beginning research in a particular area. Works in English are strongly emphasized, though major titles in other languages do appear, particularly in French and German. Monographs also predominate over articles. The guide, however, is obviously aimed at fairly serious students and will be used to best advantage by advanced undergraduate and beginning graduate students, though an effort is made to include reputable popular treatments. Allied areas such as archaeology and the history of art, literature, and philosophy are covered, and an entire section is devoted to the history of science, technology, and medicine. Notable, of course, is the increased treatment over the second edition in areas of social and cultural history; the history of women, virtually unknown as a field in 1961, is well represented in nearly every section. Full sections on medieval and modern Jewish history, or on the history of Native Americans, would not have been possible in 1961 but are included here. There doubtless will be disagreements about what works are included or excluded, or about specific fields represented. But the new edition remains a splendid achievement and is sure to be heavily consulted for years to come. It is difficult to imagine an academic library without this title; medium-size to large public libraries will also want to seriously consider purchase.

The Historical Atlas of World War I. By Anthony Livesey. Holt, 1994. 191p. bibliog. illus. index. $45 (0-8050-2651-7).

940.4'1 World War, 1914-1918—Campaigns || World War, 1914-1918—Maps [CIP] 93-47649

This work differs considerably from Oxford's *Atlas of World War I* [RBB Ja 1 94]. The Oxford work consists of maps only, with textual matter limited to a preface and explanatory sidebars. The work under review is divided into five major parts, each having an introductory essay, as well as text explaining each map. The Oxford atlas has only black-and-white maps, while the Holt book has multicolor ones, making clear by the use of colored arrows and lines just which army is moving in attack, defense, or retreat. Also, the Holt maps show variations in terrain by the use of color, with scales showing elevations in meters. The text is easy to read and closely relates to the adjoining map. There are also black-and-white contemporary photos of the trenches, armaments, troops, cavalry horses, and the like.

The American contribution to the war is rather played down, being limited to two pages of text, two small photos, and only two maps, those of the St. Mihiel and the Meuse-Argonne offensives. Surprisingly, these two text pages are not findable in the indexes, under either U.S. or under *America*, though they are identified under *Pershing* and the two place-names.

Several double-page time lines show in linear format the activities on the various fronts during each year of the war. In addition, there is a selective bibliography, as well as two indexes, one of general topics and the other of places. The endpaper maps are especially useful. One is a general map of Europe, with numbers corresponding to the pages in the book where that area is discussed; the other end-paper does the same with a map of the world, showing, for example, the area of von Spee's Pacific squadron and even the far-distant battle of the Falkland Islands.

Libraries already owning the Oxford *Atlas* might wish to supplement it with *The Historical Atlas of World War I*, which has colored maps, more explanatory text, and presents to its readers a better understanding of the event that was thought to be "the war to end all wars."

The Oxford Companion to World War II. Ed. by I. C. B. Dear and M. R. D. Foot. Oxford, 1995. 1,342p. charts. illus. maps. tables. $49.95 (0-19-866225-4).
940.53'02 World War, 1939-1945—Chronology [BKL]

This compendium was issued in commemoration of the fiftieth anniversary of World War II. Several other one-volume encyclopedias treat this topic: *The Simon & Schuster Encyclopedia of World War II* (1978), *The Historical Guide to World War II* (Greenwood, 1983), *The Dictionary of the Second World War* (Bedrick, 1990), and *World War II: America at War, 1941-1945* [RBB Ja 15 92]. The last-named book is closest in coverage to *Oxford* but was criticized for its American viewpoint.

This new work has more than 1,700 alphabetically arranged entries. More than 160 scholars contributed to the volume, most from universities in Britain. Entries range from 50 words to almost 30 pages on major countries. Almost every aspect of the war is covered, including its effect on civilians. *Children* discuss the war's impact on children in many nations. Lengthy essays cover *Women at War* and *Religion*. The many biographical entries include both political and military persons. By far the most exhaustive essays are reserved for countries, all of which have standard subsections such as "Domestic Life, Economy, and War Effort" and "Government." The entry for the U.S. includes 27 pages of text and eight statistical tables. Briefer entries treat countries that were neutral during the war, for example, Sweden and Turkey.

In addition to statistics within entries, there are special tables accompanying articles. Unfortunately there is no index or table of contents for these tables. Cross-references within entries are noted by asterisks; there are limited *see also* references at the ends of articles. Like other Oxford companions, there is no index.

More than 100 line-drawn maps provide battle information as well as sites of death and concentration camps and the Manhattan Project. A separate section of color maps shows territorial changes between 1939 and 1945, the British and French empires, and other themes. A chronology begins in 1931 with Japanese troops occupying Manchuria and lists events under five geographic regions to the formal surrender of the Japanese on September 2, 1945. A list of place-name changes shows current and wartime names (e.g., Gdansk and Danzig).

Other titles give more detailed coverage of specific aspects of this period in history, for example, *The D-Day Encyclopedia* [RBB Ja 1 94] and the *Encyclopedia of the Holocaust* [RBB Mr 1 90]. But *The Oxford Companion to World War II* is an excellent overview for public and academic libraries that need to supplement other works in their reference collections.

The Cambridge Encyclopedia of Russia and the Former Soviet Union. Ed. by Archie Brown and others. Cambridge, 1994. 604p. bibliog. illus. index. maps. $49.95 (0-521-35593-1).
947'.003 Russia—Encyclopedias || Soviet Union—Encyclopedias || Former Soviet republics—Encyclopedias [OCLC] 94-24668

Referred to in the preface as "a successor volume" to the 1982 *Cambridge Encyclopedia of Russia and the Soviet Union*, this work has the unenviable task of covering the many changes that have occurred in the world's largest country while not ignoring the earlier history that shaped it. Two of the editors from the earlier edition remain (Archie Brown and Michael Kaser, both from Oxford) and of the 132 contributors listed in the opening pages of the volume, 83 worked on the earlier work. Like other volumes in the Cambridge Encyclopedia series, this one is arranged thematically (history, cultural life, the sciences, etc.) rather than alphabetically. The editors acknowledge that "while there are a number of entries—for example, on earlier Russian history and literature—which are carried over from the previous book, the greater part of the text is published for the first time."

The volume covers events through the elections of December 1993 that catapulted Vladimir Zhirinovsky and the Liberal Democratic Party into the spotlight. Not surprisingly, the section *Politics* underwent perhaps the most change, though updates are evident throughout the volume. The only oversight spotted by the Board is the lack of any mention in *Sciences* section of the *Vega 1* and *Vega 2* spacecraft that photographed Halley's Comet in 1986.

Perhaps the most noteworthy change to this volume is its visual appeal. Although the earlier work had several color illustrations, the present volume has close to 500 of its more than 700 illustrations in color. Many illustrations that appeared in black and white in the previous edition now are in color. The *Art and Architecture* section of the 1982 volume, for example, featured 45 black-and-white and 34 color illustrations. In the new volume, the same section has only 10 black-and-white and 86 color illustrations. Even charts—such as one on Indo-European languages—that were black and white in the old edition look more appealing in the new with the addition of color. Another noteworthy change is a variety of sidebars that concentrate on famous individuals and stand out nicely from the accompanying text. Boris Yeltsin, Aleksandr Rutskoy (Yeltsin's vice president), and Andrey Gromyko are among the individuals featured this way. The work concludes with a brief glossary (primarily to initialisms and acronyms used), a 10-page up-to-date bibliography, and a detailed index—which fortunately no longer appears at the front of the work, as it did in the 1982 volume.

The Cambridge Encyclopedia provides an excellent summary of Russian history and present politics. Readers looking solely for information about Russia today will be somewhat disappointed, as there remains a sizable amount about the Soviet Union and Russian history in general, but the editors make clear that this is the intent of the work. All public and academic libraries should welcome this reasonably priced, superbly illustrated volume.

Chronology of 20th-Century Eastern European History. Ed. by Gregory C. Ference. Gale, 1994. 475p. bibliog. illus. index. $49.95 (0-8103-8879-0).
947.000904 Europe, Eastern—Economic conditions || Europe, Eastern—History—20th century || Europe, Eastern—Politics and government—20th century [OCLC] 94-77453

Dictionary of East European History since 1945. By Joseph Held. Greenwood, 1994. 500p. bibliog. illus. index. maps. $59.95 (0-313-26519-4).
947.08'03 Europe, Eastern—History—1945- —Dictionaries [CIP] 93-35840

Both of these volumes take on the unenviable task of trying to capsulize the history of an important, volatile region of the world that played a significant role in both World Wars and has been plagued with numerous ethnic and social-class conflicts.

Chronology of 20th-Century Eastern European History is "intended to provide the reader with a concise look at the major political, economic, and cultural events that have shaped the history of Eastern Europe from the turn of the century to the end of 1993." After an introductory time line on the entire region, the book is divided into nine chapters covering Albania, Bulgaria, Czechoslovakia, East Germany, Hungary, Poland, Romania, the Soviet Union, and Yugoslavia, each written by a scholar in the field. Ference, on the faculty at Salisbury State University, states that the Soviet Union is included "due to its immense influence in the region."

Each chapter begins with a brief (two pages or so) overview of the history of the country in question, a few maps, and a year-by-year, day-by-day history of the country. Most entries are relatively brief, seldom more than a paragraph or two. The chronologies all begin at different times, depending on the country (Albania, for example, starts in 1900, but Bulgaria begins in 1886), but all go through December 1993. Albania and Czechoslovakia run just over 60 pages; Romania's is the briefest at under 40.

The volume concludes with a section of 75 biographies of noteworthy individuals, a bibliography, and an index. Interestingly, there is no entry in the biographical section for Khrushchev. Also, Tito is listed under the letter B as *Josip Broz (Tito)*, though the index has a *see* reference from *Broz* to *Tito*. The volume has some 80 black-and-white photographs scattered throughout. Although the photographs are captioned, they seldom indicate the date the event shown took place, requiring the reader to scan several entries. For example, a photo captioned "President V clav Havel meets U.S. president George Bush on a trip to Washington, D.C." fails to note the date. The event is, in fact, described on the preceding page. The maps are not a strong point; several are obvious duplications of CIA maps, some even including virtually illegible descriptions that were on the originals. Although the necessary brevity of entries may often leave readers wishing for more detail, the excellent and up-to-date bibliography should help.

Dictionary of East European History since 1945 covers the same countries as the chronology, with the exception of the former Soviet Union. Author Held, who recently edited *The Columbia History of Eastern Europe in the Twentieth Century* (Columbia, 1992) and is from Rutgers, states that the volume "is intended as a guide for serious students of East European history . . . [and] deals with major events, personalities, and policies in the region on a country-by-country basis." The work is current through June 1993.

History

An introductory essay discusses the religious and nationalist background of the region as well as brief pre-Communist histories of each country with a general chronology. The rest of the volume devotes a chapter to each country. For each, there is general information on the country (population, geography, etc.), a brief chronology (four pages or so) from 1945 to the present, followed by alphabetically arranged entries covering names, organizations, events, etc. Entries are usually about a page in length, though one (*Economic Policies in Communist Poland*) is seven pages. Each entry concludes with a brief bibliography of usually no more than four or five items.

Although the entries are generally well written, they are often inconsistent across all eight countries. For example, five countries have entries discussing education, but Poland, Romania, and Yugoslavia do not. Most countries have an entry on economic policies, but Bulgaria and East Germany do not. The chapter on Hungary has the most entries (69), Bulgaria (31) the fewest. The volume also has two sections of photographs for a total of 34 photos. The 10 maps scattered throughout the volume are rather sparsely labeled line-drawn maps. The volume concludes with an index.

Of the two, the dictionary will prove to be of greater reference value. It provides enough information on various events to satisfy those with an interest in the subject. The chronology will prove to be a useful supplementary work. Its country-by-country bibliography, however, is helpful for those wishing to learn more about each region. Both reference works are useful but are likely to leave many yearning for more. A more detailed reference work on this significant area of the world must still be written.

The Facts On File Asian Political Almanac. Comp. by Chris Cook. Facts On File, 1994. 264p. bibliog. index. tables. $35 (0-8160-2585-1).
950.4'2 Asia—Politics and government—1945– [CIP] 93-26319

Cook, compiler of *The Facts On File World Political Almanac* (3d ed., 1994), follows a similar format with this work. Asian studies collections at the high-school level and above that need a digest of the most important political facts, names, and events of the past 50 years will need to consider this book. It also merits consideration for general reference collections in public and academic libraries.

Important facts difficult to find outside of larger, more expensive sources (*Statesman's Yearbook*, *Europa World Year Book*, *Encyclopedia of the Third World*) are presented here in compact form. The design is for quick reference; entries are mostly lists, tables, or a few sentences rather than pages of extended narrative. The work does not attempt to be comprehensive, but rather convenient, providing the information the reader needs on historical and political facts since World War II.

The first chapter on 23 nations of Asia includes a list of about a dozen general facts for each country such as area, population, etc. Next, a chronology of major political events from 1945 through mid-1993 includes brief entries for each year. "Heads of State and Government" lists leaders from 1945 through September 1993 when Sihanouk returned as king in Cambodia. A chapter on constitutions provides summaries of the organization of governments. Five major organizations (e.g., UN, ASEAN) are described, and "major treaties and agreements" are listed by country with dates. Also listed chronologically are wars, coups, and assassinations. Brief information is supplied on the largest political parties in each country. Election results, which are often difficult to find, are included but are not always reported consistently—the Thai elections of 1988 list the translated English names (Thai Nation Party, Rightous Force), while the 1992 elections use the transliterated Thai names for the same parties (Chart Thai and Palang Dharma). Other facts concern population and urbanization by country, refugees, natural disasters, and rice production. A glossary and a chapter of brief biographies are followed by an appendix listing new nations of Asia and important name changes. A bibliographic note provides an up-to-date list of histories and statistical sources to flesh out the facts outlined here.

Persian Gulf War Almanac. By Harry G. Summers. Facts On File, 1995. 301p. bibliog. charts. illus. indexes. maps. $35 (0-8160-2821-4).
956.7044'2 Persian Gulf War, 1991 [CIP] 94-28450

This almanac brings together the major details on a war that lasted less than 100 days. Background to the conflict is provided in several essays that discuss the historical and geographic realities of the area. A retired military officer, Summers is also the author of Facts On File's *Korean War Almanac* (1990) and *Vietnam War Almanac* (1985).

A chronology with day-by-day entries starts on February 19, 1990, with Iraq's additional reparations claims in the Iran-Iraq War, and ends with Iraq's surrender at the end of the ground war on March 5, 1991. The main body of the work is in dictionary arrangement and is illustrated with 20 maps and charts and 68 black-and-white photographs. Maps include information on topics such as the "Iraqi Defense in Depth." Several tables supply interesting details. For instance, one shows air-to-air victories, detailing the date, shooter aircraft, type downed, and weapon used; another lists the coalition-force countries with the type and number of aircraft furnished to the war effort. The 200 entries cover military units, key battles, issues, people, and weapons. Some of the essays are controversial. For example, *Casualties* discusses the inaccuracies of casualty reports from Iraq, where the number of casualties cited ranged from 100,000 killed to as few as 1,500. Other entries are technical in nature, such as HMMWV (*High-Mobility Multipurpose Wheeled Vehicle*). There are also political entries such as *Iraqgate* and biographies that treat the military leaders of the campaign. Each entry has *see also* references, as well as suggestions for further reading. A 400-item bibliography of both monographs and periodical articles is followed by subject and armaments indexes. *Persian Gulf War Almanac* is recommended to libraries of all sizes for its detailed chronology of the war, its extensive topical essays, and valuable bibliographies.

Vietnam War Films. Ed. by Jean-Jacques Malo and Tony Williams. McFarland, 1994. 480p. bibliog. illus. index. $55 (0-89950-781-6).
959.7 Vietnamese Conflict, 1961–1975—Motion pictures and the conflict [CIP] 92-56662

Malo and Williams have produced a work of comprehensive scope and international outlook. According to the subtitle, they list *Over 600 Feature, Made-for-TV, Pilot and Short Movies, 1939–1992, from the United States, Vietnam, France, Belgium, Australia, Hong Kong, South Africa, Great Britain and Other Countries*. Their criteria for inclusion are far-ranging and not limited to films about the French and American involvement in Southeast Asia (Vietnam, Cambodia, Laos) and veterans of these wars; they also include images of the antiwar movements in France and the U.S. and of Southeast Asian refugees displaced by the conflict, as well as films dealing with the region after the French and American presence.

This extensive filmography is preceded by two essays, "Southeast Asia in the French Cinema" and "The War and Vietnamese Films." Entries are listed in alphabetical order by title. Each lists the year, country, studio, color or black-and-white note, running time, major credits, and synopsis. An asterisk after the running time indicates the availability of the film on VHS in the U.S. There are also indications for French and British video formats. Themes and keywords typifying the nature of the film (e.g., *male friendship*, Special Forces, antiwar demonstration) are listed, followed by "Comments," a mini-essay addressing the film's artistic concerns and relevance to Vietnam. Contributing reviewers, listed in the front matter, are from the U.S., Vietnam, and France and represent a variety of academic disciplines. More than 100 black-and-white stills add interest to the text.

The filmography is followed by several helpful appendixes, such as a chronology of films and a list of films by country of origin other than the U.S. There are also separate lists of directors, writers, and actors and their films. The ample index includes subjects, personal names, and film titles with references to entry, not page, numbers. A well-chosen bibliography is a useful addition.

While there have been several books on films about Vietnam in recent years—for example, Dittmar and Michaud's *From Hanoi to Hollywood* (Rutgers, 1990) and Walker's *Vietnam Veteran Films* (Scarecrow, 1991)—none is as extensive as *Vietnam War Films*. Its international approach, careful organization, and many special features make it a worthy selection for history, film, and popular-culture collections.

Africa in Literature for Children and Young Adults: An Annotated Bibliography of English-Language Books. By Meena Khorana. Greenwood, 1994. 313p. indexes. $59.95 (0-313-25488-5; ISSN 0742-6801).
016.96 Children's literature—Bibliography || Young adult literature—Bibliography || Africa in literature—Bibliography [CIP] 94-34223

This annotated bibliography of books set in Africa "reflects how Africans and others have defined, interpreted, and promoted Africa, its cultures and peoples, its religions and beliefs." The author, a professor of English at Morgan State University, is also the author of *The Indian Sub-*

History

continent in *Literature for Children and Young Adults* [RBB Ap 15 92].

Here she has annotated 697 books published from 1873 to 1994, with an additional 120 mentioned in the annotations. Titles provide a representative selection from various African countries, genres, authors, and literary trends and reflect the "multiplicity of viewpoints, from nineteenth-century books by Europeans to contemporary literature by both African and Western writers." Two hundred of the titles are from African publishers.

The introductory essay provides a valuable analysis of Africa in children's literature, through three stages of development: colonial, with its Eurocentric bias; postcolonial Western, in which bias took new forms; and postcolonial Africa, which in the 1960s began to seek its own identity.

The entries are arranged according to region. Each chapter is further divided by genre: traditional literature, fiction, poetry, drama, biography and autobiography, and informational books. Annotations ranging from 100 to 400 words contain thematic and literary analysis. Quality and appropriateness of illustrations are noted. Books are evaluated for sensitivity to multicultural issues: "what purports to be a charming animal fantasy set in West Africa is, in reality, a racist book denouncing Africans and their institutions" (Lofting's *Doctor Doolittle's Post Office*). Literary awards and grade level are noted. Author, illustrator, title, and subject indexes make material easily accessible. A list of Afrocentric book distributors is appended.

Our Family, Our Friends, Our World: An Annotated Guide to Significant Multicultural Books for Children and Teenagers [RBB My 1 92] devotes one chapter to books set in Africa. *Cultures outside the United States in Fiction: A Guide to 2,875 Books for Librarians and Teachers, K-9* [RBB D 15 94] also has a section on Africa. Neither book lists titles published in Africa, and the latter book's annotations are nonevaluative. This new book will be useful for school and public librarians needing a critical evaluation of older material on their shelves and help in collection development. Its overview of informational books can help with selection from series.

Chronology of Native North American History: From Pre-Columbian Times to the Present. Ed. by Duane Champagne. Gale, 1994. bibliog. illus. index. $49.95 (0-8103-9195-3).

970.004'97 Indians of North America—History—Chronology [CIP] 94-18455

Native North American Almanac. 2v. Ed. by Cynthia Rose and Duane Champagne. UXL/Gale, 1994. 192p./vol. illus. index. $75 (0-8103-9820-6).

970.004'97 Indians of North America—Juvenile literature [BKL]

With a starting date of 50,000 B.C., the *Chronology of Native North American History* gives an overview of historical and cultural events of the native peoples of North America. Events range from the emergence of the Bering land bridge over which the first Americans came from Asia to the Indian Country Tourism Conference in March 1994. The book opens with brief chronologies of two dozen tribes, noting relocations, establishment of tribal government, etc. The lengthy introduction is an in-depth history of Native American peoples. At the beginning of the chronology, a time line notes important world events and the most significant events in Indian America. Noted is the fact that 1993 was designated the International Year of Indigenous Peoples. The chronology is in three parts: 50,000 B.C.–A.D. 1492, 1500–1959, and 1960–1994. Events are listed sequentially; there are no subdivisions for arts, politics, etc. Each section is handsomely supplied with pictures, photographs, and maps. At the end of the chronology are brief biographies of American Indian orators and summaries of important historical documents and legal cases. The text concludes with an extensive general bibliography and an index. This detailed chronology wil be useful in public, academic, and high-school libraries.

The Native North American Almanac is intended for middle-school students and should not be confused with the book for adults with the same title [RBB My 1 94]. This work opens with a glossary of terms that relate to the history and culture of native peoples, followed by essays on their history and demography. Chapters then treat major cultures in the various geographic regions. Volume 2 has chapters on religion, languages, education, health, art, literature, media, and activism. Interlaced throughout the volumes are black-and-white photographs and maps. Each volume concludes with an index to the set. A good overview of contemporary Native Americans for public and middle-school libraries.

Indian Terms of the Americas. By Lotsee Patterson and Mary Ellen Snodgrass. Libraries Unlimited, 1994. 275p. bibliog. illus. indexes. $35 (1-56308-133-4).

970.004'97 Indians—Terminology || Indians—Dictionaries || Reference books—Indians—Dictionaries [CIP] 93-47170

Based on terms concerning Native Americans drawn from children's and adult literature, this work lists names of objects, methods of doing things, and names of significant people, places, and events in fact and fiction. It is written in a manner that is accessible to all ages from elementary school through adult. The entries are for everyday activities in the home (*cache*), games (*ring and pin*), healing (11 pages listing native sources), tools (*bola*), hair styles (*roach*), and tribal specialties (*mounds*). Persons listed include significant Native Americans, those who illustrated their lives in words or pictures, as well as figures taken from myth, media, or fiction.

Each entry usually includes pronunciation (an *h*-based system commonly used in children's literature); a key appears at the bottom of every page. Variant forms or spellings are followed by the definition. Wherever dates or places may be an aid, they are included in the definition or italicized in the illustrative sentence at the end. Extensive cross-referencing to related terms is included as well as the use of boldface type to indicate other entries. An example of excellent cross-referencing is under tribal nation names such as *Algonquin*, where ancestral tribes, individual tribes, the most powerful chiefs, and terms are listed. Internal cross-references and a bracketed *see also* reference give the reader more than 30 leads for further research. Attractive line drawings are placed in the margins of pages. Appended are a bibliography of fiction and nonfiction sources, a general index, and one that groups entries by topic (e.g., *Clothing, Dance, Transportation*).

The authors say that "we have compiled our facts, drawings, maps, and narratives out of curiosity, wonder, and enjoyment." Patrons and librarians in school and public libraries will have that same sense as they explore this recommended source book.

Native America in the Twentieth Century: An Encyclopedia. Ed. by Mary B. Davis. Garland, 1994. 787p. bibliog. charts. illus. index. $95 (0-8240-4846-6).

970.004'97 Indians of North America—Encyclopedias [CIP] 94-768

More than 300 signed articles by 282 contributors make this a first-stop reference source for material about contemporary Native Americans. It is important to note that more than 40 percent of the articles were written by Native Americans. Overview articles appear on such topics as art, education, government, and health, which contain *see also* references. Other articles cover such topics as the Alaska Native Claims Settlement Act, the Bureau of Indian Affairs schools, the National Congress of American Indians, and Red Power from an Indian perspective. The largest number of articles are on individual tribes; these are often accompanied by charts and graphs and vary in length from less than one-half page for *Nanticoke* to five pages for *Navajo*. Extensive bibliographies accompany every entry. In addition, there are more than 20 full-page line maps and many black-and-white photographs. All entries are signed, and the authors' credentials are provided. At the beginning of the work, a classified list of articles lists them under such headings as *Art, Government Policy, Law,* and *Religion*. The detailed index provides subject access.

This is an easy-to-use reference work. It is an excellent source for hard-to-find information about lesser-known such tribes as the Hoh and the Tunica-Biloxi, but it has limited coverage of individuals. The editor indicates that biographical material is beyond the scope of the work, as is coverage of Canadian Natives. Since this work provides up-to-date information on tribal groups, it could easily replace books with limited coverage. *Native American Almanac* [RBB Ja 15 94] is a more popular treatment of the topic and does not provide detailed information on individual tribes. The *Native North American Almanac* [RBB My 1 94] has both historical and contemporary coverage. It also contains biographies and directory information. Libraries, high school and up, in need of a scholarly treatment of this topic will want to consider *Native America in the Twentieth Century*.

Word Dance: The Language of Native American Culture. By Carl Waldman. Facts On File, 1994. 290p. bibliog. illus. $27.95 (0-8160-2834-6).

970.004'97 Indians of North America—Dictionaries [CIP] 94-10311

This dictionary is a beginning reference point for terms encountered

History

in Native American cultural studies. It covers the social sciences, science, religion, and the arts, focusing on words that relate to the language and culture of the American Indian. Waldman is the author of many books on Native Americans, such as *Who Was Who in Native American History*.

Word Dance is excellent in its coverage of names of tribes, legendary beings, and common terms that add to the reader's understanding of Native American culture. Terms from anthropology, such as *berdache*, are defined. Expressions and slang in American English that are related to Native Americans, such as *bury the hatchet, happy hunting ground,* and *Indian giver,* are included. About 35 terms from Native American languages that are not used in English are defined. Definitions for such terms as *how, white,* and *resistance* give a distinctive perspective into the cultural history of this society. Most entries are one to three sentences in length, but those for culture areas (e.g., *Circum-Caribbean Culture Area*) are half a page. People, battles, and organizations have been omitted since they can be found elsewhere. Cross-references set off in small capitals allow for further exploration, and *see* and *see also* references are abundantly used. A categorical appendix classifies the entries under such headings as *Archaeology, Food Production,* and *Tools, Utensils, and Weapons*. An excellent current bibliography completes this work. Line drawings illustrate selected entries.

Indian Terms of the Americas [RBB O 15 94] is very similar to *Word Dance,* though it contains entries for people. Either book will be useful in public or academic libraries as a supplemental source or as a beginning point of reference. Many of the terms are defined in more depth in other sources, but the basic approach of these books in bringing words from many disciplines together is helpful.

American Popular Culture: A Guide to the Reference Literature. By Frank W. Hoffmann. Libraries Unlimited, 1995. 286p. indexes. $37.50 (1-56308-142-3).
016.973 Popular culture—U.S.—Bibliography || Reference books—Popular culture—Bibliography [CIP

Television Research: A Directory of Conceptual Categories, Topic Suggestions and Selected Sources. Comp. by Ronald L. Jacobson. McFarland, 1995. 138p. bibliog. index. paper $32.50 (0-7864-0033-1).
016.79145'0973 Television broadcasting—Research—U.S. || Television broadcasting—Research—U.S.—Bibliography [CIP] 94-44118

Hoffmann, editor of *Popular Culture in Libraries,* briefly defines popular culture, then relates it to its role in libraries. Even libraries eschewing inclusion of pop culture material may provide reference tools such as price guides and catalogs. Hence this bibliography was compiled. Books were chosen by "traditional evaluative criteria," availability, and currency (mid-1993 was the cutoff).

This book is a potpourri of genres and sources; among the genres covered are comic books, TV, horror fiction, rock 'n' roll, and UFOs. Among source listings are those for the Association for the Sexually Harassed, the Museum of Church History and Art (Mormon), *Stephen Collins Foster: A Guide to Research,* and *Union List of Film Periodicals*. Arrangement is a mixture of genres and type of source (e.g., "Journals," "Societies"). The genre chapters are divided by format (e.g., handbooks); the type-of-source chapters are divided by topic (religion, sports). Subject and author-title indexes refer readers to the 1,215 entries. Annotations generally note scope; arrangement and critical comment may be noted.

American Popular Culture's contribution is in the convenience of a list of mainline sources relating to popular culture and in broadening the understanding of what pop culture encompasses. Large public and academic libraries would be well served by the source.

Jacobson, a professor at Fordham University, arranged *Television Research* by 29 categories such as advertising, women, movies, and education. Each category is discussed in a few paragraphs, followed by a list of possible research/lecture topics and a bibliography of related sources (mostly books). A final chapter listing additional sources is followed by an index. The unannotated lists of additional sources are standard, the topic selections sensible (e.g., "Comparative analysis of lighting techniques in two or more television programs"), if sometimes very broad ("Is there a significant relationship between reading skills and television viewing behavior?"). The title, however, is misleading, because *Television Research* is really about possible course paper topics. Students who want lists of topics will appreciate this tool and the relative accessibility of the sources listed, but they will find better coverage of reference tools in the television section of *American Popular Culture*. High-school and college libraries where TV is studied can consider purchase.

International Dictionary of Historic Places: Americas. v.1. Ed. by Trudy Ring. Fitzroy Dearborn, 1995. 800p. illus. index. $125 (1-884964-00-1); 5v. set $500 (1-884964-05-2).
973 Historic sites [CIP] 94-32327

This five-volume set aims to provide information on places of historical importance—cities and towns, battlefields, archaeological sites, museums—around the world. Canby's *Encyclopedia of Historic Places* (Facts On File, 1984) identifies 100,000 historic places as to location and historical significance. This identification however, is usually quite brief, ranging from a sentence or two to a page. Its usefulness is, therefore, primarily as a quick-identification source. The *International Dictionary,* on the other hand, is to include only about 1,000 sites worldwide, of which 186 (130 U.S. and 56 in Canada and Latin America) are in volume 1. Sites are arranged alphabetically by name. An index by country precedes the entries; 17 nations are represented. The introduction gives no hint of how sites were selected. While many are obvious choices (*Tikal, Gettysburg*), one wonders, for example, why New Harmony and the Shaker community at New Lebanon were included and not the Amana Colonies. The U.S. sites tend to be clustered in the northeast amd southwest. Several states have no sites represented.

The signed entry for each site, compiled from books, periodical and newspaper articles, and source material from site headquarters, explains the events that occurred there and their historical significance, as well as what the site offers contemporary visitors. Headnotes for each essay provide the site's specific location, a brief description, and the address of an information/contact office. One or more black-and-white photos or other illustrative matter is provided. Each entry concludes with a critically annotated bibliography. The strength of the essays lies in the fullness of the treatment of events and the inclusion of personalities associated with the site. For example, the four-page entry for Vincennes, Indiana, mentions Lincoln's connection to this city and the fact that the Gimbel Brothers department store began here. One of the six essays on New York City is devoted solely to the United Nations.

The usefulness of this first volume is enhanced by the inclusion of an index replete with personal names, buildings, organizations, and places mentioned within essays. The book concludes with the credentials of the contributors—librarians, professors, and freelance writers. The endpapers locate the sites on maps, respectively, of the U.S. and Canada, and Latin America.

Volume 2, on Northern Europe, was published in March; forthcoming volumes in the set are to cover Southern Europe, the Middle East and Africa, and Asia and Oceania. Because of the amount of detail in the essays and their appended bibliographies, this set will well serve its stated audience of students, teachers, librarians, historians, and anyone interested in historic places.

African American Historic Places: National Register of Historic Places. Ed. by Beth L. Savage. Preservation Press, 1994. 623p. illus. indexes. paper $25.95 (0-89133-253-7).
973'.0496073 Afro-Americans—History || Historic sites—U.S. [CIP] 94-33218

After decades of neglect, the places associated with African American history are becoming the subject of reference works. Indeed, librarians have a bounty of titles to choose among. First there was George Cantor's *Historic Landmarks of Black America* (Gale, 1991), a travel guide to more than 300 sites in 45 states and Ontario, followed by Henry Chase's *In Their Footsteps* (Holt, 1994), another travel guide. Chase identifies more sites than Cantor; he covers 46 states, Ontario, and Nova Scotia. Both books note access policies, hours, admission cost, location, and phone number. Cantor tells motorists how to reach sites open to the public.

Significance as judged by the compilers was the primary consideration in selecting sites for Chase's and Cantor's books. In *African American Historic Places,* the significance of sites has been certified by their inclusion in the National Register of Historic Places, a standard that necessarily limits coverage to the U.S. The criteria whereby more than 62,000 sites have been listed in the National Register are explained briefly in the introduction. From these were selected some 800 that relate to African American history. All three guides organize sites by state. However the other two employ a regional progression, suitable to trip planning. African American Historic Places organizes 41 states (plus the District of Columbia, Puerto Rico, and the Virgin Islands) alphabetically. As in its parent publication, the two-volume National Register of Historic Places (U.S. Department of the Interior, 1976), state sections are organized by county. Site descriptions are somewhat more thorough than the thumbnail sketches in the National Register. Because it is designed as an identification tool rather than as a trip planner, African American Historic Places lists only addresses and does not note telephone numbers, access policies, or admission charges. The introduction, however, notes that approximately three-fourths of the properties are privately owned and not open to the public. Black-and-white photographs are provided for some of the sites.

Eight introductory essays provide context for understanding the historical significance of the sites. Representative sites include Brown Chapel African Methodist Episcopal Church in Selma, Alabama, which figured prominently in the 1965 voting-rights campaign; the Chicago home of the founder of the Chicago Defender newspaper; and Langston Hughes' house in Harlem. There are indexes by state and city, by occupations, by names of individuals or organizations, and by subject. Since the National Register of Historic Places does not single out sites related to African American history, this is a very useful tool. Given its strict criteria for inclusion of sites, African American Historic Places complements Cantor's and Chase's travel guides.

The African American Resource Guide. By Anita Doreen Diggs. Barricade Books, 1994. 224p. bibliog. paper $12.99 (1-56980-006-5).
016.973'0496073 Afro-Americans—Directories || Afro-Americans—Bibliography [CIP] 93-47551

This inexpensive book attempts to be all things to all people. It is a guide to African American literature, colleges and universities, and financial aid. It lists cultural organizations, places to go and things to do, professional associations, as well as videotapes.

How does it measure up? In the 65-page bibliography of fiction and nonfiction, some important writers do not appear. Most works represent the current popular literary scene, though dramatist August Wilson is not included. This is a starting place for a reader who is interested in the African American experience. The second chapter lists all black colleges and universities, with descriptive information and contact data. The Black Student's Guide to College Success [RBB N 15 93] is a more detailed treatment of this subject. Following this listing is a guide for finding money for college, both undergraduate and graduate studies. This section does not begin to compare with the data in Directory of Financial Aid for Minorities (Reference Services Press, 1993). The 34 cultural organizations listed do not include African American Greek-letter organizations, nor such groups as the Links, the Girlfriends, or 100 Black Women. "Places to Go" is a directory of African American cultural sites, arranged by state. Chapter 6 lists black professional associations. The Black Caucus of ALA is not mentioned. The listing of popular videos includes such films as Do the Right Thing, The Color Purple, and Shaft, but such documentaries as Eye on the Prize are not listed.

This work does many things but none of them in any depth. Other reference books address each facet separately and more thoroughly. But for small high-school and public libraries that don't own other more specialized tools, The African American Resource Guide may be a useful purchase.

The Asian American Encyclopedia. 6v. Ed. by Franklin Ng. Marshall Cavendish, 1994. 1,818p. bibliog. charts. illus. indexes. $449.95 (1-85433-677-1).
973'.0495 Asian Americans—Encyclopedias [CIP] 94-33003

Notable Asian Americans. Ed. by Helen Zia and Susan B. Gall. Gale, 1995. 468p. $65 (0-8103-9623-8).
920'.009295073 Asian Americans—Biography [CIP] 94-33638

Marshall Cavendish, traditionally associated with reference works from Britain, offers a new encyclopedia on Asian Americans, with more than 2,000 entries and more than 1,100 illustrations. Heavily biographical, it also has lengthy articles on each major Asian ethnic group in the U.S., Canada, and Latin America as well as such topics as historical events, places, religion, publications, laws, court cases, and concepts (e.g., the leasehold system in Hawaii). Coverage extends from the Asian subcontinent to the Far East and the Pacific Islands. Many foreign events, places, and people, such as the Long March in China, the Khmer Rouge, Salman Rushdie, and Corazon Aquino, are treated. This is almost as much an encyclopedia of Asia as Asian Americans.

Articles range in length from a couple of sentences to several pages. Writing is clear, if not very colorful. No pronunciation helps are provided. Only long articles are signed; annotated bibliographies are found at the ends of longer entries. About 15 percent of the volume is comprised of black-and-white illustrations, maps, statistical tables, and diagrams. Liberal use is made of cross-references. Volume 6 contains a chronology and lists of organizations, museums, libraries, Asian American studies programs in colleges, and videos. A 40-page bibliography is arranged by ethnic group and by topic. One index classifies all the entries by ethnic group and by topic; this is followed by a traditional subject index.

Treatment is generally balanced, even with such controversial topics as Korean American-African American Relations and Model Minority. This wide-ranging set should be particularly useful for high-school and public libraries.

Notable Asian Americans features 250 role models, most of whom are contemporary. Coverage includes Asian Indians, those from Southeast Asia and the Far East, Pacific Islanders, and Hawaiians. The largest number of biographees are of Chinese or Japanese descent. Typical entrants include Judge Ito, author Deepak Chopra, cellist Yo Yo Ma, actor Bruce Lee, comedian Margaret Cho, and sculptor Isamu Noguchi. Fewer than half the people here are found in The Asian American Encyclopedia, and the biographies there are much briefer.

The signed entries are usually two pages in length, and most are accompanied by black-and white photographs. Personal background and public achievements are discussed engagingly and often anecdotally. Most entries include quotations from interviews. Further sources of information are also noted for each entry. Occupation and ethnicity indexes introduce the volume; a comprehensive subject index (with cross-references) concludes it. The occupation index has many overlapping categories, such as Authors and Writers, Academicians and Scholars, and Musicians and Violinists. There are no cross-references from a category to related ones, though some people are listed under more than one occupation.

Accessible to high-schoolers and up, Notable Asian Americans is an interesting place to start reading about these personalities. Gale's Who's Who among Asian Americans [RBB O 1 94] covers far more people but in less detail.

Great Dates in United States History. Ed. by André Kaspi. Facts On File, 1994. 272p. index. maps. tables. $25.95 (0-8160-2592-4).
973'.02 U.S.—History—Chronology [CIP] 93-42889

This 1989 French publication has been translated and updated through 1992. Its aim is to provide a "comprehensible, accessible source of information on the events, people and ideas that have shaped the American experience."

The information is arranged by spans of years from the discovery of the North American continent to the end of 1992. Within each chapter, brief listings are arranged under such topics as Economy and Society, Science and Technology, and Religion, Education and Culture. There are a detailed index and 10 maps (e.g., "Native Tribes," "Free and Slave Areas," "Women's Suffrage"). Sources for the boxed tables of statistics are not always provided.

This work will not be satisfactory for users seeking specific dates of events. It is not until 1758 that the particular days of some events are included. Even after this, specific dates are not always provided; for example, the execution of anarchists Sacco and Vanzetti is listed simply as 1927.

The Encyclopedia of American Facts and Dates by Gorton Carruth (9th ed., Harper, 1993) provides much more detailed information. Because Great Dates in United States History is current, easy to use, and inexpensive, it will be useful in school and public libraries, but collections that own Carruth will find it sufficient for their needs.

Historical Statistics of Black America. 2v. Ed. by Jessie Carney Smith and Carrell Peterson Horton. Gale, 1994. 2,420p. bibliog. charts. indexes. tables. $125 (0-8103-8542-2).
973' 0496073 Afro-Americans—History—Statistics [CIP] 94-29718

This hefty two-volume set will interest researchers and browsers alike. The editors have compiled more than 2,300 tables of statistics describing black American life from 1619 to 1975. The set is designed to be a companion to their Statistical Record of Black America [RBB F 15 91], which covers 1975 to the present.

Numbered consecutively, the tables, charts, graphs, and short narratives cover a wide range of topics—including agriculture, business, military affairs, politics, religion, and the expected population and vital statistics. Much of the information comes from government documents, but significant amounts are extrapolated from works not widely available—early publications of African American institutions and from African American authors. The Negro Year Book and The Negro Handbook gathered and expounded on black data long before the Civil Rights movement. W. E. B. DuBois' The Negro in Business (1899) and The Negro Church (1903) and Leo Favrot's Study of Country Training Schools for Negroes in the South (1923) are examples of early monographs that provide insight into the realities of black American life. Many tables include whites as well as blacks, and all cite their source. The tables are indexed by subject and by date.

Browsing the 79-page table of contents points the reader to such diverse entries as "Average Acreage & Yield Corn on Black Farms in the South, 1909," "Merchants of Athens, Georgia, 1899," "Rates by Race: Racial Criminality in 1904," "Academic Honors: Colleges & Universities with Black Inductees into Phi Beta Kappa, 1874–1916," "Actors in Broadway & Off-Broadway Shows, 1960–61—1964–65," and "Slave Prices British America and West Africa, 1638–1775." In the chapter "Sports and Leisure" one learns that "the first Negro intercollegiate [football] game was played on Tuesday, December 27, 1892, between Biddle University and Livingstone College on the Livingstone campus in Salisbury, North Carolina." The "Education" chapter reports a survey done by ALA in 1943 that showed that "one-half of the 34 accredited library schools admit Negro students who meet their admission requirements. . . . The total of 17 accredited library schools includes the Schools of Library Service, Atlanta University (colored) and 16 library schools outside the Southern States."

This monumental compilation of information allows readers to comprehend the facts of black life in America over more than 300 years and should be considered by academic and public libraries.

The New York Public Library Book of Popular Americana. By Tad Tuleja. Macmillan, 1994. 451p. $27.50 (0-671-89987-2).
973'.03 Americana—Dictionaries || Americanisms—Dictionaries || English language—U.S.—Terms and phrases [OCLC] 94-22672

The New York Public Library Performing Arts Desk Reference. Macmillan, 1994. 585p. illus. index. $35 (0-671-79912-6).
791'.03 Performing arts—Encyclopedias [OCLC] 94-22673

Here are two more titles in Macmillan's (formerly Prentice Hall's) New York Public Library series. Like the other books in the series, they were written by freelance writers, not by library staff.

The publisher describes the eclectic Book of Popular Americana as an "A-to-Z of American popular culture, from Nathaniel Hawthorne to the Oreo cookie." Included are nearly 4,000 entries representing "those facets of culture that are at once distinctively American and broadly recognizable." In his introduction, Tuleja is careful to point out that his aim is "to cover not what every American *needs* to know, but what the average American once knew and has since forgotten." Entries arise from many arenas, among them literature, history, music, art, sports, commerce, media (newspapers, radio, films, television), common parlance, and slang. The chronological scope is broad enough to include the "Penman of the Revolution" Samuel Adams (1772–1803), as well as Magic Johnson's HIV status.

The author reports a longtime interest in popular culture, and according to the jacket biography, is currently a Ph.D. candidate in American folklore. He is also the author of a number of more specialized compilations of popular culture, among them Fabulous Fallacies: More Than 300 Popular Beliefs That Are Not True (McGraw-Hill, 1987).

The grab-bag quality of the contents of the Book of Popular Americana is what makes it a useful compendium, as it brings together items readily found in a wide variety of sources, but not easily found in any single volume. It is recommended for the general reference collections of public and academic libraries.

Although governmental funding for the performing arts is waning, public interest has never waxed fuller. The weekend editions of local newspapers carry listings for everything from community theater presentations to touring shows of Broadway hits, from small musical and dance-group performances to those of professional opera and ballet companies and symphony orchestras. Video stores and libraries stock videocassettes of performances, and public and cable television devote a considerable amount of airtime to the performing arts.

Intended as a source of "accurate, introductory information" on the performing arts, Performing Arts Desk Reference is divided into three main sections: theater, music, and dance. A basic vocabulary in the performing arts is necessary for understanding them, so each of these three parts begins with a glossary of related terms that will help the reader become conversant in the shoptalk of show business. Various topics are then addressed; surveys of movements in the arts' development are provided as well as biographies of their major figures. Attention is paid to several non-Western traditions, specifically Asian theater and the musical traditions of different ethnic groups. Each section concludes with lists of awards, funding sources, and additional sources of information. While it is easy enough to locate the glossaries, biographies, and other subsections through the table of contents, an index helps increase this book's reference readiness.

There is a wealth of information in these pages: a list of major works to include when starting a classical music library, synopses of major plays, and explanations of dance terminology. The bibliographies at each section's end have been carefully compiled and should prove useful. The "Libraries and Museums" section of the dance section of the book contains incorrect addresses for the Los Angeles Public Library and the Chicago Public Library's Visual and Performing Arts Division. As a survey of the performing arts, this "college of one" for the culturally impaired may help turn a few of them into cognoscenti. Recommended for most general-reference collections.

The Timetables of African-American History: A Chronology of the Most Important People and Events in African-American History. By Sharon Harley. Simon & Schuster, 1995. 400p. illus. index. $35 (0-671-79524-4).
973'.0496073 Afro-Americans—History—Chronology [CIP] 94-22571

This book chronicles significant events, figures, and movements in the lives of African Americans from 1492 to 1992. It highlights many firsts: in 1940, for example, Booker T. Washington was the first black American to appear on a postage stamp, and Richard Wright's Native Son was the first literary work by a black American to become a Book-of-the-Month Club selection. The work is arranged by year; under each date events are listed across the page under such categories as Education; Laws and Legal Actions; Religion; Arts; Science, Technology, and Medicine; and Sports. Nonblack persons are identified by an asterisk except when their racial or ethnic designation is obvious. A few black-and-white portraits of prominent African Americans illustrate the volume. The detailed index notes not only the page number but also the column under which topics are found.

This is another in the growing list of chronologies. The two-volume African American Chronology [RBB F 15 94] is aimed at middle-schoolers and is also illustrated. It is based on the more detailed Chronology of African-American History [RBB D 1 91]. Timelines of African-American History [RBB O 15 94] is an inexpensive paperback chronology. For libraries that don't own one of these other chronologies, the reasonably priced Timetables is a must item.

Timelines of African-American History: 500 Years of Black Achievement. By Tom Cowan and Jack Maguire. Perigee, 1994. 346p. bibliog. index. paper $15 (0-399-52127-5).
973'.049673 Afro-Americans—History—Chronology [CIP] 94-12771

In an era when interest in African American history and culture is at its zenith, here is a detailed chronology of this experience. Starting with the year 1492, it notes the appearance of Africans in the so-called New World as explorers. The first bondsmen were indentured servants who arrived in America in 1619 at Jamestown, Virginia. The time line ends in 1993, noting that "Clara 'Mother' Hale, founder of the Hale House for HIV-infected babies in Harlem, dies December 18 in New York." The events of each year are divided into subject categories, such as politics and civil rights, sports, literature and journalism, the military, and the visual arts. Many telling details are included in this work; for example, "1939: Of the 774 libraries in the 13 southern states, 99 admit African Americans." A brief list of contemporary events in the wider American community is given for each year. An index of proper names (but not subjects) aids access.

Think of this book as an introduction: behind every fact listed is a story of a useful life, a creative act, a blow for freedom, or an event that made a historical difference. This popularly priced work will be of use in public libraries, secondary media centers, and undergraduate and community college libraries, especially those that didn't purchase the two-volume *African American Chronology* [RBB F 15 94].

Voices of the Spirit: Sources for Interpreting the African-American Experience. By Denise M. Glover. ALA, 1995. 211p. indexes. paper $25 (0-8389-0639-7).
016.973'0496073 Afro-Americans—History—Bibliography [CIP] 94-29139

This annotated bibliography on African American history includes several types of resources, including books, traveling exhibits available from the Smithsonian Institution, and videotapes. Classic works by nineteenth-century pioneers in African American history are listed, as well as those by such contemporary scholars as John Blassingame, Darlene Hine, and John Hope Franklin. The books were published from 1883 to 1993. Glover is a librarian who has specialized in collection development with an emphasis on African American materials.

Six chapters are arranged by genre and historical period. In chapter 1 are reference books, while chapter 2 addresses collective biography and genealogy. Chapter 3 includes historiographic works. Surveys of general history comprise chapter 4, and historical works by chronological period are in chapters 5 and 6. Within each chapter, materials are alphabetized by the author or producer's last name. Books of primary documents appear at the end of each chapter in a separately alphabetized section. Each section has introductory notes, giving its scope, purpose, and focus. The letters P, E, and V are used to denote photographic books, exhibits, and videotapes. The lengthy annotations (sometimes more than a page) are evaluative and often refer to other books on the subject. Closing the work are author-title and subject indexes.

Voices of the Spirit was developed to assist in the establishment of African American collections for secondary and undergraduate schools. It will be useful in school media centers and community college libraries; public libraries will want a copy, too.

The Young Reader's Companion to American History. Ed. by John A. Garraty. Houghton, 1994. 920p. illus. index. maps. $39.95 (0-395-66920-0).
973'.03 U.S.—History—Encyclopedias—Juvenile literature [CIP] 94-22759

Similar in concept to *The Reader's Companion to American History* [RBB Ja 1 92], this book is meant for the student 11 years old and up. More than 150 historians and children's writers were commissioned to convey history with insight and understanding, and with Columbia University historian Garraty's editorial skills, this was accomplished.

The topics in this encyclopedia start with *Abolitionist Movement* and end with *Florenz Ziegfeld*. Entries range from one-quarter page to six pages (*Civil War*). All entries are signed and conclude with cross-references; some have references for further reading. The entry *Racism* describes the experience of the first European settlers, racist attitudes, and how racism is countered; in addition, *see also* references lead to different ethnic groups, related historical struggles, and organizations. Drugs, rock music, and various sports are handled in a similar manner with black-and-white illustrations that enhance the text. Several color inserts of photographs are provided for such topics as *Architecture* and *Painting*. Full-page maps show "American Colonies in the Early Eighteenth Century" and "Major Events of the Revolutionary War." Biographies are numerous and cover the presidents and such people as Eugene Debs, Ruth Bader Ginsburg, and Elvis Presley. Topics such as *Expansion, Territorial* and *Treaty of Paris*, as well as those with student appeal, such as the history of *Comics* and *Fashion*, can all be found here. Appendixes include a map of the U.S. and facts about the states. A detailed index leads to topics within entries.

The Young Reader's Companion to American History is highly recommended for school and public libraries reference collections in view of its reading level, comprehensive coverage, and attractive design. It will be an effective source for middle-school and high-school homework assignments and research.

James Madison and the American Nation 1751-1836: An Encyclopedia. By Robert A. Rutland. Simon & Schuster, 1994. 509p. bibliog. illus. index. $95 (0-13-508425-3).
973.4 Madison, James—Encyclopedias || U.S.—History—Colonial period, ca. 1600–1775—Encyclopedias || U.S.—History—Revolution, 1775–1783—Encyclopedias || U.S.—History—1783–1865—Encyclopedias [CIP] 94-12322

Originally conceived by Charles E. Smith, former publisher of many of Macmillan and Simon & Schuster's award-winning reference sets, this one-volume alphabetically arranged encyclopedia focuses on the life and times of James Madison, fourth president of the U.S. (1808-17). Its 400 articles provide detailed coverage of Madison's life, his interpreters, his writings, his political environment, foreign affairs, and his family and contemporaries.

Capably edited by Rutland, former editor-in-chief of Madison's presidential papers and professor emeritus at the University of Virginia, it includes signed articles from 88 Madison scholars, mostly historians, but also including political scientists, librarians, archivists, economists, and philosophers. Each article incorporates the most recent research on Madison and his contemporaries and includes a brief bibliography. The volume contains numerous black-and-white illustrations drawn from the Prints and Photographs Division of the Library of Congress as well as documents from the James Madison Papers at the Library of Congress and numerous maps.

Since Madison's life spans eight decades, from 1751 to 1836, the encyclopedia provides coverage of most of the key events and personages involved in American history from the Continental Congress up through the Louisiana Purchase and the War of 1812. Madison knew all of the presidents prior to 1837 (he served as Secretary of State to Thomas Jefferson) and corresponded with many of them during his retirement to Montpelier in Virginia.

The most detailed coverage in the encyclopedia is of Madison himself and includes seven articles covering his life and career. Separate articles cover his wife, Dolley, who married Madison in 1794 after an introduction by Aaron Burr, and numerous other family members. Illustrations of Madison include photographs, miniatures, silhouettes, engravings, portraits, and etchings. Articles on Madison's contemporaries tend to be succinct and focus on their relationship to him. Thus the 1-page article on George Washington describes Madison's role as his adviser. That on John Adams focuses on their profound disagreements about the nature of government. An article on the University of Virginia describes Madison's role as rector from 1826 to 1834.

Appendixes include the texts of several documents drafted by Madison, such as the Constitution of 1787. A detailed chronology contrasts key events of Madison's life with other events in America and the world and ends with the death of Dolley Madison in 1849. A synoptic outline of contents provides an overview of the conceptual scheme of the encyclopedia and makes it easy to explore related topics. There is a detailed index. Overall, this is an excellent example of a one-volume encyclopedia that should prove useful to a broad audience, from high-school students to professional historians.

The American Civil War: A Multicultural Encyclopedia. By the Civil War Society. 7v. Grolier, 1994. 100p./vol. illus. index. $179 (0-7172-7348-2).
973.7 U.S.—History—Civil War, 1861–1865 || U.S.—History—Civil War, 1861–1865—Encyclopedias, Juvenile [OCLC]

Written for middle-schoolers and up, this seven-volume set illustrates in more than 300 entries the major battles, important military figures, and fundamental concepts of a key event in American history. The unique feature of this work is its multicultural emphasis, with entries on the participation in the war of various racial, religious, and ethnic groups: for example, African, French, Irish, Italian, Jewish, Mormon, Native, and Scandinavian Americans. The set was compiled by the Civil War Society, an association of scholars, students, writers, collectors, and reenactors with a mission of furthering historical research and preserving historic sites.

The volumes are arranged alphabetically, beginning with *Abolitionists* in volume 1 and ending with a discussion of the *Zouaves* regiments of the North and South in volume 7. Although the entries are brief, ranging in length from one to four pages, they provide well-written and easily understood coverage of topics for the student. Cross-references are noted in small capital letters. There are illustrations on almost every other page: black-and-white photographs, historic prints, cartoons, and maps. Following the last entry in volume 7, the reader finds charts on the distribution of various ethnic populations in Confederate and Union territory at the time of the 1860 census. The brief bibliography doesn't appear to list any books especially for younger readers. An index covering all seven volumes concludes this work.

The American Civil War reflects a unique approach to a period in U.S. history. Entries may not provide sufficient information for a report on any one topic, but this set will be a useful companion to other works

History

on the Civil War. Middle-school libraries and public libraries will want to consider this encyclopedia for their collections.

The Atlas of the Civil War. Ed. by James M. McPherson. Macmillan, 1994. 223p. bibliog. illus. index. $40 (0-02-579050-1).
973.7'3 U.S.—History—Civil War, 1861-1865—Campaigns—Maps [CIP] 94-16962

Pulitzer Prize-winning author McPherson is Edwards Professor of American History at Princeton. In addition to the prizewinning *Battle Cry of Freedom*, his books include *Struggle for Equality* and *Marching toward Freedom*. The contributors to *The Atlas of the Civil War* are academics and military-park historians.

The 200 maps in this specialized atlas show troop movements (first and second positions, retreats), physical features, and the location of towns and counties. Clearly defined symbols indicate army hierarchies (corps, division, brigade), topographic features, and battle lines (encampments, siege lines, batteries). Thus, the reader gets a "comprehensive overview of the warfare which was destined to affect Americans for centuries." Arranged around the maps as sidebars and inserts are hundreds of photographs, eyewitness accounts, letters, and news clippings.

The atlas is divided into five sections, each one highlighting a war year from 1861 to 1865. A typical example, the 1864 "Total War," begins with a full-page photograph of General Grant accompanied by a 1,200-word article that provides a context for the two dozen maps that follow. The writing is colorful and engaging. Also presented here is a double-page color lithograph of the battle of Kennesaw Mountain, Georgia.

Since the pages measure 9 by 12 inches, the maps are fairly large. Line clarity, color, and detailing are excellent. The photos could almost stand alone as a photographic essay of the war. They strengthen the impact of the maps tremendously. For example, accompanying the map of the Spotsylvania Campaign is a photo of a dead Confederate soldier, captioned, "So devastating had been the Union fire that many of the Confederate dead lay in orderly rows, the alignment of their ranks perfectly preserved." The volume concludes with a brief bibliography and indexes of personal names and place-names.

The four-volume *Encyclopedia of the Confederacy* [RBB F 1 94] contains 67 maps, most of them on military matters. But with a reasonable price of $40, *The Atlas of the Civil War* is an excellent buy and will be valued by public and academic libraries serving serious Civil War researchers.

The Historical Atlas of the Congresses of the Confederate States of America, 1861–1865. By Kenneth C. Martis. Simon & Schuster Academic Reference, 1994. 157p. bibliog. index. tables. $75 (0-13-389115-1).
973.7'022 Confederate States of America. Congress—Maps || Confederate States of America. Politics and government—Maps || U.S.—History—Civil War, 1861-1865—Politics and government—Maps || U.S.—Historical geography—Maps [CIP] 93-46478

As proclaimed by its author, this atlas "examines the Civil War in a way never before attempted." It is the first Civil War atlas not to focus on military affairs. Martis has produced three atlases dealing with the U.S. Congress: *The Historical Atlas of U.S. Congressional Districts, 1789–1983* (Free Press, 1982), *The Historical Atlas of Political Parties in the United States Congress, 1789–1989* (Macmillan, 1989), and *The Historical Atlas of State Power in Congress 1790–1990* (Congressional Quarterly, 1993). He now turns his attention to documentation of the Congress of the Confederacy.

This work contains 45 maps (most of them in color) and 48 statistical tables, along with considerable accompanying text that explains the significance of the maps. The work is divided into six chapters, including introductory and concluding ones. Of the remaining chapters, one documents the provisional Confederate Congress of 1861–62. Another explores the characteristics of the Confederate districts, including such factors as slave population, land value, prior political sentiment, and extent of Union occupation during the course of the war. Yet another chapter illustrates electoral behavior; since there were no formal political parties in the Confederacy, Martis looks at such factors as the return of incumbents, or the prior political affiliation and support for succession of the various congressmen. A final chapter documents and illustrates a number of key votes, as well as patterns of high or low support for the key issues of conscription, impressment, and the support of the government of Jefferson Davis. There are four appendixes, including one that presents the complete extant Confederate electoral returns.

This is an impressive and meticulously documented work. The maps are attractive and easy to read; at times, however, reference to the text is necessary to make complete sense of them. The maps labeled "Confederate Support," for example, illustrate high or low support for efforts by Davis and the Central Confederate government to expand their power in response to wartime conditions. The text carefully documents the history and the various characteristics of the Confederate Congress, particularly those aspects subject to geographic analysis. For example, Martis shows how the large number of representatives from occupied districts was an important element of the Confederate Congress. These representatives, sheltered from retaliation from their constituents who were behind Union lines, supported many drastic measures by the Confederate government that may have prolonged the war.

The only other reference work to focus on the Confederate Congress is the *Biographical Register of the Confederate Congress* (Louisiana State Univ., 1975), which, despite a few simple maps and some tables, serves a very different purpose. The recent *Encyclopedia of the Confederacy* [RBB F 1 94] documents political aspects of the Confederacy but does not provide detailed analysis of the Congress and has relatively few maps not dealing with military matters. This work is highly recommended for large public libraries and academic libraries and for any library with a serious interest in the Confederacy.

America in the 20th Century. 11v. Marshall Cavendish, 1995. bibliog. illus. index. maps. $399.95 (1-85435-736-0).
973.9 U.S.—Civilization—20th century [CIP] 94-10854

The decade-by-decade approach used here is well-suited to the popular chronicling of American history in images and words. *America in the 20th Century* devotes one volume of approximately 144 pages to each of the century's 10 decades and an eleventh volume to a multifaceted index. Contrary to the 1994-95 Marshall Cavendish catalog, which gives the impression that the entire set contains some 100 illustrations, each volume actually contains about that number of photographs, maps, diagrams, cartoons, posters, advertisements, and other high-interest illustrations. Those in the volumes on the most recent decades tend to be in color. Also contrary to the publisher's catalog, this series focuses not on "the 20th century history of North America" but on the U.S. Popular culture is especially strongly represented. The clear and lively text is especially suited for junior-high and high-school audiences, but nonspecialist adults might also learn much. The set also features more than 200 capsule biographies, with photos, of individuals ranging from Elizabeth Cady Stanton and Ty Cobb to Jane Alexander and Dr. Jack Kevorkian. Quotations in sidebars are found on many pages.

Among the general topics covered in each of volumes 1–10 are social policy, politics, foreign relations, the economy, business and industry, literature and the arts, sports, education, family life, crime, and demographic change. Also highlighted are "the role and struggles of women, indigenous peoples, those with handicaps, and racial and other minorities." Of the roughly 10 chapters in each volume, the first summarizes the previous decade and provides a context for the decade under discussion, while the last chapter summarizes that decade. Each volume concludes with a list of key dates, suggestions for further reading, and an index.

The index volume begins with a list of key dates 1900–94 that is often taken verbatim from the lists in each volume. Following a glossary and cumulative list of further reading are a general index and indexes to people, science and scientists, places, civil rights and social issues, women and minorities, laws and treaties, and popular culture and the arts.

America in the 20th Century compares favorably with the recently reissued Time-Life series, *This Fabulous Century*, which also takes a decade-by-decade approach but stops with 1970. Volumes in the latter set contain a much higher proportion of illustration to text. The outstanding quality and lack of overlap in illustrations recommend both sets.

Dictionary of Twentieth-Century Culture: American Culture after World War II. Ed. by Karen Rood. Gale, 1994. 393p. illus. index. $60 (0-8103-8481-7).
973.92 U.S.—Civilization y 1945– [OCLC] 93-51505

The editorial plan for the *Dictionary of Twentieth-Century Culture*, of which this is the first volume, claims that it will have entries on "people, places, terms, art forms, and organizations associated with creative expression, those forms of creativity that seek to describe and interpret the human condition." The set is to be in 20 volumes, published at the rate of three volumes a year. Culture is defined in narrow terms to mean the arts; the sciences, government and politics, and religion are generally not included. Some political material creeps in; the Cold War made late twentieth-century America what it was and thus has an entry. John F. Kennedy and Martin Luther King, both formidable icons as well as political figures, have entries, although Malcolm X does not. Insider trading and the Chicago 8 are covered, but the Keating Five isn't.

The criteria for inclusion are not spelled out in the introductory matter, and they are not clear. Why do Mikhail Baryshnikov and Erik Bruhn both have entries, but not Rudolf Nureyev? Why isn't Fred Astaire included, when Gene Kelly is? Progressive music, New Age music, *auteur* theory, and many other movements, schools, or groups get thumbnail sketches that will probably disappoint practitioners but will be useful to laypeople seeking information. For that reason, the book merits some consideration for those who are outside the charmed circle of culture mavens and literati whose spiritual if not physical home is New York City. One of the circle doubtless wrote the insulting explanation of how a *New Yorker* cover is full of subtle allusions that have to be explained to the ignorant. Some in Pumpkin Centre (to use Robertson Davies' term) not only know who Eustace Tilley is but have even seen punk rockers.

If one can get past the tone of metropolitan superiority and many inexplicable omissions—Harlan Ellison, spaghetti Westerns, among others—the work has some merit. The sketches on periodicals such as the *New York Review of Books* and terms such as *serial music* are certainly useful, as are the brief biographies. (More than three-quarters of the entries are biographies.) There is a lot of good material on Broadway performers, producers, directors, and writers. Much of the information is available elsewhere, but this concise form would be helpful for ready-reference questions. Black-and-white photographs ranging in quality from professional to reproductions of home candid shots accompany some entries. Pop music in its various forms gets a lot of space, and while articles do not provide discographies, they do place groups in time and in style. There is some coverage of television, motion picture actors (Elizabeth Taylor gets a longer article than Richard Burton), and assorted entertainment phenomena like drive-in theaters and chain bookstores.

A topical table of contents at the beginning of the volume lists articles under such headings as *Art*, *Literature*, *Drama and Film*, and *Music and Dance*. A time line from 1945 through 1993 lists, in parallel columns, historical events and highlights in dance, drama, literature, TV, etc. The articles are well laid out in dictionary format and are easy to read. Cross-references are in boldface type. Articles are signed with initials, but the key to contributors does not give their credentials. Most articles have some references to further readinjg. There is a detailed index.

At $60 per volume, the full series, to include volumes on postrevolutionary Soviet culture, North African and Middle Eastern culture, and Western European culture since World War II, will not be a necessary purchase if all volumes are as idiosyncratic in their selection as is this one. Academic and large public libraries with a strong interest in the arts may want to purchase selected volumes in their areas of primary interest as they are published.

The Historical Atlas of New York City: A Visual Celebration of Nearly 400 Years of New York City's History. By Eric Homberger. Holt, 1994. 192p. bibliog. illus. index. $45 (0-8050-2649-5).
974.7'1 New York (N.Y.)—History || New York (N.Y.)—History—Maps || New York (N.Y.)—History—Pictorial works [CIP] 94-18992

This atlas surveys the history of New York City in more than 50 double-page spreads combining a map with brief text, illustrations, and other graphics. Each spread focuses on a particular theme such as "Stuyvesant's City," "From Iron Age to Skyscraper," "Broadway," and "Latest Arrivals" (the new immigrants). Each of the seven chapters into which the atlas is divided covers a particular historical period and is introduced by a brief illustrated overview of the period. An illustrated chronology follows the atlas proper, providing a conspectus of the city's history. Other supplementary features at the back include a section of short biographies of more than 50 outstanding individuals associated with the city, a bibliography keyed to the chapters, and a page with two lists: "New York in American Literature" (a book list) and a selective listing of museums.

An informative and visually attractive introduction to the history of the city, this atlas is quite selective in its coverage and has limited reference value compared with more comprehensive guides to the city. A spot check of the index turns up no references to Mayor Jimmy Walker and no mention of the Metropolitan Museum of Art or the Museum of Modern Art, although they do appear on maps. Babe Ruth and Mickey Mantle are mentioned on the "Our Team" pages, but not Joe DiMaggio. Among other famous New Yorkers that fail to appear in the index are Caruso, Toscanini, Joe Papp, and Woody Allen. James Baldwin is not on the literature book list, and some classic sources on the city are not cited in the bibliography, such as *The Columbia Historical Portrait of New York*. Nonetheless, many fascinating aspects of the rich history of the city are explored in the atlas: its geology, Harlem, Central Park, the rise of the great department stores, the subway, and public housing, to mention a few.

Many public and academic libraries may prefer to add this title to their circulating collection rather than to the reference shelves.

North Carolina History: An Annotated Bibliography. Comp. by H. G. Jones. Greenwood, 1995. 796p. indexes. $95 (0-313-28255-2; ISSN 1060-5711).
016.9756 North Carolina—History—Bibliography [CIP] 94-37085

In his preface, the compiler reminds us that "all bibliographies are but starting points for researchers." *North Carolina History* provides a strong starting place for serious research, not only in North Carolina history, but also in the history of early America, the American South, genealogy, Native and African Americans, women in America, and more.

Jones is former state archivist and director of the North Carolina State Department of Archives and History. He was also for many years the curator of the University of North Carolina's North Carolina Collection, reputedly the largest repository of information on a single state in the country.

North Carolina History features 11,399 entries for books, pamphlets, articles, theses, and dissertations. It includes publications about the state from the first description of Cape Fear in 1524 through 1992. An earlier volume by Mary L. Thorton, *A Bibliography of North Carolina*, 1589-1956 (Univ. of North Carolina, 1958), does not include articles, theses, or dissertations, although it does contain fiction, which Jones does not. Jones' volume opens with a chronology of North Carolina history. Entries in the first chapters are categorized in four major areas: the environment, including the state's natural features, flora and fauna, climate, and natural disasters; prehistory and archaeology; North Carolina Indians, arranged by major tribes; and exploration and attempted settlement. The rest of the work is divided into chronological periods, with each subdivided into 12 subjects, such as religion, ethnic and racial groups, economic history, science, and medicine. The largest chapter, a county-by-county breakdown, includes unique local histories. A final chapter describes historic sites and museums. Due to the number of entries, annotations are necessarily brief, usually one line. Jones masterfully makes the most of limited space, such as in this entry: "Coggins, James Caswell. *Abraham Lincoln, a North Carolinian; with Proof*. . . The myth survives."

This volume is the third in the Greenwood Bibliographies of the States of the United States series; volumes are available for Illinois, Kansas, and South Dakota. *North Carolina History* is recommended for all medium-size and large North Carolina libraries, as well as for large academic and public library research collections regardless of geographic location.

The Cowboy Encyclopedia. By Richard W. Slatta. ABC-Clio, 1994. 474p. bibliog. illus. index. $60 (0-87436-738-7).
978'.003 Cowboys—America—Encyclopedias || Cowboys—West (U.S.)—Encyclopedias || Frontier and pioneer life—America—Encyclopedias || Frontier and pioneer life—West (U.S.)—Encyclopedias || America—Social life and customs—Encyclopedias [CIP] 94-19824

This past year brought forth a spate of cowboy reference books, notably a reediting of Ramon Adams' classic work of 1936, *The Cowboy Dictionary* (Perigee, 1993), *Cowboys and the Wild West* [RBB Ja 1 95], and several books of Western slang. Now we have an encyclopedic work, embodying many slang words; famous cowboy names; broad subjects, such as *Food* or *Horses* (entries of five or six pages), and narrower topics, such as *Holster* or *Levi's* (a column or so). Biographies of cowboys or of movie cowboys usually run to four or five pages. Required accent marks are printed in headings such as *latigo* and *patron* unlike Adams' work, which omits all Spanish accents.

There is generous use of *see* references, though in some cases the reference is to a long article, with no hint as to the precise location of the term referred from. Thus, the entry *Coffee Grinder* says "see Rope." The term is to be found in the middle of the fourth column of text: "coffee grinding" is what a novice vaquero does when he wraps his lariat the wrong way around his saddle horn.

Many black-and-white illustrations supplement the text. Those copied from tintypes or other early processes, such as one of Billy the Kid, may be excused for poor quality, but a few photos of modern artists or of their work are disappointingly dark.

Though primarily concerned with the cowboy of the western U.S., the book does not ignore Argentina or Canada. The article *Gaucho* runs to six pages, with several cartoons of F. Molina Campos, who affectionately lampooned gauchos for several decades with his popular illustrations for commercial calendars.

There are several appendixes: a list of film and videotape sources, a list of cowboy museums, an annotated list of periodicals dealing with cowboys, a calendar of "western cultural happenings," a 24-page bibliography, and a detailed index.

This work is recommended for any library with an interest in the West, even if it already has one or more dictionaries of cowboy slang. *The Cowboy Encyclopedia* is broader in scope, easy to use, and written in a clear, convincing style.

Cowboys and the Wild West: An A-to-Z Guide from the Chisholm Trail to the Silver Screen. By Don Cusic. Facts On File, 1994. 333p. bibliog. illus. $40 (0-8160-2783-8).
978'.003 Cowboys—West (U.S.)—Encyclopedias ‖ Frontier and pioneer life—West (U.S.)—Encyclopedias ‖ West (U.S.)—Encyclopedias [CIP] 93-45584

This work differs from other dictionaries of western terms and topics in that it is largely concerned with persons who have recently, rather than historically, lived as cowboys in the West, or who have appeared in movies or on television in westerns. The entries range from brief (sometimes only a few words of definition of a colloquial expression) to quite long; the entry *Art*, for example, runs to nearly eight pages. The average length of a biographical entry or of a description of a movie is about one-third page.

The chief feature of the work is the wide variety of its entries: definitions of terms; locations of geographic or topographic names; biographies; plots of movies and TV shows, with a listing of the cast; photographs (more than a hundred of them) of famous people in the West or in the movies; and much miscellanea, such as Indian tribes, the Ghost Dance, etc. Recency of biographical data is sometimes rather poor; Gene Autry is carried forward only to 1969, and Roy Rogers only to 1976. There are *see also* references at the end of significant articles, a feature not found in Thrapp's three-volume *Encyclopedia of Frontier Biography* [RBB Ja 15 89]. Most biographical articles in these two works supply similar factual material, but the book under review is at times more detailed. However, it does not cite authorities, which Thrapp does regularly. At the end of the book is a valuable 13-page, double-column bibliography.

This work does not replace or duplicate any previous western dictionary, though its contents may be found in several of them. But it combines in one volume a succinct answer to questions about words, places, tribes, old-timers, gunslingers, outlaws, heroes, and above all, the movies and the TV series that made them all famous. Recommended for almost any library.

The Cambridge Encyclopedia of Australia. Ed. by Susan Bambrick. Cambridge, 1994. 384p. bibliog. charts. illus. index. maps. $54.95 (0-521-36511-2).
994'.003 Australia—Encyclopedias [BKL] 94-24669

This book draws on the expertise of more than 900 scholars to describe the world's smallest continent (or its largest island). This comprehensive reference covers not only modern Australia, but its aboriginal heritage, physical makeup, history, economy, government, and cultural contributions. Similar to other titles in this series (*Cambridge Encyclopedia of China, Cambridge Encyclopedia of Latin America and the Caribbean*), it is intended to introduce the reader to the continent of Australia and provides facts, figures, and 250 colorful photographs to enhance the understanding of its society and culture.

Sections cover such topics as the Great Barrier Reef, the legal system, agriculture, religion, health, and aboriginal art. Although topical entries throughout the volume are brief, the contributors add information in brief boxed essays. For example, in the "Media" section, a brief insert on foreign ownership is included. All articles are signed with intitials keyed to a contributors list at the front of the book. Almost all the contributors are Australian. More than 40 maps and charts are scattered throughout the volume. A bibliography of suggested readings and video recordings is arranged in the same order as the text. The detailed index uses italics to denote illustrations and bold type to indicate a major reference to a subject.

The Cambridge Encyclopedia of Australia, with its readable format and attractive illustrations, provides an overview of topics related to this continent and is appropriate for undergraduate, public, and high-school libraries.

Index to Type of Material

ALMANACS
  Almanac of State Legislatures, The. 132
  Facts on File Asian Political Almanac, The. 140
  Global Trends. 129
  Hispanic American Almanac. 47
  Native North American Almanac. 141
  Persian Gulf War Almanac. 140

ANNUALS
  Congressional Yearbook, 1993, The. 53

ATLASES
  Atlas of Classical History. 130
  Atlas of Contemporary America. 133
  Atlas of Russia and the Independent Republics. 132
  Atlas of Shipwrecks and Treasure. 129
  Atlas of Western Art History. 101
  Atlas of Westward Expansion. 130
  Atlas of World War I. 130
  Atlas of the Civil War, The. 146
  Atlas of the Mysterious in North America. 74
  Body Atlas, The. 92
  Children's Atlas of Civilizations, The. 130
  Children's Atlas of the Human Body, The. 92
  Complete Atlas of the World, The. 131
  Dorling Kindersley World Reference Atlas, The. 131
  Encyclopedic World Atlas. 131
  Eyewitness Atlas of the World, The. 131
  Historical Atlas of New York City, The. 147
  Historical Atlas of World War I, The. 138
  Historical Atlas of the Congresses of the Confederate States of America,. 146
  Human Body, The. 93
  Kingfisher First Picture Atlas, The. 131
  My First Atlas. 131
  New Viking Children's World Atlas, The. 131
  Penguin Atlas of Diasporas, The. 44
  State of the U.S.A. Atlas. 133
  Women's Atlas of the United States, The. 47

BIBLIOGRAPHIES
  Africa in Literature for Children and Young Adults. 140
  African American Genealogical Sourcebook. 136
  American Choral Music since 1920. 109
  American Historical Association's Guide to Historical Literature, The. 138
  American Military History. 57
  American Popular Culture. 142
  Anatomy of Wonder 4. 118
  Bibliographic Checklist of African American Newspapers. 60
  Classical Singers of the Opera and Recital Stages. 107
  Cloak and Dagger Fiction. 124
  Cultures Outside the United States in Fiction. 118
  Data Sources for Business and Market Analysis. 87
  Fantasy Literature for Children and Young Adults. 118
  Fieldwork in the Library. 42
  500 Great Books By Women. 45
  Good Reads. 118
  Great New Nonfiction Reads. 28
  Guide to the Zoological Literature, A. 88
  Guides to Library Collection Development. 28
  Handbooks and Tables in Science and Technology. 83
  Health Industry QuickSource. 91
  Hispanic American Genealogical Sourcebook. 136
  Historical Figures in Fiction. 124
  Homelessness in America, 1893-1992. 64
  Hooray for Heroes!. 69
  Humanities, The. 28
  Immigrants in the United States in Fiction. 118
  Information Sources in Science and Technology. 83
  International Business Information. 56
  Introduction to Reference Sources in the Health Sciences. 92
  Kaleidoscope: A Multicultural Booklist for Grades K-8. 48
  Kister's Best Encyclopedias. 31
  Literature of Rock III, The. 107
  Native Americans in Fiction. 118
  North Carolina History. 147
  NoveList. 118
  Recreating the Past. 119
  Reference Sources in Science, Engineering, Medicine, and Agriculture. 82
  Research Guide to Human Sexuality, A. 49
  Rock Stars/Pop Stars. 107
  Sourcebook on Parenting and Child Care. 98
  Television Research. 142
  Thematic Atlases for Public, Academic, and High School Libraries. 132
  Third World Resource Directory 1994-1995. 127
  This Land is Our Land. 122
  Unites States Congress, The. 53
  Voices of the Spirit. 145
  Women Artists. 103
  Young Adult Literature and Nonprint Material. 27

BIOGRAPHICAL DICTIONARIES
  American Women in Science. 86
  100 Great Africans. 134
  African Biographical Dictionary, An. 134
  Art Book, The. 102
  Biographical Dictionary of Film, A. 110
  Cambridge Dictionary of American Biography, The. 134
  Chronicle of Classical Music, The. 104
  Concise Dictionary of American Jewish Biography, The. 135
  Dictators and Tyrants. 135
  Dictionary of Contemporary American Artists. 102
  Dictionary of Literary Biography, v.137. 122
  European Immigrant Women in the United States. 136
  Explorers and Discoverers. 130
  First Century of Film. 112
  Great Leaders, Great Tyrants?. 135
  Great Lives from History. 45
  Great Women Mystery Writers. 124
  Great Women Writers. 121
  Guide to the Blues, A. 107
  Heads of States and Governments. 135
  Jewish American Women Writers. 122
  Larousse Dictionary of Scientists. 86
  Legends in Their Own Time. 136
  Leonard Matlin's Movie Encyclopedia. 110
  Marching to a Different Drummer. 43
  Native North American Literature. 122
  Notable Twentieth-Century Scientists. 86
  On the Trail of the Buffalo Soldier. 62
  Oxford Children's Book of Famous People, The. 134
  Performing Artists. 102
  Science Fiction, Fantasy, and Horror Writers. 123
  Sports Stars. 114
  Supreme Court Justices, The. 59
  Twentieth-Century Brass Soloists. 109
  Who's Who among Asian Americans. 48
  Who's Who in the Bible. 39
  Who's Who of Sports Champions, A. 114. 114
  Women and the Military. 62
  World Leaders. 136

CD-ROM
  American Heritage Talking Dictionary, The. 76
  American Sign Language Dictionary on CD-ROM. 75
  Classroom Prodigy. 27
  Companies International. 57
  Dr. Ruth's Encyclopedia of Sex on CD-ROM. 49
  Encyclopedia of Careers and Vocational Guidance. 55
  Exegy. 128
  Gale's Quotations. 33
  Her Heritage. 45
  InfoPedia. 31
  McGraw-Hill Multimedia Encyclopedia of Science & Technology. 83
  Microsoft Bookshelf '94. 28
  Physicians GenRx/Merck Manual. 93
  Poem Finder on Disc. 117
  Primary Search. 32
  Random House Unabridged Electronic Dictionary on CD-ROM. 78
  Science Navigator. 84
  USA Unzipped. 71
  Viking Opera Guide on CD-ROM, The. 108
  Wilson Applied Science & Technology Abstracts. 82
  Wilson Author Biographies. 120
  Wilson General Science Abstracts. 82

CATALOGS
  Millennium Whole Earth Catalog, The. 70

CHRONOLOGIES
  African American Breakthroughs. 134
  America in the 20th Century. 146
  Chronolgy of 20th-Century Eastern European History. 139
  Chronology of Native North American History. 141
  Chronology of Women's History. 45
  Great Dates in United States History. 143
  Great Events from History II. 54
  Notable Corporate Chronologies. 54
  Peopling of America, The. 48
  Timeline of the Arts and Literature. 101
  Timelines of African-American History. 144
  Timelines of War. 126

149

Timetables of African-American History, The. 144
Timetables of Women's History, The. 46
Your Hit Parade & American Top Ten Hits. 106

CRITICISM
Classical Music. 104
Larousse Dictionary of Writers. 121
Masterpieces of Latino Literature. 125
Modern Black Writers. 121
Twentieth-Century Children's Artists. 119
Twentieth-Century Young Adult Writers. 119

DICTIONARIES
Adventure Heroes. 100
Agricultural Entomology. 96
American Heritage Children's Dictionary, The. 79
American Heritage First Dictionary, The. 79
American Heritage Picture Dictionary, The. 79
American Heritage Student Dictionary, The. 79
Black Talk: Words and Phrases from the Hood to the Amen Corner. 80
Body, Mind & Spirit. 42
Book of Art, The. 102
Book of Food, The. 97
Bulfinch Illustrated Encyclopedia of Antiques, The. 104
CD's, Super Glue, and Salsa. 100
Chambers Dictionary, The. 76
Columbia Dictionary of Modern Literary and Cultural Criticism, The. 26
Companion to Literary Myths, Heroes and Archetypes. 74
Comprehensive Country Music Encyclopedia, The. 106
Cyberspace Lexicon, The. 27
Dictionary of Banking. 56
Dictionary of Baptists in America. 40
Dictionary of Counseling. 63
Dictionary of East European History since 1945. 139
Dictionary of Film Terms. 111
Dictionary of Fundamental Theology. 39
Dictionary of Literary Pseudonyms in the English Language, A. 116
Dictionary of Military Abbreviations. 61
Dictionary of Twentieth-Century Culture. 146
Dictionary of the Arts. 102
Divining the Future. 35
Dorling Kindersley Children's Illustrated Dictionary, The. 77
Dorling Kindersley Ultimate Visual Dictionary. 78
Dr. Ruth's Encyclopedia of Sex. 49
Encyclopedia Mysteriosa. 121
Encyclopedia of Eastern Philosophy and Religion, The. 40
Encyclopedic Dictionary of Gears and Gearing. 95
Facts on File Dictionary of Television, Cable, and Video, The. 72
Film Quotations. 111
From Afar to Zulu. 48
From aristotelian to Reaganomics. 42
Goddesses, Heroes, and Shamans. 41
Great Food Almanac, The. 97
Happy Trails. 80
Harcourt Brace Student Thesaurus, The. 77
Historical First Patents. 90
Illustrated Encyclopedia of Victoriana, The. 103
Indian Terms of the Americas. 141
Jones Cable Television and Information Infrastructure Dictionary. 71
Kingfisher Illustrated Children's Dictionary, The. 77
Kingfisher Illustrated Thesaurus, The. 77
Language of Banking, The. 56
Language of Small Businesses, The. 78
Large Print Computer Dictionary, The. 26

Larousse Dictionary of Beliefs and Religions. 40
Larousse Dictionary of Literary Characters. 121
Larousse Dictionary of World History, The. 127
Macmillan Dictionary of Measurement, The. 73
Macmillan Visual Dictionary, The. 78
Major Characters in American Fiction. 123
Merriam-Webster's Encyclopedia of Literature. 115
Metaphors Dictionary. 33
My Big Dictionary. 79
NTC's Dictionary of Acronyms and Abbreviations. 77
New York Public Library Book of Popular Americans, The. 144
Oxford Companion to Women's Writing in the United States, The. 123
Oxford Companion to World War II, The. 139
Oxford Dictionary of English Grammar, The. 82
Oxford Dictionary of Music, The. 104
Oxford Dictionary of Philosophy, The. 34
Oxford Dictionary of Quotations & Modern Quotations, The. 34
Random House Historical Dictionary of American Slang. 81
Real Life Dictionary of American Politics. 51
Richard Baker's Companion to Music. 104
Science Dictionary. 85
Shakespeare Dictionary, The. 124
Since Eve Ate Apples. 97
Succulents: The Illustrated Dictionary. 96
Thesaurus of Slang, The. 80
Travel Dictionary, The. 59
Visual Dictionary of American Domestic Architecture, The. 103
Visual Encyclopedia of Science. 32
Voyages in Classical Mythology. 41
War S!ang. 80
Word Dance. 141
World History. 126
World Music. 105

DIRECTORIES
African American Resource Guide, The. 143
America's Black and Tribal Colleges. 70
American Jobs Abroad. 99
Art & Design Scholarships. 68
Athletic Scholarships. 70
Best Hospitals in America, The. 63
Black American Colleges and Universities. 70
Choose to Reuse. 65
Directory of U.S. Military Bases Worldwide. 63
DistanceLearn. 69
Education Career Directory. 67
Encyclopedia of Education Information, The. 66
Exhibit Review, The. 71
Ferguson's Guide to Apprenticeship Programs. 54
Film and Video Career Directory. 67
Fitzroy Dearborn Directory of Venture Capital Funds, The. 57
Free and Inexpensive Career Materials. 55
Gale Guide to Internet Databases. 71
Games & Entertainment on CD-ROM. 113
Government Affairs Yellow Book. 52
Guide to National Professional Certification Programs, The. 47
HIV/AIDS Resources. 64
Historical Dictionary of Refugee and Disaster Relief Oragnizations. 65
Hoover's Guide to Private Companies. 59
Internet Access Provider. 72
Internet Compendium: Subject Guide to Social Sciences, Business and Law. 71
Internet Resource Directory for K-12 Teachers and Librarians, The. 68
Job Hunter's Yellow Pages. 99

Job Seeker's Guide to Socially Responsible Companies, The. 99
Librarian's Guide to Public Records, The. 60
MVR Book Motor Services Guide, The. 66
Marketing Information. 100
Music, Dance & Theater Scholarships. 68
National Directory of AIDS Care 1994-95, The. 95
National Directory of Internships, The. 69
National Directory of State Business Licensing and Regulation. 59
National Service Corps: A State-by-State Guide. 61
Net Games. 113
Net Money. 72
Opera Companies and Houses of the United States. 108
Opportunities for Vocational Study. 54
Oryx Guide to Distance Learning, The. 70
Performing Arts Career Directory. 67
Peterson's Guide to Nursing Programs. 92
Peterson's Internships 1995. 99
Peterson's Professional Degree Programs in the Visual and Performing Art. 101
Physical Sciences Career Directory. 67
Public Administration Career Directory. 67
School-to-Work Programs. 54
Sourcebook of Public Record Providers, The. 65
Sourcebook of State Public Records, The. 65
Specialty Occupational Outlook. 56
Tony Award, The. 113
Youth Exchanges. 67

DISCOGRAPHIES
All Music Book of Hit Singles, The. 105
All Music Guide to Jazz. 105
Building a Classical Music Library. 106
Cash Box Pop Singles Charts, 1950-1993. 106
Classical Music on CD. 106
Green Book of Songs by Subject, The. 109
Guide to Classic Recorded Jazz, The. 107
Guide to Native American Music Recordings, A. 106
Joel Whitburn's Top Pop Singles, 1955-1993. 106
Television Theme Recordings. 105

ENCYCLOPEDIAS
ABC-Clio Companion to the American Peace Movement in the Twentieth Centu. 52
Allergies A-Z. 95
Alternative Health & Medicine Encyclopedia, The. 94
Alternative Realities. 36
Amazing Animals of the World. 88
American Civil War, The. 145
American Film Comedy. 110
Asian American Encyclopedia, The. 143
Britannica Online. 29
Cambridge Encyclopedia of Australia, The. 148
Cambridge Encyclopedia of Russia and the Former Soviet Union, The. 139
Children's Television, 1947-1990. 111
China Business. 54
Complete Vampire Companion, The. 36
Computers: A Visual Encyclopedia. 26
Concise Columbia Encyclopedia, The. 30
Concise Encyclopedia Chemistry. 87
Continuum Encyclopedia of Symbols, The. 43
Cowboy Encyclopedia, The. 147
Cowboys and the Wild West. 148
Crime. 66
Dictionary of Cristian Art. 39
Dictionary of Military History and the Art of War, A. 61
Dictionary of Native American Literature. 125
Encyclopedia of Advanced Materials, The. 95
Encyclopedia of Afterlife Beliefs and Phenomena. 36

Encyclopedia of Agricultural Science. 96
Encyclopedia of American Architecture. 103
Encyclopedia of American Indian Costume. 73
Encyclopedia of American Industries, v.1. 58
Encyclopedia of American Industries, v.2. 58
Encyclopedia of Bioethics. 38
Encyclopedia of Claims, Frauds, and Hoaxes of the Occult and Supernatura. 35
Encyclopedia of College Basketball. 114
Encyclopedia of Creation Myths. 41
Encyclopedia of Endangered Species. 87
Encyclopedia of English Studies and Language Arts. 81
Encyclopedia of Home Care for the Elderly. 65
Encyclopedia of Human Behavior. 36
Encyclopedia of Human Intelligence. 37
Encyclopedia of Memory and Memory Disorders, The. 37
Encyclopedia of Plague and Pestilence. 93
Encyclopedia of Psychology. 37
Encyclopedia of Social Work. 63
Encyclopedia of Time. 87
Encyclopedia of Traditional Epics. 74
Encyclopedia of th Environment, The. 65
Encyclopedia of the American Military. 62
Encyclopedia of the Cold War. 128
Encyclopedia of the Horse, The. 97
Encyclopedia of the Musical Theatre, The. 108
Encyclopedia of the United States Congress, The. 53
Ethics. 38
Ethnic Relations. 47
Film Encyclopedia, The. 111
Great Scientific Achievements. 85
Grolier Student Encyclopedia of Endangered Species, The. 88
Hispanics in Hollywood. 112
Homelessness: A Sourcebook. 64
International Book Publishing. 33
International Dictionary of Theatre, v.2: Playwrights. 112
James Madison and the American Nation 1751-1836. 145
Junior Judaica. 42
Kingfisher First Encyclopedia of Animals, The. 88
Kingfisher Young World Encyclopedia, The. 31
Larousse Encyclopedia of Wine. 98
Man, Myth & Magic. 35
McGraw-Hill Concise Encyclopedia of Science & Technology. 84
McGraw-Hill Illustrated Encyclopedia of Robotics & Artificial Intelligen. 95
Mexico Business. 54
Native America in the Twentieth Century. 141
New Encyclopedia of Zionism and Israel. 51
New York Public Library Performing Arts Desk Reference, The. 144
Notable Asian Americans. 143
Official NBA Basketball Encyclopedia, The. 115
Older Americans Almanac. 44
Oxford Companion to Wine, The. 98
Oxford Encyclopedia of the Modern Islamic World, The. 127
Oxford Medical Companion, The. 92
Pirates and Privateers of the Americas. 129
Pirates!. 129
Professional Sports Team Histories. 114
Quintessential Cat, The. 90
Reader's Digest Illustrated Book of Dogs, The. 97
Taylor's Master Guide to Gardening. 96
UFO. 26
Vampire Book, The. 36
Van Nostrand's Scientific Encyclopedia. 85
Viking Opera Guide, The. 108
World Encyclopedia of Contemporary Theatre, The. 113
World of Tennis. 115
Worldmark Encyclopedia of the Nations. 126
Worldmark Encyclopedia of the States. 126
Young Oxford Companion to Maps and Mapmaking, The. 132
Young Reader's Companion to American History, The. 145

FILMOGRAPHIES
Animals on Screen and Radio. 110
Images in the Dark. 112
Vietnam War Films. 140

GAZETTEERS
American Places Dictionary. 133

GUIDEBOOKS
African American Historic Places. 142
Aquariums of North America. 89
Atlas of Sacred Places, The. 41
Atlas of Wild Places, The. 41
International Dictionary of Historic Places. 142
National Directory of Haunted Places, The. 35
Pop Culture Landmarks. 134
Used Car Reliability & Safety Guide, The. 72
Weissman Travel Planner for Western and Eastern Europe, 1994-1995. 133

HANDBOOKS
Bird's Eggs. 90
Birds of North America, The. 89
Birds of South America, The. 89
Business Plans Handbook. 100
CQ's Desk Reference on American Government. 51
Cambridge Encyclopedia of the English Language, The. 75
Congressional Quarterly's Guide to U.S. Elections. 52
Consumer's Medical Desk Reference, The. 64
Dorling Kindersley History of the World, The. 126
Favorite Hobbies and Pastimes. 110
Forms of Address. 73
Foxes, Wolves and Wild Dogs of the World. 90
Gay and Lesbian Rights. 52
Genealogist's Handbook, The. 136
Geneaology Online. 137
Geneaology in the Computer Age. 137
Guidelines for Bias-Free Writing. 116
Handbook of Alternative Education. 67
Handbook of Current Health & Medicine. 91
Handbook of Over-the-Counter Drugs and Pharmacy Products. 94
Handbook of the Birds of the World. 89
In Search of Your Canadian Roots. 137
In Search of Your European Roots. 137
In Search of Your German Roots. 137
Information Please Women's Sourcebook, The. 46
Jimmy Cornell World Cruising Handbook. 115
Legal Problem Solver. 60
Life's Big Instruction Book. 32
MLA Handbook for Writers of Research Papers. 116
Multicultural Clients. 64
NASDTEC Manual, 1994-1995, The. 67
New York Public Library Writer's Guide to Style and Usage, The. 117
Now Read On: A Guide to Contemporary Popular Fiction. 125
PDR Family Guide to Women's Health and Prescription Drugs, The. 43
Parents' Resource Alamanac, The. 98
Scientific Style and Format. 117
Special Education Sourcebook, The. 68
State Names, Seals, Flags, and Symbols. 138
Swallowtail Butterflies of the Americas. 89
Universe Explained, The. 86
Usage and Abusage. 81
Whales, Dolphins and Porpoises. 90

INDEXES
Barnhart New-Words Concordance, The. 80
Film Anthologies Index, The. 111
Holidays and Festivals Index. 73
Hollywood Song. 108
Index to Fairy Tales, 1987-1992. 75
Proper Names Master Index. 79
Science Experiments and Projects Index. 85
U.S. Government Periodicals Index. 27

SOURCEBOOKS
American Population Change Annual. 44
Congressional Voting Guide. 53
Consumer Health USA. 94
Datapedia of the United States 1790-2000. 51
Divorce Help Sourcebook. 59
Gale City & Metro Rankings Reporter. 50
Gale State Rankings Reporter. 50
Great Health Hints & Handy Tips. 93
Health On File. 93
Health and Environment in America's Top-Rated Cities. 50
Historical Inventions on File. 91
Historical Statistics of Black America. 143
International Holidays. 91
Martial Arts Sourcebook, The. 115
Masterworks of Man & Nature. 126
New Interpreter's Bible, The. 38
Presidents Speak, The. 61
Rating Guide to Life in America's 50 States, The. 49
Sanders Price Guide to Autographs, The. 137
Second to None: A Documentary History of American Women. 46
Small Business Profiles. 58
Sourcebook for Earth's Community of Religions, A. 40
Statistical Record of Children. 44
Statistical Record of Health and Medicine. 91
Top 10 of Everything, The. 30
Women's Rights in the United States. 46
World Market Share Reporter. 56

Subject Index

AIDS
National Directory of AIDS Care 1994-95, The. 95

AIDS (DISEASE)
HIV/AIDS Resources. 64

ACRONYMS
NTC's Dictionary of Acronyms and Abbreviations. 77

AFRICA
100 Great Africans. 134
African Biographical Dictionary, An. 134

AFRO-AMERICAN SOLDIERS
On the Trail of the Buffalo Soldier. 62

AFRO-AMERICAN UNIVERSITIES
America's Black and Tribal Colleges. 70
Black American Colleges and Universities. 70

AFRO-AMERICANS
African American Breakthroughs. 134
African American Genealogical Sourcebook. 136
African American Historic Places. 142
African American Resource Guide, The. 143
Historical Statistics of Black America. 143
Timelines of African-American History. 144
Timetables of African-American History, The. 144
Voices of the Spirit. 145

AFRO-AMERICANS NEWSPAPERS
Bibliographic Checklist of African American Newspapers. 60

AGED
Encyclopedia of Home Care for the Elderly. 65

AGRICULTURE
Encyclopedia of Agricultural Science. 96

ALLERGY
Allergies A-Z. 95

AMERICAN LITERATURE
Jewish American Women Writers. 122
Native North American Literature. 122
Oxford Companion to Women's Writing in the United States, The. 123

AMERICANA
New York Public Library Book of Popular Americans, The. 144

AMERICANS
American Jobs Abroad. 99

AMERICORPS (U.S.)
National Service Corps: A State-by-State Guide. 61

ANIMALS
Amazing Animals of the World. 88
Kingfisher First Encyclopedia of Animals, The. 88

ANIMALS IN MASS MEDIA
Animals on Screen and Radio. 110

ANONYMS AND PSEUDONYMS
Dictionary of Literary Pseudonyms in the English Language, A. 116

ANTIQUES
Bulfinch Illustrated Encyclopedia of Antiques, The. 104

APOLOGETICS
Dictionary of Fundamental Theology. 39

APPRENTICESHIP PROGRAMS
Ferguson's Guide to Apprenticeship Programs. 54

AQUARIUMS, PUBLIC
Aquariums of North America. 89

ARCHITECTURE
Encyclopedia of American Architecture. 103

ARCHITECTURE, DOMESTIC
Visual Dictionary of American Domestic Architecture, The. 103

ART
Art & Design Scholarships. 68
Atlas of Western Art History. 101
Book of Art, The. 102

ARTISTS
Art Book, The. 102
Dictionary of Contemporary American Artists. 102

ARTS
Dictionary of the Arts. 102
Timeline of the Arts and Literature. 101

ASIA
Encyclopedia of Eastern Philosophy and Religion, The. 40
Facts on File Asian Political Almanac, The. 140

ASIAN AMERICANS
Asian American Encyclopedia, The. 143
Notable Asian Americans. 143
Who's Who among Asian Americans. 48

ASTRONOMY
Universe Explained, The. 86

ATHLETES
Sports Stars. 114
Who's Who of Sports Champions, A. 114. 114

ATLASES
Dorling Kindersley World Reference Atlas, The. 131
Encyclopedic World Atlas. 131
Eyewitness Atlas of the World, The. 131
Thematic Atlases for Public, Academic, and High School Libraries. 132

AUSTRALIA
Cambridge Encyclopedia of Australia, The. 148

AUTHORS
Larousse Dictionary of Writers. 121
Wilson Author Biographies. 120

AUTOGRAPHS
Sanders Price Guide to Autographs, The. 137

AUTOMOBILE DRIVER'S RECORDS
MVR Book Motor Services Guide, The. 66

BANKS AND BANKING
Dictionary of Banking. 56

BAPTISTS
Dictionary of Baptists in America. 40

BASKETBALL
Encyclopedia of College Basketball. 114
Official NBA Basketball Encyclopedia, The. 115

BIBLE
New Interpreter's Bible, The. 38
Who's Who in the Bible. 39

BIBLIOGRAPHIES
Guides to Library Collection Development. 28
Homelessness in America, 1893-1992. 64
Humanities, The. 28

BIOETHICS
Encyclopedia of Bioethics. 38

BIOGRAPHY
Oxford Children's Book of Famous People, The. 134

BIRDS
Bird's Eggs. 90
Birds of North America, The. 89
Birds of South America, The. 89
Handbook of the Birds of the World. 89

BLUES (MUSIC)
Guide to the Blues, A. 107

BRASS INSTRUMENT PLAYERS
Twentieth-Century Brass Soloists. 109

BUSINESS ENTERPRISES
Companies International. 57
Hoover's Guide to Private Companies. 59

BUSINESS INFORMATION SERVICES
International Business Information. 56

CABLE TELEVISION
Jones Cable Television and Information Infrastructure Dictionary. 71

CANADA
In Search of Your Canadian Roots. 137

CARTOGRAPHY
Young Oxford Companion to Maps and Mapmaking, The. 132

CATS
Quintessential Cat, The. 90

CELEBRITIES
Legends in Their Own Time. 136

CETACEA
Whales, Dolphins and Porpoises. 90

CHARACTERS IN LITERATURE
Larousse Dictionary of Literary Characters. 121
Major Characters in American Fiction. 123

CHEMISTRY
Concise Encyclopedia Chemistry. 87

CHILDREN
Cultures Outside the United States in Fiction. 118
Great New Nonfiction Reads. 28
Immigrants in the United States in Fiction. 118
Statistical Record of Children. 44
This Land is Our Land. 122

CHILDREN'S ATLASES
Complete Atlas of the World, The. 131
Kingfisher First Picture Atlas, The. 131
My First Atlas. 131
New Viking Children's World Atlas, The. 131

CHILDREN'S ENCYCLOPEDIAS
Kingfisher Young World Encyclopedia, The. 31

CHILDREN'S LITERATURE
Africa in Literature for Children and Young Adults. 140
Fantasy Literature for Children and Young Adults. 118
Recreating the Past. 119

CHILDREN'S PERIODICALS
Primary Search. 32

CHILDREN'S STORIES, AMERICAN
Native Americans in Fiction. 118

CHINA
China Business. 54

CHORAL MUSIC
American Choral Music since 1920. 109

CHRISTIAN ART AND SYMBOLISM
Dictionary of Cristian Art. 39

CINEMATOGRAPHY
Dictionary of Film Terms. 111

CITIES AND TOWNS
Gale City & Metro Rankings Reporter. 50
Health and Environment in America's Top-Rated Cities. 50

CIVILIZATION
Children's Atlas of Civilizations, The. 130

COLD WAR
Encyclopedia of the Cold War. 128

COMEDY FILMS
American Film Comedy. 110

COMPACT DISCS
Classical Music on CD. 106

COMPOSERS
Chronicle of Classical Music, The. 104

COMPUTER GAMES
Games & Entertainment on CD-ROM. 113
Net Games. 113

COMPUTERS
Computers: A Visual Encyclopedia. 26
Large Print Computer Dictionary, The. 26

CONFEDERATE STATES OF AMERICA
Historical Atlas of the Congresses of the Confederate States of America,. 146

CORPORATIONS
Notable Corporate Chronologies. 54

COUNSELING
Dictionary of Counseling. 63

COUNTRY MUSIC
Comprehensive Country Music Encyclopedia, The. 106

COWBOYS
Cowboy Encyclopedia, The. 147
Cowboys and the Wild West. 148

CREATION
Encyclopedia of Creation Myths. 41

CRIME
Crime. 66

CRITICISM
Columbia Dictionary of Modern Literary and Cultural Criticism, The. 26

CURIOSITIES AND WONDERS
Top 10 of Everything, The. 30
Visual Encyclopedia of Science. 32

DETECTIVE AND MYSTERY STORIES
Encyclopedia Mysteriosa. 121
Great Women Mystery Writers. 124

DEVELOPING COUNTRIES
Third World Resource Directory 1994-1995. 127

DICTATORS
Dictators and Tyrants. 135

DISTANCE EDUCATION
DistanceLearn. 69
Oryx Guide to Distance Learning, The. 70

DIVINATION
Divining the Future. 35

DIVORCE
Divorce Help Sourcebook. 59

DOG BREEDS
Reader's Digest Illustrated Book of Dogs, The. 97

DRUGS, NONPRESCRIPTION
Handbook of Over-the-Counter Drugs and Pharmacy Products. 94

ECONOMIC HISTORY
Global Trends. 129
Great Events from History II. 54

EDUCATION
Education Career Directory. 67
Encyclopedia of Education Information, The. 66
Hooray for Heroes!. 69

ELECTIONS
Congressional Quarterly's Guide to U.S. Elections. 52

ENCYCLOPEDIAS AND DICTIONARIES
Barnhart New-Words Concordance, The. 80
Britannica Online. 29
Concise Columbia Encyclopedia, The. 30
InfoPedia. 31
Kister's Best Encyclopedias. 31
Microsoft Bookshelf '94. 28

ENDANGERED SPECIES
Encyclopedia of Endangered Species. 87
Grolier Student Encyclopedia of Endangered Species, The. 88

ENGINEERING
Wilson Applied Science & Technology Abstracts. 82

ENGLISH FICTION
Now Read On: A Guide to Contemporary Popular Fiction. 125

ENGLISH LANGUAGE
American Heritage Children's Dictionary, The. 79
American Heritage First Dictionary, The. 79
American Heritage Student Dictionary, The. 79
American Heritage Talking Dictionary, The. 76
Black Talk: Words and Phrases from the Hood to the Amen Corner. 80
Cambridge Encyclopedia of the English Language, The. 75
Chambers Dictionary, The. 76
Dorling Kindersley Children's Illustrated Dictionary, The. 77
Guidelines for Bias-Free Writing. 116
Happy Trails. 80
Harcourt Brace Student Thesaurus, The. 77
Kingfisher Illustrated Children's Dictionary, The. 77
Kingfisher Illustrated Thesaurus, The. 77
Language of Small Businesses, The. 78
Metaphors Dictionary. 33
New York Public Library Writer's Guide to Style and Usage, The. 117
Oxford Dictionary of English Grammar, The. 82
Proper Names Master Index. 79
Random House Historical Dictionary of American Slang. 81
Random House Unabridged Electronic Dictionary on CD-ROM. 78
Thesaurus of Slang, The. 80
Usage and Abusage. 81

ENGLISH PHILOLOGY
Encyclopedia of English Studies and Language Arts. 81

ENTERTAINERS
Performing Artists. 102

ENVIRONMENTAL SCIENCES
Encyclopedia of th Environment, The. 65

EPIC LITERATURE
Encyclopedia of Traditional Epics. 74

EPIDEMICS
Encyclopedia of Plague and Pestilence. 93

ETHICS
Ethics. 38

ETHNIC RELATIONS
Ethnic Relations. 47

ETHNOLOGY
From Afar to Zulu. 48
Peopling of America, The. 48

EUROPE
In Search of Your European Roots. 137
Weissman Travel Planner for Western and Eastern Europe, 1994-1995. 133

EUROPE, EASTERN
  Chronolgy of 20th-Century Eastern European History. 139
  Dictionary of East European History since 1945. 139
EXHIBITIONS
  Exhibit Review, The. 71
EXPLORERS
  Explorers and Discoverers. 130
FAIRY TALES
  Index to Fairy Tales, 1987-1992. 75
FAITH
  Larousse Dictionary of Beliefs and Religions. 40
FAMILYSEARCH (COMPUTER FILE)
  Geneaology in the Computer Age. 137
FICTION
  Good Reads. 118
  NoveList. 118
FINANCE
  Language of Banking, The. 56
FOLKLORE
  Atlas of the Mysterious in North America. 74
FOOD
  Book of Food, The. 97
  Great Food Almanac, The. 97
FOOD HABITS
  Since Eve Ate Apples. 97
FORMER SOVIET REPUBLICS
  Atlas of Russia and the Independent Republics. 132
FOXES
  Foxes, Wolves and Wild Dogs of the World. 90
FUTURE LIFE
  Encyclopedia of Afterlife Beliefs and Phenomena. 36
GAYS
  Gay and Lesbian Rights. 52
GEARING
  Encyclopedic Dictionary of Gears and Gearing. 95
GENEALOGY
  Genealogist's Handbook, The. 136
GENEAOLOGY
  Geneaology Online. 137
GEOGRAPHY
  Worldmark Encyclopedia of the Nations. 126
GEOGRAPHY, ANCIENT
  Atlas of Classical History. 130
GERMANY
  In Search of Your German Roots. 137
GHOSTS
  National Directory of Haunted Places, The. 35
GOVERNMENT PUBLICATIONS
  U.S. Government Periodicals Index. 27
HANDBOOKS, VADE-MACUMS, ETC.
  Life's Big Instruction Book. 32

HEADS OF STATE
  Heads of States and Governments. 135
HEALTH
  Great Health Hints & Handy Tips. 93
  Health On File. 93
HEALTH STATISTICS INDICATOR
  Statistical Record of Health and Medicine. 91
HEROES IN MASS MEDIA
  Adventure Heroes. 100
HISPANIC AMERICANS
  Hispanic American Almanac. 47
  Hispanic American Genealogical Sourcebook. 136
HISPANIC AMERICANS IN PICTURES
  Hispanics in Hollywood. 112
HISTORIC SITES
  International Dictionary of Historic Places. 142
  Masterworks of Man & Nature. 126
  Pop Culture Landmarks. 134
HISTORICAL FICTION
  Historical Figures in Fiction. 124
HISTORY
  American Historical Association's Guide to Historical Literature, The. 138
  World History. 126
HISTORY, MILITARY
  Timelines of War. 126
HISTORY, MODERN
  Exegy. 128
HOBBIES
  Favorite Hobbies and Pastimes. 110
HOLIDAYS
  Holidays and Festivals Index. 73
  International Holidays. 73
HOLISTIC MEDICINE
  Alternative Health & Medicine Encyclopedia, The. 94
HOMELESSNESS
  Homelessness: A Sourcebook. 64
HOMOSEXUALITY IN PICTURES
  Images in the Dark. 112
HORSES
  Encyclopedia of the Horse, The. 97
HOSPITALS
  Best Hospitals in America, The. 63
HUMAN ANATOMY
  Children's Atlas of the Human Body, The. 92
HUMAN PHYSIOLOGY
  Body Atlas, The. 92
  Human Body, The. 93
IMMIGRANT WOMEN
  European Immigrant Women in the United States. 136
INDIAN LITERATURE
  Dictionary of Native American Literature. 125
INDIANS
  Indian Terms of the Americas. 141

INDIANS OF NORTH AMERICA
  Chronolgy of Native North American History. 141
  Encyclopedia of American Indian Costume. 73
  Guide to Native American Music Recordings, A. 106
  Native America in the Twentieth Century. 141
  Native North American Almanac. 141
  Word Dance. 141
INDUSTRIES
  Encyclopedia of American Industries, v.1. 58
  Encyclopedia of American Industries, v.2. 58
INSECT PETS
  Agricultural Entomology. 96
INTELLECT
  Encyclopedia of Human Intelligence. 37
INTERNET (COMPUTER NETWORK)
  Gale Guide to Internet Databases. 71
  Internet Access Provider. 72
  Net Money. 72
INTERNET (COMPUTER NETWORK)
  Internet Resource Directory for K-12 Teachers and Librarians, The. 68
INTERNSHIP PROGRAMS
  Peterson's Internships 1995. 99
INTERNSHIPS
  National Directory of Internships, The. 69
INVENTIONS
  Historical Inventions on File. 91
ISLAMIC COUNTRIES
  Oxford Encyclopedia of the Modern Islamic World, The. 127
JAZZ
  All Music Guide to Jazz. 105
  Guide to Classic Recorded Jazz, The. 107
JEWS
  Concise Dictionary of American Jewish Biography, The. 135
  Junior Judaica. 42
JOB HUNTING
  Job Hunter's Yellow Pages. 99
JOB HUNTING
  Job Seeker's Guide to Socially Responsible Companies, The. 99
JOURNALISTS
  Dictionary of Literary Biography, v.137. 122
JUDGES
  Supreme Court Justices, The. 59
KINGS AND RULERS
  Great Leaders, Great Tyrants?. 135
  World Leaders. 136
LANDSCAPE GARDENING
  Taylor's Master Guide to Gardening. 96
LATIN AMERICAN LITERATURE
  Masterpieces of Latino Literature. 125
LAW
  Legal Problem Solver. 60
LETTER WRITING
  Forms of Address. 73

LICENSES
National Directory of State Business Licensing and Regulation. 59

LITERATURE
Great Women Writers. 121
Merriam-Webster's Encyclopedia of Literature. 115
Modern Black Writers. 121

LOBBYISTS
Government Affairs Yellow Book. 52

MADISON, JAMES
James Madison and the American Nation 1751-1836. 145

MAN
Penguin Atlas of Diasporas, The. 44

MANUFACTURERS
CD's, Super Glue, and Salsa. 100
Millennium Whole Earth Catalog, The. 70

MARKETING
Data Sources for Business and Market Analysis. 87
Marketing Information. 100
World Market Share Reporter. 56

MARTIAL ARTS
Martial Arts Sourcebook, The. 115

MATERIALS
Encyclopedia of Advanced Materials, The. 95

MEDICAL CARE
Health Industry QuickSource. 91

MEDICINE
Handbook of Current Health & Medicine. 91
Oxford Medical Companion, The. 92

MEDICINE, POPULAR
Consumer Health USA. 94
Consumer's Medical Desk Reference, The. 64

MEMORY
Encyclopedia of Memory and Memory Disorders, The. 37

MEXICO
Mexico Business. 54

MILITARY ART AND SCIENCE
Dictionary of Military Abbreviations. 61
Dictionary of Military History and the Art of War, A. 61

MILITARY BASES, AMERICAN
Directory of U.S. Military Bases Worldwide. 63

MINORITIES
Kaleidoscope: A Multicultural Booklist for Grades K-8. 48

MOTION PICTURE ACTORS
Biographical Dictionary of Film, A. 110
Leonard Matlin's Movie Encyclopedia. 110

MOTION PICTURE INDUSTRY
Film and Video Career Directory. 67

MOTION PICTURE MUSIC
Hollywood Song. 108

MOTION PICTURES
Film Anthologies Index, The. 111
Film Encyclopedia, The. 111
Film Quotations. 111
First Century of Film. 112

MULTIMEDIA SYSTEMS
Cyberspace Lexicon, The. 27

MUSIC
Building a Classical Music Library. 106
Classical Music. 104
Music, Dance & Theater Scholarships. 68
Oxford Dictionary of Music, The. 104
Richard Baker's Companion to Music. 104
World Music. 105

MUSICALS
Encyclopedia of the Musical Theatre, The. 108

MYTHOLOGY
Companion to Literary Myths, Heroes and Archetypes. 74
Goddesses, Heroes, and Shamans. 41

MYTHOLOGY, CLASSICAL
Voyages in Classical Mythology. 41

NAMES, GEOGRAPHICAL
State Names, Seals, Flags, and Symbols. 138

NATIONAL SERVICE
School-to-Work Programs. 54

NATURAL HISTORY
Atlas of Wild Places, The. 41

NEW AGE MOVEMENT
Body, Mind & Spirit. 42

NEW YORK (N.Y.)
Historical Atlas of New York City, The. 147

NON-FORMAL EDUCATION
Handbook of Alternative Education. 67

NORTH CAROLINA
North Carolina History. 147

NURSING
Peterson's Guide to Nursing Programs. 92

OCCULTISM
Encyclopedia of Claims, Frauds, and Hoaxes of the Occult and Supernatura. 35
Man, Myth & Magic. 35

OCCUPATIONAL TRAINING
Opportunities for Vocational Study. 54

OLD AGE
Older Americans Almanac. 44

OPERA
Viking Opera Guide on CD-ROM, The. 108
Viking Opera Guide, The. 108

OPERA COMPANIES
Opera Companies and Houses of the United States. 108

PAPILIONIDAE
Swallowtail Butterflies of the Americas. 89

PARAPSYCHOLOGY
Alternative Realities. 36

PARENTING
Parents' Resource Alamanac, The. 98
Sourcebook on Parenting and Child Care. 98

PATENTS
Historical First Patents. 90

PEACE MOVEMENTS
ABC-Clio Companion to the American Peace Movement in the Twentieth Century. 52

PERFORMING ARTS
New York Public Library Performing Arts Desk Reference, The. 144
Performing Arts Career Directory. 67
Peterson's Professional Degree Programs in the Visual and Performing Art. 101

PERSIAN GULF WAR, 1991
Persian Gulf War Almanac. 140

PHARMACOLOGY
Physicians GenRx/Merck Manual. 93

PHILOSOPHY
Oxford Dictionary of Philosophy, The. 34

PHYSICAL SCIENCES
Physical Sciences Career Directory. 67

PICTURE DICTIONARIES
Dorling Kindersley Ultimate Visual Dictionary. 78
Macmillan Visual Dictionary, The. 78

PICTURE DICTIONARIES, ENGLISH
American Heritage Picture Dictionary, The. 79
My Big Dictionary. 79

PIRATES
Pirates and Privateers of the Americas. 129
Pirates!. 129

POETRY
Poem Finder on Disc. 117

POPULAR CULTURE
American Popular Culture. 142

POPULAR MUSIC
All Music Book of Hit Singles, The. 105
Cash Box Pop Singles Charts, 1950-1993. 106
Green Book of Songs by Subject, The. 109
Joel Whitburn's Top Pop Singles, 1955-1993. 106
Your Hit Parade & American Top Ten Hits. 106

PRESIDENTS
Presidents Speak, The. 61

PRODIGY
Classroom Prodigy. 27

PROFESSIONAL EMPLOYEES
Guide to National Professional Certification Programs, The. 47

PROFESSIONAL SPORTS
Professional Sports Team Histories. 114

PROFESSIONS
Specialty Occupational Outlook. 56

PSYCHOLOGY
Encyclopedia of Human Behavior. 36
Encyclopedia of Psychology. 37

PUBLIC ADMINISTRATION
Public Administration Career Directory. 67

PUBLIC RECORDS
Librarian's Guide to Public Records, The. 60
Sourcebook of Public Record Providers, The. 65
Sourcebook of State Public Records, The. 65

PUBLISHERS AND PUBLISHING
International Book Publishing. 33

QUALITY OF LIFE
  Rating Guide to Life in America's 50 States, The. 49
QUOTATIONS, ENGLISH
  Gale's Quotations. 33
  Oxford Dictionary of Quotations & Modern Quotations, The. 34
REFERENCE BOOKS
  American Military History. 57
  Fieldwork in the Library. 42
  Information Sources in Science and Technology. 83
  Introduction to Reference Sources in the Health Sciences. 92
  Reference Sources in Science, Engineering, Medicine, and Agriculture. 82
REFUGEES
  Historical Dictionary of Refugee and Disaster Relief Oranglzations. 65
RELIGIONS
  Sourcebook for Earth's Community of Religions, A. 40
REPORT WRITING
  MLA Handbook for Writers of Research Papers. 116
ROBOTICS
  McGraw-Hill Illustrated Encyclopedia of Robotics & Artificial Intelligen. 95
ROCK MUSIC
  Literature of Rock III, The. 107
ROCK MUSICIANS
  Rock Stars/Pop Stars. 107
RUSSIA
  Cambridge Encyclopedia of Russia and the Former Soviet Union, The. 139
SACRED PLACES
  Atlas of Sacred Places, The. 41
SALVAGE (WASTE, ETC.)
  Choose to Reuse. 65
SCHOLARSHIPS
  Athletic Scholarships. 70
SCIENCE
  Great Scientific Achievements. 85
  Handbooks and Tables in Science and Technology. 83
  McGraw-Hill Concise Encyclopedia of Science & Technology. 84
  McGraw-Hill Multimedia Encyclopedia of Science & Technology. 83
  Science Dictionary. 85
  Science Experiments and Projects Index. 85
  Science Navigator. 84
  Van Nostrand's Scientific Encyclopedia. 85
SCIENCE FICTION
  Anatomy of Wonder 4. 118
  Science Fiction, Fantasy, and Horror Writers. 123
SCIENCES
  Wilson General Science Abstracts. 82
SCIENTISTS
  Larousse Dictionary of Scientists. 86
  Notable Twentieth-Century Scientists. 86
SEX
  Dr. Ruth's Encyclopedia of Sex. 49
  Dr. Ruth's Encyclopedia of Sex on CD-ROM. 49
  Research Guide to Human Sexuality, A. 49

SHAKESPEARE, WILLIAM
  Shakespeare Dictionary, The. 124
SIGN LANGUAGE
  American Sign Language Dictionary on CD-ROM. 75
SIGNS AND SYMBOLS
  Continuum Encyclopedia of Symbols, The. 43
SINGERS
  Classical Singers of the Opera and Recital Stages. 107
SMALL BUSINESS
  Business Plans Handbook. 100
  Small Business Profiles. 58
SOCIAL REFORMERS
  Marching to a Different Drummer. 43
SOCIAL SCIENCES
  From aristotelian to Reaganomics. 42
  Gale State Rankings Reporter. 50
  Internet Compendium: Subject Guide to Social Sciences, Business and Law. 71
SOCIAL SERVICE
  Encyclopedia of Social Work. 63
SOLDIERS
  War Slang. 80
SPECIAL EDUCATION
  Special Education Sourcebook, The. 68
SPY STORIES
  Cloak and Dagger Fiction. 124
STUDENT EXCHANGE PROGRAMS
  Youth Exchanges. 67
SUCCULENT PLANTS
  Succulents: The Illustrated Dictionary. 96
TEACHERS
  NASDTEC Manual, 1994-1995, The. 67
TECHNICAL WRITING
  Scientific Style and Format. 117
TEENAGERS
  Young Adult Literature and Nonprint Material. 27
TELEVISION BROADCASTING
  Facts on File Dictionary of Television, Cable, and Video, The. 72
  Television Research. 142
TELEVISION MUSIC
  Television Theme Recordings. 105
TELEVISION PROGRAMS, CHILDREN
  Children's Television, 1947-1990. 111
TENNIS
  World of Tennis. 115
THEATER
  International Dictionary of Theatre, v.2: Playwrights. 112
  World Encyclopedia of Contemporary Theatre, The. 113
TIME
  Encyclopedia of Time. 87
TONY AWARDS
  Tony Award, The. 113
TOURIST TRADE
  Travel Dictionary, The. 59

TRANSCULTURAL MEDICAL CARE
  Multicultural Clients. 64
TREASURE-TROVE
  Atlas of Shipwrecks and Treasure. 129
U.S.
  Almanac of State Legislatures, The. 132
  America in the 20th Century. 146
  American Civil War, The. 145
  American Places Dictionary. 133
  American Population Change Annual. 44
  Atlas of Contemporary America. 133
  Atlas of Westward Expansion. 130
  Atlas of the Civil War, The. 146
  CQ's Desk Reference on American Government. 51
  Cambridge Dictionary of American Biography, The. 134
  Datapedia of the United States 1790-2000. 51
  Dictionary of Twentieth-Century Culture. 146
  Encyclopedia of the American Military. 62
  Great Dates in United States History. 143
  Real Life Dictionary of American Politics. 51
  State of the U.S.A. Atlas. 133
  Worldmark Encyclopedia of the States. 126
  Young Reader's Companion to American History, The. 145
U.S. CONGRESS
  Congressional Voting Guide. 53
  Congressional Yearbook, 1993, The. 53
  Encyclopedia of the United States Congress, The. 53
  Unites States Congress, The. 53
UNIDENTIFIED FLYING OBJECTS
  UFO. 26
USED CARS
  Used Car Reliability & Safety Guide, The. 72
VAMPIRES
  Complete Vampire Companion, The. 36
  Vampire Book, The. 36
VENTURE CAPITAL
  Fitzroy Dearborn Directory of Venture Capital Funds, The. 57
VICTORIANA INTERIOR DECORATION
  Illustrated Encyclopedia of Victoriana, The. 103
VIETNAMESE CONFLICT, 1961-1975
  Vietnam War Films. 140
VOCATIONAL GUIDANCE
  Encyclopedia of Careers and Vocational Guidance. 55
  Free and Inexpensive Career Materials. 55
WEIGHTS AND MEASURES
  Macmillan Dictionary of Measurement, The. 73
WINE AND WINE MAKING
  Larousse Encyclopedia of Wine. 98
  Oxford Companion to Wine, The. 98
WOMEN
  500 Great Books By Women. 45
  Chronology of Women's History. 45
  Great Lives from History. 45
  Her Heritage. 45
  Information Please Women's Sourcebook, The. 46
  PDR Family Guide to Women's Health and Prescription Drugs, The. 43
  Second to None: A Documentary History of American Women. 46
  Timetables of Women's History, The. 46
  Women's Atlas of the United States, The. 47

WOMEN SCIENTISTS
American Women in Science. 86

WOMEN ARTISTS
Women Artists. 103

WOMEN SOLDIERS
Women and the Military. 62

WOMEN'S RIGHTS
Women's Rights in the United States. 46

WORLD WAR, 1914-18
Atlas of World War I. 130

WORLD WAR, 1914-1918
Historical Atlas of World War I, The. 138

WORLD WAR, 1939-1945
Oxford Companion to World War II, The. 139

WORLD HISTORY
Dorling Kindersley History of the World, The. 126
Larousse Dictionary of World History, The. 127

YACHTS AND YACHTING
Jimmy Cornell World Cruising Handbook. 115

YOUNG ADULT LITERATURE
Twentieth-Century Children's Artists. 119
Twentieth-Century Young Adult Writers. 119

ZIONISM
New Encyclopedia of Zionism and Israel. 51

ZIP CODE
USA Unzipped. 71

ZOOLOGY
Guide to the Zoological Literature, A. 88

Title Index

100 Great Africans. 134.
500 Great Books By Women. 45.
ABC-Clio Companion to the American Peace Movement in the Twentieth Century. 52.
Adventure Heroes. 100.
Africa in Literature for Children and Young Adults. 140.
African American Breakthroughs. 134.
African American Genealogical Sourcebook. 136.
African American Historic Places. 142.
African American Resource Guide, The. 143.
African Biographical Dictionary, An. 134.
Agricultural Entomology. 96.
All Music Book of Hit Singles, The. 105.
All Music Guide to Jazz. 105.
Allergies A-Z. 95.
Almanac of State Legislatures, The. 132.
Alternative Health & Medicine Encyclopedia, The. 94.
Alternative Realities. 36.
Amazing Animals of the World. 88.
America in the 20th Century. 146.
America's Black and Tribal Colleges. 70.
American Choral Music since 1920. 109.
American Civil War, The. 145.
American Film Comedy. 110.
American Heritage Children's Dictionary, The. 79.
American Heritage First Dictionary, The. 79.
American Heritage Picture Dictionary, The. 79.
American Heritage Student Dictionary, The. 79.
American Heritage Talking Dictionary, The. 76.
American Historical Association's Guide to Historical Literature, The. 138.
American Jobs Abroad. 99.
American Military History. 57.
American Places Dictionary. 133.
American Popular Culture. 142.
American Population Change Annual. 44.
American Sign Language Dictionary on CD-ROM. 75.
American Women in Science. 86.
Anatomy of Wonder 4. 118.
Animals on Screen and Radio. 110.
Aquariums of North America. 89.
Art & Design Scholarships. 68.
Art Book, The. 102.
Asian American Encyclopedia, The. 143.
Athletic Scholarships. 70.
Atlas of Classical History. 130.
Atlas of Contemporary America. 133.
Atlas of Russia and the Independent Republics. 132.
Atlas of Sacred Places, The. 41.
Atlas of Shipwrecks and Treasure. 129.
Atlas of Western Art History. 101.
Atlas of Westward Expansion. 130.
Atlas of Wild Places, The. 41.
Atlas of World War I. 130.
Atlas of the Civil War, The. 146.
Atlas of the Mysterious in North America. 74.
Barnhart New-Words Concordance, The. 80.
Best Hospitals in America, The. 63.
Bibliographic Checklist of African American Newspapers. 60.
Biographical Dictionary of Film, A. 110.
Bird's Eggs. 90.
Birds of North America, The. 89.
Birds of South America, The. 89.
Black American Colleges and Universities. 70.

Black Talk: Words and Phrases from the Hood to the Amen Corner. 80.
Body Atlas, The. 92.
Body, Mind & Spirit. 42.
Book of Art, The. 102.
Book of Food, The. 97.
Britannica Online. 29.
Building a Classical Music Library. 106.
Bulfinch Illustrated Encyclopedia of Antiques, The. 104.
Business Plans Handbook. 100.
CD's, Super Glue, and Salsa. 100.
CQ's Desk Reference on American Government. 51.
Cambridge Dictionary of American Biography, The. 134.
Cambridge Encyclopedia of Australia, The. 148.
Cambridge Encyclopedia of Russia and the Former Soviet Union, The. 139.
Cambridge Encyclopedia of the English Language, The. 75.
Cash Box Pop Singles Charts, 1950-1993. 106.
Chambers Dictionary, The. 76.
Children's Atlas of Civilizations, The. 130.
Children's Atlas of the Human Body, The. 92.
Children's Television, 1947-1990. 111.
China Business. 54.
Choose to Reuse. 65.
Chronicle of Classical Music, The. 104.
Chronolgy of 20th-Century Eastern European History. 139.
Chronology of Native North American History. 141.
Chronology of Women's History. 45.
Classical Music. 104.
Classical Music on CD. 106.
Classical Singers of the Opera and Recital Stages. 107.
Classroom Prodigy. 27.
Cloak and Dagger Fiction. 124.
Columbia Dictionary of Modern Literary and Cultural Criticism, The. 26.
Companies International. 57.
Companion to Literary Myths, Heroes and Archetypes. 74.
Complete Atlas of the World, The. 131.
Complete Vampire Companion, The. 36.
Comprehensive Country Music Encyclopedia, The. 106.
Computers: A Visual Encyclopedia. 26.
Concise Columbia Encyclopedia, The. 30.
Concise Dictionary of American Jewish Biography, The. 135.
Concise Encyclopedia Chemistry. 87.
Congressional Quarterly's Guide to U.S. Elections. 52.
Congressional Voting Guide. 53.
Congressional Yearbook, 1993, The. 53.
Consumer Health USA. 94.
Consumer's Medical Desk Reference, The. 64.
Continuum Encyclopedia of Symbols, The. 43.
Cowboy Encyclopedia, The. 147.
Cowboys and the Wild West. 148.
Crime. 66.
Cultures Outside the United States in Fiction. 118.
Cyberspace Lexicon, The. 27.
Data Sources for Business and Market Analysis. 87.
Datapedia of the United States 1790-2000. 51.
Dictators and Tyrants. 135.

Dictionary of Banking. 56.
Dictionary of Baptists in America. 40.
Dictionary of Contemporary American Artists. 102.
Dictionary of Counseling. 63.
Dictionary of Cristian Art. 39.
Dictionary of East European History since 1945. 139.
Dictionary of Film Terms. 111.
Dictionary of Fundamental Theology. 39.
Dictionary of Literary Biography, v.137. 122.
Dictionary of Literary Pseudonyms in the English Language, A. 116.
Dictionary of Military Abbreviations. 61.
Dictionary of Military History and the Art of War, A. 61.
Dictionary of Native American Literature. 125.
Dictionary of Twentieth-Century Culture. 146.
Dictionary of the Arts. 102.
Directory of U.S. Military Bases Worldwide. 63.
DistanceLearn. 69.
Divining the Future. 35.
Divorce Help Sourcebook. 59.
Dorling Kindersley Children's Illustrated Dictionary, The. 77.
Dorling Kindersley History of the World, The. 126.
Dorling Kindersley Ultimate Visual Dictionary. 78. . . . .
Dorling Kindersley World Reference Atlas, The. 131.
Dr. Ruth's Encyclopedia of Sex. 49.
Dr. Ruth's Encyclopedia of Sex on CD-ROM. 49.
Education Career Directory. 67.
Encyclopedia Mysteriosa. 121.
Encyclopedia of Advanced Materials, The. 95.
Encyclopedia of Afterlife Beliefs and Phenomena. 36.
Encyclopedia of Agricultural Science. 96.
Encyclopedia of American Architecture. 103.
Encyclopedia of American Indian Costume. 73.
Encyclopedia of American Industries, v.1. 58.
Encyclopedia of American Industries, v.2. 58.
Encyclopedia of Bioethics. 38.
Encyclopedia of Careers and Vocational Guidance. 55.
Encyclopedia of Claims, Frauds, and Hoaxes of the Occult and Supernatural. 35.
Encyclopedia of College Basketball. 114.
Encyclopedia of Creation Myths. 41.
Encyclopedia of Eastern Philosophy and Religion, The. 40.
Encyclopedia of Education Information, The. 66.
Encyclopedia of Endangered Species. 87.
Encyclopedia of English Studies and Language Arts. 81.
Encyclopedia of Home Care for the Elderly. 65.
Encyclopedia of Human Behavior. 36.
Encyclopedia of Human Intelligence. 37.
Encyclopedia of Memory and Memory Disorders, The. 37.
Encyclopedia of Plague and Pestilence. 93.
Encyclopedia of Psychology. 37.
Encyclopedia of Social Work. 63.
Encyclopedia of Time. 87.
Encyclopedia of Traditional Epics. 74.
Encyclopedia of th Environment, The. 65.
Encyclopedia of the American Military. 62.

Encyclopedia of the Cold War. 128.
Encyclopedia of the Horse, The. 97.
Encyclopedia of the Musical Theatre, The. 108.
Encyclopedia of the United States Congress, The. 53.
Encyclopedic Dictionary of Gears and Gearing. 95.
Encyclopedic World Atlas. 131.
Ethics. 38.
Ethnic Relations. 47.
European Immigrant Women in the United States. 136.
Exegy. 128.
Exhibit Review, The. 71.
Explorers and Discoverers. 130.
Eyewitness Atlas of the World, The. 131.
Facts on File Asian Political Almanac, The. 140.
Facts on File Dictionary of Television, Cable, and Video, The. 72.
Fantasy Literature for Children and Young Adults. 118.
Favorite Hobbies and Pastimes. 110.
Ferguson's Guide to Apprenticeship Programs. 54.
Fieldwork in the Library. 42.
Film Anthologies Index, The. 111.
Film Encyclopedia, The. 111.
Film Quotations. 111.
Film and Video Career Directory. 67.
First Century of Film. 112.
Fitzroy Dearborn Directory of Venture Capital Funds, The. 57.
Forms of Address. 73.
Foxes, Wolves and Wild Dogs of the World. 90.
Free and Inexpensive Career Materials. 55.
From Afar to Zulu. 48.
From aristotelian to Reaganomics. 42.
Gale City & Metro Rankings Reporter. 50.
Gale Guide to Internet Databases. 71.
Gale State Rankings Reporter. 50.
Gale's Quotations. 33.
Games & Entertainment on CD-ROM. 113.
Gay and Lesbian Rights. 52.
Genealogist's Handbook, The. 136.
Geneaology Online. 137.
Geneaology in the Computer Age. 137.
Global Trends. 129.
Goddesses, Heroes, and Shamans. 41.
Good Reads. 118.
Government Affairs Yellow Book. 52.
Great Dates in United States History. 143.
Great Events from History II. 54.
Great Food Almanac, The. 97.
Great Health Hints & Handy Tips. 93.
Great Leaders, Great Tyrants?. 135.
Great Lives from History. 45.
Great New Nonfiction Reads. 28.
Great Scientific Achievements. 85.
Great Women Mystery Writers. 124.
Great Women Writers. 121.
Green Book of Songs by Subject, The. 109.
Grolier Student Encyclopedia of Endangered Species, The. 88.
Guide to Classic Recorded Jazz, The. 107.
Guide to National Professional Certification Programs, The. 47.
Guide to Native American Music Recordings, A. 106.
Guide to the Blues, A. 107.
Guide to the Zoological Literature, A. 88.
Guidelines for Bias-Free Writing. 116.
Guides to Library Collection Development. 28.
HIV/AIDS Resources. 64.
Handbook of Alternative Education. 67.
Handbook of Current Health & Medicine. 91.
Handbook of Over-the-Counter Drugs and Pharmacy Products. 94.
Handbook of the Birds of the World. 89.
Handbooks and Tables in Science and Technology. 83.
Happy Trails. 80.
Harcourt Brace Student Thesaurus, The. 77.
Heads of States and Governments. 135.
Health Industry QuickSource. 91.
Health On File. 93.

Health and Environment in America's Top-Rated Cities. 50.
Her Heritage. 45.
Hispanic American Almanac. 47.
Hispanic American Genealogical Sourcebook. 136.
Hispanics in Hollywood. 112.
Historical Atlas of New York City, The. 147.
Historical Atlas of World War I, The. 138.
Historical Atlas of the Congresses of the Confederate States of America,. 146.
Historical Dictionary of Refugee and Disaster Relief Oragnizations. 65.
Historical Figures in Fiction. 124.
Historical First Patents. 90.
Historical Inventions on File. 91.
Historical Statistics of Black America. 143.
Holidays and Festivals Index. 73.
Hollywood Song. 108.
Homelessness in America, 1893-1992. 64.
Homelessness: A Sourcebook. 64.
Hooray for Heroes!. 69.
Hoover's Guide to Private Companies. 59.
Human Body, The. 93.
Humanities, The. 28.
Illustrated Encyclopedia of Victoriana, The. 103.
Images in the Dark. 112.
Immigrants in the United States in Fiction. 118.
In Search of Your Canadian Roots. 137.
In Search of Your European Roots. 137.
In Search of Your German Roots. 137.
Index to Fairy Tales, 1987-1992. 75.
Indian Terms of the Americas. 141.
InfoPedia. 31.
Information Please Women's Sourcebook, The. 46.
Information Sources in Science and Technology. 83.
International Book Publishing. 33.
International Business Information. 56.
International Dictionary of Historic Places. 142.
International Dictionary of Theatre, v.2: Playwrights. 112.
International Holidays. 73.
Internet Access Provider. 72.
Internet Compendium: Subject Guide to Social Sciences, Business and Law R. 71.
Internet Resource Directory for K-12 Teachers and Librarians, The. 68.
Introduction to Reference Sources in the Health Sciences. 92.
James Madison and the American Nation 1751-1836. 145.
Jewish American Women Writers. 122.
Jimmy Cornell World Cruising Handbook. 115.
Job Hunter's Yellow Pages. 99.
Job Seeker's Guide to Socially Responsible Companies, The. 99.
Joel Whitburn's Top Pop Singles, 1955-1993. 106.
Jones Cable Television and Information Infrastructure Dictionary. 71.
Junior Judaica. 42.
Kaleidoscope: A Multicultural Booklist for Grades K-8. 48.
Kingfisher First Encyclopedia of Animals, The. 88.
Kingfisher First Picture Atlas, The. 131.
Kingfisher Illustrated Children's Dictionary, The. 77.
Kingfisher Illustrated Thesaurus, The. 77.
Kingfisher Young World Encyclopedia, The. 31.
Kister's Best Encyclopedias. 31.
Language of Banking, The. 56.
Language of Small Businesses, The. 78.
Large Print Computer Dictionary, The. 26.
Larousse Dictionary of Beliefs and Religions. 40.
Larousse Dictionary of Literary Characters. 121.
Larousse Dictionary of Scientists. 86.

Larousse Dictionary of World History, The. 127.
Larousse Dictionary of Writers. 121.
Larousse Encyclopedia of Wine. 98.
Legal Problem Solver. 60.
Legends in Their Own Time. 136.
Leonard Matlin's Movie Encyclopedia. 110.
Librarian's Guide to Public Records, The. 60.
Life's Big Instruction Book. 32.
Literature of Rock III, The. 107.
MLA Handbook for Writers of Research Papers. 116.
MVR Book Motor Services Guide, The. 66.
Macmillan Dictionary of Measurement, The. 73.
Macmillan Visual Dictionary, The. 78.
Major Characters in American Fiction. 123.
Man, Myth & Magic. 35.
Marching to a Different Drummer. 43.
Marketing Information. 100.
Martial Arts Sourcebook, The. 115.
Masterpieces of Latino Literature. 125.
Masterworks of Man & Nature. 126.
McGraw-Hill Concise Encyclopedia of Science & Technology. 84.
McGraw-Hill Illustrated Encyclopedia of Robotics & Artificial Intelligenc. 95.
McGraw-Hill Multimedia Encyclopedia of Science & Technology. 83.
Merriam-Webster's Encyclopedia of Literature. 115.
Metaphors Dictionary. 33.
Mexico Business. 54.
Microsoft Bookshelf '94. 28.
Millennium Whole Earth Catalog, The. 70.
Modern Black Writers. 121.
Multicultural Clients. 64.
Music, Dance & Theater Scholarships. 68.
My Big Dictionary. 79.
My First Atlas. 131.
NASDTEC Manual, 1994-1995, The. 67.
NTC's Dictionary of Acronyms and Abbreviations. 77.
National Directory of AIDS Care 1994-95, The. 95.
National Directory of Haunted Places, The. 35.
National Directory of Internships, The. 69.
National Directory of State Business Licensing and Regulation. 59.
National Service Corps: A State-by-State Guide. 61.
Native America in the Twentieth Century. 141.
Native Americans in Fiction. 118.
Native North American Almanac. 141.
Native North American Literature. 122.
Net Games. 113.
Net Money. 72.
New Encyclopedia of Zionism and Israel. 51.
New Interpreter's Bible, The. 38.
New Viking Children's World Atlas, The. 131.
New York Public Library Book of Popular Americans, The. 144.
New York Public Library Performing Arts Desk Reference, The. 144.
New York Public Library Writer's Guide to Style and Usage, The. 117.
North Carolina History. 147.
Notable Asian Americans. 143.
Notable Corporate Chronologies. 54.
Notable Twentieth-Century Scientists. 86.
NoveList. 118.
Now Read On: A Guide to Contemporary Popular Fiction. 125.
Official NBA Basketball Encyclopedia, The. 115.
Older Americans Almanac. 44.
On the Trail of the Buffalo Soldier. 62.
Opera Companies and Houses of the United States. 108.
Opportunities for Vocational Study. 54.
Oryx Guide to Distance Learning, The. 70.
Oxford Children's Book of Famous People, The. 134.
Oxford Companion to Wine, The. 98.
Oxford Companion to Women's Writing in the United States, The. 123.

159

Oxford Companion to World War II, The. 139.
Oxford Dictionary of English Grammar, The. 82.
Oxford Dictionary of Music, The. 104.
Oxford Dictionary of Philosophy, The. 34.
Oxford Dictionary of Quotations & Modern Quotations, The. 34.
Oxford Encyclopedia of the Modern Islamic World, The. 127.
Oxford Medical Companion, The. 92.
PDR Family Guide to Women's Health and Prescription Drugs, The. 43.
Parents' Resource Alamanac, The. 98.
Penguin Atlas of Diasporas, The. 44.
Peopling of America, The. 48.
Performing Artists. 102.
Performing Arts Career Directory. 67.
Persian Gulf War Almanac. 140.
Peterson's Guide to Nursing Programs. 92.
Peterson's Internships 1995. 99.
Peterson's Professional Degree Programs in the Visual and Performing Arts. 101.
Physical Sciences Career Directory. 67.
Physicians GenRx/Merck Manual. 93.
Pirates and Privateers of the Americas. 129.
Pirates!. 129.
Poem Finder on Disc. 117.
Pop Culture Landmarks. 134.
Presidents Speak, The. 61.
Primary Search. 32.
Professional Sports Team Histories. 114.
Proper Names Master Index. 79.
Public Administration Career Directory. 67.
Quintessential Cat, The. 90.
Random House Historical Dictionary of American Slang. 81.
Random House Unabridged Electronic Dictionary on CD-ROM. 78.
Rating Guide to Life in America's 50 States, The. 49.
Reader's Digest Illustrated Book of Dogs, The. 97.
Real Life Dictionary of American Politics. 51.
Recreating the Past. 119.
Reference Sources in Science, Engineering, Medicine, and Agriculture. 82.
Research Guide to Human Sexuality, A. 49.
Richard Baker's Companion to Music. 104.
Rock Stars/Pop Stars. 107.
Sanders Price Guide to Autographs, The. 137.
School-to-Work Programs. 54.
Science Dictionary. 85.
Science Experiments and Projects Index. 85.
Science Fiction, Fantasy, and Horror Writers. 123.
Science Navigator. 84.
Scientific Style and Format. 117.
Second to None: A Documentary History of American Women. 46.
Shakespeare Dictionary, The. 124.
Since Eve Ate Apples. 97.
Small Business Profiles. 58.
Sourcebook for Earth's Community of Religions, A. 40.
Sourcebook of Public Record Providers, The. 65.
Sourcebook of State Public Records, The. 65.
Sourcebook on Parenting and Child Care. 98.
Special Education Sourcebook, The. 68.
Specialty Occupational Outlook. 56.
Sports Stars. 114.
State Names, Seals, Flags, and Symbols. 138.
State of the U.S.A. Atlas. 133.
Statistical Record of Children. 44.
Statistical Record of Health and Medicine. 91.
Succulents: The Illustrated Dictionary. 96.
Supreme Court Justices, The. 59.
Swallowtail Butterflies of the Americas. 89.
Taylor's Master Guide to Gardening. 96.
Television Research. 142.
Television Theme Recordings. 105.
Thematic Atlases for Public, Academic, and High School Libraries. 132.
Thesaurus of Slang, The. 80.
Third World Resource Directory 1994-1995. 127.
This Land is Our Land. 122.
Timeline of the Arts and Literature. 101.
Timelines of African-American History. 144.
Timelines of War. 126.
Timetables of African-American History, The. 144.
Timetables of Women's History, The. 46.
Tony Award, The. 113.
Top 10 of Everything, The. 30.
Travel Dictionary, The. 59.
Twentieth-Century Brass Soloists. 109.
Twentieth-Century Children's Artists. 119.
Twentieth-Century Young Adult Writers. 119.
U.S. Government Periodicals Index. 27.
UFO. 26.
USA Unzipped. 71.
Unites States Congress, The. 53.
Universe Explained, The. 86.
Usage and Abusage. 81.
Used Car Reliability & Safety Guide, The. 72.
Vampire Book, The. 36.
Van Nostrand's Scientific Encyclopedia. 85.
Vietnam War Films. 140.
Viking Opera Guide on CD-ROM, The. 108.
Viking Opera Guide, The. 108.
Visual Dictionary of American Domestic Architecture, The. 103.
Visual Encyclopedia of Science. 32.
Voices of the Spirit. 145.
Voyages in Classical Mythology. 41.
War Slang. 80.
Weissman Travel Planner for Western and Eastern Europe, 1994-1995. 133.
Whales, Dolphins and Porpoises. 90.
Who's Who among Asian Americans. 48.
Who's Who in the Bible. 39.
Who's Who of Sports Champions, A. 114.. 114.
Wilson Applied Science & Technology Abstracts. 82.
Wilson Author Biographies. 120. .
Wilson General Science Abstracts. 82.
Women Artists. 103.
Women and the Military. 62.
Women's Atlas of the United States, The. 47.
Women's Rights in the United States. 46.
Word Dance. 141.
World Encyclopedia of Contemporary Theatre, The. 113.
World History. 126.
World Leaders. 136.
World Market Share Reporter. 56.
World Music. 105.
World of Tennis. 115.
Worldmark Encyclopedia of the Nations. 126.
Worldmark Encyclopedia of the States. 126.
Young Adult Literature and Nonprint Material. 27.
Young Oxford Companion to Maps and Mapmaking, The. 132.
Young Reader's Companion to American History, The. 145.
Your Hit Parade & American Top Ten Hits. 106.
Youth Exchanges. 67.